Explorations In Macroeconomics

STUDENT STUDY GUIDE INCLUDED

FOURTH EDITION

Richard R. Bryant

Gregory M. Gelles

Eun Soo Park

Michael Davis

Missouri University of Science and Technology

James F. Willis

San Jose State University

M. Manfred Fabritius

Centre College

CAT PUBLISHING

ISBN 978-1-56226-665-3

To Marianna and Jim

J.F.W.

To my mom, Ann

M.M.F.

Table Of Contents

Preface .... **xvii**

Section I:
Introduction to a Market Economy **1**
A Brief Background to Americas Market Economy 2
The dimensions of a market economy 2

Chapter 1: Getting Started **5**
Join Us in the Fun 5
Contribution of Economists to Society 6
The Economic Way of Thinking 7
Mathematical Skills 9
Qualifications 13
Economists and Economic Models 14
Summing Up 15
Key Terms 15

Chapter 2: Scarcity, Efficiency, and Growth **17**
Adam Smith and The Invisible Hand 18
The Unavoidable Implications of Scarcity 19
A Scarcity-Free World? 19
Scarcity Leads to Three Basic Economic Questions 20
Analyzing the Choices Resulting From Scarcity: The Production Possibilities Model 21
Graphing the PPF for Newburgia 24
Productivity of Resources in Production and the Shape of the Production-Possibilities Frontier . 25
Efficiency and Choice 25
Attainable (but Inefficient) Points 26
Idle and Inefficiently Used Resources 26
From Unattainable to Attainable: Economic Growth, or What Causes the PPF to Move Over Time?. 27
Economic Institutions and Policies: Important Determinants of the Rate of Output Growth 29
Summing Up 29
Key Terms 31

Chapter 3: Resource Allocation through the Forces of Supply and Demand-An Overview **33**
Competitive Markets 34
The Principles of Demand 34
Why are Demand Curves Downward Sloping? 38
Changes in Demand and Changes in Quantity Demanded 39
Expressing Demand Mathematically 40
Adding Demand Curves for Analysis 41
The Principles of Supply 42
A Word of Caution 43
Supply Shifters 44
Aggregating Supply 45
Equilibrium in a Competitive Market 46
Applying Supply/Demand Analysis 48
The Rising Costs of Higher Education 48
Some Other Supply and Demand Illustrations 50
Price Controls 50
Summing Up 53
Key Terms 55

Chapter 4: Components of an Economic Society **57**
The Circular-Flow Model 57
The Simple Model 57
The Complex Model 59
What Does The Model Show? 59
The Sources of Income: Functional Distribution 61
The Way Households Allocate Their Income 62
The Way Family Income Is Distributed 62
Other Caveats About Income Inequality 63
Economic Implications of Inequality in Income Distribution 65
Sole Proprietorships 66
Advantages of a Sole Proprietorship 66
Disadvantages of a Sole Proprietorship 66
Partnerships 67
Advantages of a Partnership 67
Disadvantages of a Partnership 67
Corporations 67
Advantages of a Corporation 68
Disadvantages of a Corporation 68
Big Business and the American Corporation 69
Expenditures: What Do They Spend All That Money On? 72
Taxation 72
Principles of Taxation 72
Types of Tax Rates 73
Composition of Taxes 75
Who Pays the Tax? 76
Government and the Rules of the Game 76
Government and Regulation 76
The Rest of the World 77
Application I: Business Firms, Profit Maximizers or Agents of Social Responsibility? 78
The Effect of Competition on Business Morals 78
Responsible to Whom? 78
Maximizing Profits: Serving Private or Public Interests? 79
Maximizing Profits: Competition and the Invisible Hand 80
When May Markets Punish Socially Responsible Behavior? 81
Can or Should Firms Decide What is in Society's Interest? 81
Summing Up 82
Key Terms 85
Questions 85

Section II: The Basics of the Macroeconomy 87

Chapter 5: Measuring Domestic Income and Product **89**
Background: Why is National Economic Accounting Important? 90
The Expenditure and Income Approaches 91
Gross Domestic Product and Gross Domestic Income 92
Gross Domestic Product (GDP) 92
Gross Domestic Income (GDI) 95
Changes in U.S. Income Accounting: From GNP to GDP 96
Gross Domestic Product Contrasted With Gross National Product 96
Which is Greater: GDP or GNP? 97
Current, Constant, and Per Capita Real GDP 97
Output Excluded from GDP 99

Economic Transactions Excluded from GDP ... 100
Net National Product and Net National Income ... 100
Net National Product (NNP) ... 100
Net National Income (NNI) ... 101
National Income (NI) ... 102
Personal Income (PI) ... 102
Disposable Income (DI) ... 103
Final-Value and Value-Added Methods ... 105
Application I: Does GDP Growth Measure Improving Human Well-being? ... 107
What GDP Does Not Include ... 107
Cost of Pollution ... 108
What Does Contribute to Well-being? ... 108
Is Further GDP Growth Desirable? ... 109
Measures of Economic Welfare: A Caveat ... 110
Summing Up ... 110
Key Terms ... 112
Questions ... 113

Chapter 6: Economic Fluctuations, Unemployment and Inflation ... 115
Fluctuations: Characteristics and Clues ... 116
Types of Economic Fluctuations ... 116
Phases of a Business Cycle ... 117
Do Business Cycles Follow a Regular Pattern? ... 117
Durable-Versus Nondurable-Goods Industries ... 117
Some Causes of Economic Fluctuations: A Preliminary Look ... 119
Leading Economic Indicators ... 120
Unemployment ... 121
Kinds of Unemployment ... 121
Problems That Accompany Unemployment ... 123
Economic Costs of Unemployment: The GDP Gap ... 123
Psychological and Social Costs of Unemployment ... 125
Prices and the Problem of Inflation ... 125
Theories of Inflation ... 125
Effects of Inflation and Deflation ... 127
Employment and Prices ... 131
Application I: Defining Full Employment ... 133
What is the "Natural Rate" of Unemployment for the U.S.? ... 133
What is the Natural Rate for the U.S.? ... 134
Can We Lower the Natural Rate? ... 135
Has the Natural Rate Fallen? Evidence from the 1990s ... 135
Summing Up ... 135
Key Terms ... 138
Questions ... 139

Chapter 7: Aggregate Demand and Aggregate Supply ... 141
Aggregate Demand: Its Definition and Determinants ... 143
I. Consumption Expenditures ... 143
II. Investment Expenditures ... 144
III. Government Expenditures ... 144
IV. Net Exports (Exports Minus Imports) ... 144
Aggregate Demand: A Summary ... 145
Why Does the Aggregate Demand Curve Slope Downward? ... 145
Aggregate Supply: Its Definition and Determinants ... 146
Why Does the (Short-Run) Aggregate Supply Curve Slope Upward? ... 147

Equilibrium and Full Employment May Not Be the Same 148
When Real Income and the Price Level Change 149
Shifts in Aggregate Demand and Aggregate Supply 149
Aggregate Demand Shifts: Their Effects and Some Causes 149
Aggregate Supply Shifts: Their Effects and a Cause 150
Ranges of Aggregate Supply 151
Supply-Side Economics 152
Measuring the Aggregate Price Level: Price Indexes' 152
Indexes of Prices 152
Computing the GDP Price Index or Deflator 153
The Consumer Price Index: Its Importance 154
Application I: Demand and Supply Shocks: OPEC in the 1970s and 1980s, a War on Terrorism and a New Supply Shock in the 21st Century 155
The OPEC Shocks 155
Minimizing the Supply Shock 157
A Reverse Supply Shock 158
Oil Prices in the Late 1980s? The 1990s? The Twenty First Century? 158
2001: The Economics of a War on Terrorism 158
Rising Oil Prices Since 2004 158
A War Economy 158
Negative Economic Effects 159
Positive Economic Effects 159
What Really Happened: Summing Up and A Few Caveats 160
A few caveats 160
Summing Up 161
Key Terms 165
Questions 166

Chapter 8: Aggregate Spending in the Macroeconomy 169
Say's Law 170
Savings, Investment, and Money Markets 171
Wage-Price Flexibility 173
What About Say's Law? 174
The Abstinence Theory of Interest: Not True Said Keynes 175
Lack of Wage-Price Flexibility 176
Aggregate Supply: The Keynesian Assumptions 177
Consumption, Savings, and Investment 179
The Savings Function 182
A Change in Consumption and Savings 183
The Intended Investment Function 185
What Determines Autonomous Investment? 185
How Much Investment Will People Make? 186
Instability of Investment 186
How Does Investment Fit Into Our Model? 188
Summing Up 189
Key Terms 192
Questions 192

Chapter 9: Equilibrium in the Macroeconomy 195
Stage I: No Government Spending Or Taxes 196
The Basic Model 196
Savings Equals Intended Investment 196
Planned and Actual Investment 199
Aggregate Demand Equals Aggregate Supply 199

Average and Marginal Propensities to Consume and Save ... 201
How Changes in Aggregate Demand Affect Changes in Income: Multiplier Effects ... 205
Why a Multiple? ... 206
The Multiplier Formula ... 206
Instantaneous Multipliers Versus Periodic Multipliers ... 207
The Paradox of Thrift ... 210
Adding Government Expenditures to the Basic Model ... 211
One Approach: Savings Equals Intended Investment Plus Government Expenditures ... 212
Another Approach: Aggregate Quantity Demanded Equals Aggregate Quantity Supplied ... 214
Adding Taxes to the Basic Model ... 215
One Approach: Savings Plus Taxes Equals Intended Investment Plus Government Expenditures 216
Another Approach: Aggregate Quantity Demanded Equals Aggregate Quantity Supplied ... 217
Deflationary and Inflationary Gaps ... 219
The Deflationary Gap ... 219
An Inflationary Gap ... 220
The Balanced-Budget Multiplier ... 221
Fiscal Policy ... 222
Is There a Self-Correcting Mechanism for the Economy? ... 222
Application I: The Modern U.S. Economy: A Record of Growth, Recession, and Depression ... 226
The Roaring 20s ... 226
The Great Depression: Phase I ... 227
Weak Recovery: 1933-1937 ... 228
The Recession of 1937-1939 ... 228
The Early Forties and World War II ... 229
The Postwar Boom: 1945-1948 ... 229
The Recession of 1949 and the Expansion of 1950-1953 ... 229
The Recession of 1954 and the Expansion of 1955-1957 ... 230
The Recession of 1958 ... 230
Weak Recovery in 1960-1961 Followed by the Expansion of 1962-1969 ... 230
Inflation and Unemployment in 1970-1971: Wage and Price Controls in 1971-1973 ... 231
Inflation and Unemployment Again: 1974 to 1976 ... 231
Recovery: 1977 to 1979 ... 232
Recession Followed by Growth and Deficits: 1980-1989 ... 232
1991-2007 ... 232
2008-2011 ... 232
A Judgment About Stability ... 233
Summing Up ... 233
Key Terms ... 237
Questions ... 238

Chapter 10: Fiscal Policy, Deficit Financing, and the National Debt ... 241
Discretionary Versus Automatic Fiscal Policy ... 242
Keynesian Arguments About Fiscal Policy ... 242
Deficit Finance and the Public Debt ... 242
Deficits and the Gross National Debt ... 243
Growing Concerns About the Federal Deficits ... 245
What are the Major Concerns? ... 245
Unfounded Concerns About the Debt and Deficit ... 248
Will Federal Deficits and Growing Debt Bankrupt the Nation? ... 248
Will Federal Deficits and Growing Debt Burden Future Generations? ... 248
Debts, Deficits, and the Balance of Trade ... 249
Traditional Arguments About Budget Deficits and Trade Deficits ... 251
An Alternative to the Traditional View ... 251
Rethinking the American Fiscal System Since the 1990s ... 252

Efforts at Change Already Made ... 252
Budget Legislation Since the 1990s ... 252
Proposals for Further Change ... 253
What Should be Government's Share of the GDP Pie? ... 254
A Recap ... 254
Application I: The "Share Economy," A Replacement for Keynesian Demand Management? ... 255
  A Two Wage System ... 255
  Critiques of the Share Economy ... 256
  What is the Status of the Share Economy? ... 257
Application II: The National Debt: Where are we Headed? ... 257
Summing Up ... 258
Key Terms ... 261
Questions ... 261

Section III: Economic Policy in the Macroeconomy ... 265

Chapter 11: Money in the Modern Economy ... 267
Barter: An Early System of Exchange; ... 268
Money: A More Modern System of Exchange ... 268
The Functions of Money ... 269
Characteristics of a "Good" Money ... 270
The Supply of Money: How to Define and Measure It ... 270
Coins and Gresham's Law ... 271
Money Is Debt ... 272
Measures of the Money Supply ... 272
  M1 ... 272
  M2 ... 273
  M3 ... 273
Summing Up the Money Supply ... 273
  Near Monies, Liquidity, and Credit Cards ... 274
  Credit Cards ... 274
  The Origins of Commercial Banking: Goldsmith Banking ... 274
The Future of Money, or Can the Computer Replace Currency and Coin? ... 275
The Economy and the Supply of Money ... 276
The Equation of Exchange ... 276
The Velocity of Exchange (V) ... 277
Output, Prices, and M (for Money): A Simple First Look ... 278
The Demand for Money: An Alternative ... 279
Summing Up ... 280
Key Terms ... 282
Questions ... 282

Chapter 12: Commercial Banking and the Creation of M1 Money ... 283
The Simple Economy: Four Assumptions About a Simple Model ... 283
Money Creation in the Simple Model ... 285
Enter Currency and Coin ... 286
Enter the Government ... 288
Reserve Requirements ... 289
Enter Many Other Banks ... 291
The Federal Reserve and Clearing Checks ... 291
Lending by Individual Banks: A Little Goes a Long Way ... 292
But What About Leakages That Restrain Demand Deposit Creation? ... 295
The Role of Excess Reserves ... 296

A Final Word About Excess Reserves 296
Application I: First Steps in Banking..... 297
Summing Up 299
Key Terms..... 301
Questions..... 301

Chapter 13: Monetary Policy 303
The Structure of the Federal Reserve 304
General Powers of the Federal Reserve 306
Open-Market Operations 306
The Discount Rate 309
The Required Reserve Ratio..... 310
A Review: How the Fed Nudges the Banking System 311
Specific Powers of the Federal Reserve 311
Margin Requirements on Stocks 311
Regulations X and W..... 312
Regulation Q..... 312
Deregulation and Financial Markets: The 1980s 312
The "Deregulatory Act" of 1980 312
How well has deregulation worked?..... 313
How Sound Are America's Financial Institutions? 313
Are the Nation's Financial Institutions Still in Trouble?..... 314
Further Reform of Financial Services..... 315
A Further Movement Toward Competition? Interstate Banking..... 315
Financial Institutions: A Summing Up 315
The Powerful Fed: A Summary of Its Functions..... 315
The Fed Regulates the Supply of Money..... 315
The Fed Acts as a National Clearinghouse for Checks 316
The Fed Issues Paper Currency 316
The Fed Regulates and Examines Member Banks 316
The Fed Acts as a Banker's Bank..... 316
The Fed Is a Fiscal Agent and Bank for the U.S. Treasury..... 317
The Fed Is a Fiscal Agent for Foreign Central Banks and Treasuries..... 317
Monetary Policy..... 317
Varying the Supply of Money 317
Varying Interest Rates 317
Some Recommendations on Monetary Policy..... 318
What to Do When Recession Hits 318
The Monetary Transmission Mechanism: Credit Markets in a Recession 319
A Recession: Enter the Fed 320
Short-run Effects..... 320
Long-run Effects 321
What to Do When Inflation Hits 322
The Monetary Transmission Mechanism: Credit markets in Inflation 323
The Main Point..... 324
Weaknesses of Monetary Policy 324
Monetarism 327
Application I: How Much Does Money Matter? Monetarists Versus Keynesians..... 327
The Monetarists' Position..... 327
The Keynesian Defense..... 328
A Conclusion 329
Keynesian and Monetarist Views: A Summary of Differences..... 330
Monetary Policy and International Markets Monetary Policy 330
Summing up 331

Key Terms ... 334
Questions ... 334

Chapter 14: Economic Policy Controversies ... 337
Aggregate Supply and Aggregate Demand: A Review ... 338
How Do We Stimulate Aggregate Supply? ... 338
Fundamentals of Supply-Side Views ... 339
Tax Policy, Keynesian Expenditure Reductions or Supply-Side "Wedges?" ... 339
The Tax Cuts of 1981: How Well Did They Work? ... 340
Supply-Side Economics: Why So Controversial? ... 340
The Laffer Curve: Too Much Taxation Reduces Revenue ... 341
Can Discretionary Policy Changes Alter Growth Anyway? Rational Versus Adaptive Expectations 342
How Influential is Rational Expectations Theory? ... 343
Beyond Traditional Keynesian and Classical Policy Arguments ... 343
The Post-Keynesians, Today's Contrarians ... 344
Summing Up ... 344
Key Terms ... 346
Questions ... 346

Chapter 15: Economic Growth ... 349
Statics versus Dynamics ... 349
Sources of Extensive Growth ... 350
Increasing Productivity and Growth ... 351
Decreasing Productivity and Growth ... 352
The Classical View ... 353
Has the Malthusian Nightmare Occurred in Some Places? ... 353
Technological Change ... 354
Population Increase ... 355
The Importance of an Educated Populace: Human Capital Formation ... 356
Slowing Productivity Growth in the United States? ... 356
What is the Implication: A Contrary View ... 358
Technological Change Again: The Answer to Faster Growth? ... 358
Has the U.S. Growth Rate Really Fallen? ... 358
Growth Rate Implications ... 359
What Could We Do to Increase the Growth Rate? ... 360
Application I: Will Declining Military Spending Cut Our Growth Rate? ... 361
Do Wars Keep the Economy Healthy? ... 361
What About Reaching Potential? ... 363
Defense Spending: Does It Encourage or Retard Technological Change? ... 364
What About the Early Twenty First Century? ... 365
Application II: Must We Sacrifice Growth to Have a Clean Environment? ... 365
The Economists' View ... 365
How Population Enters the Picture ... 366
As Some Ecologists Have Seen It ... 367
As Many Economists Have Seen It ... 367
Growth and the Environment: A New Consensus? ... 368
Summing Up ... 368
Key Terms ... 372
Questions ... 372

Section IV:
International Trade And Finance ... 375

Chapter 16: Patterns of International Trade ... 377

What Makes Up Trade? 377
How Important is Trade to America? 378
America's Balance of Trade and Net Foreign Trade 378
But is Trade as Important to us as to others? 380
The Gains from Trade 381
Trade and Comparative Advantage 382
The Terms of Trade 383
Gains from Trade 384
What Determines Comparative Advantage? 385
Demand Considerations 386
Increasing Costs and Other Cautions 387
The Means of Protection 388
Tariffs 388
Elasticity and the Burden of the Tariff 390
Import Quotas 392
Export Quotas: Rational Ignorance by Consumers? 392
Arguments in Favor of Protection 393
The Infant-Industry Argument 393
The National-Security Argument 393
The Cheap-Foreign-Labor Argument 394
The Macroeconomic-Employment Argument 395
Retaliation for "Unfair" Trade Practices 396
The Rustbelt: Protecting Declining Industries 396
International Trade Policy Since World War II 397
Regional Trade Agreements 397
Current Regional Trade Arrangements 397
Multilateral Free Trade: Its Future 398
Free Trade: A Reprise 398
Application I: Does Trade Create Development? 398
The Relation Between Trade and Development 399
The Classical View 399
Reservations About the Traditional View 400
Those With Reservations: Modify Free Trade 402
Debt Problems of the LDCs and NICs 403
Implications for Trade Policies 403
Application II: Steel Tariffs 404
Summing Up 405
Key Terms 409
Questions 410

Chapter 17: Paying for International Trade 413
An Example of Trade Involving Different Domestic Currencies 413
A Workable International Monetary System 414
Foreign Exchange Markets: Determining Equilibrium Exchange Rates 415
Freely Floating Exchange Rates 415
Advantages and Disadvantages of Floating Exchange Rates 417
Fixed Exchange Rates 418
Exchange Rate Market Intervention 418
Adjusting Economies to Fluctuations in the Exchange Rate 419
Means of Adjustment 419
The Gold Standard 421
Postwar International Exchange Arrangements 423
The Managed or "Dirty" Float: Whither the Future? 424
The Mexican Peso in December 1994: How the International System Works in Crisis 425

The Balance of Payments ... 426
The Accounts of the Balance of Payments ... 426
The Current Account ... 426
The Capital Account ... 426
The Financial Account ... 427
The Balance of Payments: Deficits and Surpluses ... 427
An Actual BOP: The U.S. in 2008 ... 427
Deficits to be Financed: Current and Capital Account Balances ... 430
Application I: Politics and the Balance-of-Payments Problem ... 430
Reasons Behind Import Restraints ... 430
Protectionism: Costs and Benefits ... 431
America's Trade Problem: The Myths ... 432
Protectionism: Will It Triumph or Fail? ... 433
Lessons to Be Learned ... 433
Summing Up ... 434
Key Terms ... 438
Questions ... 438

Chapter 18: Economic Systems—How Many in the Twenty-First Century? ... 441
Basic Economic Choices: A Reminder ... 441
Evaluating an Economic System ... 442
Static Efficiency ... 442
Dynamic Efficiency ... 442
Property Rights: Should They be Vested in Individuals or in the State? ... 442
Private Property Rights ... 442
Public Property Rights ... 443
Why Do Property Rights Matter? ... 443
Market Capitalism ... 444
Economic Advantages of Market Capitalism ... 444
Economic Criticisms of Capitalism ... 445
Planned Socialism ... 445
What is Planned Socialism? ... 445
Advantages of Planned Socialism ... 445
Criticisms of Planned Socialism ... 446
Marx and Socialism ... 446
Dialectical Materialism ... 447
Class Conflict ... 447
Falling Profits and the Reserve Army of the Unemployed ... 447
Recurring Business Cycles ... 448
Marx's Prediction: The Collapse of Capitalism ... 448
What Happened to the Collapse? ... 448
Efficiency of Central Planning: The "Fatal Conceit" Problem ... 449
The End of Planned Socialism? ... 450
Transition from Planned Socialism to Market Capitalism: How Long and How Difficult? ... 450
Key Reforms ... 450
Secure Private Property Rights ... 451
Prices that Reflect Relative Scarcity ... 451
A Monetary System that Permits Price Stability ... 451
Institutional Reform ... 452
Mixed Economies: A Third System? ... 452
The End of Socialism: A Disclaimer ... 452
Economic and Political Freedom: Are They Related? ... 453
Faster Growth ... 453
Political Freedom: Does it Follow from Economic Freedom ... 453

China: A Test Case? 454
Summing Up 455
Key Terms 457
Questions 457

Glossary 459

Index 487

Student Study Guide 503

Preface

An educated person is one who has finally discovered that there are some questions to which nobody has the answers.

Anonymous

From our own observations as teachers and from recent developments in the field, two facts about the principles of economics course are apparent. First, enrollments are growing, and second, they are growing not just because students want to learn about economics, but also because they are *required* to take the course.

On the one hand, this boom gives those of us who teach economics a greater opportunity to expose students to our way of thinking, to economists' ideas on how to approach the understanding and solution of problems. On the other, it means that we have to provide students with some good reasons for learning about the subject, especially if we expect them to retain what they learn. It is our hope that this book will help students understand how economists think, and how applicable an economic perspective is to the problems of the real world. Furthermore, the basic questions facing our students, as political creatures in a democracy, are economic ones. This text should prepare them to understand policy debate in such areas as economic stabilization, the crisis of the cities; poverty, and agricultural policy. Obviously, an understanding of economics is also useful, if not necessary, for careers in such areas as business administration, sociology, psychology, history, and the administrative end of many types of engineering.

We have therefore tried to do two things. First, we have reduced the principles of economics in both volume and complexity to the point at which our students can grasp (and, we hope, *retain*) them. Second, we have applied the basic principles to problems that our students can recognize. We have tried to address particularly those students who are more concerned with a J.O.B. than a Ph.D. Many of the problems these students will face concern economics to some degree. And, although there are some questions in economics to which nobody knows the answers, there are even more for which there are *many* answers. Our students need to be able to analyze the alternatives, choose the most feasible one, and—perhaps most important—*know the basis on which the choice rests.*

Scope and Approach

In our experience, the greatest criticism of the principles of economics course is that we instructors try to do too much. Using the average textbook of 1,300-plus pages crammed with solid, valuable materials, the instructor naturally has to race in order to cover the ground. Furthermore, students tend to become swamped with the detail and diversity of the subject matter. They often become confused about what is most important. We have tried to avoid this situation.

Of necessity, we could not include in this text everything that our colleagues wanted us to—although we are grateful to them for their suggestions. We included those principles and problems that seemed most important *to us*, including what we did because both of us are teachers. In other words, we put in materials that work with our students. We have included the essential materials dealing with income determination, banking and money, government stabilization policy, supply and demand, the theory of the firm, and pricing of factors of production. In addition to this basic core, we have added materials on economic development, international trade, and other economic systems. We realize, however, that different instructors may wish to delve more deeply into an issue or expand on a problem in a particular chapter. Therefore, we have listed, at the end of chapters, a number of additional sources.

We feel that this principles of economics text has several distinct advantages over many others in the field:

1. It is not an encyclopedia of economics but, rather, contains enough theory to equip the student with a permanent level of economic literacy.

2. Most theoretical chapters contain extended applications that use the economic principles just covered to analyze practical economic problems. For example, an application, new to this edition, deals with the financial crisis of 2008-2009 and how we have moved beyond the recession. That application illustrates how the principles of macroeconomic equilibrium may be used to understand the background, causes, and controversies surrounding efforts to combat a recession that began in December 2007.

3. The use of mathematics has been limited to the practical minimum by avoiding complex algebraic manipulations and difficult derivations of relationships, and by using, instead, simple two-dimensional diagrams to illustrate principles.

4. Every attempt has been made to communicate in the everyday language of the student rather than in the technical language of the economic journal.

5. Special attention has been given to chapter summaries, end-of-chapter materials, and the glossary in order to help the student review and to reinforce the concepts presented in each chapter.

The Study Guide

To help students obtain some drill in economic problem solving and find out how well they are grasping the material, we have prepared a study guide. Each unit of this guide starts with a review of key terms and essay questions and problems that are designed to make students rethink the material just learned. It ends with a self-test consisting of true/false, multiple-choice, and matching questions. After the self-test are all self-test answers and occasional problem answers.

We regard the study guide as an important supplement to *Explorations in Macroeconomics*. Since economics requires a lot of concentration and going over material again and again, we strongly advise that students arm themselves with this learning aid.

Acknowledgments

We have benefited from the advice and assistance of many people in preparing the seven editions of *Explorations in Macroeconomics*. While our indebtedness extends to too many economists to acknowledge each one individually, we would especially like to thank those who have contributed formal reviews to the first four editions—James V. Koch of Illinois State University, R. D. Peterson of Colorado State University, Joseph M. Perry of the University of North Florida, Joseph Domitrz of Western Illinois University, Anthony L. Ostrosky of Illinois State University, and Kirk A. Blackerby of San Jose State University.

We are especially indebted to four economist colleagues who contributed formal reviews for this sixth revised edition. Professors Thomas Nickels of Mount Mercy College, H. Shahidi of the College of the Desert, Richard McCormac of American River College, and James Lee of Ohio University made many useful suggestions that have been incorporated into the text. As usual, we accept responsibility for any errors that remain.

The management and staff of CAT Publishing have been exceptionally accommodating and helpful in the lengthy process of preparing and polishing the new manuscript. While that has been true of all at CAT, we want to express our particular gratitude to our publisher, Leslie Gawain.

James F. Willis
M. Manfred Fabritius

SECTION I:
Introduction to a Market Economy

SECTION I

Introduction to a Market Economy

A Brief Background to Americas Market Economy

Over the more than two centuries of our existence as a nation and economic society, much as changed. From a small but prosperous nation of two and a half million citizens in the 1790s, we have grown to a nation of more than 300 million citizens in the early 21st century. From a rural, overwhelmingly agricultural society, we have experienced the tremendous structural changes that came to be known as the industrial revolution. By 1900, the U.S. was the world's largest industrial economy with its society ever more urban. This transformation has continued into the 21st century. In 2010, we are often described as a post-industrial society.

Change of this magnitude inevitably engenders resistance and controversy. Landowners for example resisted the transfer of resources to industrial uses. Property owners resisted government regulation. Throughout the process we continued to rely primarily on markets and market prices to allocate and reallocate resources.

In 2010, we are in a serious economic downturn, one of many in our history. We will have much to say about the controversies arising from efforts to find solutions to the contemporary problems of the economy. These problems include the crisis of financial markets, high unemployment rates, and excessive risk taking by private financial firms. In addition, the very large federal deficit continues to add to the federal debt. These along with the declining strength of the U.S. dollar in global markets are concerns.

The dimensions of a market economy

The U.S., like the vast majority of today's economic societies is a market economy, one in which private buyers and sellers interact to make choices about what to produce, and to create the prices at which voluntary exchanges between the two groups will occur. The study of how this individual disaggregated (exchange) economy works is called *microeconomics*. It is based on assumptions about human behavior as well as on assumptions about the constraints humans face in seeking to solve economic problems. It is with that background to the "economic way of thinking" that we begin this text and the course in *macroeconomics* or aggregate economics in which you are enrolled.

Microeconomics study of a disaggregated market economy.

Macroeconomics: The study of an aggregated market economy.

Why, you may well ask, should we begin with some microeconomic fundamentals rather than plunging straight into macroeconomics or the "big picture" of a market economy in its aggregated form? Put simply, it is for two reasons: (1) We cannot understand the macroeconomy fully without first understanding its underlying microeconomic processes—inflation; or significant increases in overall prices, for example, cannot be understood or the problems of inflation dealt with unless we understand how the individual prices that add up to inflation are determined, and (2) the models of the macroeconomy that are developed in this book and course are only as valid as the microeconomics on which they are built.

This microeconomic introduction to the macroeconomy is developed in four chapters. In Chapter 1, you are introduced to the most fundamental of economic problems, scarcity, or the inability of societies to satisfy all material wants. In Chapter 2, you will see how attempts to solve the problem of scarcity have resulted in widely varying levels of economic development among nations. In Chapter 3, you will see how markets, the institutional arrangements through which buyers and sellers make exchanges, allocate a society's scarce resources through the guidance of prices. Finally, in Chapter 4 you will see who are the players in both the microeconomy and the macroeconomy. The economic roles of households, business firms, and governments are examined. The role of international trade, or that of exports and imports, is briefly introduced as well.

Chapter 1: Getting Started

Join Us in the Fun

How would you answer the following questions?

1. Does a ceiling on rents reduce the quantity and quality of housing available?

2. Do tariffs and import quotas reduce general economic welfare?

3. Are direct cash payments superior to transfers in kind, such as food stamps and rent subsidies?

4. Does a minimum wage increase unemployment among young and unskilled workers? Does it reduce income inequality?

5. Are excise and sales taxes always paid by the buyers of the taxed good?

6. Does teamwork result in lower cost per unit than individuals working in isolation?

7. Should everyone be entitled to basic medical coverage?

8. Should a particular item be produced using the most technically efficient process?

After you have thought about these questions, engage in the following mental exercise. Suppose you were debating one side of one of these issues. How would you prepare for the debate? We suggest you should write down the evidence you have observed that supports your conclusion. To understand what we mean by evidence and assumptions, think about this situation. When you say it will take you two hours to drive from Rolla to St. Louis, you are basing this assertion on your past experience—past trips to St. Louis, or discussions with people who have made the trip. You are assuming there will not be a traffic jam, or a typical

Missouri thunderstorm that will force you to stop. You are also assuming there will be no major accidents, or road construction that will delay your trip. The idea is that a good debate will provide evidence and argue for a particular point of view based on that evidence and a set of assumptions consistent with that evidence.

If you have followed the instructions given in the previous paragraph, you have been acting like an economist, or at least like a beginning economist. You have been thinking about some serious economic questions. You have built a model and you have made clear your assumptions. Perhaps you have used data that you observed in the past in making your assumptions and your model. Finally, you have reached a conclusion that has allowed you to make a comment on each statement. Each student in the class may have reached different conclusions, because each has made different assumptions, has observed different data, and thinks differently. Although you have been acting as an economist, your analysis and writing will still sound nontechnical and nonrigorous to a professional economist. This is because you do not yet know the language of economics.

This textbook will guide you through the thinking process applied by many economists to important economic issues. The models, assumptions, and conclusions we will see are agreed upon by many economists, have been studied for several decades, and have, in some cases, been successfully applied to reaching conclusions about the economy. You will see as we go on that although professional economists are trying to do what you were doing above—answering questions regarding economic issues—they are doing so in what will seem to you a different language, and by using a different methodology than yours. An important goal of this course is for you to learn to present your opinions about economic issues with a degree of economic professionalism.

Contribution of Economists to Society

To give you an idea of the contribution economists make to society, we list below some of the jobs economists do. You will see that the economist is involved in all areas of society, complementing the analyses done by other disciplines, and contributing to making decisions that will enhance the wellbeing of society.

After studying a course like this, and a few more courses in economics, economics majors end up applying their knowledge in many areas of the economy. The list of areas in which economists and others with a background in economics can work is long and varied: law, marketing, investment banking, commercial banking, securities brokerage, corporate finance, government, and business accounting. The greatest number of economists work for private business firms. The next-largest group holds teaching or research positions, primarily at colleges and universities. The third largest group of economists are employed by state, local, or federal government agencies. The median base salary is nearly $74,000 per year. Let's look at each group of economists separately.

Business economists interpret and forecast the general economic climate in which firms operate: What will happen to consumers' taste, how will consumer confidence react to price increases, and how do changes in general income affect consumer demand or future sales? They analyze survey data for consideration of a new product by assessing demand conditions in a potential market. Economists working for business firms have three sets of skills. First, they must have a good grasp of economics. Second, they need to be able to use and interpret sophisticated, quantitative models, which requires an understanding of statistics and mathematics. Third, they must be able to communicate effectively one-on-one, to groups, and in written reports. Banking, manufacturing, communications, and consulting firms are the primary employers of business economists.

Economists also work in government positions. In general, most economists agree that the market, left largely to itself, does a good job of allocating goods and services. At the same time, though, the surest way to generate jobs for economists is to have extensive government regulations. For example, it is hard to find economists who support the maze of regulations and programs the government has introduced in a purported effort to help farmers, but the U.S. Department of Agriculture—the agency that administers those programs—employs more economists than any other institution in the world.

The range of jobs for economists in government is as broad as government itself. One of the major policymakers for President Bush is Edward Lazear, an economist from Stanford University, who serves as chair of the Council of Economic Advisors. Economists are instrumental in the decisions the Justice Department and the Federal Trade Commission make about whether corporate mergers or other corporate actions should be opposed. They are at the center of cities' decisions on the impact of particular development projects on the city fiscal structure answering questions such as "How much government revenue will a particular development project bring in?" and "How much will it cost?" An economist trained in natural resource economics will probably conduct cost-benefit analyses of programs ranging from highway planning to human migration. They may conduct economic and environmental impact analyses of road building in ecologically sensitive mountain environments, or the impact of population growth on water demand and supply in Utah. Most resource economists study how market incentives guide environmentally compatible resource use. They analyze the implications of energy policy proposals. Many work for government agencies such as the Environmental Protection Agency (EPA). Economists with backgrounds in relevant natural science disciplines are particularly in demand.

Being an actuary is another possibility for an economist. An actuary projects the financial effects of various human events—birth, marriage, sickness, accident, fire, liability, retirement, and death—on insurance and other benefit plans. Actuaries work for large insurance companies, for the government (Internal Revenue Service or the Social Security Administration), for other private business, or as independent consultants.

The Economic Way of Thinking

Economics
The study of the allocation of scarce resources through the process of exchange.

What is **economics**? Economics is the study of how people make choices among the multitude of alternatives available to them. It is a study of choices made by individuals, business firms, and the government. All of us go through life faced with choices in all areas of our existence and economists examine the techniques and criteria we use in making those choices.

Economics of course is not the only discipline concerned with the analysis of individual choice. Sociologists, psychologists, and anthropologists (to name a few) are also disciplines where individual choice is important. What is different in the study of choice as done by economists? Some of the factors that are important and somewhat unique to economist's analysis of choice include:

Opportunity Cost
The value of the next best alternative to any activity.

1. The importance of costs and how they are defined. Economists consider that how individuals make choices is influenced by the value or benefits of alternatives that are foregone when any choice is made. Economists refer to these foregone values as **opportunity costs** and they argue that an understanding of such costs is essential in any examination of individual choices.

Marginal Analysis
Analysis based on the effects of small changes in an economic variable.

2. Individuals are motivated by the concept of optimization or maximization. Economists argue that the primary motivation for individuals to make choices is through the pursuit of self-interest through maximization of some objective subject to the constraints they invariably face. For instance, economists assume that consumers make choices in consumption based on the goal of maximizing their satisfaction subject to constraints on their income. Firms are assumed to choose output levels that maximize their profits and so firm behavior is analyzed under this assumption.

3. Optimization occurs as the result of the application of marginal principles. Economists believe that individuals make choices on the **margin**; that is, individuals make choices based on the effects of small changes in an economic variable. For instance, when a consumer is deciding how many apples to buy, economists maintain that the decision is based on marginal principles. The consumer will buy an additional apple (a marginal apple) if the additional benefit they expect to receive from that apple (called the marginal benefit, MB, of the additional apple) is greater than the benefit gained by the best alternative that could be purchased with the price of the apple (called the opportunity cost or the marginal cost, MC, of the additional apple). The rule is to engage in an additional unit of an activity if the marginal benefit of the activity is greater than the marginal cost of the activity. In this way, total benefits (TB) are increased more than total costs (TC), thus increasing total net benefits (TB-TC). Total net benefits are maximized when MB=MC, and a further increase in the activity, e.g., buying an apple, would cause MB to be less than MC. This idea can be explained mathematically if you have had some calculus. Don't be concerned if you don't have a calculus background; this is just another way to express the idea described in the previous paragraph. Periodically, throughout the text, we will introduce an exhibit referred to as a **Calculus Parallel**. These exhibits are intended to show those who are taking their first course in calculus how a particular economic concept would be treated using calculus. Again, do not be concerned if you are not taking a calculus course–the exhibits are just another way to view economic concepts.

Calculus Parallel 1-1
We are maximizing the quantity (TB - TC). Let Q represent our activity level, such as the number of apples purchased. In order to maximize the quantity (TB - TC) with respect to Q, we take its derivative and set it equal to zero; (dTB/dQ) - (dTC/dQ) = 0. Since (dTB/dQ) is simply MB and (dTC/dQ) is MC, (TB - TC) is maximized when MB - MC = 0, or MB = MC.

Economic Way of Thinking
The conceptual idea that behavior can be explained as a desire for optimization through use of marginal principles.

In the preface to this book, we noted that professional economists see microeconomics as a unified theory of human behavior, a theory centered around the concept of optimization through the application of marginal principles. This is what we economists refer to as the **economic way of thinking**. It is a problem solving approach or paradigm that allows economists to reduce many seemingly diverse and unrelated problems and phenomena (such as those we listed at the very beginning of this chapter) into a similar framework for analysis. It is not too much of an exaggeration to say that from an economics perspective there is really only one economic problem: How to optimize through careful use of marginal principles coupled with a good understanding of costs as opportunities foregone. We hope you will keep this in mind as we analyze a host of economic problems throughout this course.

Mathematical Skills

Economics can be a very mathematical discipline. It borrows a great deal from calculus and algebra and the diagrammatic analysis that goes with them. Proficiency in these areas will help you to understand how economists model economic phenomena. However, you don't need to be a math guru in an introductory macroeconomic course. You need to be able to use the most elementary methods which, in large part, you learn along the way and master by the end of the course. The two major methodological issues you will face are presented in this section via examples. Study these examples carefully and try to refer to them in your calculus and algebra courses in order to see that we are applying mathematical principles to the specific field of economics.

Example 1: Equations and meanings of lines, diagrams of lines, intersection of lines

Put yourself in algebra mode and think of a relation between a variable X and a variable Y. Call Y "wage" and denote it by W and call X "quantity of labor" and denote it by Q_S or Q_D, depending on whether we are referring to quantity demanded or quantity supplied. Think of the equation for a straight line and its diagram. In this example, we will be doing what you do in algebra when: a) given the equation of a line, you put X as a function of Y, or vice versa; b) you draw the line on a diagram with Y on the vertical axis and X on the horizontal axis; and c) you solve a system of simultaneous equations in two unknowns, X and Y.

Suppose an economist has observed that as the wage for work study students at UMR increases, the number of hours UMR wants students to work per week decreases. After some empirical analysis, the economist concludes that this relationship could be modeled by the following algebraic equation:

$$\mathbf{Q_D = 1000 - 20W} \qquad \text{(Equation 1.1)}$$

where Q_D is the number of hours of work study labor UMR wants to hire per week and W is the wage rate per hour. An alternative way of expressing the same linear equation is to put W as a function of Q_D, i.e.,

$$\mathbf{W = 50 - (1/20)Q_D} \qquad \text{(Equation 1.2)}$$

This equation is saying that the wage rate depends on the quantity demanded. We should interpret this as expressing how much UMR is willing to pay per hour when the amount of work study labor hired is Q_D.

Slope
The mathematical measure of the steepness of a curve, defined as the change in the dependent variable divided by the change in the independent variable.

It is conventional in economics to use the expression $W = 50 - (1/20)Q_D$ to draw the relation between wage and quantity on a graph. We draw the equation as a two-dimensional graph with Q_D being the X variable on the horizontal axis, and W being the Y variable on the vertical axis. The diagram for this curve can be seen in Figure 1-1 below, and corresponds to the curve denoted by D, used by economists to represent demand.

The **slope** of this curve is: rise/run = -1/20. Notice that the slope is the coefficient that goes before the Q_D in equation 1.2, and that it is the inverse of the coefficient on W in equation 1.1. The slope measures the rate of change of

W as Q changes by an infinitesimal amount. Along a straight line, this rate of change is constant, but varies along an equation that is not a straight line.

In general, monetary values such as price, costs, wages, interest rates, etc., when they are present in the discussion, will be represented on the Y (vertical) axis. Physical quantities per unit of time, such as hours of labor per week, quantity of land per year, quantity of apples per month, etc., will be represented on the X (horizontal) axis.

To continue with our example, consider that the economist also observes that as the wage increases, students want to offer more hours of work. This relationship is observed to be:

$$\mathbf{Q_S = 500 + 30W} \qquad \text{(Equation 1.3)}$$

where Q_S is the number of work study hours students want to work per week and W is the hourly wage rate. An alternative way of expressing the same linear equation is to put W as a function of QS i.e.,

$$\mathbf{W = -500/\ 30 + (1/30)Q_S} \qquad \text{(Equation 1.4)}$$

This equation says that the wage rate depends on the quantity supplied. We should interpret this as expressing the minimum students would want to receive per hour in order to offer Q_S hours of labor.

It is conventional in economics to use equation 1.4 to draw the relation between price, or in this case, the wage rate, and quantity. We draw the equation as a two-dimensional graph with Q_S being the X variable on the horizontal axis, and W being the Y variable on the vertical axis. The diagram for this curve can be seen in Figure 1-1, and corresponds to the curve denoted by S for supply. The slope of this curve is: rise/run = 1/30. Notice the slope is the coefficient that goes before the Q_S in equation 1.4, and the inverse of the coefficient that goes before W on equation 1.3.

We observe in Figure 1-1 that the two curves intersect. Notice that economists typically say "curve" even when the expression is a straight line. The economist would like to find out where exactly they intersect. We can find this out algebraically, or diagrammatically. We will do it algebraically in two equivalent ways.

1. Using the expression for the quantity demanded and supplied equations:

$$\mathbf{Q_D = 1000 - 20W \text{ and } Q_S = 500 + 30W}$$

notice that where the two curves intersect, quantity demanded equals quantity supplied, $Q_D = Q_S$ and the price, W, is the same in both curves.
Thus, it is true at the intersection that

$$\mathbf{Q_D = 1000 - 20W = Q_S = 500{+}30W}$$
$$\mathbf{\text{or } 1000 - 20W = 500{+}30W}$$

Figure 1-1
An Illustration of Graphing

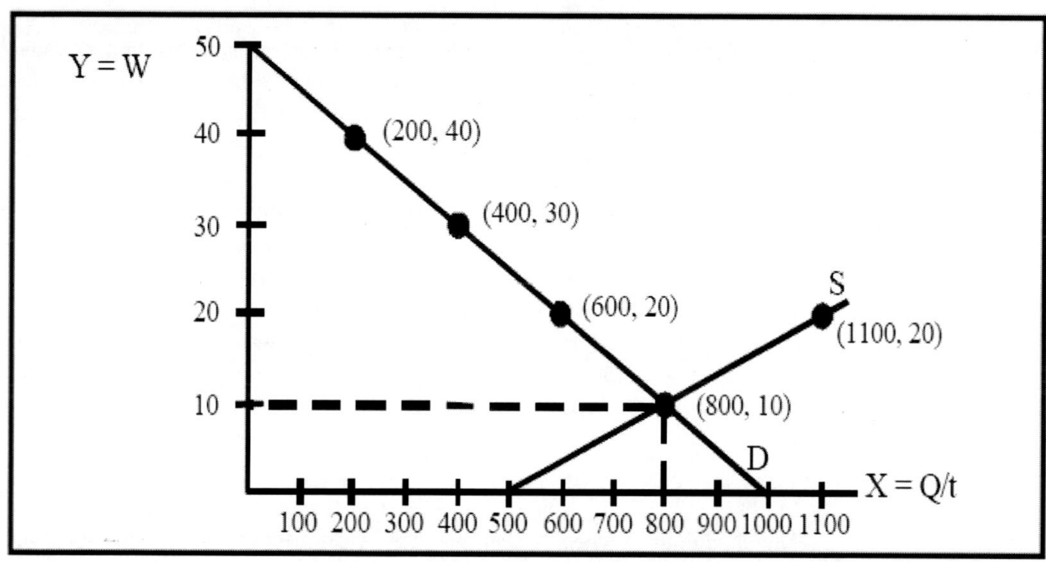

This allows us to solve for the common W:

$$\begin{aligned} 1000 - 500 &= 30W + 20W \\ 500 &= 50W \\ W &= \$10 \end{aligned}$$

Substituting this value into the demand or supply equation will give us the common $Q_D = Q_S$, that is,

$$Q_D = 1000 - (20 \times 10) = Q_S = 500 + (30 \times 10) = 800$$

This ends the problem using the quantity demanded and quantity supplied expressions.

2. Using the expression for the wage equations:

$$W = 50 - (1/20)Q_D, \text{ and } W = -500/30 + (1/30)\, Q_S$$

we can now find the same values using the alternative expressions for the price or the wage. Note that, at the intersection point, W is the same on both curves.

$$W = 50 - (1/20)Q_D = W = -500/30 + (1/30)Q_S$$

Since we know $Q_D = Q_S$, use just one name for both when solving for the intersection, Q:

$$\begin{gathered} W = 50 - (1/20)Q = W = -500/30 + (1/30)Q \\ Q = 800 \end{gathered}$$

Substituting this value into any of the equations gives us:

$$W = 50 - 1/20(800) = W = -500/30 + (1/30)(800) = \$10$$

Thus, the hourly wage rate is \$10. It should not surprise you that the answers with approach (2) are the same as with approach (1). The two approaches are equivalent, since they are based on equivalent forms of the same equations. What both say is that in the market for UMR work study students, supply and demand interact to yield a hourly wage of \$10 and quantity of hours of 800 per week. You will learn more about supply and demand in chapters to follow.

Example 2: Slopes or rates of change vs large changes in variables
The most important concept borrowed from calculus by economists is the slope or rate of change of a curve. The slope of a line was discussed in Example 1. Consider now a nonlinear equation. If the relation between a variable X and a variable Y is expressed by the equation:

$$Y = 10 - 25X^2$$

The change in Y when X also changes by an infinitesimal amount is given by the equation:

$$\Delta Y/\Delta X = 2 * (-25x)$$

whereΔ, delta, is the symbol to denote change, and the single * represents multiplication. This is the slope of the equation. It is itself an equation which tells us that as X increases, the rate of change of Y decreases (because 50 has a negative sign in front of it). Try to draw both $Y = 10 - 25X^2$ and $dY/dX = 2*(-25X) = -50X$ in two separate diagrams.

Calculus Parallel 1-2
The derivative of Y with respect to X is given by $dY/dX = 2*(-25X) = -50X$. This is the slope of the equation.

For those who have had the first course in calculus, review your calculus book for rules used in the differentiation of polynomials. We will from time to time use simple differentiation to provide illustrations of economic concepts. For those who haven't had your first calculus course yet, don't worry—everything done in this course with calculus can also be done using algebra. If you become concerned about the math, or anything else in the course for that matter, talk to your instructor, who is here to help you.

To offer an example related to microeconomics, consider what economists call a production possibilities frontier, given by the equation:

$$Y = 3L^2 + 4K^2 - 0.1X^2$$

where Y and X are outputs, L is available labor units and K is capital. Suppose L = 500 and K = 50. Upon substituting the values of L and K in the equation, we obtain:

$$Y = 760{,}000 - 0.1X^2 \qquad \text{(Equation 1.5)}$$

Draw this curve on a diagram with X on the horizontal axis and Y on the vertical axis.

This curve tells us that, given L and K, the production of Y declines when the production of X increases. Specifically, the rate of decline is given by the equation $\Delta Y/\Delta X = -0.2X$

Marginal Cost
The addition to total cost of engaging in an additional unit of an activity.

> **Calculus Parallel 1-3**
> The rate of decline is given by the derivative of Y with respect to X, $dY/dX = -0.2X$.

We know it is a rate of decline because the slope (derivative) is negative whenever X is positive. The curve you drew should also reflect this by being bowed out, or concave to the origin. In our course, this particular rate of decline will be called marginal opportunity cost or just marginal cost.

In general, the slope or rate of change of any curve, given by the derivative of the curve, will be given a name in microeconomics that will start with "marginal." We use the phrase "marginal cost" to refer to the slope of the total variable cost curve, "marginal revenue," to refer to the slope of the total revenue curve, and so on. When you see the word "marginal" remember that we are referring to the slopes or rates of change of some curve. It is important that you are able to identify the original curve, and not confuse the original curve and the curve that is given by the slope. They measure different things, as we have seen.

It is also important to distinguish between the concepts of marginal and average. While marginal is measured by the slope and tells us the rate of change of one variable Y with respect to another variable X, average can be thought of as the amount of Y per X. As discussed above, mathematically marginal can be thought of as $\Delta Y/\Delta X$ while average is measured as Y/X. The relation between the two concepts can be expressed as: average is increasing (decreasing, constant) when marginal is greater than (less than, equal to) average. The intuition is simple. Consider a case where you have a series of numbers whose average is given as M. Consider adding an additional number x (the marginal number) to the series. Clearly, the new average is less than (greater than, equal to) M as X is less than (greater than, equal to) M.

Qualifications

Sometimes we may give you the equation of a relation, and yet we may ask you to consider only big chunks of changes. For example, given the previous equation, we may ask you to consider how Y changes as X changes by a relatively large amount. Consider, for example the following points on the production possibility frontier obtained from equation 1.5.

Table 1-1

Point	X	Y
A	0	760,000.00
B	552.36	729,600.21
C	1102.72	638,400.86
D	2205.441	273,602.999
E	2756.809	0

Table 1-1 tells us how much Y decreases as X increases by 552.36. We can see that when X increases from zero to 552.36, Y decreases by 30,399.79, the difference between 760,000 and 729, 600.21. We may not be satisfied with this result, and may want to know what the average decrease is in Y as X increases from zero to 552.36. In that case, we compute:

$$\Delta Y \Delta X = -30{,}399.79 / 552.36 = -55.036$$

We can continue doing this along the curve, for example, until we reach the next 552.36 (i.e., passing from 552.36 to 1102.72 would result in a decrease in Y of 91,199.35). In this case, the average decrease in Y as X increases by another 552.36 is

$$\Delta Y/\Delta X = -91{,}199.35 / 552.36 = -165.108$$

which is larger in absolute value than the previous one. And so on. The ratio just found is not strictly the "marginal opportunity cost" although we call it that for convenience. It is actually an average of the "marginal opportunity costs" over an interval of change. If we made the interval of change very, very small, close to infinitesimal, then the expressions above for the average "marginal cost" would become the slope or rate of change that we compute using the derivative. For example, at point B, $dY/dX = -0.2X = (-0.2)*(552.36) = 110.472$, which is between the two "average" marginal costs we calculated above. Keep all this in mind. When you see tables of numbers, they come from some equation that has a derivative. When we compute changes in the numbers in the table, we are just approximating the infinitesimal changes implied by the derivative. We do that because sometimes it makes more sense to talk in terms of discrete quantities. After all, in the real world, we make our choices in a discrete fashion (one movie, two courses, etc.), although we live in a continuum.

Economists and Economic Models

The economy is a very complicated system. There are hundreds of millions of buyers and millions of businesses. Each economic relationship is somewhat unique. Economists try to get a handle on the key common factors and then try to predict what will happen in a given situation. That is, we not only try to understand how the economy operates but also to use that understanding to predict what will happen in a given situation. Toward that end, economists build models of the economy and its various parts that allow them to focus on the key relationships. The models are not intended to be complete pictures, but are instead designed to allow us to analyze the most important aspect of a particular situation. Building a model requires us to simplify the real world. Much of this course will consist of building and analyzing simple economic models based on assumptions that are only approximated in the real world.

Many students are disturbed by the prospect of making such economic assumptions. But this is really no different from many physical sciences you study, in which laboratory experiments are conducted while controlling for the variation in certain influential factors. The purpose of these experimental exercises, whether they are in economics, physics, chemistry, or another field, is to get at the basic truths that operate in a particular situation. Once the basic relationships are established, economists can modify the results to account for factors specific to that particular situation. Please bear with your instructor throughout the semester as he or she leads you through these models, and think about how the models apply to specific situations.

SUMMING UP

1. **Economics** may be defined as the social science that studies decisions under conditions of scarcity. Economists perform their functions by identifying alternative means through which people can provide for their material well-being.

2. When economists identify the alternative solutions to economic problems, they also point out the costs and benefits of each.

3. Economists are not necessarily more materialistic than other people. They do, however, insist on recognizing that most solutions to noneconomic questions require material resources (land, labor, capital, and entrepreneurship). Thus, these solutions are based in economic reality.

4. Economists interpret the problem of individual choice as a theory centered around the concept of optimization through the application of marginal principles. This is what economists refer to as the **economic way of thinking**.

5. This book contains some algebra and many graphs to help you visualize certain concepts. We also provide for those taking their first course in calculus, "calculus parallels," which shows how in particular economic concept would be treating using calculus.

6. The book makes a strong effort to avoid the use of "economese," or complex ways of wording economic principles. When technical terms first occur, they are defined and highlighted in margin notes.

KEY TERMS

Economics
Economic way of thinking
Slope
Economic models
Opportunity costs
Marginal costs
Marginal Analysis

Chapter 2: Scarcity, Efficiency, and Growth

In Chapter 1 we gave you a general introduction to economics, stated why we think studying economics is important for all students (not just economics majors), and explained a bit about what economists do and how they do it. Given these general ideas, you are now ready to begin thinking about how an economic system works. We begin with a basic assumption about the type of economy we have in mind. You have heard the phrase "free enterprise," which refers to an economy in which the factors of production, including land, labor, capital, and entrepreneurial skills, are privately owned. Individuals are free, within some limits set by society, to use the factors of production under their control as they see fit. That is, the economy's resources are allocated among all possible uses through private decisions, with little interference from the government. (Contrast this to "command" economies in which decisions are made by some centralized organization.)

Market System
The full set of means by which goods and services are exchanged.

In order to understand how these decisions are carried out in a free enterprise economy, you must first have a general idea of what is meant by the term **market system**. Whether you realize it or not, you are a frequent participant in markets. Perhaps your earliest exposure to the term was when you went to "the market" (i.e., the supermarket) with your family. It's likely that you also heard about the "stock market" at an early age. As a result, you probably think of a market as a physical location where things are bought and sold. While many markets are, in fact, single physical locations where buyers meet sellers, the term market actually applies to a much broader range of ways for buyers and sellers to interact. For example, you have probably purchased items from catalogs using a toll-free telephone number or through the World Wide Web. A market is therefore any arrangement that permits exchanges between buyers and sellers to take place, and a market system is the full set of means by which individuals or organizations offer or seek goods and services. Markets are the basic organizational feature of a free enterprise economy.

Adam Smith and The Invisible Hand

A key feature of markets is that participants act, for the most part, in their own interest. Sellers try to obtain the largest possible difference between the cost of acquiring the goods (either through production or from some other seller) and the amount of revenue taken in from the buyers of the goods. Buyers are trying to choose goods that will bring them the greatest possible benefits while staying within the limits imposed by their income or wealth.

You might think that because both buyers and sellers are looking out only for their self-interest, exchanges between a buyer and seller always yields one winner and one loser. That is not the case, as can be demonstrated fairly easily. If we assume that buyers act in their self-interest, we must conclude that voluntary exchanges with sellers makes buyers better off. Why would buyers buy something if it did not make them better off? Why would they give up something that is more valuable to them than what they receive in return? Similar reasoning applies to sellers. Therefore, assuming that both buyers and sellers are "rational" (more on this idea later in the book), and that the exchange does not involve fraud (i.e., each person knows what is being obtained in the exchange), a voluntary exchange makes *both* parties better off–or at least, no worse off. Furthermore, if society's goal is to achieve the greatest possible benefits for all participants, it should try to maximize the number of voluntary exchanges. As we shall see in the chapters to come, under the right conditions, a market system does just that.

Make no mistake–the phrase "under the right conditions" is very important in this context. Economists agree that markets can be used to achieve the most *efficient* result, a concept that we will define and explore in detail later in this chapter, but many recognize that it is not possible to force markets to recognize everything that is important to society. For example, the notion of equity or fairness is important in many situations, and it may be necessary to surrender some efficiency in order to obtain additional fairness. Some people claim that any market outcome is automatically equitable, while others believe that markets can never be made fair. Most economists reject both of these positions as being too extreme, concluding instead that some market outcomes are more fair than others; and that there is, in most cases, a trade-off between equity and efficiency. One job for economists is to determine the nature of the equity-efficiency trade-off so that society can arrive at what it believes to be the proper mix of the two.

A corollary argument is that markets move things toward those participants placing the greatest monetary value on them, and that things are put to their highest valued (by the market) uses. Why does farmland at a city's edge become a subdivision? Simply put, because that particular piece of land is more highly valued by the market as a place to live than as a source of crops. This important idea–that markets push our resources toward their highest-valued uses–will also be discussed in greater detail as the semester progresses. Once again, however, you must be mindful of the fact that markets may not be able to fully include everything that a society finds important.

Invisible Hand
The idea that a market system benefits society when individuals act in their self-interest.

Perhaps the most interesting aspect of these results of market activity is that they benefit society as a whole *even though the individual participants are simply promoting their self-interest, with no intention of "doing good" for society.* Adam Smith, whose milestone work, *The Wealth of Nations*, was published in 1776, was one of the first observers to note this tendency of markets. This observation has since become known as the **invisible hand** argument: markets benefit society as if some invisible hand were guiding them to do so. Of course, there is no actual guidance in a free market–just the interactions of self-interested individuals. These are important ideas to keep in mind as we study the details of the operation of markets and the market system. But we should first address a more basic question: "Why does it matter that resources get moved into their most highly-valued uses?" This question will occupy us for the remainder of this chapter.

The Unavoidable Implications of Scarcity

Scarcity
The condition caused by individuals' wants exceeding the capacity of available resources to satisfy them.

Resources
Things (inputs) used to make other things (outputs).

All societies, regardless of whether their economies are organized around free markets or are centrally controlled, must face a (frequently unpleasant) fact of life–the existence of **scarcity**. The essence of what economists mean when they use this term derives from two basic truths of our existence as humans. These are 1) there is a limited amount of **resources** available to society as it produces goods and services; and 2) human beings, acting individually or in groups, have desires for goods and services that are unlimited, or (perhaps more accurately) are much less limited than the available resources. Notice that we avoid using the word "need," which is much harder to pin down than "want." Of course, we know that humans have basic needs–food, clothing, and shelter–but most people in higher income countries are able to meet these needs. But do you need a steak dinner, or a $40 Tommy Hilfiger t-shirt, or a vacation condo at the beach? Certainly someone has said to you "Oh, you don't really need that!" Your likely response, whether or not you made it out loud, was "Of course I don't *need* it, but I sure do *want* it."

Before continuing our discussion of scarcity, let's first be sure you understand what is meant by "resources." A broad definition is that resources are the inputs we use to make or provide outputs of goods and services. More specifically, resources can be categorized as land, labor, capital, and entrepreneurial skills. Land includes everything you may think of as "natural resources"–land itself, on which we raise crops and build homes and factories; mineral resources, such as oil and metals; and all of free Goods the other things found in association with land, such as water and trees. Labor is human effort, including intelligence and the application of knowledge. Capital should be thought of as machinery and equipment used to make other things–factories and other buildings, tools, computers, etc. Entrepreneurial skill is essentially the ability to put the other resources together to produce a good or service desired by some members of society. We can collapse the four categories into two, by including land as a kind of capital, and entrepreneurial skills as a form of labor; the logic of doing so should be clear. In addition, some aspects of labor, such as education, can be included in capital, and is, in fact, referred to as "human capital." For our purposes, however, precise categories are not as important as an understanding of what is meant by the term "resources."

The clash between limited resources and relatively unlimited wants is what economists mean when they use the word "scarcity." Another way to think of scarcity is our inability to satisfy all human wants with our limited resources. A very important implication of scarcity is that in order to get one thing we must give up or forego something else. And it is equally important to understand that this idea applies not just to individuals, but to society as a whole.

A Scarcity-Free World?

To begin thinking about this implication, first consider a (hypothetical, of course) world in which scarcity does not exist. What would be true in such a world? Everyone could have everything he or she wanted, without having to give something up. **Free goods** are those which can be had in unlimited quantities at a zero price; that is, without having to give up something else.

Free Goods
Things that can be obtained in unlimited quantities at a zero price, or without having to give up something else.

You may be thinking that such goods are not hypothetical, citing perhaps air, or water. And you would be nearly correct. In most areas (not Los Angeles or Mexico City or Beijing), healthy air is in fact a free good. So is water, if you're willing to limit your drinking and bathing to rainy days, or if you live near an unspoiled river (not the lower Snake, or the Missouri). Or you may remember a free lunch, or ice cream served at the beginning of the school year. While that ice cream was "free" to you, it was not free to society. The resources devoted to producing it were no longer available to produce other things.

It is safe to say that there are few truly free goods; in almost every situation, you must forego one thing in order to get another. Put another way, "You can't have your cake and eat it, too," or, "There's no such thing as a free lunch." Let's now look at the implications of these facts of life.

Scarcity Leads to Three Basic Economic Questions

We have just concluded that few (if any) goods and services can be obtained without giving up something else, since resources are limited but wants are relatively unlimited, and we have used the term "scarcity" to describe that situation. Given this condition of scarcity, societies must find a way to answer a basic set of questions. These questions arise regardless of the type of economic organization used by a society, and the questions are answered differently in different systems. Although we will be concentrating this semester on the market system approach, do not think that only market economies must address these questions. Any kind of economic system faces scarcity, which means it must decide how its scarce resources are to be used.

Society must decide how to bridge the gap between individuals' unlimited wants and the limited resources available to satisfy them. There must be some way to determine how scarce resources ought to be used.

This requires that answers to the following questions be found:

1. **What to produce?** Which goods and services, and in what quantities, should we choose to produce with our limited resources? How many CDs, concerts, pizzas, restaurant meals, pencils, accounting services, computers, automobiles, haircuts, and so on, should be produced? We are limited in our choices by the available resources, as mentioned earlier, but also by the technology of production we have at our disposal.

2. **How to produce?** At a basic level, we must decide what sort of economic system to use–decentralized markets, or more centralized government controls. Also we need to decide how large the productive entities (firms, in a market system) will be and the types of productive technologies to be used. Will there be large firms with large factories or will a significant amount of production occur in backyards and garages? At the firm level, choices must be made, e.g., how many workers to hire, what technology to employ, etc.

3. **For Whom to produce?** How will we divide up the things that are produced? Will everyone get an equal share or will we tolerate large differences between rich and poor? While the other two questions have a political aspect, this one can be the most ontentious, since it involves notions of distributive justice or equity.

Use care in your understanding of the word "produce" in these questions. While we certainly include traditional production–making things, such as the examples listed in question 1–in the meaning, we also refer to something broader. For example, we generally do not think about "making" mean water, but if society chooses to maintain a higher level of water cleanliness in its rivers and lakes, doing so in most cases will require sacrificing some other things. For purposes of these three basic economic questions, you should therefore think of "production" in a broader sense: what we do with our scarce resources.

It is obvious that the answers to these questions are related to one another. For example, we will see that in a market system consumers are the ultimate authorities deciding which items get produced, and these decisions will have a large bearing on who gets the fruits of production. Furthermore, the production technologies chosen will determine how much of each item we will be able to produce with a given set of resources. An important purpose of this textbook, and the Econ 121 course, is to help you understand how our society chooses to answer these questions, and to understand the implications of the answers for economic efficiency and for the fairness of the results.

Analyzing the Choices Resulting From Scarcity: The Production Possibilities Model

Let's now take a more rigorous, quantitative look at the choices confronting society by using a numerical example stated in the context of, what economists call, the production possibilities model. Recall, from Chapter 1, that economists analyze many problems by constructing mathematical models that, while abstracting somewhat from reality, nevertheless capture the essence of the problem under consideration. We are about to do just that.

Our model is a simplified version of reality because it assumes that 1) there are only two products, or outputs produced by our hypothetical society, Newburgia; 2) Newburgia has only two resources at its disposal; and 3) technology is fixed. Our assumed possible outputs are wheat (denoted by "Y") and a composite of all other goods, which we will cleverly call AOG (all other goods, or "X"). Our inputs are labor (L) and capital (K); for simplicity, we'll include entrepreneurial capabilities and land under labor and capital, respectively, as was suggested in our earlier discussion of resources. Think of the capital input as machinery and equipment, or things that are not directly consumed but are instead used to make other things. These assumptions are obviously a simplified version of the real world, in which there are literally millions of possible outputs and a much wider variety of inputs. We could build our model to reflect these real-world numbers, but doing so would only complicate the model without allowing us to gain much (if any) additional insight.

Production Possibilities Frontier
A relationship showing the combinations of goods that can be produced in a given time period if an economy's resources are fully employed, using the best available technology.

In our model, then, Newburgia must select how much wheat and AOG to produce, given the capital and labor available to it, by using the best available technology of production. These possible combinations of outputs can be stated mathematically in the form of a **production possibilities frontier**, or **PPF**, which gives the combinations of outputs that Newburgia can produce in a given period of time when it is fully employing all of its resources and using the best available technology. The PPF is an equation, which for our purposes we will assume takes the following form for Newburgia for the current year:

$$Y = 2.5\ L^2 + 5\ K^2 - 0.3X^2 \qquad \text{(Equation 2.1)}$$

where Y is bushels of wheat per year, X is units of AOG per year, and L and K are the labor and capital resources described above. The coefficients of the equation effectively capture the technology, and the coefficients will change as technology changes (more on this point later in the chapter). The PPF thus describes the set of combinations of X and Y that can be produced using the available resources. We can also think of the PPF as telling us the maximum amount of one output that can be produced when we are producing a given amount of the other output.

To extend our example, assume that Newburgia has at its disposal a total of 200 units of labor (L = 200) and 200 units of capital (K = 200). Inserting these values into the PPF and performing the calculations yields a simpler version of the equation:

$$Y = 300{,}000 - 0.3X^2 \qquad \text{(Equation 2.2)}$$

Notice first that there is a negative relationship between X and Y; this means that along the PPF, as we increase the amount of X produced, we must produce less Y, or that to produce more X, there is a cost in terms of some amount of Y given up.

Notice also that the relationship is not linear. Using the tools discussed in Example 2 of the "Mathematical Skills" section of Chapter 1, we find that the rate of change of Y as X changes infinitesimally (the slope of the tangent at a given point along the curve) is given by the equation

$$\Delta Y/\Delta X = -\ 0.6X \qquad \text{(Equation 2.3)}$$

Equation 2.3 shows that the rate of decline of Y increases in absolute value as X increases. In graphical terms, the curve is bowed out, not linear. (See Figure 2-1 and the related discussion below.)

Marginal Opportunity Cost or Marginal Cost
How much of one good must be foregone or given up in order to obtain a small increment of another.

We call the absolute value of the slope of the PPF, or infinitesimal rate of decline of Y as X increases, the **marginal opportunity cost** or **marginal cost** of X in terms of Y, or, what is the same, how much Y must be given up in order to obtain an infinitesimal amount of X with the given resources and technology. In general, the "marginal opportunity cost" of any action, A, we take (be it sleeping, eating, going to a movie, working, studying) is the value of the best alternative foregone because we do A. Although we often drop the word "opportunity" and refer just to "marginal cost," it is important to remember that in economics "cost" is the value of the best opportunity given up.

In the particular context of the PPF, the marginal opportunity cost is given by the absolute value of the slope. Note that we could, as well, compute the rate of decline of X as Y changes, or the inverse of the slope. This would tell us how much X must be given up in order to obtain one infinitesimal increment in Y.

Calculus Parallel 2-1
The rate of decline in Y as X increases is given by the derivative of Y with respect to X, $dY/dX = -0.6X$ The rate of change in X as Y increases is given by the inverse of the derivative of Y with respect to X, $dX/dY = -1/0.6X = -5/(3X)$.

The rate of decline in Y as X increases is given by the derivative of Y with respect to X, dY/dX = -0.6X The rate of change in X as Y increases is given by the inverse of the derivative of Y with respect to X, dX/dY =-1/0.6X = -5/(3X).

We also pointed out in Chapter 1 that we are used to dealing with discrete quantities, so it would perhaps make more sense for us to talk about, say, four bushels of wheat rather than an infinitesimal increment in the amount of wheat produced. For this reason, we often use chunks of increments in the variables X and Y, with the understanding that these chunks are just intervals of the continuous curves, and that, in the limit, when the chunks become infinitesimal, the average rates of change they measure become the slope or derivative that we mentioned earlier. For convenience, in the context of the PPF, we also call those chunks "marginal opportunity costs," although they are really the average of the marginal costs of the different points in a discrete interval considered.

Table 2-1

Current Year Production Possibilities for Wheat and AOG for Newburgia

Point Label on Fig 2-1	Production of X (units of AOG)	Production of Y (bushels of wheat)	Marginal Cost of 200 more units of X	Marginal Cost of 1 more unit of X
A	0	300,000	n/a	n/a
B	200	288,000	12,000	120
C	400	252,000	36,000	
D	600	192,000		360
E	800	108,000	84,000	480
F	1,000	0		

Table 2-1 shows some calculations based on the PPF equation (2.2) given above, at intervals of 200 units of X. The fourth column (Marginal Cost of 200 more units of X) tells us how much Y we must give up to gain an additional 200 X; it is calculated by subtracting adjacent values of Y. The last column (Marginal Cost of 1 more unit of X) shows the amount of Y given up to gain 1 unit of X, and is calculated using the slope equation 2.3. To be sure you understand the calculations, fill in the blank cells in the last two columns of Table 2-1.

We can make some important observations based on Table 2-1. First, think about these numbers as illustrating a set of trade-offs between wheat and AOG. Compare point B to point A. This shows that when Newburgia produces 200 AOG, it can produce only 288,000 bushels of wheat, instead of 300,000. If the country wants to move from A to B, it will have to reduce wheat production by 12,000 bushels. If Newburgia wants to increase the production of AOG from 200 to 400, it will have to give up 36,000 bushels of wheat. If Newburgia wants to expand production from 400 to 600 AOG, it will have to reduce wheat output by 60,000 bushels. Notice that as the amount of AOG produced increases, the number of bushels of wheat that must be given up to get the same increment (200 units) increases. This means that the production of AOG is done at an opportunity cost that increases as production of AOG increases. Recall from our earlier discussion that this is the same information conveyed by equation 2.3–the slope, or marginal cost, increases as X increases.

One thing that we cannot determine from this table is exactly which point along the PPF will be chosen by Newburgia. If Newburgia operates under the market system, the choice would be made through the expression of consumers' relative preferences for wheat and AOG in the markets for these goods. Without information about these references, we cannot determine which point is chosen. We do know, however, that each of the points is efficient in the sense that Newburgia is getting the largest possible quantity of one good for a given output level of the other. We will discuss this particular property of the points on the PPF later in the chapter, but for now, let's engage in one of economists' favorite activities– drawing and analyzing graphs.

Graphing the PPF for Newburgia

A graph is simply a picture. As this semester proceeds, you will see many graphs, some of which will display data that is also presented in a table. An advantage of graphs is that it is often easier to see patterns in the data. Figure 2-1 is a graph of the data given in the first three columns (including the labels) of Table 2-1.

Figure 2-1

Newburgia Production-Possibilities Frontier, Current Year

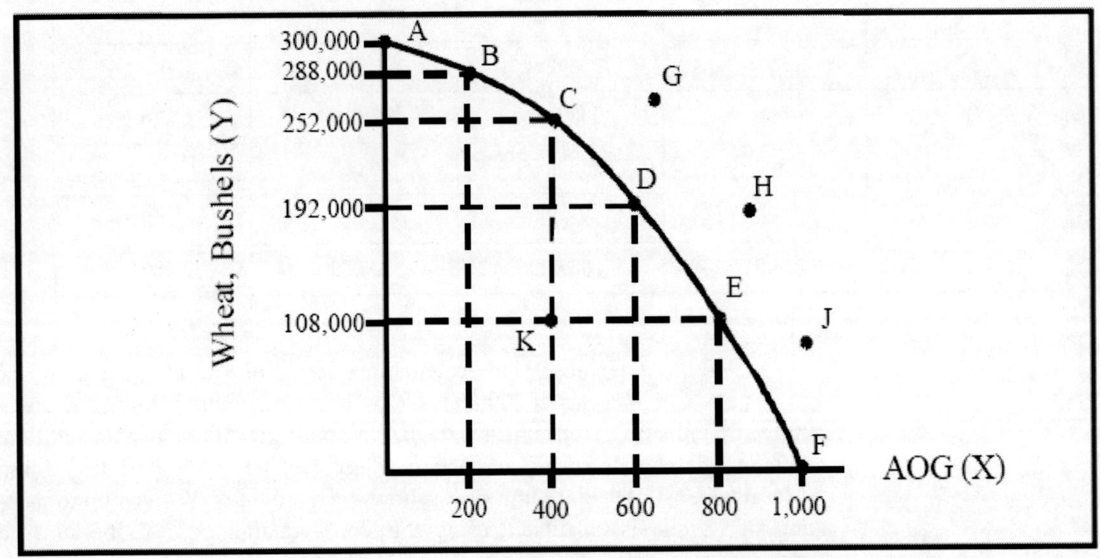

Point C in Figure 2-1, for example, represents a point on the PPF: 252,000 bushels of wheat and 400 AOG. Each of the combinations, A, B, C, D, E, and F is possible for Newburgia. The curve that passes through these points is called the production possibilities frontier (PPF), and is based on equation 2.2. Notice that the curve has a "bowed out" shape, or s concave with respect to the origin. In algebraic language, as we saw in Chapter 1, this means that the slope of the curve (the rise over the run) increases in absolute value as more AOG is produced. And as we saw earlier, the shape of this country's production-possibility frontier reflects the existence of increasing marginal opportunity costs. (Remember–the negative slope shows that opportunity costs exist, while the bowed-outward shape shows that they are increasing.) But why do marginal opportunity costs increase as more AOG is produced? This is the question to which we now turn.

Productivity of Resources in Production and the Shape of the Production-Possibilities Frontier

We have stated that marginal opportunity cost of one good (output) in terms of the other good (output) increases as we increase the production of either good, and we have incorporated this idea into Table 2-1 and Figure 2-1. The reasoning behind increasing marginal opportunity cost is fairly simple: most resources are more productive in some uses than in others. For example, although we speak of "land" as a single resource, it is clear that different parcels of land have different characteristics making it better for some uses than for others. Suppose we wanted to move along the PPF of Figure 2-1 from the upper left to the lower right, producing less wheat and more AOG. Suppose further that the production of AOG requires land for factories. We must therefore remove some land from wheat production. If we are smart, and we'll assume that we are, we will first convert land that is the least well-suited to wheat production, causing the smallest possible reduction in wheat output. But as we further increase AOG production, we will use land that is more and more productive for growing wheat. Therefore, each successive increase in AOG requires land that is more suited to wheat production than the land required by the previous increase in AOG production. The key to explaining increasing marginal opportunity costs is that a given unit of a resource has relative productivities in alternative uses that differ from other units of the same general resource type.

To be a bit more realistic, it is probably true that many units of a particular resource type are perfect substitutes in a number of uses. In an extreme case, if all units of all resources were perfectly substitutable for all uses, the PPF would be a linear function with respect to X and Y, and the PPF would be a straight line rather than bowed outward. (There would still be opportunity costs, but they would be "constant" rather than "increasing,"and our PPF would still have a negative slope.) We will simplify things by assuming that resources are either less than perfectly substitutable in each use over the entire range of output, as in our wheat-AOG example in Figure 2-1, or, that they are perfectly substitutable, and the PPF is linear throughout in all uses. See Chapter 4 for an example that uses fully linear PPF's.

Efficiency and Choice

As mentioned above, the process of decision making in a mixed (that is, free-enterprise with some influence from government) economy is quite complex, but we can give you an idea of the way economists view the process. What makes one outcome, or choice, better or worse than another? For most of us, at the personal level, the question is not hard to answer. A "C" on the first Econ test is better than a "D." An "A" is best of all. An enjoyable evening with the person of your choice is better than sitting at home watching sitcoms, even if they are your favorite shows. For society, however, choices are much harder to evaluate. Is point C in Figure 2-l with production of 400 AOG per year and 252,000 bushels of wheat per year better than or worse than point D, with more AOG and less wheat? Economists use the criterion of **Pareto efficiency** to judge such choices. "Pareto efficiency" was named in honor of the Italian sociologist and economist Vilfredo Pareto, who wrote about this problem around the turn of the century.

Pareto Efficiency or Efficiency
A situation in which no one can be made better off without making at least one other person worse off.

We define Pareto efficiency as the "inability to make someone better off without someone else being made worse off." Other terms used by economists for Pareto efficiency are "allocative efficiency," or just "**efficiency**." Notice that, by this definition, any combination of AOG and wheat that lets us increase production of one good without decreasing the production of the other is inefficient (like point K in Figure 2-1). An increase in wheat production (and consumption) without any decrease in AOG production clearly opens up the possibility of making someone better off without making someone else worse off. So, any point not on the frontier of the PPF is Pareto inefficient and judged bad by economists.

A comparison of points on the frontier, such as points C and D, is more difficult. Economists judge efficiency when there are gains and losses by adding the gains and losses across all persons affected. The move from C to D increases the production of AOG, but decreases the production and consumption of wheat. This move will surely offend some, but be praised by others. The economist asks those who favor the move, who might include persons allergic to wheat, "How much are you willing to pay for your gain?" Of those who would lose by the move–fans of Panera, owners of Subway franchises, or the wheat farmers of western Kansas–the economist asks, "How much compensation is needed to agree with the move?" If benefits, measured by the maximum gainers are willing to pay for their gains, exceed costs, measured by the minimum compensation losers need to offset their losses, the economist will judge the move from C to D efficient and thus good for society. If the gainers cannot bribe the losers, then the move is judged inefficient and bad for society. Note that for a move to be considered good by economists, it is not necessary that compensation actually be paid, just that there is the potential for making full compensation and having something left over. There remains much to be said, and explained, about efficiency, and the topic will come up again and again throughout the text, but for now let's return to the production-possibilities model.

Attainable (but Inefficient) Points

Although we have concentrated thus far on points that are on the PPF, and therefore represent the maximum possible production of one good given a production level for the other, it is entirely possible for an economy to produce inside the curve, at point K, for example. Point K represents the same level of AOG production as point C, but far less wheat production, or the same level of wheat as point E, but far less AOG. Of course, it would be possible for Newburgia to produce more of each good relative to point K. In fact, any point that lies "inside" the PPF shares this characteristic with point K. Obviously, Newburgia is not maximizing one of the outputs given the level of output of the other good–at point K, Newburgia is being inefficient. Why might this be true?

Idle and Inefficiently Used Resources

Employment
For a resource, a state of being used in the production of output.

Before continuing our discussion of how an economy might be at a point like "K," which we have just called an inefficient point, we should first define a few terms. Economists use words in fairly precise ways that may or may not reflect their meanings in common usage. First consider the concept of **employment**, which to most people has something to do with a person working at a job. Our definition is broader than that, because we are interested in the use of all resources, not just labor. Accordingly, we define employment to be the state of being used in the production of output. If you have a job, you are employed. If land is under agricultural cultivation, or even if it just has a parking lot on it, it is employed.

To be on the production possibility frontier, it is not necessary for all resources to be fully employed in a literal sense. After all, we could work more if we wanted to, but we value our leisure time too, and everyone needs at least a few hours of sleep each day. In fact, we could use a PPF model to analyze the choice between leisure time and everything else. All retail stores could remain open 24 hours a day, but we do not require that before we consider the building to be fully employed.

Let's look at the labor resource, for example. The labor force is defined loosely as those 16 years or older who work for pay (the employed) and those who are not working for pay but are actively seeking work (the unemployed). Since in a dynamic economy some people are always in the process of moving from job to job, economists consider labor to be fully employed when the unemployment rate (the percent of the labor force that is unemployed) falls to some minimum value. There is no consensus about the precise minimum value, but most would agree that it is greater than zero and less than 5 percent. When we experience an unemployment rate of 24.9 percent as we did in the Depression year of 1933 we are clearly in the interior of our production possibilities. The second most dramatic instance of being inside the PPF occurred in the period 1980-82 when the unemployment rate reached a high of 9.5 percent. And while people who have become discouraged (for whatever reason) and stop searching for a job are not counted in official labor statistics as unemployed, they would work if given the opportunity. In this sense, the official unemployment rate may understate the true extent of unemployment of the labor resource.

Unemployment
For a resource, a state of not being used in the production of output.

Underemployment
For a resource to be underemployed, they must be employed at a use less valuable than they could be.

In contrast to employment, **unemployment** is the state of not being used to produce output. It is possible for any resource to be unemployed, but society is most concerned about labor. This is in part because of the human suffering that frequently accompanies unemployment, but it is also because once we fail to use a unit (hour) of labor, it is gone forever. This is in contrast to a unit of a raw material, such as coal, which will be there tomorrow if we don't use it today. Similar to unemployment is **underemployment**, which means that some units of the nation's resources are not fully employed or, they are not employed at their most valued use. For example, suppose people who want to work full-time can only find part-time jobs or, suppose they are employed full time, but their hours would be more valuable with another job. Although employed, these people would be more productive if used in more appropriate job opportunities; therefore, underemployment can exist even though the nation may attain what appears to be full employment.

In order to learn more about these issues, take Principles of Microeconomics or Labor Economics. For our purposes in this course, you should understand that the presence of either unemployment or underemployment means that society is not producing its maximum possible output–it is not on its Production Possibilities Frontier. While it is difficult to always be on the PPF, we'd like to stay as close as possible. That is, we want the economy to operate as closely as possible to a Pareto efficient level.

From Unattainable to Attainable: Economic Growth, or What Causes the PPF to Move Over Time?

Points G, H, and J in Figure 2-1 lie outside the current PPF for Newburgia. This means that these combinations of wheat and AOG cannot be produced given Newburgia's current level of available resources and technology. Is there anything Newburgia can do to allow it to reach these points in the future? What might make them fall on or inside the PPF in the future? There are three basic possibilities, each of which would cause an outward shift in the PPF:

1. The amounts of resources (land, labor, capital, and entrepreneurship) at Newburgia's disposal increase.

2. The technology with which Newburgia converts its resources into outputs improves, allowing the country to get more outputs from the same number of resources.

3. The country chooses to produce more capital, both physical capital such as machines, and human capital through education, and fewer other goods. This decision to increase the capital stock at the expense of other goods will allow Newburgia to produce more of all things in the future. Since this action results in having more resources available in the future, it is quite similar to the first item on this list.

Economic Growth
An increase in the potential output of all goods and services.

Any of these occurrences or actions will allow Newburgia to increase its outputs of both goods in the future. Outward shifts in the PPF are also known as **economic growth**. In terms of our example PPF equation 2.1, increases in resource amounts are increases in the K and L values, which will, in turn, increase the value of the "intercept" of equation 2.2. Improvements in production technology will affect the coefficients on the K and L variables in 2.1, or perhaps will affect the coefficient on the X term in 2.1. In any case, the result of any of these three items on Figure 2-1 will be to shift the PPF outward, thus increasing the area under the curve, and making more choices of wheat-AOG combinations (such as G, H, and J) available to Newburgia.

It should be noted that if the reverse of any of the three factors occurs, the PPF will shift inward, reducing Newburgia's choices. What real-world events might lead to such an inward PPF shift? An obvious example is the European Black Plague of the 1300s, which killed about one third of the population–drastically reducing the availability of labor resources. Another is a devastating natural catastrophe such as an earthquake, which destroys factories and office buildings–"capital" resources. The flood of 1993 on the upper Mississippi River that wiped out, at least temporarily, many capital resources–acres of farmland and flood plain structures is another example. It is important to distinguish these events, which cause the entire PPF to shift inward, from unemployment and underemployment, which do not shift the PPF but instead put the economy at an inefficient point inside it.

The third item on our list–shifting production toward capital goods and away from consumer goods–brings up a question we addressed earlier, namely, which point on the PPF will (should) be chosen. Suppose that we replace wheat in Table 2-1 and Figure 2-1 with capital goods. As we pointed out above, increasing the production of capital goods today will increase the rate at which the PPF shifts outward. Some commentators believe that the U.S. saves far too little of its national income. Put another way, it is feared that the U.S. channels too little of its output into capital goods, especially in comparison to Japan, which has a relatively high savings rate. These fears are correct in the sense that lower capital goods production leads to a slower outward shift in the PPF for the U.S. over time. But it may be that our combination of capital and consumer goods is correct, given the relative strengths of our preferences for consumption today versus consumption tomorrow. So, one valid reply to the critics of the low savings rate in the U.S. is, "So what?" Remember, as long as we are producing on (or very near) our PPF, we can consider ourselves efficient in the Pareto sense. Of course, these commentators may understand this and are actually criticizing the U.S. preference for current over future consumption. (That is a valid discussion, but the appropriate role for economists in the debate is to determine how much future consumption is being foregone.) Economists are no more knowledgeable than others in deciding what is the appropriate level of willingness to exchange present consumption for future consumption.

Economic Institutions and Policies: Important Determinants of the Rate of Output Growth

Growth of output will occur as the PPF shifts to the right, or as the economy moves from a point like K in Figure 2-1 to a point on or closer to the frontier. Newburgia is, of course, a fictional society but choices such as point K are all too frequent according to a 1996 article by economist Mancur Olson, Jr. Olson, in his survey of evidence on why per capita incomes in the richer countries are more than twenty times as high as in the poorest, contends the cause is not lack of resources or technology, but the lack of a structure of incentives that lead to a location on the frontier. The nature of a country's incentive structure depends on the economic policies chosen in each period, and on the society's **economic institutions**: a legal system that enforces contracts and protects private property, a viable political system, constitutional provisions, and the extent of special interest lobbies.

Economic Institutions
Social arrangements governing decision making in production and consumption.

The most important institutional factor affecting economic incentives is a society's policies governing **property rights**, which are defined as the ability to exercise control over the use of objects or ideas. If a society has a set of rules that allows people to possess such rights, and to buy and sell them if they so choose, resources will tend to flow to their most highly valued uses, as determined by the interaction of supply and demand in the market. And if resource owners (or potential purchasers) are given the opportunity to profit from the way they manage their resources, they will have the incentive to manage them in the fashion that brings the greatest benefit to the owners. One implication of this is that if a resource owner can obtain a greater benefit by selling the resource than by retaining ownership, the resource will go to its highest valued use. And as we suggested earlier in our discussion of the invisible hand concept, this attempt by individuals to get the greatest possible benefit for themselves will, in many situations, lead to the greatest benefit to society as a whole. (In Chapters 8, 9, and 10 we will examine situations in which the pursuit of private gain does not lead to the greatest social good.)

Property Rights
The ability to exercise control over the use of objects or ideas.

As Professor Olson has suggested, countries that do not fare very well, especially those who do poorly despite having rich resource endowments, are likely to benefit from changes in institutions that lead to more individual control over those resources. On the other hand, changes in institutional arrangements that erode individual incentives can have a deleterious effect on efficient resource management. The ultimate impacts are on an economy's position relative to its current PPF and the speed with which the PPF shifts outward over time.

SUMMING UP

1. A private-enterprise economy based on the **market system** is one in which individual owners decide how to use the **resources** they own. By allowing such

decentralized decision-making, which is generally motivated by self-interest considerations, we create a tendency for the **invisible hand** property of markets to yield the greatest social benefit.

2. **Scarcity** arises as a result of the clash between a society's limited resources and its members' (relatively) unlimited wants. It requires society to choose how to use its limited resources, since producing one thing means that something else must be foregone. This leads in turn to the concept of **opportunity cost**, or **marginal opportunity cost**, which is the highest valued alternative that is foregone when choosing to produce something from the limited resources.

3. Scarcity forces a society to answer three fundamental economic questions about how to use its scarce resources: (a) What (and how much of each) to produce? (b) How to produce (which economic system and technology)? and (c) For whom to produce? These are not independent questions, since our answer to one will likely limit our possible answers to the others.

4. A tool used by economists to analyze the tradeoffs resulting from scarcity is the **production-possibilities frontier (PPF)**. This analytical device shows us all of the feasible combinations of outputs that a society can produce given its current resources (when fully **employed**) and best available technology. The negative relationship between outputs along the PPF illustrates the existence of **marginal opportunity cost** (or simply, marginal cost)–what we give up of one good in order to produce an additional increment of another. The curve is usually drawn under the assumption of increasing marginal opportunity cost–as additional units of a good are produced, increasing amounts of another good must be foregone for each additional unit of the good whose production is increased. This is another way of saying that resources are generally more productive in some uses than in others, and as we increase production of a good, we must use resources that are relatively less suited to its production. Graphically, this yields a PPF that is bowed outwards from (concave to) the origin.

5. A society may be operating at a point that is on the PPF. We say that all such points are **efficient** relative to points inside the PPF, but the PPF alone cannot tell us which point will actually be (or should be) chosen by a given country. An economy may also produce at a point inside the PPF, a situation caused by the **unemployment** or **underemployment** of resources.

6. **Economic growth** (shown as an outward shift of the PPF) occurs as a society experiences an increase in the amounts of resources available, an improvement in technology (allowing it to get more out of a given amount of resources), or by shifting current production toward more capital goods and fewer consumer goods.

7. How well an economy functions, in the sense of how close to the PPF it operates and how rapidly the PPF shifts outward, depends critically on a society's **economic institutions** and other economic policies. Economic performance can be enhanced by a good institutional structure or retarded by a poor one. One important element of institutions and policy is an economy's treatment of **property rights**.

KEY TERMS

Market System
Invisible Hand
Scarcity
Resources
Free Goods
Production-Possibilities Frontier
Marginal Opportunity Cost
Marginal Cost
Pareto Efficiency
Employment
Unemployment
Underemployment
Economic Growth
Economic Institutions
Property Rights

Chapter 3: Resource Allocation through the Forces of Supply and Demand-An Overview

Chapter 2 made the point that scarcity is a fact and we are forced to make choices. The chapter also argued that efficiency is an important criterion for evaluating decisions that must be made. Now, we introduce two principles that are very important in understanding how decisions are made, and whether the choices are efficient. These two principles are supply and demand. Supply and demand analysis is a fundamental tool for explaining how decisions are made, and for evaluating the efficiency of these decisions. We make many decisions at the personal level almost intuitively. What should we have for dinner tonight? Should I go to the movie this evening, or study for my econ exam? Other personal decisions are more carefully thought out primarily because the stakes are higher. Should I go to college or not? Is engineering really what I want to do? If I ask the big question, what will she (or he) say?

Other decisions are collective in that they require collective action–members of a club must decide whether to raise fees; a local neighborhood wonders whether incorporation into an existing city is in their interests; citizens wonder whether to vote for or against a proposed school bond, or which candidate to support in the next election.

These decisions, both personal and collective, involve consideration of opportunity costs and expected benefits. As we will see, these are the backdrops of the concepts of supply and demand respectively. To illustrate the basic principles of supply and demand, we will use a hypothetical market–the market for hours of student assistant work. To keep the discussion as simple as possible without losing sight of our objective of understanding the basics of supply and demand, we will focus on a competitive market, and four participants–two buyers and two sellers.

Competitive Markets

Competitive Markets
The market form in which neither the buyer nor seller has significant influence over the terms at which the product is sold.

Markets are institutional arrangements where people can trade to their advantage. Originally, the term was taken to mean a gathering place where people could trade their wares usually through a barter system, one unit of my good for so many units of your good. Today, markets typically symbolize exchanges of goods or services at agreed upon prices, so many dollars or Euros, and provide the framework for the analysis of the forces of supply and demand, that, together determine the quantities exchanged per period and the terms of the exchange.

Throughout this chapter, we will assume that markets are competitive, by which we mean neither buyer nor seller has much influence on the terms of trade that we summarize into a single value called the price. We will also assume the market under consideration, here the market for hours of student assistant work, is without government influence and governed solely by the informed self-interest of the participants–the buyers and sellers.

Our assumption that individual buyers or sellers have little or no influence on price is not too far off the mark in many instances. For example, as a buyer, for most purchases, you are rarely in a situation where you can influence the price by your decision to buy or not. You go to the store and decide to buy, or not buy, so many units of a specific good at a specified price. The haggling that may take place as you consider whether to buy a used car, or a dresser at a yard sale, is the exception rather than the rule. On the other hand, sellers are typically in a position whereby they can influence the price. After all, they are the ones that attach price tags to the items they sell. Often, however, the ability to attach prices does not translate into a significant influence on those prices.

For example, the downtown gas station posts its per gallon price perhaps daily, but knowing there is significant competition has little flexibility in their decision. For our discussion in this chapter we also assume buyers and sellers are informed and motivated solely by their self-interest without any constraints imposed collectively. In the context of our hypothetical market for hours of student assistance, these assumptions mean the professors who are willing to pay for these hours are informed about the quality of work performed, how much they will have to pay, when students will be available, and so on. Students who offer their hours are also informed about the consequences of their decision. They know what type of work is expected, the periods they will be called on to work, the pay they will receive, and the value of the opportunities given up if they decide to work.

The assumption of no constraints imposed collectively means that, for now, we will ignore such complexities as taxes that would have to be paid on student earnings, or price controls such as a minimum wage law. Later in this chapter, we will look at the consequences of price controls.

The Principles of Demand

Demand
A relationship between the quantity of an item demanded per period and the price of that item, or the relationship between an item and the willingness to pay for that item, ***ceteris paribus***.

The most common definition of "demand" as given in a standard dictionary is "to claim as a right." This is emphatically not what we mean by demand in economics. Depending on the context, we will speak of individual demand or market demand. We will talk about the law of demand, a demand curve, or a demand schedule. In economics, regardless of context, **demand** refers to either a relationship between price and quantity demanded per period, or a relationship between a particular good or service and a person's willingness to pay for that good or service. To be precise as possible we make another assumption, the **ceteris paribus** assumption. *Ceteris paribus* is Latin for "other things being equal," but it is used to mean we are assuming a relationship between specific variables when all other important influences are held constant. In effect, we are making an effort to mimic the scientist and their method of controlled experiments.

Ceteris Paribus
The (other things being equal) assumption that involves holding other significant factors constant while permitting a key variable to change.

Table 3-1 shows the demand schedule for one of our two professors, let's call him Professor Bob, in our hypothetical student assistant market. The demand schedule displays the number of hours per week Professor Bob is willing to hire at a number of different wages holding constant all other relevant variables, i.e., the *ceteris paribus* assumption.

Table 3-1
Professor Bob's Demand Schedule

Price (Wage) per Hour	$6	$4	$2	$0
Quantity (Hours) Hired per Week	0	4	8	12

Demand Schedule
A table showing the quantity of a good consumers are willing to buy over a period at each of several prices, *ceteris paribus*.

Law of Demand
There is an inverse relationship between the quantity demanded and price *ceteris paribus*. That is, a greater quantity of the good is demanded at lower prices and a smaller quantity at higher prices.

There are a number of things about Professor Bob's demand schedule that illustrate the principles of demand.

1. There is an inverse relationship between the price and quantity demanded. This relationship is so systematic it is referred to as the **law of demand.**

2. The relationship is time specific. In this case, the period is a week.

3. The relationship may be viewed in two equally valid ways: as the quantity demanded at a given price; or as the maximum a person is willing to pay for a given unit. For example, at $2, Professor Bob is willing to hire students for eight hours of work, or Professor Bob is willing to pay a maximum of $2 for the eighth hour of work.

4. There is a price above which the person is not interested in buying. Bob would not be in the market if the wage were to rise to $6.

5. The demand schedule shows a ceteris paribus relationship. That is, everything affecting Professor Bob's demand, other than the student wage, is held constant as the wage rate changes.

Calculus Parallel 3-1
The slope of the demand curve is given as the derivative of price with respect to quantity demanded, dP/dQ. The Law of Demand can be stated as $dP/dQ < 0$.

What are some of the factors that are being held constant as we examine Professor Bob's demand for student assistance? Bob's demand for student assistant hours is the relationship between the hours he is willing to hire and the price he must pay, but surely there are other factors that affect this relationship. There is likely to be a host of variables that are relevant in determining the demand for a good or service, but we will single out five for special consideration. Perhaps most important is Bob's available funds. How much does he have to hire students? Typically, a person's income, or wealth, will affect their demand for goods and services.

Substitutes
Two goods related in such a way that there is a direct relationship between the price of one good and the demand for the other. If the price of one good goes up, the demand for the related good goes up, *ceteris paribus*.

Complements
Two goods related in such a way that there is an inverse relationship between the price of one good and the demand for the other. If the price of one good goes up the demand for the related good goes down, *ceteris paribus*.

Demand Equation
An equation that demonstrates the relationship between the quantity demanded of a good and all hypothesized determinants of that good.

Demand Curve
A representation of a demand schedule graphically with price measured on the vertical axis and quantity demanded per period on the horizontal axis.

Further, since this money is probably available for other things, another factor in influencing Bob's demand for student hours is his consideration as to how important these other things are relative to the work the student will do for him. We refer to these types of considerations under the heading of tastes or preferences. Often the mark of a good economic researcher lies in his or her ability to find measurable variables to proxies for tastes or preferences. For example, a researcher may use temperature as a stand in for taste if investigating the demand for ice cream.

These other things, e.g., travel, books, etc., that Professor Bob could buy with his available funds have a price, so it is likely the price of these other things will affect Bob's demand for student hours. Whether a higher price for a good such as a book affects Bob's demand for student hours, depends on how Bob views the relationship between student hours and the other commodity. When an increase in the price of some related good raises the demand for the good under examination, we say the goods are **substitutes**. When an increase in the price of a related good lowers the demand for the good under examination, we say the goods are **complements**.

A last general factor likely to influence the demand for a good or service is the consumer's expectations. If the price is expected to increase in the near future, this may induce consumers to buy now, an increase in demand. If Bob feels students next semester will be willing to work for less than they are willing to work for today, he may postpone his research and lower his demand for student assistant hours.

These five factors: income, tastes, prices of substitute goods, prices of complementary goods, and expectations are important considerations affecting a person's demand for a specific good or service, however, we are usually more interested in the demand by a group of persons–the market demand– rather than an individual's demand. To account for the size of the market, we often use population, or the number of consumers. An easy way to remember the important factors affecting market demand is by the acronym PINTE. Using this acronym, the market **demand equation** for a particular good, x, may be written:

$$\mathbf{Q_{DX} = Q(PINTE)}$$

That is, the per period quantity demanded of Q_{DX}, is a function of, or depends on the factors represented by the symbols **P**, **I**, **N**, **T**, and **E**, where **P** stands for Prices (the price of the good itself, the price of substitutes for the good, and the price of complements to the good), **I** stands for income, **N** for the number of buyers, **T** for tastes or preferences, and **E** stands for expectations about future prices and market conditions.

Figure 3-1 represents Bob's demand schedule as a **demand curve** symbolized by $\mathbf{d_{Bob}}$. Notice the lowercase "d." We use lowercase to distinguish individual demand curves from market demand curves symbolized by uppercase "D." Before we go on, there are a couple of things to note about the relationship between the demand schedule shown in Table 3-1 and the demand curve shown in Figure 3-1. First, the demand schedule is discrete, but the curve is continuous. This says that, strictly speaking, only points E, C, O, and N are identified on the demand curve, so the demand curve drawn from the data in Table 3-1 would be represented by four points rather than a line. We use continuous curves because they are easier to work with mathematically, particularly if the curve is a straight line, or linear.

You remember the equation for a straight line, $\mathbf{y = mx + c}$, where c is a constant, and $\mathbf{m}$ is the amount of rise or fall of the dependent variable, y, per unit of the independent variable, x. A straight line demand curve can be represented by the equation:

$$\mathbf{q_{dx} = a - bP_x}$$

Figure 3-1

Professor Bob's Demand Curve

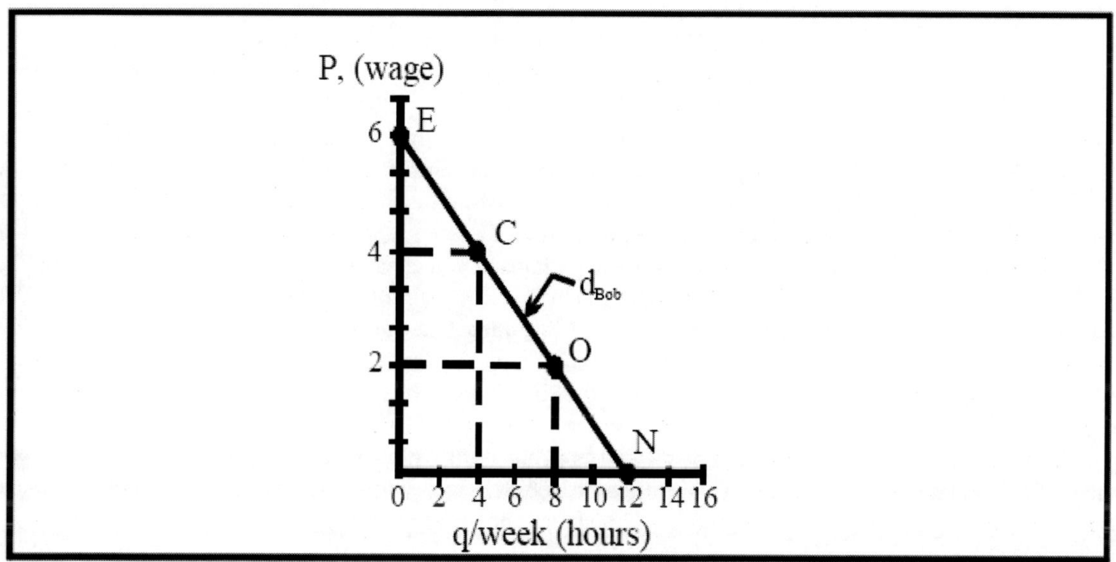

where $\mathbf{q_{dx}}$ is the quantity demanded of x per period (week in this case),**a** is the horizontal intercept (12 hours per week) that represents the number of units that would be purchased due to considerations other than the price, and **b** is the slope, or the change in the quantity demanded due to an infinitesimal change in price, $\mathbf{P_x}$. For the example given in Figure 3-1, the equation is:

$$\mathbf{q_{dx} = 12 - 2.0P_x}$$

Plug in some prices from the demand schedule given in Table 3-1 to see that the equation works.

The second thing to note about the demand curve representation of Figure 3-1, is the labeling of the axes. Usually, mathematicians put the dependent variable, y, on the vertical axis and the independent variable, x, on the horizontal axis. Isn't the quantity demanded dependent on price, and so should go on the vertical axis? Yes and No. The quantity demanded is dependent on price, but we can also view the demand curve as revealing the maximum amount a person will pay for the first, second, and subsequent units of a good per period. In this interpretation, we have a price equation with price as the dependent variable.

The fact that the demand curve in Figure 3-1 slopes downward to the right reflects the law of demand. *Consumers buy more of a product at relatively low prices than at relatively high prices, ceteris paribus.* This is one of the few economic phenomena that economists refer to using the word "law." Although there are theoretical exceptions, economists have yet to find a good for which a higher price today leads to higher consumption today, ceteris paribus. You might be tempted to conclude that this law is violated, for example, in the stock market—after all, isn't there such a thing as a buying frenzy, in which a rising price for a given company's stock leads people to buy more of the stock? While that does occur, it really doesn't violate the law of demand because the rising stock price is changing people's expectations about the stock's future price. As we pointed out earlier, expectations about future prices are one of the many factors held constant—that is, not allowed to change—when we draw a demand curve.

Why are Demand Curves Downward Sloping?

What is the basis for the law of demand? Let's first consider an individual demander. Why do you buy something? Economists would say that you buy something because you derive more satisfaction from that product (or service) than you could get from any other use of the amount of money in question. Furthermore, as you get additional units of a particular good in a given period (say, pizzas per week), the additional amount of satisfaction you derive from yet another unit of the good is less than the additional amount of satisfaction you received from the previous unit.

That is, the eighth pizza you consume this week, while increasing your total satisfaction, does not increase your total satisfaction as much as the seventh pizza did. Now, we are assuming that you are rational, so we would conclude that you would be willing to give up less to get the eighth pizza than you would have to get the seventh. Put another way, your willingness to pay for the eighth unit is less than that for the seventh. Therefore, your demand curve for pizza, which can be viewed as a **marginal willingness to pay curve** slopes downward. In the case of Professor Bob, we are assuming he feels the fourth hour of student assistant work will be more valuable to him than the fifth, so he is not willing to pay as much for the fifth hour as for the fourth hour. Economists use the phrase "diminishing marginal utility" for this idea that satisfaction decreases with additional purchases.

Marginal Willingness to Pay Curve
A view of the demand curve vertically, that is, the maximum any person is willing to pay for each successive unit.

What about a product that most people buy only once in a given period? Many principles of economics students have difficulty with the idea of an individual's demand curve, because they think about products that are bought only infrequently. They say, "I only want one car or personal computer, given my current lifestyle; I wouldn't buy two or three cars in a year no matter how low the price is." Suppose that the consumer's decision is whether to buy one or zero personal computers in the time specified. Then, we can identify each consumer's maximum willingness to pay for one computer, which would be the price above which the consumer would not buy the item this period. It is almost certain that each consumer will have a different maximum willingness to pay. As the market price of the computer falls, it will fall below more and more consumers' willingness to pay. Therefore, more computers will be sold as the price falls—consistent with the law of demand. In this instance we need to think in terms of the entire market demand for the product rather than just an individual's demand. Later in this chapter you will learn how to derive the market demand curve for a product of which each consumer buys more than one in the relevant period.

Change in Demand
A shift of a good's demand curve due to a change in any factor other than the price of that good.

Change in Quantity Demanded
A movement along a good's demand curve caused only by a change in the price of that good.

Changes in Demand and Changes in Quantity Demanded

A **change in demand** occurs only when a demand determinant **other than** the price of the good itself changes. At each price, demand is either more or less. Graphically, the demand curve shifts to the right for an increase in demand and to the left for a decrease in demand. When the price of the good itself changes, we move along a given demand curve and refer to these changes as **changes in the quantity demanded**. Let's use our demand acronym, **PINTE**, to see how changes in various demand determinants lead to a change from point A in Figure 3-2.

Figure 3-2
Changes in Demand versus Changes in Quantity Demanded

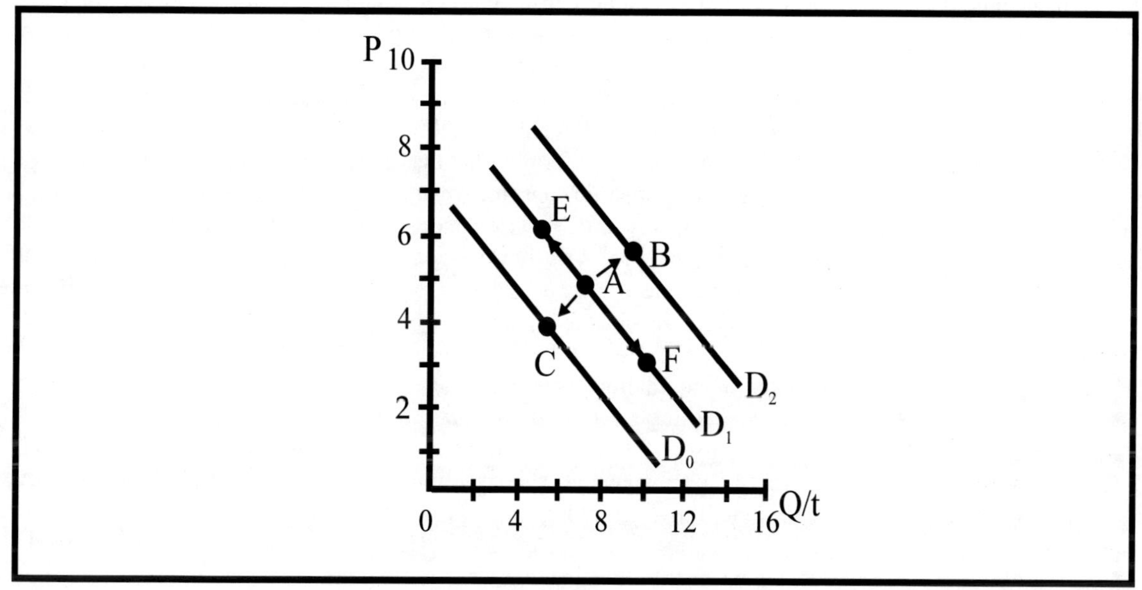

P: Change in Prices–There are three prices we typically want to consider: the price of the item itself; the price of things that may be used instead of the item whose demand we are investigating–substitutes; and the price of things that may be used with the item whose demand we are investigating–complements. As we mentioned earlier, economists define **substitutes** and **complements** in terms of the direction demand changes when the price of some related item changes. If the price of a substitute increases, by definition the demand for the substitute item increases, whereas, if the price of a substitute falls, the demand for the substitute item falls as well. For example, most persons consider Fords and Chevrolets fairly good substitutes. If in Figure 3-2 the demand for Fords is $\mathbf{D_1}$ and price and quantity demanded are represented by point A, and the price of Chevrolets were to increase, which of the four options for changes shown in Figure 3-2 would you expect? Did you select A to B? If so, correct. The increase in the price of Chevrolets would be expected to increase the demand for Fords, *ceteris paribus*. Suppose, however, the price of gasoline were to increase significantly, which change would you expect? If you aid A to C, again correct. Gasoline and automobiles are used together–they are complements and an increase in the price of one would be expected to lead to a decrease in the demand for the other.

Normal Good
A good whose demand changes in the same direction as income-an increase in demand when income increases and less when income decreases, *ceteris paribus*.

Inferior Good
A good whose demanded changes in the opposite direction from the income change-an increase in demand as income falls and less as income rises, *ceteris paribus*.

I: Changes in Income. Will an increase in income lead to an increase in the market demand for goods and services? Usually this is the case: income and demand are directly related. If income were to rise, always invoking the all other important variables held constant, or ceteris paribus assumption, the demand for different goods should also increase. If income were to fall, demand would fall. Even though most goods are **normal goods**, there are exceptions. There are some goods, called **inferior** goods, the demand for which falls as consumer incomes increase. Perhaps the use of the word "inferior" is unfortunate here, since it implies something about the quality of the product that may not be true. Beans and rice are often cited as examples of inferior goods, but there is clearly nothing "bad" about either–they are good sources of many nutrients we need and can form the basis of a very healthy diet. But as a consumer's income increases, he or she tends to buy smaller quantities of beans and rice, instead buying (more expensive) meat products. We classify a good as normal or inferior depending on market demand; however, there can be quite a bit of variation among consumers. Take hamburger, for example. For people with very low incomes, hamburger may be a normal good–they will buy more hamburger as their incomes increase from "very low" to "low." But as incomes increase further, hamburger purchases will be replaced by purchases of more expensive cuts of meat–hamburger thus becomes an inferior good. A good's status as "normal" or "inferior" may therefore vary across consumers at a point in time and for a specific consumer over time. In any event, be sure to be careful about drawing any quality inferences from the name "inferior." Remember simply that purchases of a normal good change in the same direction as the change in incomes, and purchases of an inferior good change in the opposite direction from the change in income.

N: Number of buyers. As the size of the market changes due to changes in population, or perhaps age distribution so too will demand. One factor concerning Levi Strauss is that the share of the teenage population in the United States is falling and is expected to continue to fall for the foreseeable future. Since teenagers are the largest group of buyers for their blue jeans, they see a trend illustrated in Figure 3-2 as a move from $\mathbf{D_1}$ to $\mathbf{D_0}$.

T: Tastes or Preferences. "Green" products–those manufactured in less environmentally damaging ways–have done quite well in the last few years even though they typically cost more. One explanation for this would lie in a change in consumers' taste. Their demand for environmentally friendly goods has shifted as shown by the move from D1 to D2.

E: Expectations. Clear evidence of changes in demand is available in the days before a pending hurricane on the East Coast. In any event, to estimate demand carefully requires considerable thought be given not only to the variables that are available and relatively easy to measure, but to other more complicated determinants we have grouped under the classifications of expectations and tastes.

Expressing Demand Mathematically

Above we showed how the demand for a good, x, could be expressed as a linear equation with the price as the independent variable. This can be expanded to include other demand factors such as income and other prices. For example, the demand for student assistant hours may be expressed through the following demand equation,

$$q_{dx} = a - bP_x + cI - eP_w + fP_z$$

where $\mathbf{q_{dx}}$ refers to a person's quantity of student assistant hours demanded per week, $\mathbf{P_x}$ the price, or wage, **I**, income, and $\mathbf{P_w}$ and $\mathbf{P_z}$ prices of two other goods. The parameters that need to be estimated are **a**, **b**, **c**, **e**, and **f**. As the equation is written, **b**, **c**, **e**, and **f** are all positive; **a** can be either positive or negative. The parameter a represents other factors that affect the quantity of hours demanded not otherwise included in the equation, e.g., tastes **(T)** and the size of the market **(N)**. Notice that the signs in front of the other parameters tell us what we expect about the relationship between the quantity of hours demanded and the other variables—the negative sign before **b** asserts our confidence in the Law of Demand; the positive sign attached to parameter **c** implies we believe student work is a normal good (when income increases *ceteris paribus* so will the quantity of ours demanded); the negative sign of **e** says that when the price of good **W** increases, we expect the quantity of hours demanded to fall; and the positive sign attached to **f** implies a positive relationship between the price of **Z** and the number of hours demanded. The signs attached to the estimated parameters allow a precise definition of normal goods, inferior goods, substitutes, and complements. If the sign of the parameter of the income variable is positive, the good is a normal good, but if the sign is instead negative, the good is defined as an inferior good. In a similar fashion, if the sign of the parameter of another price variable is negative, the two goods are defined as complements, but if the sign is positive the two goods are said to be substitutes.

Our next step is to derive demand from the above demand equation. This is done by assigning fixed values to all the determinants other than the price of the good itself, P_X

Adding Demand Curves for Analysis

Supply and demand analysis uses aggregations of supply and demand most often estimated statistically. Data are collected on relevant demand or supply determinants, sometimes at the individual level, but more often at an aggregate level. For example, we may have need to study the demand for gasoline and do so by collecting data at the state level, e.g., average state per capita income, number of cars licensed, number of highway miles, the average price of gasoline in the state, and so forth. Ultimately, however, aggregate demand curves rest on individual demand curves or schedules and we need to see how individual demands are "summed up" to get market demand. The application of statistical analysis to economics is fully explored in an Introduction to Economic Statistics class, and in Econometrics.

Let's introduce a second consumer to our market for student assistant hours. Figure 3-3 reproduces Professor Bob's demand curve from Figure 31 as well as a demand curve for a second professor, Professor Janet. Professor Janet's demand is represented as the linear equation:

$$\mathbf{q_{d,J} = 28 - 2.8P}$$

where $\mathbf{q_{d,J}}$ stands for the per week quantity demanded by Janet, and **P** is the per hour wage. As would be expected, the two demands differ. Janet demands more hours than Bob at any price, perhaps because the Dean, or Department Chair has favored Janet with more funds, or perhaps Janet feels student assistance is more valuable for her during this period than Bob. However, notice Janet is more responsive to a change in price than Bob. The coefficients attached to the price variable in the two demand equations show that if the price increased by $1, Janet's quantity demanded (not demand) would decrease by 2.8 hours whereas Bob's quantity demanded would drop by two hours.

To find the market demand with two consumers, we simply add horizontally. That is, at any price we add the quantity demanded by each consumer. Quantity demanded at a wage $10 or higher is zero, and from $10 to $6 the only consumer in the market is Professor Janet, so the market demand is her demand. From $6 to $0, both professors are willing to hire students. Since both demand curves are linear, we can go to zero price and add the quantity demanded: 12 plus 28 equals 40.

Figure 3-3
Aggregating Demand

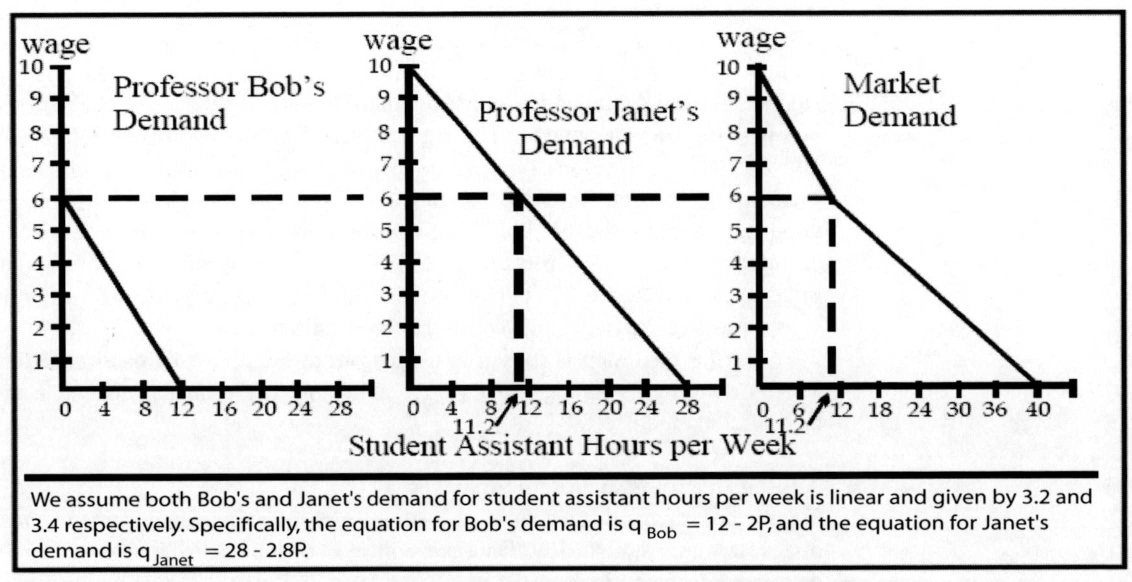

We assume both Bob's and Janet's demand for student assistant hours per week is linear and given by 3.2 and 3.4 respectively. Specifically, the equation for Bob's demand is $q_{Bob} = 12 - 2P$, and the equation for Janet's demand is $q_{Janet} = 28 - 2.8P$.

A word of caution, unless all demand curves have identical vertical (price) intercepts you cannot add the equations algebraically. In fact, the algebraic sum of the two equations were ($Q_D = 40\ 4.8P$) is the lower straight line segment, but the market demand is on inear with a "kink" at the price of $6.

The Principles of Supply

Supply
The relationship between the quantity of an item supplied per period and the price of that item, *ceteris paribus*.

Just as we are able to construct a demand curve from a demand schedule, we are able to do the same for **supply**. Still using our hypothetical student assistant market the sellers of time are students. For specificity consider the **supply schedule** of student Becky shown in Table 3-2.

Table 3-2
Student Becky's Supply Schedule

Price (Wage) per hour	$6	4	2	0
Quantity (Hours) Willing to Work per Week	11	7	3	0

It is worthwhile to pay attention to a number of things shown by the supply schedule.

Supply Schedule
A table showing the quantity of a good sellers are willing to sell over a period at each of several prices, *ceteris paribus*.

1. Becky's supply schedule shows a positive relationship between the price, several prices, ceteris or wage, and the number of hours per week she is willing to work. This paribus. positive relationship between price and quantity supplied is typical, particularly when the period is short, but there are noteworthy exceptions. Consequently, we refer to this positive relationship as a **tendency of supply.**

Tendency of Supply
Typically, but not always, sellers will offer to sell more only at a higher price, *ceteris paribus*.

2. The relationship is time specific. In this case, the period is a week. to sell more only at a

3. The supply relationship may be viewed in two equally valid ways: at each higher price, ceteris price there is an associated quantity supplied; and for each quantity sup-paribus. plied there is a corresponding price. For example, at $4, Becky is willing to work seven hours a week, and to work the seventh hour, $4 is the Marginal minimum compensation she will accept, her **marginal willingness to accept.**

Marginal Willingness to Accept
The minimum compensation necessary to induce a person to supply an extra unit.

4. There is a price below which the person is not interested in supplying. In Becky's case, we can see that at a price between $2 and $0 she is not willing to lease her time.

5. The supply schedule shows a *ceteris paribus* relationship.

Calculus Parallel 3-2
The slope of the supply curve is given as the derivative of price with respect to quantity supplied, dP/dQ. The tendency of supply can be stated as dP/dQ > 0.

Supply Curve
A representation of a supply schedule graphically with price measured on the vertical axis and quantity supplied per period on the horizontal axis.

Changes in Supply
Shifts in a supply curve caused by changes in any factor affecting supply other than a change in the price of the item being supplied.

Changes in Quantity Supplied
Movement along a supply curve caused only by changes in the price of the item being supplied.

From the supply schedule we can derive the supply curve. Figure 3-4 shows Becky's **supply curve, s_1**, assuming the relationship is linear along with two other hypothetical supply curves,s_0 and s_2. The remarks made about the relation between the demand schedule and the demand curve are appropriate for the supply schedule and curve as well. First, the schedule is discrete, but the curve is drawn continuous and may be expressed as a linear equation. Second, although quantity supplied depends on price, we place price on the vertical axis. We can do so if we interpret the supply curve as showing the minimum compensation necessary for the seller to supply a given unit of the good. Third, it is important to distinguish between a **change in supply**, and a **change in quantity supplied**. The move from A to B or from A to C along Becky's original supply curve is called a change in the quantity supplied and is due solely to a change in the wage she would receive. Becky's supply reflects the **tendency of supply** in that she is willing to work more only if her wage compensation increases and vice versa. The move from A to E represents a decrease in supply, a change in the entire price-quantity relationship, whereas the move from A to F represents an increase in supply.

A Word of Caution
Be careful in drawing new demand and supply curves. An increase in demand is a shift to the right, and a decrease in demand is a shift to the left. It would also be correct to say an increase in demand is a shift up, and a decrease in demand is a shift down, but this will get you into trouble when you shift the supply curve. As

with demand, an increase in supply is a shift to the right, and a decrease in supply is a shift to the left. But, an upward shift in supply is not an increase in supply; it is a decrease. Similarly, a downward shift in supply is an increase in supply, not a decrease.

Figure 3-4
Changes in Supply versus Changes in Quantity Supplied

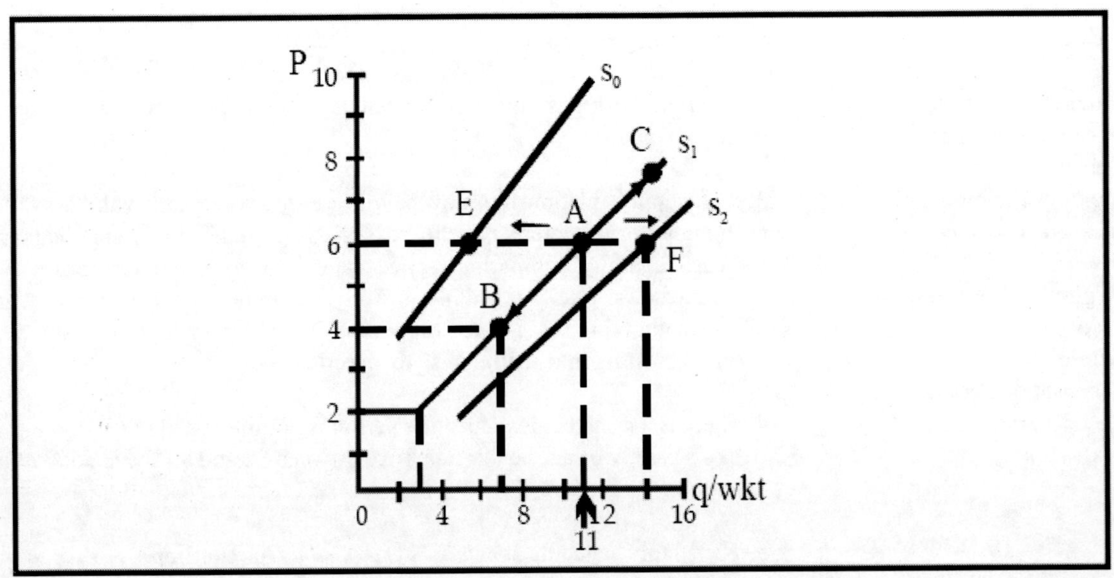

Supply Equation
An equation that demonstrates the relationship between quantiy supplied of a good and all hypothesized determinants of that good.

Supply Shifters

There are a number of factors that influence supply in addition to the price of the item supplied. In general, we specify five variables that are likely to be important, and as with demand, you may remember the important supply factors by a word, in this case **PENT**, and the **supply equation** may be written:

$$Q_{SX} = Q(PENT).$$

That is, the supply of good x is a function, or depends on the factors represented by the symbols **P, E, N,** and **T** where **P** stands for prices (the price of the item itself, the price of other items that could be supplied, and the price of inputs), **E** stands for expectations, **N** for the number of sellers, and **T** for technology, or the state of the art of production.

Let's talk briefly about each of these in the context of Becky's supply of hours of work and supply typically.

P: Prices. Supply refers to the relationship between the price of the item and the quantity supplied. For Becky, the price is the hourly wage and the supply schedule reflects this relationship, ceteris paribus. In manufacturing, the seller will supply more or less depending on the price he or she is able to get for their product. Other prices being held constant for the supply schedule include the price of other items that could be supplied and the price of resources, or inputs, necessary to the supply. In Becky's case, she might require a babysitter in order for her to perform her work. Then, the price of the babysitter would be a significant variable in determining her supply schedule. If she had to travel a distance to perform the work, the cost of transportation would be important. The supplier of manufactured goods will supply more or less depending on the wage of labor, the cost of fuel, etc. The price of other items that could be supplied refers to the fact that student assistant work requires giving up valued alternatives. If Becky "just needs to" get a good grade in her next Econ exam, the price (cost) of working has increased since the work is apt to take her away from her study time. A farmer's supply of corn is likely to depend on the price of wheat if it is the case the supply of corn precludes the planting of wheat.

E: Expectations. As with demand, a person's expectations is likely to affect their willingness to supply.

N: Number of sellers. The larger the number of students willing to work, or sellers in the market, the larger the market supply.

T: Technology. The state of technology provides the raw list of ingredients required to provide a given supply. An improvement in technology refers to the fact that fewer ingredients, or inputs as we referred to them above, are needed to produce a given quantity. Fewer inputs, given their prices, means lower costs and a greater willingness to supply than before.

Aggregating Supply

Just as with demand, economic analysis uses aggregate supply rather than individual supply. Individual supply curves are added horizontally to arrive at market supply. Figure 3-5 shows the story. The left most diagram shows Becky's supply curve derived from Table 3-2, along with the supply curve of student Ivan in the middle diagram, and the market supply in the right diagram. Neither student is willing to work for less than $2 an hour, but Becky will offer three hours at $2. The market supply is zero for prices less than $2, and at $2, three hours are offered. Becky is the only supplier until the price rises to $3 where she offers five hours, and Ivan starts to offer hours of work. When the market price is $6 per hour, Becky is willing to offer 11 hours and Ivan 10.5, so the market quantity supplied is 21.5, the horizontal sum at $6.

For practice, take the linear portion of the market supply curve in Figure 3-5, between the coordinates (5, $3) and (21.5, $6), and express it as an equation:

$$\mathbf{q_{SX} = g + hP_x \text{ for } \$3.00 \leq P_x \leq \$6.00}$$

where **x** stands for weekly student assistant hours, **g** represents autonomous supply, that supply not explained by price, and **h** represents the response of the quantity supplied to a unit change in price. The statement after the equation tells us that the range for which the equation describes the supply curve is from a price of $3.00 to $6.00. To be complete, we should have expressions for other prices. For example, we should say: for $P_x < \$2.00$, $q_{SX} = 0$. Often we will not state these expressions explicitly, but you should understand they are in effect.

Figure 3-5

Aggregating Supply

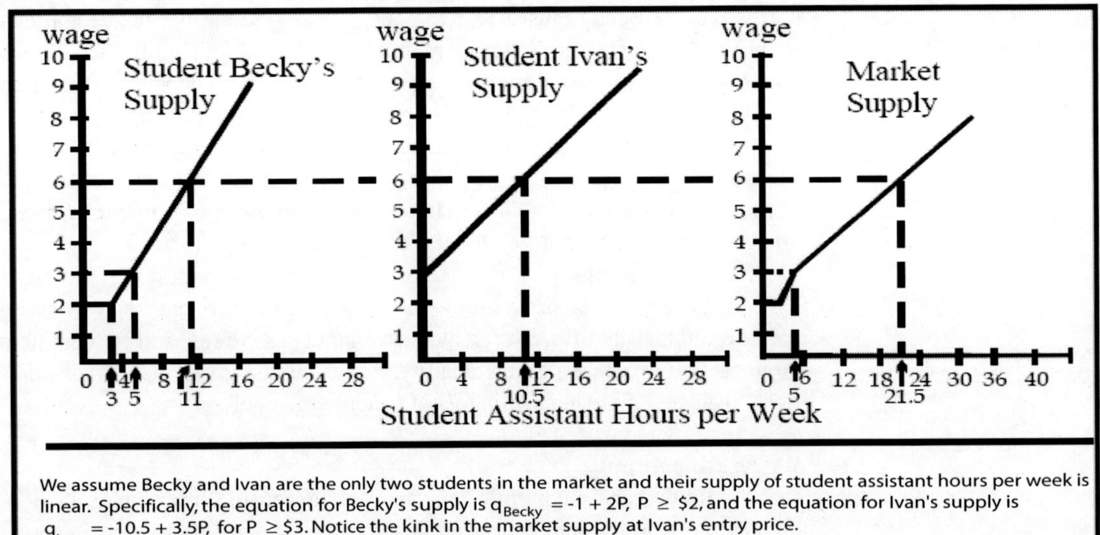

We assume Becky and Ivan are the only two students in the market and their supply of student assistant hours per week is linear. Specifically, the equation for Becky's supply is $q_{Becky} = -1 + 2P$, $P \geq \$2$, and the equation for Ivan's supply is $q_{Ivan} = -10.5 + 3.5P$, for $P \geq \$3$. Notice the kink in the market supply at Ivan's entry price.

Now, use the equation for a straight line and data shown in Figure 3-5 to find the values for **g** and **h**. Did you find, **g** = -11.5, and **h** = 5.5? Good! Notice that 1/h is the slope of the supply curve, 1/5.5 = 0.182. Assuming a linear relationship beyond \$3, the equation for market supply given by:

$$\mathbf{Q_{Sx} = -11.5 + 5.5P \text{ for } P_x \geq \$3}$$

It is time to bring supply and demand together.

Equilibrium in a Competitive Market

In this instance, the dictionary definition of equilibrium is appropriate for our purposes: "a state of rest or balance due to the equal action of opposing forces." The opposing forces in a competitive market are supply and demand. The supply of sellers willing to sell more or less at alternative prices and the demand of buyers willing to buy more or less at alternative prices. In a competitive market, price acts as a rationing mechanism and as a signaling device. When price is relatively high, only those who value the good or service relatively highly will be willing to buy (price rations available supply to those willing to pay the most). Also, when price is relatively high, sellers are eager to supply. A high price acts as a signal that the good or service is relatively scarce. In turn, relative scarcity provides an incentive for buyers to be careful with use–it's expensive, look for alternatives. Relative scarcity also provides an incentive for sellers–a good profit may be had by offering more for sale.

Equilibrium in a competitive market occurs when the market clears. That is, we are in equilibrium when the quantity buyers are willing to buy at the prevailing price, equals the quantity sellers are willing to sell at the prevailing price. We have a "balance," or "state of rest," when price adjusts so the quantity demanded equals the quantity supplied. The prevailing price where the forces of supply and demand are balanced is referred to as the **equilibrium price**.

Equilibrium Price
The price at which quantity demanded equals quantity supplied. It is the market clearing price.

Excess Supply, or Surplus
A quantity supplied larger than the quantity demanded at a given price.

Table 3-3 shows the demand schedules of our two hypothetical professors, Bob and Janet, their aggregate demand at various prices, the supply schedules of our two suppliers, students Becky and Ivan, and their aggregate supply. The equilibrium price is $5 an hour. Only at $5 an hour are supply and demand balanced. The professors are willing to hire 16 hours per week, Bob 2 and Janet 14, and the students are willing to offer 16 hours, Becky 9 and Ivan 7. At prices above $5 there is excess supply, or a surplus. More hours are offered than would be hired. For example, if the wage were $6, the students would offer 21.5 hours, but the professors would buy only 11.2. If the market is competitive, we would expect downward pressure on price as students competed to offer their hours at the above equilibrium price.

Table 3-3

Table 3-3: Market Demand and Supply for Student Assistant Hours per Week

d_{Bob}	d_{Janet}	D	P($/hr)	S	s_{Becky}	s_{Ivan}
0.0	0.0	0.0	10.0	43.5	19.0	24.5
0.0	5.6	5.6	8.0	32.5	15.0	17.5
0.0	11.2	11.2	6.0	21.5	11.0	10.5
2.0	14.0	**16.0**	**5.0**	**16.0**	9.0	7.0
4.0	16.8	20.8	4.0	10.5	7.0	3.5
6.0	22.4	28.4	2.0	3.0	3.0	0.0
12.0	28.0	40.0	0.0	0.0	0.0	0.0

Note: Entries in the Professor demand columns are from the equations given in Figure 3-3, and entries in the Student supply columns are from the equations given in Figure 3-5.

Excess Demand, or Shortage
A quantity demanded larger than the quantity supplied at a given price.

On the other hand, the market may not be in equilibrium if the price is too low. If the wage were $4 an hour, there would be **excess demand**, or a **shortage**. Students would want to work a total of 10.5 hours per week but professors would want to hire 20.8 hours. The shortage should lead to upward pressure on price as the buyers compete for the limited number of hours available. Only at $5 per hour where quantity demanded equals quantity supplied is the market in equilibrium. The forces of supply and demand are balanced.

We can also determine the equilibrium price and quantity bought and sold mathematically. First, let's look at the problem graphically. Figure 3-6 shows the market demand and supply derived from the schedules in Table 3-3. Prices above the equilibrium price create excess supply and downward pressure on price. Prices below the equilibrium price create excess demand and upward pressure on price. As price adjusts to clear the market, buyers respond by changes in their quantity they demand, and sellers respond by changing the quantity they supply.

Figure 3-6
The Market for Student Assistant Hours

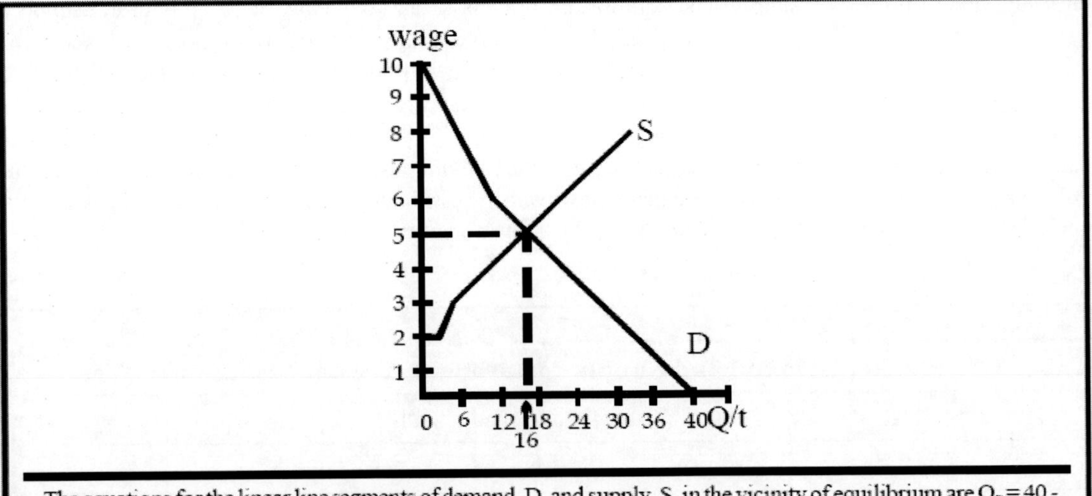

The equations for the linear line segments of demand, D, and supply, S, in the vicinity of equilibrium are $Q_D = 40 - 4.8P$ and $Q_s = -11.5 + 5.5P$ respectively.

From the demand and supply schedule, and the equation for a straight line, we can find the following linear demand and supply equations:

$$\mathbf{Q_{Dx} = 40 - 4.8P_X, \text{ and } Q_{Sx} = -11.5 + 5.5P_X}$$

where **x** refers to hours of work per week. In equilibrium the quantity demanded equals the quantity supplied so set $\mathbf{Q_{Dx} = Q_{Sx}}$ and solve for the price, $\mathbf{P_x}$.

$$\mathbf{Q_{Dx} = Q_{Sx}}$$
$$\mathbf{40 - 4.8P_x = -11.5 + 5.5P}$$
$$\mathbf{-10.3P_x = -51.5}$$
$$\mathbf{P_x = \$5}$$

Now, substitute the price into either the demand or supply equation and determine that the equilibrium quantity is 16 hours per week.

Applying Supply/Demand Analysis

Given we cannot have everything we want, how do we decide on what we want, and how do we get what we want? Simple questions, but the answers are often quite complex. While never providing a complete answer, no answer is complete without supply and demand analysis. The easiest application of supply and demand analysis occurs when market outcomes, price and quantity exchanged, are observable. If the market is competitive and in equilibrium, economists believe the observed price and quantity are the result of demand and supply forces.

The Rising Costs of Higher Education

The cost of higher education has been rising sharply for the past 25 years. The General Accounting Office recently reported that average tuition costs at public universities have increased since 1980 by 234 percent, much faster than earnings and general inflation. Tuition expenses at private universities have increased even more rapidly over the same period. These increases have outstripped the general increase in prices as measured by the Consumer Price Index (CPI), which has increased by 85 percent since 1980, and the average family's ability to pay for college as measured by household income, which has increased only 82 percent since 1980. While the price of higher education, using tuition as a proxy has increased, the percentage of our labor force that have completed four or more years of college has increased from 14 percent in 1970 to 27 percent in 2000. Can these facts be explained by supply and demand analysis?

Figure 3-7 shows a price and quantity axes with an observed equilibrium price and quantity combination P1 and Q1, and four partitioned quadrants, **A**, **B**, **C**, and **E** delineated by dashed lines. If P_1 and Q_1 represents 1980 equilibrium in the market for higher education, where is the equilibrium now? If you answered "in the quadrant marked **B**," you are right. In fact, our analysis of supply and demand leads us to the conclusion that when price and quantity exchanged both increase from one period to another, the dominant factor must have been an increase in demand. Supply could have changed, for example the dot in quadrant **B** shown by lower case **b**, is reached by an increase in demand and an increase in supply. But, if the new equilibrium is in quadrant **B**, the dominant factor must have been an increase in demand. When a new equilibrium is observed, we can see whether the dominant force in the change was an increase or decrease in demand or supply, and we are ready for the next step-- isolating the demand or supply factor, or factors, that lead to the observed change.

Figure 3-7
Using Supply and Demand Analysis to Explain Market Outcomes

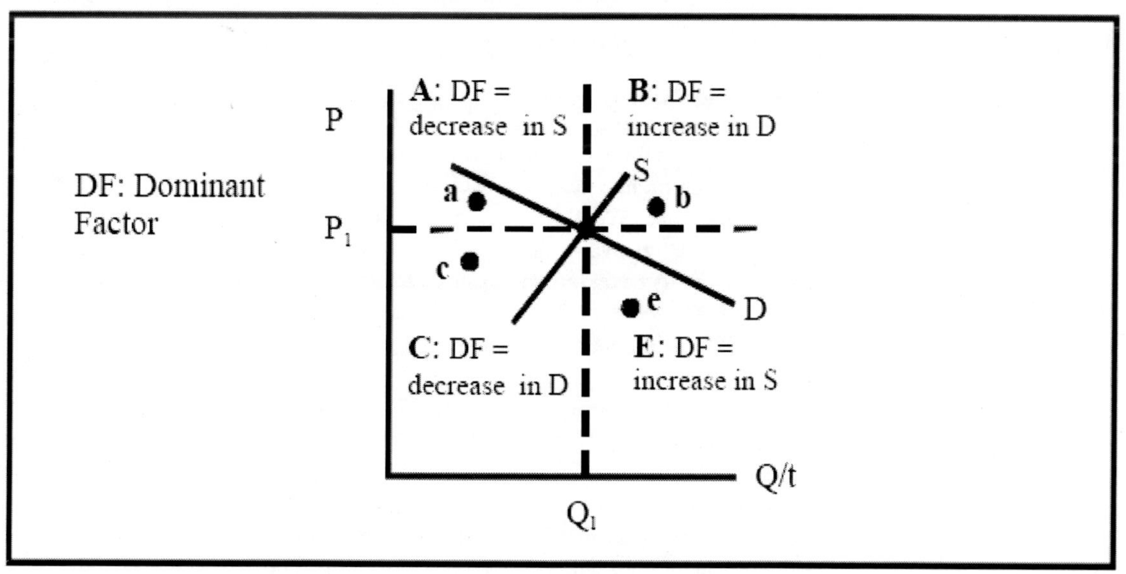

Which demand factor, or what combination of demand factors led to the change in the higher education market equilibrium from a price and quantity like P1 and Q1 in the early 1980s, to a point like **b** in the late 1990s? We mentioned above that household income hardly changed over the period compared to prices (82 versus 85 percent), so a change in income is an unlikely candidate. Market size increased, but we account for that by measuring quantity in terms of the percentage of the labor force that has a college degree. One item that has changed is the relative return to a college education. Over the period, average real wages (corrected for inflation) for high school graduates fell by11.7 percent while the average real wage of college graduates increased by 5.6 percent.

Some Other Supply and Demand Illustrations

Computing power has increased dramatically over the past decade. Prices have fallen, and more people have personal computers than ever before. In terms of Figure 3-7 we moved from a price and quantity equilibrium like P_1 and Q_1 to an equilibrium in quadrant **E**. What accounts for the change? Technological advance has lowered costs and the supply curve has shifted to the right. Has demand increased? Surely, but the dominant factor has been the increase in supply.

Per capita consumption of eggs has fallen as has the price of a dozen Grade A Large eggs since 1970. Why? A drop in demand due to a greater awareness of the ill effects of cholesterol on health has outweighed the lower cost of egg production due to mechanization of poultry farms. An example of two contemporaneous, but different equilibria are gasoline markets in Europe and the United States. We consume more gas and pay less at the pump. Why? Gasoline taxes in Europe are about four times what they are in the United States. These taxes are collected by the retailer, and partly passed on to consumers. As a result, the higher the tax, the higher the price, and the less bought.

As practice, draw axes for price and quantity and illustrate these four cases. Use a downward-sloping demand and upward sloping supply and locate an initial equilibrium. Identify a demand factor and a supply factor that have changed for each case, and show that the new equilibrium in the one of the four quadrants a, b, c, and e is due to either demand or supply dominating.

Price Controls

Most markets have a degree of government intervention that effect the forces of supply and demand. Among the numerous forms of intervention, we find labeling requirements, regulations to insure fair weights and standards, restrictions imposed on methods of production, product recall provisions, prohibitions, license requirements, taxes imposed on transactions, and subsidies legislated for various activities. We will have occasion to evaluate the efficiency of many of these measures in later chapters, but now we will use our tools of supply and demand to analyze the effects of price controls–the legislating of prices in markets.

Price Ceiling
A legally binding maximum price. To be effective, the price must be below the market equilibrium price.

Price Floor
A legally binding minimum price. To be effective, the price must be above the market equilibrium price.

Prices are akin to a two-edged sword. For buyers, prices are typically "too high," while for sellers they are "too low." Although price controls are sometimes imposed in times of national emergency, e.g., during World War II, they are usually enacted and maintained at the bequest of special interests In any event, legally imposed maximum or mini-maximum price. To be mum prices, **price ceilings** or **price floors**, are only effective if they are effective, the price must lower or higher than the one buyers are willing to pay in view of suppliers' be below the market willingness to accept. Legislators may legislate a maximum rent for a particular equilibrium price. type of apartment, but unless this price ceiling is less than the market equilibrium price, it will have no effect.

Maximum prices have a long history dating back to "usury" laws (laws Price Floor prohibiting the lending of money at "high" rates) of the 12th century. Rent A legally binding controls enacted in the United States during World War II are still present in a number of American cities, most notably New York. Gasoline prices were effective, the price must frozen in the early 1970s, and currently, medical procedures provided under be above the market government programs are subject to price limits.

Although legislation passed in 1996 promised to phase out price supports for farm products, U. S. agriculture policy since the 1930s has been characterized by price floors for numerous farm products, sugar, tobacco, wheat, cotton, dairy products among others. Another minimum price is the minimum wage. The "right" price for labor is a perennial issue of Congressional debate. To be effective, however, price floors, or support prices must be above the market clearing price. Congress may mandate the price of No. 1 wheat to be \$3.00 a bushel, but if the market price is \$3.22, the price support is ineffective.

Figure 3-8 shows two markets with effective price controls. In the left diagram, the price floor is set at \$60 while the market equilibrium price is \$40.

Figure 3-8
Price Controls

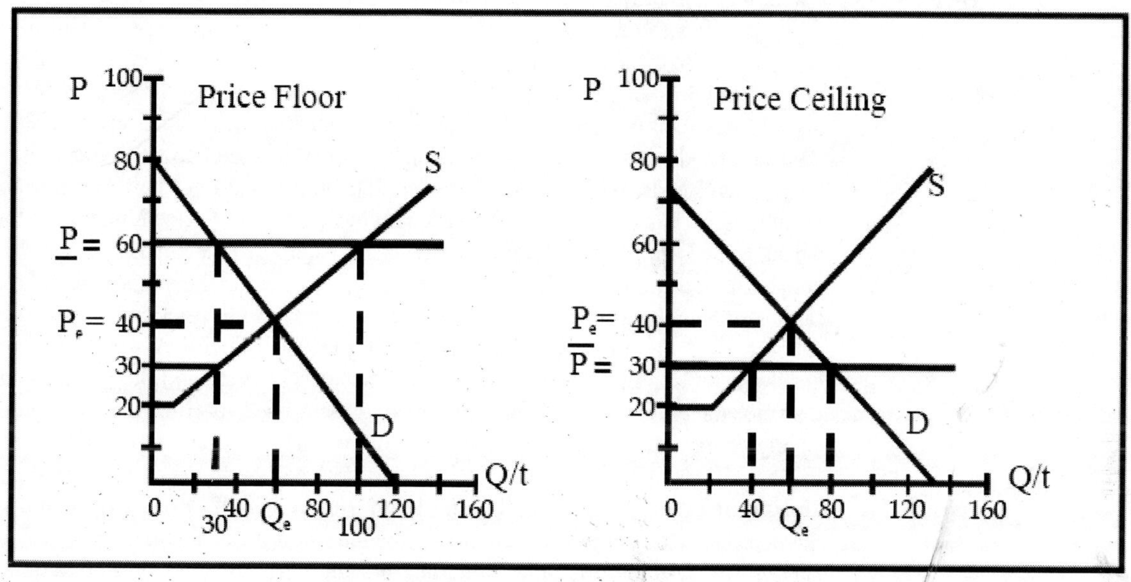

In the absence of the price floor, the market would clear with 60 units exchanged per period at \$40 a unit. The legal minimum price creates excess supply of 70 units. At a price of \$60, sellers want to sell 100 units, but buyers are prepared to buy only 30. Since sellers can't sell what buyers won't buy, only 30 units will be sold and there is an excess supply of 70 units. In the diagram to the right, an effective price ceiling is set at \$30 while the market equilibrium price is \$40. At the legal maximum price, there is excess demand of 40 units per period (Q_D = 80; Q_S = 40), and only 40 units bought.

At this stage of our supply and demand analysis we want to note a couple of implications of price controls:

1. As shown in Figure 3-8, price controls lead to excess demand or supply.

2. Since demand and supply represent the interests of buyers and sellers, a nonmarket equilibrium price imposed through price controls, creates incentives to avoid the circumstances created by the condition of excess demand or supply. Controlled prices may send incorrect signals about relative scar-

cities leading to inefficiencies in markets other than the market where price is controlled.

3. If the controls are strictly enforced, the amount bought and sold is limited to a level below the market equilibrium level, and denies exchanges that in the absence of the price controls would benefit both buyer and seller.
In the diagram to the left in Figure 3-8, the amount bought and sold at the support price of $60, 30 units per period, is less than at the market equilibrium price of $40. Transactions are prevented that would benefit both buyer and seller. Consider the purchase and sale of the 31st unit. The demand curve states there is a buyer willing to pay about $60 (a little less than $60 due to the law of demand), the supply curve states there is a seller willing to accept about $30 (a little more due to the upward-sloping supply). The would be buyer and seller of the 31st unit forego an exchange that would benefit both. In later chapters, we will see how this loss to potential buyers and sellers may be measured and how the sum of society's efficiency losses due to price controls exceeds any gain to society from these price controls.

These three points may be illustrated by the U. S. sugar program started in 1934 as part of a general program to aid agriculture during the Depression, a period of relatively low prices for farm products. Since the early 1980s, domestic producers of sugar cane and sugar beets provided about 85 percent of U. S. sugar needs, with beet production contributing just over half of domestic sugar supply. The current sugar program includes a support price higher than the world price, implemented through loans to sugar producers using sugar as collateral, and import quotas. If the market price exceeds the support price, the farmer sells their crop and repays the loans. If the market price is less than the support price, the crop is forfeited. In effect, the government buys the sugar. To ensure the U.S. sugar price is higher than the support price and the government does not have to buy any sugar, import quota are used to eliminate the excess supply (point one above). You will be looking at international trade and quotas in Chapter 4, but for our purposes import quota may be defined as a maximum amount of a good that may be imported during a specific period. The import quota reduces the supply sufficiently so the market price is at least as high as the support price. In the price floor diagram of Figure 3-8, the imposition of a quota shifts the supply curve to the left.

Generally, U. S. sugar price is supported at about twice the world price. The artificially high sugar price sends incorrect signals about the relative scarcity of sugar, point two above. Prior to 1980, sugar imports were about 50 percent of domestic consumption, but the high price of sugar induced the development of an alternative, high fructose corn syrup, to use as a sweetener in soft drinks. Now, corn syrup has replaced sugar as the soft drink sweetener, but this alternative is profitable only because we have chosen to support sugar prices at about twice the level prevailing elsewhere. Today, corn producers supply approximately 600 million bushels of corn annually to be used as a sweetener for soft drinks resulting in higher corn prices. All well and good, except the signals sent by supported sugar prices are incorrect. Efficiency would require less U. S. sugar and corn production leading to lower prices for sugar products.

In 1993, the General Accounting Office, the investigative arm of Congress, provided a study that estimated the annual cost of the sugar program to U.S. consumers at $1.4 billion per year. For practice, use a supply and demand graph and show the 1994 situation with the following data:

U.S. production	15.4 billion pounds
U.S. consumption	18.4 billion pounds
Imports	3.0 billion pounds
U.S. price	22 cents per pound
World Price	12 cents per pound

Using this data and estimated demand and supply curves, Robert Pindyck and Daniel Rubinfeld in their 1998 intermediate microeconomic theory textbook, Microeconomics, calculates U. S. consumer annual loss at $1.965 billion, that is, about $30 a year for a family of four. Notice that the consumer loss is not merely the difference between the U. S. and world price times the amount consumed (= $1.84 billion = [18.4] x [0.22 - 0.12]). In Chapter five, you will see the reason for the difference and we point to it in point three above, but the common sense of the matter is that at the lower world price, consumers would have found sugar a sweeter deal than at the higher U. S. price and the loss of these foregone benefits are taken into account by Pindyck and Rubinfeld.

Efficiency considerations takes into account not just the loss to consumers, but the gain to producers as well. The sugar program and other price support programs sustain themselves because they provide sizeable gains to producers, but there is a loss in efficiency only if consumer losses exceed the gains to domestic producers. Pindyck and Rubinfeld estimate producer gains to be about $1 billion per year. In estimating producer gains, you should note that you can not take as the gain the difference between the U. S. price and world price times domestic production (= $1.54 billion = [15.4] x [0.22 0.12]). The correct estimate is $1 billion, not $1.54 billion. In Chapter 6 we will discuss the basis for the lower estimate, but the simple reason is the fact U. S. sugar supply curves are upward sloping reflecting rising marginal costs of production.

The consensus opinion among economists is that price controls, such as price ceilings and price floors, are inefficient since the gains to those who favor such programs do not exceed the losses the programs impose on others. In the case of the sugar program, it appears it costs consumers $2 for every $1 of benefit that goes to U. S. sugar producers. One reason why we might be willing to suffer the cost of this inefficiency is equity. In fact, the initial thrust of farm programs in the 1930s was in large part motivated by our concern for the well being of farmers. We thought it fair then that something be done to alleviate the plight of the farmers, and today there is still sentiment for helping farmers. Witness the durability of Willy Nelson's annual "Farm Aid" program. If this is so, economics can point to more efficient policies to protect the farmer than current price support programs. In addition, there is evidence that the current program even with its cost to society in terms of efficiency losses, does not accomplish much in terms of helping farmers most in need. For example, the General Accounting Office 1993 study referred to above estimated that 42 percent of all sugar grower benefits went to 1 percent of all sugar farms in 1991. We can do better.

SUMMING UP

1. Studying the principles of supply and demand help us understand how decisions are made in the face of scarcity, and in evaluating decisions using the criterion of efficiency.

2. The forces of supply and demand are introduced in the context of **competitive markets**–markets in which no buyer or seller has significant influence over the price at which the product sells, is without government influence, and is governed solely by the informed self-interest of the participants, buyers and sellers.

3. **Demand**, a **demand schedule**, or a **demand curve**, represents a relationship between **marginal willingness to pay** and the quantity demanded over a period, ceteris paribus.

4. The *ceteris paribus* assumption, holding all other relevant variables constant, is critical in economic analysis. It is the mental equivalent of the scientist's controlled experiment.

5. The **law of demand** assert there is an inverse relationship between price and quantity demanded. People will buy more at low prices than at high prices and vise versa. A logical basis for the law of demand is diminishing marginal utility. A person gets less satisfaction from the third pizza a month than they get from the second pizza. Since marginal satisfaction, or utility, declines as they consume more, their marginal willingness to pay also declines.

6. It is important verbally to distinguish between a **change in quantity demanded** and a **change in demand**. A movement along a demand curve is a change in quantity demanded. A change in demand is a shift of the demand curve, and can result from a change in any of the other factors affecting the quantity demanded, e.g., income, tastes, the prices of substitutes and complements, and expectations.

7. Estimation of market demand equation allows classification of goods as **substitutes** or **complements**, and as **normal** or **inferior goods**.

8. General factors that determine the quantity demanded are summarized by the acronym **PINTE** where **P** refers to the price of the item being considered and the prices of items substitutable or complementary to the item being considered, **I** refers to income, **N** stands for the size of the market, **T** refers to tastes or preferences, and **E** stands for expectations.

9. Demand curves used for analysis are aggregate curves. This requires the horizontal summation of individual demand curves.

10. Similar points may be made for supply:
    a. **Supply**, a **supply schedule**, or a **supply curve**, represents a relationship between **marginal willingness to accept** and the quantity supplied over a period, ceteris paribus.
    b. The **tendency of supply** asserts there is typically a direct relationship between price and quantity supplied, *ceteris paribus*. People will usually sell more only if prices are higher. A logical basis for the tendency of supply is increasing marginal cost. If the cost of supplying an item increases at an increasing rate, sellers **marginal willingness to accept** must also increase.
    c. As with demand, it is important verbally to distinguish between a **change in quantity supplied** and a **change in supply**. A movement along a supply curve is a change in the quantity supplied. A change in supply is a shift of the supply curve, and can result from a change in any of the other factors affecting the quantity supplied, e.g., the price of inputs, expectations, the

size of the market, and technology. d. General factors that determine supply are summarized by the acronym **PENT** where **P** refers to the price of the item being considered, the prices of items that could be supplied, and the price of inputs necessary to the supply, **E** refers to expectations, **N** stands for the size of the market, and **T** refers to the state of technology.
e. Supply curves used for analysis are aggregate curves. This requires the horizontal summation of individual supply curves.

11. Self-interest promotes a market equilibrium, establishing a price at which the market clears, an **equilibrium price** and quantity. At the equilibrium price, the quantity demanded equals the quantity supplied.

12. If markets do not clear, there is **excess demand** or **excess supply**.
When the quantity demanded exceeds the quantity supplied, the excess demand should create incentives for sellers to raise their price. When the quantity supplied exceeds the quantity demanded, the excess supply should create incentives for sellers to lower their price.
13. Supply and demand analysis may be used to explain or predict changes in prices and quantities bought and sold.

14. Supply and demand analysis may also be used to explain the effects of price controls, either **price ceilings** or **price floors**.

KEY TERMS

Competitive Markets
Demand
Ceteris Paribus
Demand Schedule
Law of Demand
Substitutes and Complements
Demand Equation
Demand Curve
Marginal Willingness to Pay
Changes in Demand vs. Changes in Quantity Demanded
Normal Good
Inferior Good
Supply
Supply Schedule
Tendency of Supply
Marginal Willingness to Accept
Supply Curve
Changes in Supply vs. Changes in Quantity Supplied
Supply Equation
Equilibrium Price
Excess Supply, or Surplus
Excess Demand, or Shortage
Price Ceiling
Price Floor

Chapter 4: Components of an Economic Society Households, Business Firms, Governments, the Rest of the World

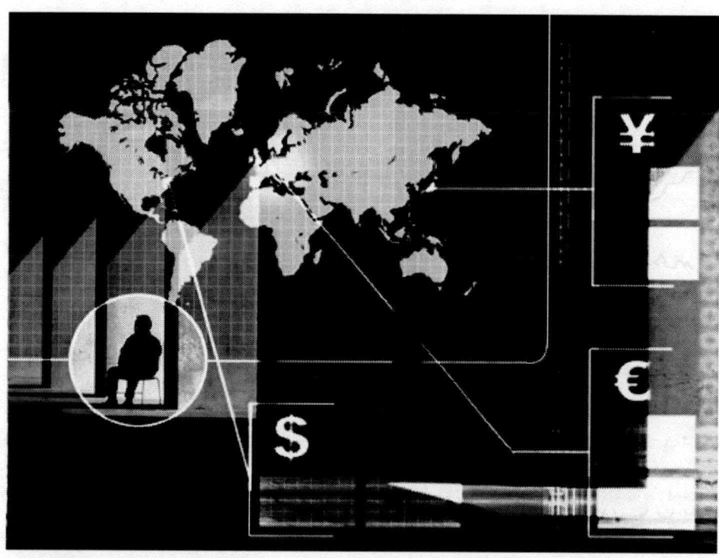

What are the basic parts of our economy, and how are they interrelated? One basic view is that the economy is made up of three sectors: (1) *households*, which provide all the factors of production and in return buy the output of the firms; (2) *business firms*, which employ these factors of production and produce goods and services; and (3) *governments*, which buy part of the output of firms, take away some of the income of households in the form of taxes, and make transfer payments to individuals. Governments also provide various forms of goods and services. These three sectors mesh in a system of flows of income and production called the *circular-flow model* of economic activity. The combined economic activities of these three sectors constitute a **closed economy**, one in which all economic flows occur within its boundaries. In this chapter we will see how this circular flow of economic activity works and then describe the characteristics of each of the three interrelated sectors. Finally, trade with the rest of the world is incorporated into our economic society. We see how exports and imports affect the flow of economic activity for a nation. This chapter concludes with an application on the important question: Are businesses committed simply to the pursuit of profits or do they also have a sense of social responsibility that transcends profits?

Closed Economy
An economy that does not trade with other economies. One in which all economic activity is domestic.

The Circular-Flow Model

The Simple Model

Let us begin by simplifying things, and assume for the moment that there is only a private sector in the economy we are examining. Thus, there are only two components of the economy: households (consumers) and producers (business firms). Consumers *own* all the factors of production; that is, the resources necessary for production to take place. Firms *hire* all the factors of production, produce the goods and services consumers use, and pay a return (income) to the factors. Figure 4-1 illustrates this.

Households provide factors of production to business firms. In return, business firms pay households income for the use of those factors of production. Labor, as a factor of production, receives its reward in the form of wages and salaries. Owners of land receive their payments in the form of rent; owners of capital receive interest; entrepreneurs receive profits. Firms utilize the factors of production to produce goods and services for the use of the households. Households, with incomes obtained from firms' use of their factors of production, pay firms for goods and services. Firms now have incomes so they can pay the factors of production to produce more goods and services. And so the process continues.

Factor Markets
Those markets in which the supply of and demand for factors of production interact to determine wages and other factor prices.

Product Markets
Markets in which the flows of goods and services are established and in which the prices of goods and services are determined.

The circular-flow model and the world of economic production have no beginning. You may start the analysis at any point. Only the amount of resources available (factors of production) limits the level of production. Firms use these resources because households use all the income they receive to buy the output firms produce by employing the resources.

The upper half of Figure 4-1, showing the flow of resources and the reverse flow of income, portrays the **factor markets**, in which the supply of and demand for factors of production interact to determine wages and other factor prices. The bottom half, which shows flows of product output and reverse flows of payments for goods and services, portrays the **product markets**. In these, the supply of goods and services, and the demand for them, interact to determine prices of goods.

Figure 4-1
Simple Circular-Flow Model With Only a Private Sector

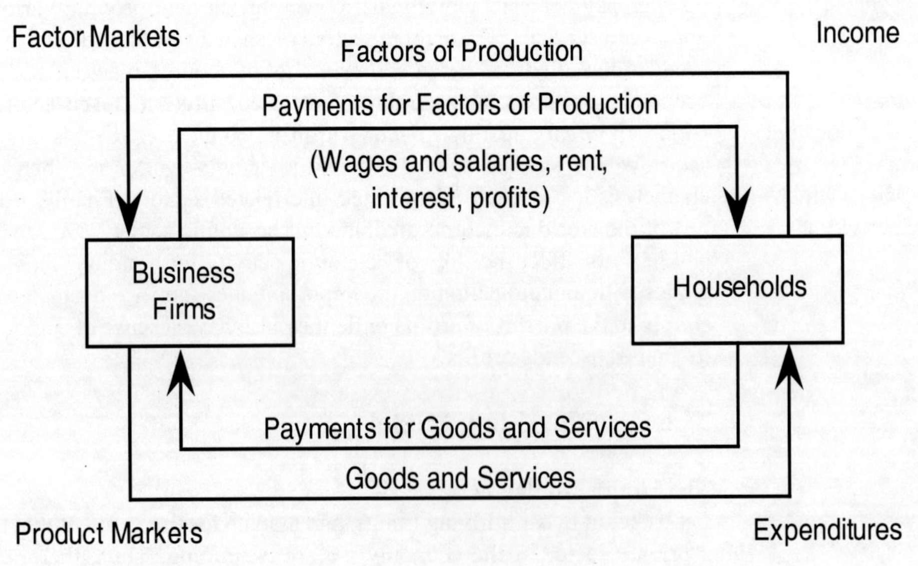

The flow of resources, products, and income between firms and households is circular in nature.

The Complex Model

Figure 4-1 is a simplification of our closed economic system. Let us now examine a more complex, more realistic circular-flow model of such an economy.

Figure 4-1 assumes that households spend all their income on buying the goods and services firms produce. This is not realistic, because people do manage to save some of their income, and also must pay some of their income to governments in the form of taxes, both of which reduce the demand for goods and services (see Figure 4-2). Since saving and paying taxes both mean *not* consuming, these two factors reduce households' demand for firms' output.

Figure 4-1also assumes that all output goes to households in the form of goods and services. Again, this is unrealistic. This more complete model includes two other sources of demand for firms' output:

1. *Other firms*. When firms demand output from other firms, this is not counted as part of the flow of goods and services to households, but as capital goods that aid in the production of other goods and services.

2. *Governments*. Federal, state, and local governments demand output from firms.

In both more complex and simple circular-flow models of the closed economy, the flow of income to households consist of wages, rent, interest, and profits. However, in the complex model, households spend their incomes not only on consumption, but also on savings and taxes. Governments enter the picture with spending for goods and services, and so do business firms themselves, with expenditures for investment. So the flow of funds is still circular. The money that taxes siphon from households' incomes becomes part of the purchasing power governments use for their expenditures. In addition, financial institutions make available for investment the money they obtain from people's savings. This keeps the money flowing. (By *financial institutions*, we usually mean commercial banks and other financial institutions including stock exchanges, though there are many other financial institutions.)

It should be apparent to you that the domestic American economy is a great deal more complex than even our so-called complex model shows. Not only do households save, but firms save also. Firms also have to pay taxes to various governments, especially if the firms are incorporated and have, so to speak, a life of their own. Governments also provide goods and services to households (for example, public schools). Governments, furthermore, provide households with income. By this, we don't mean just social security and welfare payments. Governments provide jobs and governments hire labor from households. And not only do firms invest (demand capital from other firms); so do households. The main form their investments take is home buying. (A house is considered an investment.) The list of activities that could be added to the model is endless. But the complex model gives us enough of a picture to approximate the vast complexity of reality.

What Does The Model Show?

The model in Figure 4-2 tells us that there are three sources of demand for the output of firms: households, other business firms, and governments. There are, therefore, as many different levels of demand as there are combinations of spending patterns by these three parts of society.

Figure 4-2
Complex Circular-Flow Model With Private and Public Sectors

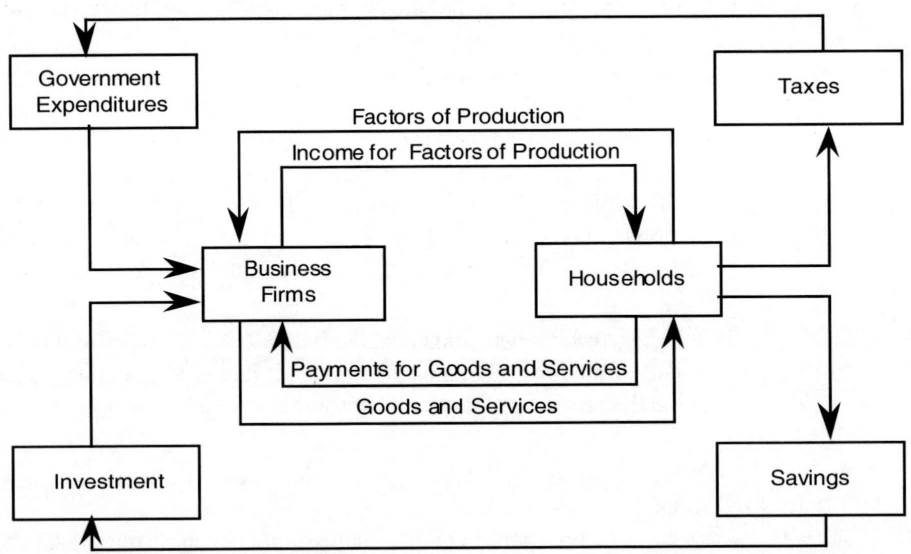

Savings and taxes drain off households' purchasing power and thus reduce their demand for consumer goods. Investment and government expenditures increase the demand for firms' output. These additions are also part of the flow, in that taxes become part of the government's purchasing power. And financial institutions such as banks make savings available for investment.

This more complex system of economic flows doesn't necessarily result in a socially desirable level of demand, one that creates full employment and a low rate of inflation. In subsequent chapters, we will examine the relationships between these flows and the overall level of income and employment and prices. At this point let us just note that households, because they have to set aside money for savings and for taxes, reduce their demand for consumer goods. Firms, by their investments, and governments by buying output of business firms, may take up some of the slack, but not all. So you may have a decrease in demand for goods and services and, eventually, unemployment. (The size of the circular flow decreases.)But if governments and business firms spend *more* than households have saved and have paid in taxes, then demand for products and services increases (the size of the circular flow increases) and inflation may result. While this is an oversimplification, you can get the general and important idea that as these flows change, the level of economic activity in a society increases or decreases with various effects on incomes, prices, and employment;. In the remainder of this chapter, we will look intensively at each of the three sectors in order to show what determines its pattern of demand for goods and services.

HOUSEHOLDS

www.bls.gov
For more information on wages and income visit this web site.

Three important questions about households and their role in economic flows are: (1) Where do they get their income? (2) How do they use it? (3) What is their share of total income?

Table 4-1
Percentage Functional Distribution of Income, 1929 – 2011

	1929	1941	1950	1960	1974	1988	1996	1999	2003	2011 *
Wages and salaries	60	62	69	71	75	73	71	71.2	73.0	69.2
Proprietors' income	17	16	13	10	6	8	8	8.8	8.8	9.3
Corporate profits	12	15	13	11	10	8	12	11.9	12.4	10.9
Rental income	6	3	4	4	2	1	2	2.0	2.0	2.8
Interest income	5	3	1	2	6	10	7	6.2	3.7	7.8

Source: Survey of Current Business, 2011
* 1st quarter

Answers to these questions will give you an insight into the probable effects of the economic decisions of households on total output and income and on the level and composition of output.

The Sources of Income: Functional Distribution

Functional Distribution of Income
The distribution of income that shows how each factor of production derives income according to its economic function(s).

When we talk about sources of income, we speak of the distribution of income as a **functional distribution**. Households, in other words, people receive their income from the wages and salaries they obtain from working; owners of land obtain theirs from rent; owners of capital obtain theirs from interest; businesses, both corporations and unincorporated firms, obtain theirs in the form of profits that are a result of their entrepreneurial activity. Economists look at these sources of income in terms of the functions they perform. It is convenient to view this functional distribution in relative terms, using percentage shares, as in Table 4-1.

Labor receives the largest portion of the money income, in the form of wages and salaries. Labor's share increased from 60 percent at the end of the 1920s to nearly 70 percent in 2011. Labor's increase is due mainly to the decline in the share that went to owners of unincorporated firms (proprietors' income), which fell by more than half during the same time span.

Corporate profits, which ran about 8 to 15 percent of total income during this period, vary according to the state of the economy. They go down in times of recession and go up when times are good. The share of income that comes from rent has been fairly steady (between 1 and 4 percent), while the share of income that comes from interest declined between 1929 and 1970 because of falling interest rates. However, in the 1970s and the late 1980s the share of interest income went up to 10 percent and more because of the revival of high interest rates. By the late 1990s, however, interest income had declined to less than 7 percent.

Many factors contributed to the changing ratios. Chief among them are changing market demand and supply for different resources, government's enlarged role in maintaining high levels of employment, efforts by unions to raise wages (at least for their members), growth in the number of corporations, and continued concentration of economic activity in corporate enterprise. You can see that both market and nonmarket forces play a role in determining the functional distribution of income.

Table 4-2
Households' Allocation of Income, Januray 2011

	Billions of Dollars	Percent
Consumption	10,596	82.3
Savings	627	4.9
Taxes	1,293	10.1

Source: Survey of Current Business, July 2011

The Way Households Allocate Their Income

How do people spend their money? A typical pattern is shown in Table 4-2 in which about 80 percent is spent on personal consumption.

Householders pay about 10 percent of their income in taxes to the various levels of government, a figure that has grown in both absolute and relative terms from only 3 percent of their income in 1929. A substantial part of this increase has, until recently, been due to the increase in funding for government expenditures for military goods and services. There have also been big increases in government social services: social security, Medicare, aid to education and housing, welfare and unemployment relief, highway construction, expansion of the park service, the list is a long one. Many of these have continued to grow under the "stimulus" plans of 2009-2010.

Table 4-3
Distribution of Before-Tax Family Income in the United States for Selected Years

Families by income quintile	1929	1960	1970	1980	1992	2008	2011
Lowest fifth	3.5%	4.8%	5.5%	5.2%	4.4%	4.2%	3.8%
Second fifth	9.0	12.2	12.2	11.5	10.5	9.7	9.3
Third fifth	13.8	17.8	17.6	17.5	16.5	15.4	15.1
Fourth fifth	19.3	24.0	23.8	24.3	24.0	23.2	23.0
Top fifth	54.4	41.3	40.9	41.5	44.6	47.5	48.9
Top 5%	30.0	15.9	15.6	15.3	17.6	23.5	21.3

Source: U.S. Census Bureau, Current Population Survey, Annual Social and Economic Supplements.

The Way Family Income Is Distributed

How is income distributed throughout the United States? Who has much, and who has little? Table 4-3 gives us a general idea and shows the unequal nature of the distribution before taxes are paid and without considering the effects of government transfer payments

Lorenz Curve
The difference between the actual distribution of income and a perfectly proportional distribution as shown graphically.

When you convert the data on income distribution in Table 4-3 into a graph, you get a curve of the inequality of income. This curve has a special name. It is called a **Lorenz curve** (Figure 4-3). It shows the difference between the actual distribution of income and a perfectly equal distribution. By comparing the Lorenz curves for various countries, you can also compare the relative inequality in the distribution of income between one country and another. However, before you draw any conclusions, remember that Lorenz curves frequently show before-tax money income only and not non-cash production, such as food that farmers grow for their own tables. Therefore, comparisons between countries, especially when non-cash incomes are significant, may be misleading.

Other Caveats About Income Inequality

The Lorenz curve is not an entirely accurate measure of the degree of inequality in a nation's income distribution. For one thing, the data in Table 4-3 on which the Lorenz curve in Figure 4-3 is based represent cash incomes before taxes are paid. Table 4-4 shows that when personal taxes are paid, the percentage shares of the lowest fifth, second fifth, and third fifth of family income earners are increased, while incomes of the fourth and top fifth of family income earners are reduced.

Figure 4-3

Lorenz Curve: Distribution of Family Income in the United States, 2008

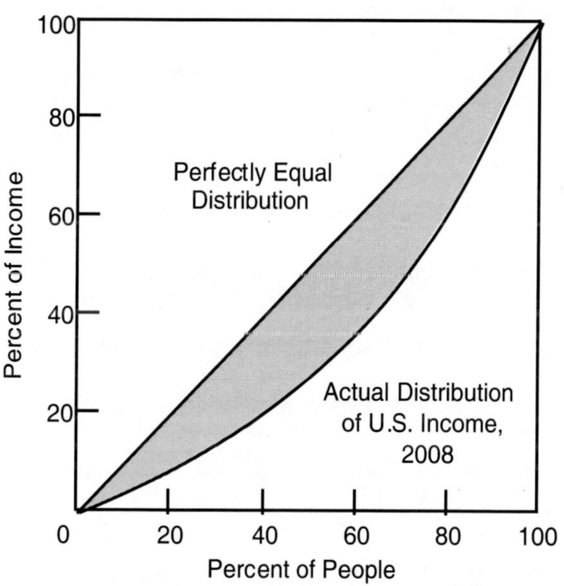

The straight 45 degree diagonal line shows what a perfectly equal distribution of income would look like. The difference between the actual (unequal) and the perfectly proportional distribution, represents the inequality of income.

Note that the bottom fifth of income earners saw their income share raised by 0.4 percent, while the top fifth saw their income share reduced as a result of personal taxes in 2008. Economist Edgar Browning[1] has argued that an accurate distribution of income must reflect the changes in real, disposable incomes resulting from government transfer programs, as well as personal taxes. Table 4-3 shows that in 2005 the top fifth of income earners received almost fifteen times as much family income as the bottom fifth (50.4 percent versus 3.4 percent).

1. Browning, Edward K. *Redistribution and the Welfare System*. Washington, D.C., American Enterprise Institute, 1975.

Table 4-4

Impact of Personal Taxes on the Distribution of Income, 2008

Income quintile	Change in percentage income share after taxes
Lowest fifth	+ 0.9
Second fifth	+ 1.2
Third fifth	+ 0.6
Fourth fifth	– 0.4
Top fifth	– 2.4

Source: U.S. Bureau of the Census, Current Population Reports, *Measuring the Effects of Benefits and Taxes on Income and Poverty: 1989*, U.S. Government Printing Office, Washington, DC, 2009, and earlier issues.

Figure 4-4

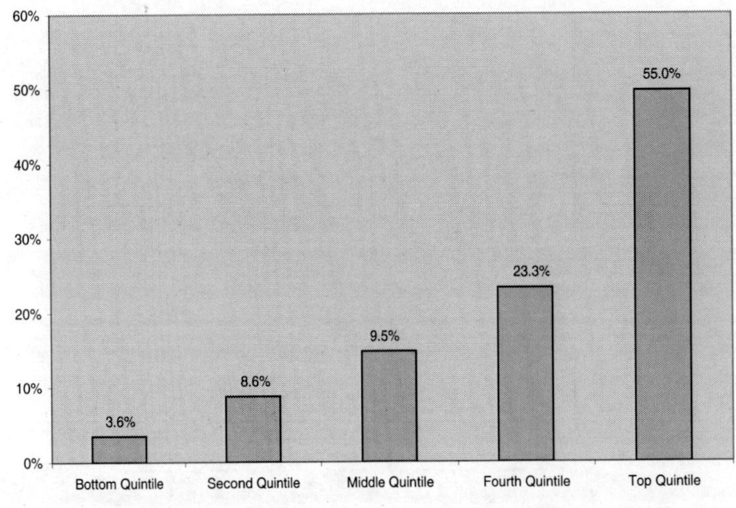

Source: U.S. Bureau of the Census, Current Population Survey for 2008

The distribution of income has become a major issue in American economic and political life. In the early 2000s that discussion focused on "two Americas, one rich, one poor." Recent research only partially supports the view that over time the distribution of income including the effects of taxes, transfer payments and other considerations has grown more and more unequal.

A recent report by Robert Rector and Rea Hederman[2], Jr. shows that when all factors are taken into consideration such broad conclusions are difficult to draw. Figure 4-4 and Figure 4-5 are based on the Rector-Hederman study.

2. Rector, Robert, and Rea Hederman, Jr. *Two Americas: One Rich, One Poor* and *Understanding Income Inequality in the United States*. Washington, D.C., The Heritage Foundation. August 2004.

Figure 4-5

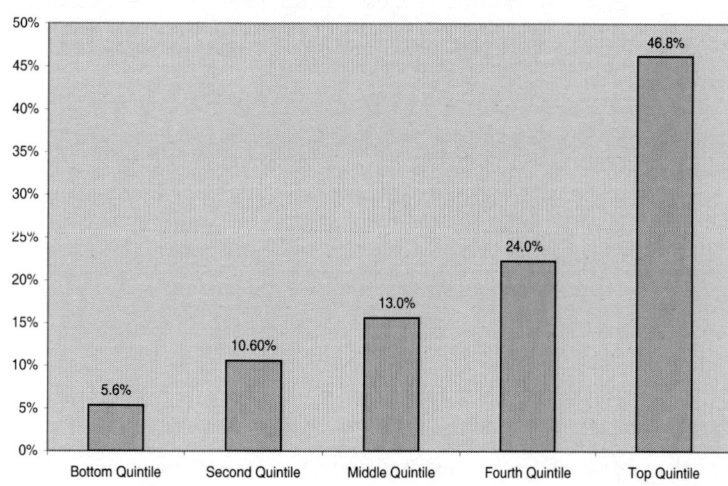

Source: U.S. Bureau of the Census, Current Population Survey for 2008

For example Figure 4-4 shows the differences in the distributions of pre-tax income uncompensated for tax payments or other factors The top quintile received 50.4 percent of income and the bottom quintile 3.4 percent. Figure 4-5, on the other hand, shows the changes in the distribution once tax payments, capital gains, health insurance and non cash government benefits are included. The top quintile received 46.2 percent of income and the bottom quintile received 5.4 percent. Equity in the distribution is made more difficult to assess when we observe that in 2002, taxpayers in the top quintile paid more than 82 percent of taxes and those in the bottom quintile more than 3 percent.

Economic Implications of Inequality in Income Distribution

Although the ethical implications of inequality in distribution of income are fascinating, we will restrict ourselves to the economic implications.

In underdeveloped countries, the main problem is to increase the economy's output so that all citizens can have a higher standard of living. These countries need increased resources, especially capital, to shift the production-possibilities curve outward and increase economic growth. Forming new capital requires increased savings. Increasing savings withdraws resources from the production of consumer goods, thus making these resources available for investment, and the production of capital. So to increase the formation of capital and to foster more rapid economic growth, a higher rate of savings is needed. The rich save a larger percentage of their income than the poor because the poor spend all their income to maintain their standard of living. A more uneven distribution of income would increase the income of the rich and might increase savings. Thus, apart from other considerations, an underdeveloped country, in order to increase savings and the rate of formation of new capital, might require a less equal income distribution than it already has.

On the other hand, in a developed economy, a central problem is how to maintain full employment and keep the large industrial system growing. To do this, you want consumers to demand all the goods and services that business firms can produce. Here one may reverse the argument of the preceding paragraph and say that a developed country ought to have *its* income more evenly distributed. That way, the rich would get a smaller slice of the pie. Savings would be less and consumer demand higher. This view, though prevalent in the 1950s, '60s, and '70s, was challenged by supply-side economists beginning in the 1980s who have argued that increased savings are needed in developed economies also.

Two qualifications are necessary to the above. The problems of economic growth and full employment are much more complex than the above brief sketch indicates. Second, economic *efficiency* (maximizing output with a given set of resources) is not the same thing as economic *equity* (what we think, normatively, is right or wrong in a moral sense). The implications for distribution of income may differ, depending on whether our goal is efficiency or equity and on what weight we give to each.

BUSINESS FIRMS

Today there are more than 10 million companies in the United States, from the corner grocery store to such corporate giants as AT&T. We can classify business firms primarily under three legal headings: (1) *Sole Proprietorships*, (2) *Partnerships*, and (3) *Corporations*.

Sole Proprietorships

Sole Proprietorship
A business firm owned by one individual who has full responsibility for it.

The most common form of business organization is the **sole proprietorship**, an enterprise owned by one person, who is solely responsible for it. There are more than 9 million sole proprietorships in the United States, chiefly in agriculture, retail trade, pharmacy, law, and medicine. They are usually small in scale and have an average life span of five to seven years. Although hundreds of thousands cease production each year, even larger numbers begin each year.

Advantages of a Sole Proprietorship

1. You can easily form a sole proprietorship; it doesn't take much cash. In many areas, just the act of beginning production is all that is necessary.

2. The sole proprietor is the only one to receive benefits when the firm succeeds, and is the only one responsible for its activity, so there is a close correlation between effort expended and reward. Thus, the incentives for efficiency are great.

Disadvantages of a Sole Proprietorship

1. The sole proprietorship has **unlimited liability**. This means that there is no differentiation between the assets of the business enterprise and the personal wealth of the proprietor. If the business incurs losses, the proprietor is responsible for them.

2. Sole proprietors must rely on themselves for all management skills, and since no one person can be a specialist in all managerial functions, the business may suffer. Inadequate management is one of the chief cause of failure in small, sole-proprietor businesses.

3. The sole proprietorship often has limited capital, since the proprietor has to depend primarily on his or her own resources, and since an individual's borrowing capacity is limited. Sole proprietors also tend to have lower credit ratings than partnerships or corporations.

4. The sole proprietorship has *limited life*, in the sense that the lifetime of the business may be limited to the working lifetime of the proprietor.

Partnerships

Partnership
A form of business organization in which two or more individuals combine to operate an enterprise.

A second form of business organization is the **partnership**, in which two or more individuals combine to operate a business enterprise. There are several kinds of partnerships, but the following is a general description.

Advantages of a Partnership

1. Because there are two or more people involved in the ownership, the partner-owned business has access to more capital. The enterprise can draw on the wealth and borrowing power of its several partners.

2. A business with more than one owner can count on specialized skills in management. One partner can be in charge of production; another of accounting; a third, of sales; and so on. Specialization of management functions strengthens a business greatly.

Disadvantages of a Partnership

1. A partnership, like a sole proprietorship, has unlimited liability. Each individual partner's personal wealth can be tapped to pay debts. Each partner is responsible not only for his or her own mistakes, but also for the mistakes of all the rest of the partners.

2. Partnerships have limited life, which fosters instability. Partnership agreements are automatically dissolved whenever a partner dies, or whenever one withdraws from the partnership because of a disagreement. The remaining partners may draw up a new partnership agreement, or they may not.

3. Partnerships have limited access to capital. Various devices that the corporation can use to raise financial capital are not available to the partnership.

Corporations

Corporations
Business firms whose existence and function is apart from that of their owners.

Corporations are legal entities that function separately from their owners. There are fewer corporations by far than there are sole proprietorships or partnerships, but corporations produce more, employ more people, and have more assets than all other business forms combined.

Advantages of a Corporation

Limited Liability
In a corporation, the fact that individual owners are responsible only for the value of their shares purchased and not other debts.

1. A corporation's owners have **limited liability**. This means that the people who own it, the stockholders, are not responsible individually for its debts. They can lose only the money they paid for their stock. The risks of the firm, thus, are not only spread over a larger group of owners but limited to the value of the individuals' shares.

Obviously, the situation is not that simple. The owner-manager of a small corporation may very well have to pledge her or his own credit and take on a personal liability. For example, in order to raise additional funds, the manager may become personally liable by signing a personal note for a loan for the corporation. The discussion that follows, however, relates more to the larger corporation than the smaller.

2. Because a corporation is a legal entity, it can be sued (or it can sue) without the owners, the stockholders, becoming involved.

3. A corporation has **unlimited life**; it can continue to exist no matter who owns stock in it. Stockholders continually buy and sell their ownership instruments (shares of stock) with no effect on the life of the company.

Bonds
Debt instruments issued by corporations.

Preferred Stock
Stock issued by a corporation that has no voting rights but has a preferred right to dividend payments.

Common Stock
Stock issued by a corporation that has voting rights but no preference in the distribution of dividends.

4. A corporation has easier access to financial capital because of its ability to use a variety of financial instruments: bonds, preferred stock, and common stock. **Bonds** are instruments of debt; the corporation has to pay interest on them regularly, and counts this as a cost of production. Stocks, on the other hand, are equities or instruments of ownership, and the company is not required to pay dividends on them regularly. **Preferred stock** is called preferred because the company has to pay dividends on it *before* it pays dividends to holders of **common stock**. Owners of preferred stock have no voting privileges, however, and usually there are limits on the amount of dividends the company can pay to them. Owners of common stock have full voting rights and no limitations on the amount of dividends that the company can pay them.

5. Because stockholders need not be managers of a corporation, and because the corporation can raise large amounts of financial capital, it can afford to hire efficient managers, capable of taking on very specialized management functions.

Disadvantages of a Corporation

1. Forming a corporation may take a long time and be very expensive, depending on the nature of the proposed firm. People involved in the formation of a new corporation have to follow state and federal laws, pay fees of incorporation, and pay lawyers' fees and other expenses.

Double Taxation
The fact that a corporation pays taxes on its gross earnings and its shareholders pay taxes again when corporate earnings are distributed as dividends.

2. A corporation has to pay taxes to both the state and federal governments (corporate income taxes, property taxes, and so on). This leads to **double taxation**, which means that the corporation pays taxes on the gross income it earns, and distributes parts of the remaining income as dividends to stockholders; then the stockholders have to pay taxes on the dividends, since this money constitutes personal income.

3. State and federal governments pass laws that restrict the behavior of corporations. Some of these restrictions do not apply to sole proprietorships or partnerships.

4. The larger the corporation, the more ownership may become separated from control, and the greater the possibility of conflict of interest between managers and owners. Large corporations may have thousands of stockholders. The largest corporations, such as AT&T, General Motors, and Exxon/Mobil, may have millions. Stockholders who hold only a few shares have neither the time nor the incentive to take an active part in controlling the corporation by their votes.

When management sends out its annual report, containing a glowing description of what it has done for the stockholder this year, it includes a proxy card. This proxy card, if the stockholder signs and returns it, gives the company's management the right to vote his or her stock. If the corporation has paid the usual dividend, the stockholder generally mails the proxy card back. In this way management tends to become self-perpetuating and often may regard its stockholders as being, in a sense, the recipient of corporate welfare (after all, they get their regular dividend checks). Stockholders, busy people placated by regular payments of money, may become lethargic and uncritically accept the policies of management. Management may orient its policies first and foremost toward its own continued control of the corporation. In brief, we are implying that, in many large corporations, the stockholders may find it hard to control the management. If this occurs, the self-interest of these independent managers may conflict with the self-interest of the stockholders

Readers will note that even when management policies diverge from the interests of stockholder-owners, market discipline may occur in the form of takeover bids. Should management decisions result in lower profits and reduced prices of a firm's stocks, financial entrepreneurs may initiate a "takeover" of the firm in the belief that present share prices "undervalue" the firm, and that with new management, the firm can be made more profitable.

Big Business and the American Corporation

Americans have a long history of concern about firms that engage in monopolistic behavior. This concern is evidenced by U.S. acceptance of the antimonopoly provisions of English Common Law and by the many antimonopoly or antitrust laws that Congress has passed since the Sherman Antitrust Act of 1890.

People have feared that large monopolistic firms would interfere in a competitive economy and even try to subvert the democratic political system, and that these firms would increase prices while reducing output, and slow the rate of adoption of improved technology. In addition, some people have been afraid that firms of great size and wealth could encourage decisions by government that would be unduly favorable to them, and that would ignore the public good.

www.whitehouse.gov/fsbr/esbr.html
For more information on production visit this web site.

Although corporations are a minority of business firms, they are the dominant form of business organization. Table 4-5 shows that the four largest automobile corporations had more than 90 percent of the sales of the industry, not including imports, in 2002 alone. Concentration, though, becomes much smaller in other industries such as food preparation in which the four largest firms made 32 percent of sales. We will consider the implications of such concentration in later sections of this book. Figure 4-4 shows how dominant the corporate form of business is in the modern American economy. Although accounting for only 20 percent of the number of firms, corporations accounted for over 90 percent of sales in 2002. On the other hand, single proprietorships dominated the number of firms (70 percent) but accounted for only 6 percent of sales. Partnerships made up the remainder in both categories (10 percent of firms, only 3 percent of sales).

Table 4-5
Concentration of Manufacturing Production: Sales Ratio for Selected Industries, 2008

Industry	Percentage of Sales by Four Largest Firms
Motor vehicles	87
Malt beverages	77
Aircraft engines and parts	70
Soap and detergents	55
Metal cans	41
Food Preparation	34

Source: U.S. Bureau of the Census, Census of Manufactures, 2008 (data are for 2007).

Figure 4-6
Number of Firms and Percent of Sales by Types of Firms, 2007

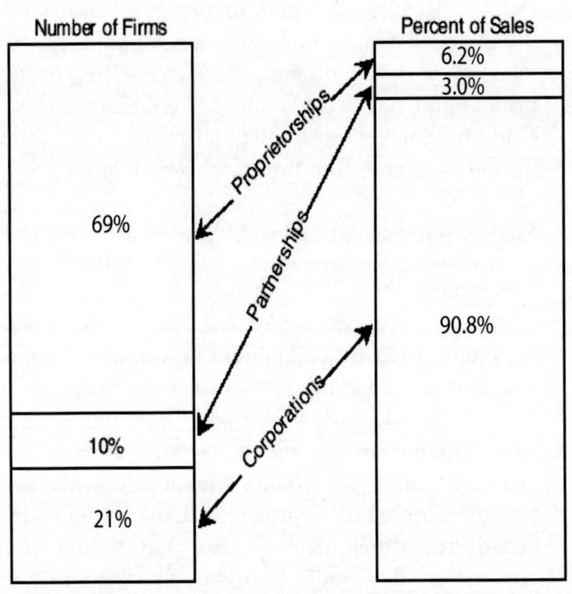

Source: Statistical Abstract of the United States, 2008.

Some critics, as we noted earlier, have criticized corporations for their dominance of the economy and feared their ability to exert undue influence both politically and economically in American society. As we have seen, though, this form of business organization offers great advantages in its ability to raise capital and bring together the larger quantities of resources, including organization and management, that modern technology dictates for the sake of efficiency. Critics mistakenly equate bigness with the ability to restrict competition or to exercise monopolistic influences over both the economy and its political processes. There will be much more about these subjects in the microeconomics portion of your principles of economics course.

Multinational Corporations
Those that buy resources as well as produce and sell products in many countries and throughout parts of the world.

It is worth noting that many modern corporations have crossed national boundaries in this century. Indeed, since World War II, there has been a major growth of **multinational corporations,** those that buy resources as well as produce and sell products in many countries throughout the world. Though fear was expressed early on that such corporations would lie beyond the control or oversight of individual nations, and thus potentially destabilize economic relations, international competition and growth in market sizes seem to have greatly diminished that concern. Clearly, the multinationals have performed a useful role in enhancing the movement of resources as well as goods and services throughout the globe. In other words, they have helped to create a more integrated international economy.

Table 4-6
Expenditures of the Federal Government, for 2012

Item on Which Money is Spent	Percentage of Total	Expenditures (Billions of Dollars)
Defense (military)	19	677
Medicare & Medicaid	21	748
Income security	12	428
Social security	22	784
Net interest (public debt)	6	214
All other	20	712
Total	100.0	3,563

Source: Congressional Budget Office Historical Tables.

Figure 4-7
Direct Expenditures of State and Local Governments 2010

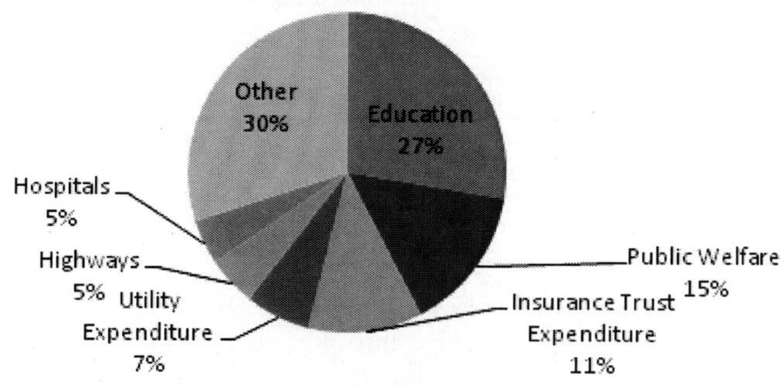

Source: U.S. Census Bureau, 2010 Annual Surveys of State and Local Government Finances.

GOVERNMENTS

Governments, federal, state, and local, affect economic activities through many means: (1) expenditures, (2) taxation, (3) enactment of laws, and (4) regulatory activities.

Expenditures: What Do They Spend All That Money On?

The expenditures of the federal government for all sorts of things, from guns to butter, stimulate output in the economy, both directly and indirectly. These expenditures stimulate output directly by creating a demand for goods and services; they stimulate it indirectly by income transfers that do not require an immediate good or service in return, such as educational grants, social security, and interest on the national debt.

When you look at Table 4-6, you will notice the figures for income security, Social Security, Medicare and Medicaid, which together accounted for about 55 percent of expenditures in 2012. Defense expenditures came third, with around 19 percent. In addition, some of the expenditures for international affairs and finance, as well as interest on the national debt, are attributable to previous national defense efforts.

Figure 4-7 shows the way state and local governments generally spend their money. For these two levels of government, the two major direct items in 2010 were education (27.7 percent) and public welfare (14.7 percent). These two added up to over 42 percent of the states' budgets.

Taxation

Taxes drain off; (that is, consumes) purchasing power that households could otherwise use to buy consumer goods. Thus, taxation reduces consumer demand. Let us look briefly at the way taxation affects this demand.

Principles of Taxation

Who should pay for government services? And how much should they pay? There are two ways of looking at this problem: (1) benefits received and (2) ability to pay.

Benefits-Received Principle
That argument that tax payments should be commensurate with the benefits received from government services.

Benefits Received: According to the **benefits-received principle**, people should pay taxes commensurate with the benefits they receive from government services. School taxes are a hypothetical example: a family with two children in public schools would pay twice as much as a family with only one in public school, and a family with no children in public school would pay no school taxes.

This view looks at government services as services that the taxpayer buys, much as she or he buys shoes or tomatoes in the market. It reverses the old adage that "you get what you pay for" to "you pay for what you get." The people who receive government services pay for them with taxes. By this reasoning, the more services you receive, the more taxes you should pay.

In reality, there are limitations to applying the benefits-received principle. First, it is practically impossible, in many cases, to figure out a fair basis for taxes by this principle. For example, how could national security expenditures be distributed on the basis of benefits received? Even the distribution of school taxes is not simple, because a person who never has children benefits from living in a society of better-educated citizens. Second, if one applied the benefits-received principle strictly, it would place heavy burdens on the poor and disadvantaged members of our society, who would be denied access to most government services because they could not pay for them. The point is that the benefits-received principle may be more appropriate in some areas than others, and in some areas it may not be appropriate at all.

Notwithstanding these two drawbacks, the government has sources of tax revenue based substantially on benefits received:

1. *State and federal excise taxes on gasoline*. These taxes are frequently earmarked for construction and maintenance of highways; the more you use the highways, the more gasoline you must buy and the more taxes you must pay to maintain the highways. It is true, however, that tax revenues are increasingly being used to fund mass transit systems that are not based on the benefits-received principle.

2. *Payroll taxes*. These are put into various funds, out of which social security, Medicare, and other benefit payments are made. As the social security program is expanded and as the average age of Americans increases, the government increases these taxes to pay for the added benefits, and to compensate for inflation. (Although social security benefits do vary somewhat, according to variations in how much one has paid into the program, these differences are fairly limited and thus weaken this example.) In fact, recent studies suggest that there is little relationship between social security benefits and taxes paid by individuals.

Ability-to-Pay Principle
The argument that, as peoples' incomes grow, they can afford to pay a larger part of their incomes in taxes.

The **ability-to-pay principle** of taxation assumes that those who have a larger income are capable of paying not only a larger tax, but also of paying a larger percentage of their income in taxes than those who have smaller incomes. According to this argument, when a person has a very low income, all of it goes to buy necessities. As the person's income increases, some of it can be devoted to non-necessities. The higher a family's income, the more it can afford to spend on nonessentials and the larger percentage of its income it can pay in taxes, while still being able to buy essentials.

One tax based on the ability-to-pay concept is the graduated income tax. The taxpayer, after deducting for size of family and for certain expenditures (health-care expenses, interest payments, charity, and so on), pays a percentage of net income in taxes. The higher the net income, the higher the percentage. A real flaw in this system is the near impossibility of enacting tax laws that are equitable to all and of arranging the deductions in such a way that families are taxed at a comparable rate. For a long time there has been controversy about these deductions and about other rules relating to what is considered taxable income. Many people charge that tax loopholes benefit higher-income groups. One big loophole which you have probably heard discussed, is the **capital gains tax**. It used to work this way: If you bought an asset and held it for at least one year and sold it for a gain, only 25 percent of the difference, or capital gain (that is, the increase in value of the asset), was considered taxable income. In 2003, capital gains taxes were again treated differently. The gains in asset values are now taxed at a rate of 15 percent. Proponents argue that this will lead to increased saving and investment while opponents say that the change simply reinstates a loophole that primarily benefits those with high incomes.

Types of Tax Rates

Tax Rate
The percentage of income paid in taxes.

The **income tax rate** is the percentage of income a person pays in taxes. We can classify taxes in relation to the tax rate and what happens to it as our income increases. From this point of view, taxes are either progressive, regressive, or proportional.

Progressive Tax
A tax in which the rate increases as income increases.

A **progressive tax** is one in which the rate increases as income increases. The best example of it is federal income tax. As a person's taxable income gets larger, the rate of taxation increases also.

Regressive Tax.
A tax in which the rate decreases as income increases.

A **regressive tax** is one in which the rate declines as income increases. A sales tax is an example: When you pay a sales tax on clothes, you pay it on the basis of how much you buy. The *rate* does not change as the amount you buy increases. However, the higher your income, the larger the percentage of income you put into savings, and the smaller the percentage of income you put into clothes. So the percentage of your income that the government takes for sales taxes declines as your income increases.

Here is how this works in figures. Suppose that the sales tax is 5 percent. Adams has an income of $100 a week and spends all of it on taxable items. Thus Adams spends 5 percent of income on sales tax. However, Bloggs makes $200 a week. Being "richer," Bloggs saves $50 and spends only $150 on sales-taxable items. The sales tax Bloggs pays, as a percentage of income, is only 3.75 percent. *Note:* Some sales taxes have a stronger impact on low-income groups than others. A sales tax on bread would be much more regressive than a sales tax on swimming pools. In fact, if a sales tax is properly selective, it need not be regressive at all.

Figure 4-8
The Three Types of Tax Rates

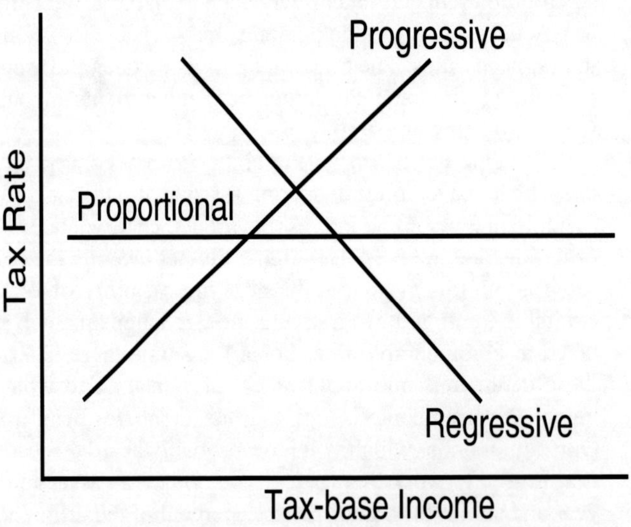

Proportional Tax
A tax in which the rate remains constant as income changes.

A **proportional tax** is one with a rate that remains the same as the taxpayer's income changes. Social Security taxes fit this concept. The percentage tax rate (6.2 percent) stays the same up to the cap of around $113,700 for 2013. Beyond this limit the tax becomes regressive since you continue to earn more income and pay no additional taxes. Some states have proportional taxes on incomes[3].

Figure 4-8 shows that the progressive curve slopes upward, so that the tax rate increases (up the vertical axis) as the tax-base income increases (out the horizontal axis). The regressive curve slopes downward, so the tax rate decreases (down the vertical axis) as the tax-base income increases (out the horizontal axis). The proportional curve is horizontal, since the tax rate remains unchanged as the ax-base income increases (out the horizontal axis).

Table 4-7
Estimated Federal Government Revenues by Source, est 2012

Source	Amount of Revenue (Trillions of Dollars)	Percent of total
Personal current taxes	1.13	46
Corporate income tax	.245	10
Other taxes	.221	9
Social insurance receipts	.858	35
Total	2.45	100.0

Source: Economic Report of the President, 2011

Table 4-8
Sources of State and Local Revenues, 2010

Source	Billions of Dollars	Percent
Property taxes	893	35
Sales and gross receipts taxes	867	34
Individual income taxes	510	20
Corporation net income taxes	77	3
Motor vehicle	51	2
All other	153	6
Total	2.56	100.0

Source: U.S. Census Bureau, 2011.

Composition of Taxes

Table 4-7 shows where the federal government obtains its revenues. As you would expect, personal income taxes are the most important source, bringing in 45.4 percent of the total in 2006. Payroll tax dollars (social insurance receipts), which mostly go to pay for social security and Medicare, are next, with 36.6 percent. Corporate income taxes come third, with 10.8 percent of the 2006 total.

Table 4-8 gives the same information about state and local governments combined. Note that these governments tend to get a large percentage of their tax money from sales taxes: 34 percent. Only about 20 percent of state and local revenues come from personal income taxes. Local governments, alone, collect most of their tax revenue from property taxes: about 68 percent of the total in 2010. It should be noted that by May, 2009, transfers

3. The definitions used in this section are followed by most economists. These definitions of progressive, regressive and proportional taxes are slightly different from the definitions one would find in a dictionary.

from the federal government under its stimulus program were the largest source revenue for state governments.

Who Pays the Tax?

Usually, you cannot shift the responsibility for paying your personal income taxes to another person. Most of us lack the economic power to pass on these taxes by making others pay higher rates for our service or products. Property taxes are, in effect, paid by those who use the property. For example, renters usually pay the property tax, indirectly, as part of their rent unless their building has many vacancies, in which case the landlord may not be able to charge high enough rents to shift all the tax to the renters.

But what about corporate income taxes? Does the corporation pay them, or can they pass these taxes along to their customers through higher prices? If the corporation is operating in a field in which there is a lot of competition, the competition prevents it from passing the tax along to customers. If a corporation is in an industry in which there is little competition (for example, large firms that make a product for which there are few good substitutes), the firm may be able to shift at least part of the burden of the tax to the customer.

Is the tax structure as a whole, federal, state, and local, progressive or regressive? Federal income taxation, because of the large share coming from personal income taxes, is probably somewhat progressive. Tax loopholes (such as the exemption from taxes of the interest from tax-free municipal bonds) cancel some of the progressiveness of the personal income tax. State taxes, because of the predominance of sales taxes, are probably regressive, whereas local taxes are probably closer to proportional, because of the predominance of property taxes.

Government and the Rules of the Game

Governments, by enacting and enforcing various laws, set the rules for economic activity. To begin with, the Constitution itself sets some of the rules, and the Supreme Court has backed these up through its interpretations of the Constitution. Also there have been many statutes passed, plus countless laws relating to contracts. Virtually every business transaction involving a contract is limited by these laws. The many antitrust laws indicate how anxious Congress is to keep large corporations from exercising monopoly power. Bear in mind that labor unions, and the government itself, also have monopoly power, though labor unions are exempted from the provisions of the antitrust laws.

Government and Regulation

To set limits for the nation's industries, many federal and state commissions regulate economic activities to varying degrees. For example, in every state, there are public utility commissions that set prices and set other guidelines for telephone, electricity, gas, water, and transportation services. Some argue that these utility commissions are politically biased and even in some cases have anti-competitive effects. Perhaps so, but their intended purpose is to prevent the utility companies from taking advantage of the public through their power over prices.

Some of the principal federal government agencies charged with economic regulations are:

1. *The Interstate Commerce Commission*. Established in 1887, it was responsible for overseeing rail, bus, and truck transportation; sets rate schedules, routes,

and various conditions of competition. Its powers have diminished with the substantial deregulation of recent decades.

2. *The Federal Trade Commission.* Established in 1914 to prevent unfair practices by firms (such as false and misleading advertising).

3. *The Food and Drug Administration.* Acts as watchdog against harmful or disease-carrying foods, cosmetics, and drugs; also checks the efficacy of drugs and the validity of drug advertising.

4. *The Federal Communications Commission.* Regulates TV and radio; grants and revokes licenses to broadcast.

5. *The Securities and Exchange Commission.* Supervises the stock exchanges, the over-the-counter stock market, and the issuance of new securities; tries to prevent manipulation of stock prices; tries to ensure truthful and adequate information on stocks to stockholders, both present and potential.

6. *The Departments of Agriculture; Housing; Transportation; and Health and Human Services* have branches that perform overseeing and regulatory functions.

With all these agencies to help protect consumers and businesses, is the public well protected? There is doubt; many people feel that in spite of this network of regulatory agencies, the consumer is often short-changed. Some people charge that many of the people serving on the commissions, in fact, are "captured," that is, they favor the industries they're supposed to regulate, a case of the wolves guarding the sheep. This may be true, at least in some cases, since many of them were executives in these very industries before they were appointed, and many of them, after their term of office, become executives in the same industries they have been regulating. On the other hand, the agencies are sometimes so "captured" by consumer interests that they fail to leave firms with revenues that permit them to compete for capital. Again, these are subjects that will be treated more extensively in the microeconomic principles of economics course in which the regulatory functions of governments are examined in more detail.

The Rest of the World

In the absence of trade with other nations, the components of an economic society would consist of its households, business firms, and its government(s). Throughout history, however, societies have exchanged goods and services as well as resources with each other. In doing so, an economic society becomes an open economy, one whose levels of income and product are influenced both by domestic and foreign economic activities.

Open Economy
One whose levels of income and product depend on both domestic and foreign economic activities.

In an **open economy**, the circular flow diagram shown in Figure 4-2 must be modified to incorporate the effects of (1) exports, those goods and services sold to other nations, and (2) imports, those goods and services purchased from other nations. Business firms, households, and governments are all involved in these flows. Businesses export goods and services and earn incomes from factors of production such as capital investments abroad. Conversely, foreign businesses export goods and services to our domestic economy and earn factor incomes from factors such as capital employed in the domestic economy. Households buy imported goods and sell factors of production such as financial capital. Governments not only regulate these international flows but also collect import tax revenues and, through domestic international financial institutions, influence the monetary flows and currency exchange rates that play an important role in the open economy's international transactions. Much more will be said about these activities and their importance to the domestic economy in the chapters on international trade and finance.

Application I: Business Firms, Profit Maximizers or Agents of Social Responsibility?

The Effect of Competition on Business Morals

In Western Europe in the Middle Ages, the moral prescriptions of the church affected the economic behavior of merchants. The concepts of a just price and a just wage, plus the widespread idea that anyone who charged interest on money was guilty of usury, were intended to limit employers and merchants in setting prices.

By the time Adam Smith[4] wrote *The Wealth of Nations*, in 1776, the dictates of the church that restrained merchants were replaced by the dictates of competition, which surprisingly enough exerted an even stronger effect, and in the same direction. Adam Smith's "Invisible hand" was *competition.* According to Smith, businessmen (as well as consumers) were selfish and concerned primarily with their own personal gain. Self-interest ruled economic behavior, but competition restrained this behavior, this desire to maximize one's own economic good, and channeled it into maximizing the public good. Why?

Each firm had such a small part of the total market that it could not control the price of a given product and thus gain an advantage over others. Each small firm seeking customers had to produce at the most efficient level, turn out the kinds of products and services the consumer wanted, and sell them at the lowest price commensurate with staying in business. The selfishness of these small producers was guided, as if by an invisible hand (competition), to maximize the welfare of society at large.

However, today, although many industries do have to cope with fierce competition, many others are dominated by a few giant firms (though even these may be restrained by foreign competition or by competition from firms in other industries). So the tenets of the medieval church no longer exercise the force of law over the people, and monopoly power may have weakened Adam Smith's invisible hand of competition.

How should corporate producers behave? Should they produce goods and services and price them with only the goal of maximizing their own profits, using every advantage their size and market dominance affords? Or should the corporation, like a good citizen, consider the social and economic needs of the society as a whole? In other words, what are the social responsibilities of business?

Responsible to Whom?

Business decision makers, including corporate managers, have many responsibilities. In recent years, the notable corporate scandals involving firms such as Enron and Worldcom have reinforced the importance of reexamining these responsibilities. The financial crisis of 2008 - 2011 has exposed extensive risk taking and its impact on the economy as indications of a lack of social responsibility as well. Among these are responsibilities to stockholders, to employees,

---

4. Smith, Adam. *An Enquiry into the Nature and Causes of the Wealth of Nations*. London, Metheun and Co. 1904. Fifth Edition.

and, of course, to their own self-interests. An interesting and important question to ask is: Does the pursuit of profit by firms, especially in a competitive market environment, necessarily lead to the serving of the broader interests of society? Adam Smith clearly believed that this coincidence of interests (those of individuals and society) would occur through the invisible hand of competitive pressure even though it was through "no intent" of those making the business decisions. In more recent times, however, questions have been raised about whether and under what conditions the coincidence occurs. Further questions have arisen as to whether firms *should* act out of a sense of social responsibility as well as one of responsibility to shareholders. In a fundamental sense, these two sets of questions (*are* society's interests served by individual firm decisions, and *should* firms try to serve social interests) are bound up together. Let's look at the arguments on both sides.

Maximizing Profits: Serving Private or Public Interests?

Corporate directors and the managers who report to them have a responsibility to the firms' owners, its stockholders. That responsibility to enhance the value of their shares is consistent with making decisions that maximize the firms' profits (the difference between its revenues and costs). Critics of decisions made on this basis say that while it satisfies one narrow set of (stockholder) interests, it can result in actions that are socially irresponsible or that impose costs on many others in society. While it may, for example, be possible to produce a passenger vehicle at lower costs by failing to make it "crash-safe," or to equip it with tires or other systems that are unsafe, the extra profit gained merely transfers costs to others and, in the judgment of such critics, is unethical or immoral. More to the point, say critics, it creates a need for government regulation to ensure that public health and safety standards are adequately represented where profit maximizing decisions do not lead to those results.

Critics of profit maximizing decisions frequently argue, thus, that the public's representatives (government) should constrain profit maximizing decisions by (1) limiting how products can be produced (e.g., crash resistant construction of cars, non-polluting insecticides) and (2) What products can be marketed (e.g., banning such "noxious" products as marijuana, cocaine, asbestos, and the like). Also government has a responsibility, say critics, to regulate the behavior of the firm not only in producing its products, but also in marketing them. While deceptive advertising, for instance, *might* be profitable for a firm, government agencies (e.g., the Federal Trade Commission and the Securities and Exchange Commission) help prevent consumers from being misled by narrowly focused profit-seeking firms.

Of course, there are many others who say that many business firms, while concerned with profits, also *do* act out of a sense of social responsibility. Why else, say proponents of this view, would corporations sponsor medical research or make donations to public broadcasting or voluntarily recall defective products. If nothing else, say those with this view, the "immoral" and abusive actions that profit maximizing firms might undertake would be deterred by the fear of a reaction from the public. Such corporate actions might lead to public insistence that governments strictly regulate firm behavior and do so in a way contradictory of the firm's and its stockholders' interests.

Cartoon Feature Syndicate

"I figure someone has to hold the line."

Maximizing Profits: Competition and the Invisible Hand

There is evidence that the American economy has become substantially more competitive in recent decades. According to an important study in the 1980s by William Shephard[5], increased competitiveness has been due to (1) deregulation (removal of government controls) of several industries, (2) increased competition from other countries (imports), and (3) antitrust (antimonopoly) legal actions by governments. Thus, although market power remains significant in some U.S. industries (e.g., computers, soups, cereals, drugs, and the like) there has been a major resurgence of competitive forces in almost all others. While these are subjects that you will explore more fully in the microeconomic principles course, for our purposes, it suffices to ask: How is competition related to socially responsible behavior by firms?

The answer to the above question turns heavily on the kind of business behavior considered. Firms in a competitive industry all sell at the same price. We would not, therefore, expect a single firm to make production decisions that raise its costs above those of other firms for to do so would lower the firm's profit. The market, in other words, would punish such behavior. On the other hand, the competitive market will also punish firms that produce inferior or unsafe products for such firms will lose customers to the many other firms whose (superior or safe) products are very good substitutes for those of the "greedy" firm.

Where monopoly exists, that is where consumers do not have good alternatives to buying from "greedy" firms or those that produce unsafe or inferior products, markets may not punish or at least may not punish as quickly or surely a firm's "profits at any cost" strategy. Under these market circumstances, many argue for government regulations that may take such forms as product safety standards or even government licensing of products. Even in

---

5. Shepherd, William G. "Causes of Increased Competition in the U.S. Economy, 1939-1980." *Review of Economics and Statistics* 64. November, 1982.

many of these cases, however, it may be more advantageous for government policy to encourage competition than to engage in regulation.

When May Markets Punish Socially Responsible Behavior?

Even competitive markets will not necessarily encourage socially desirable behavior or punish undesirable behavior in all cases. One of the clearest examples is the case of environmental pollution. A firm that voluntarily undertook costly pollution reduction decisions (e.g., smokestack scrubbers) in producing its products while other firms did not would see its relative profit fall. The market, in other words, might well punish socially desirable behavior. To ensure that such behavior is forthcoming, therefore, may well require government action or intervention. As environmental problems have become more apparent and in many instances more severe, pressure for government intervention to cause firms to use scarce environmental resources (e.g., air, water) in ways compatible with social goals has increased. As a result, air quality goals and standards have been developed in many areas. Emissions controls have been mandated and other actions taken that affect products produced and the techniques used to produce them. While these actions have not changed the basic nature of profit maximizing decisions by firms, they have altered the constraints within which those decisions are made. In the twenty-first century, there are calls for government to engage in regulatory and other programs that will reduce the environmental effects of "greenhouse" emissions. This may result in effects that change production processes and prices, although how and to what extent is not clear yet.

Can or Should Firms Decide What is in Society's Interest?

The idea of Smith's invisible hand was not that business people either intended to promote the public's interest or, in fact, even *knew* necessarily what that interest was. Doubtless, there are instances in which decision makers realize that certain actions would even be counter to the interests of many other citizens. Selling products that are known to be harmful and deceiving consumers into believing them to be beneficial falls into this category. In other cases, though, firms may simply not have either the information or the perspective to judge what is or is not in society's interest as opposed to their own (profit maximizing) interest. A single competitive firm in Los Angeles, for example, may have no idea what *its* production technology contributes to the environmental pollution of that "air shed." As a result, it could make no rational choice, even if it wanted to act in a socially responsible manner, about how much it should spend on modifying its plant. All firms acting in this same manner, though, may significantly pollute the air. A decision about socially desirable air purity standards, thus, must be made socially rather than privately. The main point here is that, in instances such as the hypothetical one above, it is not always greed or selfishness that creates the lack of correspondence between private and social interests; rather, it is at least sometimes the lack of information or perspective that creates the problem. Where those circumstances exist, society must, through some means, create the perspective and provide the information upon which firms are expected to act. In 2009, the federal government assumed much larger responsibility for circumscribing private firms behavior. Its actions included limiting cooperate salaries for executives whose firms received "bailout" funds and even determining which executives would be retained and which fired.

SUMMING UP

1. In the basic circular-flow model of the national economy, households provide firms with all the factors of production. Firms, in turn, pay to employ these resources, which they use to produce goods and services for the households. To complete the circle, households use the income from selling their resources to pay for the goods and services. Firms using the income from the sale of goods and services pay for still more factors of production to produce still more goods and services. And so on.

2. The more complex model of the national economy takes into account the fact that people do not spend all of their incomes. They save some and pay some out to governments as taxes. This reduces the public's demand for business firms' goods and services. The household's savings go to financial institutions, which make them available for investments. The household's tax dollars go to the government, which uses them to buy goods and services, and thereby becomes industry's biggest customer. However, these flows of money from investment and from government to business firms, to buy industry's goods and services, are not always at a level that make possible full employment and stable prices.

3. The concept of *functional distribution of income* has to do with the sources of income. In 2011, 69.2 percent of income in the United States came from wages and salaries; about 10.9 percent was corporate profits; about nine percent was proprietors' income; eight percent was interest income; and three percent was rental income.

4. In 2011, Americans spent about 82 percent of their income on personal consumption and about 10 percent on taxes; they save about 4.9 percent. Of the amounts spent on consumption, they spend about 14 percent on durable goods, 35 percent on nondurable goods, and 51 percent on services.

5. The distribution of income in the United States is unequal. The 20 percent of families receiving the lowest incomes receive only about 4.1 percent of the total U.S. income, while the 20 percent receiving the highest incomes get about 52.5 percent of it. When one diagrams the data on income distribution for a given period, one sees that the resulting curve which economists call a *Lorenz curve*. The distribution after taxes and transfer payments, if drawn, is less unequal.

6. The three main forms of business organization are the *sole proprietorship*, the *partnership*, and the *corporation*.

7. The advantages of a *sole proprietorship* are that (a) it is easy to form, and (b) there are high incentives to succeed. The disadvantages are that (a) its owner has *unlimited liability*, (b) it is difficult for a person working independently to specialize management functions, (c) access to capital is limited, and (d) it has limited life.

8. The advantages of a *partnership* are that (a) it has increased access to capital, and (b) it offers management more chances to specialize functions. The disadvantages are that (a) its owners have unlimited liability, (b) it has limited life, and (c) its access to capital is less than that of a corporation.

9. The advantages of a *corporation* are that (a) its owners have *limited liability,* thus the risks of the firm are spread over a larger group of owners, (b) it constitutes a legal entity, (c) it has *unlimited life*, (d) it has greater access to capital than a sole proprietorship or a partnership, and (e) its management can specialize functions because of its larger size. The disadvantages are that (a) the process of forming a corporation takes a long time and is expensive, (b) corporate profits are double-taxed, (c) there are special laws directed at corporations, and (d) there is a danger of separation of ownership and control.

10. Many industries in the United States are dominated by corporations. Some people charge that these large firms prevent competition and bias political decision-making although large firms, including multinational firms, are an efficient means for raising capital and enhancing resource mobility.

11. The dictates of the church, about just prices and wages, in the Middle Ages were intended to restrain business pricing. These dictates have been replaced in recent centuries by the "invisible hand" of competition has caused the private pursuit of self-interest to result in socially desirable outcomes. Development of monopoly power in some markets, though, may have limited the effect of the "invisible hand."

12. A firm's decision makers have responsibilities to the owners of the firm and profit-maximization is consistent with serving the owners' interests. Adam Smith argued that competition would make selfish (profit-maximizing) decisions by individuals consistent with the interests of society.

13. Arguably, efforts by firms to minimize cost and maximize profit may lead to the production of products that are harmful and that impose costs on many members of society. This has led critics of profit-maximizing decisions to argue that government should constrain such decisions by limiting how some products may be produced and even, in some instances, *which* products may be marketed.

14. Some say that business firms *do* act with a sense of social responsibility, which tempers their profit-maximizing decisions. If nothing else, according to proponents of this view, strict profit maximizing decisions are not always undertaken because of a fear that public insistence would lead to government strictly regulating firms' decisions.

15. Evidence suggests that the American economy has become substantially more competitive in recent decades, though market power continues to exist in some industries. The way in which competition is related to firm behavior depends on the type of behavior considered.

16. Competitive markets will punish firms that incur costs not incurred by other firms since all sell at the same price. Competitive markets also will punish firms that produce inferior or unsafe products. Monopolistic markets are not as certain to punish the latter type of behavior.

17. Socially desirable behavior, such as reducing the environmental pollution effects of production, will not likely be undertaken by competitive firms. To insure such behavior probably requires government intervention and constraining profit-maximizing behavior. That intervention may result from increasing calls to fight the environmental effects of "global warming."

18. In some instances, the invisible hand may not lead to socially desirable behavior by firms not because of greed, but because of lack of knowledge of what is socially desirable and also because of lack of social perspective.

19. The federal government spends about 19 percent of its money on defense and defense-related activities and 47 percent on income and social security. States spend 40 percent of their money on education and highways.

20. There are two main principles of taxation: (a) benefits received, and (b) ability to pay. According to the *benefits-received principle*, one should pay taxes on the basis of the amount of benefits one receives from government expenditures. According to the *ability-to-pay principle*, the tax rate should be higher percentage for higher incomes.

21. A *tax rate*, the percentage of income one pays in taxes, can be either *progressive*, *regressive*, or *proportional*. When a tax is *progressive*, the tax rate increases as income increases (for example, the graduated federal income tax). When a tax is *regressive*, the tax rate decreases as income increases (for example, some sales taxes). When a tax is *proportional*, the tax rate remains unchanged as income increases (for example, property taxes).

22. Personal income taxes are most important at the federal level, since they account for 43.8 percent of total revenues. Sales and excise taxes are most important at the state level, bringing in 49 percent of the states' monies. Property taxes are most important at the local level, because they are the source of 70 percent of total revenues.

23. Governments, by passing laws, set the rules for economic activity. Two important areas of law are those that deal with (a) contracts, and (b) antitrust legislation. Governments also affect economic activities through various regulatory commissions and agencies.

24. Closed economies, those that do not engage in trade with other nations, have their economic flows determined exclusively by domestic activities of households, firms, and governments.

25. Open economies, those that do engage in trade with other nations, have their economic flows determined not only by domestic activities, but also by the effects of exports, sales to other nations, and imports, purchases from other nations.

KEY TERMS

Ability-to-pay principle
Benefits-received principle
Closed economy
Corporation
Factor markets
Functional distribution of income
Lorenz curve
Multinational corporations
Open economy
Partnership
Product markets
Progressive tax
Proportional tax
Regressive tax
Sole proprietorship
Tax rate

QUESTIONS

1. Using the complex circular-flow model, show how changes in (a) efforts to save, (b) efforts to invest, (c) payments of taxes, and (d) spending by government all affect total output and employment. Show these changes in factors one at a time.

2. How has the functional distribution of income changed since 1929?

3. How do Lorenz curves permit comparing a number of countries in terms of the level of equality in their respective distributions of cash income? What effect(s) may taxes and transfer payments have on the equality of income distribution?

4. If you were in charge of a firm, what would be the advantages and disadvantages of operating as a sole proprietorship, as a partnership, or as a corporation? What are the disadvantages of each form of operation?

5. What is meant by saying that the "invisible hand" leads self-interest serving private individuals to make decisions that are "through no intent of their own" consistent with society's interests?

6. What are some types of profit maximizing behavior by firms that may be socially irresponsible? Should governments intervene where such behavior takes place?

7. If governments do intervene to constrain private business decisions in (6) above, what types of constraints may be imposed?

8. Even if firms are tempted to engage in narrowly "greedy" behavior, what fear might cause them not to maximize their narrow self interests?

9. What has happened to the competitiveness of the American economy in recent decades? What factors has contributed to this change?

10. What types of behavior by firms will competitive markets punish? Reward?

11. Can a society rely totally on the "invisible hand" to solve its environmental problems including "global warming?"

12. Why may it be difficult for firms that seek to behave in a socially responsible way to do so?

13. In general, which principle of taxation do you prefer: benefits received or ability to pay? Why?

14. Look at the taxes listed in Tables 4-8 and 4-9 and decide which are progressive, which regressive, and which proportional. What determines who ultimately pays each of the taxes?

15. "Economic activity is heavily influenced by the way governments define the rules of the game." Do you agree? Why?

16. "With all the government regulatory commissions and agencies, the consumer is amply protected from improper business activity." Do you agree? Why?

17. You are the economic adviser for a federal commission studying taxes. You have been given the task of recommending comprehensive changes in the composition of taxes. What recommendations on tax changes would you make? Since any changes in the composition of taxes would shift the incidence of taxes (change the people who would be paying taxes), clearly state what changes in the incidence of taxes would occur. Explain your recommended changes from an economic point of view; from a moral or ethical point of view.

SECTION II:
The Basics of the Macroeconomy

Section II

The Basics of the Macroeconomy

Section I gave you an introduction to the workings of a market economy including the fundamental ways in which markets work to allocate resources. It also introduced you to the economy's players, that is, its consumers, producers, and governments.

With that background in mind, we are going to shift focus in Section II to begin building an understanding of macroeconomics or of the economy operating at its highest level of aggregation. In Chapter 5, we will first build the empirical basis for understanding the macroeconomy by examining the measurements that are made of aggregate income flows in a society. In Chapter 6, we will lay out the relationships between those flows, the level of overall economic activity, and fluctuations in that level that create recessions and "booms" about a trend of economic growth. Chapter 7 is a discussion of how aggregate demand and supply are determined and interact to create an aggregate price level as measured by price indexes and an aggregate level of real income. Chapter 8 develops the rudiments of a model of aggregate demand and its determinants in a market economy. Chapter 9 completes this section by (1) tracing the controversies concerning the role of government verses private market forces in creating full employment equilibrium in a society, and (2) developing in stages a "Keynesian" model of the macroeconomy in which managing aggregate demand is seen as the key to income growth and full employment with stable prices.

Chapter 5: Measuring Domestic Income and Product

Gross Domestic Product: The market value of all final goods and services produced in any particular year within a country.

For reasons you will examine closely in this course, it is extremely important to measure (or estimate) how much the American economy is producing in any particular period of time. The largest such measure now in common use is called the **Gross Domestic Product (GDP)** or the market value of all final goods and services produced in any particular year within a country. All attempts to estimate national income flows go back to the 1930s and are regarded as indicators of the nation's economic health. They are also vital information in the making of national economic policy and the policies of firms throughout the economy as well as the policies of government.

In this chapter, we will look at a broad range of these estimates and also at ongoing efforts to coordinate them across the many different national economies. As we will see, changes in our national income accounting system have been made, and more changes seem likely to come as the world's economies become increasingly interdependent.

As you read, it is important to remember that GDP and the other concepts contained in this chapter are *estimates*, not precise measures. The following anecdote illustrates some of the reasons why this "caution" is necessary.

Way back in 1971, President Nixon unveiled the GNP[1] (Gross National Product) clock in the lobby of the Bureau of the Census building. The machine had been preset, according to the predictions of statisticians, to tick off the value of output produced. When the President showed the clock to reporters, it was recording a $1-trillion GNP. It didn't seem to bother anyone that (1) the machine had been running for some time, waiting for the proper moment to be revealed, (2) actual GNP was a good bit less than the $1 trillion predicted at the time, and (3) the $1-trillion GNP was in part achieved by increased prices rather than by increased output.

But despite the gadgetry and the "slight" distortions of politicians, GDP and the concepts of national income accounting are important to a better understanding of the economy. Changes in the amount of the output of an

1. The difference between Gross Domestic Product and Gross National Product is small and is explained in the next few pages.

economy can affect the material levels of well being of everyone within that economy. In this chapter we shall discuss some of the most important concepts and estimates of economic performance.

An important question is: Even if the level of output in the economy increases, does it really mean that the individual member of the economy is better off? With all these urgings for increases in GDP, do such increases really improve material life? The application in this chapter will discuss that question. But first we need some basic understanding of the national economic accounts.

Background: Why is National Economic Accounting Important?

Although most of these concepts were, as indicated before, worked out during the depression of the 1930s, especially by Nobel Laureate Simon Kuznets, economists greatly improved and expanded the national economic accounts during World War II to meet the government's needs for wartime planning. Government agencies had to have measures of economic performance in order to make the best allocation of output and to formulate policies that would keep the economy stable. A British economist, Richard Stone, who made a major contribution to this effort, was also awarded the Nobel Prize in Economic Science for his efforts. A difficult problem for the United States was how to shift all those resources to fight the war and still minimize inflation. Data provided by the national economic accounts gave information about how much production could be used for consumption and how much income people would have for consumption. Now, knowing how much excess income people had, the government could estimate the size of government programs, taxes, savings, and government bond sales. The government needed to soak up consumers' excess income and reduce demand, so that prices could be kept down. Sales of government bonds were an important way to keep people from spending their incomes on the reduced supply of consumer goods available during the war.

The national economic accounts, like a family's account books, give government policy makers the information necessary to formulate economic policies that are appropriate to prevailing economic conditions as well as those that are expected. This information is also important for business groups and consumers, who also have to make economic decisions. Do you buy your house now or next year? What you think the economy is going to do next year is important because, along with many other things, it not only affects your own income, but also the income of others, and *their* level of demand and prices. The totals of these accounts, especially when we compare one year with another, give us all indications as to whether the economy is changing, and if so, how.

The Expenditure and Income Approaches

Expenditure Approach An approach to national income accounting that measures the goods and services people buy, or the expenditures they make.

Income Approach An approach to national income accounting that measures the incomes generated in producing the national output.

People look at the national economic accounts from two points of view: (1) the **expenditure approach**, which measures the value of the goods and services that people buy, that is the kinds of expenditures they make and (2) the **income approach**, which measures the incomes that are generated by the output of the economy. To sum it up, the expenditure approach deals with kinds of output, while the income approach deals with kinds of income generated in the production of that output.

In effect the two approaches are two sides of the same coin, and the statistical results of each are (indeed *must be*) equal. Suppose that the only output of an economy were one car, one machine to produce the car, and one schoolhouse. The expenditure approach to measuring economic performance would entail totaling the value of those three items of production. But the value of that output would be apportioned to the factors of production as income. The income approach would entail recording how much of that income is apportioned to each of the different factors of production. The two results, that obtained from the expenditure approach and that from the income approach, must be equal. *The value of what is produced is equal to the income distributed.*

We see how these two approaches lead to the same result in Table 5-1. The expenditure approach is concerned with what is produced. In Table 5-1, the total value (column (4)), the value of the labor and other costs, is $19,000. The income approach is concerned with the income generated. The total income, the sum of columns (1), (2), and (3), is $19,000. The two approaches lead to the same numerical results. In each case, the income generated must be equal to the value produced.

Cartoon Feature Syndicate

"Remember when one billion was such a frightening figure?"

Table 5-1
Income and Expenditure Approaches

	Expenditure Approach			
Income Approach	**(1) Car**	**(2) Machine**	**(3) Schoolhouse**	**(4) Total Value**
Labor	$10,000	$3,000	$6,000	$19,000
Interest	5,000	750	1,000	6,750
Rent	2,500	400	750	3,650
Profits	7,500	500	1,000	9,000
Depreciation	2,500	250	1,150	3,900
Indirect business taxes	2,500	100	100	2,700
	$30,000	$5,000	$10,000	$45,000

Gross Domestic Product and Gross Domestic Income

Gross Domestic Product (GDP)

Gross domestic product, as mentioned earlier, measures the total dollar value of all final goods and services produced in a particular period, in a given economy. Two elements of that definition need explaining.

1. When we say that only the value of *final goods and services* is included in the GDP, we avoid the possibility of counting output more than once in the GDP statistic. Most manufactured products use materials from several firms. These intermediate products become part of the final product, so the value of the final product also covers the cost of these intermediate products. To include the intermediate products separately would mean that we would be counting them twice, once when we included them separately and again when we listed the final product.

For example, suppose that the intermediate products that go to make up our $30,000 car in Table 5-1 include $500 worth of steel and $100 worth of rubber, which the automobile producers buy and then incorporate into the car. When the manufacturer sells the car, the price must be high enough to cover the cost of all the intermediate products. Economists, to avoid counting a unit of output twice in the GDP, therefore list only the final value of the car, the price to the ultimate user.

This policy, however, creates a problem. Work in progress and inventory on hand at the end of the year represent output for that year, and should be included in the GDP for that year. At the same time, work that was in progress the year before and inventory that was produced the year before are also included in the final product, and they should not be included in the current year's output. Economists resolve this by subtracting from the GDP the inventory at the beginning of the year and adding to the GDP the inventory at the end of the year. Formally, this is accomplished by including in investment a net inventory figure (beginning inventory subtracted from ending inventory).

Let's look at our car again. At the beginning of the year, it was only partially completed and was worth about $10,000. That was output from last year, which should not be included in this year's GDP. But the car is completed this year, and sold to a consumer. Also, this year, more than just one car is produced. Half of the second car is made, say, $15,000 worth. That $15,000 in partially completed car should be counted as part of this year's output. Solution: Subtract the $10,000 work-in-progress car that was on hand at the beginning of the year (beginning inventory) from the $15,000 work-in-progress car that is on hand at the end of the year (ending inventory). Net inventory (part of the investment) is +$5,000.

2. The GDP contains the total dollar value of goods and services for a specific time period only, usually one year. Only output for that year is included, and none from any prior period.

The three major groupings of expenditures on goods and services that are counted in the gross domestic product are (1) expenditures for personal consumption, (2) expenditures for investment, and (3) expenditures by the government.

Personal Consumption Expenditures (C)
Expenditures by consumers for durable goods, nondurable goods, and for services.

When we talk about expenditures for Personal Consumption; **personal consumption expenditures** (C), we're actually talking about three kinds of expenditures: (1) When you buy a refrigerator or a car, you're buying a *durable good* (durable because is takes a long time to use it up). (2) When you buy food or clothes, you're buying a *nondurable good* (it is used up quickly). (3) When a barber cuts your hair or a waiter brings you a pizza, you're buying *services*. But remember that although the waiter who brings you that pizza is giving you a service, the pizza itself is a nondurable good.

Gross Private Domestic Investment (I)
Capital creating activities that are private (nongovernmental) in a domestic economy.

Investment expenditure is really a simplified way of referring to **gross private domestic investment** (I). *Gross* means all investment output is counted, including investment that replaced depreciated and obsolete capital. *Private* means that only *non government* investment is counted. *Domestic* means that only investment made within the United States is counted. So, when Toyota builds a new plant for its Camrys in South Carolina, this is included in investment because it represents output of U.S. resources. However, when Toyota builds an assembly plant in Mexico, it is not part of our GDP. Even if it were owned by a company based in the United States, the employment generated and production capacity created directly benefit the Mexican economy, not the U.S. economy. *Investment* is the act of creating capital, manufactured producer goods that aid in the production of other goods and services.

Gross investment is divided into (1) equipment and machinery, (2) business and residential construction, and (3) net changes in inventory. Remember that one subtracts beginning inventory from ending inventory. The balance is part of investment.

Government Expenditures (G)
Purchases of goods and services by all levels of government.

Government expenditures (G) include only government purchases of goods and services. These are divided into three types: services, goods, and investment. *Services* include the salaries the government pays to its employees, such as soldiers and county agents. *Goods* are products used up in the operation of the government (paper, gasoline used in government cars, and so on). Government *investment*, like private investment, is the creation of physical things that aid in the production of goods and services and exist for at least one year (computers, school buildings, and so on). Of course, when we say government, we mean *all* levels of government: local, state, and federal. GDP measures only the output of the economy, and therefore, includes only those expenditures for goods and services (these are output of the economy) by the government. However, the government also spends money for things other than output that it buys, and these are not included in GDP for example people receive government transfer payments without an immediate obligation to do something in return. The administrative assistant in the Department of Commerce provides a service (labor) for a paycheck. The assistant's salary *is* included in GDP. The family on welfare does not give goods or services in return for its check, nor does the jobless worker who receives unemployment compensation, nor does the wheat farmer from Kansas who receives agricultural subsidy payments. These government expenditures, since they do not involve concurrent production of either goods or services, are not included in GDP.

However, several adjustments still have to be made. Imports are included in these expenditures, and since imports were produced outside the United States, we must subtract them from GDP. Also, the United States produces goods that are not included in our expenditures for consumption, investment, and government; our exports. Exports, however, represent output of the U.S. economy, so we must add them to GDP. The plus exports and minus imports can be shortened to **net exports** (X_N). In other words, we subtract imports from exports. If exports are larger, net exports are positive; and if imports are larger, net exports are negative.For example, the United States imports Toyota automobiles from Japan. They are part of our consumption, because Americans buy them. But the autos are not part of our output. Therefore, they must be subtracted from our GDP. On the other hand, we export wheat to Japan. It is not part of our consumption, because we do not consume it, the Japanese do. But it *is* part of our output and must be added to our GDP. In other words, we subtract the imports (such as Toyota Corollas) and add the exports (such as wheat sold to Japan).

Net Exports (X_N)
The difference for an economy between its exports and its imports. Net exports are positive when exports > imports, negative when exports < imports.

Table 5-2 contains a breakdown of the GDP for 2008 and the first quarter of 2009. The sharpness of the 2008-2009 recession can be seen in the figures for 2008 and the first quarter of 2009 (annualized). GDP for 2008 was $14,264 trillion while the annualized GDP data for 2009 are $11,340.9, a decline of about 21 percent. The formula for GDP is thus:

$$GDP = C + I + G + X_N$$

Table 5-2
Gross Domestic Product (GDP) for 2012 (billions of dollars)

	2012
Personal consumption expenditures (C)	11,119
Gross private domestic investments (I)	2,062
Government expenditures (G)	3,063
Net exports (X_N)	-520
Gross Domestic Product (GDP) equals	15,685
$GDP = C + I + G + X_N$	

Source: Bureau of Economic Analysis, 2013

Gross Domestic Income (GDI)

Gross domestic income measures the total income at market prices generated in the production of all final goods and services during a given period, in a given economy. The term *at market prices* simply indicates that we compute the measure at the market level for goods and services and that this measure must cover all costs incurred through that market. You can keep this straight if you remember that GDP shows total output, while GDI shows how the income generated by that output is distributed. The two must be equal for the same time period.

Table 5-3
Gross Domestic Income (GDI) for 2011 (billions of dollars) - 1st quarter

Wages and salaries (W)	8,154.8
Rent (R)	325.2
Interest (P_C)	925
Profits (P)	818.8
Capital Consumption Allowance (D)	1,460
Indirect Business Taxes (T)	1,075.5
Net Factor Income From Abroad (Y_N)	-120
Gross Domestic Income (GDI)	14,830

Source: Bureau of Economic Analysis May 26, 2011
*Items do not add to total because of omissions

Wages and Salaries (W) The income payments to labor.

Rent (R) The income payments to owners of land.

Interest (P_C) The income payments to owners of capital.

Table 5-3 shows the breakdown for GDI in 2011. Naturally this summation includes the income earned by the factors of production (labor, capital, land, and entrepreneurship). Wages and salaries encompass all income earned by labor, including social security taxes paid by employees and employers. **Wages and salaries** are the income payments to labor. **Rent** is the income payments to owners of land; this figure includes an estimated rent for homes occupied by their owners. **Interest** is the income paid to owners of capital. Only interest paid by private business is included; the interest on government debt and on consumer debt is not. **Profit**; is the payment to entrepreneurship for the function of organizing and taking the risks of business. *Proprietors' income* is the return to entrepreneurship in firms that are *not* incorporated. (Another term for proprietors' income is *profits of unincorporated businesses.*) *Corporate profits* are the return to entrepreneurship in forms that *are* incorporated.

Profit (P) The payments to entrepreneurship in incorporated and unincorporated firms.

Capital Consumption Allowance (D) (Depreciation): A measure of the wearing out of capital through use or obsolescence.

Indirect Business Taxes (Taxes on goods and services that are passed on to consumers.

Besides the five income items listed for GDI in Table 5-3, there are two costs that must be covered by the final value of the product, but cannot be apportioned to the factors of production. **Capital consumption allowance** (D), or **depreciation**, is a legitimate expense, since it measures the wearing out of capital each year, either through use or obsolescence. The other non-income cost in **indirect business taxes** (T), or taxes on goods and services that are passed on the consumer. Two main forms of these are excise and sales taxes. The firm pays excise taxes (for example, cigarette and liquor taxes) and passes them on to the consumer in the form of higher prices. These taxes are covered by the final value and must be listed separately in gross domestic income.

A final income factor is net factor income from abroad. It is computed by totaling income received from U.S.-owned factors of production in other nations and then subtracting income paid to foreign-owned factors of production in the U.S. This result may be positive or negative. In 2011, as Table 5-3 shows, net factor income from abroad was negative (-$120 billion). In other words, this nation paid $120 billion more for foreign-owned factors used in the U.S. than it earned from U.S. factors of production employed abroad.

In brief, then, we see from Table 5-3 that the formula for gross domestic income is:

$$GDI = W + R + P_C + P + D + T + Y_N.$$

Changes in U.S. Income Accounting: From GNP to GDP

System of National Accounts (SNA) A system of measuring national income and product that is standardized across nations.

For many years, the United States used a system of income accounting different from that of most other nations. Gross National Product was the focal measure of overall economic activity in this country. Most other nations, however, had shifted to a **System of National Accounts (SNA)** devised by the United Nations, and intended, in part, to standardize such measures across a vast range of economies. The range is from those with extensive central planning and government ownership of resources to market economies with an emphasis on market allocations of resources and private ownership.

In 1991, the United States began shifting to the SNA framework. As a result, changes have occurred in the reporting and measuring of national income and product. The most important such change is to move away from the use of GNP as the primary measure of U.S. economic output. The new measure, instead, is GDP.

Gross Domestic Product Contrasted With Gross National Product

Although we have, as a nation, moved largely to use of GDP data, GNP continues to be useful for some purposes. Thus, it is useful to explain briefly differences between the two concepts. Gross National Product (GNP) is a measure of the current value of output from the use of factors of production owned by a country's residents. Even if production occurs outside the borders of the U.S., it is included in our GNP as long as the output occurs from the use of U.S. owned resources. As we have seen, Gross Domestic Product (GDP), on the other hand, is a measure of the value of output that occurs *within* a nation's borders. The GDP of the U.S., thus, is a measure of economic activity occurring in this country, regardless of who owns the domestic resources that give rise to the output. Since part of U.S. output is from foreign-owned resources, GDP includes income payments to foreigners, but does not include payments to U.S. residents from abroad. GDP, thus, is conceptually different from GNP.

Included in our exports are receipts of factor income from the rest of the world. These are largely receipts of interest, dividends and reinvested earnings of foreign affiliates of U.S. corporations. While these are included in exports, they are not, in reality, part of the domestic output. Thus, they need to be subtracted from gross national output. Included in imports are payments to foreign investors of interest and dividends and reinvested earnings of U.S. affiliates of foreign corporations. In reality they represent value of domestic production and should be included in gross domestic product.

The difference thus between gross domestic and gross national product or income is the net difference between receipts and payments of factor income from or to the rest of the world. As we saw in Table 5-3, this difference, called net factor income from abroad, may be positive or negative. For the rest of the accounts GNP and GNY provides the bases of the accounts, not GDP and GDI.

Which is Greater: GDP or GNP?

Finally, it is worth noting that GNP is now most useful as a measure of income rather than output. As we saw earlier in this chapter, this involves estimating the incomes generated in producing the nation's product.

Current, Constant, and Per Capita Real GDP

Back in the 1960s a Republican Senator (Barry Goldwater) and a Democratic Secretary of Labor (Arthur Goldberg), debated on educational TV with each using extensive statistics concerning the national economic accounts. With these statistics, each of the speakers proved that the only time Americans were well off was when his own party was in power. Who was lying, the statistics or the statisticians? In a sense, neither, because the debaters were using different measures, sometimes including, sometimes excluding the effects of prices on GDP. It would have been "fairer" if they had made clear to the onlookers what measures they were using. When statistics are being bandied about, much skepticism is needed, especially concerning whether price changes are or are not included. As Disraeli said, "There are three kinds of lies: lies, damn lies, and statistics." With our new emphasis on GDP, let's see what the differences are between nominal or money GDP, and real or constant GDP.

Gross domestic product may change because of changes in (1) prices and (2) level of real output. But only the changes in real output (that is, in number of products produced) affect material well-being. To obtain GDP data for comparative purposes, therefore, you need to do away with price changes. Here's how you do it:

Money (Current) GDP The value of final goods and services produced expressed in the prices of the period in which they are produced.

Real (Constant) GDP The value of final goods and services produced expressed in terms of a base year's prices.

Statistics on GDP before the data are adjusted for price changes are called **money** or **current GDP**, which is the output of a given year valued in the prices of that year. (In 1940 you could buy a brand-new Chevrolet or Ford for less than $1,000. But at that time many people were paid only $25 a week, and the best hamburger was 25 cents a pound.)

Real or **constant GDP** is the output of a given year adjusted for price changes. Converting money to real GDP involves the use of a *price index*, or now often called the implicit GDP deflator, which is a measure of changes in the price levels. The index used is called implicit price deflation as noted in Table 5-4.

There are various kinds of price indexes, depending on what you're measuring. Two well-known indexes are (1) the *consumer price index*, compiled and published by the Bureau of Labor Statistics, which measures price changes for a certain market basket of goods purchased by a family of four in an urban area, and (2) the *wholesale price index*, or now often called the producer price index, which measures changes in wholesale prices. In addition, the national income division of the Commerce Department has developed an index called (3) the *general price index* (or more formally the *GDP implicit price deflator*), by which you can convert current to constant GDP.

Now let's see how this works. Pick a specific year as the base year, and assign the value 100 to the price level in it; then compare the prices that prevailed in all other years to the prices that prevailed during the base year. Let's say that in year 2, prices increased by 20 percent over the base year, so, the price index for year 2 is 120. Let's say that in year 3, prices were 10 percent lower on the average than prices in the base year. Then the price index for year 3 is 90. By the same token, a price index of 132 means that prices in general have increased by 32 percent over the base year. A price index of 84 would mean that prices had declined by 16 percent from the base year.

Table 5-4
Inflating and Deflating Nominal GDP to Adjust for Changes in the Price Level (billions of dollars)

(1) Year	(2) Nominal, or unadjusted, GDP	(3) Price level index,* percent (2000 = 100)	(4) Real, or adjusted, GDP, 2000 dollars
1960	$527.4	22.37	$2,357.6 (= 527.4 ÷ 0.2237)
1970	1,039.7	29.29	$3,549.6 (= 1,039.7 ÷ 0.2929)
1980	2,789.5	57.38	$4,872.1 (= 2,795.6 ÷ 0.5738)
1990	5,803	86.83	$6,683.4 (= 5,803 ÷ 0.8683)
2000	9,953.6	100.00	$9,953.6 (=9,953.6 ÷ 1.00)
2005**	12,479.4	110.231	11,321 (=12,479.4 ÷ 110.231)
2009	14,075.6	118.2	11,280 (=14,075.6 ÷ 118.2)
2012	15,685	133.33	11,764 (=15,685 ÷ 133.33)

Source: Economic Report of the President, 2013
*U.S. Department of Commerce implicit price deflators.
** Annualized third quarter data.

To convert money GDP to real GDP, divide money GDP by the price index and multiply by 100. For example, if you take 2000 as the base year (in other words, 2000 = 100), and if the price index today is 130, to find the real or constant GDP for the year, you divide this year's money GDP by 130 and multiply by 100. That gives you this year's GDP in terms of 2000 dollars; in other words, *real GDP*.

Real GDP does not account for changes in population, so when you divide real GDP by population, you have *per capita real GDP*. This is the best-known statistic for comparing a nation's relative material well-being at one time with its material well-being at another time. Again, because almost all nations now use GDP as their domestic output indicator, such comparisons are made more accurate.Table 5-4 gives a sampling of real GDP, with the accompanying price index. The year 2000 is the base year for this particular set of statistics. Therefore its price index is 100; money GDP in 2000 is equal to real GDP. You can see that the ratio of money GDP to the price index for that year multiplied by 100, equals real GDP. Although prices dropped in some years before 1960, they have risen since

If the price index is less than 100, this means that prices are lower than for the base year. So when you convert money GDP to constant GDP, the amount increases. This is known as *inflating current GDP* to obtain a real figure that compensates for lower prices. When the price index is greater than 100, it indicates that prices are higher than the base year, so money GDP is greater than constant. The conversion is known as *deflating current GDP* to account for increases in price. Real or adjusted GDP is shown in column (4) and reflects the inflating or deflating of nominal or unadjusted GDP.

Output Excluded from GDP

The national economic accounts are *definitional* concepts. The people responsible for computing the accounts define what will be considered output, and, for various reasons, including the difficulty of computation, they do not include everything produced. By definition, they exclude the following kinds of output from the national income accounts.

1. *Services by homemakers*. If one had to buy these services on the market, children's nurses, house cleaner, cook, chauffeur, companion, the cost would be high. The services of a homemaker, for example, would cost hundreds of dollars per week if bought in market. National income accountants, though, exclude these services when they are figuring the national income because homemakers don't get paid in money.

2. *Illegal goods and services*. These illegal activities involve production, supply, demand, and market prices. Economists exclude them, however, because it is impossible to estimate their monetary value. You can't ask the local pushers how much heroin or cocaine they sold last year, or the owners of gambling establishments what their takings were. (Imagine a president analyzing the way GDP had increased in the nation because drug sales had increased 10 percent.)

3. *Labor of children in the household.* If your daughter or son mows the lawn, it doesn't add to the GDP. But if he or she mows the *neighbor's* lawn and is paid $40.00, economists count it in (or at least attempt to).

4. *The labor in do-it-yourself projects*. When you buy wood and brackets to build bookshelves in your living room, economists include the materials you bought in GDP. But the labor it takes you to build them doesn't count.

5. *Volunteer help to nonprofit organizations*. For example, the Red Cross has a paid staff; their wages *are* counted. But if you donate your services, even though you work very hard for long hours, this volunteer help isn't counted in the GDP.

Economic Transactions Excluded from GDP

Just as economists exclude certain types of production, they also exclude the following types of economic transactions:

1. *The buying and selling of intermediate products*. This is excluded because intermediate products are included in the final value of the products. This exclusion prevents counting them twice.

2. *The buying and selling of used items* such as cars and homes. This is excluded because the production of these items took place and was included in a prior time period. Their resale now constitutes only a change in ownership, not an increase in production of goods and services.

3. *The buying and selling of financial securities such as bonds and stocks*. This is excluded because production has not taken place, only the transfer of ownership of debt (though the value of the services involved in the transfers are counted).

Net National Product and Net National Income

Net National Product (NNP)
For an economy, the net value of all final goods and services produced in a particular period of time

Net National Product (NNP)

GNP includes depreciation or the amount of capital used up in producing output. Because economists find it useful to have a measure of output that does *not* include this depreciation, so that they can measure only net additions to total production, they use the expenditure approach to compute **net national product**, which is the net dollar value of all final goods and services produced during a given period. We speak of GNP as being; "total value," indicating that depreciation *is* included, while we speak of NNP as being "net value," indicating that depreciation is *not* included.

Your car is not considered an investment, but part of consumption. (A salesperson's car would be an investment.) However, to give you an understanding of what is meant by depreciation, let us think about your car as an investment. After your new car is one year old, it is less valuable than when it was new. Its value has gone down for the following reasons: (1) It has been driven, and there is only just so much mileage one can get out of the car. Let us say that you can get 100,000 miles of driving out of the car. If you drove 20,000 miles the first year, the car is one-fifth used up. (2) The car is no longer new, styles have changed, and, most important, manufacturers have made improvements in cars since this one was made. This aspect of depreciation is called *obsolescence*.

Just as a car, a consumer durable, decreases in value over time, investment goods, the capital people produce to aid in production, such as machines and factory buildings, depreciate by being used up and becoming obsolete, unless they have the most up-to-date improvements. One can say that depreciation is excluded in calculating the net national product because to count the value of capital used up in the process of current production would be to count something made in previous income periods.

Table 5-5
Net National Product (NNP) for 2009 (billions of dollars.)

Consumption (C)	11,370.9
Net private investment (I_N)	233.4
Government expenditures (G)	1,444.3
Net exports (X_N)*	1,331.0
Net National Product (NNP) equals	14,379.6
$NNP = C + I_N + G + X_N$	
NDP = GDP - D	

Note: The difference between NNP/NNI and GDP/GDI is capital consumption allowances (depreciation).

*Does include net flows of factor income from and to the rest of the world.

Net National Income (NNI)
For an economy, the net income at market prices that is generated in producing all final goods and services in a particular period of time.

Note:
When gross investment exceeds depreciation, net investment is *positive.*

Note:
When gross investment is less than depreciation, net investment is *negative.*

Net National Income (NNI)

By the same token, economists use the income approach to compute **net national income**, which is the net income (at market prices) generated in the production of all final goods and services during a given period. Once again, we speak of GDI as being total income, indicating that depreciation *is* included and we speak of NNI as being net income, indicating that depreciation is *not* included.

Table 5-5 contains a breakdown of NNP for 2009. For NNI, the only change from GDI (Table 5-3) is that depreciation is not included. For NNP,.gross private domestic investment becomes net private domestic investment. The difference between gross and net is measured by the amount of depreciation, or capital consumption allowance. Net investment, therefore, measures only the additions to the capital stock of the economy. If the value of gross investment is greater than depreciation, then more capital is being created than is being lost through depreciation. Net investment is then *positive*, and the economy generally expands because its stock of capital is expanding. Depreciation may be greater than the value of gross investment. If so, net investment is *negative*. In this case, the stock of capital is contracting because more capital is being lost than is currently produced. Capital stock, and thus the ability of the economy to produce, is contracting. This situation of a negative net investment has occurred during severe depressions (1930-1933) and during wars (World Wars I and II) when the need to produce war goods was greater than the need to produce investment. During the years 1917-1918, while the United States was fighting in World War I, total real output declined because the United States was at full employment when it entered the war. But during World War II, in 1942, 1943, and 1944, real output increased substantially (despite a negative net investment) because of the large amounts of unemployed labor and unused plant capacity remaining from the depression of the 1930s, and because employers used both labor and plants more intensively through the device of overtime.

Table 5-6
National Income (NI) for 2008, First Quarter, 2009 (billions of dollars) (Annualized)

Net national product	14,075.6
Less indirect business tax and other statistical adjustments	85.0
National income (NI) equals	13,090.6
NI = W&S + R + I + P	
NI = NNI – IBT	

Note: National income includes only the income generated by the factors of production. The difference between net national product and national income is indirect business taxes.

National Income (NI)
For an economy, the net income at factor prices generated in the production of all final goods and services.

National Income (NI)

The third major measure of the value of economic output is **national income**, which is a measure of income generated only by the factors of production (labor, land, capital, and entrepreneurship). National income is net income at factor prices generated in the production of all final goods and services in a given time period. As before, *net income* means that depreciation is not included. *At factor prices* means prices obtained in the factor market for the factors of production, and therefore we are excluding indirect business taxes, which are paid as a part of market prices. For example, an excise tax is levied on cigarettes by the federal government and is collected not at the retail level, as with a sales tax, but at the manufacturing level. The market value for cigarettes for inclusion in GDP and NNP includes the excise tax. The income generated by the production of cigarettes at the factor market does not include excise tax.

Table 5-6 shows the breakdown of national income for 2005. There is no comparable way to measure it using the expenditure approach.

Personal Income (PI)
For an economy, all incomes received by individuals in the production of final goods and services as well as from transfer payments.

Personal Income (PI)

Our first measure of economic performance was GDP-GDI, the second measure was NNP-NNI, and the third was NI. Our fourth measure of a nation's economic performance is **personal income**. Personal income consists of all income received by *individuals*, whether from production or by transfer payments. It is computed by deducting from national income those income flows that do not accrue to individuals, as distinct from corporations and governments, and by adding those income flows to people that are not included in national income.

First, to compute personal income (see Table 5-7), subtract that part of national income that does not accrue to persons. Corporate profits consist of corporate taxes, the savings of corporations or retained earnings, and dividends. Dividends are distributed to the stockholders (persons) and are retained in Personal income. Corporate taxes and retained earnings (undistributed corporate profits) are not income to persons and are subtracted from national income. Social security taxes are included in wages and salaries. These are transfer payments to the government and must also be subtracted from national income to derive personal income.

Table 5-7
Personal Income for 2009 (billions of dollars) (Annualized Third Quarter Estimates)

National income (NI)	9,488.6
Less:	
Corporate profits and capital consumption (CT)	1,234.8
Net interest (NT)	497.6
Contributions for social insurance (CS)	872.0
Wage accruals less disbursements (W)	0.0
Plus:	
Personal income receipts in assets (PIR)	1,234.8
Personal current transfer receipts (PD)	32.9
Equals personal income (PI)	12,142.9
PI = NI – CT – NT - CS - W + PIR + PD	

Source: Economic Report of the President, 2009

Note: One can compute *personal income* by subtracting from national income that part that is not income to persons and by adding incomes accruing to persons that are not part of national income.

Second, add income persons receive that is not included in national income. These are personal interest income and personal dividend income. Transfer payments *from* the government include such things as unemployment compensation, welfare payments, social security payments, and interest on government debt. Although interest on government debt is not really a transfer payment, since it is a payment for the use of borrowed funds, we included it here by definition. Also included as an addition to personal income are business transfer payments to persons. (Remember that the accounts are definitional concepts, depending for their definition on the decisions of the authority responsible for computing the accounts.)

The computation can be condensed by deriving a figure for net transfer payments. Subtract the transfer payments *to* the government from the transfer payments *from* the government. If the latter is larger, it is a plus figure. If the former is larger, it is a negative figure. Table 5-7 shows the breakdown of personal income for 2005. Once again, there is no comparable measure using the expenditure approach.

Disposable Income (DI)

Disposable Income (DI) For an economy, those personal incomes over which individuals have control as to their uses.

The fifth and last measure of economic performance is personal **disposable income**. This is the portion of people's incomes that they have control over; that is, they can control where and how this portion is spent. (See Table 5-8). People do not have control over the part of their income paid to the government in taxes, such as personal taxes and property taxes. So personal *disposable* income is personal income less personal taxes.One can also look at disposable income from the point of view of how people apportion it. They can either spend it (consumption), save it (personal savings), or use it to pay interest on consumption loans. Disposable income is an important measure in the national economic accounts. It is, in effect, the measure of purchasing power of the consuming public. Changes in DI result in changes in total consumer demand. Government economic policy must keep a close eye on this measure. How would tax changes affect it? How would changes in government expenditures affect it? The federal government made tax cuts for the 1974 and 1975 tax years precisely for the purpose of increasing personal disposable income to stimulate consumer demand.

Table 5-8
Disposable Income for 2009 (billions of dollars) (First Quarter 2009 Annualized Estimates)

Personal income (PI)	12,142.9
Less personal taxes (PT)	1,073.7
Equals disposable income (DI)	11,069.7
DI = PI – PT	
or	
Consumption (C)	11,370.9
Personal savings (PS)	490.3
Interest on consumer loans (ICL)*	1156.5
Equals disposable income (DI)	11,069.2
DI = C + PS + ICL	

Note: One can compute *personal disposable income* by subtracting personal taxes from personal income, or by adding consumption, personal savings, and interest on consumer loans.

*Contains some other minor accounts

Table 5-9
Summary of the National Economic Accounts

1.	GDP= $C + I + G \pm X_N$
	GDI= $W + R + I + P + D + T$
2.	NDP= $C + I_N + G \pm X_N$
	= GDP - D
3.	NNI= $W + R + I + P + T$
	= GDI - D
4.	NI= $W + R + I + P$
	= NNI - T
5.	PI= NI - CT - UCP ± NPT
6.	PDI= PI - PT
	= C + PS + ICL

.*Note:* This summary of the formulas for the National Economic Accounts uses the notations contained in Table 5-2 through 6. If you have any problem in interpreting the notation, refer to the appropriate table. Also, net exports for GDP are adjusted for net international flows of earnings on foreign investment.

Table 5-8 shows the breakdown of disposable income for 2003. Table 5-9 summarizes the formulas for the national economic accounts. Figure 5-1 shows the relationships between the major income and product accounts so that they may be readily visualized.

Figure 5-1
Comparative U.S. National Income and Product Accounts, 2009 (billions of dollars) (Third Quarter Annualized Estimates)

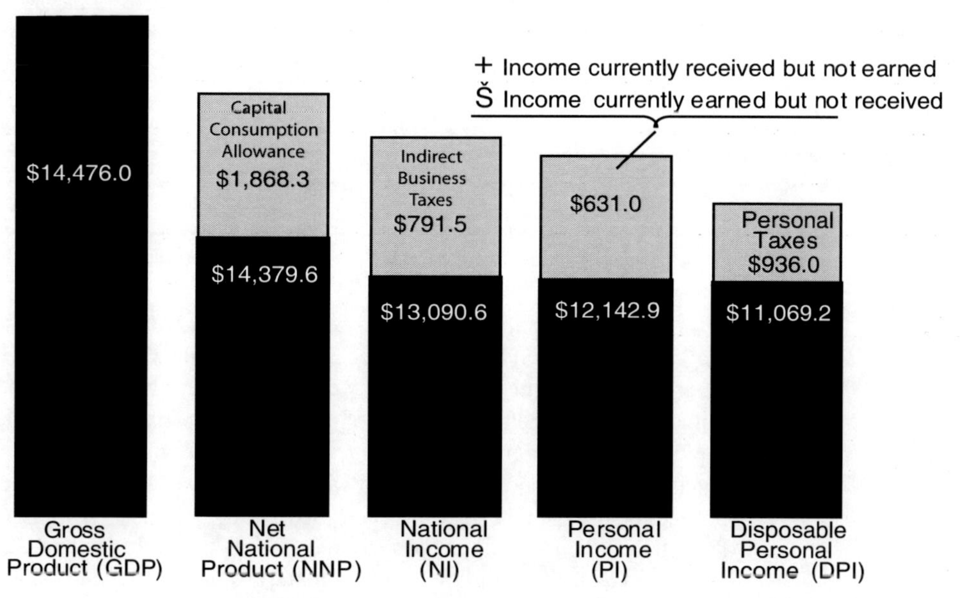

Source: *Economic Report of the President.* (Washington, D.C.: U.S Government Printing Office, 2009).

Gross domestic product plus receipts of factor income from the rest of the world minus payments of factor income to the rest of the world equals gross national product. Gross national product minus capital consumption allowance equals net national product. Net national product minus indirect business taxes equals national income. National income plus income currently received but not earned (transfer payments, personal interest, dividend income) minus income currently earned but not received (corporate profits, net interest, social security taxes) equals personal income. Personal income minus personal taxes equals disposable personal income.

Final-Value and Value-Added Methods

Final-Value Method A method of computing the GDP in which only the prices of goods sold to final users are added.

We have been defining the various national accounts and what goes to make them up. But how does one compute the values for domestic product? By two methods: the final-value method and the value-added method.

1. *The **final-value method**.* The sum of prices to the ultimate users of goods and services produced. These final values include all values added at substages of production. To avoid double counting, one does not list intermediate products.

Value-Added Method A method of computing the GDP in which the values added at each stage of production are summed.

2. *The **value-added method**.* Commodities go through many stages of production. As an unfinished product moves from one firm to another, it is changed in form or location or is stored. Each of these functions adds value. The sum of these additions to value equals the final value of the product.

Table 5-10
Stages of Production of a Desk

Stages	Value of Product Sold	Value Added
1. Lumbering	$2.50	$2.50
2. Sawmill	4.50	2.00
3. Furniture factory	10.00	5.50
4. Retailer (the final value)	20.00	10.00
Final value		$20.00

Note: The value added does not include values from prior stages. When one adds all of the values at each stage, the total equals the final value.

Let us examine Table 5-10 where we have used a desk as an example. *Stage 1*: Lumbermen cut down a tree and transport it to the sawmill. By the time the tree arrives at the sawmill, it is worth more than when it stood in the forest. Value has been added to it, say, $2.50, because of the expenditure of labor, land, capital, and entrepreneurship. *Stage 2*: The sawmill cuts the tree into lumber. Again, value is added, say $2.00, and again it is equal to the cost of the factors of production used at that stage. At each succeeding stage (the furniture factory and the retailer) the expenditure of resources means that value is being added. The furniture factory takes $4.50 worth of materials, applies resources, and sells the resulting product for $10.00. Value added was $5.50. The values added at each stage are equal to the final value, or the price to the ultimate user ($20.00).

Table 5-11 shows how this value-added method of computation works. The left-hand side shows how the income produced by the added value was distributed during production by the furniture factory, Atlas Furniture Company. Labor (one factor of production) received wages plus social security taxes, or $865,000. Land ownership received rent, or $250,000. Corporate profits earned were $150,000. However, the factors of production are not the only contributors to value added. Depreciation and business taxes also contribute, $300,000 and $150,000 respectively, because the company has to count these costs into the expense of making furniture.

Because ending inventory was less than beginning inventory, the total production figure must be reduced by that difference (-$100,000). Last, and most important, not all the value was created at this stage of production (the fashioning of wood into furniture). The raw materials bought by the firm acquired their value at prior stages of production. Value added, according to both the final-value method and the value-added method, was thus $1,915,000. The British (and several other European countries) use *value-added taxes* to raise tax money although the tax rates vary from one nation to another. The British call it the VAT. The French have a similar tax, which they call a *turnover tax*. Thus far the United States does not have a value-added tax, although a proposal to enact one has been discussed in Congress in recent years.

Table 5-11
The Atlas Furniture Company, Statement of Value Added

Income Generated by Value Added		Sources of Value Added	
Wages	$850,000	Net sales to U.S. government	$600,000
Social security taxes	15,000	To Smith Company	600,000
Rent	250,000	To Jones Company	800,000
Interest	200,000	To business firms	400,000
Depreciation	300,000	To exports	250,000
Taxes other than corporate income taxes	150,000	Inventory increase or decrease	
Corporate profits	150,000	Inventory decreased	–100,000
Income generated by value added	$1,915,000	Value of production	$2,550,000
		Cost of raw material	–635,000
		Value added	$1,915,000

Application I: Does GDP Growth Measure Improving Human Well-being?

In the years 2007 through 2011, as we have seen, America has experienced recessions or periods of slow GDP growth together with continued higher rates of unemployment and underemployment. It is probable that most Americans regard faster GDP growth as not only desirable but necessary to reduce the countries unemployment rate.

There is a temptation to view the various measures of national income as measures also of material well-being. Many people, economists among them, view increases in per capita real GDP as evidence for widespread improvement in people's well being. Until a few years ago, most people went along with this idea. But since then, we are less certain of the relationship between income growth and human welfare. You may well ask, "Am I *really* better off as GDP increases?" If the nation increases the annual output of cars and flat screen television sets, will we all be happier for it?

Setting aside the problem of measuring human happiness, the attack on the use of GDP growth as a measure of human well-being is threefold. First, since GDP doesn't include *all* output and costs, it is not as accurate a measure of output contributing to well-being as we would like. Second, there is a large amount of counted output that may not contribute to material well-being, and may even detract from it. Third, the very process of increasing GDP may possibly decrease well-being.

What GDP Does Not Include

As we have noted, not all output is included in GDP. Remember that the labor of homemakers, illegal production, labor on do-it-yourself projects, labor by children in the household, and volunteer labor are all excluded from GDP. But when comparing the *change* in output from one year to the next, one tends to think that these exclusions don't really matter or that these exclusions don't vary.

The women's liberation movement has long argued for concrete recognition of work in the home by placing dollar values on household chores. However, the amount of housework as a percentage of GDP does not *change* much from one year to the next.

As for illegal production, such as gambling (where illegal), prostitution and dope peddling, who is going to convince anybody that this sort of thing adds to the well-being of the public or that the level of it changes from one year to the next?

As for the other excluded items, do-it-yourself work, children's work in the household, and volunteer work, no one can measure them accurately enough to give us statistics, so they are excluded in the measurement of GDP for very practical reasons.

Cost of Pollution

In addition, GDP statistics fail to take into account many costs outside the realm of the marketplace itself, such as pollution. The air, the rivers, the oceans, and the land can be, in many circumstances, free dumping grounds for the wastes that are by-products of the production and consumption of goods. This pollution, however, does cost society something, because pollution affects the aesthetic quality of the environment, causes physical discomfort, threatens health, disrupts the food chain, and unbalances the atmosphere.

The cost of all this pollution is not borne by either the producers or consumers of the products that create the pollution, but by those who are hurt by it. Since this kind of cost is not reflected in GDP or in the cost of specific products, we cannot make completely informed choices in the marketplace about what to produce and how much to produce. If the costs of pollution were reflected in the price of the products we buy, the composition of our output would probably be quite different from what it is now. This in spite of efforts to include the effects. Ongoing efforts to incorporate these costs into the price of production may lead to significant future changes in the composition of output.

The problems of estimating the costs of pollution are hard to overcome. It would be much like subtracting depreciation from gross investment to get net investment. After one had subtracted the external costs from the final value, one would have "net economic product," a phrase coined by Nobel Laureate Paul Samuelson.

If you measured the net economic value of production in these terms, some products would add less to the country's well-being than their value. In fact, some kinds of output might even detract from the country's well-being. How much do people benefit from the output of a chemical plant in Cincinnati after you deduct the destructive effects of the millions of gallons of waste the plant pours annually into the Ohio River? What is the contribution to public well-being of a new car after you deduct the car's pollution of the air with hydrocarbons and carbon monoxide?

What Does Contribute to Well-being?

One can also attack GDP as a measure of well-being by challenging the contributions to social welfare of some parts of output that are included in GDP figures. Does the flood of advertising to which we are all exposed make us healthier, happier, or wiser? We don't have space here to go into the pros and cons of advertising. There seems little doubt, however, that some of the resources spent on advertising are wasted, as far as material improvement is concerned. Advertising that does not give information on which to base an economic decision or that actually gives wrong information is not a benefit to consumers.

And then there are defense expenditures. While such expenditures do add to security, or the protection of our lives and property, there is an optimal outlay on this as well as other activities. We may sometimes exceed this level. For example, do expenditures that make it possible for U.S. military forces to kill each human being on earth several times over increase security or well-being.

The forms of output that increase GDP but not human well-being, and certainly you can add more to the few mentioned here, use up resources of the economy that could have been used to produce other things that do add to material well-being. In other words, the opportunity costs of these "wasted" resources are the goods we could have produced by using the resources in other ways.

Is Further GDP Growth Desirable?

In an article written in the 1970s, Robert Heilbroner[2] seemed to take the view that continued growth would lead not so much to the exhaustion of the earth's natural resources as to the destruction of its environment. He said that the exponential curves of growth, human and industrial "would sooner or later overtake the finite capabilities of the biosphere," and bring about a terrible reduction in the quality of life. Heilbroner's recommended solution was public (government) control over family size and consumption habits and over the volume and composition of industrial and agricultural output.

There are probably few today, including few economists, who concur with this extreme or "doomsday" view. Our space here is too limited to permit us to survey the large amounts of literature on the economics of pollution. However, we do not believe that growth per se causes pollution. The problem lies in the signals by which production and consumption take place. We believe that industry can control pollution by various devices and incorporate the cost of controlling it into the market price of the products. How to eliminate pollution or even *how much* of it to eliminate (the question of opportunity cost enters in) are the questions. But it is highly probable that we *can* control pollution and still maintain growth. In fact, we need continued growth to be able to create the resources necessary to do many things including control of pollution.

2. In Passell, Peter and Leonard Ross, *The Retreat from Riches*. Viking. 1972.

Measures of Economic Welfare: A Caveat

There is likely no measure of economic welfare that will not be highly controversial. Nonetheless, such attempts are not only interesting but useful. If nothing else they focus our effort to relate economic production and human well-being. A noted economist, Arthur Okun[3], once observed that caution is advisable in these regards. According to Okun:

> *I know you will not ignore the GNP[4]. I urge that you not try to "fix" it, to convert GNP into a purported measure of social welfare. You are doing your job so well that people are asking you to take on a different and bigger job. Resist at all costs, for you can't do that job; indeed, nobody can. Producing a summary measure of social welfare is a job for a philosopher-king, and there is no room for a philosopher-king in the federal government.*

SUMMING UP

1. The national economic accounts are measures of economic activity. They are definitional concepts, and in each country the economists who compute the accounts define what is to be included and what excluded.

2. The *expenditure approach* to economic accounts analyzes the kinds of output the economy produces. The *income approach* looks at the kinds of income generated by the economy's output.

3. There are five main yardsticks used to measure national economic accounts. The first consists of *gross domestic product*, computed by the expenditure approach, and *gross domestic income*, computed by the income approach. The second is *net national product*, the third is *domestic income*, the fourth is *personal income*, and the fifth is *disposable income*.

4. *Gross domestic product* is the total value *at market prices* of all *final goods and services* produced in a given economy during a given period. GDP is made up of *consumption*; *gross private domestic investment*, *government expenditures*, and *net exports*.

5. *Gross domestic income* is the total income at market prices generated in the production of all final goods and services produced during a given period. GDI is made up of *wages and salaries, rents, interest, ' proprietors' income, corporate profits, capital consumption allowances, indirect business taxes,* and *net factor income from abroad.*

6. The second measure of economic performance consists of *net national product*, computed via the expenditure approach, and *net national income*, computed via the income approach. Both exclude capital consumption allowances.

---

3. Okun, Arthur. "Should GNP Measure Social Welfare?" *Survey of Current Business*, July, 1971.
4. Recall that GNP was the preferred measure of total national output before GDP.

7. *Net national product* is the net value of all final goods and services produced in a given period. NNP is made up of consumption, net private domestic investment, government expenditures, and net exports.

8. *National income* is the net income at market prices generated by the production of all final goods and services produced in a given period. NNI is made up of wages and salaries, rent, interest, proprietors' income, corporate profits, and indirect business taxes.

9. The third measure of a nation's economic accounts is Income: *national income*, which is the net income *at factor prices* generated in the production of all final goods and services in a given period. NI is made up of wages and salaries, rent, interest, proprietors' income, and corporate profits.

10. The fourth measure is *personal income*, which is all income received by private citizens. PI is made up of national income, less corporate taxes, less retained earnings, plus or minus net transfer payments.

11. The fifth measure, *disposable income*, is the income that people can dispose of, that is, use to make purchases or save. DI is made up of personal income less personal taxes, or in other words, consists of consumption, personal savings, and interest on consumer loans.

12. Economists use two methods, the *final-value method* and the *value-added method,* to compute the values of the gross domestic product. When they use the final-value method, they add all the prices paid by the ultimate consumers of all goods and services produced. When they use the value-added method (the second method), they first compute the value added at each stage of production, and second, total all the values added.

13. The U.S. has switched its reporting of national output to the System of National Accounts (SNA) devised by the United Nations. GNP is no longer the main measure of output. Rather, Gross Domestic Product (GDP) is now used. GDP measures the current value of output that occurs within a nation's borders. It includes income payments to foreigners but excludes payments to U.S. residents from abroad.

14. *Money* or *current GDP,* for a given year is GDP valued in the prices of that year. *Real* or *constant GDP* is the output of a given year adjusted for changes in prices. One computes real or constant GDP by dividing money GDP, by the *price index* and multiplying by 100. However, currently, the best single measure of comparative well-being is *per capita real GDP,* which one finds by dividing the real or constant GDP by the total population.

15. The following output is excluded from gross domestic product: (a) services by homemakers, (b) illegal goods and services, (c) labor of children in the household, (d) labor on do-it-yourself projects, and (e) volunteer help to nonprofit organizations.

16. The following transactions are excluded from gross domestic product: (a) the buying and selling of intermediate products, (b) the buying and selling of used items, and (c) the buying and selling of financial securities.

KEY TERMS

Capital consumption allowances
Disposable income
Expenditure approach
Final value method
Government expenditures (G)
Gross domestic income (GDI)
Gross domestic product (GDP)
Gross national income (GNY)
Gross national product (GNP)
Gross private domestic investment (GDI)
Income approach
Indirect business taxes
Interest
Money (current) GDP
National income
Net exports
Net factor income from abroad
Net national income
Net national product
Personal consumption expenditure
Personal income
Profits
Real (constant) GDP
Rent
System of National Accounts (SNA)
Value added method
Wages and salaries

QUESTIONS

1. Economists in the former Soviet Union did not include services as output when they computed national income accounts. If you were creating an income accounting system, would you include services as part of the national income accounts?

2. From the following data (next page) for a hypothetical nation, compute:

   a. gross domestic product.
   b. net national product.
   c. national income.
   d. personal income.
   e. disposable income.

3. Gross domestic product must be equal to gross domestic income, and net national product must be equal to net national income. Why?

4. Of the two methods of computing the national economic accounts, the final-value method and the value-added method, which do you think is easier to use? Why?

5. If you were listening to a politician quote income statistics, what role would price changes play in helping you to understand the statistics?

	Billions of Dollars
Consumption	300
Gross private domestic investment	150
Government expenditures	200
Imports	35
Exports	30
Capital consumption allowances (depreciation)	50
Indirect business taxes	25
Social security taxes	20
Transfer payments from the government	35
Corporate taxes	20
Retained earnings	10
Personal taxes	100

6. What is the difference conceptually between GNP and GDP? What are the advantages of GDP as a measure of national output?

7. Compute the *real* GDP of a hypothetical nation from the following data:

Year	Money GDP	Price Index
1929	103.1	50.6
1940	99.7	43.9
1950	284.8	80.2
1960	503.7	103.3
1980	974.1	135.3
2000	1075.0	150.7
2008	1,430	160.0

8. The national economic accounts are definitional concepts and do not include all output or economic transactions. What kinds of output and transactions are excluded from the national economic accounts? Why?

9. What is the basis for the argument that GDP measures fail to include many things that are part of human welfare?

10. Do GDP measurements correct for the social costs of environmental pollution?

11. Why are economists skeptical of the argument that continued GDP growth will lead to the exhaustion of non-reproducible resources?

12. How is the Nordhaus-Tobin calculation of *measured economic welfare* made? What is the fundamental problem with all such measures?

Chapter 6: Economic Fluctuations, Unemployment and Inflation

During its more than two centuries of existence, the United States has achieved an enviable record of economic growth as we noted in the introduction, the nation was probably never "poor," except for the earliest year if its colonial period. It has evolved from a small agricultural nation into the largest economy in the world. Today, its people enjoy one of the globe's highest standards of living.

This impressive record of growth by America's market economy has conveyed widespread benefits for almost all Americans in terms of real income and economic well-being. Nonetheless, the upward tide of growth has not been smooth. Throughout our history, there have been 13 sharp and sometimes lengthy periods of growing unemployment and declining real incomes. At other times, growth has been so rapid in nominal terms that it has been accompanied by the effects of large price increases or inflation.

This chapter will assay the causes of these deviations from the trend of rising real growth. The deviations from the smooth historical trend of 3 percent real growth per annum are called economic fluctuations or business cycles. We will examine not only the causes of these fluctuations but also look at what can be done to reduce or avoid the costs they impose upon this nation's people. In an extended application, we will look at how far we can push down unemployment without triggering the costs of inflation. The American economy has endured a recession that began in December 2007 and officially ended in June of 2009. For more information on this financial crisis, read the Application entitled "The Financial Crisis of 2008-2009" which is the first application in Chapter One.

First, though, let's look at the characteristics of these fluctuations.

Fluctuations: Characteristics and Clues

Types of Economic Fluctuations

Economists identify four types of fluctuations in economic activity. We see these phases represented in Figure 6-1.

Figure 6-1
Phases or Fluctuations of Economic Activity

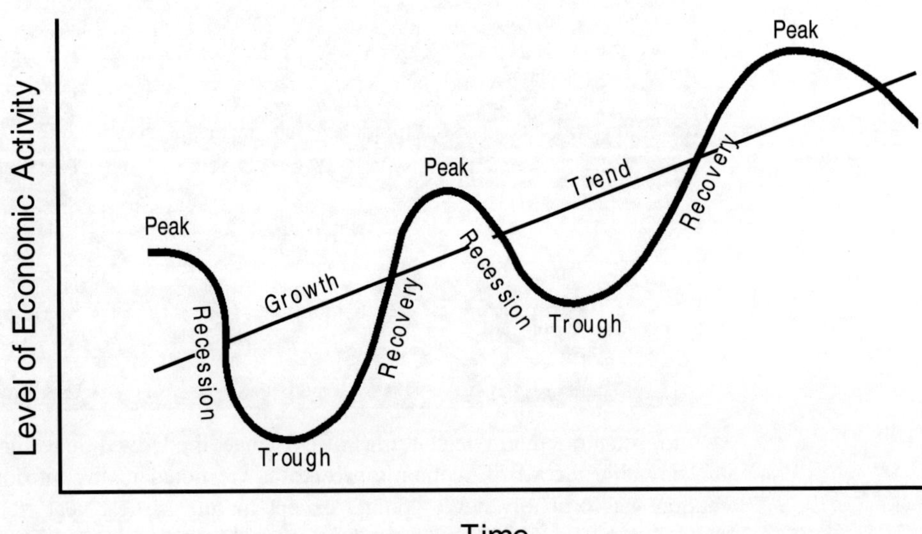

Economists distinguish four phases of economic activity: Peaks, Recessions, Troughs, and Recoveries. Although these phases are represented here as smooth deviations from the long-term upward trend of growth in economic activity, we must recognize that each phase is unique in its length, severity, amount of unemployment, and degree of inflation.

Secular Trend
The long-term expansion or contraction of an economy's business activities.

1. The **secular trend**, represented by the upward sloping growth trend line in Figure 6-1, represents the expansion of an economy over very long periods of time. These trends may occur over fifty to a hundred years. Within these long-run trends, shorter fluctuations occur. These are called business cycles.

Business Cycles (or fluctuations)
Reoccurring non-periodic fluctuations in economic and business activities.

2. **Business cycles (or fluctuations)** are reoccurring non-periodic fluctuations in economic and business activities. They happen over and over again, but not necessarily in any regular or periodic way, and take place over a period of six to eight years. These business cycles will be the main topic of this chapter. Within these business cycles, regular seasonal variations occur.

Seasonal Variations
Regular variations in economic activity that occur within a year.

3. **Seasonal variations** are fluctuations that occur regularly within each year. For example, employment in agriculture increases in the summer as harvest time approaches, and retail sales increase just before Christmas and Easter. To judge the significance of these seasonal increases or decreases in economic activity, you must compare them to the levels of activity at the same time in other years. In other words, to analyze various other influences on business activity, you must make allowances for seasonal activity and "filter out" the seasonal effects.

Random Variations
Irregular variations in economic activity that cannot be accounted or planned for.

4. **Random variations** are irregular variations that one can't account or plan for, since they don't follow any regular pattern. Examples of random variations are the depressed agricultural output caused by the drought of 1936; the steel strike of 1959; and the stock market downturn when President Reagan was shot in 1981.

Phases of a Business Cycle

Recession Phase
That downward part of the business cycle in which output and employment fall for at least six months, and inflation tends to decrease.

In the beginning of the **recession phase** of a business cycle, the level of economic activity begins to fall. (See Figure 6-1). Output and employment start to sag, and investment and consumption start to shrink. Inflation tends to creep downward. As the recession continues, unemployment may become high, investment and consumption low and sluggish. A great deal of plant capacity sits idle, and price drops may occur. Profits fall. By definition, a recession is a downturn that lasts at least six months.

Recovery Phase
That upward part of the business cycle in which output and employment rise and ultimately, as capacity approaches, prices tend to rise.

In the **recovery phase**, unemployment begins to diminish and unused plant capacity begins to be put into operation again, while income, output, and consumption rise. At this stage, prices may stay relatively stable. As the recovery continues, the nation approaches full employment and full utilization of capacity. Investment and consumption rise, and because of high levels of demand, so do prices. Profits typically rise.

Do Business Cycles Follow a Regular Pattern?

The very word *cycles*, the concept of phases, and such as those in Figure 6-1 seem to imply regularity or uniformity. However, history shows that although business cycles do recur, there is little or no regularity or uniformity to them. Because of this lack of uniformity, many economists say that the terms *business fluctuation* or *economic instability* are more appropriate than *business cycle*.

www.nber.org
For more information on business cycles visit this web site.

For example, in Figure 6-2, there is no uniformity in the length of time from one peak to another. It took nine years for the United States to go from the peak in 1960 to the next peak in 1969, but only two years to go from the peak in 1953 to the next peak in 1955. And there is no uniformity in the contraction phases, either. In the Great Depression, the contraction phase lasted from 1929 to 1933, about three and a half years. In the recession of 1949, the contraction phase was about one year. In the early 1990s, the contraction or recession phase lasted a short time. Similarly, there is no uniformity in the expansion phases. You can also see that there has been no uniformity in the *intensity* of the various phases of the business cycles.

Durable-Versus Nondurable-Goods Industries

Not only do the cycles differ from one to another, but also each cycle differs in the way it affects various kinds of economic activity. The biggest differences are those in price and output in industries that produce durable goods and industries that produce nondurable goods. Over the whole cycle, in the durable-goods industries, output varies widely. Prices vary much less. In the nondurable-goods industries, prices vary, but output tends to be more stable.

In the durable-goods industries (heavy equipment and machines, major appliances), the main effect of declining demand during the recession and depression phases is reduced output and employment. In the nondurable-goods industries (food, clothing, furniture), the main impact of declining demand is on prices. To learn why this variation occurs, let's think about the differences between durable and nondurable goods, and the differences between these industries in the nature of competition.

1. People can postpone buying new durable goods for a long time. When times are bad, the consumer repairs the old car or washing machine rather than buying a new one. A manufacturer faced with falling demand and dwindling profits repairs the machines on hand rather than buying new ones. And, with plenty of idle plant space, the manufacturer sees no point in building a new plant or a new wing on the old one.

Figure 6-2
Business Activity in the United States 1860 - 1990

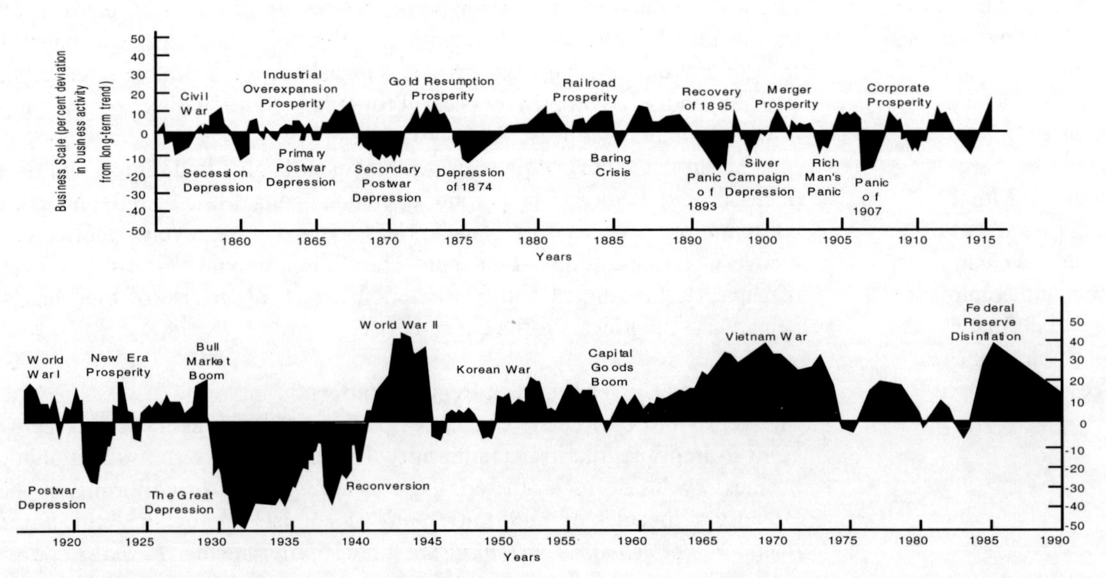

Source: Cleveland Trust Company.

Here we see the ups and downs of business activity in the United States from before the Civil War until 1990. The prosperity during the 1960s and that during the 1980s were the longest periods of sustained rise in business activity during this period. The ups and downs in business activity are measured as a *percentage change* compared with the long-range trend.

2. Industries that make consumer and producer durables (cars, steel, electrical equipment) tend to be more concentrated industries, with just a few large companies and less competition than in other industries. Various forms of monopoly power are manifest, so the big firms tend to protect their prices. Unless faced with intense international competition, they sometimes react to decreases in demand by cutting back on the quantity they produce.

During a recession, when decreased consumer buying is combined with decreased production by the large durable-goods companies, supply decreases. Prices may also go down, but at a slow rate. In the recession of 1958 and the ones in 1969 and 1970, prices rose rather than fell. The likely reason is that the concentrated durable-goods industries prevented their own prices from falling.

3. People can't easily postpone buying nondurable goods (such as food, clothing, furniture) because there is a recession. Thus the demand for the output of these industries is more stable. But it still falls off in a recession.

4. In the nondurable-goods industries, there are many small companies and more competition. These firms can't stabilize prices by cutting supply because they lack power. Their prices, thus, fluctuate more with the business cycle.

Some Causes of Economic Fluctuations: A Preliminary Look

Many economists have advanced theories about the causes of the irregular fluctuations in economic activity that have occurred throughout our history. We will devote much of the chapters that follow to these theories. As an introduction, however, it is useful to summarize some of the more important arguments:

1. *Innovations*. Some economists have focused on the role of innovations (new products, new technologies, new supplies of resources, new markets, and the like) in economic growth and development. A famous economist at Harvard, Joseph Schumpeter, is especially associated with this line of thought. Though innovations ultimately result in rising productivity and economic growth (a movement upward along the growth trend line in Figure 6-1), they occur irregularly and in "swarms." Throughout our history, major innovations such as the railroad, the automobile, and micro-chips and processors have caused bursts of economic activity pushing the economy to a new peak. But as their effects ultimately diminish, firms fail and a recession moves the economy toward a new trough. Thus, the theory suggests that fluctuations are an inherent part of the dynamic of economic progress in a market economy.

2. *Political and Random Events*. An examination of Figure 6-2 will show that many peaks and troughs in American history have been associated with political events, especially wars. The Civil War, World Wars I and II, and the Vietnam War are all examples of this association. Some wars have been associated with severe inflation or with wage and price controls and with inflation that followed their removal. Some economists believe there is a "political business cycle" in the sense that government expenditures may be timed to maximize re-election prospects of incumbent politicians and thus timed irregularly to produce or at least accentuate peaks and troughs. Still others believe that government monetary policy and its irregularities are largely responsible for economic fluctuations.

3. *Aggregate Demand.* Many economists believe that, at least in the short term, the most important influence on the level of economic activity in a market economy is aggregate spending. Firms produce goods and services in order to obtain profit. We presume that they produce what is expected to be the most profitable amounts of these goods. When aggregate demand or expenditure is low, firms produce less and employ fewer resources, including labor. In reverse, when aggregate spending increases, firms find it profitable to employ more resources and hire more labor. As we will see in this and in upcoming chapters what happens to overall prices is also related to aggregate spending. If, beyond some point, spending rises and little or no additional output can be produced, because output is at or near capacity, prices rise sharply and inflation results.

4. Constancy of government policy. Nobel-prize winning research has led to the conclusion by many economists that the lack of constancy in government policy (especially monetary policy) and failure to commit to rules rather than short-run variations in policies has led to failures of the economy to respond in the desired ways to those policies! This has contributed to "boom and bust" periods[1].

---

1. Editorial, "American, Norwegian Win Nobel." *The Wall Street Journal.* October 12, 2004.

Leading Economic Indicators

As we have seen, the general level of economic activity moves with the business cycle. However, there are exceptions. In 1974, for example, real GDP fell by about 5 percent. Inflation increased at a two-digit rate and business profits in some industries were high, yet unemployment increased. In the recession phase, the general level of activity goes down. With the recovery phase, it goes up. Changes in output and price vary in degree as well as timing in different kinds of activity. Some measures of economic activity, called **leading indicators**, lead the business cycle by decreasing or increasing before the rest do. They are, thus, commonly used as tools for forecasting changes in economic activity.

Leading Economic Indicators
A monthly index of eleven economic indicators which tends to lead changes in GDP. When an upward or downward trend of several months appears on this indicator, the economy tends to eventually move in that same direction.

The Department of Commerce has put together a composite or weighted average index called the *index of leading indicators (ILI)*. It is composed of eleven key statistics. They are:

1. *Average workweek.* If the average workweek falls, policymakers expect future reductions in output by manufacturing firms.

2. *Initial claims for unemployment insurance.* Rising first time claims suggest fewer jobs and future reductions in output.

3. *New orders for consumer goods.* If manufacturing firms receive fewer new orders, a future reduction in output and GDP is likely.

4. *Stock market prices.* Falling stock market prices reflect several important changes in economic activity. They (a) portend expected falling profits, (b) reflect reductions in consumers' wealth, and (c) reflect less attractive opportunities to issue new stock. For all three reasons, GDP may fall.

5. *Orders for new plants and equipment.* When such orders decline, they signal falling investment and likely future reductions in GDP.

6. *Permits to build new houses.* Home building is a major form of investment and the construction industry is a bellweather of the economy. A significant decline in permits to build new houses portends a likely fall in GDP.

7. *Vendor performance.* There is an irony in this indicator's performance. As sellers of resources used to produce final output do a more efficient job, it is because there is a slowing demand for their services. Improved vendor performance, thus, may indicate a future fall in GDP.

8. *Changes in amounts of unfilled orders for durable goods.* If the volume of unfilled orders diminishes, a falling level of aggregate demand is indicated with a subsequent decline in GDP.

9. *Changes in key raw materials prices.* Some raw materials prices lead but move directly with GDP. A decline in these prices, thus, often leads a decline in GDP.

10. *The supply of money.* For reasons we will examine closely in other chapters, changes in the supply of money are directly correlated with changes in GDP. Thus, a falling money supply is associated with a falling future GDP.

11. *Consumers expectations index.* The University of Michigan's Survey Research Center compiles an extensive index of consumer expectations. If this index declines, it indicates a likely future decline in consumer spending and, ultimately, a falling GDP.

We have discussed each of these indicators as predictors of recession. The direction of prediction can exactly be reversed to see how each might contribute to a prediction of recovery. Each of the eleven indicators is assigned a weight which may change with the changing structural characteristics of the economy. It is important to note that it is the *composite* or *weighted average* index that is the forecasting indicator rather than any individual component. As a rule of thumb, when the index moves in a particular direction for three consecutive months, the economy tends to soon turn in that same direction.

The index, however, is not infallible. While its movements have correctly forecast several recessions, as well as recoveries, it has also incorrectly forecast both on occasion. As a macroeconomic policy tool, it is useful only when its forecasts are correct and timed such that policy adjustments can be put into effect. On a few occasions, the ILI has forecast recessions that occurred so quickly thereafter that policy adjustments could not be made in time to mitigate the effects of the recession.

Nonetheless, the ILI is a useful tool in forecasting cyclical downturns and upturns. It is useful not only to the executive and legislative agencies of the government but also to private firms and research institutes. A major reason for making such forecasts is because of the effects of cyclical changes in economic activity on the level of employment and unemployment. In the next section we will examine the various concepts and definitions of employment and unemployment.

Unemployment

Full Employment
A concept of the employment goal to be attained in an economy. As such, it must be defined and redefined as the structure of an economy changes.

Full employment is a main goal of any country's national economic policy. Though it may seem an obvious concept, defining and measuring it is, in fact, fraught with difficulties. *Full employment* doesn't mean that every person in the nation has a job. The term refers to the labor force in general, which, by definition, includes anyone in the United States age sixteen or over who is permitted to work and who has a job or is actively seeking one. In 2011, the civilian labor force of the United States comprised almost 154 million people. Full employment doesn't even mean that all the labor force is employed. Allowances are made for people who are temporarily between jobs or are in the process of changing jobs. In other words, some amount of unemployment is a normal condition in a market economy that is continually reallocating its resources.

Kinds of Unemployment

You may think that unemployment is unemployment, and that's that. But economists have identified different *kinds* of unemployment according to their sources:

Frictional Unemployment
The measure of unemployment of those who are moving from one job to another (also called transitional unemployment).

Frictional or Transitional Unemployment occurs among those people who are unemployed for a while as they search for new jobs or await taking new jobs. There are imperfections in all labor markets that necessarily result in *frictional unemployment*:

1. Labor immobility of one kind or another, such as inability or unwillingness to commute or relocate.

2. Workers' inadequate knowledge of the job market.

3. The impossibility of instantly matching job-hunting people with job vacancies.

Cartoon Feature Syndicate

"Merry Christmas, Staff!"

The amount of frictional unemployment depends on the degree of these imperfections. As we noted before, it may be desirable to the extent that it reflects labor mobility in moving from less productive to more productive employment. When everybody in the labor force is employed except for people who are frictionally unemployed, we say that full employment exists.

Cyclical Unemployment
The amount of unemployment associated with deficiencies in aggregate demand during recessions and troughs.

Cyclical unemployment. During recessions and business cycle troughs, the aggregate demand of the public for goods and services may not be enough to create a full-employment demand for members of the labor force. We sometimes refer to the resulting unemployment as "demand-deficient unemployment." Although frictional unemployment is a fact of life in all phases of a business cycle, unemployment due to lack of demand is a direct result of the "downward" phases of business cycles. Consequently, to get rid of this kind of unemployment, a government will try to achieve economic growth or at least stability and to reduce business fluctuations.

Structural Unemployment
Unemployment caused by a mismatching of jobs and workers skills.

Structural Unemployment. Changes in the structure of the economy are what cause *structural unemployment*. These changes in structure may come about because of changes in technology or because of changes in the composition of consumer demand and output, which lead to shifts in the pattern of demand for labor. Such structural changes affect both skilled and unskilled workers. In the 1950s and early 1960s, for example, the shift from coal to oil for heating homes left massive unemployment in the anthracite coal mines in eastern Pennsylvania. In Minnesota, many workers became jobless when iron ore deposits in the Mesabi Range were exhausted. On the West Coast, in the late

1960s, large numbers of engineers who worked in the aerospace industries lost their jobs because of the government's cutback in its aerospace program when the Vietnam War caused reallocation of defense expenditures. All these events are examples of structural unemployment. In the 1990s, we saw major changes in employment as defense spending was reduced and as firms "downsized" and adopted new technology to increase their "competitiveness" in international markets.

Seasonal Unemployment
Unemployment that occurs during specific seasons of the year.

Seasonal Unemployment. Unemployment caused by seasonal shifts in labor supply and demand during the year is called *seasonal unemployment.* It often occurs in industries such as construction, agriculture and tourism, where the weather affects the demand for labor.

Problems That Accompany Unemployment

A particularly disturbing aspect of structural unemployment involves low skilled workers. Since World War II, with the advent of computers and countless technologically sophisticated instruments of production, the demand for low skilled labor, as a percentage of total demand for labor, has dropped greatly, even though the percentage of low skilled laborers in the labor force has remained constant. Many jobs for the less skilled have disappeared entirely. One problem of the last forty years, is that our educational system has failed to impart to some students the skills they need to make them employable. The needs of inner city minority groups, in particular, remain inadequately met.

www.bls.gov
For more information on unemployment visit this Bureau of Labor Statistic web site.

Unemployment due to lack of demand is a serious problem. However, if we can maintain economic growth or at least greater stability in the business cycle, we seem to have some tools to control it. Structural unemployment, though, is much more difficult to control. We must find ways to ensure that the hard-core unemployed obtain the new skills they need to survive in today's internationally competitive economy. Job-training programs, in the last thirty years have, for the most part, fallen short of their goals. Minimum-wage laws, originally introduced to help unskilled workers and young people entering the job market for the first time, may actually be hurting them, although the magnitude of the job loss is disputed by some economists. These laws have caused wages to rise beyond the productive ability of some low skilled workers and some teenagers. Some people argue that a reduction in these minimum-wages, at least for certain categories of workers, especially the young entering the labor force, would increase employment among teenagers. The minimum wage law that went into effect in 1990 provided for a training wage for several months and its effects were a source of controversy, the most recent increase in the Federal minimum wage was enacted in 2009.

We should also mention the discouraged-worker effect. Workers who have been rendered unemployed by so-called structural changes may eventually give up seeking work and just drop out of the labor force. Teenagers especially suffer from this discouragement. Those who never find jobs in the first place, disappear from the labor force and from our GDP statistics, as if they had become invisible, and form a hidden cost of unemployment.

The continuously high unemployment rate among minority groups, and among teenagers indicates the magnitude of our failure to deal with structural unemployment among those who are least skilled.

Economic Costs of Unemployment: The GDP Gap

The costs of unemployment to society are both economic and psychological. Obviously we can measure the economic costs in terms of goods and services the unemployed could have produced if they had jobs. One economist, Sherman Maisel, in a book called *Fluctuations, Growth, and Forecasting*, estimated that unemployment in the depression of the 1930s cost the economy $650 billion in foregone product (using 1957 prices as a basis). This was more than enough to pay for World War II, to provide every family in the United States with a new home and two cars, or to give all who qualified a college education.

GDP Gap
The difference between full-employment GDP and actual GDP achieved.

We can also measure economic costs of unemployment as the difference between actual GDP achieved and potential GDP, or the GDP that could have been obtained with full employment. Figure 6-3 shows actual and potential GDP (assuming 4 percent unemployment). The difference between the two is called the **GDP gap**. The gap, in other words, measures the opportunity cost or foregone output that is forever lost when all who are able and willing to work do not find jobs.

Figure 6-3
Output Gap: Real GDP Compared to Potential GDP, 2000-2013

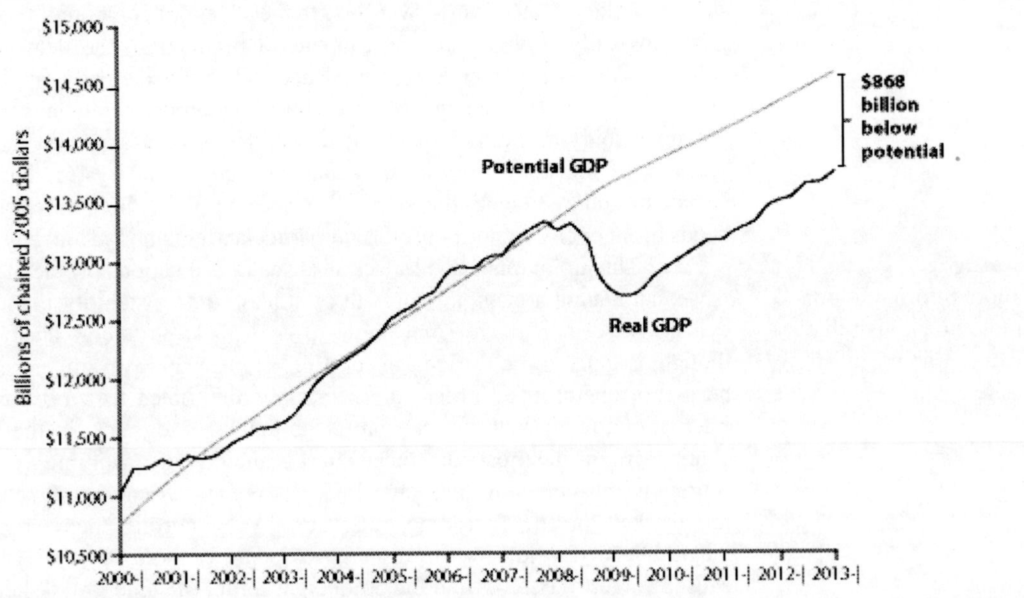

Source: Bureau of Economic Analysis National Income and Product Accounts and Congressional Budget Officet, updated April 26, 2013.

Okun's Law
The rule that for each 1 percent that the actual unemployment rate exceeds the natural rate, a 21/2 percent GDP gap results.

One way the relationship between the unemployment rate and the GDP gap can be analyzed is known as **Okun's law** after macroeconomist Arthur Okun who formulated it. The law indicates that for each 1 percent that the actual unemployment rate exceeds the natural rate, a $2^1/2$ percent GDP gap results. If in 1994, for example, the natural rate of unemployment was 5 percent and the actual rate was 6 percent, there should have been an approximate $2^1/2$ percent gap between potential GDP and actual GDP. In other words, according to Okun's Law, the 1994 GDP should have been $2^1/2$ percent greater if the unemployment rate had been 5 percent instead of 6 percent.

www.gpo.gov/eop
For more information on the GDP gap visit this web site.

The GDP gap, the amount of output sacrificed when the economy does not fully use its existing resources, was marked between 1957 and 1965. Between 1965 and 1968, unemployment fell below 4 percent[2] and actual GDP exceeded the 4 percent potential. This GDP surplus was helped because of the 1965 tax cut, plus high government expenditures for the war on poverty and the escalation in Vietnam. This period of full employment was brief, and the gap reappeared by the end of 1969. You can see that it is extremely difficult to utilize

2. Historically, many politicians and economists have argued that 4 percent unemployment is basically full employment.

the labor force fully and hold unemployment down to the 4 percent level. In the late 1980s, we approached this potential with an unemployment rate between 5 percent and 6 percent. In early 1995, the unemployment rate was about 5.4 percent and the economy was again approaching its potential or full-employment GDP. By the beginning of the 21st century we saw the unemployment rate drop below 4 percent though the actual GDP remained below the potential GDP.

Psychological and Social Costs of Unemployment

In a society basically still ruled by the work ethic, to be out of work, especially to be unemployed for a long time, causes acute mental suffering. Two extreme examples, which appeared in the newspapers in the mid-1980s, were the cases of two individuals, one who lost his job and shot himself, and another who hung himself in the steel mill from which he had become unemployed.

In addition to mental anguish, prolonged unemployment causes insecurity about one's self-worth. It creates family strain that goes beyond economic privation. In the past, and even more so today, prolonged unemployment has placed the individual psychologically, as well as economically, beyond the pale of normal society.

High levels of unemployment also put social and political stress on society at large. In a very real sense, a less affluent group may become pitted against a more affluent group. To paraphrase Abraham Lincoln, a society that is half affluent and half deprived, cannot long endure, or, at least, cannot expect to have social tranquility.

Prices and the Problem of Inflation

Inflation
A general rise in the level of prices.

During various phases of a business cycle, the level of employment changes. Thus a nation must not only maintain economic growth but also try to maintain full employment. Another serious problem an economy faces is **inflation**, or a general rise in the level of prices. During various phases of a business cycle, the level of prices changes. Since World War II, prices have primarily been rising. This, as we know, is inflation.

As prices of goods and services increase, the amount of these goods that a dollar will buy decreases. Thus, inflation causes a decrease in the purchasing power of the dollar. Figure 6-4 shows the rates of unemployment and inflation in the United States between 1960 and 2009.

Theories of Inflation

Demand-Pull Inflation
The rise in aggregate prices that occurs when demand increases more rapidly than supply.

There are two basic types or causes of inflation.

1. ***Demand-pull inflation***. Remember that in our discussion of supply and demand, we said that when demand increases (for a given supply of a good), the price of that good will increase. The same sort of phenomenon occurs for the entire economy. When the economy is at full employment, output, over a short period of time, cannot increase because there are no resources (especially labor) available to increase it. When demand for goods and services increases, there are not enough productive facilities to increase output in order to meet this increased demand. Consequently, markets ration out their goods or services, causing increased prices.

www.bls.gov
For more information on inflation visit this web site.

Let's look at an example of a demand-pull situation: In 1966, President Johnson escalated the war in Vietnam by increasing our troops there to more than 500,000 men. To maintain these troops in combat half a world away, the U.S. government had to buy billions of dollars worth of equipment and supplies.

The government had also sharply increased its expenditures on antipoverty programs, and there had been tax cuts in 1964 and 1965. As a result of this combination of events, the economy had reached full employment. Unemployment had actually dropped below 4 percent. Thus, the economy was able to meet the increased demand for armaments only by drawing resources away from the production of other commodities.

Figure 6-4

Rates of Unemployment and Inflation (Unemployment 2003 - 2013; Inflation 2003 - 2013)

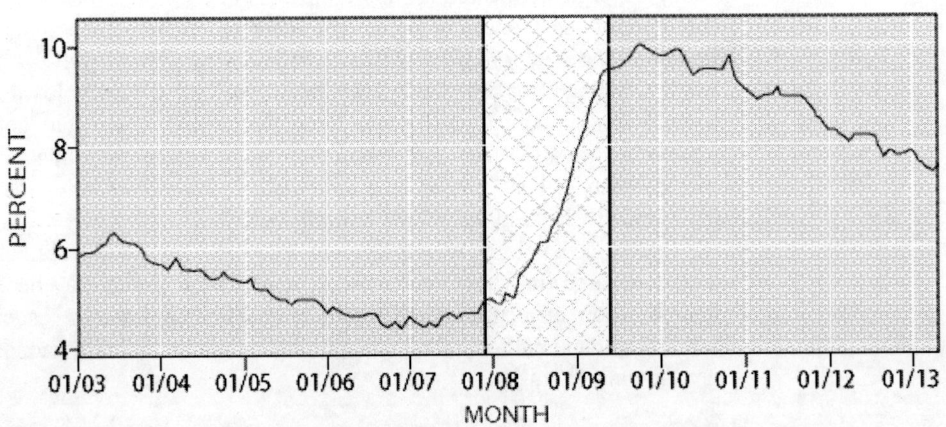

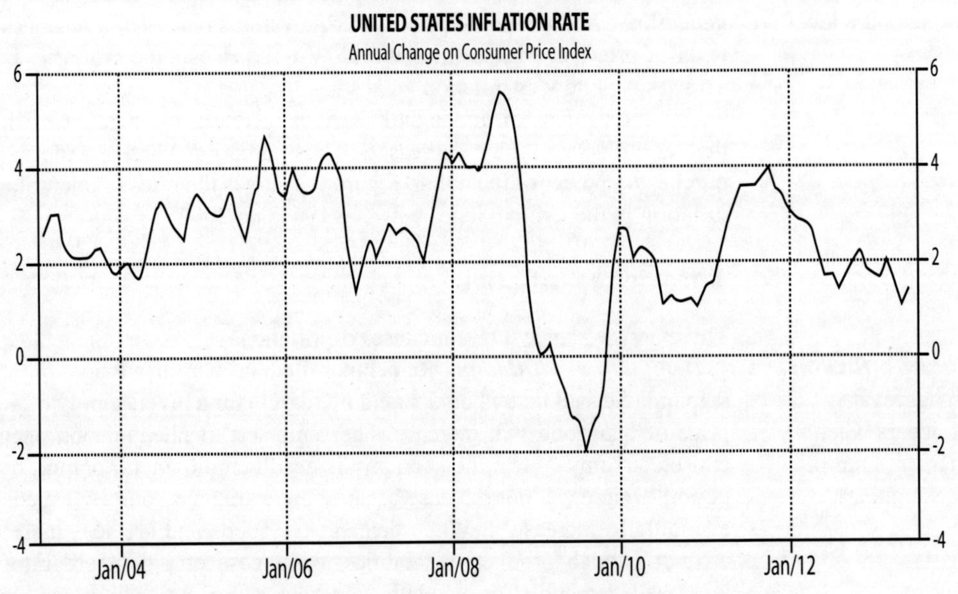

Source, Bureau of Labor Statistics, Current Population Survey.

It did this by increasing the prices of resources used to make nonmilitary goods. Then prices of resources used to make armaments increased, which increased the price of the finished products. At the same time, the supply of resources to other markets declined, decreasing supply and increasing prices. That is what we mean when we say that the marked inflation of 1967-1969 was primarily due to demand-pull inflation.

In brief, then, demand-pull inflation occurs when an economy's demand exceeds the ability of that economy to supply at existing prices. Too many dollars are chasing too few goods. The effect is to pull prices up.

Cost-Push Inflation
The rise in aggregate prices that occurs when resource prices and costs increase more rapidly than factor productivity.

2. ***Cost-push inflation***. When the suppliers of resources increase their prices faster than their productive efficiency increases, cost-push inflation occurs. When resource costs go up faster than increases in productivity, a company's production costs per unit increase. These increased production costs are ultimately reflected, at least in part, in higher prices.

The usual example people give of cost-push inflation is that of wage push. When unions force industry to give workers wage increases and the workers do not produce correspondingly more output, cost-push inflation occurs. Suppose that workers in the carpet industry increased their productivity 3 percent and the union obtained wage increases of 4 percent. You can see that the carpet manufacturer's labor costs per yard of carpet go up. (Increased productivity reduces labor costs per unit by 3 percent, while wage increases raise costs per unit 4 percent; net cost increase is 1 percent.) Right after World War II (between 1945 and 1949), labor unions staged a real drive to increase wages. They argued that wage rates had stayed at about the same level during the war, while both productivity and company profits had risen dramatically.

The labor unions naturally wanted workers' wages to catch up. On the whole, industry leaders did not fight this move to increase wage rates, because a strong demand-pull inflation was already under way because of the ending of the depression and war-postponed consumption. It was easy to pass the wage hikes on to the consumer in the form of higher prices.

In the 1970s, the whole world experienced two singularly agonizing cases of cost-push inflation through supply shocks. At the beginning of the 1970s, the world's major oil-producing and oil-exporting countries formed an association: OPEC. Among them, the OPEC countries control the bulk of the world's oil. And between 1971 and 1974, they quintupled the price of crude oil. The industrialized world is heavily dependent on oil. It is primarily oil that keeps the wheels of industry turning, that generates electricity for our power plants, that gets most of us to work. Therefore, the OPEC countries' two increases in oil prices quickly increased the costs of production generally and set off a worldwide inflation and economic crisis. We will examine the effects of this inflationary experience along with the deflationary experience of falling oil prices in the mid-1980s in another chapter.

Money Income
The current flows of money incomes to individuals.

Real Income
The current flows of money incomes to individuals expressed in terms of purchasing power.

Effects of Inflation and Deflation

When prices go up or down, this movement has a financial effect on all of us. It affects the economy in three ways: (1) by redistributing real income, (2) by redistributing real wealth, and (3) by changing the level of output.

1. *Redistribution of real income*. First, we should make a distinction between *money* and *real income*. **Money income** is the number of dollars a person receives in income, or the number of dollars in the paycheck, for most people. **Real income** is what can be bought with money income. You can see that your real income can change when there is either (a) a change in your money income, or (b) a change in the general level of prices and the purchasing power of your dollar. In the following discussion, we shall assume that the total pie (the level

of output) remains constant; that is, that the total level of output is unaffected by changes in prices.

In terms of income, there are two broad classes of people: people whose incomes are fixed, or semifixed, and those whose incomes are variable. When there is inflation, the people with fixed or semifixed incomes suffer because their money income does not increase as fast as prices do; their real income, therefore, declines. People with fixed incomes are usually nonunion workers, those living on welfare or pensions, and those with income based on interest; that is, the widows and orphans, the elderly and the poor, and the unorganized.

The money incomes of people with variable incomes often increase faster than prices go up, for example, the incomes of the people whose earnings come from the profits of a business. Some elements of cost for the business may tend not to increase as fast as prices. In industries where this occurs, profit margins increase. In general, (although there are exceptions), the money incomes of those who obtain their incomes from profits tends to increase faster than prices increase.

Historically, organized labor generally has had enough clout to increase wages at least as fast as prices rise, and often more so, so organized labor usually has enjoyed increased real income, at least for a time. This is particularly true when unions make their contracts for short periods and adjust them quickly to inflation rates.

Real Interest Rate
The nominal interest rate minus the rate of inflation.

Savers are frequently hurt by unanticipated inflation. To begin with, the real value or purchasing power of accumulated savings will decline as prices rise. This is true of savings accounts, fixed value paper assets and a wide variety of other forms of savings. Additionally, rising interest rates on savings often lag the growth in other prices, so that the **real interest rate** (nominal interest rate minus the rate of inflation) may become negative. As the experience of the late 1970s and early 1980s shows, this results not only in a redistribution of real income but is also a powerful disincentive to saving.

Deflation
A general fall in the level of prices.

During a **deflation**, when prices fall, those with fixed incomes temporarily enjoy increases in their real income, because a dollar buys more. This often does not apply to unorganized labor, because unorganized labor does not have enough economic power to prevent wage cuts. ("Times are hard. You will just have to take less per hour.")

"You've no idea what's happened to prices, you'll have to pull a really big job the first thing when you get out!"

What happens to people with variable incomes during a deflation? Those with income from profits tend to suffer losses in real income. Suppose you are living on the income from stock you own in one company. The company has to lower its prices because of the deflation. But the company still has to pay for resources (labor and materials), and the costs of these resources lag behind the fall in prices. Thus, the margin of profit gets narrower and narrower, and presently the company is unable to pay dividends to its stockholders.

Often for organized labor in a deflation, it has the economic power to keep employers from cutting back wages, (though not jobs) in spite of falling prices.

2. *Redistribution of real wealth.* In terms of real wealth, there are three categories: debtors (who borrow money), creditors (who lend it), and savers (who save it).

www.cbo.gov
For more information on interest rates visit the Congressional Budget Office at the web site listed above.

During an inflationary period, debtors benefit. But creditors and savers lose real wealth; that is, their wealth does not buy as much as it used to. In our example, suppose you are the debtor. Let's say that you borrowed $100 from your brother a year ago and he is not charging you interest, and suppose that there has been a 10 percent inflation during the year. Prices in general were 10 percent lower a year ago, and thus purchasing power of each dollar was 10 percent higher. If you repay the loan today, you're 10 percent richer, assuming that you didn't pay interest. But your brother, the creditor, is 10 percent poorer. He lent you the money when prices were lower and purchasing power higher. If he spends that $100 today, he'll get 10 percent less for it than he would have a year ago.

Now suppose that your brother had saved the $100 instead of lending it to you. Unless he earned interest on it, he would still have lost 10 percent, because a year ago when he saved the money, its purchasing power was 10 percent higher than it is today. (The creditor and saver would not be hurt by inflation if the rate of interest increased enough to compensate for the inflation and to pay them back for the risk, for the loss of liquidity, for the fact that they could not use the money themselves, and for all the other sacrifices people make in order to earn interest on their money.)

During a deflationary period, just the reverse holds true: Creditors and savers benefit, and debtors lose real wealth. Creditors lent money when prices were higher and each dollar was worth less, but they are paid back when prices are lower and thus the dollar's purchasing power is greater. Savers, too, are better off. They saved money when prices were higher and each dollar bought less. But now that prices have come down, their savings have higher purchasing power. Debtors, on the other hand, are hurt, because they borrowed money when prices were higher and purchasing power lower, but now they have to pay it back when prices are lower and dollars have greater purchasing power.

3. *Changed level of output due to changed prices.* We have been assuming that the economy's output was unchanged as prices changed and that as prices changed, some groups gained at the expense of others. What happens, though, if the total output changes? Relative redistribution of wealth still takes place, but its adverse effects may be lessened or accentuated. Let us see why.

A strong inflation can lead to recession and unemployment for a number of reasons: (a) Since all prices do not increase at the same rate, a sharp inflation may quickly cause structural distortions. Some firms' costs rise faster than they can raise prices of their output, so their profits are reduced. They could possibly take losses. They reduce their output, they lay off workers, and they may even go bankrupt. (b) Rapidly rising prices confuse both producers and consumers, so that people hesitate to make decisions. This causes a decrease in demand for output. On the other hand, rapidly rising prices may lead to **inflationary expectations**, or the belief that prices will continue to rise and cause decreases in real income. This may lead to increased current demand and further inflationary pressure. (c) Consumers may revolt against rising prices and refuse to buy. This again causes a decrease in demand. (d) People who are hurt by the redistributive effect of higher prices have to cut back on their buying, again decreasing the demand for output. The lucky ones who actually benefit from higher prices may step up *their* buying, but their increased demand may not compensate for the decreased demand on the part of those who are caught in the squeeze of higher prices.

Inflationary Expectations
The belief that inflation is inbuilt and will continue, thus, leading to falling real income.

The net effect of all this is a decrease in total demand for the economy's output, which means that output falls off and so does employment. The result is *recession.*

We have been discussing sharp increases in prices. But some economists argue that *moderate* increases in prices can actually be beneficial to output, for the following reasons: (1) When inflation is slight, business and industries can see in advance that the costs of their resources (labor and materials) are going to go up by a certain amount next year, so they can raise their own prices slightly and thus counter the structural effects of varying rates of price changes. (2) The prices of products may increase faster than the prices of resources, so that the profits of business and industry actually increase. When business people are making high profits, they are more inclined to invest. Thus, more jobs open up, employment rates rise, and the rate of economic growth increases.

However, if a moderate inflation continues for a long time, it may accelerate and become built-in or what is called *creeping inflation.* This may become a threat to the economy for three reasons: (1) Creeping inflation can accelerate until it becomes a severe inflation, with all its potential for causing recession. (2) Creeping inflation can generate inflationary expectations and lead to a wage-price spiral, resulting in serious inflation. Unions demand wage increases to compensate for past inflation and often add an extra margin for anticipated future inflation. During a prosperous period, business people are reluctant to face a strike, so they agree to grant the unions their wage hikes, which in turn, increase the costs of production. Businesses pass these higher costs on to consumers through higher prices, which often reflect an extra profit margin for the firms. (3) In due course, creeping inflation results in redistribution of wealth and puts serious economic strain on disadvantaged groups. The result may be *recession.*

A moderate deflation, bringing about a gradual fall in prices, may also contribute to increases in output. Deflations in the twentieth century, however, have been rare, especially since World War II. During the prosperous part of the 1920s (1922 to 1929), prices sloped gently downward because of increases in productivity without corresponding increases in workers' wages. (The unions had a hard time surviving during the 1920s.) The general population enjoyed increases in their real income as prices fell. At the same time, businesses had larger profits, since productivity increased faster than prices fell. Both factors kept the demand for capital goods high. More recently, there was a moderate slowing of inflation in 1982-1983, when, in the face of restrictive monetary policy, prices slowed down.

But deflation, too, can create problems. When the decrease in prices is very rapid, it tends to reduce the level of output. The following sequence occurs:

(1) Retail prices fall faster than prices of *factor inputs* (the resources an industry uses to manufacture things). This squeezes out profits and introduces losses. (2) Since prices do not fall uniformly, the structure of prices becomes distorted. Some firms have their profits wiped out entirely. (3) Business people, when faced with falling prices, become very pessimistic and tend to withhold further investment. All these conditions lead to decreases in output. The result is *recession.*

Employment and Prices

To prevent the economy from continually plunging down and climbing up, governments try to initiate policies of stabilization, aimed at maintaining full employment and stable prices. It is difficult to attain both objectives at the same time, since they are sometimes contradictory.

Figure 6-5
Prices and Employment

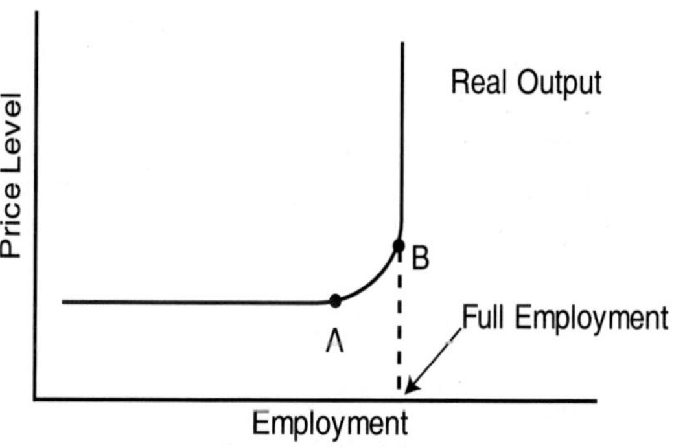

As output increase, industry starts using resources that were formerly unemployed, and prices remain stable. At point A, some resources start to be in short supply; this forces prices up. At point B, there is full employment. Further increases in demand only result in still higher prices.

Figure 6-5 shows that as output increases, more people get jobs, so unemployment is reduced while prices remain stable. At this stage, there is still some unused space and unemployed labor that industry can use without raising its prices. However, as output reaches point A, industry can achieve further increases in output only by raising its prices. Although point A is reached before there is full employment of all labor, certain categories of skilled labor and other resources may be in short supply. Beyond point A, the ever expanding output creates an ever greater demand for resources, which means that the prices of these resources will increase still further and inevitably the general level of prices will also rise. At point B or full employment), any further effort to increase output will result in continued demand-pull inflation; prices increase but real output cannot. In other words, demand-pull inflation occurs before the economy reaches full employment because some forms of labor and resources are in shorter supply than others. More expensive resources force up the prices of products before full employment is achieved.

Phillips Curve
A function that depicts the tradeoffs between unemployment and inflation.

From this we can see that there is a tradeoff between employment and prices. Beyond some point of resource use, if you want to reduce unemployment you most likely will have to accept some increases in prices. We can diagram this tradeoff between employment and prices. The resulting curve, called a **Phillips curve** after A.W. Phillips looks like the one in Figure 6-6.

Figure 6-6
A hypothetical Phillips Curve

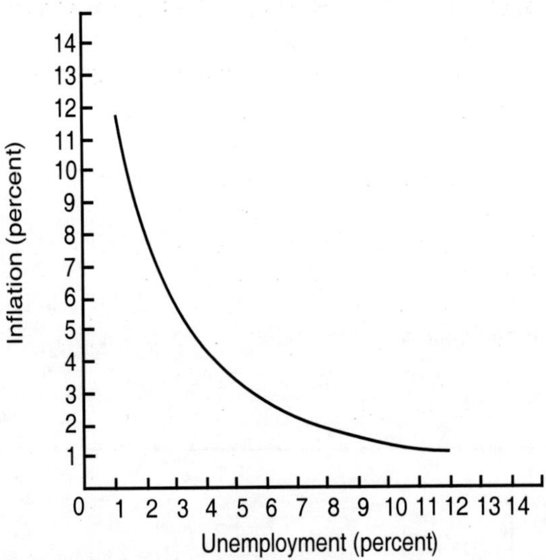

The horizontal axis is the percentage of unemployment; the vertical axis, the percentage rate of inflation. The Phillips curve shows the relationship between the two.

When we examine Figure 6-6, which covers the period since World War II, we see a Phillips curve representing a relationship that many considered politically acceptable until the 1970s: unemployment at 4 to 4.5 percent, inflation at 4 to 5 percent. If the government then had tried to force the unemployment rate below 4.5 percent, prices would have increased too much. According to this Phillips curve, before the 1970s, the tradeoff between inflation and unemployment was a politically acceptable one.

Now lets see what has happened to the Phillips curve since 1970. During the recession of 1970-1971, unemployment of about 6 percent was coupled with an inflation rate of about 7 percent, making the government's policy of economic stabilization much harder to carry out. The economy seemed to be in a period of **stagflation**, or a combination of inflation and economic stagnation. In other words, the economy seemed unable to move down the Phillips curve. In the recession of 1974-1975, the tradeoff was even less acceptable. In 1974 unemployment reached 9 percent, while inflation was nearly 12 percent. Our experience with unemployment-inflation in the late 1970s and early 1980s did not seem to invite optimism about the prospects of achieving lower rates of unemployment and inflation at the same time. The period since 1982, however, has seen relatively low rates of inflation and unemployment compared to the 1970s. Some, though, continue to worry about a resumption of stagflation.

Stagflation
A combination of inflation and economic stagnation.

Other economists doubt that stagflation will recur. Nonetheless, if stagflation resumes, whenever the government tries to reduce unemployment, it will have to stimulate output, which increases demand, which in turn might increase prices. On the other hand, whenever the government tries to reduce inflation, it will have to reduce demand, which reduces output, which can increase unemployment. When the tradeoff between inflation and unemployment is politically unacceptable, any effort the government makes to reduce unemployment just increases an already politically unacceptable level of inflation and vice versa.

Application I: Defining Full Employment

What is the "Natural Rate" of Unemployment for the U.S.?

The rate of unemployment in the first few years of the twenty first century was around 4 to 6 percent though in 2011, it was over 9 percent. In the early 1980s it was just under 10 percent, the highest since 1941. Since World War II, and especially since the Employment Act of 1946 and the Humphrey-Hawkins Act of 1978, various efforts have been undertaken to spell out a national employment goal. Humphrey-Hawkins asserted that goal to be 4 percent unemployment. Can we construct a set of macroeconomic policies that will permit us to reach that goal? As you will learn in this course in macroeconomic principles, there are various policy tools available to government that permit it to try to influence the level of employment. One problem or constraint in executing employment policy, however, is the set of tradeoffs between unemployment and inflation that we have observed and which is represented in the Phillips curve.

How far, then, can economic policy move the economy in the direction of full employment without causing an unacceptable rate of inflation? What, in other words, is a reasonable definition of full employment and a target for policy makers to attempt to reach?

For many years, it was thought that unemployment could not be pushed below the rate of *frictional unemployment*. Since that rate was widely assumed to be about 4 percent, policy goals (such as Humphrey-Hawkins) centered on that figure. As a result of the experience of the 1970s and 1980s, there is, today, less concern for frictional unemployment (indeed, economists rarely focus on the term now) and more concern for identifying a **natural rate of unemployment**, a rate at which the economy tends to produce neither an acceleration nor a deceleration in inflation (i.e., the inflation rate is stable).

Natural Rate of Unemployment
The rate of unemployment at which inflation neither accelerates nor decelerates (i.e., the inflation rate is stable).

A major problem with identifying the natural rate of unemployment for the American economy is *shifting inflationary expectations*.The Phillips curve tradeoffs between unemployment and inflation, even if identifiable, are unstable. We see this instability in Figure 6-7. In this hypothetical example of the natural rate argument, the economy is initially in equilibrium at point A on a short-run Phillips curve that is based on an expected inflation rate of 3 percent. The natural rate of unemployment is assumed here to be 6 percent. Point A is stable because there is no tendency for inflation or deflation to occur. Now, suppose that a public policy decision is made to lower the (unacceptable) rate of unemployment below 6 percent at point A. By whatever set of means (government expenditures, tax changes, money supply changes), the economy is stimulated and total spending rises. Employers, facing a growing demand for output, try to hire more people and other resources and, in doing so, bid up resource prices (wages, etc.) and, thereby, cause firms' costs to rise.

In the short run, the response to the stimulation of the economy is to move to point B with a lower (4 percent) rate of unemployment and a higher (5 percent) rate of inflation as prices rise in response to cost increases. Some workers, though, whose wage agreements were based on an expected inflation rate of 3 percent, see a decline in their real incomes. As those agreements expire, new wage agreements, based on a new higher expected rate of inflation are negotiated. These new higher wage cost agreements, though, lead to a new round of inflation and a higher *expected* level of price increases. The Phillips curve, in other words, shifts to a new (6 percent) expected inflation rate and equilibrium is restored at point C with the economy again at its natural unemployment rate of 6 percent. The long-run Phillips curve is a vertical line parallel to the inflation rate axis from the natural rate of unemployment. Points A and C are on this vertical Phillips curve. That is, they consist of points at which (at different inflation rates) there is no tendency for further inflation or deflation.

Figure 6-7
A Hypothetical Example of the Short-Run and Long-Run Tradeoffs Between Inflation and Unemployment: The Natural Rate Argument

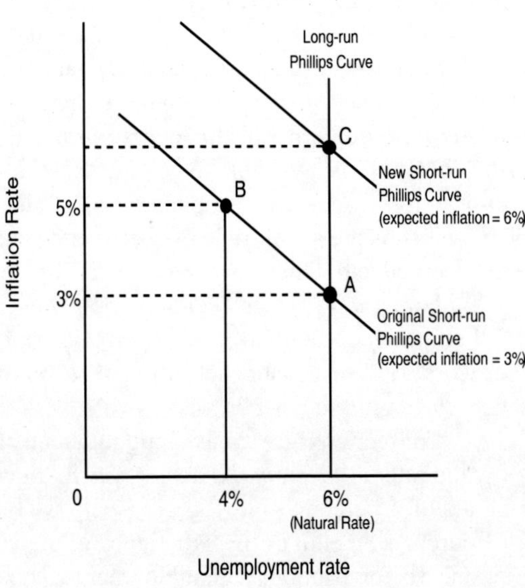

Source: From Stuart Weiner "The Natural Rate of Unemployment: Concepts and Issues." *Economic Review.* Federal Reserve Bank of Kansas City. January, 1986.

The key points of the natural rate of unemployment argument are, (1) It is difficult, if not impossible, to push the actual unemployment rate of an economy in the long run below its natural rate, and (2) attempts to do so merely result in higher rates of inflation rather than lower unemployment.

What is the Natural Rate for the U.S.?
According to research done by macroeconomist Robert J. Gordon, the U.S. has rarely been able to lower unemployment to its natural rate since 1945. More importantly for this application, the natural rate trended upward from less than 5 percent to about 6 percent in the forty years between 1945 and 1985. A major reason for this rise in the natural rate appears to be the change in the composition of the American labor force. In 1945, men comprised the overwhelming part of the labor force, whereas in recent years, women and teenagers have constituted a large and growing portion. The latter groups have higher structural as well as frictional rates of unemployment. Thus, as Economist Stuart Weiner[3] notes, the "overall unemployment rate consistent with constant inflation has risen." Weiner estimated the natural rate in 1994 was 6.25 percent and could go higher in the next twenty-five years.

3. Weiner, Stuart E. "The Natural Rate of Unemployment: Concepts and Issues." *Economic Review.* Federal Reserve Board of Kansas City. January, 1986.

Can We Lower the Natural Rate?

Can we find ways to lower the natural rate of unemployment? Can we, in other words, shift the long-run Phillips curve in Figure 6-7 to the left so that points such as B involve stable relationships with a 4 percent unemployment rate as well as acceptable inflation rates and lower inflationary expectations? Weiner argues that doing so will involve making labor markets work more perfectly and will involve some combination of the following:

1. Creating a better match between skills of available workers and job openings (better educational and vocational programs).

2. A better match between locations of jobs and available workers (worker relocation subsidies and a more efficient national employment service). Also, programs such as "enterprise zones" in cities to keep firms from leaving urban areas.

3. Eliminating or reducing institutional barriers. (Laws and practices such as minimum wage laws, union membership restrictions, and racial or sexual discrimination are examples).

Weiner also notes that lowering the natural rate below the currently estimated range of 5 to 6 percent is desirable. Opportunity costs to society of having such a large part of its labor force unemployed are very high. It is not desirable to eliminate all unemployment for we need the labor mobility of people *moving* from less productive to more productive employment that is reflected in *transitional* unemployment. Nonetheless, a 4 percent natural rate is far more desirable, socially, than a 5 to 6 percent rate.

Has the Natural Rate Fallen? Evidence from the 1990s

In the mid 1990s, the natural rate estimates were under attack. The estimate is increasingly important because it influences monetary policy as well as in other ways. With unemployment rates falling in 1994 from 6.7 percent to 5.4 percent, inflationary pressures should have been building according to Gordon's earlier estimate. Today, Gordon says, the natural rate could be as low as 5 percent. Caution remains, however, as some fear that a lengthy lag may exist between declining unemployment and a rising rate of inflation.

SUMMING UP

1. There are four types of economic fluctuations: (a) The *secular trend*, which is the expansion or contraction of the economy over very long periods of time; (b) *business cycles*, which are repetitive but not regular variations in general economic activity; (c) *seasonal variations*, which happen regularly at the same time each year; and (d) *random variations*, which have no regular pattern or recurring cause.

2. The two phases of the business cycle are: (a) the *contraction phase*, often leading to a recession, when unemployment and unused capacity are high and investment and consumption are low; and (b) the *expansion phase*, when investment, consumption, and employment are high and prices may be rising.

3. In business cycles, there is no regularity in the length of the cycle or any of its phases, nor is there regularity in the intensity of activity. Many consider the term *business fluctuation* more descriptive than *business cycle.*

4. Prices in durable-goods industries tend to be more stable over a given business cycle than prices in nondurable-goods industries. (a) During a contraction in economic activity, people postpone buying new durable goods such as automobiles and washing machines; they tend to repair and keep using the goods they have. But they must continue to buy nondurable goods, such as food and clothing. (b) Nondurable-goods industries are more competitive than durable-goods industries; thus individual firms cannot limit the drop in their own prices.

5. *Leading economic indicators* are measures of economic activity that point the way to coming increases or decreases in economic activity shortly before there is an actual rise or fall. Economists use these leading indicators (stock-market prices, building permits, average workweek, and so on) as tools with which to forecast economic activity.

6. There are several kinds of unemployment: (a) *Frictional unemployment* includes people who are unemployed only for short periods of time as they move from one job to another. (b) *General Unemployment* or *Unemployment due to lack of demand* occurs when there is not enough total demand for industry's output for full employment to be attained. (c) *Structural unemployment* which is due to structural changes in the economy, which take place because of changes in technology and the composition of output, with resulting changes in the pattern of demand for labor. (d) *Seasonal unemployment*, which reoccurs regularly during the same time of the year.

7. The *GDP gap* reveals the economic costs of unemployment by showing the difference between potential and actual gross domestic product. The cost of unemployment in economic terms may be high, but the individual psychological and social costs, plus social and political tensions, may be even higher. According to *Okun's Law*, for each one percent that the actual unemployment rate exceeds the natural rate, a 21/2 percent GDP gap results.

8. There are two types of inflation: (a) *demand-pull inflation*, in which total demand for an economy's output exceeds the ability of the economy to supply at existing prices, and prices rise to ration the scarce supply; (b) *cost-push inflation*, in which suppliers of resources increase their prices faster than workers increase their productivity, which pushes cost of production up, forcing companies to increase their prices.

9. Cost-push inflation and administered-price inflation exist because of the dearth of competition in certain industries and can interact to cause an upward spiraling of prices.

10. During periods of inflation, *redistribution of real income* occurs, because those with fixed or semifixed incomes cannot increase their *money income* to compensate for rising prices. Those with variable incomes can usually increase their real incomes, since their money incomes might go up faster than prices do. The reverse occurs during a period of *deflation*, when prices fall.

11. There is also redistribution of real wealth during a period of inflation, as debtors benefit from inflation because they borrow high-purchasing-power dol-

lars and pay back low-purchasing-power dollars. Creditors and savers lose in an inflation because they lend (or save) high-purchasing-power dollars and are paid back low-purchasing-power dollars. The opposite occurs during a deflationary period, when prices fall.

12. A strong inflation may ultimately lead to recession, as cost distortions put pressure on some firms, confuse both producers and consumers, and weaken the consumer's willingness and ability to buy. Moderate inflation may increase output and income by stimulating investment. *Creeping inflation* (or moderate inflation over a fairly long period) may eventually have bad effects on the economy. Savers may be hurt during inflation as real interest rates (nominal rates minus the rate of inflation) may even become negative.

13. It is difficult for a government to readily achieve both full employment and stable prices at the same time, especially in a noncompetitive economy. As the economy increases its output, some resources run out before full employment is attained. The prices of these resources will increase, and prices in general will increase, before full employment is reached.

14. A diagram of the tradeoff between unemployment and higher prices is called a *Phillips curve*. Some economists question whether a valid Phillips curve tradeoff may be established. To the extent that it is a valid concept, the Phillips curve for the pre-1970 period appeared to be stable and had politically acceptable levels of tradeoff between unemployment and inflation. After 1970, the Phillips curve reflected higher levels of tradeoff between unemployment and rising prices. In recent years, however, the economy has achieved relatively low rates of inflation consistent with relatively small GDP gaps.

15. Unemployment in the U.S. in the early 2000s was about 5 percent. Most national goals or targets have set 4 percent as the desirable rate. Macroeconomic policies can influence the actual rate of unemployment.

16. There are tradeoffs between unemployment and inflation (or price instability). Economists, in assessing these tradeoffs, have sought to define and measure a *natural rate of unemployment*, one in which inflation tends neither to accelerate or decelerate (the inflation rate is stable).

17. Phillips curve tradeoffs have been unstable in the short run because of changing inflationary expectations. As macroeconomic policies are applied to lower the actual unemployment rate below the natural rate, inflation rises and there is a shift upward of inflationary expectations.

18. Rising inflationary expectations cause rising wage and other resources costs that become reflected in higher prices and increasing inflation. As a result, the economy returns to its natural rate of unemployment but with a higher rate of inflation than before.

19. The natural rate argument leads to the conclusion that (1) in the long run, an economy cannot be pushed below its natural rate of unemployment, and (2) attempts to push unemployment below that level simply raise inflation.

20. Studies indicate that the natural rate of unemployment in the U.S. has (1) rarely been reached since 1945, (2) tended upward since the 1960s time period, and (3) is currently somewhat more than 5 percent.

21. A changing composition of the labor force is thought to be the major reason for the increase in the natural rate of unemployment (more women and teenagers participating in the labor force). The labor force now exhibits more structural as well as frictional unemployment.

22. Lowering the national rate of unemployment is desirable. Doing so will require changes in labor markets that include (1) better matches between skills and job vacancies, (2) better matches between job locations and available workers, (3) eliminating institutional barriers in labor markets.

23. Transitional unemployment remains desirable because the economy needs the labor mobility that is reflected in people moving from less productive to more productive jobs.

KEY TERMS

Business cycle
Contraction phase
Cost-push inflation
Cyclical unemployment
Deflation
Demand-pull inflation
Expansion phase
Frictional unemployment
Full employment
GDP gap
Inflation
Inflationary expectations
Leading indicators
Natural rate of unemployment
Okun's Law
Random variations
Real interest rate
Seasonal variations
Secular trend
Stagflation
Structural unemployment

QUESTIONS

1. Some economists have said that the term *business cycle* is not accurate, and they advocate using such terms as *business fluctuation* or *economic instability*. What is the basis of their objection? Do you agree with them?

2. Define the following terms:
   a. Secular trend
   b. Concentrated industries
   c. Leading indicators (LI)
   d, Frictional unemployment
   e. Structural unemployment
   f. The GDP gap
   g. Inflation
   h. Demand-pull inflation
   i. Cost-push inflation
   j. Administered-price inflation
   k. Stagflation
   l. Inflationary expectations

3. Compared to clothing prices, washing machine prices tend to be stable, although there are wide variations in production over a given business cycle. Why is that?

4. Unemployment due to the public's lack of demand for industry's output fluctuates as business activity fluctuates, while structural unemployment may not. Why is this so?

5. How does the existence of monopoly power affect the level of prices?

6. How does the level of prices affect the distribution of real income? The distribution of real wealth?

7. What are real as opposed to nominal interest rates? What effects result from negative real interest rates?

8. In a market economy, some argue that it is difficult to have full employment and stable prices at the same time. What is the argument?

9. The natural rate of unemployment seems to be higher than previously. What implications does this have for an economic policy that will stabilize the economy? Why did this change occur?

10. You are a member of the President's Council of Economic Advisers in 2012. You have just told the President that the country cannot have full employment and stable prices at the same time. Furthermore, inflation in 2012 is 2 percent and unemployment is over 7 percent. The President charges you to advise him which should be decreased: inflation or unemployment. Which would you counter with government policy: inflation or unemployment? Give *economic* justification for the one you've chosen. Since some groups are hurt by inflation and others by unemployment, your decision hurts some and helps others. Give ethical and moral justifications for your decision.

11. What is meant by the term "natural rate of unemployment"?

12. What is the difference between identifying the natural rate and the actual rate of unemployment for an economy? Which has typically been higher in the American economy?

13. What may cause the tradeoffs between inflation and unemployment shown in a Phillips curve to be unstable?

14. Why, according to the natural rate of unemployment argument, is it difficult to keep an economy below its natural rate of unemployment? What happens, according to this argument, when efforts are made to push the unemployment rate below the natural rate?

15. What has happened to the natural rate of unemployment in the U.S. since 1945? What seems to have caused this effect?

16. Is it desirable to lower the natural rate of unemployment in the American economy? Why?

17. Of the various things necessary to lower the natural rate of unemployment, which do you favor? Which will probably be most difficult?

Chapter 7: Aggregate Demand and Aggregate Supply

We have seen that, in spite of long-term real economic growth, price levels, employment-unemployment rates, and real income levels have varied greatly in uneven cycles of American history. In this and succeeding chapters we will build a framework for determining what creates not only aggregate price levels, employment levels, and growth rates but also how we may understand and explain the fluctuations in those key macroeconomic variables that were examined in the chapter covering supply and demand.

Let us begin with an explanation of the aggregate price level and changing levels of price. First, however, remember that we are not talking about a single price, like that of a particular good. Rather, we seek to explain the average level of all prices in an entire economy. In the chapter on supply and demand, we saw that in individual markets for commodities and services, prices are established by equilibrium forces that clear markets at levels that equate quantity demanded and quantity supplied.

The single product equilibrium-price model of chapter three on supply and demand is very useful for understanding and predicting how the price of a good such as personal computers is determined. It is also useful for explaining relative prices such as those of diamonds and water, or oil and gasoline. In addition, the model is helpful in explaining large changes in relative prices such as the change in gasoline prices relative to microcomputers in the early twenty first century.

Figure 7-1
Aggregate Level of Prices and Real Income for the Entire Economy

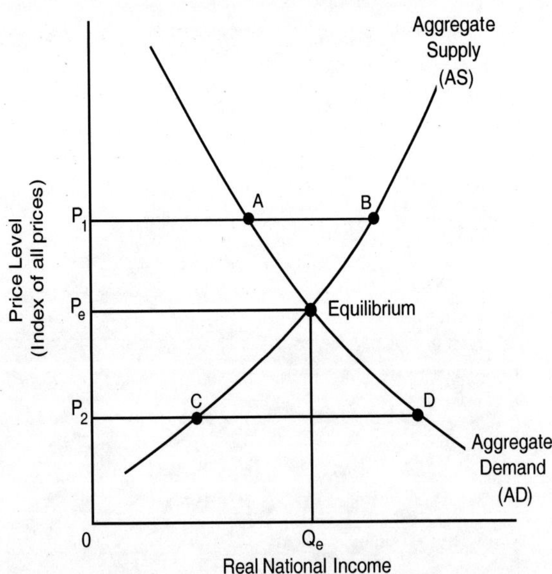

Aggregate demand and aggregate supply determine, in equilibrium, the level of prices and the level of real income for the economy. Aggregate demand is negatively sloped; as the price level falls, quantity demanded increases. Aggregate supply is positively sloped; as the price level rises, quantity supplied increases. Equilibrium national income and the equilibrium price level are where aggregate quantity demanded = aggregate quantity supplied or at equilibrium quantity Q_e and price level P_e. At any disequilibrium price level, (such as P_1 or P_2), there would be excess supply or excess demand forcing prices downward or upward to eliminate shortages or surpluses.

Useful as it is, the single-good supply and demand-based pricing model does not provide insights into important macroeconomic questions. Why did overall prices in the early twenty-first century rise so slowly and now are rising more rapidly? What conditions might trigger a return to the double digit inflation of the late 1970s and early 1980s? These are but two of many aggregate price questions which require a different framework for their understanding. This framework is called an aggregate demand- aggregate supply model of the overall level of prices and real national income in an economy. We see in Figure 7-1, a picture of a hypothetical economy's price level using this model.

On the vertical axis of Figure 7-1 are the economy's various possible price levels or indexes of prices. Later in this chapter, we will explain how such price indexes are constructed and measured. For the moment, think of the index as a measure of the weighted average of the prices of all important commodities and services being traded in the economy. On the horizontal axis, we measure the various levels of real national income for the same economy. The model explains how the equilibrium level of prices and the equilibrium level of real national income is established. Equilibrium here has the same meaning as in the chapter on supply and demand; it is the level of prices and real income toward which the economy is moving given the aggregate demand for and the aggregate supply of its commodities and services.

Aggregate demand and aggregate supply determine, in equilibrium, the level of prices and the level of real income for the economy. Aggregate demand (AD) in Figure 7-1 is negatively sloped; as the price level falls, the quantity demanded of real national income increases. Aggregate supply (AS) is positively sloped; as the price level rises, the quantity supplied of real national income increases. We will shortly examine the reasons why AS is positively sloped and AD negatively sloped.

Equilibrium national income and the equilibrium price level are established where aggregate quantity demanded = aggregate quantity supplied or at income Q_e and price level P_e. We should note again, for emphasis, that this equilibrium real income is simply the level toward which the economy tends given the underlying AD and AS schedules. It is not a target or even necessarily a desirable level of real income. Q_e might be a level associated with severe recession and high unemployment or it might be associated with over- full employment and a high rate of inflation.

At any disequilibrium price level (P_1 or P_2) there would be excess supply (AB) or excess demand (CD) causing producers to adjust prices downward or upward to eliminate shortages or gluts.

Equilibrium Level of Prices and Equilibrium Level of Real National Income
A level that is established where aggregate quantity demanded equals aggregate quantity supplied.

*The **equilibrium level of prices** and the **equilibrium level of real national income** is established where the aggregate quantity demanded equals the aggregate quantity supplied.*

Only at P_e, in Figure 7-1, the equilibrium level of prices, are the plans of producers to offer commodities and services for sale made equal to the plans of buyers to purchase commodities and services.

Aggregate Demand: Its Definition and Determinants

Aggregate Demand
A measure of the entire planned spending on final goods and services at different price levels.

Aggregate demand (AD) is a measure of the entire desired or planned spending on final goods and services at different price levels. As there are four sources of such planned spending, there are four corresponding determinants of AD. When we examine the "Keynesian" model of income determination, we will see that managing or influencing AD involves influencing one or more of these four components.

I. Consumption Expenditures
The largest element of AD, consumption spending and variations in consumption spending, are subject to determination and variation by the many things that influence consumer behavior. Economists believe that the major elements or components which influence that behavior are:

1. ***Disposable income.*** Disposable income may be used for consumption or saving. From our individual gross incomes, what we may dispose of in these ways depends on taxes, and private and public transfer payments. If, for example, social security payments are taxed, disposable incomes of retired persons will decline and so will the contributions of such households to aggregate demand.

2. ***Cost and availability of credit.*** Durable, often expensive, consumer goods are usually purchased with loans. The cost of this credit and its availability heavily influence consumer expenditures on automobiles, housing, and other such goods. If the (interest rate) cost rises, the availability of such credit diminishes and this important component of AD will fall. Of course, if the cost of credit falls as it did during much of the early 1990s, aggregate demand will rise.

3. ***Expectations.*** All of us have expectations about future economic events that will affect us. Will we have a job? If so, will our incomes rise? These

expectations are influenced by both public and private actions. If our expectations worsen, if we expect declining income or even unemployment, our purchases of many goods will decline. Consumer confidence surveys are often taken as a measure of these expectations.

II. Investment Expenditures

The most volatile element of AD is investment spending on plant and equipment, inventories, and research and development. Firms' investment decisions appear to be influenced by the following four factors:

1. ***Interest rates***. Whether investments are financed by borrowing in capital markets or by the use of retained earnings, firms use interest rates as the benchmarks against which to measure the expected profitability of an investment. Thus, if interest rates rise, the profitability of an investment must be higher to induce a firm to make the investment, and fewer investments will be made.

2. ***Government policy***. Present government policies as well as expected future policies influence investment choices. Will there be investment tax credits? Will tax breaks be given to firms that locate in a particular area? These and many other aspects of government policies affect the profitability of an investment strategy.

3. ***Expectations***. Many investments have long-term payoffs. While the future is uncertain for firms as well as for consumers, both groups must establish expectations about future market conditions as well as future public policies. Present investment decisions, therefore, are partly a function of expected future events.

III. Government Expenditures

The second largest element of aggregate demand in the United States, government spending, is quite variable but difficult to ascribe to a simple set of influences since it is the result of a complex political process. There are various levels of government and various factors that seem to influence the expenditure policies of each. Among the factors which may be influential are efforts to secure re-election by public officials, automatic stabilizer programs which are tied to varying economic conditions, changes in political philosophy (the proper role of government), and national emergencies such as war and depression.

IV. Net Exports (Exports Minus Imports)

Currently, the smallest element of aggregate demand; net exports has nonetheless become increasingly important in recent years. Net exports can be positive or negative. If positive, net exports add to aggregate demand. If negative, net exports decrease aggregate demand. Net exports are most influenced by three basic factors:

1. ***Trade policy***. If China "voluntarily" limits its exports of textiles to the United States, Americans will probably spend less on such goods and the net imports of the United States will tend to fall. If nations impose or raise tariffs on U.S. goods, our net exports will tend to decrease as a result of the decrease in the quantity demanded of our exports.

2. ***Exchange rate changes.*** If, for example, the dollar buys fewer Euros, European imports tend to cost more in the United States, and U.S. exports to Europe tend to become cheaper. Rising U.S. sales to Europe and decreasing European sales to the United States tend to increase our net exports.

3. ***Politics.*** Politics always plays an important role in trade between nations. If the government of Japan will not allow U.S. firms to bid for construction contracts in Japan, then our net exports tend to decrease. On the other hand, if Japan opens its markets to free trade, our net exports will tend to grow.

AGGREGATE DEMAND: A SUMMARY

Aggregate demand is the sum of intended spending on consumption expenditures, investment expenditures, government expenditures, and net exports at each overall price level. AD thus may be expressed as the sum of consumption expenditure (C) + investment expenditure (*I*) + government expenditure (G) + net exports (X_n).

$$AD = C + I + G + X_n$$

Why Does the Aggregate Demand Curve Slope Downward?

The aggregate demand curve shown in Figure 7-1 has a negative slope. That is, the lower the price level, the higher the quantity demanded, the higher the price level, the lower the quantity demanded. It may be tempting to think that this is simply a restatement of the law of demand. However, that is not so! Recall that the law of demand dealt with the effects of a change in the price of a single good, holding other prices (and income, taste, etc.) constant. Clearly such a *ceteris paribus* assumption cannot be made in the case of the aggregate demand curve which deals with changes in the (weighted average) prices of all goods on the level of real national income. If the aggregate price level falls, substitution effects will explain nothing for there are no substitutes for all goods and services (including savings).

Basically, there are *three reasons* why AD in Figure 7-1 has a *negative slope*. Although we will develop each more fully in other chapters, let us summarize these three causes:

1. *Effects of interest rate changes* on aggregate spending. Consider what happens when the price level rises. Households and firms need to hold more money to cover their transactions between receipts of income, thus increasing the demand for money. The increased money demand will cause interest rates to rise. As these rates rise, the demand for both consumer goods and non-consumer goods decreases, causing a decline in the quantity demanded of the economy's output.

2. *The effects of changes in wealth* on aggregate spending. Asset values are expressed in monetary (dollar) terms. When the price level changes, the real purchasing power of these assets, such as bonds and balances in banks, moves in the opposite direction. If prices double, for instance, the value of a $10,000 bond is halved. Therefore, if prices go up, individuals will have to save more to restore their real wealth positions. The increase in savings will tend to reduce the quantity demanded of current output.

3. *Relative price changes between foreign and domestic goods.* An aggregate demand curve includes all sources of demand for domestically produced goods, including foreign sources. When the price level in the United States increases (*ceteris paribus*), American goods become more expensive relative to foreign goods. Americans substitute foreign goods for those domestically produced and foreigners substitute their own domestically made goods for American goods. Both substitution effects tend to decrease the quantity demanded of U.S.-made commodities and services.

For all three reasons, we may assume the following:

As the aggregate price level rises, the quantity demanded of the output of an economy decreases; as the price level falls, the quantity demanded of the output of an economy increases.(Aggregate demand curves slope downward.)

Aggregate Supply: Its Definition and Determinants

Aggregate Supply
A measure of the entire desired output of final goods and services at different price levels.

Aggregate supply (AS) is a measure of the entire desired output of final goods and services at different price levels. All of the things that may influence business decisions about production rates are potential determinants of aggregate supply. Included in such a list would be the following six basic factors:

1. ***Cost and availability of resources***. Firms making profitable supply decisions consider not only revenue but also cost in deciding what and how much to produce. If resource prices rise, firms' costs do as well and AS tends to decrease. In this chapter's application, we will look at what sharp increases and decreases in oil prices in the 1970s and 1980s did to output decisions as well as real income and price levels. As oil prices rise in the early 21st century we should remember that increases in resource prices work their way through the economy and its supply of goods quickly in comparison with other determinants of aggregate supply.

2. ***Capacity and investment plans***. In any short-run period, an economy has only so much *capacity*; its stock of plants and equipment, skilled laborers, and other resources. Naturally, the economy cannot produce beyond the limits imposed by this stock. Investment spending, however, will in the long run result in a shift of, or increase in, this capacity and a greater aggregate supply. Since investment also creates jobs and income, it will stimulate aggregate demand.
Most investment spending is undertaken by private firms. Government spending, however, may directly or indirectly raise the capacity of the economy. In wartime, governments may actually build plant and equipment. Ordinarily, though, the effects are indirect; government spending on activities such as roads, ports and airport facilities increases the productivity of private investment and results in a larger capacity.

3. ***Technology***. Technological change raises the productivity of all resources and increases aggregate supply. As an example, the U.S. automobile industry, finding itself threatened by the inroads of Japanese cars in recent times, has invested billions of dollars in developing and implementing new technology including robotics.

Technological changes not only result from investments, they also cause new investments. While much technological change is gradual, the big changes, such as microchips in the 1970s, come from intensive processes of research and development. These changes occur with significant time lags before implementation and are often subsidized by government.

Investment in Human Capital
Expenditures made on training, education, and increasing the skill levels of individuals

4. ***Productivity***. The *productivity* of resources, the output produced by each unit of input, depends on many things. The productivity of labor, for example, depends on the productivity of the capital with which it is employed. Labor's productivity also depends heavily on training, education, and on increasing skills. Economists refer to these three factors as **investment in human capital**.

Productivity growth has become a major issue in the United States in recent years, particularly since it has at times grown at a faster rate in some other industrial nations than in this country. There have been calls for more investment in human capital as well as in new plant and equipment to raise the joint productivity of labor and capital and thereby increase the aggregate supply of commodities and services.

5. ***Expectations***. Firms, like consumers, form expectations. Payouts on many investments is often long term. In making investment and production decisions, firms must form expectations about prices for their products as well as expectations of future overall price levels in order to assess the present value of such decisions. If expectations change, we would expect firms to re-evaluate their decisions and alter both the mix and amount of investments and planned production rates.

www.commerce.gov
For more information on commerce policies visit the Department of Commerce at the web site listed above.

6. ***Government policies***. Government policies affect aggregate supply decisions in numerous ways. Such policies affect the availability and cost of resources. Will the United States allow exploration for oil in offshore sites? The policy decision will likely affect the price of oil and energy costs of firms. Will government policy tend toward further deregulation of transportation? The result will certainly affect the transport costs of firms in producing and distributing goods and services. These are merely illustrative of the myriad of government policies and changes in policy that influence firm's supply decisions.

Why Does the (Short-Run) Aggregate Supply Curve Slope Upward?

The aggregate supply curve in Figure 7-1 is positively sloped. Indeed, we will assume the following:

As the aggregate price level rises, the quantity supplied or produced will rise; as the aggregate price level falls, the quantity supplied or produced will decrease. (Short-run aggregate supply curves slope upward.)

Recall that we assume that the supply curve of a firm is based on cost and that in the short run, rising costs associated with ultimately diminishing productivity result in firms offering more for sale, only at higher prices. The AS curve for the entire economy in Figure 7-1 is based on the same assumption. In the short run, it is reasonable to assume that input prices (wages, interest rates, etc.) are constant and that it is rising real cost that explains the upward-sloping (short-run) aggregate supply curve. Of course, the process works in reverse. If private firms reduce output rates, they will lay off less efficient resources, and their (unit) costs will fall, making them willing to offer smaller rates of output for sale at lower prices.

It will be important to the reader to know that if the overall price level rises, there will ultimately be pressure to increase factor prices, including wage and salary rates as well as interest rates. The ultimately increasing costs associated with rising factor prices create supply shocks and affect equilibrium income and price levels. This interaction will be addressed more fully in another chapter.

Figure 7-2
Equilibrium Income, Actual Income, and the GDP Gap

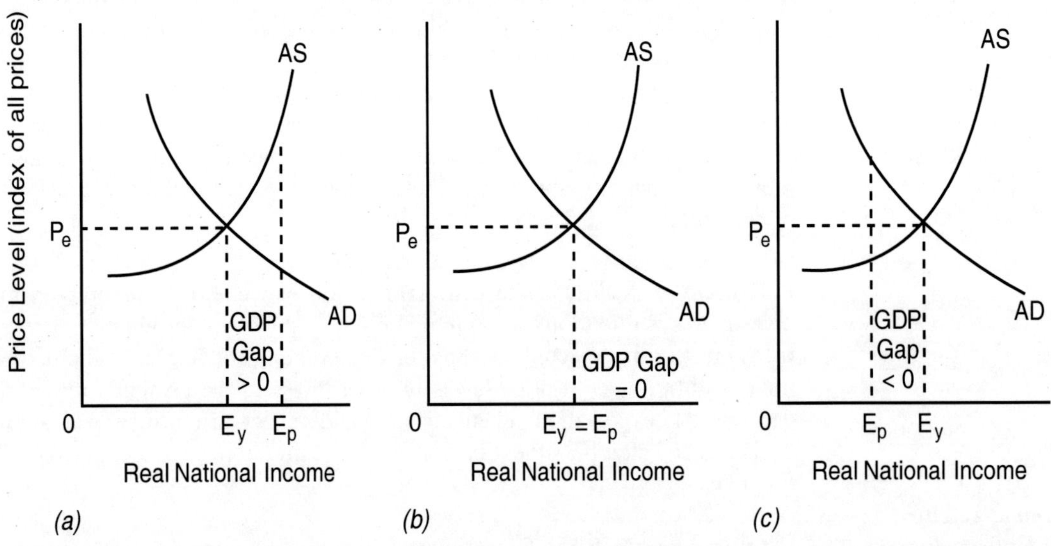

In *(a),* the equilibrium level of income, E_y, is less than the potential or full employment level of income, E_p. The GDP gap $E_p - E_y$ is positive. In *(b),* the equilibrium level of income, E_y, equals the potential or full employment level of income and employment, E_p. The GDP gap is zero, the economy is producing at its potential with only a natural rate of unemployment. In *(c),* the equilibrium level of income, E_y is greater than the potential or full employment level of income, E_p. The GDP gap $E_y - E_p$ is temporally negative.

Equilibrium and Full Employment May Not Be the Same

We have seen that there is a potential or capacity GDP that a nation is capable of producing if it fully employs its resources, especially its labor force. We also have seen that the full employment level, though rarely reached, does not correspond to zero unemployment. The actual level of unemployment is the one that the current economy produces. The natural rate is the one at which inflation tends neither to accelerate or decelerate. (Explained by frictional unemployment or people seeking to move to new jobs.) In recent times, this natural rate has been estimated to be about 5 to 6 percent of the labor force, though recent estimates suggest it may be lower.

Equilibrium income, therefore, may be greater than full employment, less than full employment, or correspond to full-employment income. We see all three of these possibilities represented in Figure 7-2. In (*a*), the equilibrium level of income, E_y is less than the potential or full employment level, E_p. The GDP gap, $E_p - E_y$ is positive and the economy is operating with an unemployment rate above the natural rate. In (*b*), the equilibrium level of income corresponds to the potential or full employment level ($E_y = E_p$). The economy is reaching its potential and operating at its natural rate of unemployment. In (*c*), the equilibrium level of income, is above the potential level ($E_y > E_p$), and the GDP gap is less than zero. The economy is operating at above its natural rate of unemployment.

When Real Income and the Price Level Change

What we have seen is that aggregate demand and aggregate supply determine, in equilibrium, the level of real income together with the level of prices. Now let's see what happens when either aggregate demand or aggregate supply changes.

Shifts in Aggregate Demand and Aggregate Supply

Aggregate Demand Shift
The term used to describe an increase or decrease in aggregate demand.

Aggregate Supply Shift
The term used to describe an increase or decrease in aggregate supply.

Aggregate Demand Shift is the term used to describe an increase or decrease in aggregate demand. A shift to the right is called an increase in aggregate demand and means that more real income will be demanded at each price level. A shift to the left is called a decrease in aggregate demand and means that less real income will be demanded at each level of prices.

Aggregate Supply Shift is the term used to describe an increase or decrease in aggregate supply. An increase in aggregate supply means that more real product will be supplied at each price level. A shift to the left, on the other hand, means that less real product will be supplied at each price level.

The most important point to remember about this is:

When either an aggregate demand or an aggregate supply shift occurs, there will be a change in the equilibrium level of income and product for an economy as well as a change in its level of prices.

Figure 7-3
The Effects of Aggregate Demand Shifts

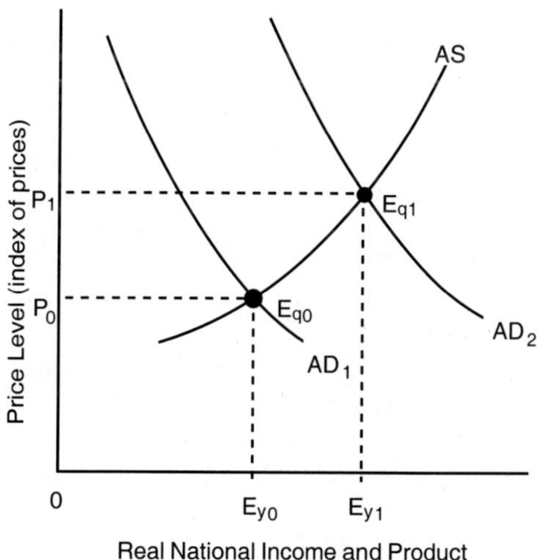

An increase in aggregate demand shifts the AD curve to the right from AD_1 to AD_2. Equilibrium income increases from E_{y0} to E_{y1} in a movement along the upward sloping short-run aggregate supply curve, as prices rise from P_0 to P_1. The reverse occurs with a decrease in aggregate demand, decreasing equilibrium income to E_{y0} and prices to P_0.

Aggregate Demand Shifts: Their Effects and Some Causes

We see in Figure 7-3 the effects of aggregate demand shifts. If AD increases, as from AD_1 to AD_2, both income and the price level increase as well (from $E_y{}^0$ to E_{y1} and from P_0 to P_1). If AD decreases, as from AD_2 to AD_1, both income and the price level decrease (from E_{y1} to E_{y0} and from P_1 to P_0). Both directions of change involve a movement along the short-run aggregate supply curve. For example, in the early 1980s, the United States faced "double-digit" inflation which was perceived to be a serious problem threatening the growth and stability of the economy. In response, the monetary authorities contracted the money supply sharply, reducing AD_1 and helped create a severe recession with almost 10 percent unemployment and sharply falling inflation rates. In 1983, AD increased in the face of tax cuts, budget deficits, and increased confidence. This resulted in growing income and declining unemployment, which fell to less than 4 percent by 2000. Anything which causes households and firms to spend more at all price levels can shift AD to the right. Conversely, anything that causes households and consumers to spend less at all price levels can shift AD to the left.

Figure 7-4
The Effects of Aggregate Supply Shocks

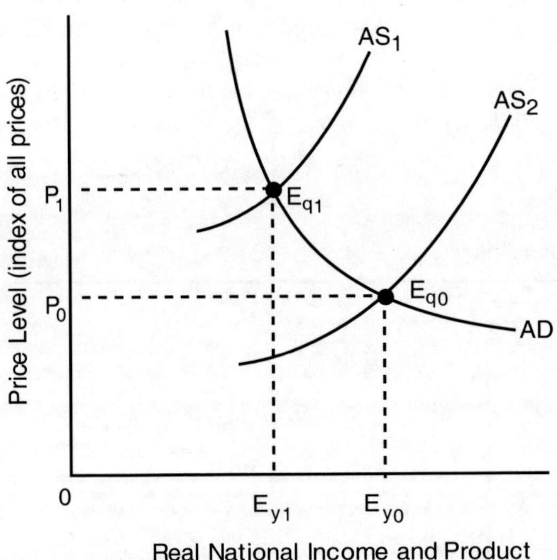

A decreasing aggregate supply shifts the AS curve to the left as from AS_2 to AS_1. Equilibrium income decreases from E_{y0} to E_{y1} and the level of prices increases from P_0 to P_1. The movement from E_{q0} to E_{q1} is a movement along the aggregate demand curve, AD. An increasing aggregate supply shifts the AS curve to the right as from AS_1 to AS_2. Equilibrium income increases from E_{y1} to E_{y0} and the level of prices decreases from P_1 to P_0. The movement from Equilibrium (E_{q1}) to Equilibrium (E_{q0}) is a movement along the aggregate demand, AD.

Aggregate Supply Shifts: Their Effects and a Cause

In Figure 7-4, we can see the effects of aggregate supply shocks. If AS decreases, as from AS2 to AS1, equilibrium income decreases from E_{y0} to E_{y1} and the price level rises from P_0 to P_1. If aggregate supply increases, as from AS1 to AS2, equilibrium income rises from E_{y1} to E_{y0} and the price level declines from P_1 to P_0. Both directions of change in AS result in movements along the aggregate demand curve, AD. As we have seen, there are many things that can cause changes in aggregate supply.

In the early to mid-1970s, there was a dramatic and largely unexpected increase in energy prices, especially in the price of imported crude oil. As a result, the costs of producing virtually all commodities and services increased. This influence shifted aggregate supply to the left and contributed to reduced income, rising unemployment, and rising prices, a condition that came to be known as stagflation. We will look at this in more detail in the application to this chapter for this shift came about because of influences outside the domestic economy.

Note: The different ranges of aggregate supply are: (a) unemployment with many unemployed resources, (b) bottlenecks with fewer unemployed resources and a movement toward full employment, and (c) full employment, in which real output cannot rise.

By the early to mid-1980s, oil export prices began to grow more slowly and then to decline in absolute terms. Falling energy prices reduced the costs of supplying commodities and services, shifting aggregate supply to the right and contributing to rising real income and a declining price level. (Inflation rates actually became negative for a very short period in 1987.)

Ranges of Aggregate Supply

The aggregate supply curves seen in Figures 7-1 through 7-4 were all upward sloping, showing that increasing quantities of commodities and services were associated with rising levels of prices. Clearly, however, the general state of the economy will determine whether production costs rise and how sharply they rise as output expands. We can identify three possible ranges of aggregate-supply price-level relations. These three sections of aggregate supply we will call (a) unemployment, an economy with large quantities of unemployed resources, (b) bottlenecks, the economy approaching full employment, and (c) full employment, the economy at capacity. We see all three conditions represented in Figure 7-5.

Figure 7-5
Ranges of Aggregate Supply

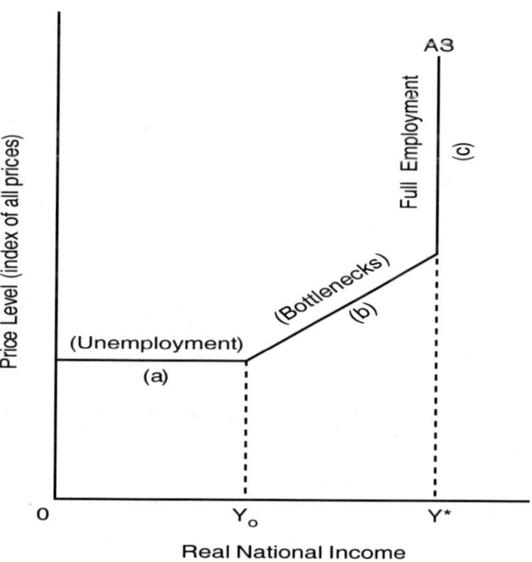

Range (a) represents an economy with large quantities of unemployed resources, an economy in recession or even depression. Range (b) represents an economy moving toward full employment and bidding less efficient resources into use as output grows; i.e., an economy with bottlenecks in supply responses. Range (c) represents an economy at full employment income (Y*); i.e., an economy that cannot increase real output, only prices.

In Figure 7-5, we see that in range (a), the economy's real income can grow in response to changes in aggregate demand, and this growing income can be accomplished without an increase in overall prices. This stable price level growth can be maintained up to income level Y_0. In range (b), the economy's real income can grow but presumably only with the rising costs associated with bottlenecks and drawing less productive resources into use. This growth with rising prices can be maintained up to income level Y*. In range (c), at full employment, Y*, the economy can respond to further increases in demand only with rising prices. The economy at Y* has reached its production-possibilities frontier and until that frontier shifts outward from increasing endowments of resources or from improvements in technology, real output cannot grow.

The most important implication of these ranges is that efforts to increase real output, reduce unemployment and maintain stable price levels through changes in aggregate demand are crucially influenced by aggregate supply responses. If, for example, taxes are cut and disposable incomes increase, we would expect aggregate demand to increase. If the responding economy is in range (a), real income will grow with stable prices. In range (b), real income will grow but there will also be rising prices. In range (c), real output cannot grow and the consequence of an aggregate demand increase will be inflation.

Supply-Side Economics

From the end of World War II to the early 1980s, national policies, including monetary and fiscal policies, focused on trying to change aggregate demand in the appropriate direction and amount necessary to create acceptable levels of employment and real income in the United States. Such efforts were designed to create growing real income at relatively stable price levels. All such efforts seemed to grow, at least in part, from the commitments in the Employment Act of 1946, but stopped short of a commitment to full employment such as that in the Humphrey-Hawkins Act of 1978. The implicit assumption in all these efforts seemed to be that changes in aggregate quantities supplied would adjust to whatever level was required to create stable prices in the face of growing aggregate demand. In other words, the assumption seemed to be that the economy's supply responses would occur in range (a).

In the early 1980s, we began to hear from "supply-siders" who said that tax cuts and other incentives to increase aggregate supply were the recipe for economic growth with acceptable price stability. Some even argued that cutting tax rates could not only shift aggregate supply to the right and increase income at lower prices levels but also produce increases in tax revenues with which to deal with budget deficit problems. Supply-side advocates and supply-side skeptics are far from resolving their differences and we shall have much more to say about these arguments in another chapter.

Measuring the Aggregate Price Level: Price Indexes'

We said earlier that we would come back to the levels of prices in Figure 7-1 and show how those levels are computed or measured. There are two basic reasons why such measurements are important to both public and private decisions in the American economy. First, the real national income or product (GDP) is a vast heterogeneous mix of goods and services that has to be reduced to a common monetary measure in a given year as well as between different years. Second, changes in GDP from one year to another are measures of rising prices (inflation), falling prices (deflation), or price stability. It is crucial that the common denominator, dollar values, be constant as we track aggregate prices through time. Doing this requires the construction of price indexes.

Indexes of Prices

An aggregate price level is calculated as an index number. To measure or calculate an index requires identifying a collection of goods and services called a "market basket" in a specific time period. The level of prices of the goods and services in that "basket" in a particular year can be compared with the prices of the same or a similar "basket" in a base year or reference period. In recent years, federal government agencies charged with computing such indexes have often chosen 2000 as the base or reference year. Thus, the price index in 2013, for example, may be expressed as:

Price index in 2009	=	Price of the market basket in 2013 / Price of the same market basket in 2000	x 100

Multiplying the price ratio $\left(\frac{P2013}{P2000}\right)$ by 100 is a convention of national income accountants. It permits a simple expression of the result. Let's illustrate that hypothetically. Suppose that the price of the basket in 2013 is twice that of the same basket in 2000. The ratio $\left(\frac{2}{1} = 2\right)$ when multiplied by 100 is expressed as an index number of 200. Thus, as inflationary pressures move prices upward, the index of prices rises above 100. Similarly, suppose the price of the market basket in 2009 is half that of the same basket in 2000. The ratio $\left(\frac{1}{2} = 0.5\right)$ when multiplied by 100 results in an index number of 50. Thus as deflationary pressures push prices downward, the index of prices falls below 100.

Consumer Price Index A measure of a market basket of about 300 goods and services commonly purchased by urban consumers. It is published quarterly.

The federal government computes and reports several important price indexes. Most familiar of these measurements is the **Consumer Price Index** (CPI). A measure of a market basket of about 300 goods and services commonly purchased by urban consumers, its quarterly report is watched closely by many who seek to analyze changes in consumer welfare. A far better measure, however, of the *overall* price level represented in Figure 7-1 is the GDP price index or GDP deflator.

Computing the GDP Price Index or Deflator

Let's follow through the calculations in Table 7-1 to see how a hypothetical GDP price index may be calculated for 2009 using 1987 as the base or reference period. From column (1) we see that the economy produces only four goods, hamburgers, computer diskettes, gasoline, and books. Let's suppose that the quantities produced of the goods are 1, 1, 2, and 1 units. Column (3) tells us that the per unit prices of the four goods are $4.00, $10.00, $1.50, and $20.00 respectively. Column (4) shows that total expenditures on the goods (columns (3) x (2)) are $4.00, $10.00, $3.00, and $20.00 for a total expenditure of $37.00.

Using 1987 as the base or reference year, we see in column (5) that the prices of our four goods in that year were $3.00, $7.00, $1.00, and $15.00. A comparison of columns (5) and (3) shows that prices of each of the goods rose between 2000 and 2009. More significant to our index is that the total cost of our "basket" was $27.00 in 1987 and $37.00 in 2009. In other words, if prices in 2009 were the same as in 1987, the basket in the current year would cost $27.00. To compute the 2009 price index, we will divide the 2009 price of the market basket ($37.00) by the 1987 price of the same basket of goods ($27.00).

Table 7-1
A Hypothetical GDP price index for 2009

(1) Produce	(2) Quantities in 2009 market basket	(3) Prices of market basket items in 2009	(4) Expenditures on market basket in 2009 (3) X (2)	(5) Prices of 2009 market basket in 1987 (base period)	(6) Expenditures on 2009 market basket in 1987 (5) X (2)
Hamburgers	1	$ 4.00	$ 4.00	$ 3.00	$ 3.00
Computer diskettes	1	10.00	10.00	7.00	7.00
Gasoline	2	1.50	3.00	1.00	2.00
Books	1	20.00	20.00	15.00	15.00
			$37.00		$27.00

Recall that the quotient or result is then multiplied by 100 to create the simple conventional result.

$$\text{GDP price index in 2009} = \frac{\text{Price of the market basket in 2009}}{\text{Price of the same market basket in 1987}} \times 100$$

or in our hypothetical example:

GDP price index, 2009 = $37.00/27.00x 100 = 137

The price index for 2009, then, is 137. This is a short-hand way of saying that the weighted (weights in column (2)) average of the prices of goods in our market has risen by 37 percent since 1987. Similar calculations could be made for all years prior to 2009 using 1987 as the base period. As we saw in the chapter on measuring domestic income and product, this index number or price level (137) can be used to deflate the growth in nominal GDP from 1987 to 2009 to obtain a measure of the growth in real GDP over that period of time.

Remember, though, that this growth in GDP is at best, an imperfect indicator of improvement in the welfare of a nation's citizens. As Arthur Okun[1] once noted, there are many things including "peace, equality of opportunity, the elimination of injustice and violence, greater brotherhood among Americans of different racial and ethnic backgrounds...." that could make this country better off without an increase in real GDP. Also remember that there are various important things, including non-market transactions, improved quality of products, and leisure, that are excluded from GDP measures.

The Consumer Price Index: Its Importance

As mentioned earlier, the consumer price index (CPI) is the most widely reported of the government's price indexes and is considered an important measure of inflation. Determined from a 1992–1994 survey of spending patterns of urban households, it consists of about 300 goods and services. Unlike the GDP deflator, it is a "fixed weight" measure, it uses the same weights for each of the

1. Okun, Arthur M.,"Social Welfare Has No Price Tag." *The Economic Accounts of the United States Retrospect and Prospect.* U.S. Department of Commerce, July, 1971.

goods in each of the years reported. The GDP measure changes these weights each year. This is one of the reasons why critics of the CPI believe that it overstates inflation since consumers do in fact change their spending patterns, particularly over a period of several years. The fixed weight approach assumes that changes in relative prices do not induce consumers to substitute between goods or even classes of goods.

The CPI, like the GDP deflator, does not take into account qualitative changes. Medical care prices, for example, are widely reported to be rising rapidly and significantly influence increases in the CPI. Failure to account for improvements in the quality of medical care, however, cause this medical care price increase to be overstated.

COLAs
Cost of living Adjustments.

Why does this overstatement of inflation by the CPI matter? First, it contributes to the inflation itself. As many as 50 million Americans, including about 40 million social security recipients, have their payments or wages tied to the CPI. These cost-of-living adjustments (COLAs) increase the demand for goods and services and thereby, the inflationary pressure on prices. Secondly, indexing of income tax brackets, that began in 1985, tie marginal tax rates to changes in real rather than nominal income. Though this indexing is widely supported, if the CPI overstates price increases, it causes the real-tax obligations of citizens to be understated.

Application I: Demand and Supply Shocks: OPEC in the 1970s and 1980s, a War on Terrorism and a New Supply Shock in the 21st Century

In the preceding chapter, we learned that the equilibrium level of real income and the aggregate price level associated with that equilibrium are determined by aggregate demand (AD) and aggregate supply (AS). Changes in either AS or AD or simultaneous changes in both can change the equilibrium and produce a new level of prices and real income for the economic society. Such variations occur internally and arise from changes in the internal factors affecting AS and AD which we also examined in the preceding chapter. Almost continual variations in AD and AS produce new levels of income and prices. Also, cycles of expansion and contraction together with varying levels of employment and unemployment that we examined in chapter 6 result from these variations.

External Aggregate Demand and Supply Shocks
Factors external to the macroeconomy that change its equilibrium levels of income, employment, and prices.

At times, the macroeconomy, whatever are it's AD and AS driven internal equilibrium tendencies, is "shocked" by external factors, factors that can affect either AS or AD or both simultaneously. These shocks, called **external aggregate demand and supply shocks** may have important effects on equilibrium levels of income, employment, and prices.

In this application, we will examine several external shocks to the American economy that have occurred in recent decades. Those shocks in the 1970s and 1980s related to the efforts of OPEC (Organization of Petroleum Exporting Countries) to increase petroleum prices thereby enhancing foreign exchange earnings of its member nations. We will also examine the effects of a reverse shock from falling petroleum prices in the late 1980s and early 1990s when OPEC lost control of those prices. Finally, we will look at the possible effects of an ongoing shock to the American economy, that arising from the terrorist attacks of 2001 and the ensuing "war on terrorism" waged by the United States and it's allies.

The OPEC Shocks

The 1970s and 1980s were periods marked by wide variations in economic activity. Vietnam War spending, substantially financed by deficit spending, resulted in inflation and price controls (Refer to Figure 6-2 for a visual reminder of the period). The end of the war and demobilization accompanied by falling military expenditures caused a decline in Aggregate demand. Dramatic increases in oil prices (OPEC I in 1973–1975) reduced aggregate supply and resulted in a sharp recession in 1975–1976. In the late 1970s, continued inflation combined with a second sharp increase in oil prices (OPEC II) produced slow growth. In five years, the real (discounted for inflation) price of oil increased by about 600 percent.

To illustrate the effects of a supply shock, let's look at OPEC II in 1979–1980. Remember that aggregate supply curves are based on costs of production and that they slope upward because of rising costs of larger quantities supplied from existing plant and equipment.

When costs rise – in this case because of a rapid rise in oil prices – the AS curve shifts upward or to the left. As this happens, we expect the equilibrium level of real national income to decrease and the price level (index of all prices) to rise. How great these effects will be depends in large measure on how much production costs have been raised. In the case of oil prices, the two shifts appear to have been quite significant. By one estimate, almost 5 percent of the world's gross product is composed of the value of oil production.[2] Putting this in perspective, it is likely that no other energy price, indeed no other resource price, reaches that level of significance. Thus, the shift in aggregate supply costs from a major change in such a price should be expected to be large.

We see the outlines of such a process in Figure 7-6. The very large increases in oil prices from OPEC II increased short-run production costs and shifted aggregate supply from AS (1979) to AS (1980). With a smaller supply, aggregate quantity demanded decreased and real income (GDP) declined with the economy spiraling into a major recession. The recession was accompanied by a strong inflationary pressure with the consumer price index (including the price of gasoline and heating oil) rising from 217.4 to 246.8 or by 13.5 percent. America experienced "double digit" inflation for only the second time in its modern history. With a smaller aggregate supply, the demand for labor decreased and the unemployment rate among civilian laborers rose from 5.8 percent to 7.1 percent.

Was the entire set of macroeconomic effects attributable to the supply shock? Probably not, but the majority of the independent causality appears traceable to this major price-cost-supply shift. The main point is that employment, price levels, and real income can be affected dramatically not only by changes in aggregate demand, about which we will say much more in the ensuing chapters, but also by changes in aggregate supply. This introduces a very troublesome element in national economic policy when such supply changes may be caused by forces difficult or impossible to effect with domestic policy measures.

We have chosen the 1979-1980 supply shock because it was a "pure price effect," one unaccompanied by other types of external shocks. The same effects might have been shown through OPEC I (the oil price change in 1974). In that instance, though, there was also an embargo with its own price and other supply effects.

---

2. Fried, Edward R. "World Oil Markets New Benefits, Old Concerns." In McClelland, Peter D., *Readings in Introductory Macroeconomics.* New York: McGraw Hill, 1988.

Figure 7-6
Aggregate Supply Shifts Resulting From Cost Shocks of Oil Prices in 1979-1980

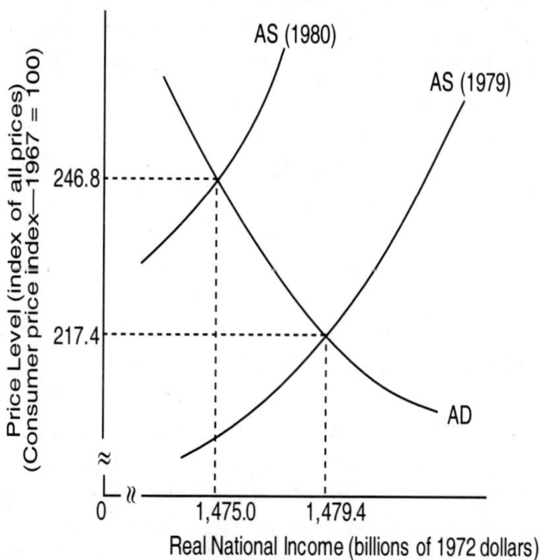

In 1979 OPEC announced major increases in oil export prices. The aggregate supply costs shifted upward (leftward) from AS (1979) to AS (1980). As a result, real national income declined from 1,479.4 billion to 1,475.0 billion and the consumer price index rose from 217.4 to 246.8.

Minimizing the Supply Shock

Many economists were surprised that income and price effects of OPEC II were not more dramatically adverse than they were. On reflection though, this should not be so surprising. Naturally, when the price of something as basic as energy increases sharply, consumers, including nations and firms, look for ways to minimize the costs to themselves. As Edward Fried has shown, in the case of OPEC II, the 1980s witnessed the following:

1. Energy use efficiency increased after the 1973-1974 shock. Energy was conserved as an input in production as well as in households.

2. Oil became less important as a source of energy. Oil became a relatively expensive source of energy; as a result, it declined from 55 percent to 45 percent of primary energy use.

3. At higher oil prices, many non-OPEC producers expanded output. For example, the fields in Mexico, the North Sea, and the coast of Alaska expanded output.

4. OPEC, as a cartel, found it increasingly difficult to maintain its monopoly prices. Lacking an effective means to discipline its members, it tried production quotas but the incentive to cheat on prices and quotas was intense.

5. Saudia Arabia, the lowest cost producer which then held 40 percent of the world's reserves, found its ability to maintain prices through adjusting its output increasing untenable.

As a consequence of the above, the quantities demanded of (OPEC and non-OPEC) oil proved to be smaller than anticipated. Quantities supplied, on the other hand, proved much larger. As a result, by the mid-1980s, downward pressures on oil prices became irresistible.

A Reverse Supply Shock

Oil Prices in the Late 1980s? The 1990s? The Twenty First Century?

Between late 1985 and April 1986, average oil prices fell from $28 to $14 a barrel (a kind of *unintended* OPEC III). Go back to Figure 7-6, but reverse the direction of change in aggregate supply. Even though oil had become less influential as a source of energy, it was, and remains, very important in that regard. A major reduction in costs and a shift downward or to the right of AS occurred tending to reduce the GDP price index or at least its rate of growth. From 1985 to 1987, these prices rose by less than 6 percent. At the same time, the aggregate quantity demanded rose as price pressures diminished and real GDP rose by 6.2 percent. It would be wrong to think that both events were caused entirely by the reverse (positive) supply shock of dramatically falling oil prices. Indeed, other things (e.g., budget deficits) were happening to stimulate aggregate demand. The point, though, is that supply shocks can have positive as well as negative effects on inflationary pressures and growth in real income. They can, in other words, help to solve problems as well as create them.

In the early 1990s, the U.S. and its allies fought a war in the Persian gulf that was at least partly undertaken to keep oil supplies and oil prices stable. Another oil price "shock" of the sort experienced earlier could, however, again reduce aggregate supply, cause inflation and plunge the nation into serious recession. However, in 2001, oil prices again fell sharply. This time, through, the "shock" occurred against a different economic setting.

2001: The Economics of a War on Terrorism

As we have seen, aggregate demand and aggregate supply shocks can, at times, be positive in their effects on the macroeconomy. Earlier we saw an example of a dramatic decline in petroleum prices-driving energy prices down in 1985–1986. A similar decline began occurring in 2001. The former occurred against a backdrop of a growing economy and, by reducing supply costs, increased AS and real income, while restraining upward pressure on prices. The latter decline however, occurred in an economy that had been slowing for months. In March, 2001, the American economy entered a recession (two consecutive quarters of decline in GDP).

Rising Oil Prices Since 2004

From 2004 to 2008, oil prices again rose rapidly though their cause, a new "supply shock" proved less dramatic than its predecessors in terms of affecting aggregate supply and aggregate demand. The severe recession starting in 2007 eventually caused oil prices to drop dramatically by 2009. Since has continued to creep upward.

A War Economy

In September 2001, America and its economy were shocked by terrorist attacks which quickly led to military mobilization and efforts to seek out and eliminate further terrorist threats to the nation. Although the outcome of those efforts is yet to be determined, they will certainly have effects on the nation's macroeconomy. Let's sketch out what (in Figure 7-7) the effects may be:

Figure 7-7
Possible Unfavorable Effects of the War on Terrorism and Declining Consumer Confidence

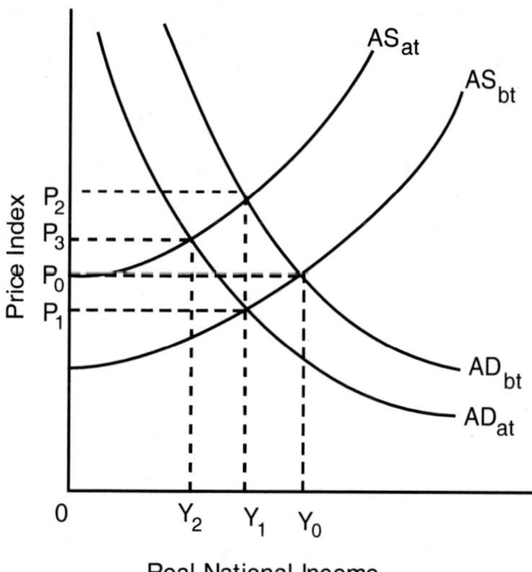

In Figure 7-7, the possible unfavorable effects associated with the period following terrorist attacks are illustrated. The pre-terrorist attack equilibrium with aggregate supply before terrorist attack (AS_{bt}) and aggregate demand before terrorist attack (AD_{bt}) is with price level P_0 and real income Y_0. As a result of rising costs of production and distribution due to counter terrorism measures, AS shifts upwards to AS_{at} and the (aggregate supply after attack) and prices rise to P_2 with real income falling to Y_1. As a result of declining Consumer Confidence, however, AD falls to AD_{at} and together with AS_{at} causes prices to fall from P_2 to P_3 and real income to fall from Y_1 to Y_2. The net effect is slightly rising prices and falling real income.

Negative Economic Effects

Those who argue that efforts to combat terrorism will have a negative effect on an economy cite the following:

a) The costs of production and distribution will increase to reflect the higher costs of added security. In December 2001, the International Monetary Fund estimated the direct costs to the U.S. at $21 Billion; at the same time it lowered its estimates of the 2002 growth of the American economy from 2.7 percent to 2.2 percent. These higher costs include such things as airport security and security of the mails; higher costs, in turn, will reduce aggregate supply. We see this in Figure 7-7, where AS shifts from AS_{bt} (Aggregate supply before terrorism) to AS_{at} (Aggregate supply after terrorism). Real income falls from Y_0 to Y_1 and prices rise from P_0 to P_2.

b) Declining Consumer Confidence causes Aggregate demand, to decline, in Figure 7-7, before terrorism (AD_{bt}) shifts to the left to AD_{at}. With a reduced Aggregate supply (AS_{at}) a new lower level of aggregate demand (AD_{at}) produces a new macroeconomic equilibrium with real income Y_2 and price P_3.

The overall impact of the War on terrorism according to this argument is to reduce real income (from Y_0 to Y_2) and to increase prices (P_0 to P_3). In other words, the war on terrorism increases the recessionary pressure on an economy that may be experiencing those pressures.

Positive Economic Effects

Those who argue that efforts to combat terrorism will have a positive effect on an economy already in recession cite the following:

a) Aggregate demand will rise because the federal government, free of the pressure to run budget surpluses and pay down the national debt, will increase both direct military expenditures and those related to international security. As a result, aggregate demand shifts upward to right as in Figure 7-8 from AD_{bt} to AD_{at}. This causes real income to increase from Y_0 to Y_1, and prices to rise from P_0 to P_2.

b) Falling oil and other energy prices will cause costs of production to decrease which increase aggregate supply from AS_{bt} to AS_{at} in Figure 7-8. This increased supply, in conjunction with increased aggregate demand (AD_{bt} to AD_{at}) creates a new equilibrium with real income rising from Y_1 to Y_2.

The combined effects of increased aggregate demand (AD_{at}) and increased aggregate supply (AS_{at}) are to increase real income with a stable level of prices. The net effect in other words, is to reduce recessionary pressure on the macroeconomy.

Figure 7-8
Possible Favorable Effects of the War on Terrorism and Declining Consumer Confidence

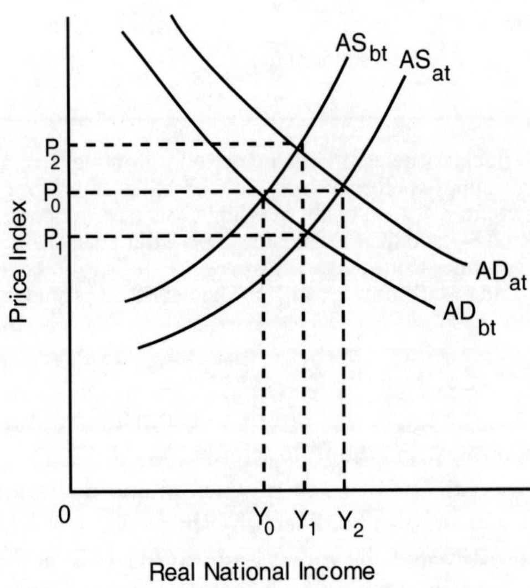

In Figure 7-8, the possible favorable effects associated with the period following terrorist attacks are illustrated. The pre-terrorist attack equilibrium with aggregate supply before terrorist attack (AS_{bt}) and aggregate demand before terrorist attack (AD_{bt}) is with price level P_0 and real income Y_0. As a result of declining energy prices, AS shifts outward to AS_{at} (aggregate supply after attack) and the price level falls to P_1 with real income growing to Y_1. Expenditures on combating terrorism increase aggregate demand to AD_{at} (aggregate demand after terrorism) and prices rise to P_0 but income rises further to Y_2. The net effect is stable prices and growing real income and employment.

What Really Happened: Summing Up and A Few Caveats

External shocks to the economy, as we have seen, can have major effects on its equilibrium levels of real income and prices. A major derived effect may be on job creation or the level of employment. A negative shock not only causes lower real income, it also reduces the demand for labor. A positive shock, on the other hand, not only causes real income to grow but also increases the demand for labor.

A few caveats

1. The long term effects of favorable shocks such as falling energy prices will depend on how long they last and whether energy prices subsequently rise as

they have since 2007. Expectations of consumers and producers which, as we have seen, influence both demand and supply, are formed out of recent experience and expectations of the future.

2. The arguments about government spending to fight a "war on terrorism" are controversial. That war, like others in American history, is likely to increase aggregate demand. This increase, if large may have major effects on an economy in recession. For example, some economic historians argue that military spending in 1942-1945 finally ended the great depression. Robert Higgs[3] points out, however, that price controls during the war make it difficult to assess the increase in real output during that period. Higgs argues that war output satisfies no consumer demands and that such output should be excluded from measures of increasing product. David Henderson[4] adds that wars lead to increased government control over the economy, and that Higgs is right in labeling war expenditures an "opportunity cost" rather than a benefit. On the other side of this argument, many economists say that war expenditures do create jobs (as they did between 1942 and 1945.)

3. Finally, it is important to remind ourselves that we are dealing with *external* influences on the equilibrium of the American economy. It is basically its internal workings, the domestic factors that influence and determine the behavior of consumers, producers, and governments that will move the economy out of recession. This, as we saw in the chapter on economic cycles, has occurred many times. Robert Parry[5], President of the Federal Reserve Bank of San Francisco, says: "The Economy *will* recover and in the long run, its fundamentals are strong." Virtually all economists would argue that it is those fundamentals, not external shocks that will determine the economy's long–run growth path.

SUMMING UP

1. In spite of substantial long-term real income growth, the U.S. has experienced movements about its "target" of growth with stable prices. In this chapter, we looked at an aggregate demand-aggregate supply model of real income and prices. This model is quite different from the single product supply and demand model of price and quantity demanded in the chapter on supply and demand.

2. Aggregate price levels and levels of real income are established by the interaction of aggregate demand and aggregate supply. The equilibrium price level and the equilibrium level of income are established where aggregate quantity demanded equals aggregate quantity supplied. Equilibrium real income does not, however, necessarily correspond to desired real income.

---

3. Higgs, Robert. "Wartime Prosperity. A Reassessment of the U.S. Economy in the 1940s." *Journal of Economic History*, 52, 1992.
4. Henderson, David R. "The Economics of War." *San Francisco Chronicle*, November 28, 2001. Also "The Joy of Freedom, An Economic Odyssey." *Financial Times*, Prentice Hall, 2001.
5. Parry, Robert T. "The U.S. Economy After September 11." Federal Reserve Bank of San Francisco, Weekly Letter, December 7, 2001.

3. Aggregate demand is a measure of the entire desired spending on final goods and services at each level of prices. The four factors that make up and determine aggregate demand are (a) consumption expenditures, (b) investment expenditures, (c) government expenditures, and, (d) net exports. Consumption expenditures depend on disposable incomes, cost and availability of credit, and expectations. Investment expenditures depend on interest rates, the expectations of producers, and government policy. Government expenditures are complex in determination but depend on such things as varying economic conditions, political philosophies, national emergencies, and efforts to secure re-election. Net exports (exports minus imports) can be either negative or positive and depend on exchange rate changes, trade policy, and politics. Thus, aggregate demand is equal to consumption expenditures (C) + investment expenditures (I) + government expenditures (G) + net exports (X_N).

4. Aggregate demand curves slope downward. The lower the price level, the greater the aggregate quantity demanded. The higher the price level, the lower the aggregate quantity demanded. The reason for the negative slope is not the same as with individual demand curves. Instead, the effects of interest rate changes, the effects of wealth changes, and the effects of relative price changes between domestic and foreign goods explain why AD slopes downward.

5. Aggregate supply is a measure of the entire desired output of final goods and services at each level of prices and real income. The factors which affect aggregate supply are (a) cost and availability of resources, (b) capacity and investment plans, (c) technology;, (d) productivity, and (e) government policy. Firms observe and act on increases in resource prices quickly, as their total costs and profitability are affected. Any economy's aggregate supply is constrained in the short run by its capacity stock of plants and equipment and other productive resources. In the long run, this capacity is increased by investment. Technological change increases the productivity of all resources and both results from and causes investment. Productivity, output per unit of input, depends on many things, including investment in human capital. Concerns have been raised about slower productivity growth in the United States than in other industrial nations. Expectations play a role in all decision making including supply plans, and changes in these expectations may importantly affect such plans. Government policy has many influences on supply plans. Tariffs, tax rates, and environmental decisions all affect costs and profitability and, thereby, supply.

6. Aggregate supply curves slope upward. As the price level rises, aggregate quantity supplied rises. As the price level falls, aggregate quantity supplied falls. The explanation for the positive slope appears to lie in the ultimately rising real cost of production from using resources of diminishing productivity as aggregate income rises. Thus, short-run aggregate supply curves slope upward on the assumption that productivity diminishes but factor prices in the short run are constant as aggregate prices rise. This assumption has to be modified to examine long-run aggregate-supply conditions.

7. Equilibrium (actual) levels of real income and prices may or may not be equal to potential (full employment) levels. At full employment, an economy operates at its natural rate of unemployment or that corresponding to frictional unemployment with inflation that neither tends to increase or decrease. Thus, equilibrium income and prices may create a GDP gap that is positive; i.e., an economy may operate with an unemployment rate greater than the natural rate.

Alternatively, the economy may operate with an unemployment rate below the natural rate. Finally, equilibrium (actual) and potential (full employment) may be equal in which case the economy operates with its natural rate of unemployment, thought to be about 5 to 6 percent or less for the United States in 2005.

8. Equilibrium, real income, and price levels are subject to changes from demand shifts (changes in aggregate demand), as well as from supply shifts (changes in aggregate supply). Both aggregate demand and aggregate supply may increase or decrease. Either change will produce a change in the equilibrium level of income for the economy as well as a change in the level of prices.

9. An increase in aggregate demand will increase equilibrium real income and the price level, and will cause a movement along the aggregate supply curve. A decrease in aggregate demand will decrease equilibrium real income and the price level, and also cause a movement along the aggregate supply curve. Many factors, including changes in the money supply and changes in government expenditure and taxation, can cause such aggregate demand shocks.

10. An increase in aggregate supply will increase equilibrium real income and decrease the price level, and will cause a movement along the aggregate demand curve. A decrease in aggregate supply will decrease equilibrium income and increase the price level, and will also cause a movement along the aggregate demand curve. Many factors, including all factors that change input prices and the costs of production, can cause such aggregate supply shocks.

11. General economic conditions determine whether and how much production costs change as output (supply) changes. The three ranges or possibilities of aggregate supply response are (a) unemployment, the economy has large quantities of unemployed resources, (b) bottlenecks, the economy is approaching full employment, and (c) full employment, the economy is operating at capacity. In range (a), aggregate demand growth will cause rising real income at a stable level of prices. In range (b), aggregate demand growth will cause rising real income but with rising levels of price. In range (c), aggregate demand growth in the short run can only result in rising prices since an increase in real income is unattainable.

12. For decades, public economic policy has focused on adjusting aggregate demand to accomplish macroeconomic objectives of income, employment, and price stability. By the 1980s, "supply-side" advocates voiced the view that public policy should center more on adjusting aggregate supply through enhanced incentives to production. The debate between the two groups continues.

13. Measurements of aggregate levels of prices in an economy are called *price indexes*. They are necessary to reduce a vast heterogeneous mix of goods and services to a common denominator, their monetary values, and to permit comparisons of price changes from one year to another.

14. Index numbers, used to measure inflation, first require establishing a "market basket" of goods and services in a particular year whose prices can then be measured. The index for a year is calculated against the prices of that same basket of goods and services in a base or reference year.

Thus the index for 2009 is:

GDP price index in 2009	=	Price of the market basket in 2009 / Price of market basket in 1987	x 100

Multiplication by 100 produces a standard conventional result which can be compared to the base year's prices.

15. Two of the most widely used indexes of the federal government are the consumer price index (CPI) and the GDP price index or GDP deflator.

16. By comparing the average of the weighted prices in the current year with those in the base year, we can see what has happened to average prices over that period. We can use this resulting index to deflate or inflate the changes in nominal or money GDP to obtain a measure of the growth or decline in real GDP.

17. There are various things affecting economic welfare that are not reflected in indexes and real GDP growth. Thus, the measure is an imperfect reflection of welfare change.

18. The consumer price index (CPI), unlike the GDP deflator, is a fixed-weight index. It assumes that the spending patterns of consumers do not change from year to year. It also ignores qualitative improvements in goods and services. For this reason, it probably overstates inflation and leads to increased inflationary pressures from cost-of-living adjustments and understatement of tax obligations where tax rates are tied to changes in real, rather than nominal income.

19. The macroeconomy may be subject to external aggregate demand shocks and external aggregate supply shocks. These are factors outside the domestic economy that alter it's income and price level. When production costs are raised sharply by an external supply shock such as oil price increases, there is a shift upward or to the left of aggregate supply. This occurred twice (1973-1974 and 1979-1980) (OPEC I and OPEC II) in the past 35 years.

20. According to economic principles, an upward shift in aggregate supply will cause a decline in the equilibrium level of real national income as well as an increase in the price level. Where the aggregate supply effect is large, the effects on income and prices will also be large.

21. In the case of OPEC II, the 1979-1980 oil prices increases were very large. As a result, prices rose by 13.5 percent and unemployment rose from 5.8 percent to 7.1 percent. Real income declined. Although it is unlikely that the entire set of effects can be traced to the supply shock, it was clearly a major factor.

22. Supply shocks, since they are often unpredictable and difficult, if not impossible, to control, introduce an element of instability into national economic policy.

23. Supply shocks can be and tend to be minimized. In the case of OPEC II, efforts to minimize the effects led to increasing efficiency in energy use, a diminishing importance for oil as a primary energy source, increased output by non-OPEC suppliers, and, finally, decreasing stability of the oil cartel and a reduced ability of Saudi Arabia to support oil prices.

24. By the mid-1980s, reductions in quantities of oil demanded and increases in quantities supplied made downward pressures on oil prices irresistible.

25. Average oil prices fell by 50 percent between late 1985 and April 1986. This helped set in motion a reverse or positive supply shock for the economy. The shift downward, or to the right, of AS helped to diminish price increases and to increase the equilibrium level of real income.

26. Supply shocks can have both negative and positive effects on the economy. They can help to solve economic problems as well as cause them. In 2001, the American economy was shocked by terrorist attacks; a "war on terrorism" has ensued.

27. Some argue that the war on terrorism, like other wars, will tend to increase output and jobs. They argue that (1) war expenditures will increase aggregate demand and (2) falling energy prices will increase aggregate supply. The combined effect of the two influences will help to pull the American economy out of recession.

28. Others argue that the war on terrorism will tend to decrease aggregate supply as (1) the costs of security increase, and (2) decreased consumer confidence decreases aggregate demand. The two influences combined will make economic recovery more difficult.

29. Long term effects of the current shocks will depend in part on how long they last. Arguments about the effects of government war spending continue. Some argue that such expenditures do not contribute to consumer welfare and should be ignored from that standpoint. Most economists concede, though, that such expenditures create jobs.

30. Although external influences or shocks can have important effects, the internal workings of the American economy are most influential in its recovery from recession. If those fundamentals are strong, the economy will recover as it has done many times.

KEY TERMS

Aggregate demand
Aggregate demand shift
Aggregate supply
Aggregate supply shift
Consumer price index
Equilibrium level of prices and real income
GDP price index or deflator
Investment in human capital
Price indexes
Ranges of aggregate supply
External Aggregate demand shocks
External Aggregate supply shocks

QUESTIONS

1. How are individual market prices for commodities and services established? How is this different from the determination of aggregate prices and real income?

2. How do aggregate demand and aggregate supply interact to create an actual level of real income as well as a price level in an economy?

3. What is aggregate demand? What four components make up aggregate demand? What factors influence each component?

4. Which of the components of aggregate demand are largest and which are most volatile?

5. What are the three explanations for the negatively sloped aggregate demand curve? Is the reason for a negatively sloped aggregate demand curve the same as the reason for a negatively sloped demand curve for an individual good? If not, why not?

6. Upward sloping aggregate supply curves are based on what explanation? On what assumption about input prices is the short-run aggregate supply curve based? Would such an assumption be warranted in the long run?

7. How is aggregate supply defined? What influences determine aggregate supply?

8. What is the difference between the actual level of unemployment and the level of unemployment at full employment with a stable inflation rate called? Can this difference be zero? Why not?

9. Can the equilibrium level of income exceed the potential (full employment) level? If so, what is the relation between the natural and actual rates of unemployment?

10. If the equilibrium, (actual) national income and the potential (full employment) income are equal, with what rate of unemployment is the economy operating?

11. What is a demand shift? What is a supply shift? What affects will such shifts have on an economy's equilibrium income and price level?

12. What is meant by saying that "changes in aggregate demand cause movements along aggregate supply"? What may cause such changes in aggregate demand (demand shocks)?

13. What is meant by saying that "changes in aggregate supply cause movements along aggregate demand"? What may cause such changes in aggregate supply (supply shocks)?

14. "When aggregate demand changes, its effects on the price level depend on the range of aggregate supply in which the economy is operating." Explain.

15. What is the heart of the disagreement between "supply-siders" and "demand-siders" over achieving macroeconomic objectives?

16. Answer the questions below based on the information about aggregate demand (AD) and aggregate supply (AS) contained in the figure below.

a. The equilibrium level of income is (Y_2), (Y_3), or (Y_1)?

b. The equilibrium level of prices is (P_2), (P_3), or (P_1)?

c. At what price level (P_3, P_1, or P_2) is there excess aggregate supply? Aggregate demand?

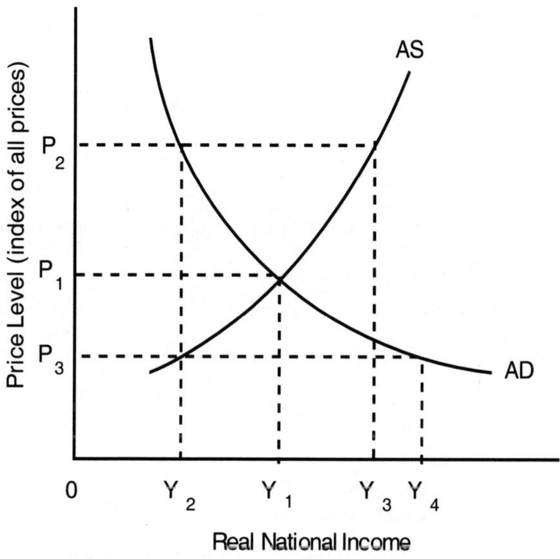

17. What is an "index number"? What is measured by the GDP index? The consumer price index?

18. What is the formula for calculating a price index for the year 2009?

19. What is meant in saying that the consumer price index is a "fixed weight" index? If the price of the CPI market basket in 1995 is $42 and the price of that basket in 1987 was $35, what is the CPI in 1995? What distortions in the economy are caused by using the CPI as a measure of inflation?

20. What are the major differences between the CPI and the GDP price index or deflator? Compute the GDP price index for 1995 based on (a) price of market basket in 1995 = $28, and (b) price of market basket in 1987 = $20.

21. What effect did the oil price increases of 1973-1974 (OPEC I) and 1979-1980 (OPEC II) have on aggregate supply?

22. According to economic principles, what macroeconomic effects will result from a decline in aggregate supply?

23. How important were the price, employment, and output effects of OPEC II?

24. Why is achieving national economic policy objectives more difficult in the face of supply shocks?

25. The price increases from OPEC II led to efforts to minimize their adverse effects. What things were done in these respects?

26. Oil prices fell dramatically in 1985-1986. From what did this seem to result? What happened to real income and employment as a result of "OPEC III"?

27. In macroeconomic terms, what should we expect to happen as a result of "positive" supply shocks such as the oil price decreases in late 2001?

28. What are external aggregate demand shocks? External aggregate supply shocks?

29. What are possible negative economic effects of a "war on terrorism"?

30. What are possible positive economic effects of a "war on terrorism"?

31. What does Robert Higgs argue about the effects of war expenditures on an economy?

Chapter 8: Aggregate Spending in the Macroeconomy Classical and Keynesian Theories

Classical Theory
A body of economic theory that concludes that full employment is the norm for a market economy and that non-intervention by government is appropriate macroeconomic policy.

Keynesian Theory
A body of economic theory that concludes unemployment is possible for a market economy and that significant government intervention is appropriate macroeconomic policy.

In the chapter on aggregate demand and aggregate supply, we obtained an overview of the macroeconomy through understanding the concepts of aggregate demand and aggregate supply. In this chapter and in the chapter on equilibrium in the macroeconomy, we will build on that foundation to show how spending and saving interact to create an equilibrium level of income and employment for a society. In doing so, we will contrast two very different theories about the structure and operation of the macroeconomy. One is **classical theory**; in its extreme form it assumes that the aggregate supply curve is vertical, or that the economy operates at capacity and that full employment is the norm. The theory suggests that laissez faire or non-intervention in the market by government is appropriate government macroeconomic policy. The other is **Keynesian theory**; in its extreme form, it assumes that the aggregate supply curve is horizontal or that unemployment and other unused resources are often found in the macroeconomy. This theory suggests that significant government intervention is called for in order to move the macroeconomy toward full employment.

As the chapter on economic fluctuations shows, a central problem of any economy is to control the destructive forces of unemployment and inflation. The classical and Keynesian views of the economy continue to fuel debates about economic policy in the U.S. While the Keynesian view has dominated those debates through much of the period since World War II, there remains much controversy, and a clear understanding of the two perspectives is important to following the policy controversies of the early twenty first century. After contrasting the two theories, we will develop the Keynesian model in stages.

In this chapter we will build the foundations of the Keynesian model. Building on these foundations, we will construct the full Keynesian model in the chapter on equilibrium in the macroeconomy. We want you to learn from these chapters the basic facts of the modern demand-based theory of income and employment. Though controversial, this theory continues to exercise great power over government policy and, thus, your money, your standard of living, and even the laws that govern you.

CLASSICAL ECONOMIC THEORY

Before Keynes wrote *The General Theory of Employment, Interest, and Money* in 1936, most economists, including Keynes, belonged to the school called *classical economics.* Many aspects of classical economics are still accepted by most economists. Indeed, the theory has been refined as we shall see in the next chapter. However, in this chapter, we are analyzing only the classical theory of income and employment. We will also see that Keynes challenged some of the basic tenets of that theory.

Classical economists[1] said that a market-oriented economy had enough built-in self-corrective mechanisms that, if left to its own devices, its income would move to that level at which its labor force would be fully employed. They also claimed that if unemployment occurred (1) it would be due to temporary over-production and would be quickly corrected by market forces, or (2) it would be due either to interference by the government or to insufficient degrees of competition, or (3) it would be due to the unwillingness of workers to adjust their wage demands downward in response to market forces.

Three theories led classical economists to this conclusion that income would of its own accord move toward the level at which full employment exists:

1. Say's law
2. Savings, investment, and money markets
3. The theory of wage and price flexibility

Say's Law

Say's Law
In its simple form, the law states that supply creates its own demand.

Jean Baptiste Say (1767-1832) was a French historian writing around 1800. Economists know him mainly for **Say's law**. The simple version of that law is: *Supply creates its own demand.* We can best illustrate Say's law by the simple 2 sector circular-flow model (Figure 8-1). Recall its basic premise that households provide all the resources, labor, land, capital, and entrepreneurship, to firms, and firms pay households for these resources. Using these resources, firms produce goods for consumption by households. In turn, households pay for these goods and services with the income they get from selling their resources to firms.

In terms of the simple circular-flow model, "Supply creates its own demand" means that firms, while they are in the process of turning out all the goods and services that constitute supply, are at the same time acting as the sources of the income that households need to buy the firms' output. We saw in the chapter on economic fluctuations that gross domestic product creates an equivalent amount of gross domestic income. The level of that income is stabilized at the point of full employment. When firms employ all the labor available, households receive enough income to buy all the firms' output produced by that labor. Say's law is stunning in its simplicity. Unfortunately, it does not hold up in real life, at least not in its simple form.

---

1. Classical economists include David Ricardo and John Stuart Mill in the nineteenth century, and Alfred Marshall and Arthur Pigou (Neo *classicals*) in the twentieth century.

Figure 8-1
Simple Two Sector Circular Flow Model

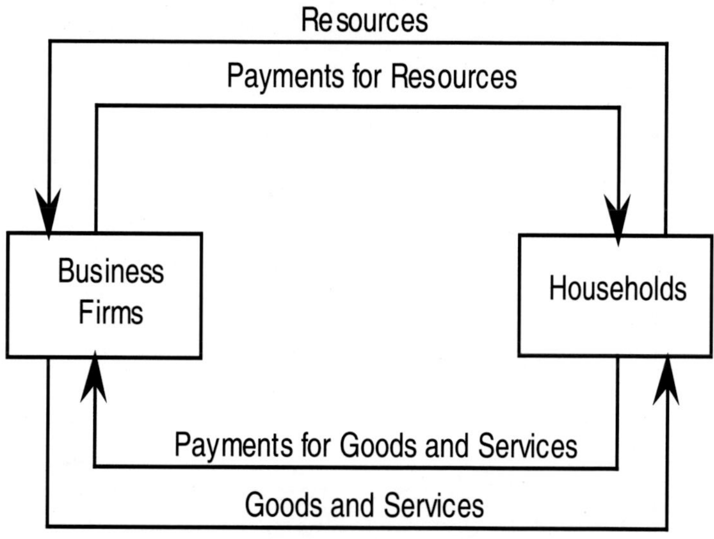

Savings, Investment, and Money Markets

Classical economists readily agreed that the simple circular-flow model illustrating Say's law was not adequate for an industrialized twentieth-century economy. However, they maintained that even a more complex circular-flow model (Figure 8-2) showed that income, left to itself, would move toward the level at which full employment would exist.

This is the classical reasoning. Households must use some of their money for savings and taxes, which means that savings and taxes siphon off some income that they would otherwise spend on consumption. Firms get most of their support, that is, demand for their output, from households. But firms *also* derive support from two other sources: government expenditures and investment. Economists of the classical school used to maintain that these four factors, taxes, savings, government expenditures, and investment, could be linked so as not to disturb the basic theory that income would adjust itself to the level at which full employment existed.

When people worried that these taxes and government expenditures would have a disturbing effect on this finely balanced model, the classicists had an answer: Just see to it that government expenditures and taxes are *equal*, and keep them both at the lowest possible levels. They'll balance each other off, and this will keep the effects of government fiscal activity to a minimum.

What about savings and investment? Would *they* balance each other off? Or would they create an imbalance and perhaps cause instability and nudge income to a level that would mean equilibrium at less than full employment?

Figure 8-2
A More Complex Circular-Flow Model

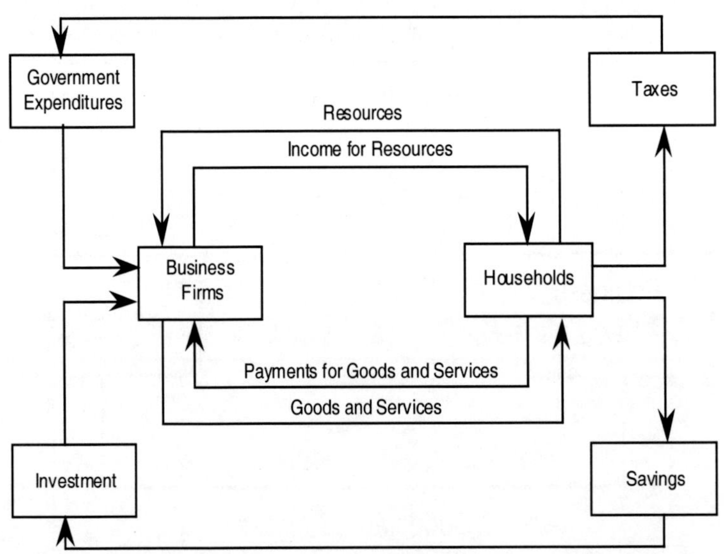

Abstinence Theory of Interest
An argument that people will save because interest payments induce them to abstain from current consumption.

Classical economists argued that savings and investment would be coordinated through interest rates established in money markets. They explained this link by using the **abstinence theory of interest**. People prefer to consume goods and services now, rather than later, because present consumption yields greater satisfaction than future consumption. If people are to be induced to save, that is, to abstain from consumption, they must be given a reward. This reward is called *interest*. Given interest, the consumer is willing to abstain from present consumption, in other words, save. Then in the future the consumer will be able to consume more because he or she will have more money (savings plus interest) with which to do so. The higher the interest rate (the reward for saving), the larger the quantity saved. Thus, the abstinence theory of interest provides the link between savings and investment.

The amount of money saved determines, in money markets, the *supply of loanable funds*. As Figure 8-3 shows, the curve for the supply of loanable funds slopes up to the right because the higher the interest rate, the larger the quantity saved. Therefore, the abstinence theory of interest explains why the supply of loanable funds slopes up to the right.

The decisions of businesses to expand their productive capacity by building new plants and equipment are what determine the demand for loanable funds. A person will make an investment when the return realized from that investment is at least equal to the cost of the interest on the money borrowed to make it. In other words, people make investments that have a rate of return equal to or greater than the interest rate. Classical economists said that the rate of return on an investment was determined by its productivity and thus, in the long run, by the state of the economy's technology. The demand curve for loanable funds in Figure 8-3 slopes downward to the right because falling interest rates make for greater profitability on investments. One could say that the interest rate is like rent paid on money. More investment is profitable at a 6 percent interest rate than at a 10 percent one, because the 6 percent rate also includes all investment that has a rate of return between 6 and 10 percent.

Figure 8-3
Supply of and Demand for Loanable Funds in Money Markets

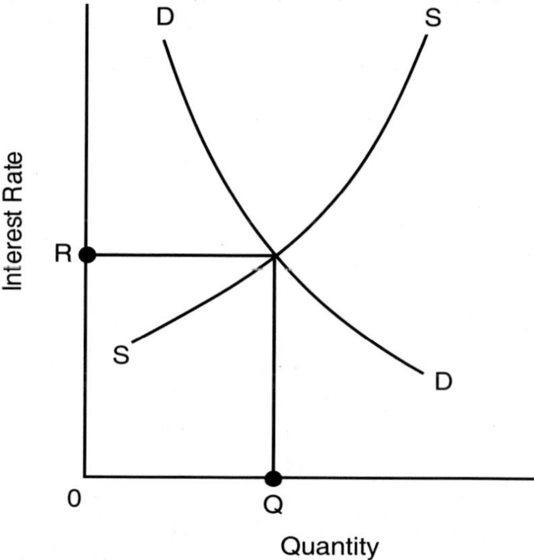

The supply of loanable funds (S) slopes up to the right because the higher the interest rate, the more people wish to save. The demand for loanable funds (D) slopes down to the right because the lower the interest rate, the more investment there is that yields a rate of return equal to or greater than the interest rate.

Thus, the interest rate links investment and savings. And the intersection between the supply of loanable funds (amount of money saved or withhold from the demand for consumption to become equal to the investment that businesses wish to add to the demand for consumption. The equality always becomes evident; demand always uses up the supply. The level of employment of resources still determines the level of income. The level of income still moves to full employment.

Wage-Price Flexibility

Classical economists recognized that there can be temporary overproduction in certain areas, because of either errors in estimating consumer demand or a failure of the interest rate to bring what people are willing to save into line with what businesses are willing to invest. Fluctuations in the market prices of labor and of products, however, quickly wipe out these temporary states of overproduction. As overproduction develops, workers lose their jobs and start to compete with workers who are still employed. This has the effect of reducing wages. As wages fall, lower costs and competition between firms forces prices down. Declining wages and declining prices together eliminate overproduction.

Elimination of overproduction is brought about by two effects of falling wages plus falling prices: (1) Total demand by workers is maintained, even though the money volume of spending declines, because prices of products fall in the same proportion as wages. Competition forces down wages, but also forces down prices. Classical economists assume that, because of competition, the decline in prices will be proportional to the decline in wages. The worker is no worse off, in effect, when wages fall 10 percent if prices also fall 10 percent. (2) The fall in prices causes those with savings to demand more goods, which eliminates excess supply. As prices fall, people with savings have greater wealth or purchasing power, their savings can buy more at the new lower prices.

Feeling richer, savers buy more, and save less. This increase in savers' consumption, as prices in general fall, is called the **Pigou effect**, after its classical originator, Arthur Pigou.

Pigou Effect
The argument that falling prices increase people's wealth or purchasing power and cause them to consume more.

To review: if the nation's budget is balanced (and balanced at a low level) so that government does not affect the market, and if there is enough competition in both the labor market and the product market, then the level of the nation's income automatically adjusts itself to the point at which there is full employment. In other words, classical economists concluded that there would not be long-term involuntary unemployment.

In the early 1930s the British government, in the throes of the Great Depression, sought answers from various classical economists. Surely these economists could work some magical cure that would revive the economy so that the level of income would rise to the point of full employment. Obviously the mechanism that ordinarily achieved this state of affairs did not seem to be working (or working quickly enough). Something was interfering with it.

Government fiscal activity was the culprit, said the classical economists. Let the government balance its budget and reduce its expenditures as much as possible, they recommended. So the British government in the early 1930s slashed expenditures and raised taxes. That will do for a start, said the classical economists, but in addition, because wage-price flexibility is not working, you must counter the influence of labor unions by forcing down wages; when the cost of wages falls, prices will fall, too, and demand will then increase.

Keynes, pondering the situation from his chair at Cambridge University, disagreed with these recommendations. He believed that they would worsen rather than lessen the depression. Keynes's ideas had been anticipated by his fellow economists, and many of them were being discussed by his contemporaries. However, it was Keynes who finally put these ideas together.

THE KEYNESIAN CRITIQUE

Keynes[2], who died in 1946, has been called the most influential economist of the twentieth century. His *general theory* disputed the classical income-determination theory, that held that the level of income would automatically move toward a position in which there was full employment. His argument largely replaced classical income theory for several decades and, as we noted earlier, dominated the theory and policies down to the 1980s. Today most, though not all, economists are Keynesians in some sense. At the least, they accept certain of his basic ideas and use his framework of analysis. Some economists today, however, regard the Keynesian system of analysis and its policy recommendations as outdated and appropriate only to depression-like conditions. But more about that after we have surveyed the Keynesian arguments.

What About Say's Law?

Keynes said that Say's law did not apply to a modern industrial society. In Say's eighteenth-century French world, production was small-scale and craft-oriented. People worked with simple machines. It did not take huge amounts of capital to repair them or replace them. Investment was therefore modest, and so was the

---

2. Keynes, J.M. *The General Theory of Employment, Interest and Money.* London/New York, McMillan. 1936.

need for savings. Households and firms (as viewed in the simple circular-flow model) were correspondingly small. Cottage industry abounded, and very often products were made to order. However, Say's law was an oversimplification even in his own day, because much of the French economy, and even more of the British, was taken over by larger-scale industries, as the Industrial Revolution accelerated during the latter part of the eighteenth century.

Classical economists replied that they recognized the oversimplification of Say's law and came up with the complex circular-flow model, which made adjustments for the more complex world.

The Abstinence Theory of Interest: Not True Said Keynes

A major feature of the classical theory of income was the *abstinence theory of interest*, which linked the desired level of savings (remember that savings always means decreased consumption) to the desired level of investment (which always means increased demand) through the interest rate. With government expenditures and taxes balanced, at the lowest possible levels, the classical view of the economic world seemed to be fairly valid.

But Keynes questioned the classical theory that desired or planned savings and desired or planned investment are always linked. He sought to invalidate the abstinence theory of interest, as follows:

1. *Savers and investors are different groups and are differently motivated.* Business groups make all the investment decisions and base them on comparative costs and on returns on investment. Profitability is the main reason for investment. Households are the main savers. They outsave businesses, even though large corporations do save great amounts in the form of undistributed profits. But in a wealthy society, households also save great amounts. Their motivation for saving, however, naturally differs from that of the business investors. But the simple fact of these differences in motivation is not important. The important point is: *Why should the interest rate link savings and investment?*

2. *The interest rate does not determine the level of savings.* People who save are going to save regardless of the level of the interest rate, and their motives vary. Some save because of custom or morality. Some save to provide security in old age; some to pay for a large purchase, such as a house or automobile. Some save to provide a fund for emergencies; some save to send their children to college. In sum, *people's motivations for savings are varied and are not merely influenced by the level of the interest rate.* Therefore, a certain rate of interest is not necessarily required to make people save. Many people would probably set aside money each month even if no interest rate existed.

3. Not only did Keynes seek to break the tie between planned investment and savings, by showing that the interest rate did not solely determine the amount of savings, but he also weakened the tie between investment and the interest rate. He said that businesses, in computing the probable returns on their investments, had to estimate future business conditions. Therefore, if you want to analyze why businesses invest, you must take into account their expectations of future conditions. This inclusion of expectations, a psychological factor that classical economists failed to give any weight to, weakened the relationship between planned investment and the level of interest rates.

So economists, according to Keynes, were left without the comforting mechanism of the interest rate that coordinated savings and investment at full employment. Without this, the economy could experience declining demand and unemployment, or increasing demand with resulting rises in employment, and possibly inflation. Let us see why.

Look at Figure 8-2 again. If planned savings are greater than planned investment, consumer demand for the firms' output of consumer goods shrinks, and investment demand does not take up all the slack. So total demand falls, and along with it, output, income, and employment fall.

Now suppose the reverse occurs. Suppose that savings are less than planned investment. This means that savings do not cause consumer demand for the output of firms to decrease as much as investment causes the firms' output to increase. As total demand increases, so does output, income, and employment. Eventually, when full employment exists, further increases in demand only generate increases in prices.

Lack of Wage-Price Flexibility

What did Keynes have to say about the classical economists' reliance on wage and price flexibility to correct any excess supply that might lead to unemployment? Remember that the classical economists said that a temporary oversupply of goods would cause unemployment, which would cause workers to compete harder for jobs, and that this would push wages down, which in turn would force prices down. Proportionate declines in wages and prices would leave real income unchanged, and thus real levels of demand for goods. People with savings would increase their level of consumption, and this would stimulate demand, and so on. Keynes said there were three factors that weakened this theory:

1. The flexibility of wages and prices is not great enough to generate these movements. Many corporations, possessing monopoly power in product markets, can keep prices from moving downward. Many labor unions also exercise monopoly power in factor markets in the same way; the unions are able to keep wages from moving downward. To Keynes's arguments, one can add that since 1936, governments have interfered more and more in the workings of the market, rendering it more inflexible. This has been true especially in areas such as minimum-wage laws and price-support systems for agriculture.

2. Even if wages and prices were both to decline, it is unlikely that real spending for goods and services would remain unchanged. After all, prices and wages never fall uniformly. Therefore, some groups would be hurt and some helped. And the two groups would never exactly offset each other. Furthermore, the burden of debt of workers would siphon away a large percentage of their incomes, thus cutting down on their spending. Finally, people are psychologically conditioned to plan their spending on the basis of money in hand rather than real income.

3. Even if one could overcome the obstacles generated by both factor 1 and factor 2, in order for the economy to expand very much as a result of increased real savings brought about by a decline in prices, there would have to be sharp drops in prices, and prices would have to stay low for a long time. There are easier ways to stimulate demand during periods of excess supply.

To summarize the Keynesian view: (1) Wage-price flexibility does not exist in sufficient amounts. (2) If it did, real spending would drop anyway. (3) Even leaving aside factor 1 and factor 2, there are easier ways to eliminate a generalized excess supply in the economy.

Aggregate Supply: The Keynesian Assumptions

The Keynesian theory we will set forth in this and the chapter on equilibrium in the macroeconomy focuses on aggregate demand and its role in determining the level of real income and employment. The model treats price levels as constants in order to center on income and employment effects of aggregate demand and changes in demand.

What kind of supply behavior would be consistent with this simple Keynesian model of demand-determined real income at stable prices? The answer can be seen in Figure 8-4. Notice that short-run aggregate supply is horizontal; planned or desired output responds to all changes in aggregate demand at a constant level of prices (up until we hit near full employment levels of output). The economic conditions that would explain this are those in the range of aggregate supply in which there is substantial unemployment or excess capacity. This supply-price relationship may be a reasonable assumption about firms offering to sell more at existing prices as long as they have idle or under utilized plant and equipment. In effect, firms have horizontal supply curves and the aggregate supply curve, as a result, is also horizontal at P*, the constant aggregate level of prices.

Note that in Figure 8-4, a change (shift) in aggregate demand, from AD_0 to AD_1, results in an increase in real income from Y_0 to Y_1. Both real incomes are consistent with the same level of prices, P*. The key point here is that:

Given the Keynesian assumption about short-run aggregate supply, aggregate demand determines real income, and that demand can be adjusted to any level required to accomplish income and employment goals with stable prices.

Figure 8-4
Determination of Real Income with a Keynesian Short-Run Aggregate Supply Function

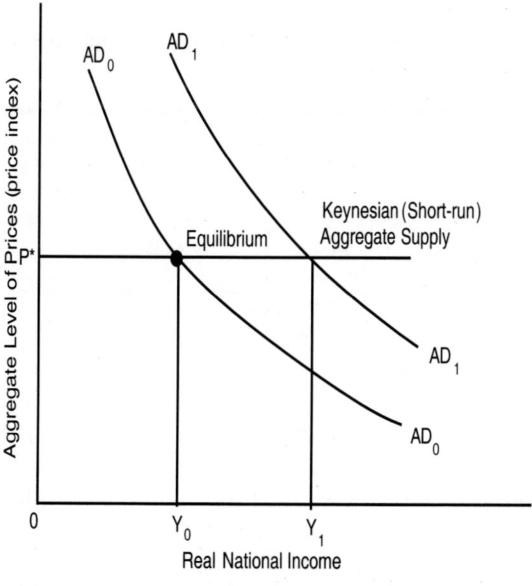

In a simple short-run Keynesian model, real income is determined by the location or amount of aggregate demand. Y_0 here is the equilibrium real income. A stable level of prices (P*) is consistent with a growing real income up to the point at which bottlenecks appear.

THE KEYNESIAN CONCLUSIONS

Classical economists, according to the Keynesian critique, were at least partially mistaken when they said that income would automatically move toward a level that would ensure full employment. Of course, the level of real national income may arrive at a position at which there is full employment and relatively stable prices, but there are no mechanisms that ensure that if this occurs, it will do so in an acceptable period of time. Therefore, it is more likely, say Keynesians, that the level of income will be either at a position at which there is unemployment or at which there is inflation. Both states are undesirable. So let's ask ourselves, what factors determine the level of income?

In the Keynesian view, as we noted earlier, it is the level of *aggregate demand*, the total demand for commodities and services, that determines an economy's level of real income. A business will produce only if it can expect profits. It can sell its goods only if there is demand for the product. In this case, what's true for one business is true for the entire economy: Output, and therefore income, will move in the same direction as aggregate demand. Increased income and employment will follow from increases in aggregate demand. Reduce demand and income and employment will suffer. But remember, according to Keynes, *there are no automatic market mechanisms that can force aggregate demand to the level at which there is full employment.*

This being so, the implication of Keynes' theory is that to achieve full employment, the government must manipulate aggregate demand. Not since the days of **mercantilism**, from the sixteenth through the eighteenth centuries, has economic theory made it the responsibility of the government to maintain economic welfare. That is why some economists have called Keyneianism modern-day mercantilism.

Mercantilism
A school of economic thought that held that government should take the responsibility for maintaining economic welfare.

Incidentally, when we talk about the level of income here, we mean the *equilibrium income.* Recall from Figure 8-4 that equilibrium real income is established where aggregate quantity supplied is equal to aggregate quantity demanded. It is the central tendency of real income that equates the plans of consumers with those of producers. It is the income we have after all the forces in the model have worked themselves out. It is a stable level of income, so long as the various factors in the model *do not* change.

There are, as we saw in the chapter on aggregate supply and aggregate demand, four factors that determine the level of aggregate demand are:

1. Consumption expenditures
2. Investment expenditures
3. Government expenditures
4. Net exports

Three of these, consumption, investment, and government expenditures, make up *effective demand.* Increases in these items increase demand; decreases in any of them reduce demand. Savings and taxes siphon off the purchasing power of people and prevent them from using this money to satisfy their consumption demands.

Because these four factors determine demand, they also determine income and employment. So let's analyze the nature of the first three, consumption, savings, and investment, and show how they relate to changes in the level of income. Then, in another chapter, we will first take a simple nongovernment model and show how these factors determine an equilibrium level of income; finally, we will make the model more complex by adding in government expenditures and taxes.

Consumption, Savings, and Investment

You are already familiar with the idea of a function or curve. In the analysis of demand and supply, you saw that demand is not a relationship between a specific price and a specific quantity of a good or service, but between various quantities at various prices. When you draw a diagram of the demand schedule, it becomes a demand curve, which shows the functional relationships between prices and quantities demanded.

The same thing is true for the **consumption function**. It is not a specific quantity consumed by people at some given income level; it is a schedule, showing the relationships between levels of income and quantities consumed during a particular period of time. A diagram of this schedule, such as that in Figure 8-5, shows the functional relationship between income levels and quantities consumed.

Figure 8-5
The Consumption Function or the Relationship Between Income and Consumption

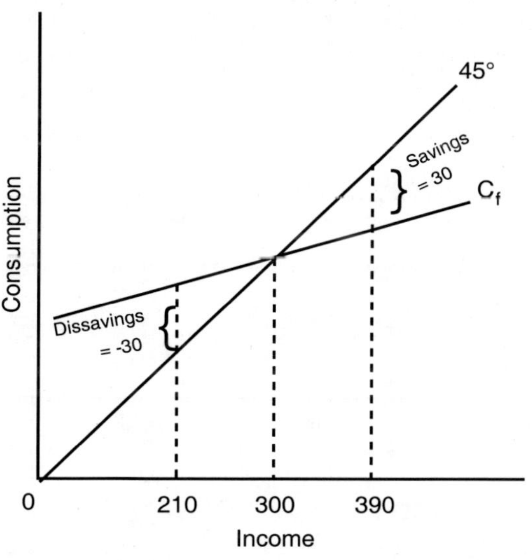

The distance from the income axis to the 45° line is the same as the distance from the 45° line to the consumption axis. Each point on the 45° line shows where income (the distance right on the axis) is equal to consumption (the distance up to the 45° line). Where the consumption function C_f, crosses the 45° line, (at income 300) consumption is equal to income. Where the consumption function lies above the 45° line (income level 210) the distance from the 45° line to C represents dissaving (30). Where the consumption function lies below the 45° line (income = 390), the distance from C_f to the 45° line represents savings (30).

Consumption Function
A schedule showing the relationships between levels of income and quantities consumed during a particular period of time.

Savings Function
A schedule showing the amounts people save at different levels of income in a particular period of time.

Investment Function
A schedule showing the amounts invested at different levels of income in a particular period of time.

The *consumption schedule*, or *function*, relates quantities consumed to levels of income. One must understand it in order to identify all the factors that influence the level of employment and income. Therefore, one must relate the various factors involved to income. So we shall deal not only with the consumption function, with how much people *consume* at different levels of income. We shall also deal with the **savings function**, the schedule showing amounts people *save* at different levels of income during a particular period of time, and with the **investment function**, the schedule showing amounts *invested* at different levels of income during a given period of time.

Let's build our income model in steps, just as we did our supply-and-demand model. First we show consumption schedules for individuals; then we add individual schedules to get an economy-wide consumption schedule. We diagram this and have a consumption function or curve for the whole economy. Again, as before, we assume that income is the only thing that changes. All other factors affecting the quantity of goods and services that people consume are fixed.

One could construct a consumption schedule for an individual in much the same way as one constructs a demand schedule for an individual. Ask each individual how much she or he would spend on consumption at each level of income and how much he or she would save. Table 8-1 shows consumption schedules for three individuals, A, B, and C. Note that each differs from the other. However, each shows that quantity consumed increases as income increases but *not as rapidly as income increases*. When one adds the consumption schedules and the income schedules of all the individuals, one obtains an economy-wide consumption schedule.

Table 8-1
Consumption Schedules for Three Individuals

A		B		C	
Income	**Consumption**	**Income**	**Consumption**	**Income**	**Consumption**
$2,000	$3,500	$2,000	$3,000	$2,000	$3,000
4,000	5,000	4,000	4,000	4,000	4,800
8,000	8,000	8,000	6,000	8,000	8,400
12,000	11,000	12,000	8,000	12,000	12,000
16,000	14,000	16,000	10,000	16,000	15,600
20,000	17,000	20,000	12,000	20,000	19,200
24,000	20,000	24,000	14,000	24,000	22,800
28,000	23,000	28,000	16,000	28,000	26,400

Table 8-2
Consumption and Savings Schedule for an Economy

Income (billions of dollars)	Consumption (billions of dollars)	Savings (billions of dollars)
210	240	–30
240	260	–20
270	280	–10
300	300	0
330	320	10
360	340	20
390	360	30
420	380	40
450	400	50

Table 8-2 is an example of a consumption schedule for an entire economy. It shows that at low levels of income, people live beyond their means by consuming more than income (income levels 210, 240, and 270). At income level 300, consumption just equals income and savings are zero. Above income level 300, consumption is less than income, so the economy can save as well as consume. Figure 8-5 is a diagram of the data in Table 8-2.

To bring our analysis into focus, we have drawn, in Figure 8-5, a line from the origin upward, at an angle of 45 degrees. We shall call that line the 45 degree line. Note that consumption and income are equal to each other at any point on the 45° degree line.

There are different theories about the exact shape of the consumption function. However, for our purposes, we make the simplifying assumption that the consumption function, C_f, is a straight line, slopes up to the right, and crosses the 45 line. Where the consumption function crosses the 45 line (at 300), quantity consumed is equal to income. Whenever the economy drops below income level 300, consumption is greater than income. For example, note in Table 8-2 that at income level 210, consumption is 240, which leaves the economy 30 in the hole (negative savings). At that point, note in Figure 8-5 that the consumption function lies above the 45 line. When that happens, economists have a word for it: **dissavings**, the opposite of savings. Dissavings means that more is being consumed than is being produced within the economy.

Dissavings
The term used to describe negative savings by people in a society.

On the other hand, if the income level is above 300 (e.g., at 390 in Figure 8-5), consumption for the economy is less than income, and the consumption function lies below the 45 line. The distance from the consumption function to the 45 line measures savings of (30).

To sum up, if the economy's C_f is *below* the 45 line (income levels over 300), positive savings take place. If the C_f lies *above* the 45 line (income less than 300), negative savings, or dissavings, take place.

Everyone knows how easy it is for private citizens to consume more than their income and wind up dissaving. They perhaps start out by drawing on their savings, until the savings are gone; then they borrow or perhaps apply for public assistance. In a fairly similar way, an entire economy can consume more than it produces, and experience overall dissavings. An economy can draw on its accumulated savings, its capital stock, by the mere fact that it does not produce enough capital to replace worn-out and obsolete capital; its net investment becomes negative, and it comes face to face with dissavings. The economy can borrow from other countries, which means that foreigners' money gets invested in one's own country. Or it can obtain foreign aid, in the form of gifts or international charity. The last two options, borrowing or accepting charity, mean that more is imported than is exported. In other words, the economy is consuming more than it is producing.

An example of dissaving occurred during the depression of the 1930s which was so severe that in the United States and several other countries net investment was negative and consumption exceeded income. Israel, several times during its brief existence, has been forced into dissavings by the necessity of maintaining a strong military stance and the need to absorb a constant flood of new immigrants. Israel has financed its excess of consumption over income in part by international borrowing, but primarily by gifts from the world's Jewish community, and especially by aid from friendly nations such as the United States.

Figure 8-6
The Savings Function

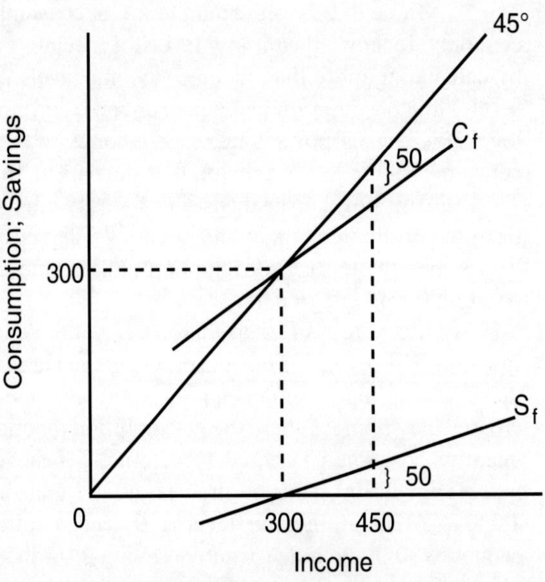

One can plot the savings function (S_f) from Table 8-2 or derive it from the consumption function (C_f). The distance from C_f to the 45° line measures savings. These distances should be marked off from the income axis to the savings function.

The Savings Function

Out of any given income, people either consume or save. So once you know the consumption schedule (see Table 8-2) or the consumption function (Figure 8-5), you can find the savings schedule and savings function, since savings is the act of *not* consuming. In brief:

income = consumption + savings.

In Table 8-2, the third column, the savings schedule, is the difference between income and consumption. Figure 8-6, expresses this savings function graphically. However, you could have used the consumption function in Figure 8-6to derive the savings function. The distance from the consumption function to the 45 line represents savings, either positive (incomes above 300) or negative (incomes below 300). If you measured off those distances on the income axis, with negative savings (dissavings) lying below the income axis, you would also have a savings function.

A Change in Consumption and Savings

When we talked about demand and supply, we stressed the distinction between a change in *quantity demanded* and a change in *demand.* The same distinction applies to other functions. A change in quantity consumed or quantity saved is a movement along a specific C_f (consumption function) or S_f (savings function) caused by a change in income. When a *non*income factor changes, it changes the entire schedule of consumption and savings and results in a shift of these functions. This constitutes a change in consumption and in savings. Let us look at the factors that can cause such shifts in consumption and savings.

Figure 8-7 shows a *change in quantity consumed* as a movement along C_1 from A to B because of a change in income. A *change in consumption* itself is a shift from C_1 to another consumption function, C_2, because of a change in one of the *non*income factors listed below:

Figure 8-7
Change in Consumption and Change in Quantity Consumed

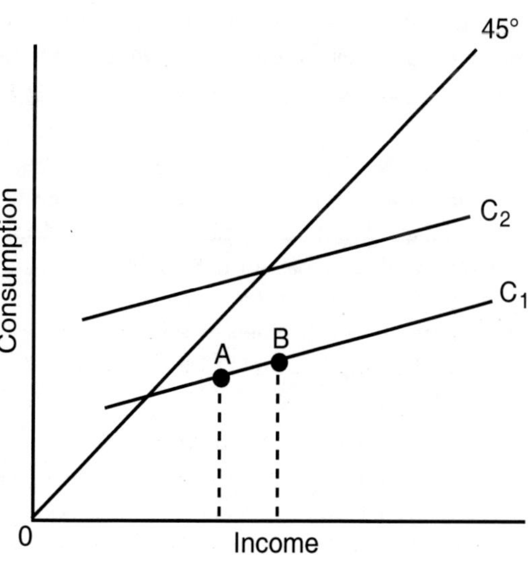

1. *Changes in social customs, mores, or attitudes toward savings.* Many of us have heard about the "Protestant ethic" hard work, thrift, and rational investment that lead to economic success. The stronger people's feelings about thrift, the higher the savings function. Today, people seem to be less concerned with personal savings, since institutional programs, such as pension funds and insurance programs, have apparently reduced the perceived need for individual saving.

2. *Changes in assets of consumers*. There are three ways of looking at people's asset positions: (a) What are their liquid assets? (b) What is their debt level? (c) What is their stock of goods (especially durable goods)?

Liquid Assets
Assets such as savings accounts or government bonds that may be quickly converted into money.

First, **liquid assets** are assets in the form of money or something that can be quickly converted into money, such as savings accounts and government bonds. People like to have some assets in liquid form for several reasons, the main one is being prepared for an emergency. Once people have accumulated comfortable amounts of liquid assets, they can use their incomes for consumption. Second, paying off debt reduces income available for consumption over a period of time. When people accumulate debt quickly, this temporarily increases their consumption. However, when people are paying off debt, they consume less, out of necessity.

Since the level of debt affects consumption, the terms of consumer debts are important factors in determining consumption. What is the interest rate? How long a time will it take for repayment? These and other conditions of consumer loans encourage (or discourage) consumers from borrowing, and thus affect their level of consumption.

When you accumulate durable goods (cars, refrigerators, and so on), your consumption in the immediate future usually drops off sharply. If today you go on a spree and buy a washer, a dryer, and a plasma television set, you will probably not need new ones for several years, and this will surely lower your spending rate.

3. *Changes in expectations about future earnings*. If people expect that their earnings will increase in the future, and if they feel secure, they are inclined to consume more now than they would if they were pessimistic about future earnings. Young couples just starting a family borrow heavily to establish a home, expecting that their income will increase over the years. However, if there is a recession and they start to feel insecure about their jobs, or if inflation is cutting into their real income, people cut present consumption and increase their savings, to hedge against future wants.

4. *Changes in taxes*. When taxes go up, the amount people have to spend on daily consumable items naturally becomes smaller, no matter what their income is. Households pay part of their taxes out of income that they would otherwise spend for consumption, and part out of income that they would save. The effect of increased taxes is to decrease both consumption (increased taxes shift the C_f down) and savings (taxes shift the S_f down).

5. *Changes in the distribution of income; changes in demographic (population) factors*. Changes in the way income is distributed have a strong effect on the consumption function. Poor people have to consume a much larger proportion of their incomes than rich people do. Therefore, if something happens to redistribute the wealth so that the poor get a larger portion of it, the consumption function will shift upward and slope upward at the same time. Changes in the age distribution of the population also affect the position of the consumption function. The larger the percentage of people in age groups that are not income earning, the more people there are who are consuming without working to finance that consumption (for instance, children and the elderly). The baby boom that lasted from 1946 through 1964 was a strong element in keeping consumption high. But the large drop in the birthrate over the period from 1955 to 1975 reduced aggregate consumption in the succeeding period.

The five factors listed above can be divided into two broad categories: objective (or economic) factors and psychological factors. We consider changes in assets of consumers, changes in taxes, and changes in distribution of income and demographic factors to be objective or economic factors. We consider the psychological factors to be changes in social customs, mores, or attitudes toward savings, and changes in expectations about future earnings.

The Intended Investment Function

Autonomous Investment
Those investments not affected by changes in people's incomes and consumption.

Induced Investment
Those investments induced or generated by changes in income and consumption.

There are two kinds of investment: *autonomous* and *induced.* **Autonomous investment** is *not* affected by changes in people's incomes and consumption. It is affected by factors outside the model. In other words, the level of autonomous investment is independent of the factors within the model. **Induced investment**, on the other hand, is induced or generated by changes within the model, specifically by changes in income and consumption. For example, if the level of income increases, the quantity consumed also increases. This increases the need for plant and equipment (that is, for capacity) to produce the increased quantity of consumer goods demanded. This increased investment needed to expand capacity to take care of increased consumption is *induced* investment. For purposes of our model here, we shall assume that induced investment is zero and that we are dealing only with autonomous investment. Later, when we have completed our model, we shall add induced investment.

What Determines Autonomous Investment?

www.whitehouse.gov/fsbr/esbr.html
For more information on investment visit this web site.

Businesses keep on investing, that is, creating capital, just as long as they expect that the returns from an investment are going to be at least equal to the cost of that investment. There are two factors that determine how much they invest. These factors are: (1) the cost of investing and (2) the expected rate of return.

1. ***The interest rate.*** When you invest your money in something, such as a machine or a building, and you put down some cash and borrow the rest. The cost of investing is not the price of the machine or building since you get this purchase price back by the device of *depreciation*, which is a legitimate cost of producing the product. Depreciation is built into the final price of any product. The *cost* of the investment is the interest that you must pay on the money you borrow to buy the thing *or* the interest you forego by using your funds instead of lending them out. In other words, if you had not bought that thing, you would have had an *opportunity* to lend your cash to somebody else and have interest payments flowing back to you.

Marginal Efficiency of Capital
The function that shows the quantity of investment made at each of several interest rates or the quantity that yields an expected return equal to or greater than each interest rate.

2. ***Marginal efficiency of capital.*** The marginal efficiency of capital is the expected rate of return on capital. In other words, it is the stream of income that businesses expect to receive over the life of the capital relative to its price. Two main items, plus a number of smaller factors, determine the marginal efficiency of capital:

a. *Productivity of capital.* The more productive the capital, the greater the profit one can expect to receive back from an investment. The productivity of capital changes with the development of new machines that reduce the costs of labor or capital, or with the development of a new process, a new product, or new markets. So it can be said that any growth in productivity means greater potential profits to investors.

b. *Expectations.* Since the marginal efficiency of capital deals with future returns, it is bound to be influenced by the future economic activity investors expect. This introduces a psychological and potentially irrational element. A President may have a heart attack, a war may occur in a part of the world that supplies petroleum, or meteorologists may predict a severe winter, and people in business may overreact. They may become more pessimistic, or more optimistic, than economic conditions warrant, and their attitudes may change almost overnight.

c. *Other factors*. Some of the other factors that affect the marginal efficiency of capital are the price of capital itself (for example, the sale price of a machine); the risks connected with the investment; taxation (especially in the case of taxes such as investment tax credits, that are directly tied to the investment); and, in the case of house construction, population growth and migration.

How Much Investment Will People Make?

Figure 8-8 shows how to go about figuring how much autonomous investment is likely to be made. The MEC (**marginal efficiency of capital**) curve shows the quantity of investment likely to yield an expected rate of return equal to, or greater than, the interest rate. The MEC curve slopes down to the right. This is so because as the interest rate falls, larger amounts of investment (capital instruments) will yield an expected return equal to or greater than the interest rate.

Figure 8-8
MEC curve

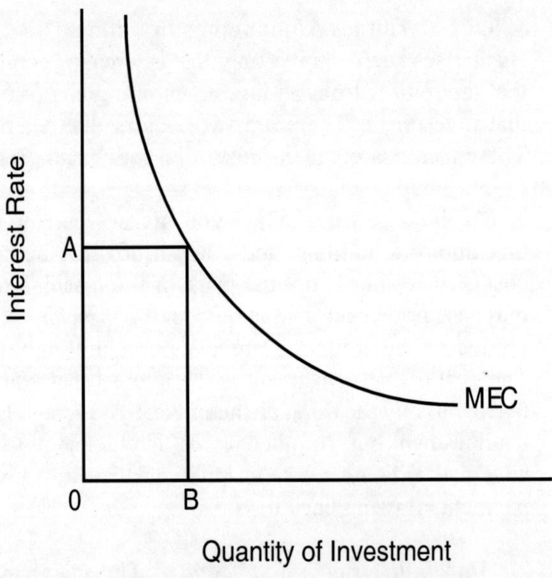

The marginal efficiency of capital (MEC) curve shows the quantity of investment at various interest rates. Investments must yield a rate of return equal to or greater than the interest rate. To find out how much investment is likely to take place, one must know the rate of interest that an investor is going to have to pay in order to borrow the money to make the investment.

Instability of Investment

In good times and bad, over the years consumption and savings have shown amazing stability. Gross private domestic investment, the other hand, has varied greatly as Figure 8-9 shows.

Figure 8-9

The Instability of Investment, Annual Changes in Real Gross Private Investment and GDP, 1958-2012

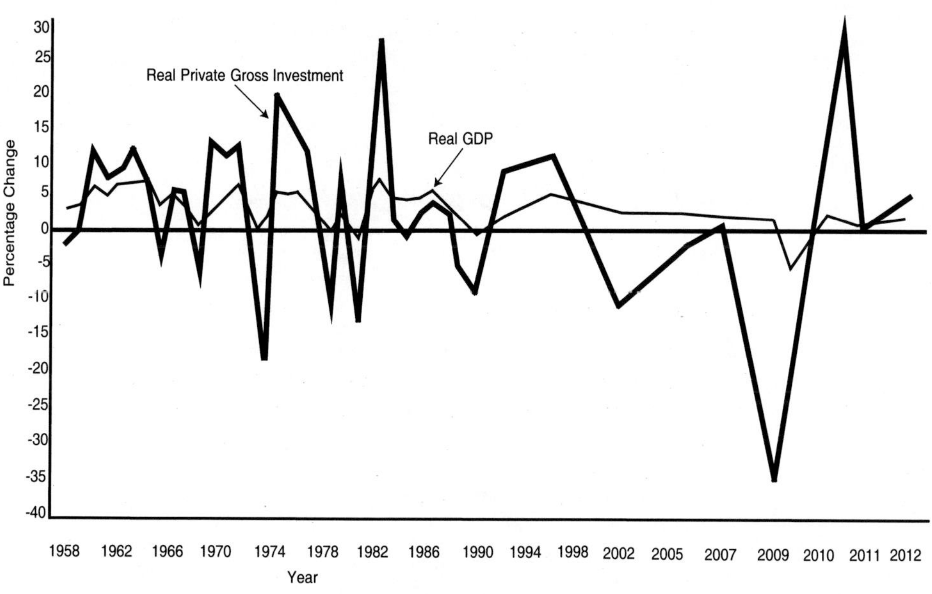

Source: Economic Report of the President.

Investment spending is highly volatile. In comparing changes in real investment and real GDP, we observe that the annual percentage changes in investment are greater than the percentage changes in GDP.

It has also, as Figure 8-9 shows, varied much more than real GDP. You can understand this pattern of investment if you just stop to think of the instability of the factors that determine the quantity invested. Interest rates fluctuate widely. The influences on people's expectations about the future are both rational and irrational. The flow of technological innovations is not even, so that industry improves its production techniques in fits and starts. Furthermore, the government itself may inject instability into the investment scene through changes in its economic policies and through loss of public confidence due to scandals.

However, since World War II, a number of changes have tended to increase the stability of investment. For one thing, the Employment Act of 1946 committed the government to economic stabilization. This has probably given business people greater confidence than they formerly had and reduced the likelihood of short-term variations in investment. Corporate retained earnings increased, so that corporations have not had to depend so heavily on the capital markets for investment funds. However, as the recession of 2008-2009 has demonstrated again, investment remains the most unstable component in the aggregate demand model of income.

Figure 8-10
Equilibrium Income: Relation Between Consumption (C_f), Savings (S_f), and Intended Investment (II)

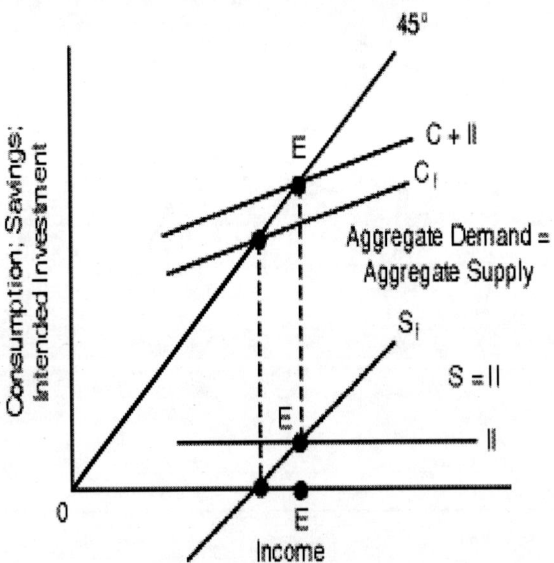

The bottom of the diagram shows intended investment in relation to savings. To find equilibrium income (E), one assumes that savings equals intended investment. Or one can add intended investment to the consumption function, so that aggregate demand equals aggregate supply. Both approaches give the same equilibrium income (E).

How Does Investment Fit Into Our Model?

We have made a number of assumptions: (1) We have assumed that the consumption function is a straight line that slopes upward to the right. This means that as people's incomes increase, they spend more on consumer goods, but they spend lower *percentages* of their incomes on these goods. (2) We are including in our category of intended investment only autonomous investment. (To review, *autonomous* investment is investment that is not affected by people's levels of income.)

Now look at Figure 8-10, which takes two different approaches to the matter of intended investment as it relates to the equilibrium level of income. (Note that II in Figure 8-10 stands for "intended investment," *not* roman numeral two!) Remember that the equilibrium level of income is the one that will not change unless one of the factors in the model changes.

Savings-Equals-Intended-Investment Approach
The determination of equilibrium income by equating savings and intended investment.

One approach, called the **savings-equals-intended-investment approach**, is located on the bottom of the diagram. This shows the relation of savings (which *reduces* consumer demand) to investment (which *adds* to consumer demand). Note that the intended investment function that intersects the savings function is parallel to the income axis. Since the vertical distance from the income axis to the II function measures intended investment, and since it must be the same at all levels of income if it is to be consistent with the fact that investment is not affected by income, the two lines are parallel.

Aggregate-Demand-Equals-Aggregate-Supply Approach
The determination of equilibrium income by equating aggregate demand and aggregate supply.

The second approach, called the **aggregate-demand-equals-aggregate-supply approach**, adds the intended investment function to the consumption function. Putting the II function here points up the relation of aggregate demand to aggregate supply. (Both these approaches will be discussed further in another chapter.) Note again that C + II is parallel to the consumption function (C_f). The vertical distance from C_f to C + II measures intended investment. Intended investment must be the same at all levels of income to be consistent with the fact that autonomous investment is not affected by income. The two lines, thus, are parallel.

SUMMING UP

1. This chapter builds on the foundation discussed in the chapter on aggregate demand and aggregate supply to show how spending and saving interact to create an equilibrium level of national income. It focuses on two theories or approaches to this subject, the *classical theory* and the *Keynesian theory.*

2. *Classical economists* theorized that the aggregate supply curve is vertical or that in a market-oriented economy the level of income would automatically move to a position at which there would be full employment and capacity. Classical theory is based on: (a) Say's law, (b) the abstinence theory of interest, and (c) the theory of wage and price flexibility.

3. *Keynesian economists* theorize that the aggregate supply curve is horizontal or that there can be unemployment in the macroeconomy and government intervention may be necessary to move toward full employment.

4. *Say's Law* states in its simple form that supply creates its own demand. In terms of the simple circular-flow model, owners of resources receive incomes generated by producing supply and use those incomes to buy the total supply of goods and services that the economy produces.

5. In terms of the complex circular-flow model, the classical economists said that taxes and government expenditures need not have disturbing effects if both factors were kept equal and balanced at as low a level as possible. The way to get rid of the disturbing effects of savings and investment is through the rate of interest, as analyzed in the abstinence theory of interest.

6. The *abstinence theory of interest* states that people would rather consume now than save now and consume later. Therefore, people need a reward, interest on savings, to make them save. The higher the reward, the larger the quantity saved. Thus, the curve showing quantities of loanable funds saved slopes upward to the right when measured against the interest rate.

7. How much people invest depends on the rate of return, which in turn depends on the productivity of technology. Thus, the curve showing the quantities of loanable funds demanded at various interest rates slopes down to the right. More investment yields returns equal to (or greater than) the interest rate at a lower interest rate than at higher interest rates.

8. The equilibrium interest rate is the rate at which the *quantity supplied* of loanable funds is equal to the quantity *demanded* for the loanable funds. Therefore, the interest rate is the stabilizer that causes the amount of savings people wish to accrue (decreasing demand) to equal the amount of investment people wish to make (increasing demand).

9. If industry produces a temporary surplus, this surplus is quickly eliminated, because industry lays off workers, and the unemployed then compete for jobs, so wages fall. Also, as firms compete to sell off excess goods, prices fall. However, the worker's real income, and in general real demand, do not fall, since wages and prices fall proportionately. Because lower prices mean that the purchasing power of each dollar is greater, people with savings feel wealthier and thus increase the quantity of goods and services they demand (the *Pigou effect*).

10. John M. Keynes, in his 1936 book, *The General Theory of Employment, Interest, and Money*, rejected the classical conclusion that income always tends toward a position at which there is full employment.

11. Keynes said that Say's law was a gross oversimplification not only of the twentieth-century industrial world but also of Say's own eighteenth-century French world.

12. Keynes felt that the abstinence theory of interest was not valid because the interest rate does not correlate intended savings with intended investment, for these reasons: (a) The people who save are different from the people who invest and have different motivations. (b) The interest rate does not determine the level of savings, since the reasons why people save are largely unrelated to the level of the interest rate. (c) Business groups' expectations of the future are not strongly affected by the interest rate. Expectations are largely a psychological factor. Yet they have a strong influence on the rate of investment. These criticisms by Keynes weakened the traditional belief in the relationship between investment and the interest rate.

13. Since the interest rate, according to Keynesians, does not correlate savings and investment, desired savings can exceed desired investment. This reduces demand, and, eventually, income. On the other hand, desired savings can be *less* than desired investment. People can spend too freely. This increases demand and income.

14. Keynes attacked the remaining support of the classical income theory, wage and price flexibility, by making the following arguments: (a) Wages and prices are not flexible enough because there is not enough competition. (b) Even if wages and prices were to be flexible enough, real spending would drop anyway. (c) Leaving (a) and (b) out of the picture, there are easier and faster ways to get rid of a general excess supply of goods and services in the economy.

15. In the Keynesian model, it is aggregate demand that determines the level of income and employment. At least in the short run, price levels are considered constants since aggregate supply is in the range in which prices do not rise as aggregate demand increases.

16. The aggregate supply behavior that is consistent with the Keynesian assumption about constant price levels is one in which the aggregate supply curve is horizontal to the real income axis. Desired output responds to all changes in aggregate demand at a constant level of prices. Firms offer more for sale at existing prices, at least up to capacity rates of output.

17. Keynes concludes: (a) There is no market mechanism to make the actual level of income coincide with the preferred level of income at full employment. The actual level may exist at full employment, at less-than-full employment, or at full employment with inflation. (b) The level of income is determined by the level of *aggregate demand*, in other words, by the total spending in the economy.

18. Several factors determine the level of aggregate demand: intended consumption, intended investment, government expenditures (these three add to effective demand), intended savings, and taxes (these two detract from effective demand.)

19. The *consumption function* shows the functional relationship between quantities consumed and various levels of income. One assumes two things: (a) that all *non*income factors affecting the quantity consumed are fixed, and (b) that the consumption function is a straight line that crosses the 45° line (consumption is equal to income at that point) and slopes upward.

20. One can derive the *savings function* from the consumption function, since income is equal to consumption plus savings. Therefore, the difference between consumption and income is savings. The savings function is a straight line that crosses the horizontal axis and slopes upward. The distance from the savings function to the horizontal axis is equal to the distance from the consumption function to the 45° line.

21. A change in the quantity consumed or saved is due to a change in income, which causes a movement along the curve of the consumption or savings function. A change in both consumption and savings is due to a change in a *non*income factor, which causes the whole consumption and savings functions to shift.

22. Nonincome factors that may cause a change in consumption and savings are (a) changes in social customs, mores, or attitudes toward savings, (b) changes in assets of consumers (both quantity and composition), (c) changes in expectations about future earnings, (d) changes in taxes, and (e) changes in distribution of income and changes in demography (the distribution and density of population).

23. In this book we deal with two kinds of investment: autonomous and induced. *Autonomous investment* is influenced only by factors other than income and consumption. *Induced investment* is determined by changes in income and in quantity consumed. To keep our model simple, we assume here that induced investment is zero.

24. People make that amount of investment for which they can expect a rate of return equal to or greater than the cost of the investment. The cost of an investment is equal to the interest paid for the funds needed to finance it. The expected rate of return is the *marginal efficiency of capital*, and it is determined primarily by increases in productivity and by expectations of future economic activity.

25. Of the three components that increase effective demand, investment is the most unstable. The reason is that there are fluctuations in the three main factors determining the volume of investment: interest rates, expectations of the future, and the flow of technological improvements.

26. If one is making a diagram of the relation between consumption, savings, and intended investment, one can put the intended investment function above

and parallel to the horizontal axis, and it will intersect the savings function. This emphasizes the relation of savings (which reduce the demand for consumption) to investment (which adds to it). This is called the *savings-equals-intended-investment approach.*

27. Alternatively, one can add the intended investment function to the consumption function; this is called aggregate demand. This function emphasizes the effect of total demand on income and is called the *aggregate-demand-equals-aggregate-supply approach.*

KEY TERMS

Abstinence theory of interest
Aggregate-demand-equals-aggregate supply approach
Autonomous investment
Classical theory
Consumption function
Dissavings
Induced investment
Investment function
Keynesian theory
Liquid assets
Marginal efficiency of capital
Mercantilism
Pigou effect
Savings function
Savings-equals-intended-investment approach
Say's law

QUESTIONS

1. Explain how a classical economist would defend the conclusion that the level of income always tends to move toward a point at which there is full employment. Include the role of Say's law, the abstinence theory of interest, and wage-price flexibility. What type of aggregate supply condition does the classical economist assume?

2. How did Keynes challenge the classical conclusion about income and employment, especially as it referred to the three foundations of classical theory: Say's law, the abstinence theory of interest, and wage-price flexibility?

3. What was Keynes' conclusion about the relationship between income and full employment? How is the level of income determined, according to Keynes?
4. What are the five factors that determine aggregate demand? How do changes in each of the five affect effective demand?

5. Which of the following factors change the quantity people consume or save, and in what direction? Why?

a. An increase in the holding of consumer durables
b. A decrease in taxes
c. An increased desire for security in old age
d. An increase in income
e. A decrease in the amount of money that people hold

6. Answer the following questions based on the figure below:

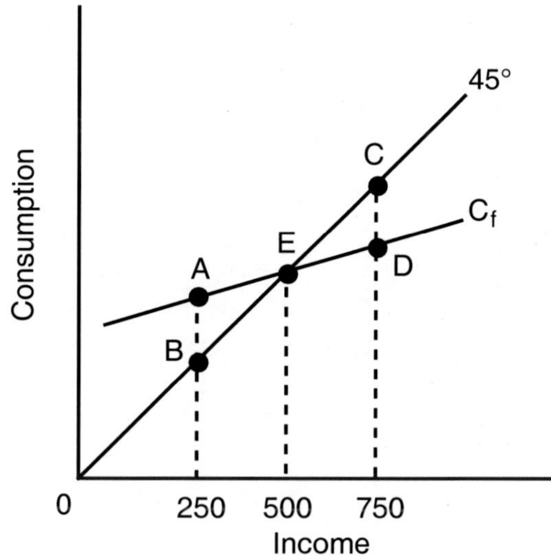

a. The equilibrium level of income in the figure above is (1) 250, (2) 500, or (3) 750?
b. Dissavings in the figure above is represented by the distance (1) CD, or (2) AB?
c. Savings in the figure above is represented by the distance (1) CD, or (2) AB?

7. Distinguish between autonomous and induced investment.

8. Does autonomous investment increase or decrease when the following things happen? Why?

a. The interest rate increases
b. A new breakthrough in science opens up new areas of technological innovation for industry
c. The stock market collapses and the general feeling is one of pessimism

9. What is the least stable element of aggregate demand as a part of GDP?

Chapter 9: Equilibrium in the Macroeconomy

In this chapter, we will see how levels of planned expenditures by consumers, investors, and government interact with planned savings and taxes to create an equilibrium level of national income. We will also account for international trade effects by factoring into that equilibrium the influence of net exports (exports minus imports). We will do this in three stages, first, and for simplicity, without government and second with the influences of government expenditures and taxation. Finally, in Stage III, we will treat the macroeconomy as open and subject to the demand influences of exports and imports.

It is useful, before we begin, to remember the distinction we drew between the classical and Keynesian positions on equilibrium in the macroeconomy. While both theories conclude that an economy whose equilibrium is disrupted will tend to move toward a new equilibrium level of income, they differ on whether that new level will tend to produce full employment. Classical economists argue that "markets work," that flexibility in factor and product prices tends to produce a new set of prices (including interest rates) that restore long run equilibrium at full employment and capacity rates of output (vertical aggregate supply conditions). Keynesian economists, however, argue that modern markets, while displaying some wage and price flexibility, have built in rigidities that prevent prices from moving to a level that will necessarily restore equilibrium at full employment. This difference creates disputes about public policy prescriptions (laissez faire versus neo-mercantilist approaches) in the relationships between government and the market macroeconomy. In this chapter, we will build a Keynesian model and begin to explore some of the policy conclusions to which it leads.

Figure 9-1
Simple Model: Savings Equals Intended Investment

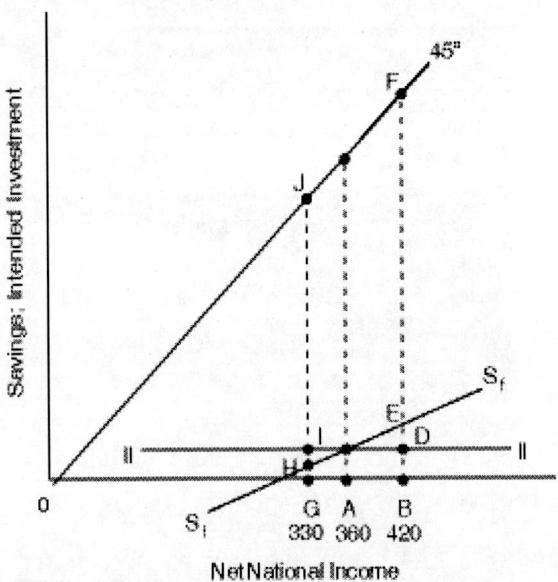

Equilibrium income is that amount of income at which savings equals investment: income A (360). Income levels above it (B = 420) yield involuntary (unplanned) additions to inventory (DE = 20). Income levels below it (G = 330) yield involuntary decreases in inventory (HI = 10).

Now we will again build a simple Keynesian model to enable us to approach a more complex model. Let's leave government and international trade out of the model for now and say that government expenditures and taxes as well as net exports are zero. This leaves us with only three factors to deal with: consumption, savings, and investment. Now let's see what happens.

STAGE I: NO GOVERNMENT SPENDING OR TAXES

THE BASIC MODEL

Savings Equals Intended Investment

Figure 9-1 shows the intended investment function (II) parallel to the horizontal axis and intersecting the savings function (S_f). This placement, which emphasizes the relation of investment to savings, is called the *savings-equals-intended-investment approach. It* shows the relation of savings, which diverts people's money away from demand (leakage) for goods and services, to investment, which supplements or adds to consumption demand (injection). For example, you save money for a down payment on a house by denying yourself many things you would like to have. Then, when you buy the house, you invest, by paying out the capital you have created to buy the house. You increase demand for output from many firms, output needed to build the house.

What is the equilibrium level of income? And what does it take to maintain it? Equilibrium *price* was previously defined as the central tendency of the market, a price that didn't change as long as supply and demand didn't change. Furthermore, any price other than the equilibrium price automatically triggers forces that push the price toward the equilibrium point. In the same way, the equilibrium level of *income* is the central tendency of the economy. That level of income will not change so long as the factors in the model (consumption, savings, and investment) do not change. Any other level of income would be unstable and would trigger economic forces that push the level of income toward equilibrium.

Now look at Table 9-1. The data are based on Table 8-2, except that we have added data on intended investment. Note that investment is constant at 20, because we include only autonomous investment, which does not change when income changes.

In the savings-equals-intended-investment approach, the equilibrium level of income is 360 (equivalent to income A in Figure 9-1).When an economy's consumption, savings, and investment are as shown in Figure 9-1 and Table 9-1, the equilibrium level of income is the level at which savings equals investment (income level A in Figure 9-1 and 360 in Table 9-1). To prove this, one must first show that the economy cannot maintain income levels above A (or 360) and then show that it similarly cannot maintain income levels below A (360).

From here on, we will cite Figure 9-1 only, and after each reference to Figure 9-1, there will be numbers in parentheses that refer to corresponding points in Table 9-1. If you follow the discussion on both the diagram and the table, you will understand the explanation better.

Table 9-1

Savings Equals Intended Investment (billions of dollars)

Income	Consumption	Savings	Intended Investment
210	240	–30	20
240	260	–20	20
270	280	–10	20
300	300	0	20
330	320	10	20
360*	340*	20*	20*
390	360	30	20
420	380	40	20
450	400	50	20

Now bear in mind that businesses produce most of their goods and services with the intention of selling them to consumers. However, they do set aside a portion of their output for investment. Let's say that at income B (420), which is above the equilibrium level, businesses produce BD (20) for investment (BD is the distance from the horizontal axis to the intended investment function, II). This leaves DF (400) remaining for the ***public to consume.***

Unplanned or Involuntary Additions to Inventory
The excess of what businesses plan to produce over what households plan to consume.

But the public has its own ideas. Let's say that people plan to save BE (40), which is the distance from point B to the savings function (S_f). This leaves a gap here, because businesses produce DF (400) for consumption, and people consume only EF (380). Business firms are left with the remainder, DE (20), as unsold output, which must be added to their inventory. This is called **unplanned** or **involuntary additions to inventory** (because inventories are defined as business investment).

Unplanned or Involuntary Reductions in Inventory
The excess of what households plan to consume over what businesses plan to produce.

Business firms that have this unwanted inventory stashed in their warehouses or on the shelves of their stores must reduce orders to the companies that supply them with raw materials. Manufacturers cut production, which reduces their income, so they must lay off workers. Gradually, the economy takes a turn downward, moving from income level B (420) back toward the equilibrium income level A (360). This happens because at any level above A (360), what businesses produce for consumption is greater than what consumers wish to consume. Note that the savings function lies above the intended investment function. Business firms are forced to hold these unwanted additions in their inventories. They react by reducing inventories, and income.

Now, at any level below the equilibrium income, such as G (330), businesses produce GI (20) for investment, which is more than the amount people save, GH (10). They also produce IJ (310) for consumption, which is less than what the public wants to consume, HJ (320). Now people are consuming more than businesses produce for consumption. When they do this, they reduce business inventories. Thus there are **unplanned** or **involuntary reductions in inventories** equal to HI (10).

When businesses find that their inventories are slipping below what they want them to be, they order more from their suppliers to replenish the inventories. Manufacturers then increase output, which increases their income, so they hire more workers. The economy moves from income level G (330) toward the equilibrium level of income A (360). Any lower income would result in unplanned decreases in inventories.

Income level A (360) is an equilibrium level because, at that level, what businesses plan to produce for investment is equal to what the public plans to save, and what businesses plan to produce for consumption is equal to what the public plans to consume. The plans of businesses mesh with the plans of the public.

In this state of balance, businesses have neither *involuntary accumulation* of inventories (in which businesses produce *more* than people consume, and their savings function lies above the intended investment function) nor *involuntary reduction* in inventories (in which businesses produce *less* than people consume, and the savings function lies below the intended investment function). What they plan in the way of inventory is what they actually realize.

To summarize: At equilibrium income, people's savings equal business firms' intended investment. At income levels *above* equilibrium, businesses want to invest *less* than what people want to save. As a result, consumers demand less than what businesses produce for consumption. So when cost-conscious citizens, intent on saving money, buy fewer consumer goods and services than businesses offer for sale, company executives watch gloomily as their warehouses fill with unwanted inventory. They must somehow dispose of this inventory. They may either reduce orders to the manufacturers or offer the goods for sale at lower prices.

At income levels *below* the equilibrium, the reverse occurs. Businesses want to invest *more* than the amount people want to save. As a result, consumers are willing to buy more than businesses have for sale. So inventories fall to such a point that businesses increase their volume of new orders. Business output increases, and so does business income.

Planned and Actual Investment

By now you can see that there is a strong relationship between savings and investment. The key aspect of this relationship is that *savings reduce demand* (by lowering the level of people's consumption), while *investment adds to demand* (that is, adds investment demand to consumer demand for the output of business). In order to arrive at an equilibrium level of income, savings and investment must balance off at a level that both businesses and consumers want. The demand of businesses for investment has to equal the demand of consumers for a given amount of savings. When these two factors are not equal, when the balance is out of kilter, businesses take steps to remedy the situation, by changing their output and their number of employees.

It is this important relation of savings to investment that calls attention to the distinction between ex-ante and ex-post investment.

Planned Investment
Planned investments by firms.

Actual Investment
Actual investments by firms.

Planned investment is the amount of investment that businesses plan to make.

Actual investment is the amount of investment that they actually do make.

To get a clear idea of this relation, look again at Figure 9-1 and Table 9-1. We are going to use the same letters and numbers we used before. (Again, after the letters from Figure 9-1, we will include the corresponding figures from Table 9-1, in parentheses.)

In Figure 9-1, at income level B (420), planned investment is equal to BD (20), while actual investment is equal to BE (40). This is because unplanned accumulations to inventory DE (20) are added to planned inventories, and inventories are considered investment. This means that business plans are not being realized. Their actual investment is twice what they planned.

At income level G (330), businesses are again in a bad spot, because their planned investment is GI (20), while their actual investment is GH (10), only half of what they planned. This is because unplanned reductions in inventory HI (10) are deducted from planned inventories.

In both cases, business firms' actual investment is equal to consumers' actual savings. This equality is due either to unplanned additions to inventories or to unplanned subtractions from them. One has to take into account the fact that *inventories*, whether planned or unplanned, *are part of investment.*

However, an economy does not achieve equilibrium income simply because it arrives at a point at which actual investment equals actual savings. Unplanned (involuntary) changes in inventory cause businesses to either reduce or increase their orders to manufacturers. These changes in orders naturally cause the level of output to either rise or fall, and with it, the level of income and employment. Each factor affects each other factor. Only at the equilibrium level does planned investment by business equal actual savings by consumers. At that point, all expectations are met. There are neither increases nor decreases in planned inventory. The level of income is in equilibrium.

Aggregate Demand Equals Aggregate Supply

Now let's approach the subject of the equilibrium level of income from another angle: Suppose we look at aggregate demand and aggregate supply (Figure 9-2). In this simple Stage I model, aggregate (in other words, total) demand is composed of (1) consumption demand plus (2) investment demand, which is represented by the line C + II in Figure 9-2; the letters stand for "consumption plus intended investment." (Remember that to simplify things we are leaving government out of the picture. There are no government expenditures and no taxes.)

Figure 9-2
Simple Model Without Government: Aggregate Demand Equals Aggregate Supply

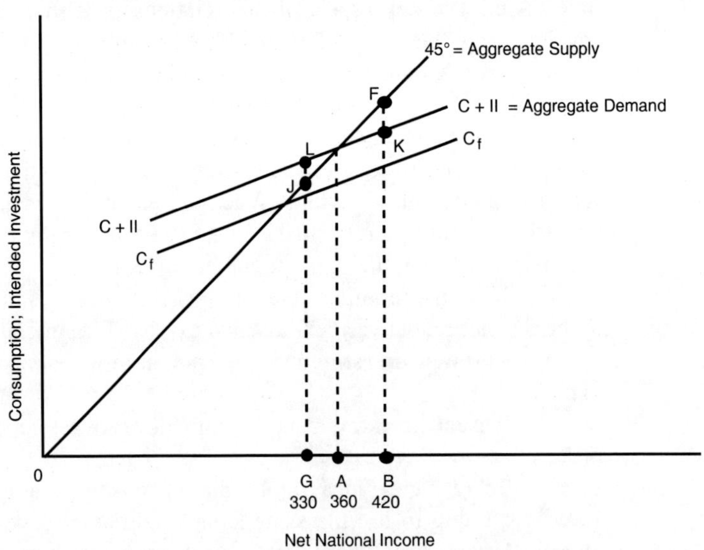

At income A (360), equilibrium income is at the level at which aggregate demand (C + II) equals aggregate supply (45° line). At income B (420), aggregate supply exceeds aggregate demand, and excess inventories KF (20) pile up. At income G (330), aggregate demand exceeds aggregate supply, and there is an inventory deficit of JL (10).

In our analysis of the national economic accounts, we concluded that the income generated in an economy is equal to the value of the economy's output. So in Figure 9-2, we could say that the 45° line that represents income also represents output. In effect, then, we are assuming that the vertical distance from the horizontal axis to the 45° line, the aggregate supply function, is the output that businesses think they can sell at that level of income. ("Small cars are moving pretty well. Let's make twenty thousand Dustrats, and see how they sell.")

Figure 9-2 shows that, at income A, aggregate demand equals aggregate supply. This is the equilibrium level of income. To establish this, one has to show that any other level of income would *not* be an equilibrium.

Look at Figure 9-2. Again, we will use Table 9-1's figures in parentheses. Note that, at any income above the equilibrium level (A), aggregate supply (the 45° line) is greater than aggregate demand (C + II). In other words, businesses plan to supply more than consumers plan to demand. In Figure 9-2, at income B (420), aggregate supply is BF (420), while aggregate demand is only BK (400, or C + II). Supply exceeds demand by KF (20), which reflects unplanned additions to inventory. ("How can we ever unload two thousand tons of chicken feathers when we've ordered more than people want to buy? Cancel our order for more.") Output, income, and employment go down. Income shrinks in the direction of A (360), the equilibrium level.

At any income below the equilibrium level, aggregate demand (C_f + II) is greater than aggregate supply (the 45° line). Consumers demand more than businesses can supply, and inventories gradually dwindle away. ("Hey, listen to this! Insomnia Motels have increased their order by ten thousand chicken-feather pillows. Phone around and see if you can locate ten thousand yards of heavy striped ticking for pillow covers.") Output, income and employment go up. At income G (330) in Figure 9-2, aggregate demand is GL (340) (C_f + II), while aggregate supply is only GJ (330). Demand exceeds supply by JL (10), which reflects unexpected reduction in businesses' inventories. When this happens, income expands in the direction of A (360), the equilibrium level.

So you see, our economy really *must* move toward equilibrium. Any unsettlement on either side of A sends the income level moving back toward that equilibrium. Note that Figure 9-3 includes both intended investment; (II) and savings (S_f). Thus we can compare the savings-equals-intended-investment and the aggregate-supply-equals-aggregate-demand approaches. Both wind up with the same equilibrium level of income: A (360).

THE KEYNESIAN MULTIPLIER

Average and Marginal Propensities to Consume and Save

At this point let's inject some definitions that will help you understand a few new concepts: (1) the *average* propensities to consume and save, and (2) the *marginal* propensities to consume and save.

Average Propensity to Consume
The percentage of a given disposable income that people tend to consume.

The **average propensity to consume** (APC) is the percentage of a given disposable income that people tend to consume (or spend for consumer goods). The formula is:

$$APC = \frac{C}{DI}$$

where DI is the level of income and C is consumption.

Figure 9-3
Simple Model: Aggregate Demand Equals Aggregate Supply, Plus Savings Equals Intended Investment

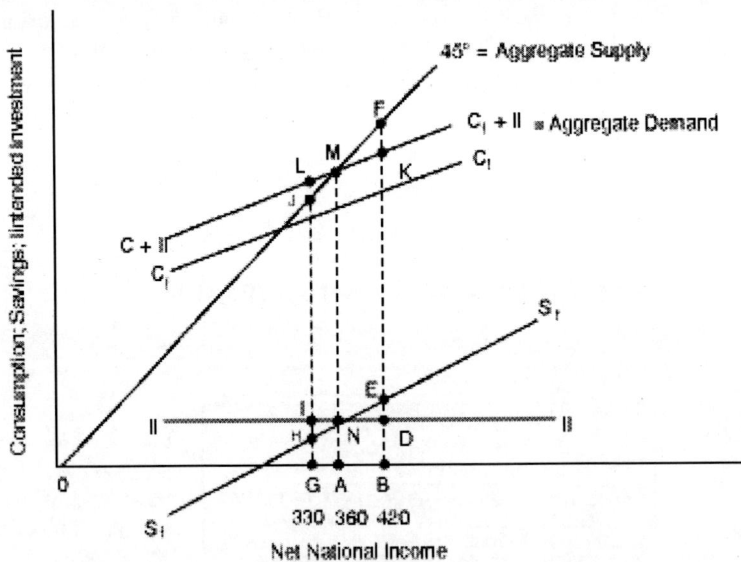

When both approaches are included in the same diagram, the same equilibrium level of income applies to both: A (360) is equilibrium.

Average Propensity to Save
The percentage of a given income that people tend to save.

The **average propensity to save** (APS) is the percentage of a given disposable income that people tend to save. The formula is:

$$APS = \frac{S}{DI}$$

where S is savings. Since income equals consumption plus savings, the average propensity to consume plus the average propensity to save equals one, or in other words, 100 percent of disposable income.

Marginal Propensity to Consume
The change in consumption associated with a change in income.

The **marginal propensity to consume** (MPC) is the *change* in consumption associated with a change in income. The formula is:

$$MPC = \frac{\Delta C}{\Delta DI}$$

Marginal Propensity to Save
The change in saving associated with a change in income.

where ΔC means the *change* in consumption and ΔDI means the *change* in disposable income. (The triangle symbol is the Greek letter delta. It means a change in some quantity.) The **marginal propensity to save** (MPS) is the *change* in saving associated with a change in disposable income. The formula is:

$$MPS = \frac{\Delta S}{\Delta DI}$$

Again, the marginal propensity to consume plus the marginal propensity to save equals one, or in other words, 100 percent of the increase in disposable income will be saved or consumed.

Remember that APC + APS = 1 and MPC + MPS = 1.

The key concept to remember here is that the *average* propensities to consume and save have to do with the *percentage* people consume and save out of a specific level of disposable income, while the *marginal* propensities to consume and save have to do with the percentages people consume and save out of *changes* in disposable income.

For example, suppose that the level of disposable income in the economy is $400 billion and the level of consumption is $300 billion. Then the *average* propensity to consume is:

$$\frac{C}{DI} \text{ or } \frac{300}{400} \text{ or } \frac{3}{4} \text{ or } .75.$$

Savings equal $100 billion (DI - C = S). The *average* propensity to save is:

$$\frac{S}{DI} \text{ or } \frac{100}{400} \text{ or } \frac{1}{4} \text{ or } .25.$$

Now suppose that the level of disposable income in the economy increases by $50 billion, the level of consumption increases by $40 billion, and the level of savings increases by $10 billion. Then the *marginal* propensity to consume is:

$$\frac{\Delta C}{\Delta DI} \text{ or } \frac{40}{50} \text{ or } \frac{4}{5} \text{ or } .80.$$

The *marginal* propensity to save is:

$$\frac{\Delta S}{\Delta DI} \text{ or } \frac{10}{50} \text{ or } \frac{1}{5} \text{ or } .20.$$

For a picture of the marginal propensity to consume, see Figure 9-4, which shows a section of the consumption function.

Figure 9-4

The Marginal Propensity to Consume (MPC)

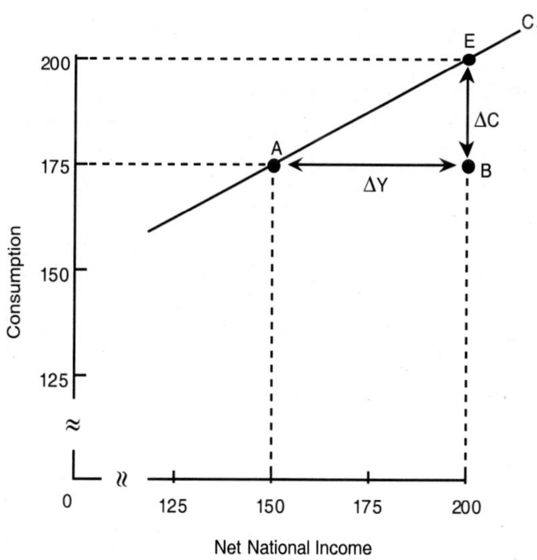

Income increases (DI) from 150 to 200 (shown by arrows from A to B). Consumption increases (C) from 175 to 200, shown by arrows from B to E. Income increases by 50 and consumption by 25. The MPC equals:

$$\frac{25}{50} \text{ or } \frac{1}{2} \text{ or } .50$$

Now look at Table 9-2. We arrived at these figures by taking the data on income, consumption, and savings from Table 9-1 and computing the marginal propensities to consume and save. Let's take an example to see how the various average and marginal propensities to consume and save are calculated. The first three columns, Income, Consumption, and Savings, are taken directly from Table 9-1. The fourth column, APC (average propensity to consume), is calculated by dividing Consumption by Income. Thus the APC at an income level of 210 = $\frac{240}{210}$ = 1.14.

At the same income level, APS (average propensity to save) = $\frac{-30}{210}$ = −0.14. The two averages must equal one or 1.14 – .14 = 1.0. The marginal propensities to consume (MPC) and save (MPS) are calculated as midpoints. Remember that they represent the *changes* in consumption and savings from a *change* in income. Thus, when income rises from 210 to 240, consumption rises from 240 to 260 and the MPC = $\frac{20}{30}$ or .67. The change in savings associated with that same increase in income is from –30 to –20 or $\frac{10}{30}$ or.33. The two marginal changes (MPC and MPS) must account for the entire change in income, thus, .67 + .33 = 1.00 or 100 percent of the change in income. To assure yourself of understanding these concepts, calculate the APCs, APSs, MPCs, and MPSs for all the remaining levels of income in Table 9-2.

Table 9-2

The Average and Marginal Propensities to Consume and Save

Disposable Income	Consumption	Savings	APC	APS	MPC	MPS	I_{I1}	I_{I2}
210	240	–30	1.14	–.14			20	30
					.67	.33		
240	260	–20	1.08	–.08			20	30
					.67	.33		
270	280	–10	1.04	–.04			20	30
					.67	.33		
300	300	0	1	0			20	30
					.67	.33		
330	320	10	.97	.03			20	30
					.67	.33		
360	340	20	.94	.06			20	30
					.67	.33		
390	360	30	.92	.08			20	30
					.67	.33		
420	380	40	.90	.10			20	30
					.67	.33		
450	400	50	.89	.11			20	30

How Changes in Aggregate Demand Affect Changes in Income: Multiplier Effects

Whenever aggregate demand shifts, as evidenced by a shift in autonomous investment or a shift in autonomous consumption, or both, it is a sure sign that the equilibrium level of income has also changed, because the additional money people are spending or investing must be coming from *somewhere*.

Figure 9-5 shows a case of aggregate demand (the sum of consumption plus investment) shifting up by 10, from AD_1 to AD_2. Perhaps this shift is due to an increase in autonomous investment or to an upward shift in the consumption function. Whatever the reason for it, this upward shift causes the equilibrium level of Income to rise from B to C, or an increase of 30. Note that this figure of 30 is three times as big as 10, which is the upward shift in aggregate demand.

The point we are trying to make is that income always changes by *more* than the initial shift in aggregate demand. This phenomenon is called the **multiplier effect**, because the amount of change in the equilibrium level of income is a multiple of the initial amount of change in aggregate demand. To define a multiplier, think backward, like this:

Multiplier Effect
The effect of change in aggregate demand on income.

Multiplier
The multiple by which income changes as aggregate demand changes or $\frac{\Delta Y}{\Delta AD}$.

The change in net national income (Y) due to a given initial change in aggregate demand (AD) is a multiple of that change in demand. This multiple is called the ***multiplier***.

Figure 9-5
The Multiplier Effect

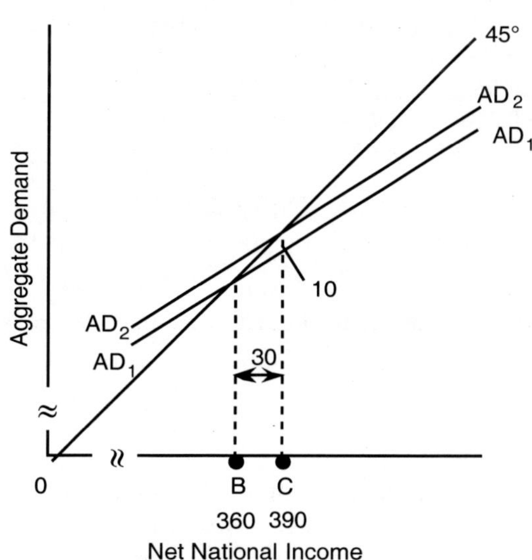

Aggregate demand shifts up from AD_1 to AD_2, an initial increase (an injection) of 10, which increases equilibrium income B to C, an increase of 30. An initial change in aggregate demand changes equilibrium income by an amount larger than the initial change in aggregate demand. Since the change in income is a *multiple* of the initial change in aggregate demand, this is called the *multiplier effect.*

There are two important points to keep in mind: (1) In order for a new level of income to be permanent, the initial upward shift of aggregate demand must be permanent. (2) The amount of increase in income is related to the amount of the initial upward shift of aggregate demand. As income increases, there is a movement up AD_2, so that in the end AD_2 is equal to income C.

In Figure 9-5, in which income changes by 30 and aggregate demand initially changes by 10, the multiplier $\frac{\Delta Y}{\Delta AD} = 3$.

Why a Multiple?

The reason why income changes by a multiple of the initial change in aggregate demand is that people's marginal propensity to *consume* is greater than zero. Or, put another way, their marginal propensity to *save* is less than one. In other words, the marginal propensities to consume and save are the keys to the multiplier concept. Table 9-3 helps explain why this is so. It shows that the public will spend two-thirds of any increase in income on consumer goods and services.

Suppose a savings bank invests $1 million in a new bank building. Even before construction starts, many people begin to earn incomes from this project, so aggregate demand increases. Workers, manufacturers, and many suppliers of goods and services start to benefit. Given that these people have an MPC of 2/3, they will spend two-thirds of this new income and save one-third. This spending generates more new income, so a second round of spending begins. The people in round 2, in their turn, also spend two-thirds of what they get and save one-third. This income generation continues, and on each round of spending, people spend two-thirds and save one-third. So during each round, one-third becomes savings. Finally all the original $1 million *winds up as savings*. But the total increase in income that has been generated by all this spending is $3 million or three times the bank's original investment. The multiplier here is, of course, three.

The Multiplier Formula $\frac{1}{1 - MPC}$

Multiplier Formula
The formula for determining the multiple change in income associated with a change in aggregate demand.

There is a simple and useful formula for computing the multiplier (M), the change in equilibrium real income from a change in aggregate demand. You would do well to memorize the **multiplier formula**:

$$M = \frac{1}{1 - MPC} \text{ or, since } 1 - MPC = MPS \text{ , } M = \frac{1}{MPS}$$

The multiplier is the reciprocal of the marginal propensity to save. Here, with a little simple arithmetic, is how the formula works when MPC equals 2/3:

$$M = \frac{1}{1 - MPC}, \quad M = \frac{1}{1 - 2/3}, \quad M = \frac{1}{1/3}, \quad M = 1 \times \frac{3}{1}, \quad M = 3$$

Remember that in order for this increase in income to be permanent, the increase in autonomous investment must remain at the new higher level. This means that more new investment has to be made to replace the $1 million that originally came from the bank.

Instantaneous Multipliers Versus Periodic Multipliers

Instantaneous Multiplier
A multiplier effect that takes effect instantaneously.

You may have the impression that the multiplier process takes place very quickly. That is, strictly speaking, not true. However, the concept of the **instantaneous multiplier** (a multiplier effect that takes place instantaneously) is useful to us at this stage, so we will use it for the time being. Whenever we introduce a different time dimension into the multiplier, we will say so.

Table 9-3
How the Multiplier Effect Works, Given That the Marginal Propensity to Consumer (MPC) Equals 2/3

		Initial Amount of Capital
Autonomous investment	⟶	\$1,000,000
Second round of spending		666,666
Third round of spending		444,444
Fourth round of spending		296,296
Fifth round of spending		197,530
Sixth round of spending		131,685
Seventh round of spending		87,781
Eighth round of spending		58,512
Total spending after n^{th} round		\$3,000,000

However, you must recognize that the process of generating and regenerating demand, output, and income takes *time*. Those people and businesses in Table 9-3 who received income as a result of the savings bank's initial investment of \$1 million had to have *time* to make the necessary decisions about spending their new incomes ("Should we pay Junior's college bills, or buy a new Dustrat?"). And then they had to have time to act on these decisions ("Good-bye, Junior, and don't forget to give this check to the college cashier"). And when the money filtered down to the people in round 2, they also had to have time to make decisions and to spend their new incomes. (Though they had less money to make decisions about, because the people in round 1 had saved one-third of their additional income.)

Periodic Multiplier
A multiplier effect that occurs over several periods of time.

So you can see that it would be much more realistic to visualize a **periodic multiplier**, a multiplier effect that takes place over several periods of time, as the money from the original investment passes down the line, from one round of expenditures to the next. It is true that an economy feels the biggest impact of a multiplier within the first few time periods (usually about eighteen months) after the initial investment, but the long-range effects of a multiplier are spread over several time periods. These long-range effects create difficulties for the people who are trying to formulate government economic policy. A government policy maker who is trying to figure out how much money the government should pump into the economy in order to stimulate demand must be aware of previous changes in demand and their continuing impact on the economy's income.

THE ACCELERATOR PRINCIPLE

When we discussed the two kinds of investment (autonomous and induced), we assumed that induced investment was zero, in order to simplify our model. We left out induced investment. Now we are going to look at it.

Whenever the equilibrium level of income increases, people consume more goods and services, and this increase in consumption brings on, or induces, new investment. If you look at Figure 9-5, you see a higher income level (c) that would intersect the consumption curve just as before, but higher up; in other words, at a point indicating a greater quantity consumed. The level of quantity demanded is higher. This increase in quantity consumed means that industry has to have an increased capacity to produce goods and services, and this in turn requires larger amounts of investment. That is what we mean by *induced* investment. Additional investment naturally follows increased consumption. Table 9-4 shows this chain of events, using the shoe industry as an example.

Let us say that you are a shoe magnate, and you own a factory that makes shoes. Each of your 100 shoe-making machines produces 1,000 pairs of shoes a year, and has a life span of 10 years. In period 1 (suppose that each period equals one year), your 100 machines are equally divided as to age, so you act as you usually do, and order 10 new machines to replace 10 that wore out. In period 2, however, the demand for shoes picks up by 1 percent, so you order an additional machine that year: 10 for replacement and one for expansion (that one machine is induced investment). You want to take advantage of that demand for 1,000 extra pairs of shoes, since you want all the business you can get.

Table 9-4
Induced Investment and the Accelerator Principle in the Shoe Industry

Time Period	Percentage Increase in Demand for Shoes	Number of Pairs of Shoes Demanded	Total Number of Shoe Machines	Demand for New Machines
1		100,000	100	10
2	1	101,000	101	11
3	2	103,020	103	12
4	3	106,110	106	13
5	3	109,293	109	13
6	2	111,479	111	12
7	0	111,479	111	10

In period 3, the demand for shoes increases by 2 percent (more than the 1 percent increase in period 2). Now you need 103 machines to meet demand. So you order 12 new machines: 10 for replacement and two for expansion (those two machines represent induced investment). In period 4, demand increases at an increased rate: 3 percent. Now you need 106 machines. You order 13 new ones, still 10 for replacement, plus three for expansion. Induced investment continues to increase. In period 5, although demand continues to increase, the rate of increase remains the same: 3 percent. You now need 109 machines. You order 13 new ones: 10 for replacement and three for expansion. Note that this year your induced investment did not increase. In period 6, demand still increases, but at a lower rate, only 2 percent. Now you need 111 machines, but you order only 12 new ones: 10 for replacement and only two for expansion. Your induced investment has decreased.

This example shows that your demand for extra new machines (your induced investment) does not depend upon the absolute level of demand for shoes. It depends on the *percentage increase in demand* for shoes. If you're going to increase your induced investment and keep expanding your plant's capacity to produce shoes, you must be able to see that there is an increasing rate of increase in demand for shoes. If the percentage increase in demand falls off, you are going to cut back your induced investment. And this also has a multiplier effect on the economy's income, only in a downward direction.

Accelerator Principle
The argument that induced investment is related to the rate of change in demand or output.

This cause-and-effect situation is called the **accelerator principle**. You can see that a small increase (1 percent) in the amount of consumer demand causes a much larger increase in induced investment. And this, in turn, has its multiplier effect on income. Higher incomes bring about an increase in demand for consumer goods and services, which has an accelerator effect on the economy.

However, this same accelerator factor introduces a strong unstable element into the growth of an economy's income. The reason is that whenever there is a decrease in the rate of growth of consumers' demands, the acceleration starts to go in the opposite direction, down. The accelerator becomes a negative one, and this causes declines in income.

Economists often use this interaction between the multiplier and the accelerator to explain business fluctuations. As an economy climbs up out of a recession, the increases in consumer demand bring the positive accelerator into play. This causes a rapid upswing in the economy. Gradually, though, the rate of growth embodied in that upswing slows down. Then the negative accelerator takes over and begins to pull the economy down.

Also, the accelerator may not take place in the earliest phases of recovery from a recession, because there is still a lot of unused capacity (that is, idle machines and empty plant space). Until that idle capacity is used up, one hardly notices that times are getting better.

Only as an economy's recovery approaches the stage at which all machines and plant space are fully utilized, does it begin to feel the effects of the accelerator.

In Figure 9-6, you see that when the accelerator is positive (that is, when induced investment is rising and both income and consumption are also rising), the curve depicting intended investment (II) slopes upward. The opposite occurs when the accelerator is negative; then the II curve slopes downward.

Bear in mind that *the multiplier relates autonomous investment* (plus any other change in aggregate demand) *to changes in income,* whereas *the accelerator relates induced investment to changes in income or output.*

Figure 9-6
Induced Investment

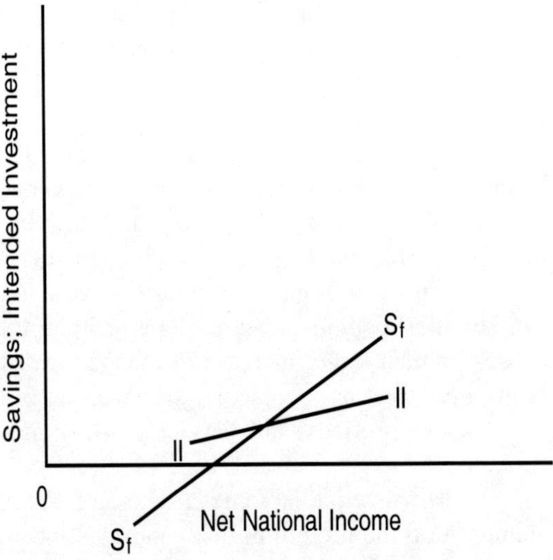

The Paradox of Thrift

Paradox of Thrift
The argument that during a recession, attempts to increase savings reduced output and at a lower level of income, savings actually fall.

During a recession, when income is falling and the newspapers are full of stories about rising unemployment, people begin to feel insecure and uncertain about their futures. Perhaps they retrench and reduce their consumption, so that they can save more. They may sleep more peacefully, knowing that their savings account is fatter. But if *everyone* does the same thing, if everyone cuts back and scrimps and saves, it may be disastrous for the economy. Eventually what happens is not an increase in savings, but a *decrease* in the quantity actually saved. This effect is known as the **paradox of thrift**.

Figure 9-7 shows this peculiar reverse effect. Suppose there is a recession, with its accompanying fall in aggregate demand and income and its accompanying increase in unemployment. The people who still have jobs nervously begin to cut back their spending so that they can save more. The line marked S_1 is the initial level of savings, before the recession. Income then stands at B, and quantity saved at C.What happens when people begin to save more? Just the opposite of what you would expect. When everybody's savings increase, the savings function shifts upward to level S_2. Intended investment is now equal to savings only at income A. This indicates that income has fallen from B to A, and that the actual quantity people are saving has decreased from C to D.

The moral of all this is that when an entire economy tightens its belt, consumer demand falls and income decreases. This conclusion rests on the assumption that the increase in intended savings is not offset by an increase in intended investment. At the least, there is no assurance that the increased investment, which results from lower interest rates associated with larger savings, will offset the larger planned savings. The quantity actually saved may decrease.

Figure 9-7
The Paradox of Thrift

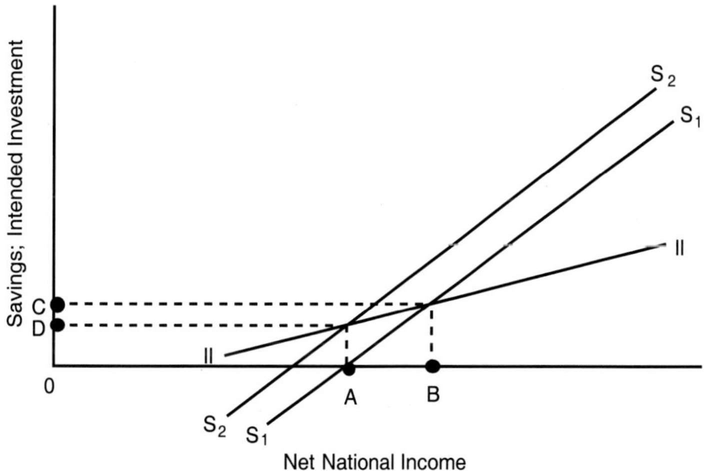

Therefore, paradoxically, during a recession if everybody is trying hard to save more, the *amount* of savings may become less. Note, though, that this argument applies only to severe recessions and depressions. It does not negate the fact that, in order to have a period of growth, an adequate supply of savings and its associated low interest rates are necessary.

STAGE II: ADDING GOVERNMENT SPENDING AND TAXES TO THE KEYNESIAN MACROECONOMY

In the late twentieth century, government expenditures and taxes collected by governments have large effects on aggregate expenditures. Expenditures directly influence (raise) aggregate demand.

Taxes, on the other hand, reduce personal and business incomes and diminish aggregate demand. Government purchases of everything from defense goods to computers used to run its agencies constitute about 25 percent of GDP. For this reason, we must add expenditures and taxes to our Keynesian model of macroeconomic equilibrium. We are still simplifying the model since we continue to assume that there are no effects on aggregate spending from foreign trade (net exports are assumed to be zero).

Adding Government Expenditures to the Basic Model

We can add government expenditures (G) an injection to our model in the same way we added intended investment to it; by seeing them in relation to (1) the savings function, and (2) the consumption function.

How do government expenditures affect savings and consumption? Recall our earlier discussion of determining the equilibrium level of income. We spoke of the two approaches to the subject: the savings-equals-intended-investment approach, and the aggregate-demand-equals-aggregate-supply approach. When we consider government expenditures in relation to the *savings* function, they become part of the savings-equals-intended-investment approach. But considered in relation to the *consumption* function, government expenditures become part of the aggregate-demand-equals-aggregate-supply approach.

Figure 9-8
Savings Equals Intended Investment Plus Government Expenditures

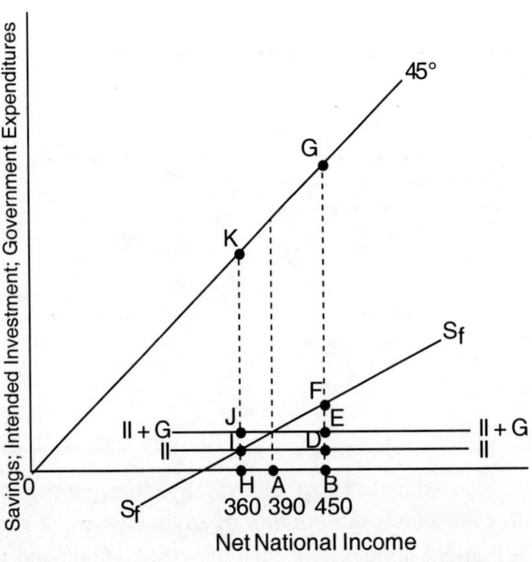

The basic Stage I model with the addition of government expenditures (G) above intended investment (II), so that G is the distance between II and II + G. The equilibrium level of income is now A, where Sf equals II + G.

One Approach: Savings Equals Intended Investment Plus Government Expenditures

Figure 9-8 shows the earlier savings-equals-intended-investment approach with government expenditures added. Savings, you recall, has a depressing effect on demand for output. But government expenditures, along with investment, add to consumer demand for the total output of firms. So government expenditures increase the demand for output. The point of equilibrium is now the point at which savings equals intended investment *plus government expenditures.* (Remember that without the existence of taxes, all these expenditures must be financed by borrowing.)

In Figure 9-8, the II + G (intended investment plus government expenditures) function is parallel to the investment II function, and also parallel to the horizontal axis. We are assuming here that government expenditures are determined only by political factors and are not affected by the level of income of the economy. This is, of course, not a realistic assumption, but the real factors involved *are* largely political, and this assumption is useful for simplifying our model. If you understand this simple model, you can experiment with your own assumptions about how government expenditures vary with the level of national income.

To repeat, with government expenditures included, a nation's equilibrium income is the income at which *savings equals intended investment plus government expenditures*. This is income A in Figure 9-8, and 390 in Table 9-5. (*Note:* Our discussion will rely mainly on Figure 9-8, but you can also follow it in Table 9-5. As earlier in this chapter, we have inserted number values after the letter symbols from Figure 9-8).[1]

Table 9-5

Government Expenditures Added to the Data in Table 9-1

Income	Consumption	Savings (S)	Intended Investment (II)	Government Expenditures (G)
210	240	–30	20	10
240	260	–20	20	10
270	280	–10	20	10
300	300	0	20	10
330	320	10	20	10
360	340	20	20	10
390*	360*	30*	20*	10*
420	380	40	20	10
450	400	50	20	10

Note: The equilibrium level of income (S = II + G) is 390 and is equal to A in Figure 9-1. Income B in Figure 9-1 equals 450, and income H equals 360.

Let's assume a level of income that is above A (390), say, the high income level of B (450). Businesses produce for investment BD (20), for government demand DE (10), and the rest for consumption EG (420). The public, however, cautiously insists on saving BF (50) and consumes only FG (400). So business is producing more for consumption (EG =420) than the public is consuming (FG = 400), creating involuntary (unplanned) additions to inventory, in the amount of EF (20). Businesses cut orders to manufacturers, and try to decrease the unwanted stockpile of goods. Manufacturers suffer dwindling output and income, so they lay off workers. Income moves to the equilibrium level A (390).

At any income below this, say at H (360), businesses produce for investment HI (20), for government demand IJ (10), and for consumption JK (330). The public saves HI (20), and consumes the remainder, IK (340). This means that businesses are producing less for consumption (JK = 330) than the public demands (IK = 340). The results are involuntary (unplanned) reductions in inventory, equal to IJ (10). Businesses increase their orders to manufacturers. Manufacturers increase their output, have a welcome surge of income, and hire more workers. Income again moves toward A (390), the equilibrium level.

It is only at the equilibrium level of income that production for investment plus government expenditures equals savings, and that the amount produced for consumption equals the amount consumed. At that level, there are neither involuntary increases nor involuntary decreases in inventory. Income

1. Please note that equilibrium is now 390 at point (A) when we add government spending to our analysis. In the earlier sections of this chapter, equilibrium point (A) was 360 without government spending.

stays at a particular equilibrium level, however, only as long as the various functions in the model are constant.

Figure 9-9
Aggregate Demand (C + II + G) Equals Aggregate Supply

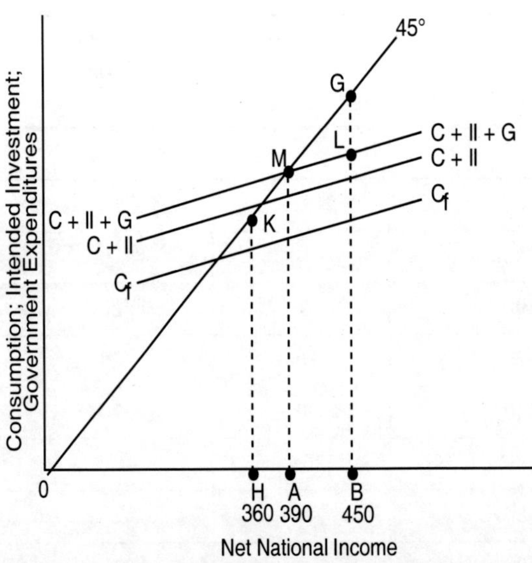

This is a basic model shown earlier in this chapter with the addition of government expenditures. Aggregate demand becomes consumption plus intended investment plus government expenditures (C + II + G). Equilibrium income is again at the level at which aggregate quantity demanded equals aggregate quantity supplied (point M) on the (45° line)

Another Approach: Aggregate Quantity Demanded Equals Aggregate Quantity Supplied

Now let's consider government expenditures and the consumption function, and how they fit into the aggregate-quantity-demanded-equals-aggregate-quantity-supplied approach to equilibrium income. Figure 9-9 shows government expenditures added to consumption plus intended investment: C + II + G, which all now add up to aggregate demand. (Aggregate supply is still the 45° line.) The equilibrium level of income is A (390), where aggregate quantity demanded and aggregate quantity supplied are equal. When income is B (450), *above* the equilibrium level, quantity demanded is less than quantity supplied. Businesses produce more than the public demands and inventories begin to pile up, so businesses cut their orders to suppliers. The results are losses in income, drops in output, rises in unemployment. The level of income moves down toward A (390), the equilibrium level.

When income is H (360), *below* the equilibrium level, quantity demanded exceeds quantity supplied. Businesses produce less than the public demands, and inventories melt away, so businesses rush new orders to suppliers. The results are gains in income and in output and rises in employment. Income moves up, toward the equilibrium level A (390).

Earlier, the equilibrium income without government was 360, because consumption (340) plus investment (20) was equal to aggregate quantity supplied at income level 360. In our new model with government, aggregate demand increases by 10 (government expenditures), and because of the multiplier the equilibrium level of income increases by 30, to 390.

Figure 9-10
Savings Equals Intended Investment Plus Aggregate Quantity Demanded Equals Aggregate Quantity Supplied

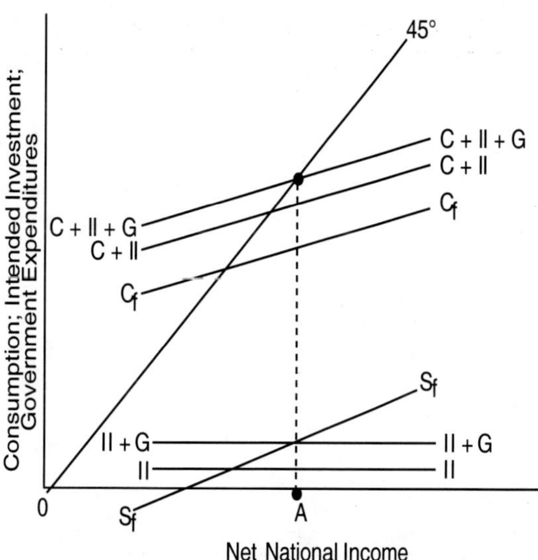

Now we combine Figure 9-8 with Figure 9-9 to get Figure 9-10. You can see that *both* approaches, savings equals intended investment, and aggregate quantity demanded equals aggregate quantity supplied, generate the *same equilibrium level of income,* A (390).

Adding Taxes to the Basic Model

Consumption, investment, and government expenditures together make up aggregate demand, Savings, as we have noted, *reduce* aggregate demand (because savings decrease consumption).

Now let's add taxes to our model. Taxes affect two components of the model: consumption and savings. You pay taxes out of income that you would have chosen to spend on consumption, or perhaps to use partly for savings.

Suppose that there were no taxes. How much of that income would you have spent on consumption and how much would you have saved? As we saw in the first part of this chapter, that would depend on your marginal propensities to consume and to save. Since taxes change our disposable income, this means that the multiplier concept applies. Suppose taxes are levied at $30 billion (Table 9-6). This would cause disposable income to shrink by $30 billion, and it would affect people at all levels of income. If our marginal propensity to consume were two-thirds (as it is in Table 9-6), our consumption function would shift downward by two-thirds of $30 billion, or by $20 billion. At the same time, since our marginal propensity to save is one-third, our savings function would shift downward by $10 billion. Figures 9-11, 9-12, and 9-13, plus Table 9-6, show what happens when taxes are included in the model.

Note that including taxes shifts both consumption and savings functions down proportionately, so that the new functions are parallel to the old. We are assuming that all the taxes are proportional taxes rather than progressive or regressive taxes. If taxes are proportional, there is no change in the distribution of income or in the marginal propensity to consume and to save; thus C_f and C_{at} are parallel in the figures, as are S_f and S_{at}.

Table 9-6
A More Complete Model of a Nation's Economy, Including Government Expenditures and Taxes

Inco me	Consumption Before Taxes	Consumption After Taxes	Savings Before Taxes	Savings After Taxes	II	G	Taxes
210	240	220	–30	–40	20	10	30
240	260	240	–20	–30	20	10	30
270	280	260	–10	–20	20	10	30
300	300	280	0	–10	20	10	30
330	320	300	10	0	20	10	30
360	340	320	20	10	20	10	30
390	360	340	30	20	20	10	30
420	380	360	40	30	20	10	30
450	400	380	50	40	20	10	30

One Approach: Savings Plus Taxes Equals Intended Investment Plus Government Expenditures

You can see in Figure 9-11 that introducing taxes into the model causes the savings function S_f to shift downward. Taxes are measured by the vertical distance from savings after taxes (S_{at}) to taxes plus savings after taxes ($T + S_{at}$).

Figure 9-11
Another Addition to the Simple Model: Savings Plus Taxes Equals Intended Investment Plus Government Expenditures

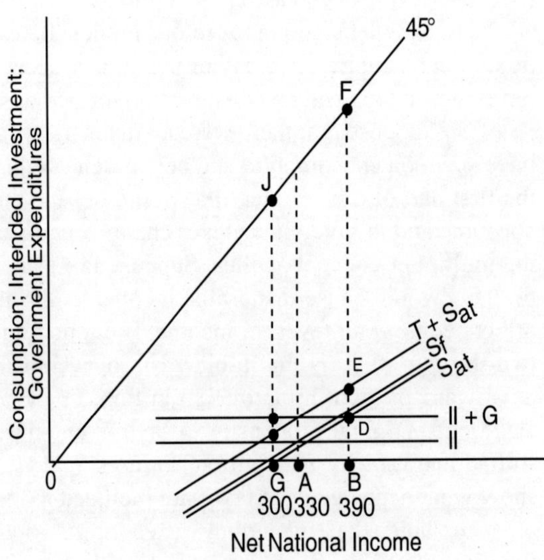

When taxes are included, the savings function drops to S_{at} (savings after taxes). S = II + G becomes S + T = II + G. Equilibrium income is now A.

Now that we have added taxes and government expenditures to the model, the savings-equals-intended-investment approach becomes the *taxes* plus savings-equal-intended-investment plus government expenditures approach. Now two main factors reduce consumption demand: taxes and savings. That elusive equilibrium level of income is now the level at which these two main factors, savings and taxes, are offset by two supplemental elements of demand: intended investment and government expenditures.
The process can be expressed algebraically:

$$C + S + T = \text{aggregate supply (income)},$$

$$C + II + G = \text{aggregate demand (for products)}.$$

In an equilibrium situation:

$$C + S + T = C + II + G.$$

When you subtract C from both sides:

$$S + T = II + G \text{ (A in Figure 9-11, or 330 in Table 9-6).}$$ [2]

Those who prefer graphic illustrations may look at Figure 9-11. The equilibrium level of income is A (330 in Table 9-6).

How does it happen that equilibrium income is only 330 now that we have added the effects of taxes? In Figure 9-8 and Table 9-5 the equilibrium level was 390. But that was when we were counting only government expenditures. Add taxes, and the level goes down by 60 points, to 330. Why? Income B (390), in Figure 9-11, is now *above* the equilibrium. At that level businesses produce BD (30) for investment and the government, and the rest (DF, or 360) for consumption. The public wishes to consume only EF (340) and use the rest (BE, or 50) for savings and taxes. This lowers the quantity of goods that businesses sell. Inventories pile up (DE, or 20), so firms cut their orders to suppliers. Manufacturers cut output, lay off workers, and lose money. The national level of income drifts downward, toward equilibrium at A (330).

The reverse happens at income level G (300), because that's *below* the equilibrium level. So businesses produce only IJ (270) for consumption, plus GI (30) for investment and the government. But the public consumes HJ (280), and uses the rest (GH, or 20) for savings and taxes. So they're consuming more than business is producing, with the usual results: unplanned reduction of inventories (HI, or 10). Businesses increase their orders, manufacturers increase their output, hire more workers, and earn more money. The national level of income drifts upward, toward equilibrium at A (330).

Another Approach: Aggregate Quantity Demanded Equals Aggregate Quantity Supplied

Now let's try a different approach, aggregate quantity demanded equals aggregate quantity supplied, and see if the same formula for equilibrium income holds, now that we have added taxes to the picture. People pay part of their taxes with money they would have spent on consumption and part out of money that they would otherwise have saved. In Figure 9-12, consumption shifts down from

---

2. Please note that with the addition of taxes to this model the new equilibrium, at point (A), is now 330.

C_f to C_{at}. As it does so, aggregate demand also shifts down, to C_{at} + II + G. This means that equilibrium income is again at the level at which aggregate quantity demanded equals aggregate quantity supplied-income level A (330).

At income B (390), aggregate demand (BK, or 370) is less than aggregate supply (BF, or 390). The excess supply of KF (20) causes business firms to cut orders to manufacturers, who in turn cut output, lose income, and then must lay off workers. National income drifts downward, toward A (330), as it did when we used the approach of savings plus taxes equal investment plus government expenditures.

At income G, or 300, aggregate quantity demanded GL (310) is greater than aggregate quantity supplied GJ (300). This excess demand JL (10) causes businesses to increase orders to manufacturers, who in turn increase output, income, and number of workers. National income drifts upward, toward the equilibrium level A (330).

By now the process should be clear. In Figure 9-13, the same equilibrium level of income (A) is reached by approaching the problem from the standpoint of savings plus taxes equal investment plus government expenditures (equilibrium point B), or by approaching it from the standpoint of aggregate quantity demanded equals aggregate quantity supplied (equilibrium point C).

Figure 9-12

The Effect of Taxes on the Nation's Economy: Aggregate Quantity Demanded Equals Aggregate Quantity Supplied

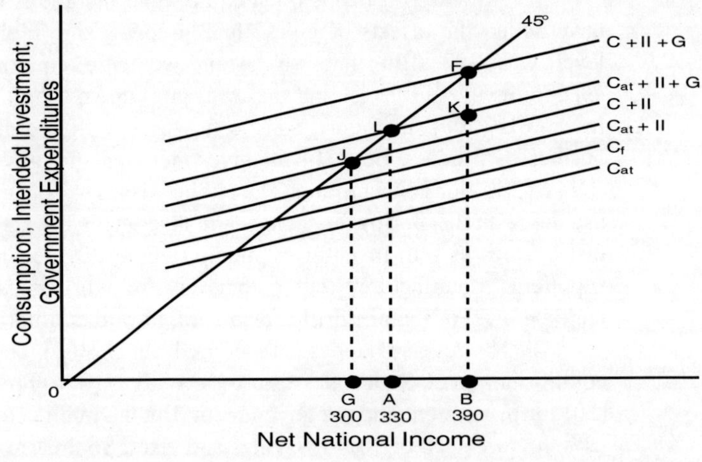

When taxes are included, the consumption function drops to C_{at} (consumption after taxes), bringing aggregate demand down to C_{at} + II + G. Equilibrium income is now A, at which level aggregate quantity demanded equals aggregate quantity supplied.

Figure 9-13
The Effect of Taxes on the Nation's Economy: S + T = II + G, and Aggregate Quantity Demanded Equals Aggregate Quantity Supplied

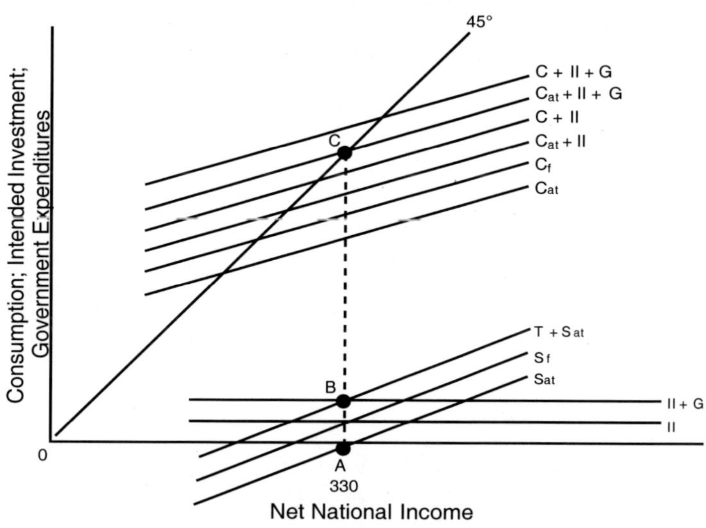

One obtains the same equilibrium level of income whether one uses savings plus taxes equals intended investment plus government expenditures, or aggregate quantity demanded equals aggregate quantity supplied.

Deflationary and Inflationary Gaps

Keynesians, as we know, conclude that a nation's economy does not always move toward a full-employment equilibrium level of income. A country could be at an equilibrium level of income and still have unemployment. *Or* it could have full employment. *Or* it could have inflation. There are not sufficient market mechanisms to bring income to full employment, that presumably is socially preferred.

The Deflationary Gap

Look at Figure 9-14. Suppose that there is full employment at B, but that the equilibrium level of income is only A. Let us suppose, as Keynesians do, that the economy's producers will respond to an increase in demand by offering larger quantities supplied at existing prices (the horizontal portion of the aggregate supply curve). It is obvious there is unemployment. To do away with this unemployment, income would have to increase by AB. However, it is apparent that the economy could not maintain an income of B. The reason is that at point B, aggregate supply would exceed aggregate demand by DE, and inventory changes would then cause income to drop back to A. An increase in demand of DE would be needed in order to achieve full employment. This gap, DE, is called the **deflationary gap**. To get rid of it and to push income up to the level B, aggregate demand would have to shift to E. How could this be achieved? There are several ways: by increasing consumption, by increasing investment, or by increasing government expenditures. It can also be done by reducing taxes and savings. In the 1980s, a combination of tax cuts and investment tax credits together with federal budget deficits increased aggregate demand. This expansionary influence was also accompanied, however, by an increase in aggregate

Deflationary Gap
The amount by which aggregate demand would have to increase to move net national income to its full-employment level.

supply which reduced any inflationary pressures that might otherwise have existed.

Figure 9-14
A Deflationary Gap

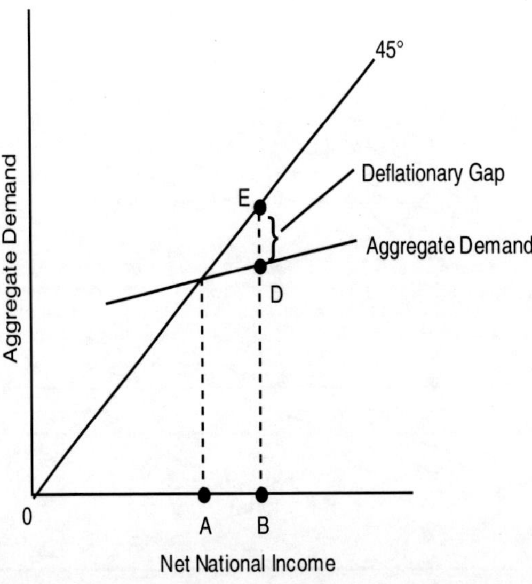

Although equilibrium income is A, the income that will achieve full employment is B. The deficit between actual demand and demand necessary to obtain full employment is DE, called the deflationary gap.

An Inflationary Gap

Figure 9-15 shows another situation, in which equilibrium income is again A, but this time the level at which there is full employment is F. If you look at that aggregate-demand curve, you will see that the economy cannot maintain the F level, because of excess demand. This excess demand will cause money incomes to go up to A. But there was already full employment at F. Manufacturers cannot hire more workers (there are none to hire), so they cannot increase output. How would you go about moving money income from F to A? If you increase prices, the result is inflation.

Clearly, the economy is operating in the capacity or vertical range of aggregate supply and the gap can only result in price increases with no increase in real output. This excess demand (GH in Figure 9-15) is called the **inflationary gap**. To keep prices from increasing, you would have to decrease aggregate demand: lower consumption, cut down investment, or cut down government expenditures. In the inflationary year of 1981, for example, consumption and investment spending were sharply curtailed by the higher interest rates resulting from a tightened monetary policy.

Inflationary Gap
The amount by which aggregate demand would have to decrease to move net national income to its full-employment (non-inflationary) level.

In brief, a *de*flationary gap is the deficit in demand that leads to unemployment, and an *in*flationary gap is the excess of demand that leads to inflation.

Figure 9-15
An Inflationary Gap

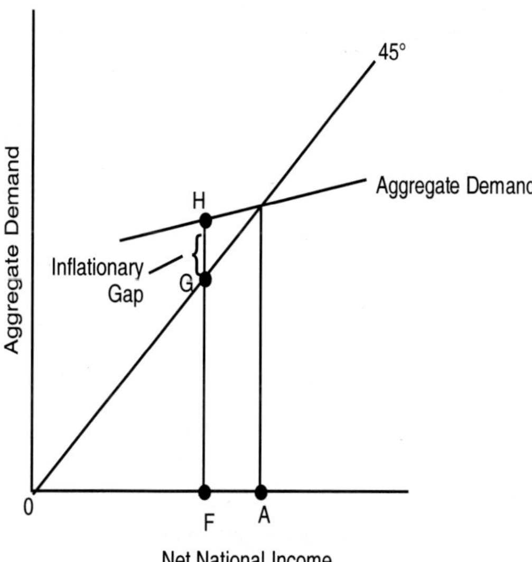

Although equilibrium income is A, the income that will achieve full employment and relatively stable prices is F. The excess demand, which causes inflation, is GH, called the *inflationary gap.*

The Balanced-Budget Multiplier

Balanced-Budget Multiplier
The change in net national income that results when both government expenditures and taxes change in the same direction and by the same amount.

The government sector includes (1) government expenditures and (2) taxes. Suppose the government decides it must increase its *expenditures* by $10 billion this year. It also decides to increase *taxes* by $10 billion at the same time. When both G and T increase by the same amount, the equilibrium level of income also increases by the same amount. When both decrease by the same amount, what happens? The opposite is true. Thus, the curious result that when governments undertake a balanced-budget decrease in taxes and in expenditures, equilibrium income falls by the amount of the decrease. The **balanced-budget multiplier** is one.

We can explain this best through an example. Suppose that government expenditures and taxes both increase by 10 and that the marginal propensity to consume is three-fourths, or .75. An increase in government expenditures of 10 means that aggregate demand goes up by 10. Now comes the difficult part. When *taxes* go up by 10, only 75 percent of that increase (remember that MPC = .75) has a depressing effect on consumption. It is assumed that people take the extra 25 percent of the tax increase out of their savings. In other words, consumption drops by 75 percent of 10, or 7.5. So government expenditures add 10 to aggregate demand, but taxes reduce aggregate demand by 7.5. The net effect on aggregate demand is thus an increase of only 2.5. Yet we have just said that equilibrium income will rise by 10. This happens because 2.5 is one-fourth of 10, so when the MPC is .75, the multiplier is four. If you multiply 2.5 by four you get 10. It looks like this:

$$M = \frac{1}{1 - MPC} = \frac{1}{0.25}$$

$$4 \text{ X } 2.5 = 10$$

(Remember that the multiplier applies to changes in aggregate demand and that the balanced-budget multiplier applies to equal and same-direction changes in taxes and government expenditures.) With aggregate demand increased by 2.5 and with a multiplier of four, total income increases by 10. In brief, when the government makes a balanced-budget increase of 10 (that means increasing both expenditures and taxes by 10), the equilibrium level of income also increases by 10. No matter what the marginal propensity to consume, the results are the same. You can test this by choosing a different MPC and using the same $10 for government spending and taxes. The important point to remember is that changes in government expenditures have a direct and more powerful effect on aggregate demand than do tax changes of the same magnitude. The existence of the balanced-budget multiplier emphasizes the fact that changes in the federal budget are not neutral, they affect the level of income even when the changes are of a balanced-budget nature.

Fiscal Policy

In the days before Keynes, the classical economists favored little government involvement in business affairs, a balanced national budget, and a government that used as few resources as possible. These tenets were based on the idea that when a market economy developed problems, it would automatically adjust itself so that the problems disappeared.

Is There a Self-Correcting Mechanism for the Economy?

We do not wish to leave you with the impression that economists since Keynes have concluded that market economies have no self-correcting mechanisms. While Keynes argued that such mechanisms could not be relied on to create full employment, evidence for the period since 1930 clearly indicates their existence. Wages and prices, in other words, are not completely inflexible. In the 1930s, for instance, wages and prices fell and this undoubtedly contributed to the slight recovery of 1936. The deep recession of 1981-1982, in another example, saw the economy operating at an estimated $265 billion below its GDP potential or capacity. Again, wages and prices fell, at least their rates of increase fell sharply. This point can be seen in Figure 9-16. Both wages and prices were growing at rates in excess of 9 percent in 1981. By 1986, their rates had been cut to 3 to 4 percent.

Most economists since Keynes, however, seem to argue that it would be unwise to simply wait for the workings of this wage-cost-price mechanism to correct either deflationary or inflationary gaps, though there are some who think all government intervention through fiscal or monetary policy or wage-price controls distorts and delays the self-correcting mechanism. The preponderance of view, however, seems to be that intervention appropriately timed and in the appropriate amounts is called for to reduce the delays in the self-correcting mechanism.

The makers of government economic policy have three aggregate demand based approaches they can use to try to make the situation better:

1. **Fiscal policy**. Raise or lower government expenditures and taxes (as in the tax cuts of the 1960s, in the early 1980s, in 1992 and in 2002 and 2003).

2. **Monetary policy**. Vary the supply of money and the rate of interest (as in the restrictive monetary policies of 1981, 1982, and 1995 and the expansionary monetary policy of 2001-2013).

3. **Incomes policy**. Fix wages, prices, and profits (as in the Nixon wage and price freeze of the early 1970s and the monetary policy of 2001-2003).

It is important to note that for these policy tools to work as intended they must be appropriately designed both in direction and timing. Some argue that the deep recession of 2008-2010 had it origins at least partially in the low interest rates maintained by the Federal Reserve System in the early 2000's.

We will explore the workings of fiscal policy more fully in the next chapter. Monetary policy, its workings and the debates about its effectiveness, will be more fully covered in the chapter after the fiscal policy chapter.

Figure 9-16
Rates of Growth in the United States. Wages and Prices, 2003-2011

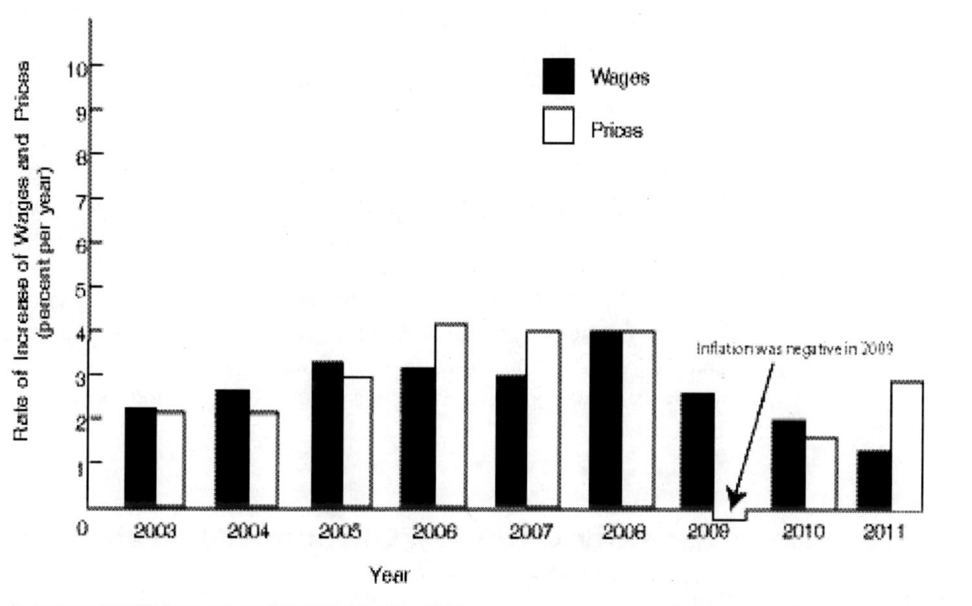

Source: Economic Report of the President and Bureau of Labor Statistics, 2012.

STAGE III: COMPLETING THE KEYNESIAN MODEL: THE EFFECTS OF NET EXPORTS

To this point, we have modeled the Keynesian macroeconomy as if it is closed, one in which aggregate demand is determined by the expenditure plans of domestic households, investors, and governments. In fact, however, all economies, including that of the United States are open; they experience a demand for their goods from other nations (export sales) and they also demand goods produced in other nations (import purchases). The difference between the value of exports (X) and that of imports (M), as we already know, is called *net exports* (X_N). Thus, where X = export and M = imports:

$$x_n = x\text{-}m.$$

Clearly, the value of exports may equal the value of imports and X_N may be zero in which case net exports have no effect on aggregate demand. The value of exports may exceed the value of imports and $X_N > 0$ means that net exports add to aggregate demand. The value of exports may also be less than the value of imports and $X_N < 0$ means that net exports reduce aggregate demand. Whichever is the case, net exports become a fourth expenditure stream that must be added to planned consumption spending (C), intended investment (II) spending, and government expenditures (G) to measure aggregate demand at various levels of national income. This aggregate demand in Stage III becomes:

$$\text{Aggregate demand (AD)} = C + II + G + X_N$$

A SIMPLIFYING ASSUMPTION ABOUT NET EXPORTS

The relationship between changes in national income and changes in net exports is complex. It seems reasonable that imports are desirable goods and that as domestic income grows, the quantities of such goods demanded rise. It is less clear that foreigners buy more of our exports as *our* incomes rise. Indeed, income growth in those other nations, together with exchange rate changes would be far clearer and more influential on the volume of our exports. On the basis of this reasoning, then, net exports probably tend to decline as domestic incomes rise, *ceteris paribus* (holding other factors such as overseas income growth constant).

For the sake of simplicity and to illustrate the basic relationship between X_N and aggregate demand, we will assume that net exports are positive and are a *constant* addition to aggregate demand at all levels of national income. The more complicated relationships can safely be left to more advanced courses in macroeconomics.

MACROECONOMIC EQUILIBRIUM WITH POSITIVE NET EXPORTS

We know that equilibrium in the macroeconomy occurs when aggregate planned spending is made equal to aggregate planned supply. In Figure 9-17, we see how that equilibrium is affected by our assumption of a constant and positive level of net exports at all possible income levels. Total expenditure is the vertical sum of consumption expenditures (C_{at}) plus intended investment expenditures (II) plus government expenditures (G) plus net exports (X_N). The resulting function (C_{at} + II + G + X_N) contains many possible income levels. In Figure 9-17, however, there is only one level at which planned spending is equal to planned output. That is at E where the aggregate expenditure function intersects the 45° line which, in the Keynesian model, represents planned output or aggregate supply. Note that at any level of national income below E, planned spending lies above or is greater than planned output. Firms respond by planning to produce more which raises national income. At any income level greater than E, planned output exceeds planned spending. Firms reduce output which reduces national income. Only at E, the equilibrium level of income and output, are expenditure plans equal to output plans.

A FINAL REMINDER: KEYNESIAN AND CLASSICAL EQUILIBRIUM

We began by comparing and contrasting classical and Keynesian assumptions about equilibrium in the macroeconomy. Both view equilibrium alike; it is the level of income toward which an economy tends to move in view of the underlying aggregate supply and demand conditions. Classical economists believe that market flexibility (changing wages and prices) will move the economy toward a full employment equilibrium in the long run. Keynesian macroeconomists believe that it is inventory adjustments or changes in planned output that will resolve equilibrium. Keynesians, however, reject the view that such adjustments will necessarily create full employment even in the long run. That leads Keynesians to argue for discretionary government expenditure policies that will raise aggregate demand and move the economy toward a full employment equilibrium level of income. We will look at such policies, called fiscal policies, in the next chapter. A third group of economists called **Post-Keynesians** or **New Keynesians** argue even more strongly for government intervention. This group, evolving since the 1930s, concludes that wages and prices are not flexible and calls for strong government intervention often in the form of an incomes policy involving wage and price controls.

Post-Keynesian ("New Keynesians")
A group who purport to build on early Keynesian theory and who argue for strong government intervention to create full employment and stable prices.

Figure 9-17
The Effect of Net Exports on the Nation's Economy: Aggregate Quantity Demanded Equals Aggregate Quantity Supplied

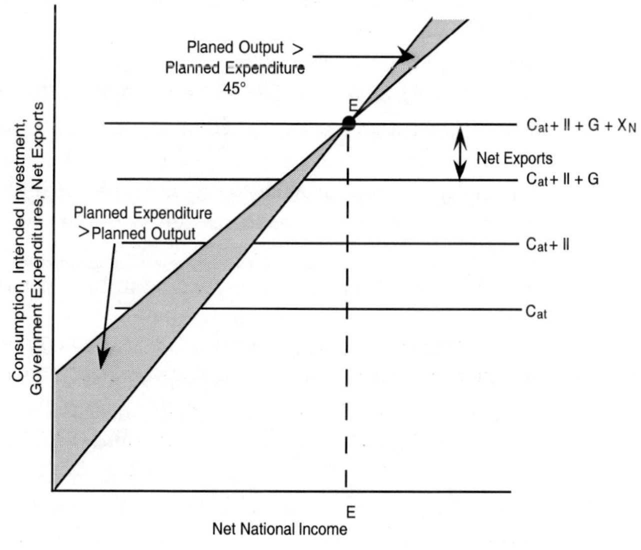

In Figure 9-17, net exports are added to domestic aggregate demand to determine total aggregate demand. C_{at} represents planned consumption after taxes, C_{at} + II represents total private spending by consumers and investors. C_{at} + II + G represents total planned domestic spending including government expenditures. C_{at} + + II + G + X_N represents total planned spending including a constant amount of net exports. E is the equilibrium level of net national income. At any smaller level of income, planned spending exceeds planned output (represented by the 45° aggregate supply line). At any greater income level, planned output exceeds planned spending. At E, aggregate quantity demanded equals aggregate quantity supplied.

Application I: The Modern U.S. Economy: A Record of Growth, Recession, and Depression

In this chapter we talked about the Keynesian system of income determination in a private-enterprise, market-oriented economy. We saw that the multiplier effect and the accelerator principle lead to expansion and contraction. According to the Keynesian and Post-Keynesian arguments, a market economy such as that of the U.S. has no in-built tendency toward full employment. How does the experience of America's market economy compare with this model? Let's look into this and discuss economic stability in our economy. We shall explore, in brief, the history of economic fluctuations in the United States since the 1920s, in order to gain a better insight into the factors that cause the irregular cycles of economic growth and recession in the last 75 years.

The Roaring 20s

From 1922 to 1929, the economy expanded rapidly from a low of $70 billion in money GDP in 1921 to a high of $104.4 billion in 1929. This expansion was marred by two mild recessions, one in 1924 and the other in 1927. Even so, there was less than 5 percent unemployment in these downturns. Prices declined somewhat between 1921 and 1929, from a price index of 52.8 in 1921 to an index of 51.3 in 1929. (1967 is used as a base year. In other words, in 1967 the index was 100.)

The two main bases of the prosperity of the 1920s were (1) the expansion of the construction industry and (2) the increase in output of a number of "new" industries, especially the automotive industry. Both residential and business construction expanded through 1926, but then residential construction began to fall off. Further expansion in business construction, however, maintained the increases into 1927, at which time they began to decline.

This development of new industries in the 1920s seen in Keynesian terms was a main cause of high aggregate demand. Radios, electric power, chemicals, telephones, motion pictures, durable consumer appliances, and cars, especially cars, contributed to the boom. Although most of these industries were not new in the 1920s, they grew up in that decade. **Primary demand** (that is, demand by those who had never owned certain goods before) was large. Automobile production went from 2.2 million per year in 1920 to 5.5 million by 1929, more than double in nine years.

Primary Demand
Demand for products created by first-time buyers.

The direct effect of this expansion was that people began to demand these new products in increasing numbers. ("I'd give anything to have a refrigerator. You never have to empty the drip pan, and you don't have to stay home to let the ice man in.") Many industries supplying goods to manufacture new products were stimulated as well. Car makers had to have vast quantities of raw materials and semifinished parts. Their needs stimulated booms in the steel, rubber, glass, textile, and petroleum industries and created a new service industry: gasoline retailing. Governments (mainly local and state) built $10 billion worth of roads for these new machines. But most important were the capital investments that auto makers had to make for plant and equipment to expand their production capacity.

Despite the general prosperity, there were some weak spots in the economy. The agricultural sector was semi-depressed throughout the decade due to many factors.

A problem that soon became more serious than the rest was developing over the international means of payments. After World War I, the German government owed huge sums of money (reparations) to the Allies. The U.S. treasury encouraged private individuals and institutions to lend more to the

German government, so that Germany might pay war reparations to England, France, and Italy, so that in turn these countries could pay to the United States the money they borrowed during World War I. This was a very circular process and in the long run dangerous to the economy. (We shall say more about this later.)

The Great Depression: Phase I

In 1929 the U.S. economy, and for that matter, the world economy, entered a recession that became the worst depression in history. Money GDP in the United States fell from about $104 billion in 1929 to about $56 billion by 1933. Unemployment in 1933 increased to the highest level ever: 25 percent of the labor force was unemployed and another 25 percent was partially employed. Prices dropped by about 24 percent. Oddly enough, the very factors that led to the prosperity of the 1920s laid the foundations for the depression.

The large primary demand for automobiles (demand by those who had never had cars before), and for the products of the other new industries, was beginning to drop off by 1929. There was a time lag before the onset of **secondary (replacement) demand** (demand for products to replace consumer goods), which was needed to prop up demand to the levels of 1929.

Secondary (Replacement) Demand
Demand that is created when consumers replace products.

Figure 9-18
Growth Curve of the Automobile Industry

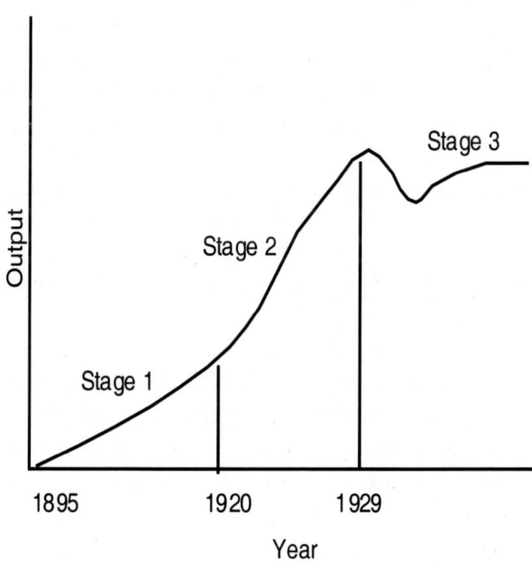

To see this, look at Figure 9-18, which is an idealized version of the life cycle of the automotive industry. During Stage I (1895-1920), people invented the automobile and worked to improve it. This stage is referred to as *the perfection of the innovation*. Note that the rate of growth of demand is relatively slow. In Stage II (1920-1929) the perfected innovation enters the primary market, and it catches on quickly. In Stage III (beginning in 1929) primary demand has become saturated.

While the shift to replacement demand is going on, excess capacity develops. Output falls from its 1929 high. As the demand for the products of the new industries fell, a negative accelerator effect appeared, and there was a fall in induced investment, both in the new industries themselves and in those industries that had been stimulated by them. By June of 1929, there was excess capacity, so people decreased their investing. Manufacturing output declined. The construction industry, the second major stimulator of the 1920s economy, had been hit by excess capacity and falling output as early as the middle of 1927. By the end of 1929, it had collapsed.

To put it in Keynesian terms: As demand fell toward the end of 1929, investment fell also. The large savings caused by the widening of the profit margins reduced consumption demand. Aggregate demand fell, and so did income.

For a year the stock market had been going up. Prices of stocks rose rapidly in relation to potential earnings. In October of 1929 the market simply collapsed. Another key function of the stock market is to mirror the psychological view of investors and during the year before the crash, it mirrored such optimism that few noted the signs of decline. After the crash, pessimism ruled and many people felt there was no hope.

From 1929 to 1933, the U.S. banking system also came close to complete collapse. When the stock market crashed, it crashed so quickly that banks were left holding large amounts of corporate stock, a huge capital loss. In addition, banks owned large numbers of mortgages. When mortgage holders could no longer make their monthly payments and real estate values plummeted, the banks were left holding innumerable chunks of illiquid property. All these factors eroded their asset position, and banks began to fail. People panicked. Long queues of frantic people lined up outside banks, waiting to withdraw deposits. This caused even secure banks to fail. By 1933, when Roosevelt took office, the banking system was in a desperate position.

As the U.S. banking system deteriorated, so did international trade, and quickly, too. The shift from government ownership to private ownership of war debts meant that private means of international payments became linked to reparations and war-debt payments. When the market collapsed in 1929, the structure of repayment of war debts crumbled also, bringing down the private system of international payments. A further blow to international trade came in 1931, when the United States started a round of retaliatory tariff increases that further reduced exports and put a damper on world production.

Weak Recovery: 1933-1937

When Roosevelt became president in 1933, government spending rose and this had the effect of creating what were, for that time, large deficits. Congress also passed a series of laws aimed at correcting weaknesses in the economy, though some, by encouraging monopoly, would be seen by many economists as counterproductive.

The national debt jumped from $19.5 billion in 1932 to $36.5 billion by 1937, an increase of $17 billion in five years. This stimulated an increase in GDP of $35 billion between 1933 and 1937. Private investment remained low, however. (In 1929 net private domestic investment was $8.3 billion. By 1933 it had dropped to *minus* $5.6 billion, and in 1937 it was still only $4.6 billion.)

The Recession of 1937-1939

President Roosevelt, concerned about the increasing federal deficits, decided that private investment should shoulder more of the task of coping with the continued depression. So in 1937 the federal government reduced deficit expenditures. At the same time, monetary policy was tightened. In the face of higher interest rates and weak demand, private investment, however, failed to take up the slack and continue the expansion. As a result, output declined and unemployment increased from about 14 percent to 18 percent. In 1938, the Social Security system went into effect. The taxes associated with this system reduced disposable incomes and probably contributed to the recession. For the first time in the history of U.S. business cycles, a second recession came along before the economy had recovered from the first.

The Early Forties and World War II

During 1940 and 1941, as the United States increased its military expenditures and its exports to its allies, who were already at war, the recovery began to quicken. Keynesians saw in this the multiplier and accelerator effects of this increased output in the form of increases in both consumption and investment.

When the United States entered the war, on December 7, 1941, the economy went all out in the war effort. However, because there was so much unemployment left over from the depression of the 1930s (unemployment was still at 10 percent in 1941), the economy did not reach full employment until the beginning of the third quarter of 1942. Until then, there had been sharp increases in output of military goods, consumer goods, and investment goods. Once full employment was achieved (the vertical range of aggregate supply), the economy had to cut back on the production of investment and consumer goods in order to continue to increase output of goods needed by the military.

Since there was full employment and plenty of overtime work, people had higher personal incomes. Yet the nation's need for more and more military goods reduced the availability of consumer goods. The government prevented excess demand by imposing higher taxes and price controls and by encouraging people to save and to buy government bonds. Thus large amounts of personal savings, plus price and wage controls and rationing, kept inflation within reasonable bounds.

The Postwar Boom: 1945-1948

At the end of the war, there was a slight dip in the economy as the United States shifted from military production to civilian production. Then, despite many people's fears that there would be a repeat of the 1930s, the economy began to expand rapidly. Even though the government cut back its military spending by more that $55 billion, the demand for consumer goods, investment, and export goods created a boom.

Because of the depression and then the war, both business investment and consumer demand had been kept low for fifteen years. After the war ended, businesses rushed to invest in plant and equipment, because of depreciation, obsolescence, and the need to reconvert to peacetime production.

Americans were not alone in their headlong rush to achieve the good life, to gratify demands they had postponed for so long. They were joined by the rest of the world. Exports rose to new highs as a war-ravaged world turned to the United States for consumer goods and for investment to rebuild the world's economy. Unfortunately, under the impact of all this demand, inflation developed.

The Recession of 1949 and the Expansion of 1950-1953

In late 1948 the economy had its first postwar recession, a short, mild downturn caused primarily by excess inventory that businesses accumulated as output temporarily outstripped demand. In June of 1950, war broke out in Korea, and the recovery from the 1949 slump accelerated and became another boom. Consumers, fearing another round of inflation and also fearing that the government would again put on controls, increased their purchases. As the Cold War became hotter, the government increased its military expenditures, both to fight the war and to increase U.S. military strength in general.

The Recession of 1954 and the Expansion of 1955-1957

When the Korean War ended, consumers stopped buying so much, and so did the government; inventories piled up. In 1954 along came a recession. This too was mild and short, however, because the government took prompt fiscal and monetary steps to ease the situation. A tax cut plus an easy money policy softened the downturn.

In 1955 a boom in residential construction and in demand for consumer durable goods, especially cars, caused U.S. national output to expand quickly. But in 1956 and 1957, the market for consumer durables, saturated by the sales of 1955, again sagged. However, the economy held steady because of increases in producer durable goods and in nonresidential construction.

The Recession of 1958

By the end of 1957 the investment boom slacked off. Demand for consumer durables was still as a low point after the saturation of the 1955 boom. And the government further restricted demand, both by cutting its expenditures and by following what many people considered a too tight money policy. The result was the most severe recession to come along since the war.

Weak Recovery in 1960-1961 Followed by the Expansion of 1962-1969

Although the recession of 1958 was severe, it was short, less than one year. Business recovered, consumer demand picked up, and so did government demand, so that 1959 saw a renewed expansion. However, this recovery was not strong enough, and the economy went through another recession in 1960 and 1961, a mild one this time.

Between 1962 and 1969 the economy expanded without interruption, the longest expansion in U.S. history until the 1980s. Yet, early in the sixties Presidents Kennedy and Johnson were both concerned about the slowness of growth, the high unemployment rates (between 5 and 6 percent between 1962 and 1964), and the perception of a problem of chronic poverty.

The government used deliberate economic policy to combat these problems. To attack chronic poverty, there was Johnson's (largely unsuccessful) "War on Poverty." The government stepped up its expenditures, which in Keynesian terms gave some stimulation to the economy. The real stimuli, however, were the Johnson tax cuts in 1964 and 1965. The 1964 tax cut alone amounted to \$11 billion, which had a marked effect on the economy: Unemployment fell from 5.2 percent in 1964 to 4.5 percent in 1965. As the tax cut worked, the economy moved toward full employment.

The 1965 escalation in Vietnam compounded our problems, as defense expenditures increased from \$50 billion in 1965 to \$80 billion by 1968. Government, all levels of government, increased spending during this period, pouring out money, especially on schools and highways. Then, too, people's demand for consumer goods continued to be enormous, which caused a spurt in the growth of the GDP. Unemployment fell to 3.5 percent by 1969.

Excess aggregate demand, however, soon lead to substantial inflation. The consumer price index rose from 92.9 in 1964 to 109.8 in 1969, 17 points in only five years, in large measure caused by the overheating of the economy; that is, by demand-pull inflation on an economy operating near capacity.

Light Ahead

Inflation and Unemployment in 1970-1971: Wage and Price Controls in 1971-1973

Toward the end of the sixties there was such a high rate of inflation that in 1969 the government, in alarm, adopted some restrictive policies. The effect was only to increase unemployment. It was a repetition of 1958. The economy suffered from the worst of conditions, **stagflation**: high unemployment and high inflation.

Stagflation
A term used to describe the combination of high unemployment and a high rate of inflation.

In 1971, although the economy was beginning to recover and GDP was expanding, prices were still rising. The balance of payments was worsening, and unemployment was still high. Existing fiscal and monetary policy seemed inadequate to policy makers to deal with all these problems at the same time. So in August of 1971 President Nixon took several steps, announcing fiscal programs designed to increase demand and employment, a 90-day wage and price freeze, and the first of a number of "phases" to control prices. Also, to help the balance of payments, Nixon floated the dollar in international exchange markets. All this took everybody by surprise. A few weeks before, Nixon had said that he did not believe in controls and that he would never devalue the American dollar.

In 1972 price increases were noticeably less, and so was unemployment. Our balance of payments improved, and GDP increased sharply. As a result, in Phase II and Phase III, Nixon loosened price controls. But in 1973 prices went up again, by about 8 percent, and the dollar depreciated by 12 percent on the international market. So one might say that Nixon's medicine did not work in the long run.

Inflation and Unemployment Again: 1974 to 1976

From 1974 to 1976 unemployment rose rapidly to more than 8 percent. Inflation passed 12 percent, for 1974, and real GDP rose very slowly after first falling. Stagflation seemed to many to have become built into the economy.

In the mid-1970s, the central problem seemed to be how an economy could combat at the same time high unemployment, falling or very slowly growing real GDP, and significant inflation. Simply using fiscal and monetary policy to expand the economy, to reduce unemployment, and to contract the economy in order to control inflation was not feasible.

Recovery: 1977 to 1979

The stagflation concerns subsided somewhat as favorable monetary policies and continuing federal deficits stimulated the economy. As unemployment fell from 7.1 percent to 5.8 percent, real GDP grew by about 8 percent. A continuing high rate of inflation (almost 20 percent growth in the CPI) led many to conclude that productivity and supply were not growing rapidly enough in the United States.

Recession Followed by Growth and Deficits: 1980-1989

The supply shocks of sharp energy price increases from OPEC II led to rising costs, declining aggregate supply and rising unemployment. Unemployment reached almost 10 percent and the economy entered double digit inflation (13.5 percent from 1979 to 1980). A change of administration in 1981 led to tax cuts and efforts to stimulate both aggregate demand and aggregate supply. Supply-side economic policies became the focus of public macroeconomic policy. To combat inflation, restrictive monetary policies were pursued with a sharp recession resulting in 1982-1983, and unemployment peaking at 9.7 percent in 1982. Thereafter, the stimulative effects of easier monetary policies, tax cuts, investment tax credits and large federal budget deficits combined to reduce unemployment (to 5 percent in late 1989) and cut inflation rates (the CPI rose only about 2 percent annually from 1985 to 1986 and at rates of 3 percent to 4 percent from 1986 through 1989). Large trade deficits to be financed and very large budget deficits remained key problems.

1991-2007

The economy lapsed into recession in 1991. By now, there was little sympathy for an incomes policy and in view of the large national debt and federal deficits, little ability to employ Keynesian stimuli to the economy. By late 1994, and following a period of cost reducing measures by firms, the economy began to grow substantially and with little evidence of inflation.

That growth continued to 2001 and the result was the longest period of such expansion in the nation's history. By late 2001, the economy slowed with a brief recession followed by slow growth. In 2004, the economy returned to its historical growth path and has continued to grow into 2007.

2008-2011

In December, 2007, the American economy moved into the great recession. That recession continued into mid 2009 and was quite sharp. By 2010, the economy experienced very slow growth and was out of the recession and into very slow growth. Some have compared this recession with the "Great Depression" of the 1930s which, as we saw earlier, did not end until 1940-1941. In 2009 and 2010, there were huge federal expenditures that were designed to restore equilibrium and growth in America's market economy. Will this effort succeed? To do so, it will be necessary not only to increase aggregate demand but to stimulate the investments necessary to increase productivity and create new jobs. While this did not happen in the 1930s, monetary policy is working in tandem with fiscal policy which may enhance the chances of success. For an update on the economy at the beginning of 2009.

A Judgment About Stability

Is American capitalism inherently unstable? You can see from this short record of the past sixty years that the U.S. economy is subject to oscillations in levels of output, employment, and prices. We have even seen that many combinations of these three can exist at the same time.

The U.S. economy can experience severe drops in prices, income, and employment (the recessions and depressions prior to 1945). It can also have stable or near-stable prices, low unemployment, and expanding output (as in the 1920s and the mid to late 1980s and the 1990s). It can have expansions accompanied by substantial inflation (1945-1948, 1950-1953, 1955-1957, 1965-1969, 1972-1973, 1977-1979). Finally, recession, with falling real incomes and high unemployment, can occur at the same time as sharp increases in prices (1958, 1970-1971, and 1974 to late 1975).

Let us sum up this overview with the following: The American economy clearly is growth oriented. Its long-term trend in terms of real income and employment has been upward. Standards of living have risen secularly and by the late 1980s, a larger percentage than ever of the potential labor force was employed. In 2004, the unemployment rate was as low as 5.4 percent and has continued at 4 to 5 percent in the years since. Yet, the nation, historically, continues to be plagued by cyclical variations that sometimes are sharp. Is there a way to have long-term growth without these cycles? Unfortunately, at this point in time, economic theory provides no clear answer to this question.

SUMMING UP

1. This chapter relates levels of planned expenditures by consumers, investors, and government to planned savings and taxes in order to understand equilibrium levels of national income in the macroeconomy. It does so in three stages, first without government expenditures and taxes, and second with those factors included. Finally, it incorporates the influence of foreign trade on the equilibrium by including the influence of net exports (exports minus imports) on the equilibrium level of incomeincome.

2. In Stage I, we build a model of an economy omitting the factors of government and taxes and using only consumption, savings, and investment. The equilibrium level of income in such an economy is at the level at which savings equal intended investment. At income levels above equilibrium, people consume less than businesses produce for consumption. Businesses face *unplanned* or *involuntary additions to inventories*, which means that they then will cut their orders to manufacturers. The results are reductions in output, employment, and income.

3. At income levels below equilibrium, people consume more than businesses produce for consumption. Businesses experience *unplanned* or *involuntary reductions in inventories*, which cause them to increase their orders to manufacturers. The results are increased output, employment, and income.

4. *Ex-ante investment* is investment that is desired or planned. *Ex-post investment* is investment that actually takes place. Ex-post (actual) investment always equals savings, because involuntary additions to or subtractions from inventories cause these two factors to be equal. An equilibrium income occurs only when ex-ante and ex-post investment and ex-ante and ex-post savings are all

equal. At that point, all expectations or plans of businesses and the public are satisfied.

5. In our simple, *non*government model, aggregate *demand* is consumption plus intended investment, and aggregate *supply* is the 45° line in our Keynesian diagram. An economy reaches equilibrium income when aggregate supply and aggregate demand intersect. When the income level is above equilibrium, aggregate quantity supplied is greater than aggregate quantity demanded, and unplanned increases in business inventory push the level of income back toward equilibrium. At income levels below equilibrium, aggregate quantity demanded is greater than aggregate quantity supplied, and unplanned decreases in business inventory push the level of income up toward equilibrium.

6. The two approaches, (a) savings equals intended investment, and (b) aggregate demand equals aggregate supply, produce the same result: the same level of income.

7. The *average propensity to consume* (APC) is the percentage of a specific level of income that people tend to spend in consumption:

$$\text{APC} = \frac{C}{Y}$$

The *average propensity to save* (APS) is the percentage of a specific level of income that people tend to save:

$$\text{APS} = \frac{S}{Y}$$

The *marginal propensity to consume* (MPC) is the percentage of any *change* in income that people tend to spend on consumption:

$$\text{MPC} = \frac{\Delta C}{\Delta Y}$$

The *marginal propensity to save* (MPS) is the percentage of any *change* in income that people tend to save:

$$\text{MPS} = \frac{\Delta S}{\Delta Y}$$

8. When aggregate demand shifts, income changes. However, a given change in aggregate demand causes income to change by an amount larger than the initial change in demand, an effect called the *multiplier effect.* The multiple that the change in income is of the initial change in aggregate demand is the *multiplier.*

9. The multiplier effect is due to the fact that the marginal propensity to consume is greater than zero. When people have an increase in income, from whatever source, they do not save all of it. They spend part of it, which generates demand for more goods, thus creating more income.

10. The *multiplier formula* is

$$\text{M} = \frac{1}{1 - MPC} \quad \text{or} \quad \text{M} = \frac{1}{MPS}$$

The multiplier is the reciprocal of the marginal propensity to save.

11. *Induced investment* is investment brought on by increases in income, which cause people to consume a greater quantity of goods and services. In turn, this increases the demand for more capacity (capital) to produce the greater quantity of goods and services.

12. By means of the *accelerator principle*, one can analyze the ups and downs of induced investment over time. An increase in the rate of growth of consumer demand causes a much larger increase in the demand for additional capacity. However, any decrease in the rate of growth of consumer demand causes a much larger decrease in the demand for additional capacity.

13. The accelerator principle introduces an element of economic instability, in that, after an economy reaches full capacity during a recovery, increases in the rate of growth of consumer demand generate large increases in induced investment. This causes income to expand rapidly. At some point, the rate of growth in consumer demand begins to slow down, and a negative accelerator (due to declining induced investment) pulls the level of income and the economy down.

14. Induced investment causes the intended investment (II) function to slope upward, so that economies with higher levels of investment have higher levels of income. (We are assuming a positive accelerator here.)

15. The *paradox of thrift* is that during a depression or recession, when the savings function shifts upward because everyone wishes to save more, income falls because of a fall in aggregate demand. This causes the quantity saved to decline. The paradox of thrift is based on the presumption that increased investment will not offset the increases in planned savings. The argument applies only to severe declines or recessions and does *not* mean that an adequate supply of savings and low interest rates is unimportant to economic growth.

16. Governments today exert a major influence on aggregate demand both directly through their expenditures and indirectly through their tax policies.

17. When one includes government expenditures in the Keynesian model, and diagrams the G *(government)* curve so that it intersects savings, the equilibrium level of income is where savings equals intended investment plus government expenditures. At incomes *above* the equilibrium level, businesses produce more for consumption than the public consumes, and therefore have involuntary additions to inventories. At incomes *below* the equilibrium level, businesses produce less for consumption than the public consumes, and therefore have involuntary reductions in inventory.

18. When one includes government expenditures in the simple model, aggregate demand becomes consumption plus investment plus government expenditures. The equilibrium level of income is still the point at which aggregate quantity demanded equals aggregate quantity supplied (the 45° line). At incomes above that, businesses supply more goods and services than the public demands, and thus have unplanned additions to inventory. Therefore, income moves down toward equilibrium. At incomes below the equilibrium level, aggregate quantity demanded is greater than quantity supplied, and businesses have unplanned reductions in inventory. Thus, income also moves up, toward equilibrium.

19. People pay their taxes in part from money they would have spent on consumption and in part from income they would have saved. So taxes shift both

the consumption function and the savings function downward. How great the shift is depends on the marginal propensities to consume and to save.

20. When one includes taxes in the Keynesian model, the equilibrium level of income becomes the level at which taxes plus savings equals intended investment plus government expenditures. At incomes above the equilibrium level, businesses produce less for investment and for the government than people save and pay out in taxes, so that businesses produce more than the public consumes. Thus, businesses have involuntary accumulation of inventories, and income moves toward the equilibrium level. The reverse occurs at incomes below the equilibrium level.

21. For equilibrium to exist, aggregate quantity demanded must still equal aggregate quantity supplied, even after taxes and government expenditures are added. Now, however, taxes push down the C_f, and thus the rest of aggregate demand. At incomes above the equilibrium level, aggregate quantity supplied exceeds aggregate quantity demanded. This excess supply causes income to fall. When incomes are below the equilibrium level, the reverse occurs.

22. When the level of demand in an economy is below that which creates a full employment income, this deficiency in demand creates a *deflationary gap*. When an economy has a greater than full employment demand, the excess of demand creates an *inflationary gap*.

23. When there is a balanced-budget change (a change in which government expenditures and taxes move in the same direction and by the same amount), the equilibrium level of income changes by the same amount and in the same direction. The *balanced-budget multiplier* is equal to one. Income changes because any change in expenditures affects aggregate demand by the full amount, while a change in taxes affects *only* aggregate demand by that portion the public takes away from consumption to pay taxes. The public dips into savings to pay part of the tax increase.

24. The experience of the 1980s suggests that there is a self-correcting mechanism in the economy, at least in the case of inflationary gaps. Wage and price growth slowed in the face of high unemployment rates. Many economists, though, would regard it as unwise to rely solely on this slow self-corrective mechanism to deal with inflationary and deflationary gaps. Governments may intervene to influence demand through the use of fiscal policy, monetary policy or through an incomes policy.

25. Completing the Keynesian model requires modeling an open economy, one in which net exports (exports minus imports) are a fourth expenditure stream.

26. Net exports (X_N) may be zero ($X = M$), positive ($X > M$), or negative ($X < M$). We model for simplicity as $X > M$ by a constant amount.

27. Aggregate demand in an open economy is now $AD = C + II + G + X_N$.

28. Equilibrium: Income in the Keynesian open economy occurs when planned aggregate demand equals planned aggregate supply. At income levels below equilibrium planned aggregate demand (expenditure) > planned aggregate supply (output). The reverse holds for income levels above equilibrium.

29. Recall that in both Keynesian and classical views macroeconomies tend toward equilibrium levels of income and to restore equilibrium when there is a change in aggregate demand or supply. Classical economists argue that wage and price flexibility will restore equilibrium at full employment in the long run and that government intervention is harmful to the workings of the markets in doing that. Keynesian economists, on the other hand, do not believe that there is sufficient wage and price flexibility to assure a full employment level of aggregate demand and national income. Keynesians and Post-Keynesians argue that government intervention (fiscal policy, monetary policy, incomes policy) is necessary to assure a movement toward full employment.

KEY TERMS

Accelerator principle
Average propensity to consume
Average propensity to save
Balanced-budget multiplier
Deflationary gap
Discretionary fiscal policy
Ex-ante investment
Ex-post investment
Inflationary gap
Instantaneous multiplier
Marginal propensity to consume
Marginal propensity to save
Multiplier
Multiplier effect
Multiplier formula
Net Exports
Periodic multiplier
Post-Keynesians
Primary demand
Secondary (replacement) demand
Stagflation
Unplanned or involuntary additions to inventory
Unplanned or involuntary reductions in inventory

QUESTIONS

1. Answer the following questions based on the figure below:

   a. The 45° line represents (1) aggregate demand or (2) aggregate supply?
   b. The C + II represents (1) aggregate demand or (2) aggregate supply?
   c. The equilibrium level of net national income is (1) 500, (2) 400, or (3) 300?
   d. The distance HI at income 500 represents (1) excess inventory accumulation or (2) an inventory deficit?
   e. The distance BJ at income 300 represents (1) excess intended saving or (2) excess intended investment?

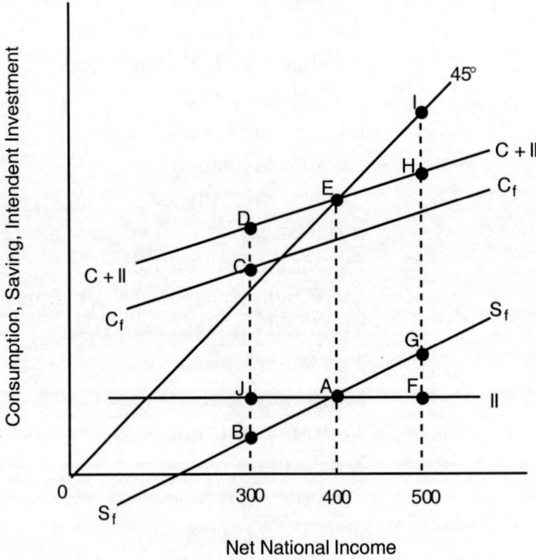

2. Assume that the MPC = 2/3 and the APC = 2/3.
   a. Suppose that the equilibrium level of income equals 300. What are the equilibrium levels of consumption, investment, and savings? Assume that government expenditures and taxes are both zero.
   b. Suppose that for the situation in part a, investment increases by 10. What are the new equilibrium levels of income, consumption, savings, and investment? Explain your answers.

3. Show how one may use a multiplier-accelerator model to explain business cycles.

4. During a recession, would it be in an individual's self-interest to increase her or his savings? Would it be in the interest of the whole economy if everybody increased savings during the recession? Why? On what assumption is this "paradox of thrift" based?

5. One economist said, "Savings always equals investment, whether the economy is at equilibrium or not." What makes that condition true? If an economy is not at equilibrium, what will occur to bring it toward the equilibrium point?

6. Using the figure below, answer the following questions:

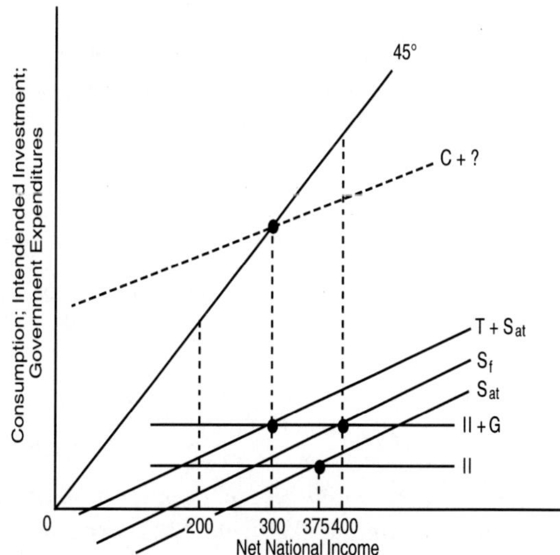

a. Equilibrium net national income using the intended investment + government expenditure approach is (a) 400, (b) 375, (c) 200, or (d) 300?

b. Equilibrium net national income using the aggregate quantity demanded equals aggregate quantity supplied approach would be (a) 400, (b) 375, (c) 200, or (d) 300?

c. The line labeled C + ?, in the figure above, represents aggregate demand including government expenditures, taxes, and net exports. What should the line be labeled (a) C + II, (b) C_{at} (c) C + II + G, or (d) C_{at} + II + G + X_N?

7. Assume that the MPC = 2/3, the APC = 2/3, and the equilibrium level of income is 300.

a. Government expenditures increase by 10. What is the new equilibrium level of income, consumption, savings, investment, and government expenditures? Explain your answers.

b. Assume that taxes increase by 10, in addition to the increase in government expenditures in part a. What is the new equilibrium level of income, consumption, savings, investment, government expenditures, and taxes?

8. Parts a and b of question 2 depict a balanced-budget increase; you should show an increase in income of 10 by the end of part b.
Use a different MPC, and recompute a and b. With different MPCs, is the balanced-budget multiplier still one?

9. How can one use a multiplier-accelerator model to explain business cycles?

10. How can one get rid of a deflationary gap? an inflationary gap?

11. If one wishes to stimulate aggregate demand by increasing government expenditures, the form in which the government makes these expenditures makes no difference. A dollar of expenditures is a dollar of expenditures! Do you agree? Explain (and be complete).

12. Do you agree with classical economists or with Keynesians and Post-Keynesians in the argument about relying on self-correcting mechanisms to solve problems of inflationary and deflation gaps? Why?

13. What influence do net exports have on the equilibrium level of national income in the Keynesian macroeconomy?

14. What factors that contributed to the expansion of the 1920s helped to lay the foundations for the Great Depression of the 1930s?

15. What were the major factors contributing to economic expansion during the 1960s? What problems did they create?

16. Trace the origins of the recession-inflation of 1974 to 1976. What economic policy do you think would have been appropriate to handle the situation? Explain your reasoning.

17. What seems to have been the state of the economy from 1977 to 1979?

18. What effects did OPEC II have on the economy in 1979-1980?

19. From 1980 to 1981 what happened to unemployment, inflation and GDP growth?

20. What factors seem to have contributed to the prolonged expansion of the economy between 1982 and 1990, as well as the long expansion of the 1990s?

21. Will Keynesian remedies to be practiced in the financial crisis of 2008-2009 be successful?

Chapter 10: Fiscal Policy, Deficit Financing, and the National Debt

The nature and extent of the federal government's role in influencing and guiding the economy toward growth, full employment, and price stability are subjects of continuing controversy. That controversy played a major role in the presidential election of 2008. In 1946, the Employment Act spelled out the federal government's macro-economic responsibility as follows:

> *"It is the continuing policy and responsibility of the Federal Government to use all practical means consistent with its needs and obligations and other essential considerations of national policy to coordinate and utilize all its plans, functions, and resources for the purpose of creating and maintaining, in a manner calculated to foster and promote free competitive enterprise and the general welfare, conditions under which there will be afforded useful employment opportunities, including; self-employment for those able, willing, and seeking to work, and to promote maximum employment, production, and purchasing power."*

Fiscal Policy
Variations in government expenditures and taxation.

For most of the period since World War II, **fiscal policy**, variations in government expenditures and taxation, has been a major tool in federal government efforts to guide the economy toward growth and acceptable levels of employment. From the previous chapter, we know that the Keynesian model suggests what that role should be. It also suggests how fiscal policy can be used to fill deficiencies in aggregate demand during recessions and restrain excessive aggregate demand during inflationary periods.

In this chapter, we will look at the various ways tax changes and expenditure changes affect the macroeconomy. We will also examine the record of modern fiscal policy as well as the federal government's budgetary process to assess the widely perceived problems of large deficits and accumulation of national debt. Finally, we will look at "supply-side" arguments that were again gaining prominence as fiscal policy was reexamined in the mid-1990s. That reexamination required looking not only at effects on aggregate demand but also at effects on aggregate supply.

Discretionary Versus Automatic Fiscal Policy

Discretionary Fiscal Policy
Deliberate changes of government expenditures and/or taxes to achieve particular economic goals.

Non-discretionary Fiscal Policy
Changes in expenditures and tax policies that reduce instability in income and employment.

Automatic Stabilizers

Most fiscal policy discussions focus on **discretionary fiscal policy** which deals with changes in expenditure and tax plans designed to achieve specific macroeconomic goals of full employment and price stability. Such changes result from decisions by Congress and the federal executive, and frequently take the form of legislation. We have seen earlier that there are also automatic stabilizers or non-discretionary changes in fiscal policy connected with fluctuations in economic activity. These include such things as automatic changes in marginal tax rates as incomes fall, and automatic increases in government transfer payments as unemployment rises. While these do not result from current discretionary decisions, they do have stabilizing effects on income and employment, though they are not strong enough to prevent periods of recession and inflation.

Keynesian Arguments About Fiscal Policy

Compensatory Fiscal Policy (Functional Finance)
The argument that fiscal policy changes can vary aggregate demand and lead to output growth with stable prices.

Keynesians argue for **compensatory fiscal policy** (or functional finance) that uses fiscal policy tools to create changes in aggregate demand. These changes, it is argued, acting through multiplier effects, will generate increased employment and growing output with stable prices. How does this work? We see in Figure 10-1 how, based on Keynesian assumptions, it works in the case of a recession.

Suppose that the Keynesian assumption about aggregate supply is warranted. In part (a), with a horizontal aggregate supply, the economy, because of recession, is operating at national income level Y_0 with aggregate price level $\bar{P}_0$. To achieve a full employment level of national income Y_1, it is necessary to augment (shift) aggregate demand from AD to AD', or by the distance AB. Whether done through tax decreases or through government expenditure increases, Y_1 can be achieved with a stable price level, $\bar{P}_0$.

Suppose, on the other hand, as in part (b), the economy, facing the need to increase national income from Y_0 to Y_1, is operating in the upward sloping portion of AS. Though compensatory finance may be employed to increase aggregate demand and induce the necessary growth in national income to reach full employment, two results differ from the Keynesian expectation. They are: (1) inflation, the price level rises from P_0 to P_1, and (2) the amount of tax or expenditure stimulus required to achieve full employment is larger (AC versus AB).

Budget Deficit
The amount by which government expenditures exceed government revenues.

Deficit Finance and the Public Debt

Budget Surplus
The amount by which government revenues exceed government expenditures

Whether seen from the Keynesian viewpoint or from the classical perspective, an important dimension of functional finance is not represented at all in Figure 10-1. Use of government tax and expenditure policies to achieve employment goals may lead to expenditures that are not financed out of current revenues. Tax reductions and expenditure increases in periods of recession mean that the government runs a **budget deficit**, the amount by which current government expenditures exceed current government revenues. Of course, if government deficits during recessions were offset by comparable **budget surpluses** (revenues in excess of expenditures) in periods of economic expansion, the budget would be balanced over the course of business cycles.

Figure 10-1
Using Compensatory Finance to Eliminate a Recession: Keynesian and Non-Keynesian (classical) AS

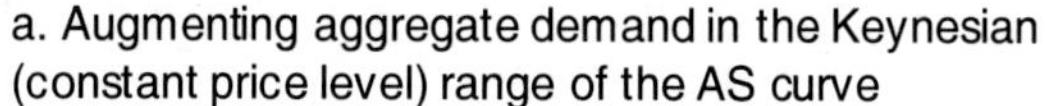

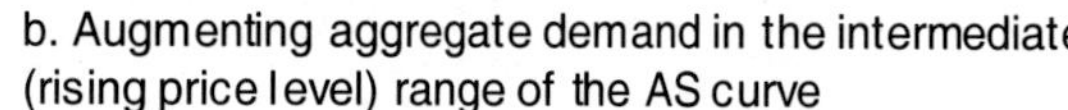

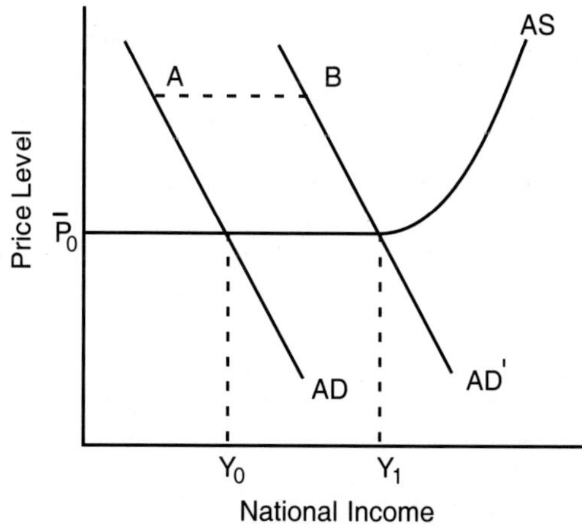

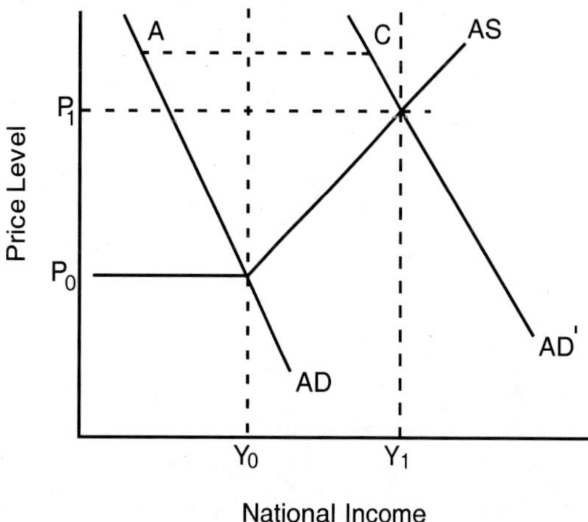

In Figure 10-1, the income level needed to eliminate a recession is Y_1 and the existing level of income is Y_0. A Keynesian fiscal policy is to increase aggregate demand (AD) from AD to AD'. In part (a), the increase in AD needed to increase national income to Y_1 with stable prices $\bar{P}_0$ is AB. In part (b), however, in the intermediate (upward sloping) range of AS, prices rise as AD increases and, because AS rises more slowly, a greater increase in aggregate demand (AC) is necessary to increase national income from Y_0 to Y_1.

Deficits and the Gross National Debt

www.census.gov
For more information on government deficits visit this web site.

Table 10-1 provides an historical overview of the results of not funding federal expenditures out of current revenues. It shows the growth of federal government debt since 1929. It also puts that debt in the perspective of the country's gross domestic product showing it as a percentage of GDP. Interest payments on the debt also are shown as a percentage of GDP, although it is important to remember that all of the data are in current dollars. Were the figures corrected for inflation since 1929, the *real* growth would be much less. In 1929, the federal debt ($16.9 billion) was 16 percent as large as GDP ($103.2 billion) and interest payments ($0.7 billion) on that debt were less than 1 percent of GDP. In 1940, at the end of the Great Depression, the federal debt ($50.7 billion) was 51 percent of GDP ($100.1 billion) and interest payments ($1.1 billion) were 1.1 percent of GDP.

Table 10-1
The Federal Debt, Its Relationship to GDP, Interest on the Debt, and interest payment as a% of GDP (selected years in current dollars)

(1) Year	(2) Federal debt, billions	(3) Gross domestic product, billions	(4) Interest payments, billions	(5) Federal debt as percentage of GDP, (2) ÷ (3)	(6) Interest payments as percentage of GDP, (4) ÷ (3)
1929	$16.9	$103.2	$0.7	16%	0.7%
1940	50.7	100.1	1.1	51	1.1
1950	256.9	286.7	4.5	90	1.6
1960	290.5	513.4	6.8	57	1.3
1970	380.9	1,010.7	14.1	38	1.4
1980	909.0	2,708.0	53.3	34	2.0
1990	3,206.3	5,513.8	177.5	58	3.2
2000	5,628.7	9,708.4	223.0	58	2.3
2005	7,509.3	12,042.4	355	62	2.9
2010	14,350	14,745	381	97	2.6
2011	14,790	15,163	454	98	2.9
2012	16,066	15,776	359	102	2.3

Source: Economic Report of the President, 2013; U.S. Department of Commerce

The federal debt grew greatly during World War II as a result of deficit financing (by sales of federal debt) of much of the war effort. In 1946, the debt reached $271 billion with the debt reaching 128 percent of GDP ($211.6 billion), and with interest payments ($4.2 billion) which were 2 percent of GDP.

After 1950, the debt grew from $256.9 billion (90 percent of GDP) to $908.5 billion (34 percent of GDP) in 1980. In other words, the debt, though growing, was a shrinking part of the GDP "pie." From 1980 to 1990, however, the debt grew more rapidly than GDP. From 34 percent of GDP in 1980, the debt increased to 58 percent of GDP in 1990. Interest on the debt grew from 2 percent of GDP in 1980 to 3.2 percent of GDP in 1990. Between 1990 and 2005, the debt rose from 58 percent of GDP to 62 percent of GDP though, with falling interest rates, interest as a percent of GDP declined to 2.6 percent by 2010.

From 2009 to 2012 the United States ran deficits above $1 trillion a year. Predictions are that the deficit for 2013 will be just under $1 trillion. The deficits are decreasing and this number should continue to decrease as the the United States economy slowly continues to expand.

Growing Concerns About the Federal Deficits

The growth of National debt in the 1980s mirrored the growth in federal deficits in that same period. That increasing expenditures, created primarily to fund increased expenditures on defense and "welfare" programs, were not paid out of current revenues can be seen in Table 10-2. From a deficit of $74 billion in 1980, the excess of federal expenditures over revenues reached $208 billion in 1983, and exceeded $200 billion in six of the fiscal years between 1984 and 1994. By the beginning of the 2000s, the growth of the debt, had created a set of major policy concerns that continue into 2010.

Table 10-2
Annual Federal Deficits (selected fiscal years in billions of dollars)

Year	Deficit
1970	$3.2
1980	73.8
1985	212.0
1990	221.0
2000	+ 236.4 (surplus)
2010	1,293
2012	1,087

Source: Economic Report of the President, 2013

What are the Major Concerns?

1. The *magnitude* of the deficits and the related debt have come to be a major concern. In the 1970s, the average federal deficit was about $35 billion annually. In the early 2000s, the average deficit was $200 to $300 billion. Thus, the tripling (in current dollars) of the federal debt can be tied directly to rapidly growing deficits. What is perhaps equally troublesome is that the deficits are actually *understated.* In all recent years, the Social Security Trust Fund (into which all social security tax receipts are paid) has accumulated large surpluses. The purpose of the fund is to pay for future retirement benefits of many "baby boomers" who are beginning to retire in the twenty-first century. To include these social security tax receipts as current revenues understates the "true" budget deficit. Many economists feel the fund should be "off budget." For example, if the surplus in social security tax revenues had not been included in 1991, the federal deficit would have been $339 billion rather than $269 billion similar results apply to the deficits down to 2010. A caution is, however, in order here. That the social security surplus is (must be) invested in U.S. government securities enhances the security of the fund and does not mean it is used to fund "overspending" by the federal government.

2. A second major concern is connected to the rising percentage of the federal budget that consists of interest payments on the federal debt. As you can see in Table 10-1, interest payments on that debt in 2010 were $381 billion, an amount that exceeds the total deficit in most years of the 1980s! (See Table 10-2). Perhaps the largest problem that follows from this is: As Congress searches for ways to reduce the huge expenditures of 2009-2013, and balance the federal

budget, it finds that it has little discretion in reducing one of the largest items in that budget, *interest on the federal debt.*

3. A third major concern is with the cyclical timing of the *deficits*. Throughout the history of the United States, federal deficits have usually occurred in periods of cyclical downturn (for example, the 1930s) or in periods of wartime or urgent defense needs (for example, during World War II). Although recessions in the early 1980s and 1990s contributed to the size of deficits, clearly, large deficits would have existed even if the economy had operated at or near full employment! The large federal tax increase in 1992 tended to reduce the 1993 and 1994 deficits. Large deficits in an economy operating at low rates of unemployment raise fears of demand-pull inflation. Deficits in 2002, 2003 and 2004 appear to have resulted, at least in part, from tax reductions designed to increase aggregate demand and aggregate supply and decrease unemployment. Deficits in 2010 to 2013 appear to reflect large federal stimulus expenditures as well as unfunded mandates in Social Security and other entitlement programs.

"Crowding-Out" Effect The decline in investment spending that may occur as deficit financing raises interest rates.

4. There is real concern that large deficits will result in a **"crowding-out" effect.** The principle concern is that financing the deficits will increase the demand for financial savings and raise interest rates which, in turn, will reduce investment spending. As this happens, net investment falls leading to a smaller future productive capacity for the economy. Whether this will happen depends on whether it is private consumption or investment that is reduced at the higher interest rates and larger government expenditures. To the extent that investment is "crowded-out," future generations bear the burden because they will "inherit" an economy with less productive capacity. To the extent that present consumption is "crowded-out," the current generation bears the burden.

With the exception of the 1992 federal tax increase, financing of deficits in the 1980s and 1990s was accomplished through sales of government debt in money markets. It appears to us, therefore, that if crowding-out has occurred, most of it was against investment goods and, thus, that the burden lies primarily on future generations' reduced ability to produce and consume. There are, however, two qualifications to this presumed burden on future generations:

a. *The nature of government expenditures.* Just as private expenditures may be on present consumption or on investment, so may government expenditures. If the expenditures giving rise to the deficit are essentially for consumption (food stamps, increased benefits for public employees, and the like), then it is investment that will be "crowded-out" and future generations bear the burden. On the other hand, if the expenditures are for public investment (harbors, dams, flood control on the Mississippi, repairing levees on the Gulf Coast, and the like), then future productive capacity may actually grow though there will be relatively more public capital and relatively less private capital.

b. *The employment effects of government expenditures.* We assumed earlier that most (deficit creating) government expenditures in the 1980s and 1990s occurred when the economy was operating at or near full employment. Some economists have concluded that much of this deficit finance actually *moved* the economy towards full employment through a set of Keynesian multiplier effects. Thus, if substantial unemployment exists when the initial government outlays take place, a movement toward the (full employment) production-possibilities curve can occur without a burden on *either* current consumption or capital investment. This is demonstrated in Figure 10-2.

In Figure 10-2, the economy represented is in recession, operating below its production-possibilities curve. The federal debt is increased through deficit financing and, as a result, interest rates rise from 6 percent to 8 percent.

With investment demand I_1, the interest rate increase causes the quantity demanded of private investment to decline from $20 billion to $15 billion. The $5 billion decrease in investment represents the "crowding-out" effect of deficit financing and leads to a burden on future generations who will "inherit" a less productive economy. As government expenditures financed by the deficit grow, however, employment increases and business profit expectations improve. Expecting higher future profits, firms increase their demand for investment from I_1 to I_2. With the higher investment demand schedule, $20 billion is again the investment demanded even at the higher interest rate of 8 percent.

The central point of this Keynesian argument is that if the "crowding-out" effect occurs it may be offset (as in Figure 10-2), more than offset, or partially offset by the stimulative effects on aggregate demand and investment demand when deficits occur in periods of recession. Research in the 1980s by economists Paul Evans and Robert Barro[1] supports the view that, in fact, government deficits do *not* lead to higher interest rates. Evans and Barro, thus, question the whole notion of "crowding-out."

Figure 10-2
The "Crowding-Out" Effect and the Investment Demand Effect of Government Expenditures

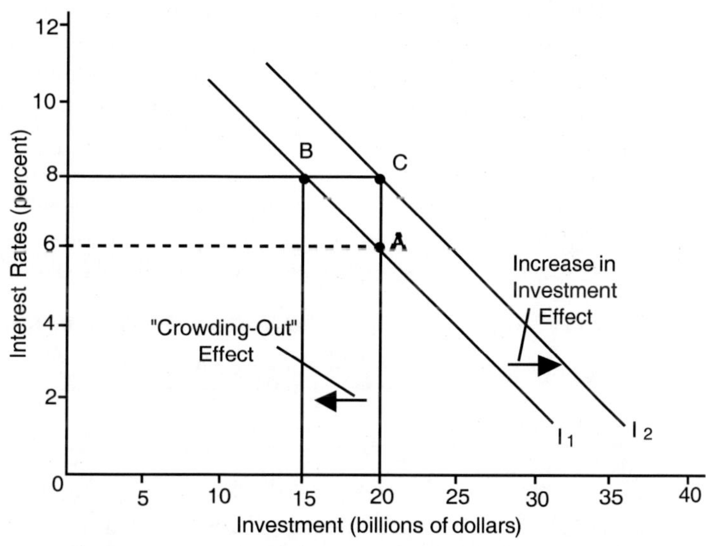

According to the "crowding-out" effect, an increase in interest rates caused by financing a federal deficit will reduce investment expenditures and the productive capacity of the economy inherited by future generations. In this illustration, I_1 is the original investment demand curve. Financing the deficit causes interest rates to increase from 6 percent to 8 percent and the quantity of investment to decline (point A to point B) from $20 billion to $15 billion with a $5 billion "crowding-out." However, the increased government expenditures stimulate the economy, improving business profit expectations and leading to an increase in investment demand from I_1 to I_2 (point B to point C). With interest rates at 8 percent and investment demand I_2, the amount of private investment is $20 billion, and the increase in the investment effect offsets the "crowding-out" effect.

---

1. Evans, Paul. "Interest Rates and Expected Future Budget Deficits in the United States." *Journal of Political Economy*, 95. February, 1987. Barro, Robert. "The Ricardian Approach to Budget Deficits." *Journal of Political Perspectives*, December 3, 1986.

Unfounded Concerns About the Debt and Deficit

There are two often expressed concerns about deficits and associated debt growth that are basically false and unfounded. The first is that the debt will ultimately grow so large that the government, unable to fund its activities, will become bankrupt. The second is that growing debt places an increasing burden on future generations. Let us look at each in turn.

Will Federal Deficits and Growing Debt Bankrupt the Nation?

Will the continued growth of debt ultimately mean the government will be unable to meet its obligations or "pay its bills" as can happen to private individuals and firms? Fundamentally, the answer is no. The reasons for this are three-fold:

1. *Raising revenues.* Under the Constitution, the federal government has the authority to impose and collect taxes. Since 1913, that authority has extended to income taxes, today the largest source of federal revenues. There is usually resistance to tax increases (one of which is the expected negative effects on investment and consumer spending), and there has been much debate in recent years about the federal tax system as well as its rates. The point, though, is that the authority to impose and increase taxes belongs to the government alone. Thus, individuals and firms may become bankrupt; the federal government *cannot.* Sovereign governments may be overthrown by revolution (the 18th century American Revolution and the 1989Russian Revolution, are examples), but they do not become bankrupt.

2. *Ability to refinance the debt.* The Treasury Department and the Federal Reserve refinance a part of the debt as it comes due each month. There is, thus, no practical reason why the debt *must* be reduced or eliminated. New government bonds can be sold to retire or repay maturing ones. Although expenditures could be cut or taxes increased to do the same thing, refinancing is a viable alternative. An important caveat, however, is that the debt must be sold to other countries (eg, China and Japan), these countries, faced with a declining exchange value for the U.S. dollar may resist greatly increasing the holding of U.S. federal debt.

3. *Control over the money supply.* At times, sovereign governments, faced with difficulty in meeting financial obligations, simply create (through the printing press or otherwise) enough money to pay their bills. This, too, is a power alone of governments. Of course, the amount of money created may greatly exceed the growth of goods and services, and inflation will result. There may be severe problems as a result of this but not, in any direct sense, the bankruptcy of the nation.

Will Federal Deficits and Growing Debt Burden Future Generations?

The per capita debt (in current dollars) grew from about $4,000 in 1980 to over $48,358 in 2011. Some in the press, as well as elsewhere, say we are placing a burden on future generations. Does each American born in the 1990s and in future decades have a simple obligation, a net debt, to pay that per capita bill? No. That would be so if the debt did not also represent an offsetting amount of assets, government bonds. While some of the debt (about 28 percent) is owed to foreigners, the vast majority of it (about 72 percent) is owed to American citizens. *The key point, thus, is that every dollar of federal debt is a dollar of credit to someone, and 72 percent of it is a credit to American bondholders.*

Could the debt be repaid? Yes. Would there be a major effect if it were repaid? Emphatically, yes! Repayment would require major increases in taxes and/or reductions in federal expenditures on non-debt service activities. Since the debt is not uniformly held by Americans (some own more than $25,000, some less, some none) repayment would result in a massive transfer of and redistribution of income. The result would not, however, be a decline in total assets or wealth in the United States but a redistribution of those assets and that wealth. Most economists believe that the debt need not be repaid, anyway.

If the burden of the debt is not on future generations, where does it lie? The opportunity cost of the debt is borne by the generation in which it is created. Some of the debt increase since the 1980s has been due to rapid growth in programs that the federal government seemed unable or unwilling, for domestic political reasons, to restrain. Many of its expenditure programs (cost of living increases for social security recipients, growth of welfare benefits, growth of Medicare benefits, stimulus expenditures, and the like) fall into this category. A significant part of the debt increase was also to fund increased defense spending during the "cold war." Now that the "cold war" is over (we won) and the Soviet Union is gone, what was the burden of this failure to fund increased government expenditures (particularly defense goods) out of current (tax) revenues? The answer will take you back to the very definition of opportunity cost. The burden lies in the myriad of other goods and services that could have been consumed if the resources used to produce the actual defense and non-defense goods had been used to produce other goods. In addition, the production of defense goods shifted resources away from capital goods so the next generation will inherit an economy with less productive capacity. There is, thus, a type of inter generational burden.

Generational accounting, developed in the 1990s by Alan Auerbach, Jagdish Gokhale, and Lawrence Kotlikoff[2], is an effort to put the federal government's budget data in a form that shows how different generations are affected (burdened) by government spending policies. It accounts for lifetime net tax rates and lifetime net tax burdens of the present and future generations. In a 1995 study, Auerbach, Gokhale, and Kotlikoff conclude that with present government policies, intergeneration balance would require raising income taxes *permanently* by 43 percent, and cutting federal transfers by 33 percent or government purchases by 32 percent in 1996! In other words, the conclusion is that present fiscal policies are significantly unbalanced in a generational sense.

Debts, Deficits, and the Balance of Trade

We have looked at both the real and the misplaced concerns about the effects on the domestic economy of accumulated federal deficits and debt. Were the United States a closed economy, the concerns could be left at that. Foreign trade (exports and imports) and its finance are not only part of the American economy, however, but an area of increasing importance. Many, though not all, economists believe that there are problems associated with federal budget deficits that make it more difficult to achieve a balance of trade (exports = imports). Paul McCracken[3], a former member of the Council of Economic Advisors, argues

2. Auerbach, Alan J., Jagdish Gokhale and Laurence J. Kotlikoff. "Restoring Generational Balance in U.S. Fiscal Policy What Will It take?" *Economic Review*, Federal Reserve Bank of Cleveland, Vol. 31, No. 1, 1995. Quarter 1.

that the currency depreciation or a weakening dollar (more dollars necessary to buy foreign currencies) experienced in 1995 is, in other words, a vote of no confidence in an American fiscal policy that has failed to move toward a balanced budget. McCracken says that the deficit problem is not that the federal government is "going broke" and that the declining dollar is not a reflection of a weak macroeconomy or of poor monetary policy. He says it is also not the work of speculators. The increased deficits, says McCracken, have caused the Treasury to compete for and take more and more of the supply of domestic savings (which are relatively small anyway) to finance and refinance federal debt. In the 1970s, financing those deficits took about 10 percent of domestic savings; in the 1980s and 1990s, that percentage rose to 20 and 25 percent, respectively and since 2005, the figure has risen to about 25 percent. This has caused a decline in the growth of the domestic capital stock and, as a corollary, a decrease in real income growth. It is true, says McCracken, that net foreign inflows of capital covered some of the difference. The net inflow of foreign *investment*, foreign savings used to finance an increased stock of productive capital, however, has become *negative* (repayments exceeding new investments). McCracken is concerned that the declining exchange rates reflect an underlying decline in confidence that foreign investors have in the future growth of an economy burdened with a low rate of savings coupled with deficit financing that is diverting both domestic and foreign savings into assets (federal government bonds) that do not contribute to increases in future productive capacity. McCracken's argument is directed to the failure of the Balanced Budget Amendment in 1995. We will have more to say about efforts to change federal budgeting in the upcoming section.

Figure 10-3

The Traditional View of Federal Budget Deficits and Balance of Trade Deficits

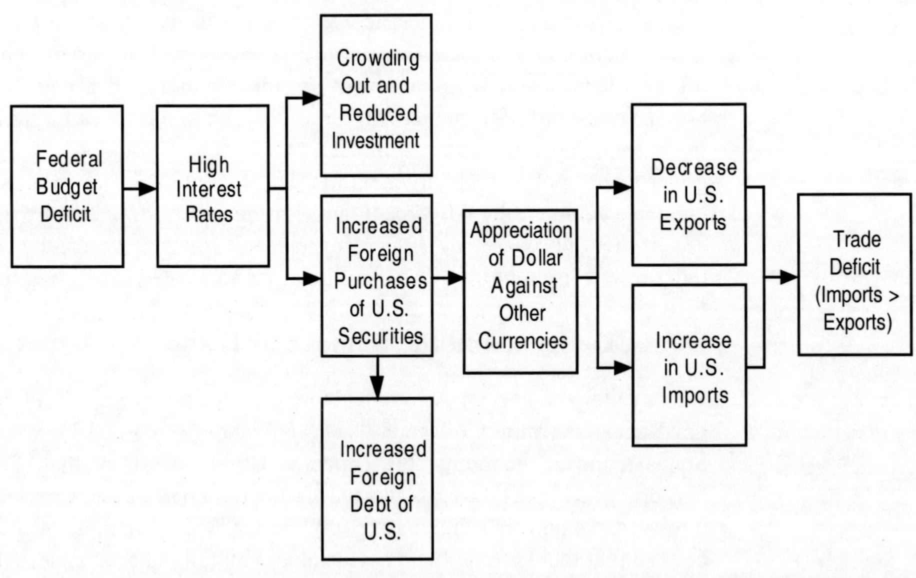

The view of many economists is that federal budget deficits lead, through a series of effects, to trade deficits. First, the deficit increases the demand for savings and leads to higher interest rates in money markets and monetary policy that is restrictive. Higher interest rates lead to "crowding-out" and less domestic investment. The higher interest rates lead to an

3. McCracken, Paul W. "Falling Dollars? Blame the Deficit" *Wall Street Journal*. April 13, 1995.

increased foreign demand for U.S. securities and, thus, to greater foreign debt. Financing the increased purchases of U.S. securities raises the exchange rate of the dollar against other currencies. U.S. exports are now more expensive; U.S. imports are cheaper. The relative increase in imports leads to a deficit in the U.S. balance of trade.

Traditional Arguments About Budget Deficits and Trade Deficits

There are traditional arguments about the relationship between federal deficits and trade deficits that focus on monetary policy, interest rate changes, dollar appreciation, and trade deficits. Though these do not seem to entirely fit the circumstances of the American economy since the early 2000s, it is important to mention them. We see the traditional chain of causality between budget deficits and trade deficits in Figure 10-3. In the first link in the chain, financing a federal budget deficit increases the demand for domestic savings and raises U.S. interest rates relative to those in other nations. It also leads to restrictive monetary policy. In the second link are two effects: (1) a "crowding-out" of domestic investment, and (2) an increased demand for (relatively high interest rate) U.S. securities. As U.S. securities are sold to foreigners, the foreign debt of the U.S. increases (the U.S. is now the world's biggest debtor nation). In the third link, foreigners buy more U.S. dollars to purchase U.S. securities, and this increased demand for U.S. dollars causes the fourth link, an appreciation of the dollar against other currencies (pound sterling, yen, German mark, etc.). Because the dollar is now more expensive, in the fifth link, there is a decrease in (more expensive) U.S. exports and an increase in (less expensive) U.S. imports. In the final link, as imports rise relative to exports, the U.S. balance of trade becomes negative (exports < imports).

It is worth noting that one conclusion of this traditional analysis is that fiscal policy of the sort suggested by the Keynesian model may not be as expansionary as its proponents claim. Deficits employed to fill demand gaps and to increase employment may be at least partially offset by a decline in exports as the dollar appreciates, and declining jobs in the export sector may offset some of the increased employment in the domestic economy.

An Alternative to the Traditional View

Ricardian Equivalence Theorem
The view that deficit finance has the same effects whether done through credit market borrowing or through current tax increases.

There are some economists, including several who are very prominent, who challenge the traditional view. They argue that even if the government goes into credit markets to finance a deficit, the increased demand for savings will not necessarily lead to higher interest rates and the set of linked effects shown in Figure 10-3. These contrarians base their argument on the **Ricardian Equivalence Theorem** which states that financing a deficit by credit market borrowing has the same economic effects as financing it through a current tax increase.

The argument is based on the reactions of individuals to current deficits that must be financed in the future. Aware that deficits today will require higher future taxes to finance the deficits, individual households cut current consumption because they anticipate a reduction in future after-tax incomes and, instead, save more to be able to pay the higher expected future taxes. If this argument is accepted, the first link in the chain of causal events in Figure 10-3 is broken. The increased domestic saving offsets entirely the increased demand for domestic savings and the rise in interest rates is avoided destroying the linkage effects that lead ultimately to a trade deficit. Adherents of the traditional view, who probably constitute most economists, believe that the experience of the American economy since 1980 contradicts the Ricardian Equivalence Theorem. Budget deficits, as we saw earlier, ballooned in the 1980s and the 1990s and are growing very rapidly in 2009-2011, and so did the trade deficits.

Rethinking the American Fiscal System Since the 1990s

In spite of some misplaced concerns, huge deficits and rising federal debt have also ignited real and well-placed concerns not only among economists but also among millions of Americans. The Congressional elections of 1994 focused on some of those concerns. The Presidential election of 2008 again focused, at least partly, on these concerns. For at least a decade, proposals have been made, even some laws passed, to change the federal fiscal system. As we write this revision, major revisions of the system seem uncertain. The complexity of the system and its web of interrelated effects on incentives to risk taking and innovation, and saving and investment, together with its effects on income distribution, promise to make the efforts at revision contentious and difficult. Let's now look at some of the revisions already undertaken as well as some of the proposals for the future.

Efforts at Change Already Made

By the mid-1980s, it was clear to many that budget deficits and the federal debt were skyrocketing. Several Congressional efforts in succeeding years have been undertaken to impose fiscal discipline that would restrain deficits and debt growth.

Gramm-Rudman-Hollings Act (GRH), passed in late 1985, the legislation was intended to produce reductions each year in federal deficits with a goal of achieving a balanced budget by 1991. In 1987, the act was revised to provide for smaller deficit reductions and the goal of a balanced budget shifted forward where it remains.

The basic intent of GRH was to encourage Congress and the president to work together toward annual deficit reductions. Failure to do so would trigger automatic spending cuts. The recession of 1991, together with the huge federal expenditures associated with the Savings and Loan bailout, made GRH unfeasible. The automatic cuts were never made and, in effect, GRH was abandoned.

Budget Legislation Since the 1990s

Passed in late 1990, the Budget Reconciliation Act of 1990 was intended to trim $500 billion of budget deficits between 1991 and 1996. This was to be done through (1) an increase in the top marginal income tax rate, (2) lower deductions, (3) new "luxury" taxes, (4) higher excise tax rates, and (5) higher payroll taxes for Medicare. Decreases in federal spending in the same period of $260 billion were to contribute to deficit reduction. In addition, the Budget Enforcement Act of 1990 required that any increases in federal expenditures (other than emergency expenditures) must be accompanied by equal-sized cuts in existing expenditures or increases in taxes. Tax reductions also were to require equal and offsetting tax increases or expenditure cuts.

These measures, together with the Budget Reconciliation Act of 1993, which raised tax rates, increased taxes on social security benefits, and imposed higher excise taxes on tobacco and other goods, reduced budget deficits in the early twenty-first century. None, however, even has as a goal a balanced budget in the 1990s. (Indeed, deficits have grown again in the early years of the twenty first century.)

Proposals for Further Change

In the 104th Congress that took office in January 1995, a flurry of activity designed to further reform the American fiscal system took place. Some of the most important actions and proposals considered were:

1. A *balanced budget amendment* to the Constitution. The most restrictive action proposed has been to amend the Constitution to require an annual balance in the federal budget. Passed by the House of Representatives in March 1995, the proposal was narrowly defeated in the Senate. Proponents of the amendment argue that only a Constitutional restraint will have sufficient force to cause Congress and the president to take responsible steps to prevent large deficits and continued growth of the debt. Opponents say that such an amendment would tie the federal government's hands in periods of recession and deny it the ability to use compensatory fiscal policy as a counter-cyclical tool. Opponents also point out that in 1993, federal debt as a percent of the GDP fell as a result of the budget actions in the 1990s that we have already discussed. The proposal for a Constitutional amendment seems likely to continue as a way to deal with the country's perceived fiscal problems.

2. *Line-item veto*. Many public finance economists believe that the president should have the authority to veto specific items in appropriations bills while signing the other provisions of the bill into law. It has long been a practice to attach special interest expenditures favorable to groups in a particular congressional or senatorial district to an appropriations bill that contains many other expenditures beneficial to the country as a whole. Without a line-item veto, the president must sign or veto the entire bill. Many see the present system as one that is prone to fiscal "blackmail" and one that makes expenditure reductions very difficult. In early 1995, line-item veto provisions were passed by both the House of Representatives and the Senate.

3. *Privatization*. Proposals continue to be made to make many government programs private. There are three ways in which this may be done: (1) contracting out government activities so that they are undertaken by private firms, (2) selling government assets (oil reserves, power plants, public lands) to private owners, and (3) providing consumers with vouchers which may be used to buy goods and services. Proposals to sell government assets such as the (quasi-public) U.S. Postal Service and Amtrak would yield revenue with which to reduce deficits. Contracting out would lower the cost of government. All such activities rely on the assumption that private firms, faced with an incentive to minimize cost, would be more efficient. Governments could establish standards for such activities but private sector incentives would reduce the amount of resources used to produce the goods and services. Vouchers would allow private individual consumers to make choices about purchases but, again, rely on private firms to produce those goods and services efficiently. Proponents say that government agencies, absent the profit motive, have less incentive to behave efficiently.

4. *Changes in budgetary procedures*. Many public finance economists believe that major changes are needed in federal budgetary procedures.

a. *Budgeting for entitlement programs*. Entitlement programs (social security, food stamps, Medicare, Medicaid, farm subsidies, and the like) pay benefits to any eligible American and have no cap on funding. Such programs, while estimated annually in cost, are not subject to expenditure limits. They are also the most rapidly growing of federal expenditures. As economist Michael Walden[4] says, "Any serious attempt to control federal spending must address the 'open-wallet system' employed with such programs." Proposals have been made to "means test" some; other proposals suggest limiting their growth to inflation and the growth of the eligible population. All such ideas promise to be difficult to enact since they are likely to be opposed by well-organized interest groups with strong preferences to preserve the "open-wallet" approach.

b. *Current account-capital account budgeting.* Current federal budgetary procedures treat all items as being on current account. We know from our earlier discussion that some federal expenditures (roads, bridges, water projects, and the like) involve capital or infrastructure building, projects whose benefits will exist for many years. Other federal expenditures (employee salaries, transfer payments and the like) are to pay for current services or current benefits. The federal government would do well, say many economists, to emulate the practices of private businesses and divide its budget into these two components. The current budget might well be constrained so that all expenditures must be paid out of current revenues. On the other hand, projects in the capital budget might be funded by borrowing just as private firms do. It would still be necessary, of course, to consider whether the resources needed to implement the capital budget would be more productive in the public or in the private sector.

What Should be Government's Share of the GDP Pie?

A fundamental question confronts Americans in 2013. With the Federal government intervening in the economy to "bail out" firms that have taken extreme risks, to "choose the winners and loosers" among unsuccessful firms, it is important to reassess the role of government with respect to businesses.

A most fundamental way to deal with governmental fiscal problems is to ask: What should be its economic role and what part of the GDP must it claim to carry out that role? If retirement programs are included, Michael Walden says this percentage now is 35 percent (28 percent without retirement programs). One could require by law or by constitutional amendment that government spending not exceed that percentage of the GDP. It would, though, be extremely difficult to decide and agree on government's role (something we have been arguing about throughout our national history) as well as its corresponding share of GDP. Even the policy statement of 1946 with which we began this chapter offers no guidance.

A Recap

Throughout our history as a nation, the role of government and its claims on resources to execute its role have been controversial. That controversy has never been more intense than in the period since the 1990s. From the 1960s to the 1980s, Keynesian fiscal policy was in ascendancy and compensatory fiscal policy was used at various times to move the economy toward lower rates of unemployment. In the 1980s, faced with (1) supply-side arguments to use tax cuts to spur economic growth, (2) rising defense expenditures to fight the "cold war," and (3) entitlement programs that were on "automatic pilot" or "open-wallet," federal expenditures grew more rapidly than federal revenues. The financing of

---

4. Walden, Michael. "How Big is Government?" and "Who Pays the Tax Bill?" Chapter 5 in *Economic Issues, Rhetoric and Reality.* Prentice Hall, Englewood Cliffs, New Jersey, 1995.

the ensuing large deficits lead to a huge increase in the federal debt. Since 1985, various efforts have been made to restrain these deficits and the growth of the debt. While some of the efforts in the 1990s produced short-term deficit reductions, no long-term approach has yet been adopted. In light of the large deficits of 2009-2013 and those that are projected through 2015, it may be likely that a combination of approaches, one that limits the rate of growth of federal expenditures, will be adopted. It is, however, by no means clear what that combination will be.

Application I: The "Share Economy," A Replacement for Keynesian Demand Management?

As we have seen in the immediately preceding chapters, the percentage of people unemployed (those who did not work last week and have been looking for work for at least four weeks) has been up and down in a near roller coaster fashion for the last 70 years. The "Keynesian revolution" ascribed this tendency of instability to a lack of wage and price flexibility in the economy. The Keynesian recipe for dealing with that perceived flaw in a modern market economy, was government management of aggregate demand, i.e.; expenditure and tax programs to push the economy toward full employment at stable prices.

From the mid-1980s to the present, there has seemed to be appreciably less enthusiasm for this type of macroeconomic policy. Faced with escalating federal debt and seemingly intractable budget deficits, Keynesian demand management would be difficult to pursue even if it enjoyed widespread political support. A number of economists have undertaken to identify ways to create a tendency toward full employment without major fiscal policy involvement by the federal government. A prominent such effort is that of Economist Martin Weitzman[5] of MIT. In a book entitled *The **Share Economy***, Weitzman argues that both inflation and unemployment problems can be solved by making wages more flexible and by tying the pay of workers at least partly to the profitability of the firms that employ them.

Share Economy
A proposal under which some of the wage earnings of labor would be tied to the profitability of firms.

A Two Wage System

Under Weitzman's proposal, wages would be separated into two components: (1) a base pay that does not vary with firms' profits, and (2) a second component that would fall as profits diminish and rise as profits increase. The current wage system in the U.S. results in lay-off of workers in a recession as firms' cut back production. The result is an increase in unemployment. Under the "share economy" proposals, the (1) non-base component of wages would fall as firms revenues decline, (2) costs of production would decrease, (3) prices could be cut to increase sales, and (4) the work force would be maintained (a scenario of wage and price flexibility similar to the classical one that Keynes sought to disprove). Weitzman thus believes that full employment could be maintained even in the face of a recession.

Weitzman argues that even if only 15 to 25 percent of workers' wages were in the form of profit sharing, this stabilizing influence on unemployment would be effective. This would happen in a "share economy" without sacrificing the resource mobility essential to any capitalist system. Workers would not be laid off when there was a declining demand for a firm's products. If the decline continued though, the firm's profitability and the wages it would offer workers

---

5. Weitzman, Martin."The Share Economy-Can It solve Our Economic Ills?" *U.S. News and World Report*, August 26, 1985.

would fall relative to those in growing industries. When the wage gap grew large enough, labor would relocate to higher wage areas of the economy. Those would be the areas where consumers apparently prefer those labor resources to be used (in view of the higher prices they are willing to pay for the growing industry's output).

When, asked if this "share economy" proposal has been tried elsewhere, Weitzman points to Asia. "Japanese workers receive 25 percent of their pay as a bonus. In South Korea and Taiwan about 15 percent of pay comes as a bonus. Even government workers in Korea have their pay tied to profitability." The proposal would of course, cause workers to assume some of the risks of business; in other words, workers would become partly venture capitalists. Because of this, Weitzman expects the greatest opposition to his proposal to come from unions whose senior member's are least vulnerable to lay off and who through seniority, command the highest wage premiums. Such workers would be asked to accept more wage variability in order to assure a higher and more stable level of employment.

Critiques of the Share Economy

It might be reasonable to suppose that Keynesian economists would oppose Weitzman's proposal for it would seem to diminish the role of demand-management in macroeconomic policy. In fact, some of the most prominent "Keynesians," while expressing doubts about the proposal, have urged that it be seriously investigated. Lawrence Summers[6] formerly of Harvard (and the U.S. departments of Labor and Treasury and economic advisor to the Obama administration) says: (1) in view of the widely held belief that a natural rate of unemployment precludes effective long-run trade-offs between inflation and unemployment, and (2) that the gains achievable by increasing the average level of employment make other macro-economic goals seem trivial. Summers believes that the system deserves study and that it would not necessarily have an inflationary bias because the tight labor markets resulting from its low rate of unemployment would not cause upward pressure on wages. Indeed, he states that, "with profit-sharing, taut labor markets and stable prices can coexist."

Nonetheless, Summers argues that there is no free lunch offered by the share economy. Negative effects could come about from two sources: (1) fellow worker problems, and (2) investment problems. The fellow worker problem derives from the incentives of workers faced with a declining revenue pie to resist hiring additional workers and an incentive to let the least productive workers go. Workers, concludes Summers, would be in competition with each other which would be exactly the opposite of the Japanese system. The investment problem comes from fixing the profit share of the revenue pie while allowing the wage component to vary. This, according to Summers, seems likely to reduce incentives to investment.

Another prominent macroeconomist, Alan Blinder[7] of Princeton University (and the Federal Reserve Board), says the Weitzman plan may be seen in two somewhat different ways. As a device for ending unemployment, it is a "bottle half full"; as ân intrusion on the business cycle (with its elimination of less productive enterprises) it is a "bottle half empty." Blinder, who sees unemployment elimination as *very* important, believes the bottle "three quarters

---

6. Summers, Lawrence, H. "On the Share Economy: Prospectus and Problems." *Challenge.* November-December, 1986.
7. Blinder, Alan S. "The Share Economy: A Bottle Half Full." *Challenge.* November-December, 1986.

full." In addition, he says, by giving workers greater job security and a greater stake in the companies they work for, there might be higher productivity and less resistance to labor-saving technical change.

Blinder refuses to reject the Keynesian idea that "shorter and shallower" recessions are better, and continues to argue that the externalities of firms' actions (effects on consumers incomes) "justify government intervention to smooth business cycles."

What is the Status of the Share Economy?

Clearly, the wage-price system of the American economy continues to be different from the share economy. Indeed, as Blinder notes, even if the Weitzman plan is socially optimal, it will not be adopted unless it is also seen as privately optimal. To this end Weitzman has argued for a tax subsidy to firms that would cause them to adopt the plan. Blinder says that there are numerous other practical problems that would have to be solved as well. Many economists, Keynesians and non-Keynesians alike, feel that the proposal is worth serious study.

Application II: The National Debt: Where are we Headed?

Our "National Debt" is comprised of all outstanding federal government securities held by agencies of the Federal Government, individuals, foreign investors, banks, local and state governments, corporations, and insurance companies.

Debt is created when the Federal Government has expenditures greater than the revenues needed to cover these expenditures. When this occurs in any given year the government runs what is known as a deficit for that year. If the Federal Government runs deficits (as it has throughout most of the past 50 years), the total value of all bonds issued to cover these deficits adds up to our national debt.

Typically, the largest budget deficits have occurred during war years and times of recession. However, deficits and the debt soared during the relatively peaceful and prosperous time period of the 1980's[8]. These deficits continued into the 1990's until 1998, when the budget turned to a surplus for the first time in almost 30 years.

The growth of the national debt over the last three decades or so is startling. In 1980 the debt was less that 1 trillion dollars, but by 2013 the gross public debt had increased to over 16 trillion dollars.

The "burden" of this debt is a topic that interests many U.S. citizens. Certainly there are several problems caused by such a large national debt. First, the interest amount on the national debt is the third largest expenditure in the federal budget. Only defense spending and income redistribution are higher. Another concern with an increasing national debt is a problem called the "crowding-out effect." The crowding-out effect occurs when the Federal Government, in financing its debt, borrows from the limited supply of loanable funds in the U.S. economy. With increased federal borrowing, banks may find that the demand for loans exceeds their supply at the current interest rate. The banks may then increase their interest rate to bring the supply and demand for loanable funds back into equilibrium. This higher interest rate may then crowd out some of our current business investments.

Another potential problem with increasing deficits, which leads to increasing debt, is that this practice may lead to misuse or what is commonly called "pork barrel spending."[9] In general, most congressmen like to spend

8. Although the 1980s were years of peace for the nation, there were major increases in spending for national defense.

federal monies in their districts. If the public is unconcerned about the deficits, the size of deficit-financed expenditures may lead to wasteful government projects.

Yet another popular argument is that the national debt places an undue burden on future generations. Most economists agree that debt incurred during wars or periods of economic hardships (recessions or depressions), is a necessary burden placed on U.S. citizens; but debt incurred during times of prosperity creates an unnecessary burden for future generations.

One thing history has shown us is that the national debt will likely continue to grow and will continue to be a subject of great debate.

SUMMING UP

1. The economic role of government has always been controversial. The Employment Act of 1946 assigned the federal government a broad responsibility, though the act stopped short of a commitment to create and maintain full employment.

2. *Fiscal policy*, variations in government expenditures and taxation, was a major counter-cyclical tool of the federal government from the 1960s to the 1980s.

3. *Discretionary fiscal policy* consists of changes in expenditures and taxes that are made to achieve specific macroeconomic goals. There are also *automatic stabilizers*, changes in taxes and expenditures that are triggered by fluctuations in economic activity that result in changes in income and employment.

4. Keynesians argue for *compensatory fiscal policy*, the use of fiscal policy (tax, expenditure) tools that will shift aggregate demand and result, during recession, in increased employment and income at stable prices. This argument is based on the Keynesian assumption that changes in aggregate quantity supplied can equal changes in aggregate demand without increased prices (the horizontal range of aggregate supply). If, on the other hand, a more classical aggregate supply (upward sloping range of aggregate supply) conditions hold, expansionary fiscal policy will lead to aggregate price rises and a larger fiscal stimulus will be required to achieve the same fiscal goal.

5. Use of fiscal policy tools in either range of aggregate supply may result in government *budget deficits* (expenditures > revenues) unless funded out of current revenues. *Budget surpluses* may result if revenues exceed expenditures.

6. The federal debt grew greatly during World War II as budget deficits financed much of the war effort through sales of federal bonds. From 1950 to 1980, the federal debt grew less rapidly than GDP and fell as a percentage of GDP from 90 percent to 34 percent. From 1980 to 1994, however, the federal debt grew much more rapidly than GDP and rose from 34 percent of GDP in 1980 to 67 percent of GDP in 1994.

7. Concerns about the post-1980 growth of the federal debt are mirrored in the size of the federal deficits in that period. The annual deficit rose from $74 bil-

---

9. Also known as earmarks.

lion in 1980 to a peak of $435 billion in 2004. Though post 1992 deficits declined through 1996, they rose again sharply beginning in 2002.

8. A major concern about the deficits is their very large magnitudes. Also troubling is that, by including Social Security Trust Fund revenues as current general revenues, the deficit is actually understated. Another concern is that interest payments on the debt which constitute a rising percentage of the federal budget, reduce discretionary expenditures, those which may be subject to reduction.
9. The timing of the deficits is a further concern. Though deficits, historically, have occurred during recessions and wartime, most recent deficits have occurred when the economy was operating with low rates of unemployment. This development leads to fears about Demand-pull inflation; demand-pull inflation.

10. An often expressed concern about deficits is that financing them in credit markets will lead to "crowding-out," a decline in net investment spending as federal demand for funds causes interest rates to rise. Future generations, thus, inherit a less productive economy. If consumption is "crowded-out," the current generation bears this burden.

11. The authors conclude that if "crowding-out" has occurred, it has been at the expense of investment with future generations bearing the burden. Two qualifications, however, are (1) government expenditures that are deficit financed may be for investments in which case, future generations will benefit from a more productive economy, and (2) government expenditures in times of significant unemployment may, through Keynesian effects, move the economy toward full employment with little or no burden on current consumption or investment.

12. An unwarranted concern about the deficits and the national debt is that the government will ultimately be unable to fund its activities and will go bankrupt. This is false because governments can (1) refinance their debts and, (2) unlike individuals can raise revenues through taxation and "printing" money.

13. Seventy seven percent of the federal debt consists of assets (bonds) owned by Americans. It is, thus, a debt of the government but mainly an offsetting credit to American citizens. While it could be repaid, doing so would result in a massive redistribution of income and wealth since the assets funding it are not uniformly held by Americans. The real opportunity cost of the; debt is on the generation in which the debt is created for that generation foregoes the goods and services that are not produced.

14. Some economists, including Paul McCracken, believe that the continuing deficits undermine the confidence of foreign investors. As the Treasury competes for a larger percentage of a (limited) supply of domestic savings, foreign investors foresee a decline in the capital stock of the U.S. and the net inflow of foreign capital becomes negative. As foreign capital leaves the country, exchange rates of the dollar against foreign currencies decline.

15. In the traditional view, federal deficits are related to trade deficits through monetary policy, interest rate changes, and dollar *appreciation.* A budget deficit leads to tight money and higher interest rates, which leads to crowding out and reduced investment, rising foreign purchases of U.S. securities, and increased foreign debt of the U.S., which causes the dollar to appreciate, which causes decreased U.S. exports and increased U.S. imports, which, in turn, leads to a trade deficit.

16. "Keynesian" expansionary fiscal policies may lead to decreased exports and trade deficits. This reduction in aggregate demand means that such policies may be less expansionary than Keynesians have argued.

17. A contrary view of the effects of budget deficit finance is seen in the *Ricardian Equivalence Theorem.* This theorem holds that financing deficits through credit market sales of bonds has the same effects as financing them through tax increases. If bonds are sold, individuals, aware that future tax increases will be required to finance the deficits, will cut consumption and save more to pay the expected higher taxes. This increased saving causes deficit financing not to lead to higher interest rates and, breaks the tie between deficit financing and trade deficits.

18. A major push to rethink and reshape the American fiscal system has occurred since the early 1990s. The system is very complex and has major effects on incentives to risk taking, innovation, saving and investment, and the distribution of income. Its revision will be difficult.

19. Changes in the fiscal system that have already occurred include (1) the Gramm-Rudman-Hollings Act of 1985 that could have lead to automatic spending cuts but has, instead, been abandoned, and (2) the Budget Reconciliation and Budget Enforcement Acts in 1990 and 1993, which require offsetting expenditure cuts or tax increases when new expenditures are authorized.

20. Proposals for future changes include (1) a Balanced Budget Amendment to the Constitution that would require an annual balance in the federal budget, (2) the Line-Item Veto which would allow the president to veto particular appropriations that serve narrow interest groups, and (3) privatization that could take the form of contracting out government activities, selling government assets, and providing consumers with vouchers to buy goods and services.

21. Many economists suggest that needed changes in federal budgetary procedures include (1) entitlement programs should be subject to expenditure caps rather than the "open-wallet" system, and (2) the federal government should adopt a current budget/capital budget format which would permit federal borrowing for capital projects but restrict payments for current services to current revenues.

22. A most fundamental fiscal reform would be to restrict the Federal government's share of the GDP to that which is necessary to carry out an agreed on role. That share is now 23 percent including retirement programs. Defining the role, however, would be very difficult.

23. The Keynesian arguments for government intervention to manage aggregate demand and reduce the severity of business cycles have been less well received since the 1980s. One of the proposals to replace this demand management is contained in the idea of a "share economy" advanced by Martin Weitzman.

24. Under the share economy proposal, there would be two components of the wage payment to workers. Most of the payment would be in the present contract form which guarantees a wage but not permanent employment. The second component would be tied to the profitability of firms, with that share rising as profits increase and falling as profits diminish.

25. Under the share economy proposal, wages would fall in a recession. This would result from falling demand and reduced profits of firms. Thus, firms will not lay off workers but will cut prices to restore sales.

26. Weitzman's plan would still retain the desirable feature of labor mobility. Declining industries would still lose labor to growing industries because of increasing wage differentials between the two.

27. Weitzman believes his plan would be akin to the systems of successful economies such as Japan, Taiwan, and South Korea. Workers would assume some of the risks of business in order to obtain job security. Unions who protect senior members from lay offs may be the strongest opponents of the plan.

28. Keynesians such as Lawrence Summers and Alan Blinder believe that the plan, while not perfect or a "free lunch" deserves to be studied. Given the view that there is a natural rate of unemployment below which the economy cannot be pushed in the long run, this may be an attainable way to achieve full employment.

29. Summers concludes that the plan may not have an inflationary bias. However, workers would be in competition with each other and the least productive workers might be let go as a result of the "fellow worker" problem. There might also be a disincentive to investment as a result of a decreasing profit share.

30. Alan Blinder regards the proposal as worthy of serious study. Not only does it help solve the *very* serious problems associated with unemployment, it gives greater job security and a greater stake in the company to workers. Both things might raise productivity and lessen resistance to labor-saving technical change.

31. The share economy will not be adopted unless it is seen as *privately* optimal. Weitzman argues for tax subsidies to firms to induce their acceptance of the system. There are, no doubt, other practical problems to be solved as well.

KEY TERMS

Automatic stabilizers
Budget deficit
Budget surplus
Compensatory fiscal policy
"Crowding-out" effect
Discretionary fiscal policy
Fiscal policy
Ricardian Equivalence Theorem
Share economy

QUESTIONS

1. What is the basic macroeconomic role assigned to the federal government by the Employment Act of 1946?

2. Explain what is meant by *fiscal policy* and what its role in economic stability was from the 1960s to the 1980s.

3. Explain the differences between *discretionary fiscal policy* and *automatic stabilizers*. What are examples of each?

4. What is the Keynesian assumption about aggregate supply during periods in which *compensatory fiscal policy* is employed? What is the classical assumption? Which of the two assumptions increases the amount of compensatory fiscal policy stimulus required to achieve employment goals?

5. What is meant by budget deficit? iB.Budget Surplus; Budget surplus? Which has been characteristic of federal budgets since 1969?

6. In what year did the federal debt as a percentage of GDP reach its maximum? What caused this maximum?

   a. What happened to the federal debt as a percentage of GDP from 1950 to 1980? From 1980 to 1994? What were the major causes of the change from 1980 to 1994?
   b. What causes budget deficits? What is the relationship between federal budget deficits and the federal debt?

7. What are the four major current concerns about federal debt?

   a. In what sense is the magnitude of the federal deficits understated?
   b. Interest on the federal debt has risen as a percentage of the federal budget. Why is this viewed by many as a problem?
   c. Deficits in recent years have frequently occurred when the economy was operating with low levels of unemployment. Why is this timing a matter of concern?

8. What is the "crowding-out" effect? How is this effect related to the burden of deficits and debt on present and future generations?

9. How do the nature of government expenditures and the employment effects of government expenditure qualify any conclusion about the burden of deficits and federal debt?

10. How, according to Keynesians, may the "crowding-out" effects of deficits during periods of recession be at least partially offset by their stimulative effects?

11. Explain why concerns about federal bankruptcy and federal debt burdens on future generations are basically unwarranted?

12. What would be the major effect of a repayment of the federal debt?

13. What was the major burden of large increases in the federal debt during the post-1980 period?

14. What are Paul McCracken's major concerns about the effects of large federal deficits on the U.S. balance of trade?

15. Explain, step by step, how a federal budget deficit may, in the traditional view, lead to a budget deficit. Why does this view support the idea that fiscal policy stimulus to the economy may be less than expected by Keynesians?

16. What is the Ricardian Equivalence Theorem? How does it break the chain of events in the traditional view of the relationship between budget deficits and trade deficits?

17. Why will it be complex and difficult in the 1990s to reshape the American fiscal system?

18. What were the provisions of (1) the Gramm-Rudman-Hollings Act (1985), (2) the Budget Reconciliation Act of 1990, (3) the Budget Enforcement Act of 1990, and (4) the Budget Reconciliation Act of 1993?

19. How would a Balanced Budget Amendment change the American fiscal system? How does Line-Item Veto change the system? Privatization of federal programs?

20. What is meant by the "open-wallet" system of budgeting for entitlement programs? What proposals have been made to change this system?

21. How would adoption of a current-account and capital-account in the federal budget change the American fiscal system? What is the rationale for adoption of this type of budgeting procedure?

22. Why would it be very difficult to limit federal government spending by limiting its share of GDP?

23. What is the Keynesian solution to the problem of the business cycle?

24. What would be the system of wage payment in a "share economy?" How does this differ from the present wage-price system?

25. If the "share economy" system were adopted, what would be the effect on wage-price flexibility?

26. Would there be labor immobility in a share economy? Explain.

27. What nations have wage systems similar to that in the "share economy"?

28. Who would you expect to strongly oppose a share economy? Why?

29. Why has the acceptance of a natural rate of unemployment heightened interest in the "share economy"?

30. What does Summers mean by fellow worker problems and investment problems associated with a share economy?

31. What might the share economy do to worker job security, labor productivity, and implementation of labor-saving technological changes?

32. Identify some of the problems in getting agreement to create a "share economy."

SECTION III:

Economic Policy in the Macroeconomy

Section III

Economic Policy in the Macroeconomy

In Section I, we laid the foundations for examining the macroeconomy. We did this through looking at the fundamental assumptions of economics and through discussing its basic methodology including its reliance on principles of supply and demand in understanding how a market economy functions. In Section II, we shifted focus from individual behavior and individual markets to examine the foundations of aggregate or macroeconomics. We looked at how aggregate income flows are measured as well as how we may understand the irregular variations or cycles in those flows. After laying out the differences between classical and Keynesian economists about flexibility in the macroeconomy, we built in stages a Keynesian model of income and employment that focuses on managing aggregate demand.

In Section III, we shall build further on this theoretical and empirical foundation by shifting from theory and measurement to economic policy. We will concentrate on two main areas of economic policy. Fiscal policy, variations in government expenditures and taxes are our first concern. We shall see what options governments have in financing their operations and what the different macroeconomic effects are of taxation and issuance of debt. After surveying the modern record of U.S. fiscal policy, we shall look at the widely perceived problems of federal budget deficits and the U.S. debt. Since the mid-1990s, the "supply-side" arguments about government policy and economic growth have reemerged and we will examine those arguments as well.

A second major focus of Section III is on monetary policy or variations in the supply of money. Since the mid-1990s, this has been the major tool of macroeconomic policy in the United States. We shall see not only how the money supply is created but also how monetary policy affects that creation

Chapter 11: Money in the Modern Economy

In this and upcoming chapters, we will examine the basic roles of money in a modern market economy. Policy debates concerning the supply of money took on even greater importance beginning in the 1990s. These have grown stronger in 2009-2013 because of the efforts of the central (Federal Reserve) bank to use monetary policy to diminish the effects of a severe recession. But before we can talk about monetary policy, it is necessary to understand what money is and what essential functions it performs.

First, let's note that, although money is an important part of an economy, the factors of production, the resources essential to producing things (land, labor, capital, entrepreneurship) do not contain money. Money does not directly produce anything although resources are required to produce money. In view of this, how does money contribute to turning out automobiles or computers, or any of the myriad of goods and services we consume each year?

Before we can trace a clear relationship between the supply of money and the production of goods and services, there are some questions we must answer in this chapter and in the next about money itself: What is money? What are its functions? How is it increased or decreased, and how is this process controlled? How does the system of banks and non-bank financial institutions work? How does money affect the level of economic activity and prices? Most important, how can monetary policy changes influence the supply of money in order to bring about a higher level of income and employment, with stable prices?

Barter: An Early System of Exchange;

People can produce goods and services without the existence of money; where there is no money, goods must be exchanged for other goods. When this happens, the system of exchange is called **barter**.

Barter
A system in which goods are exchanged for other goods.

For example, Farmer Nielson needs a hundred bushels of wheat and a pair of shoes, size eleven. He looks around his farm to see what he can barter and decides that his 250-pound pig is surely worth a hundred bushels of wheat and a pair of size-eleven shoes. He takes his pig to his nearest neighbor, Farmer Gomez, a wheat farmer, and offers to barter the pig for the wheat and the shoes. Farmer Gomez agrees that it's a fair exchange, but although he has the wheat, he doesn't have the size-eleven shoes. So Farmer Nielson goes down the road to Farmer Camilla McGrath. Her father died recently and left a closet full of size-eleven shoes, but she has no wheat. Her brother on the next farm also has some of their late father's size-eleven shoes, and he has plenty of wheat, but he doesn't want the pig. Farmer Nielson will probably make his trade eventually, but it may cost him a lot of time and effort.

Double Coincidence of Demand
A situation in which there is a mutuality of needs and in which one individual is willing to exchange goods with another.

The central requirement of the barter system is what is called a **double coincidence of demand**, or of wants. Not only must Farmer Nielson want what the other person has, but also the other person in the exchange must want what Nielson has. Establishing mutuality of needs is usually time consuming and therefore inefficient. How much easier it would be for Nielson to take the pig to the butcher in town, sell it for money, buy the wheat from the miller, and then drop by the shoe store and pick up a pair of size-eleven shoes.

Money: A More Modern System of Exchange

Modern economies are much more complex than early ones, and this creates pressure to replace barter with a more efficient system of *money exchange*. As a society specializes its labor and other resources, it must also specialize the means by which exchanges are made.

Your instructor is not only a teacher, not only a college teacher, but, even more specialized than that, an economics instructor, producing a service called education. How should he or she be paid? In a society without money, would one student barter potatoes, another mow the instructor's lawn, or another clean the classroom? Although barter was used earlier in this and other countries, it is too cumbersome today (though governments occasionally engage in barter trade with each other). The existence of money makes possible, an efficient flow of goods and resources, and a more highly developed economy.

But what is money? What is the essential ingredient that makes a thing money?

Money
Anything that people accept in exchange for goods and services.

A thing becomes **money** when people accept that thing in exchange for goods and services in general. *Money is money because people say it is money* and accept it in exchange for almost anything else. Governments may decree that something be accepted as payment for all debts, public or private. Although this *encourages* acceptance of that thing as a medium of exchange, it does not guarantee it. In the past, money consisted of gold and silver or paper backed by gold and silver. You could exchange a paper five-dollar bill for a five-dollar gold piece. This increased its acceptability as money. Today if you take a five-dollar bill to a bank, you will get in return only a new five-dollar bill. And yet you can still exchange it for goods and services.

In the long run, it is just the *acceptance* of the thing called money in exchange for goods and services that makes it money.

The Functions of Money

There are four basic functions that money performs:

1. Money acts as a *medium of exchange*. The central ingredient of money is its acceptability by others. When money is exchanged for goods and services, it is functioning as a medium of exchange and relieves a society of the need to use barter.

2. The second function is a corollary of the first. Money is a *standard of value or unit of account*. Money serves as a measure by which a value can be set on goods and services. In a barter economy, if Farmer Nielson wanted to know the value of his pig, he compared it with the value of other goods. The pig might be worth a hundred bushels of oats and the extraction of an aching tooth, and so on.

In a money economy, the pig's value is set in terms of the monetary unit of the country. The monetary unit of the United States is the dollar, so here the pig is valued in dollars. Although other nations have differing standard units (Euros, pounds, francs, and so on), in each country money functions as a standard of value or unit of account and makes it possible for people to place a value on goods and services. It is, thus, a common denominator of all goods and services.

3. Money is the most liquid of assets and acts as a *store of value*. In a barter economy, how can Farmer Nielson *save*? He can do so only by storing goods. He can stash away wheat or preserve the products of the pig (bacon, ham, sausages), or he can accumulate larger numbers of things. But it costs a lot to store these things, and such products can deteriorate over a period of time. It would be simpler if Nielson could sell his output and save the accumulated *money*. (Money occupies little space; it doesn't rot or breed weevils. It just sits there and frequently earns interest.)

But money *does* fluctuate in value, because of increases or decreases in prices. Inflation reduces the purchasing power of money and therefore reduces its value. Deflation causes the reverse to happen. This factor reduces the efficiency of money as a store of value.

4. Money is a *means of deferred payment*. Money facilitates lending and the repayment of loans. In a barter economy, borrowing is a most cumbersome affair. Suppose that Nielson's land is next to the river, and one year the river floods and destroys his wheat crop. He goes to Farmer Gomez, who lives in the unaffected uplands, and borrows wheat so he can plant a new crop. But because of the flood, wheat is now relatively scarce, that is, in short supply, with a high relative exchange value. The following year the weather is fine, and there is a bumper crop. Nielson, with plenty of wheat today, pays Gomez back for the wheat he borrowed last year. But with this year's abundance of wheat, the scarcity value of wheat has declined markedly, compared with last year, and wheat has a low relative exchange value.

It is more efficient to base credit on a general medium of exchange: money. One expects money and its scarcity value (in simple language, its purchasing power) to be less subject than barter items to variations outside people's control.

However, the value of money, its purchasing power, does vary as prices vary, and this, as we said earlier, reduces the usefulness of money. There have been times in history when the supply of money increased so rapidly that it led to monetary disaster. During the American Revolution, for example, the Continental Congress issued so much currency with no backing that the people lost confidence in it. The purchasing power of that money dropped so low that the currency was not accepted in exchange for goods and services and the expression "not worth a Continental" became a part of our language.

Characteristics of a "Good" Money

Many things have performed the function of money. During the American Revolution, in Massachusetts wheat served as money, and in Virginia tobacco was legally defined as money. American Indians used strings of colored beads called wampum as money; some African tribes have used cattle and cowry shells, and some groups in the South Sea Islands have used large stones. Apart from paper currency, gold, silver, and copper are the materials that most commonly serve as money.

What characteristics should one look for in a good money? (1) It should be portable, or easy to carry; (2) it should be easy to recognize, but hard to counterfeit or duplicate illegally; (3) it should be easily subdivided, to allow for small as well as large purchases; (4) the cost of storing it, that is, physically storing it in a safe place, or storing it in an accounting sense, should be low; (5) it should be durable, and not wear out or rot quickly; and (6) the relative supply should not vary so greatly that large variations in relative scarcity value occur, since purchasing power changes as prices vary.

The Supply of Money: How to Define and Measure It

Defining and identifying the supply of money in the United States has become more difficult in recent decades. Ideally, we would like the definition to include all financial instruments that may readily be used in the short-term exchange of goods and services. Because of institutional and legal changes in our monetary system since the early 1970s, the exact identification and measurement of those instruments has become more complex for reasons we will look at in this and the succeeding chapter. As a first approximation, however, let's define money in the following way:

Money consists of all liabilities in commercial banks and other financial institutions that are subject to demand plus currency and coin in circulation.

Demand Deposits
Accounts that are subject to withdrawal by means of a check.

Demand deposits are what you know as *checking accounts*. They are called demand deposits because you can withdraw these deposits "on demand," by presenting a check.

A *check* is merely an order to a financial institution from the holder of a demand deposit to transfer some money from the deposit and pay it to someone else. The deposit is the money, not the check. If there is no deposit, the check is worthless.

About 40 percent of our money supply, as defined, is in the form of demand deposits. This is so, because it is both more convenient and safer to make large transactions this way. Another 33 percent is in other checkable accounts. However, the economic importance of "checkbook money" is even greater than that, since about 90 percent (by value) of all economic transactions are accomplished by means of checks drawn against demand deposits.

Depository Institutions
Those institutions that hold demand deposits.

The keepers of demand deposits are called **depository institutions**. Commercial banks are the largest part of the institutions that hold our demand deposits. Since demand deposits comprise the bulk of the U.S. money supply, commercial banks hold most of the supply of money in the United States. (As we shall see later, however, many other institutions in the United States now hold and create money.) The second largest component of our narrowly defined money supply is *currency in circulation*, which means currency that is in use rather than in the vaults of banks or of the Federal Reserve. Currency; is the paper money in the U.S. economy and consists of Federal Reserve Notes that are issued by the Federal Reserve Banks.

Coins are another part of the supply of money. Though relatively small, they are a vital part of that supply. These metal tokens are minted by the Treasury, but also issued through the Federal Reserve Banks. Today both currency and coin are called **fiat money**. Their value as monetary instruments is greater than their value as commodities. The five-dollar bill as a monetary instrument is worth five dollars in goods and services.

Fiat Money
Monetary instruments that have less value as commodities than as money.

Cartoon Feature Syndicate

"I'm holding onto my cash, I think money is going to come back."

As a *commodity* (waste paper or perhaps a wall decoration) it is worth very little. The twenty-five-cent coin, if it were melted down and sold as metal, would be worth far less than twenty-five cents. Currency and coin are also defined as **legal tender**, which is any money the law says must be accepted as payment for all debt, public (owed to or owed by the government), or private (owed by one individual to another). The smallest part of our money supply is travelers checks which make up less than one percent of the total.

Legal Tender
All forms of money that, by law, must be accepted in payment of private or public debt.

Coins and Gresham's Law

Coins are a clear example of fiat money. Governments long ago discovered that they could "profit" from issuing coins that contain less precious metal (gold, silver) than their face value. Though the United States did issue non-debased coins (such as the famous gold double eagles) earlier in our history, all coins in the U.S. money supply today are debased, that is, they contain mostly base (less valuable) metal. The fact is that all of the non-debased coins today are collectors items and, depending on condition, sell for more than their face value. When sold, they end up in museums, private collections, or being melted down. This is a clear illustration of **Gresham's Law**, which asserts that debased money always tends to drive non-debased money out of circulation. In other words, coins con-

Gresham's Law
The assertion that debased money will drive non-debased money out of circulation.

taining mainly base metal will circulate while the dear (precious metal) coins will be driven out of circulation.

Each of the three different kinds of money, demand deposits, currency, and coin, has its own advantages and disadvantages. The convenience of paying for things, especially expensive items, through the medium of checks that transfer demand deposits is fairly obvious. One does not have to carry large sums in currency. Most people use demand deposits most of the time to pay for larger bills or expenses.

However, checks have two disadvantages: (1) Not everyone is willing to accept a check in economic exchange. The fear of fraud or of inadequate funds in the check payer's demand deposits, plus the trouble of collecting on bad checks, reduces the acceptability of checks as money. (2) For small purchases, a check ordering a transfer of a demand deposit is a very inefficient form of money. Imagine a child in a candy store pulling out a checkbook to pay for a fifty-cent purchase. Coins and currency are more efficient in such cases.

Money Is Debt

www.federalreserve.gov/fomc/
www.federalreserve.gov
For more information on the money supply visit the Federal Reserve web site listed above.

Demand deposits are liabilities of institutions that create them. Currency is a liability of the Federal Reserve banks. Both are non-interest-bearing debt. In effect, the supply of money is the monetization of certain forms of debt. The commercial bank or other institution that holds your demand deposit promises to pay you in money the amount of your account when you demand it. If you go into the bank and demand the deposit, the bank will give you currency. But what is currency? A ten-dollar bill says on its face that it is a Federal Reserve Note. The Federal Reserve promises to pay you ten dollars for it. Like the demand deposit, the ten-dollar bill is a promise to pay. But if you go to the Federal Reserve Bank and demand payment, you will receive only a new bill or change for the old one.

Since government will not exchange anything tangible for currency, like gold or silver, what is currency good for? What are demand deposits good for? Their worth lies in the fact that people are willing to exchange goods and services for them. Thus, by definition, currency is money. The value of money is not the gold or silver that backs it up (there is today no gold or silver backing the U.S. supply of money), but the goods and services that the money can buy. That value depends on the *prices* of the goods and services to be bought in relationship to the supply of money. The lower the prices, the more a given amount of money can buy, and thus the higher the value of money.

Measures of the Money Supply

M_1

The money supply we have talked about above, demand deposits, coin, currency and travelers checks, is a measure of money that focuses on those things that serve as a medium of exchange. That measure is referred to as **M_1** money.

M_1
A measure of money supply that includes currency, coin and travelers checks plus all deposits that are subject to checks.

M_1 = Currency, Coin, Travelers Checks and all Checkable Deposits

Remember though, that money also serves as a standard of value, a store of value, and a means of deferred payment. To focus on these functions of money and to correlate the money supply more closely with changes in GDP, we shall define the money supply two other ways.

M_2

A measure of the money supply that includes all M_1 money plus small time deposits and money market mutual funds.

Near Monies

Assets with all of the characteristics of money except that they do not circulate as a medium of exchange.

M_3

A measure of the money supply that includes all M_1 + M_2 money + large value certificates of deposits (CDs).

M_2

M_2 includes all of the components of M_1 plus savings deposits, small time deposits and money market mutual funds. These last three elements are called **near monies**, assets that have all the characteristics of money (particularly as a store of value) except that they do not circulate as a medium of exchange. To get some idea of the relative importance of M_1 and M_2 in 2001, M_1 amounted to 1.34 trillion dollars while M_2 was equal to 6.2 trillion dollars.

$$M_2 = M_1 + \text{Savings Deposits} + \text{Small Time Deposits} + \text{Money Market Mutual Funds}$$

M_3

A third, and still broader, definition of the money supply is also possible. **M_3** consists of all the components of M_2 plus negotiable certificates of deposit (CDs). This is the broadest of the three money supply measures. In 2001, its value was 4.28 trillion dollars.

$$M_3 = M_2 + \text{Large Value Certificates of Deposit}$$

Summing Up the Money Supply

For many purposes, the money supply can no longer be defined simply as currency, coins and checkable deposits (M_1). There are so many new (and ever changing) near monies in America's financial markets that we must take account of these if we are to have an adequate measure not only of the things that serve as a medium of exchange but also serve to store value, serve as a standard of value and as a means for deferred payments. The near monies we will look at are:

1. *Savings Deposits*, those that earn interest but do not mature at a specific date. These deposits are found not only in commercial banks but also in savings and loan associations, mutual savings banks and credit unions. They are not subject to routine checking demands and thus, are not included in M_1.

2. *Time Deposits*, those that have a specific maturity date that typically is as short as thirty days and range up to several years. Some financial institutions offer similar non-negotiable certificates of deposit with fixed interest rates. They are not included in M_1 because they cannot be resold and must (subject to large penalties) be held to maturity.

3. *Money Market Fund Accounts*. First introduced by Merrill Lynch in 1971, they exist in large amounts but are not included in M_1 because of restrictions on checking against them and also because minimums are established for these checks. They are, in other words, not sufficiently flexible to be included as a medium of exchange.

4. *Negotiable Certificates of Deposit* Certificates that have some of the characteristics of money but are usually denominated in large sums ($100,000+) and are not subject to checking. For these reasons, they are included neither in M_1 nor M_2.

Near Monies, Liquidity, and Credit Cards

When an economy has a large amount of near money (that is, is in a highly liquid state), the average and marginal propensities to consume tend to increase. If the economy is already in an inflationary gap, high liquidity may worsen the inflation. However, if the economy is in a recession, with a deflationary gap, high liquidity may soften or cushion the contraction.

Credit Cards

Credit Cards: Where do they fit? Are they substitutes for money? The credit card is only a quick and convenient way to *borrow* money. At the end of the month, the borrower gets a statement of purchases made with the credit card during the month and must pay in *money* for what was charged. All a credit card does is reduce the inconvenience and risk of carrying around a large amount of money. It is not a substitute for money. But credit cards do enable people to increase their purchasing power temporarily. This can affect total demand, and thus the level of income, employment, and prices. Furthermore, the public's ability to vary purchasing power temporarily by using credit cards can make it harder for the government to carry out a stabilization policy.

The Origins of Commercial Banking: Goldsmith Banking

To understand how M_1 is created, we must understand the original depository institutions and their role in creating demand. The origins of today's commercial bank lie with the goldsmiths of seventeenth-century England.

In the early 1600s in England, the safest places to store valuables were the vaults and safes of the goldsmiths of London, who made useful items out of gold. Wealthy people put their gold and silver in these vaults for safekeeping; the goldsmiths charged a fee for this watchdog service. At first, the goldsmiths had to return the same gold and silver that people had entrusted to their care. However, after a while, people said the goldsmith did not have to return the piece of gold that was deposited, just an amount of gold of equivalent value. This relaxing of the rules began a series of developments that eventually led to the modern commercial bank.

The depositor, the person who left gold with the goldsmith, received a document stating the value of the gold deposited. (This document was equivalent to your bankbook, which shows how much you have deposited.) When Lady Upton-Chase found that she needed money or wanted to buy something, she could take this document and transfer ownership of all (or any part) of the gold to a third party. She would write, "I order you, the goldsmith, to pay to the third party so-and-so much of the gold on deposit."

Thus, the modern check was born. Since the goldsmiths were internationally known, these endorsements of deposits to another person were widely accepted as a means of payment. Thus, they functioned as money. Deposits of gold at goldsmiths eventually became today's demand deposits. But the story does not end there.

The goldsmith became known as a person with money to lend, and people who needed money began borrowing from the goldsmith. At first goldsmiths lent their own gold. In time, they realized that people who stored gold with them would not want that gold back for a while. There was always a certain amount of stored gold in their vaults, so they began to lend some of it. After a while the borrowers, instead of taking the gold, accepted documents stating that they had gold on deposit with the goldsmith. The borrowers would *endorse* these documents of deposit (write checks) over to those people they wished to make payments to.

The goldsmiths were soon creating documents of deposits in amounts much larger than the amounts of gold they actually had in their vaults. Since these documents attesting to deposits were accepted as payment, they functioned as money. Thus the goldsmiths, by making loans and creating deposits (attested to by documents), were creating and increasing the supply of money.

The goldsmiths, however, had to be prepared to give gold back when people presented these documents transferring deposits (checks). Fortunately, not all of these documents were presented at the same time. Thus, the goldsmiths were able to keep a prudent supply of gold, enough to meet these demands, on hand at all times. This was the origin of the **fractional reserve principle**, that is, the need to have on hand an amount of reserves (in this case gold) smaller than the total amount of deposits, to meet possible demands for withdrawal of deposits in gold.

Fractional Reserve Principle
The need to maintain on hand a reserve less than the amount of total deposits.

So one sees in seventeenth-century English banking the *origins* of our modern commercial banking system: (1) deposits that can be withdrawn on demand; (2) the check as a means of transferring these deposits and the functioning of these deposits as money; (3) the practice of lending money by creating a deposit and increasing the supply of money; and (4) the need to keep reserves of gold in amounts that are fractions of total deposits, which make possible the lending and creation of new deposits, and thus a larger supply of money.

In another chapter you will see how commercial banks and other depository institutions today are like the goldsmiths of long ago: By their lending activities, these institutions increase and decrease the amount of demand deposits and, thus, the M_1 money supply.

The Future of Money, or Can the Computer Replace Currency and Coin?

Today, as we have seen, there are many forms of money and near money. It is possible to create a scenario in which M_1 money or at least coin and currency may lose most if not all of its importance as a medium of exchange.

Imagine an economy without currency and coin, and also without checks as you know them. Imagine a great central computer. In its memory banks are entered all expenditures and all receipts of money. All receipts of income are fed directly into the computer and added to each individual's account. No more depositing of paychecks, no more lugging around dirty, germ-covered currency and coin.

Everyone has an account. Everyone has her or his own card, perhaps keyed to the thumbprint. Every place that sells things, every place at which people make payments has terminals connected to the computer. When you buy something, you take your debit card, slip it into the terminal, and it types out the deduction to be made from your account at the computer.

No more bad checks. If you overdraw your account, lights will instantly flash, and a recorded voice from the computer terminal will say, "You're overdrawn." No more hours spent figuring your bank balance. You can obtain it on request from the computer. No more hiding income from the Internal Revenue Service. The computer knows all. Big Daddy will indeed have become a machine.

Have we not begun to see this process in the 2000s? Want to buy gasoline or groceries? No need for cash, your automatic teller machine card is used instead and the amount automatically deducted from your bank balance. A recent study by John Caskey and Gordon Sellon, Jr.[1], suggests that debit card use will grow rapidly, though there are cost barriers that limit that expansion.

The Economy and the Supply of Money

How do changes in the supply of money affect the level of economic activity? Two major factors are (1) the absolute size of the supply of money and (2) the rapidity with which the supply of money changes hands in a given period of time.

Consider a simple economy with only three people: Farmer Martinez, Mo Courington the shoemaker, and Vee Jackson the baker. The supply of money in the economy is $20. Vee Jackson buys $20 worth of sausages from Farmer Martinez. Therefore, Farmer Martinez exchanges $20 worth of output for $20 in money. Farmer Martinez buys $20 worth of shoes from Mo Courington, and again exchanges $20 in output for $20 in money. Finally, Mo Courington, buys $20 worth of bread from Vee Jackson, and there is a further exchange of $20 in output for the same $20 in money. Although the supply of money is only $20, this $20 has changed hands three times, and the total output supported through this process is $60. Figure 11-1 shows this process through a circular-flow diagram.

The Equation of Exchange

Equation of Exchange (MV = PQ). The supply of money times its velocity equals the price level times the amount of net goods and services.

One can express the circular-flow process in Figure 11-1 in the form of an equation, called the **equation of exchange**:

$$MV = PQ.$$

M stands for the supply of money and V is the *velocity of exchange*, or the number of times the supply of money changes hands in a given period. One might call MV the *effective supply of money.* Also, if P is the average price level of the goods sold, and Q is transactions in physical terms and can be restricted to include only the output of net final goods and services, then PQ (the money value of that output) is *net national product*.

$$MV = PQ = NNP.$$

Let's make an equation from our example: M, the supply of money, is $20; V, the velocity of exchange, is three (since the money changed hands three times); and Q, physical output, consists of the sausages, shoes, and bread. It can be seen that MV equals PQ, since 20 x 3= 20 x 3.

So the equation of exchange works perfectly in this extremely simple model. Although the gigantic economy of the United States, with its 300 million people and its multitude of transactions and output, is vastly more complex, it operates the same way. (We have considered PQ as being NNP and velocity, V, as being essentially the velocity of income. Now we can define Q as including *all* economic transactions. We can say that Q includes the buying and selling of intermediary products, financial instruments, and even used items. When one defines transactions, Q, that way, velocity, V, is much higher. One can call it the velocity of transactions. Here, in order to keep our analysis simple, we shall consider only the velocity of income.)

---

1. Caskey, John P. and Gordon H. Sellon, Jr. "Is the Debit Card Revolution Finally Here?" *Economic Review*, Federal Reserve Bank of Kansas City, Vol. 79, Number 4, Fourth Quarter, 1994.

Figure 11-1
The Circular Flow of Money and Output

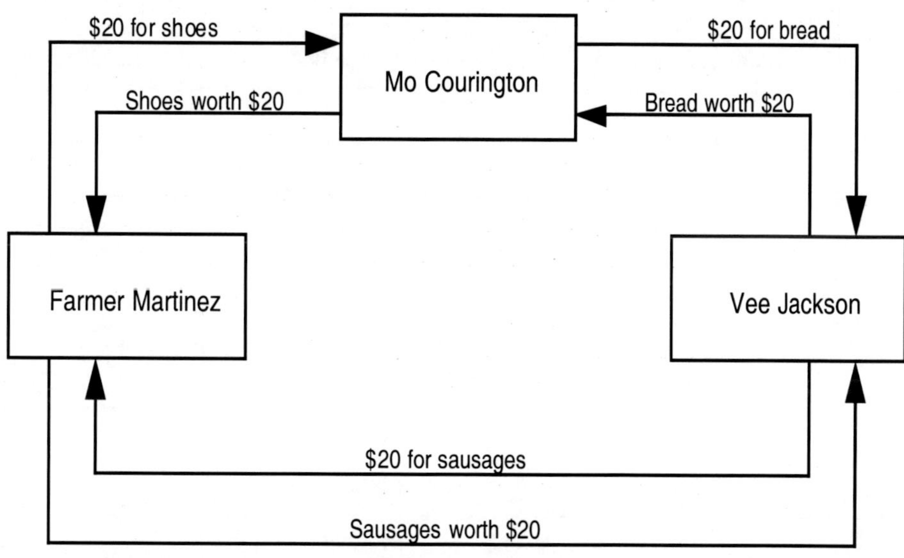

Source: Economic Report of the President, 2004, G.P.O. Washington D.C.

The Velocity of Exchange (V)

www.federalreserve.gov For more information on the velocity of money visit this web site.

You now see that the dollar value of output PQ is determined by changes in the supply of money, and also by changes in the velocity of exchange (the number of times the money supply M changes hands). The supply of money is controlled by the monetary authority responsible for doing so. (In the United States, it is the Federal Reserve.) The velocity of exchange, on the other hand, cannot be controlled. It depends on the structure of the financial system and on the actions of the public. One can easily measure velocity by dividing the net national product by the supply of money. Table 11-1 shows that measure of the velocity of exchange for recent years between 1986 and 2003.

The data in Table 11-1 show that the velocity of exchange (V) since the mid-1980s was rather constant though declining in recession years (1991–1992). It is true that V rose earlier between 1960 (3.3) and 1985 (5.7). The reasons for the increase between 1995 and 2009 seem to have been because the public was able to use the supply of money more and more efficiently for three reasons: (1) Financial institutions and financial markets have grown both more complex and more available to the public. The increased use of savings accounts, money market accounts, stocks and bonds, government securities, and various forms of private short-term commercial credit have moved money more rapidly from one use to another. (2) The public has greatly increased its use of credit cards, which has cut down its need to hold money. (3) The public has increased its use of institutions such as banks and other financial intermediaries, reducing its need to hold money for longer periods of time. We should also note that there may be a problem with M_1 as the money supply here. Other assets may be so liquid that some other measure of the money supply may correlate better with NNP than M_1. This is a complex subject of great controversy among monetary economists..

Table 11-1
The Velocity of Exchange

	M_1 (billions of dollars)	NNP (billions of dollars)	V $NNP \div M_1$
1986	724.5	3,799.2	5.24
1990	826.4	4,965.1	6.01
1991	897.7	5,114.3	5.70
1992	1,024.8	5,367.3	5.24
1994	1,149.9	6,264.7	5.4
1998	1,094.8	7,738.2	7.1
2003	1,287.1	9,835.7	7.6
2005	1,368.9	10,786.2	7.9
2009	1,684	14,399.6	8.6
2012	2,252	12,026	5.3

Output, Prices, and *M* (for Money): A Simple First Look

To examine the way changes in the supply of money affect output of goods and services and their prices, we must make a simplifying assumption: We will assume that V (the velocity of exchange) is constant (an assumption that seems warranted for recent years).

Given the equation of exchange, MV = PQ, when M (some measure of the supply of money) increases and V (the velocity of exchange) is constant, then PQ (the value of output) must increase. The important question is: Will P (prices) increase, or will Q (output) increase? There we pointed out that during a recession, when there is high unemployment and excess capacity in factories, output can increase without much increase in prices. This is because an increase in aggregate supply can occur without increases in prices from private producers. Therefore, if the United States has a recession, and the supply of money (M) increases, prices (P) will remain relatively stable and output (Q) will increase. We also said in another chapter that as an economy approaches full employment, some resources will be in shorter supply than others, and prices will begin to increase. This is because aggregate supply under these conditions is upward sloping. An increase in aggregate quantity supplied in response to an increase in the money supply occurs only with rising costs and prices. Therefore, as money (M) increases and the economy approaches full employment, prices (P) begin to rise, along with output (Q). Obviously, when the economy is at *full* employment, any increase in the supply of money (M) will only result in an increase in prices (P). Output (Q) cannot increase any further, because all resources are fully employed.

If economic policy is geared toward increasing output and employment, the appropriate monetary policy is to increase the supply of money. On the other hand, if the policy seeks to decrease inflation, the appropriate monetary policy is to decrease the supply of money.

But remember, we are assuming that the velocity of exchange (V) is constant. When V changes, it may either reinforce or counteract the effects of changes in the supply of money.

The Demand for Money: An Alternative

There is another way of looking at the way the supply of money affects output and prices. For many reasons, people need to hold part of their assets in the form of money (as opposed to real estate and other assets). People do not receive income at the same time that they have to pay for the goods and services they buy. For example, professors are paid once a month. Although they pay the usual recurring bills on the first of the month, they must keep some money on hand to buy food, gasoline, haircuts, and so forth, for the rest of the month. This is called holding money for *transaction purposes*. People also need to hold money for emergencies: The car breaks down, the water heater springs a leak, or someone gets sick. This is called holding money for *precautionary purposes*. In addition, people hold money to take advantage of economic opportunities. Stock prices may be low, or there may be a sale on coats. One needs money on hand to take advantage of these opportunities. This is called holding money for *speculative purposes*.

Whatever the reason, people want to hold certain amounts of money. How much they hold depends on their incomes, the amounts and kinds of assets they have accumulated (durable goods, liquid assets, and so on), and their personal lifestyles. If the supply of money increases, people find themselves holding more cash than they wish, and they may invest all or part of it, or they may spend all or part of it on more consumer goods and services. Therefore, when money increases, both investment and consumption demand increase.

Suppose the supply of money decreases. Then people have less cash on hand than they want, so they have to either decrease their consumption (an uncomfortable solution) or convert other assets into cash. That is why investment and consumption demand both fluctuate with the supply of money.

Because people want to hold a certain amount of their assets in the form of money, they react when their actual holdings do not correspond to their desired holdings. If they have more assets in the form of money than they want when the supply of money increases, they increase their investments. They also buy more consumer goods. This expands the economy. Income increases, which has the effect of increasing the amount of money that people wish to hold. This process continues until what people wish to hold becomes equal to the increased supply of money. When the supply of money decreases, the reverse occurs.

Thus the two monetary approaches (the equation of exchange and the demand for money) lead to the same conclusions. An increase in the supply of money increases aggregate demand and expands the economy. A decrease in the supply of money decreases aggregate demand and contracts the economy. We shall have more to say about this in the upcoming chapter.

SUMMING UP

1. This chapter examines the basic roles of money in a modern market economy.

2. When people use the *barter* system, they exchange goods for goods and do not use money. The most serious flaw in the barter system is the need for *double coincidence of demand.* That is, the person you wish to trade with must have what you want, and also want what you have.

3. When people use a *money exchange* system, they exchange goods for money and then money for goods. This is a much more efficient way to carry out the four functions money performs: (a) It is a *medium of exchange.* (b) It is a *standard of value or unit of account.* (c) It is a *store of value.* (d) It is a *means of deferred payment.*

4. The characteristics of a good money are the following: (a) It is portable, or easily carried. (b) It is easily recognized, but hard to counterfeit or duplicate. (c) It is easily subdivided. (d) It costs little to store. (e) It is durable. (f) The supply of it is relatively stable.

5. The *supply of money* in the United States has become more difficult to define and measure. One definition is that it consists of all *demand deposits* and all currency and coin in circulation. About 75 percent of the supply of money, thus defined, is in the form of demand and other checkable deposits *(checking accounts). Depository institutions* are those financial firms that hold demand deposits and honor checks written against them. *Currency* is issued by the Federal Reserve, while *coins* are minted and issued by the Treasury. *Fiat money* is any money that has greater value as a monetary instrument than as a commodity. *Legal tender* is any money that the government says is to be accepted for all debts, public and private.

6. Coins are an example of fiat money. Almost all coins today are debased (contain less valuable metal). Those that are not debased (contain valuable metal) have been driven from circulation by the debased coins. This illustrates Gresham's Law that debased money will drive non-debased money out of circulation.

7. Money is debt. *Demand deposits* are debts (liabilities) of commercial banks. *Currency* is a debt (liability) of the Federal Reserve.

8. Measuring the money supply as demand deposits, currency and coin is known as M_1, a measure of the highly liquid financial instruments that are quickly used as a medium of exchange.

M_1 = Currency, Coin, Travelers' Checks and Checking Deposits

9. Since money also serves as a standard and store of value as well as a means of deferred payment, we can broaden the money supply measurement to include those financial instruments that serve these additional purposes. This measure is known as M_2 and adds near monies, things that have all the characteristics of money except that they do not readily serve as a medium of exchange. Included in M_2 are the components of M_1 plus savings deposits, small time deposits and money market mutual funds.

$$M_2 = M_1 + \text{Savings Deposits} + \text{Small Time Deposits} + \text{Money Market Mutual Funds}$$

10. The broadest conventional measure of the Money supply, M_3 adds long-term negotiable financial instruments, especially large denomination certificates of deposit.

$$M_3 = M_2 + \text{Large Value Certificates of Deposit}$$

11. Credit cards are not money. They are simply instruments that permit individuals to borrow against future income. As such, they may affect short-term variations in demand but serve none of the four functions of money; neither are they near money.

12. Goldsmith banking in seventeenth-century England established the basic structures of modern commercial banking including the *fractional reserve principle.*

13. One can use the *equation of exchange,* MV = PQ, to describe how changes in the supply of money affect economic activity. In this equation, M is the supply of money, V is the velocity of exchange, P is the price level, and Q is actual output.

14. The *velocity of exchange* (V) is calculated by dividing NNP by M_1. Though it grew between 1960 and 1985, it has been rather constant since.

15. Assuming *velocity of exchange* (V) to be constant, when the supply of money (M) increases, PQ increases. If there is unemployment and unused plant capacity as M increases, output (Q) increases and price (P) is relatively stable. As the economy approaches full employment, price (P) begins to increase while M is still increasing, and when the economy reaches full employment, only prices increase.

16. An alternate approach to how changes in the money supply affect economic activity examines why people hold money. They hold it for purposes of *transactions, precaution,* and *speculation.* The amounts they want to hold depend on their incomes, the quantities and kinds of assets they have, and their lifestyles.

17. When the supply of money increases, people have more money on hand than they want, and they try to convert it to other assets (invest it) or they spend it on more consumption. If the supply of money decreases, people have less money on hand than they want, and they try to increase their cash on hand by cutting back on their consumption or by reducing their investments (or both).

KEY TERMS

Barter
Demand deposits
Depository institutions
Double coincidence of demand
Equation of exchange
Fiat money
Fractional reserve principle
Gresham's Law
Legal tender
M_1 money
M_2 money
M_3 money
Medium of exchange, standard of value, store of value, means of deferred payment
Money
Near monies

QUESTIONS

1. What are the four basic functions of money? How does rapid inflation affect the performance of these functions?

2. "Money is the root of all evil." Why don't we do away with it?

3. Suppose that our government suddenly printed up enough money to give everyone a new fifty-dollar bill. What would happen to output and prices? State clearly the assumptions you are making about employment and velocity of exchange.

4. Why are near monies not included in M_1?

5. How does M_3 differ from M_2?

6. In what ways did goldsmith banking create the foundations for present day banking?

7. What are the characteristics of a good money? Pick three commodities, and analyze their favorable and unfavorable characteristics as a good money.

8. "Money is money because people say it's money." Do you agree? Why?

9. Why do non-debased coins not circulate as part of the money supply?

10. What effects do credit cards have on the supply of money?

Chapter 12: Commercial Banking and the Creation of M_1 Money

In the previous chapter, we discussed the functions, the characteristics, and a little of the history of money. We mentioned that the bulk of the M_1 money supply is in the form of demand and other checkable deposits, which are held primarily by commercial banks but also by other financial institutions. So in analyzing how the supply of money is increased or decreased, and how it is controlled, we must look again at commercial banking.

The Simple Economy: Four Assumptions About a Simple Model

The U.S. financial system is complex and the best way to approach it is to abstract from that complex reality and set up a simple model. We will call it the Simple Economy and make four assumptions about its financial system to enable us to analyze the process of increasing and decreasing the supply of money in basic terms. Then we will drop these assumptions, one by one, so that the analysis will gradually become more complex and realistic. Finally, we will examine, the U.S. financial system.

Here are the four simplifying assumptions:

1. The only financial institution in the Simple Economy is a single bank. That bank, the First National Bank, is a monopoly bank, or in other words, it is the Simple Economy's banking system.

2. The government has no control over the First National Bank, so there are no regulations that restrict its banking activities.

3. There is no paper currency or coin. The Simple Economy's entire money supply consists of the demand deposits (checking accounts) in the First National Bank.

Table 12-1
The First National Bank's Balance Sheet

Assets		Liabilities and Net Worth	
Loans	$1,000,000	Demand deposits	$1,000,000
Buildings and equipment	500,000	Net worth	500,000

4. The Simple Economy is closed, that is, there is no international trade. This last assumption is the only one we will not drop later in the discussion. If we were to take international trade into account, we would make our discussion of banking transactions unnecessarily complex at this stage. We will introduce open economy banking and monetary policy in the next chapter.

First we will analyze the process of increasing and decreasing the supply of money in the simplest model. Then we will drop assumption 3 and show what effects currency and coin have on the money supply. Then we will drop assumption 2 and show what happens when the government regulates the supply of money. Finally we will drop the assumption that there is only one bank and analyze the functioning of the multibank system with many separately incorporated banks. At that point we will analyze the U.S. banking system in relation to the supply of money.

Now let's consider the First National Bank, an established and ongoing commercial bank (Table 12-1 shows its balance sheet), with *liabilities* of $1 million, all in demand deposits. In other words, the First National owes its depositors $1 million. It also has $500,000 in *net worth*, which represents the equity or ownership of the stockholders in the bank. Last, it has $1.5 million in assets, $1 million in the form of loans. The First National has loaned that $1 million to the citizens of the Simple Economy. The other $500,000 in assets is in the form of the bank's buildings and equipment. Remember that for the First National's books to balance, the bank's assets and liabilities plus net worth have to be equal, just as they must in any company's accounting balance sheet.

The following short tables will show only *changes* in the balance sheet. This will help us focus on the effects of banking transactions on the supply of money. Note that there is only $1 million in money in the Simple Economy, and remember that all of the Simple Economy's money is in the form of demand deposits (no currency and no coin).

Table 12-2
The Effect of a Loan on the First National Bank's Balance Sheet

Assets		Liabilities	
Loans	+$10,000	Demand deposits	+$10,000

Money Creation in the Simple Model

Joe Bloggs, one of Simple Economy's more ambitious citizens, has made a discovery which he hopes will make him rich. He has invented mottled-gray bubble gum that will blend into sidewalks. He goes to see Elvira Snodgrass, president of the First National Bank, to tell her of his discovery. "Wonderful!" says Snodgrass. "No more of those unsightly pink blobs on our sidewalks. You'll make a pile out of this invention, son!"

When Bloggs asks to borrow $10,000 to set up a bubble-gum factory, Snodgrass approves the loan. Table 12-2 shows what happens then.

First, Bloggs signs a promissory note, stating that he will pay the bank $10,000 in six months' time. To the bank, this promissory note is an asset, since Joe Bloggs now owes the First National Bank $10,000. The category "Loans" increases by $10,000. But now the First National must pay Bloggs that money he has borrowed. It does this by increasing his demand deposits at the bank by $10,000; by this act, it increases the supply of money in the Simple Economy by $10,000.

"But," you may say, "where did the First National Bank get the $10,000 to give Joe Bloggs?" The answer is simple. The bank created that demand deposit by simply writing on Bloggs' account, "plus $10,000." *The bank creates demand deposits to pay for the loans that it makes.* It cannot just take the demand deposit from somebody else's account, because what would *that* person do if he or she wanted to use that demand deposit? Nor can the bank take it from accounts in its own name, because that would mean that the bank owed money to itself, which is an absurdity. The point we are trying to make is that commercial banks create demand deposits when they make loans.

With that $10,000 demand deposit, Bloggs first hires a contractor to build his factory and pays the contractor $2,500. He makes this payment by writing a check on his account. So Bloggs' account goes down by $2,500 and the account of the contractor goes up by $2,500. There is no change in the Simple Economy's supply of money, for accounts are only transferred. Bloggs then buys machinery for $2,500, and writes another check to pay for it. Again his account shrinks by $2,500, while the machinery seller's demand deposits increase by $2,500. Again, there is no change in the supply of money, only transfers of demand deposits. When Bloggs buys raw materials for $2,500, the same thing happens. And it happens again when he hires workers and starts producing bubble gum.

In effect then, as Bloggs spends his demand deposit, his account is slowly transferred to those to whom he makes payments by writing checks. The supply of money changes hands as the demand deposit at the bank is transferred. (Isn't this like your own experience with commercial banks?)

Table 12-3
Decrease in the Supply of Money

Assets		**Liabilities**	
Loans	-$10,000	Demand deposits	-$10,000

Now Bloggs starts selling bubble gum to retail stores, which the store owners pay for by writing checks drawn on their own demand deposits. Bloggs deposits those checks, so his account increases while the accounts of the store owners decrease. Still no change in the *supply* of money. Joe makes profits, and eventually his demand deposits increase to $10,000.

Now Bloggs can pay off his promissory note to the bank. He goes to the office of President Snodgrass and writes a check for $10,000. Snodgrass writes "Paid" on the promissory note and deducts the amount from Bloggs's account. (In effect, Bloggs has received and paid off an interest-free loan. To keep our analysis simple, we have avoided the subject of interest on loans.)

Table 12-3 shows the transactions on the books of the First National Bank. Note that the account called "Loans" decreases by $10,000 as Bloggs pays off the note. The First National Bank's demand deposits are also decreased by $10,000 as the bank deducts the check from Bloggs' demand deposits. The Simple Economy's supply of money actually decreases by $10,000, for Bloggs's check to the bank decreases only his own demand deposit and is not transferred to any other account.

What has this analysis shown us? (1) When a commercial bank (First National Bank) makes a loan, and creates a demand deposit in order to make the loan, the supply of money is increased. (2) When a loan is paid off by means of a check that decreases demand deposits, the supply of money is decreased.

Enter Currency and Coin

We are about to drop assumption 3 because there are two basic weaknesses in this simple model: (1) For small purchases, it is very inefficient to write checks transferring demand deposits; one needs paper currency and coin. (2) The existence of currency and coin provides an automatic check on the ability of the First National Bank to expand the supply of money.

The first weakness (no currency or coin) is apparent. When a supply of money consists only of demand deposits, all transactions, no matter how small, have to be made by checks and transferring demand deposits. When you buy a newspaper, you would have to write a check for fifty cents. The cost of handling checks for these small amounts would be greater than the value of the transactions. Therefore, one important function of currency and coin is to provide a more efficient form of money for small-value transactions.

Table 12-4
The Effect of the Government's $1 Million Deposit of Currency and Coin on the Balance Sheet of the First National Bank

Assets		Liabilities	
Cash in vault	+$1,000,000	Demand deposits	+$1,000,000

The second weakness is that in this simple model without currency or coin, the bank (by lending) can expand the supply of money without limit. When we introduce currency and coin, you will see that they provide an automatic check on the ability of the bank to expand loans and thus to expand the supply of money.

We said that people in the United States find it most comfortable to hold about 25 percent of the M_1 supply of money in the form of currency and coin. (This percentage varies somewhat from place to place and from one month to another.) We will assume that the Simple Economy people are like Americans. They also want to hold 25 percent of the supply of money to be used for exchange purposes in the form of currency and coin. And we will also assume that this percentage does not vary.

Let's introduce currency and coin into the economy. The Simple Economy's government wants to spend $1 million more than it receives in taxes. To cover this deficit, it issues $1 million in currency and coin. What happens when the government deposits the currency in the First National Bank? Table 12-4 shows the effect on the First National's balance sheet.

The bank now has an asset of $1 million called "Cash in vault," and also a liability of $1 million, which is the demand deposit held by the government that represents the deposit of currency. The Simple Economy's supply of money has increased by $1 million, the demand deposit owned by the government. Remember that the actual cash in the First National Bank's vault is not yet part of the supply of money, because it is not yet in circulation.

The government spends the $1 million for various goods and services, like roads, bombers, and education. This spending transfers the demand deposit from the government to the individuals who sell these goods to the government. Remember, though, that people want 25 percent of their supply of money in the form of currency and coin. Therefore, they withdraw from their demand deposits $250,000 in cash.

Table 12-5 shows the results. Only $750,000 remains in the vault in cash, and demand deposits are only $750,000. The supply of money, however, is still $1 million consisting of $750,000 in demand deposits and $250,000 in currency and coin in circulation, in people's pockets.

Now the First National Bank has assets in a form that does not earn it any income (the $750,000 cash in its vault). The bank's officers want to put those assets to work earning income. So they lend out $1 million, which, as you already know, creates demand deposits of $1 million.

Table 12-5

The Effect on the First National Bank of a Withdrawal by Depositors of $250,000 in Cash from Their Demand Deposits

Assets		Liabilities	
Cash in vault	$750,000	Demand deposits	$750,000

Table 12-6

The Effect on the First National Bank's Balance Sheet of a Second Withdrawal of $250,000 by Depositors

Assets		Liabilities	
Cash in vault	$500,000	Demand deposits	$1,500,000
Loans	1,000,000		

Remember that the bank can lend more money than the amount of cash it holds in its vault because the depositors want to keep only 25 percent of the supply of money in the form of currency and coin.

Now the demand deposits are $1 million fatter. What happens? Well, the people still want to keep 25 percent of the country's money in the form of, currency and coin, so they withdraw *another* $250,000 in cash. Table 12-6 shows the net results. "Cash in vault" is down to $500,000 and the total of demand deposits is $1.5 million. The supply of money is now $2 million, $1.5 million in demand deposits and $500,000 in currency and coin in circulation.

The First National Bank still has assets in a form that does not earn them any income (the $500,000 "Cash in vault"). The bank's officers want to put the assets to work, so they extend *more* loans. Let's say they loan $2 million, and thereby create demand deposits of an additional $2 million. The citizens of the Simple Economy still wish to keep 25 percent of their M_1 money in the form of currency and coin. To do this they withdraw $500,000 in cash, reducing demand deposits by a like amount.

Table 12-7 shows the net results. The First National Bank's vault no longer has any cash at all. Loans and discounts are $3 million and demand deposits are $3 million. The country's supply of money is now $4 million; that is, $3 million in demand deposits and $1 million in currency and coin in circulation. If the bank extends still more loans, and thereby creates still more demand deposits, the depositors, to get the 25 percent of the total money supply in currency and coin that they want, will demand more currency than the bank has.

Table 12-7
The First National Bank's Balance Sheet When It Increases Loans to $3 Million

Assets		Liabilities	
Cash in vault	0	Demand deposits	$3,000,000
Loans	3,000,000		

In effect, *the amount of currency and coin in the vaults of the bank places a limit on the amount that the bank can lend.* Since the people want to hold 25 percent of the money supply in the form of currency and coin, the country's total supply of money is limited to four times the amount of currency and coin available, or one dollar in cash for every three dollars in demand deposits. In order to increase its lending, and thus the supply of money (demand deposits), the First National Bank would have to get more currency and coin from the government.

www.federalreserve.gov
For more information on banking regulation visit this web site.

To summarize, currency and coin perform two functions: (1) For purchases that have small value, they are a more efficient form of money than demand deposits. (2) They provide an automatic check on the ability of the bank to make loans, create demand deposits, and increase the supply of money.

Enter the Government

Let us now drop our second assumption, that there is no government regulation. The Simple Economy's government creates a Central Bank for the purpose of controlling lending by the First National Bank. The government requires that the First National Bank keep assets in the form of reserves equal to a specific percentage of its demand deposits, and gives the Central Bank the power to increase or decrease these reserves. (Bear in mind that Central Banks, such as the Federal Reserve, are only bankers' banks. They do not engage in banking activities involving the public.)

Reserve Requirements

Remember that a bank's reserves are not demand deposits, but some form of assets that the banking authority defines as reserves. The U.S. government defines *reserves* as all deposits by *depository institutions* in the Federal Reserve, plus currency and coin held in the vaults of these institutions.

Enter the Federal Reserve (Courtesy Federal Reserve System)

Table 12-8
Reserves Versus Demand Deposits for the First National Bank

Assets		**Liabilities**	
Required reserves	$200,000	Demand deposits	$1,000,000
Excess reserves	800,000		
Total reserves	$1,000,000		

Required Reserve Ratio
The minimum ratio of reserves to deposits that depository institutions are required to maintain.

Let's say that the Simple Economy's Central Bank defines reserves as the U.S. Federal Reserve does. This means that the First National Bank may count as reserves all First National Bank deposits at the Central Bank, plus all currency and coin the First National Bank holds. The law says that the First National Bank must keep a minimum quantity of reserves equal to a certain percentage of its demand deposits. This percentage is called the **required reserve ratio**. For example, suppose that the required reserve ratio is 20 percent and that the First National Bank has $1 million in demand deposits. According to law, the First National Bank must have $200,000 in reserves (20 percent of $1 million) or $200,000 in deposits at the Federal Reserve Bank, and/or in currency and coin.

Table 12-8 shows that the First National Bank has $1 million in reserves and also $1 million in demand deposits. Since there is only a 20 percent required reserve ratio, to comply with the law, the First National Bank is required to hold only $200,000 of those reserves. The other $800,000 of its reserves are not required, and are called **excess reserves**. A bank's required reserves plus its excess reserves equal its *total reserves*.

Excess Reserves
Reserves of depository institutions that are above the required reserve ratio.

Now consider the excess reserves of the First National Bank, assets it is not required to have and that are not earning income for it. What can the First National Bank do to remedy this? Table 12-9 shows the First National Bank's accounts after it lends out $1 million, which in turn creates (or increases demand deposits by) $1 million (the payment of the loan). The First National Bank's total reserves are still $1 million, because there has been no change in deposits at the Central Bank and no change in currency and coin. All that the First National Bank has done is to create a loan, and therefore to create a demand deposit. However, demand deposits are now $2 million, and the amount of reserves that are required (which must be 20 percent of demand deposits) increases to $400,000. Excess reserves decrease, to $600,000, since some of those excess reserves now become part of required reserves.

Table 12-9
The First National Bank's Accounts After It Lends an Additional $1 Million (thus increasing demand deposits by $1 million)

Assets		Liabilities	
Required reserves	$400,000	Demand deposits	$1,000,000
Excess reserves	600,000		
Total reserves	$1,000,000		
Loans	$1,000,000		

Table 12-10
The First National Bank's Accounts After It Lends an Additional $3 Million More and Reduces Its Excess Reserves to Zero

Assets		Liabilities	
Required reserves	$1,000,000	Demand deposits	$5,000,000
Excess reserves	0		
Total reserves	$1,000,000		
Loans	$4,000,000		

The First National Bank still has $600,000 worth of non-income-earning assets (the remaining excess reserves of $600,000). Table 12-10 shows that the bank's officers finally increase their loans by $3 million, which increases demand deposits by the same amount, to $5 million. Nothing has happened to the First National Bank's total reserves because there has been no change in either its deposits at the Central BankCC or its holdings of currency and coin. However, required reserves (20 percent of demand deposits) now equal total reserves, and there are no excess reserves left in the bank. So the First National Bank cannot lend another penny to anyone.

Each time a bank extends loans and creates demand deposits, its required reserves must increase by 20 percent of the increase in demand deposits. Since the act of lending and creating demand deposits does not affect total reserves, this increase in required reserves must come out of excess reserves. Now the First National Bank has reached the position (see Table 12-10) of zero excess reserves. It cannot lend any more money, because, if it tried to, the law would require it to hold more reserves than it has, and it would be violating the banking laws. The bank must have excess reserves before it can lend more and increase its demand deposits further. These excess reserves can then quickly become required reserves to comply with the law that specifies 20 percent required reserves.

In comparing Tables 12-8, 12-9, and 12-10, one can see that $800,000 in excess reserves enables the bank to create five times that amount in demand deposits. Because the required reserve ratio is 20 percent, the First National Bank can expand the supply of money by five times its excess reserves. This means that it needs only one dollar of reserves for every five dollars of demand deposits. This is the bank's **fractional reserve requirement**. If the required reserve ratio were to be increased to 50 percent, the bank would need one dollar of reserves to create two dollars of demand deposits. If the required reserves were to be increased still further, to 100 percent, the bank would have to hold one dollar for every dollar it loaned. In other words, required reserves and demand deposits would have to be equal.

Fractional Reserve Requirement
The minimum percentage of reserves against deposits that depository institutions must legally maintain.

Enter Many Other Banks

Now remember the first assumption that the First National Bank is the only commercial bank in Simple Economy. It is a *monopoly* bank; it is, in fact, the entire commercial banking system. A monopoly bank can lend money and create demand deposits (money) that are a multiple of its excess reserves. The First National Bank can do this because depositors cannot write checks and deposit them in other banks. There *are* no other banks.

The behavior of an individual commercial bank in a multibank system differs from that of a monopoly bank with respect to its excess reserves, lending, and creation of demand deposits.

Now we will drop the assumption that there is only one bank, a monopoly bank, in the economy. Let's assume that there are more than 15,000 separately incorporated, privately owned, commercial banks, and that the economy being discussed is that of the U.S. Now we can begin to analyze the U.S. banking system.

The Federal Reserve and Clearing Checks

The United States has had a Central Bank since 1913. It is called the Federal Reserve System or "Fed" for short. The nation is divided into *twelve* reserve districts, each with a Federal Reserve Bank. Federal Reserve Banks perform an important function not previously discussed, they serve as a national clearinghouse for checks. Now what does that mean?

In our system, with its many commercial banks, you can write a check on your account in one bank and have it deposited in an account in another bank. How do banks collect or receive payment for such checks from other banks? They do it through the Federal Reserve (Fed) collection process.

Table 12-11 shows what changes take place in this collection process. You write a check for $1,000 on a demand deposit in the Bank of America in California, and this check is deposited in the First National Bank of Boston. The

Table 12-11
The Effect of One Check on the Federal Reserve and Two of Its Member Banks

Bank of America		Federal Reserve	First National Bank of Boston	
Assets	**Liabilities**	**Deposits**	**Assets**	**Liabilities**
Reserves	Demand deposits	First National Bank of Boston	Reserves	Demand deposits
–$1,000	–$1,000	+$1,000	+$1,000	+$1,000
		Bank of America		
		–$1,000		

demand deposits in the First National Bank of Boston are increased by $1,000. To collect its money, the First National Bank sends the check to the Federal Reserve, which increases the First National Bank's deposits with the Fed. In other words, the reserves of the First National Bank increase by $1,000. Meanwhile, back at the Bank of America, the situation is the opposite. The Federal Reserve reduces the Bank of America's deposits with the Fed by $1,000. In other words, the reserves of the Bank of America decrease by $1,000. The Federal Reserve then sends the canceled check to the Bank of America, which reduces *your* demand deposits by $1,000.

In brief, at a multibank system, when a check is drawn on an account in Alpha Bank and deposited in Bravo Bank, there is a transfer of both demand deposits and reserves (deposits at the Federal Reserve). The Federal Reserve acts as the third party, the go-between.

Lending by Individual Banks: A Little Goes a Long Way

Now we are going to deal with a number of independent banks in the Federal Reserve System. Let's call our four representative banks Alpha, Bravo, Charlie, and Delta. An individual bank in a multibank system can lose both demand deposits and reserves overnight to other banks, through a flow of checks. Therefore, Alpha Bank, an individual bank in a multibank system, cannot lend money and create demand deposits that are a multiple of its excess reserves. Alpha Bank, following a conservative rule, lends an amount *equal only to its own excess reserves.* If it lends more, it runs the risk of losing (through a flow of checks) so much of its reserves that it cannot meet the law's reserve requirements.

Table 12-12 shows the changes in the relevant accounts for Alpha Bank as it applies this rule. Part (a) shows that Alpha Bank, before it lends $800,000, has $1 million of established demand deposits. On the basis of its past experience, Alpha Bank estimates that these deposits will remain with the bank. Alpha Bank also has $1 million in reserves, of which $200,000 are required and $800,000 are excess, since the required reserve ratio is 20 percent.

Part (b) of Table 12-12 shows Alpha Bank lending only an amount equal to its excess reserves. Suppose, however, that the worst occurs (part c) and that all these new demand deposits flow out as checks to other banks, for example, to Bravo Bank.

Table 12-12
Changes in the Relevant Accounts for Alpha Bank

(a) Alpha Bank Before it Lends $800,000		(b) Alpha Bank After it Lends $800,000	
Assets	**Liabilities**	**Assets**	**Liabilities**
Required reserves $200,000	Demand deposits $1,000,000	Reserves $1,000,000	Demand deposits $1,800,000
Excess reserves $800,000		Loans $800,000	
Total reserves $1,000,000			

(c) Alpha Bank After Checks Have Cleared		(d) Bravo Bank After Receiving Checks	
Assets	Liabilities	Assets	Liabilities
Reserves $200,000	Demand deposits $1,000,000	Reserves $800,000	Demand deposits $800,000
Loans $800,000			

Bravo Bank now has an increase in demand deposits of $800,000 (part d). It sends these checks to the Federal Reserve, which promptly increases Bravo's deposits there by $800,000 and at the same time reduces Alpha's deposits there by $800,000. The Federal Reserve then sends the canceled checks to Alpha Bank, which duly notes the fact that its demand deposits have shrunk by $800,000.

Part (c) shows us, however, that even though Alpha Bank has lost $800,000 in reserves and demand deposits, it can still meet its obligations. It still has its required reserves ($200,000 in reserves is adequate because the bank has $1 million in demand deposits and the required reserve ratio is 20 percent).

In Table 12-13, part (a) shows that Bravo Bank now has excess reserves of $640,000. Part (b) shows Bravo lending up to its limit of $640,000, thereby creating demand deposits of $640,000.

Now suppose the worst happens (part c). All the checks drawn on Bravo Bank's newly created demand deposits flow to Charlie Bank. Charlie Bank now has an increase in its demand deposit of $640,000.

Charlie Bank sends these checks to the Federal Reserve, which increases Charlie Bank's deposits with the Federal Reserve (and its own reserves) by $640,000 (part d). At the same time, the Fed deducts $640,000 from Bravo Bank's deposits at the Fed (and lowers Bravo's reserves by that amount). When Bravo gets these canceled checks back, it records the information that it has $640,000 less in demand deposits.

Bravo Bank has followed the rule and lent only as much as it held in excess reserves. Even though it has lost the newly created demand deposits and equivalent reserves, it can still satisfy the legal reserve requirement.

Table 12-13
Changes in the Relevant Accounts for Bravo Bank

(a) Bravo Bank Before it Lends $640,000		(b) Bravo Bank After it Lends $640,000	
Assets	**Liabilities**	**Assets**	**Liabilities**
Required reserves $160,000	Demand deposits $800,000	Reserves $800,000	Demand deposits $1,440,000
Excess reserves $640,000		Loans $640,000	
Total reserves $800,000			

(c) Bravo Bank After Checks Have Cleared		(d) Charlie Bank After Receiving Checks	
Assets	**Liabilities**	**Assets**	**Liabilities**
Reserves $160,000	Demand deposits $800,000	Reserves $640,000	Demand deposits $640,000
Loans $640,000			

We could continue to analyze this process at great length. At each round of lending, the excess reserves diminish (as excess reserves are reclassified as required reserves), so that excess reserves decrease only to the limit of its excess reserves, creating demand deposits (money) to pay for the loans. However, as excess reserves filter through all the banks, the whole banking system makes loans and creates demand deposits that are a multiple of the original excess reserves in Alpha Bank.

Table 12-14
Demand Deposits Created

Bank	Amount
Alpha Bank	$800,000
Bravo Bank	640,000
Charlie Bank	512,000
Delta Bank	409,600
Rest of the banks	1,638,400
	$4,000,000

Table 12-14 shows what happens. Alpha Bank created $800,000 in demand deposits. This money, by means of checks, was transferred to Bravo Bank. Bravo Bank took this $800,000 and created $640,000 in demand deposits. If we had continued our analysis, you would have seen that Charlie Bank then created $512,000 in demand deposits. And when that money got over to Delta Bank, Delta Bank created $409,600. As the money went further and further, the other banks in the system created $1,638,400. Because the required reserve ratio is 20 percent, the whole banking system could create $4 million in new demand deposits, even though each bank made loans and generated new demand deposits only up to the amount of its excess reserves. If each bank lends an amount equal to its excess reserves and uses only demand deposits to pay out money for the loans, the formula for the multiple that demand deposits may be of the required reserve ratio, the **deposit multiplier** (DM) is:

Deposit Multiplier
The formula for determining the multiple that demand deposits may be of required reserves. DM = 1/ R

$$DM = 1/R,$$

where R is the required reserve ratio. In our example, R is 20 percent. The deposit multiplier equals:

$$DM = 1/.20 \text{ or } 5$$

But What About Leakages That Restrain Demand Deposit Creation?

We have seen that it is technically possible, with a 20 percent required reserve ratio, for banks to have a maximum potential of creating new demand deposits five times the original excess reserves. However, the full multiple creation of demand deposits rarely takes place. There are what are called **leakages**, factors in the creation of demand deposits in the process, which reduce the ability of the depository institutions to expand demand deposits.

Leakages
Factors in the creation of demand deposits which reduce the ability of depository institutions to expand demand deposits.

1. *Currency and Coin (C)*. Suppose that people who borrow from the bank withdraw currency and coin from their demand deposits. This has the effect of withdrawing reserves from the banking system, thus reducing the amount of demand deposits that can be created. For example, suppose that when Alpha Bank lends out the original $800,000, one of the borrowers demands $100,000 in currency as payment, instead of a demand deposit. So, instead of $800,000 in checks being transferred from Alpha Bank to Bravo Bank, only $700,000 in checks is transferred. Reserves (deposits at the Federal Reserve) shifted from Alpha to Bravo are $700,000 (not $800,000). Bravo's excess reserves are thus $560,000, not $640,000. Bravo Bank cannot make as many new loans or create as large demand deposits, and this effect is passed on through the rest of the system. The $100,000 taken as currency in payment of loans at Alpha Bank reduces the original excess reserves in the banking system, and thus the total of new loans and demand deposits.

2. *Excess Reserves (E)*. We have assumed so far that each independent bank lends up to the limit of its excess reserves, that it lends every penny it can, provided it can maintain enough reserves to meet the legal minimum. In practice, bankers are often much more conservative and want to keep a cushion or extra reserve in case checks are drawn against them in amounts greater than the amounts of the new demand deposits. What if some depositors write checks against Alpha Bank's original deposits and this money flows into other banks? If Alpha has not kept some of its excess reserves on hand, it will not be able to meet these unexpected transfers of demand deposits and reserves. However, if

banks do lend out amounts less than their excess reserves, then the amount of the demand deposits created in the system is much less.

3. *Demand for Loans*. The fact that the banking system has excess reserves (the ability to make loans) does not mean that there are always good opportunities to lend. During a business slump, bankers may fear that some potential borrowers will not be able to repay loans. So when times are bad, bankers may not lend up to the maximum. Also, at times there may not be much demand for loans even when interest rates are low.

When we take these leakages into consideration, the formula for the deposit multiplier becomes more complex:

$$\text{DM} = \frac{1}{R + E + C}$$

where R is the required reserve ratio, E is excess reserves, those *not* used by the banking system to create loans, and C is the currency withdrawn by those receiving loans. We cannot factor loan demand conditions into the formula because it focuses only on the ability to supply loans.

The Role of Excess Reserves

In our analysis of the way money is created under government regulation, we have pointed out the crucial role of excess reserves. Without excess reserves, banks cannot extend loans and create demand deposits. Therefore, control over the amounts of reserves in the banking system means control over the amount of lending that is done, and, by extension, control over the supply of M_1 money itself. As the supply of the many near monies we looked at earlier has grown, the Fed's ability to control all forms of money has been somewhat diminished. As we saw with the sharply restrictive monetary policy of the Fed in 1981-1982, however, its power to control money and economic activity remains very great and its authority over reserve requirements was extended in the 1980s to all depository institutions, not simply commercial banks. Only the Federal Reserve has the power to increase or decrease the required amount of excess reserves in the system. If it wishes to increase economic activity it can lower deposits creating reserve requirements. On the other hand, if it wishes to restrict the growth of economic activity, it can raise reserve requirements. How it may do this is a subject we will look at in the next chapter.

A Final Word About Excess Reserves

Excess reserves can be used to create earnings for financial institutions. Though cautious, bankers naturally tend therefore, to minimize the amount of excess reserves they hold. One important way they do this is to turn them into very-short-term earning assets by lending them to other banks that are short of required or desired reserves. A market has been created in which such transfers occur. That market, the **federal funds market**, handles billions of dollars of such inter-bank transfers through brokers. If Alpha Bank is short of reserves, it contacts a broker who arranges a short-term (often overnight) transfer of excess reserves from Bravo Bank. The interest rate at which such reserve loans is made is known as the *Federal Funds Rate.* A key point, in other words, is that excess reserves do not just sit around idly in the American financial system.

Federal Funds Market
The market in which banks, through inter-bank transfers, lend their excess reserves to other banks.

Application I: First Steps in Banking

The following selection from *Punch,* the late British humor magazine, requires no introduction.

Q. What are banks for?
A. To make money.

Q. For the customers?
A. For the banks.

Q. Why doesn't bank advertising mention this?
A. It would not be in good taste. But it is mentioned by implication in references to Reserves of £249,000,000 or thereabouts. That is the money they have made.

Q. Out of the customers?
A. I suppose so.

Q. They also mention Assets of £500,000,000 or thereabouts. Have they made that too?
A. Not exactly. That is the money they use to make money.

Q. I see. And they keep it in a safe somewhere?
A. Not at all. They lend it to customers.

Q. Then they haven't got it?
A. No.

Q. Then how is it Assets?
A. They maintain that it would be if they got it back.

Q. But they must have some money in a safe somewhere?
A. Yes, usually £500,000,000 or thereabouts. This is called Liabilities.

Q. But if they've got it, how can they be liable for it?
A. Because it isn't theirs.

Q. Then why do they have it?
A. It has been lent to them by customers.

Q. You mean customers lend banks money?
A. In effect. They put money into their accounts, so it is really lent to the banks.

Q. And what do the banks do with it?
A. Lend it to other customers.

Q. But you said that money they lent to other people was Assets?
A. Yes.

Q. Then Assets and Liabilities must be the same thing?
A. You can't really say that.

Q. But you've just said it. If I put £100 into my account the bank is liable to have to pay it back, so it's Liabilities. But they go and lend it to someone else, and he is liable to have to pay it back, so it's Assets. It's the same £100, isn't it?
A. Yes, but ....

Q. Then it cancels out. It means, doesn't it, that banks haven't really any money at all?
A. Theoretically....

Q. Never mind theoretically. And if they haven't any money where do they get their Reserves of £249,000,000 or thereabouts?
A. I told you. That is the money they have made.

Q. How?
A. Well, when they lend your £100 to someone they charge him interest.

Q. How much?
A. It depends on the Bank Rate. Say five and a half per cent. That's their profit.

Q. Why isn't it my profit? Isn't it my money?
A. It's the theory of banking practice that....

Q. When I lend them my £100 why don't I charge them interest?
A. You do.

Q. You don't say. How much?
A. It depends on the Bank Rate. Say half a percent.

Q. Grasping of me, rather?
A. But that's only if you're not going to draw the money out again.

Q. But of course, I'm going to draw it out again. If I hadn't wanted to draw it out again I could have buried it in the garden, couldn't I?
A. They wouldn't like you to draw it out again.

Q. Why not? If I keep it there you say it's a Liability. Wouldn't they be glad if I reduced their Liabilities by removing it?
A. No. Because if you remove it they can't lend it to anyone else.

Q. But if I wanted to remove it they'd have to let me?
A. Certainly.

Q. But suppose they've already lent it to another customer?
A. Then they'll let you have someone else's money.

Q. But suppose he wants his too...and they've let me have it?
A. You're being purposely obtuse.

Q. I think I'm being acute. What if everyone wanted their money at once?

A.It's the theory of banking practice that they never would.
Q.So what banks bank on is not having to meet their commitments?
A.I wouldn't say that.

Q.Naturally. Well, if there's nothing else you think you can tell me...?
A.Quite so. Now you can go off and open a banking account.

Q.Just one last question.
A.Of course.

Q.Wouldn't I do better to go off and open a bank?

SUMMING UP

1. Our analysis of the banking system of the imaginary Simple Economy is based on four assumptions: (a) There is only one bank in the system, the First National Bank. (b) There are no government regulations. (c) There is no currency or coin. The economy's supply of money is limited to the amount of demand deposits in the First National Bank. (d) There is no international trade.

2. The First National Bank increases the supply of M_1 money by extending loans, which are paid to the borrower by creating new demand deposits. The borrowers pay off the loans by checks drawn on their demand deposits. This decreases the supply o M_1 money in the economy.

3. The Simple Economy banking system, limited by our four assumptions, has the following weaknesses: (a) For purchases of small value, demand deposits are a very inefficient form of money. (b) The First National Bank's ability to expand the supply of M_1 money through lending is unlimited. But we can eliminate these weaknesses by dropping our third assumption and introducing currency and coin.

4. People like to hold a certain percentage of a nation's money in the form of currency and coin. The amount of currency and coin held provides an automatic check on the bank's ability to extend loans and increase demand deposits. As the bank lends out money, it creates more demand deposits, and demand deposits are money. Then people withdraw more currency and coin from the bank in order to maintain that desired percentage of the money supply in the form of currency and coin. When the bank no longer has any currency and coin left in its vaults, it can no longer lend, and create new demand deposits.

5. Varying the quantity of currency and coin is not an efficient way to regulate the total money supply. A more efficient system is to (a) establish a central bank, such as the Federal Reserve System, (b) require commercial banks to keep assets in the form of reserves equal to a certain percentage of demand deposits, and (c) empower the central bank (the Federal Reserve in the case of the United States) to vary the amount of reserves. In the U.S. financial system, *reserves* are defined as deposits of depository institutions at the Federal Reserve plus cash in the vaults of those institutions.

6. In a one-bank (monopoly) system, loaning money creates demand deposits, but does not affect total reserves. However, in a system that has a government-imposed *required reserve ratio,* an increase in demand deposits raises the figure for required reserves. Banks must then count their *excess reserves* as part of their required reserves. When all its reserves come under the heading of "required," a commercial bank cannot extend loans, because it has no more excess reserves that it can reclassify as required reserves when demand deposits increase.

7. Because the required-reserve ratio is less than 100 percent, that is, it is *fractional*, depository institutions can create demand deposits that are a multiple of their reserves.

8. In our simple model of the banking system in the Simple Economy, the monopoly bank need not be concerned about a flow of checks and reserves to other banks because there is only one bank in the system. Therefore, a monopoly bank can expand the supply of money (create demand deposits) by lending out money equal to a multiple of its reserves. The size of the multiplier depends on the size of the required reserve ratio.

9. When we drop the assumption that there is only one bank and assume that there are 12,000 banks, with the Federal Reserve controlling all of them, we are approximating a model of the U.S. banking system. The Federal Reserve acts as a national clearinghouse for checks. When Alpha Bank receives a check from Bravo Bank, Alpha sends it to the Federal Reserve. The Federal Reserve increases Alpha's deposits (reserves) with the Federal Reserve and reduces Bravo's deposits (reserves) with the Fed. When Bravo Bank receives the check, it reduces the demand-deposit account on which it is drawn.

10. When checks flow from one bank to another, both reserves and demand deposits are transferred. To avoid letting its reserves fall below the required level, an individual bank in a multibank system makes loans (and thus creates demand deposits) only up to the level of its excess reserves. But as these excess reserves gradually filter through the banking system, the banking system creates demand deposits (money) that are a multiple of the original excess reserves.

11. In the real world, the banking system does not increase the supply of M_1 money by the full multiple of its excess reserves because of the following *leakage* effects: (a) Some borrowers want *currency and coins* instead of demand deposits in payment for their loans, which has the effect of withdrawing reserves from the banking system, thus reducing the amount of demand deposits that can be created. (b) Some banks, as a matter of prudence, will wish to keep *excess reserves* because they fear that an unexpected flow of checks to another bank might drain off reserves not only from their new demand deposits, but also from old demand deposits. (c) If there is a business slump, some banks will not lend money up to the limit of their excess reserves, because they fear that some loans will not be repaid. Sometimes, too, there is not much demand for loans, even when interest rates are low.

12. Banks, nonetheless, minimize the holding of excess reserves. Banks that have excess reserves lend them, for very short periods, to other banks that need reserves. This is done through the Federal Funds Market at a rate of interest known as the Federal Funds Rate.

KEY TERMS

Deposit multiplier
Excess reserves
Federal funds market
Fractional reserve requirement
Leakages
Required reserve ratio

QUESTIONS

1. What effects do the following transactions have on the demand deposits and reserves of Alpha Bank? On the whole commercial banking system? Why? (The required reserve ratio is 20 percent.)

   a. Ernie Jones withdraws $100 from his demand deposit account in Alpha Bank.
   b. Susan Smith borrows $500 from Alpha Bank, but puts the proceeds into Bravo Bank.
   c. Betty Cohen deposits $200 in her account at Alpha Bank by a check drawn on someone else's account at Alpha Bank.
   d. Susan Smith pays off her loan at Alpha Bank by a check drawn on her account at Alpha Bank.

2. What effects do these four transactions have on the supply of money? Why?

3. Why must a commercial bank maintain a certain level of reserves under the U.S. banking system? What are excess reserves, and what is their significance?

4. In a commercial banking system, how is the supply of money increased and decreased?

5. In a multibank system, an individual bank makes loans only up to the level of its excess reserves, while the whole commercial banking system can lend out money that is a multiple of the original bank's excess reserves. Why is there this difference?

6. What leakages can prevent a commercial banking system from lending at the full multiple of its original excess reserves?

7. What is the Federal Funds Market? What is the Federal Funds Rate?

Chapter 13: Monetary Policy
Central Banking in Financial Markets That are Deregulated and International

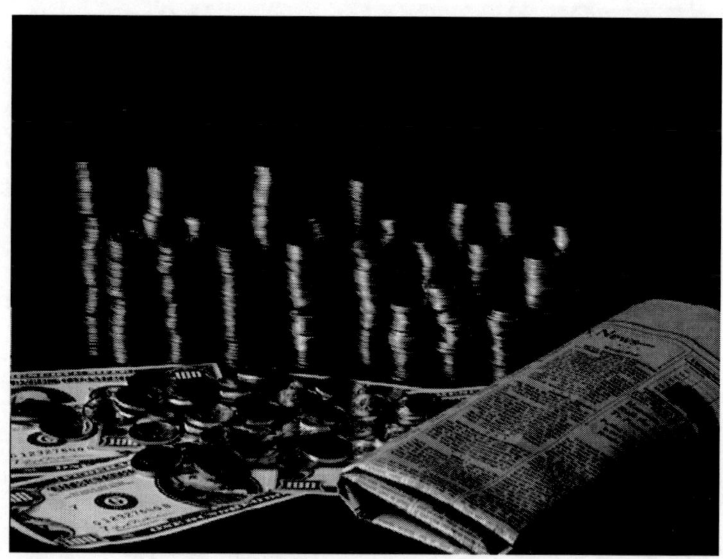

Money, as we have seen, plays a vital role in the economic life of people. The money supply and changes in the money supply affect the decisions of every consumer and producer, as well as the activities of the government. Because of the important link between money and the levels of income, employment, and prices, all modern governments exercise some degree of control over their system of financial institutions. In the United States, these controls began taking their modern form with the creation of the Federal Reserve System (the "Fed") in 1913.

Control by the Fed generally increased from its inception to the 1980s. This was especially true with the banking reforms of the 1930s. By the 1970s, it became clear to many that regulation of monetary institutions had, in some respects, gone too far. As a result, and, in response to rapidly evolving financial markets, substantial deregulation occurred in the 1980s and 1990s and continues to occur into the early 2000s. At the same time, in recognition of the macroeconomic importance of controlling the money supply, some regulatory powers of the Fed have been broadened.

How to control as well as measure the money supply remains an area filled with controversy. After we have examined the workings of the Fed, America's central bank, we will in the application in this chapter, assay some of the controversies between Keynesians and Monetarists, as well as arguments about how effective, if at all, are discretionary macroeconomic policy changes.

Figure 13-1
Boundaries of Federal Reserve Districts and Their Branch Territories

Source: Federal Reserve Bulletin. Reproduced by permission of the Board of Governors of the Federal Reserve System.

THE STRUCTURE OF THE FEDERAL RESERVE

Central Bank
A financial institution established by government to oversee a nation's monetary system.

Where do *banks* go when they want to go to the bank? They go to a Federal Reserve Bank, which is a banker's bank or a **Central Bank**, one that is established by the government to oversee the country's financial system.

When Congress passed the Federal Reserve Act of 1914, it did not create just one bank. It divided the country into 12 Federal Reserve Districts, with a Federal Reserve Bank in each. Figure 13-1 shows the 12 districts and the location of the 12 Federal Reserve Banks. For example, the first Federal Reserve District takes in all of New England. Its Federal Reserve Bank is in Boston. The twelfth district consists of seven western states plus Alaska and Hawaii. Its bank is in San Francisco.

National Banks
Commercial banks chartered by the federal government.

State Banks
Banks chartered by state governments.

www.federalreserve.gov
For more information on the structure of the Federal Reserve visit this web site.

All **national banks** (commercial banks chartered by the federal government) are required to be members of the Federal Reserve System. **State banks** (commercial banks chartered by the various state governments) can join it if they wish. Not all commercial banks are members of the Federal Reserve System. Those that are, however, comprise the larger commercial banks in the United States, and control more than 70 percent of U.S. banking assets. It is important to note that the Depository Institutions Deregulation and Monetary Control Reform Act of 1980, while permitting all depository institutions to offer checkable deposits, imposed uniform reserve requirements on all depository institutions, bank and non-bank alike. The distinction between members and non-members has, thus, become much less important.

Each Federal Reserve Bank is technically owned by the commercial member banks in its district. On becoming a member, each commercial bank must buy stock in its District Federal Reserve Bank, the amount depending on the size of its capital surplus. It receives a fixed annual dividend on these shares.

The main policy-making body of the Federal Reserve is the board of governors, in Washington, D.C. There are seven governors including the chairman, who are appointed for terms of 14 years by the President, with the advice and consent of the Senate. Though not a separate branch of government, the Board of Governors of the Federal Reserve is substantially independent of the executive branch of government. Only rarely has a President had the chance to appoint a majority of the board of governors, since a President ordinarily appoints a new member only once every two years. Therefore, a President who wanted to try to play God with the nation's money supply would not be able to do so unless all seven members of the Board of Governors of the Federal Reserve died or resigned at the same time. Some regard this as a built-in safety valve.

There are two main committees that help the board of governors formulate policy:

1. *The Federal Open Market Committee (FOMC)* controls decision making about the most important weapon the Fed has in controlling excess reserves, lending, and the supply of money: open market operations, which we will say more about later. This committee is made up of the members of the Board together with five of the Presidents of the District Reserve Banks.

2. *The Federal Advisory Council* consists of 12 prominent bankers, one from each of the 12 boards of directors of the Federal Reserve Banks. They meet periodically with the Board and advise the governors about problems in the various districts of the system. The Council, however, has no policy-making authority.

Each of the 12 Federal Reserve Banks has a nine-member board of directors. Three are appointed by the board of governors in Washington, to represent the national interest. Three are elected by the member commercial banks, one from the large banks, one from the medium-size banks, and one from the small banks; they represent banking interests in the particular district. These six appoint the remaining three, who represent the general economic community.

So we see a mixture of both quasi-public and pure public elements in the Federal Reserve System. The national board of governors, with its two main support committees and its three appointed members on each board of directors of the 12 Federal Reserve Banks, is the public element. The ownership of the 12 district Federal Reserve Banks by the commercial banks in that district, plus the fact that the commercial banks appoint three members to the board of directors of their district Federal Reserve Bank, is the quasi-public element. Unquestionably, however, the pure public element is the dominant influence in monetary decision making, and it is important to remember that the Fed is not a profit-making institution. Early in our history, the Congress created two "almost" Central Banks that were both public and private in their functions. The Fed was an effort to create a true Central Bank or "bankers' bank."

General Powers of the Federal Reserve

In the previous chapter we pointed out that commercial banks must have excess reserves in order to make loans and create demand deposits, and that as a bank increases its demand deposits, it must transfer or reclassify excess reserves as required reserves. Also, in a multibank system, the individual commercial bank needs a prudent margin of excess reserves in case its customers decide to write an unexpectedly large number of checks, thereby transferring demand deposits and reserves to other banks. Its ability to participate in the Federal funds market helps it to maintain this margin.

The device we used earlier to explain the Central Bank was a hypothetical economy, the simple economy, with one Central Bank that had the power to vary the amount of excess reserves held by commercial banks. This power is called the **general power** because it enables a central bank to increase or decrease the excess reserves that a commercial bank must have in order to make any kind of loan.

General Power
The authority of the central bank (Fed) to increase or decrease the required reserve ratio.

The U.S. Federal Reserve has three means at its disposal to influence excess reserves: through open-market operations, through the discount rate, and through the required reserve ratio.

Open-Market Operations

What is for sale in the open market? There are many instruments, including debt instruments that are short term (maturing in 90 days to one year), highly liquid (easily sold for a cash return), and relatively free of risk. Examples are *prime commercial paper* (promissory notes of large secure corporations), *banker's acceptances* (short-term debt of banks), and *Treasury bills* (short-term debt of the federal government).

In the open market, the Federal Reserve (FOMC) is an important customer. It buys and sells already issued federal government debt (primarily Treasury bills), which has the effect of increasing or decreasing excess reserves in the commercial banking system. This effect makes open-market operations the most important of the Fed's three weapons. The added advantage of this weapon is that it can be applied selectively. Remember that in open-market operations, the bonds are not bought directly from the Treasury.

1. *Increasing reserves.* To increase a depository institution's excess reserves, the Federal Reserve buys government-debt securities on the open market, as shown in Figure 13-2.

Figure 13-2
Changes in Assets and Liabilities of both the Federal Reserve Bank and the Commercial Bank When the Commercial Bank Sells Government Securities to the Federal Reserve

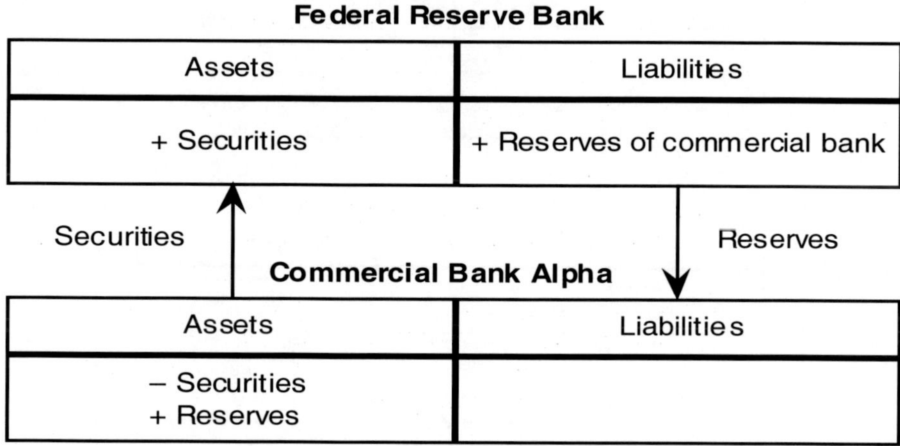

Let's say that a certain commercial bank, Alpha Bank, has customers begging for loans, but Alpha does not have enough excess reserves to lend any more money or to create any more demand deposits. Instead of going to the Federal Funds Market, let's suppose that the Fed comes along and buys some assets, government securities, from Alpha Bank. To pay for these assets, the Fed increases Alpha Bank's deposits with the Federal Reserve. This means that the Fed is taking on a liability. Alpha Bank is exchanging its government securities for a deposit at the Federal Reserve Bank. So Alpha's total reserves increase, and thus its excess reserves also increase.

But what happens when the Federal Reserve buys government securities from private individuals? (See Figure 13-3). Along comes an ordinary citizen, Joe Reed. The Fed buys a government security from him and gives him a check in return. Reed deposits the check in his account at his commercial bank, Alpha Bank. Alpha sends the check to the Federal Reserve, which increases Alpha's deposit with the Fed. That is, it increases Alpha Bank's reserves. The Federal Reserve; has an increase in its assets (the government security it bought from Joe Reed) and an equal increase in its liabilities (the deposits of the commercial bank at the Fed). Joe Reed's total assets are unchanged. The decrease in his holdings of government securities is exactly equal to the increase in his demand deposits. The effect of all this on Alpha Bank is an increase in assets (its reserves increase because its deposits with the Federal Reserve increase), and an increase in liabilities (Reed's demand deposit account). Thus Alpha Bank's total reserves have increased and, therefore, so have its excess reserves.

Figure 13-3
Changes in Assets and Liabilities of the Federal Reserve Bank, Plain Citizen Joe Reed, and Commercial Bank Alpha When the Federal Reserve Bank Buys Government Securities from a Private Citizen

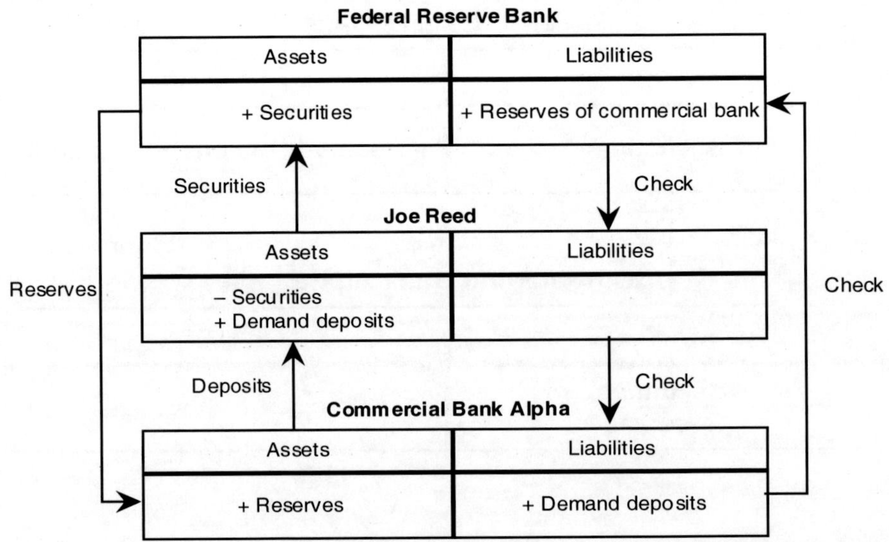

2. *Decreasing reserves.* To decrease depository institutions' excess reserves, and also to decrease their total reserves, the Federal Reserve sells government securities. Figure 13-4 shows how this works.

First, lets say that the Federal Reserve sells the government security to a commercial bank (Bravo Bank). When Bravo Bank buys a government security from the Fed, it pays for it by accepting a reduction in its deposits with the Federal Reserve. The Fed's assets decrease (by the amount of the securities sold to Bravo Bank). Its liabilities also decrease, because Bravo Bank's deposits with the Fed decrease. This means that Bravo Bank's total reserves decline. Therefore, Bravo Bank's excess reserves decline.

Figure 13-4
What Happens to Assets and Liabilities of the Federal Reserve Bank and Commercial Bank Bravo When the Fed Sells Government Securities to Commercial Bank Bravo

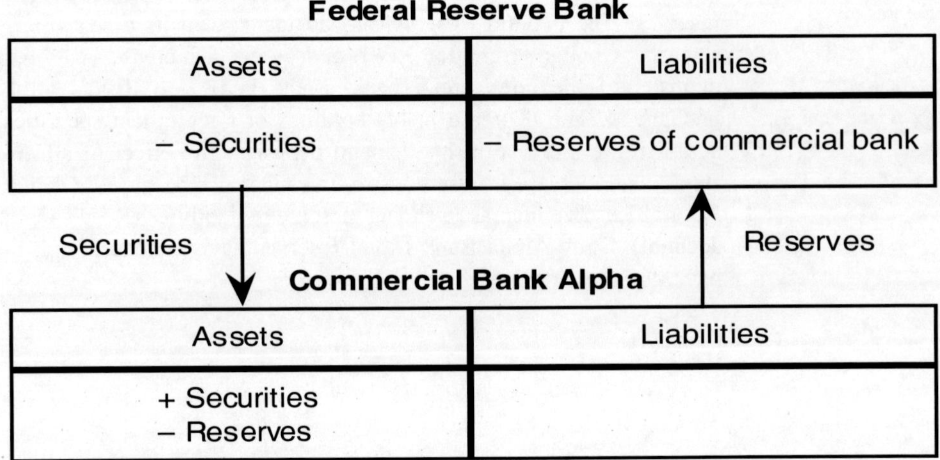

How does it affect excess reserves and the supply of money when the Federal Reserve sells government securities to *non*-commercial banking institutions, or to private individuals? Figure 13-5 shows what happens.

Figure 13-5
What Happens to Assets and Liabilities of the Federal Reserve Bank, Maria Deluca, and Commercial Bank Charlie When the Fed Sells Government Securities to a Private Citizen

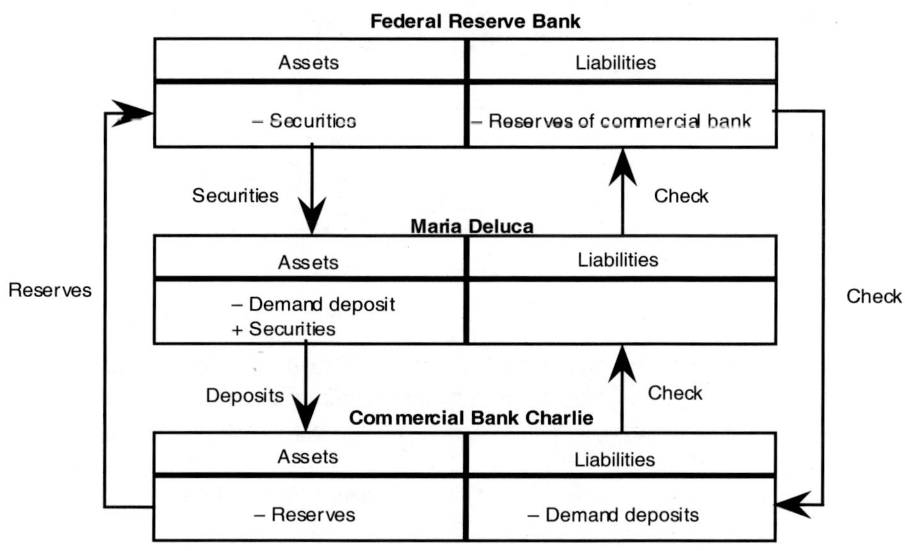

Here is Maria Deluca, citizen, who buys a government security from the Fed and gives a check in return. The Fed collects on the check by reducing the deposits with the Fed of Charlie Bank, the commercial bank that holds Deluca's demand deposits. The Fed sends Deluca's check to Charlie Bank, which reduces the amount of demand deposits in her account. The Fed's assets decrease by the amount of the securities sold to Deluca. There is an offsetting decrease in the Fed's liabilities (Charlie Bank's deposits with the Federal Reserve). The total assets of Maria Deluca are unchanged. Her holdings of government securities increase and her demand deposits decrease by equal amounts. Charlie Bank's assets decrease (its reserves, that is, its deposits at the Federal Reserve, are less) and there is an equal decrease in its liabilities (the demand deposits of Maria Deluca).

Therefore, when the Federal Reserve sells government securities, the effect is to reduce total reserves, and thus to reduce excess reserves of the whole commercial banking system. Because of this decrease in the excess reserves of commercial banks, their lending ability decreases, and so does their power to increase demand deposits (the supply of money).

The Discount Rate

The Federal Reserve Bank, as we have said, is a banker's bank to depository institutions: It holds deposits for them and helps collect or clear checks between institutions. The Fed also makes loans to member commercial banks and other thrift institutions by buying either their promissory notes or by buying from the banks IOUs of nonbanking corporations or individuals defined as acceptable by the Fed. When the Fed buys such promissory notes, it deposits the proceeds in the depository institution's Federal Reserve account, increasing the bank's total reserves, and thus increasing its excess reserves.

Depository institutions do not get all these services free. The Federal Reserve Bank charges interest for making these loans. It is called a *discount* rather than interest, because the Fed collects the interest charge when it makes the loan.

Discount Rate
The rate of interest charged by the Fed when it makes loans to member banks and other depository institutions.

For example, a commercial bank, Delta Bank, sells the Fed a $1,000 promissory note that matures in three months. The **discount rate** (interest rate) is eight percent per year, a two percent discount for the three-month period. Delta Bank actually receives from the Fed only $980, or $1,000 less two percent. Delta's deposits at the Federal Reserve increase by $980. In other words, Delta pays the Fed $20 for the privilege of using $1,000 for three months.

If the Federal Reserve wants to encourage depository institutions to increase their reserves this way (that is, to increase their deposits with the Fed), it can reduce the cost of borrowing by *lowering the discount rate.* If the Fed wants to discourage institutions from increasing reserves this way, it can increase the cost of borrowing by *increasing* the discount rate.

Note: The Federal Reserve cannot reduce the reserves of depository institutions by this device. It can only use the discount rate to *encourage* or *discourage* the increasing of reserves. In addition, the Federal Reserve in recent years has restricted its lending through discounting to situations in which depository institutions are in temporary need of reserves. Remember, though, institutions can borrow each other's excess reserves through the Federal Funds Market.

Note: There is a difference between discount-rate policy and discount policy. *Discount-rate policy* has to do with variations in the discount rate and their effects. The *discount policy* has to do with the availability of discounts. As a means of power over excess reserves, the Fed's ability to manipulate the discount rate is not as important as its operations in the open market.

However, through the responses of the depository institutions, the Federal Reserve discount rate controls interest rates on loans of all sorts: mortgage loans, car loans, and so forth. When the Fed raises its discount rate, this is a sequence of repercussions in the economy: (1) Everybody knows the higher rate is a signal that the Fed is tightening credit. (2) The higher rate discourages institutions from increasing their reserves, and thus keeps them from making as many loans. (3) The higher discount rate pushes up all other interest rates.

The Required Reserve Ratio

When a depository institution makes a loan, as you know, the essential ingredient is excess reserves. The institution cannot loan more money and create more demand deposits once it reaches the bottom of its excess-reserve barrel, because it might risk dropping below its required reserves. The final and most powerful tool which the Fed can employ to affect the banking system is that it can change the **required reserve ratio**, the percentage of reserves against deposits that financial institutions are required to maintain.

Required Reserve Ratio
The percentage of reserves against deposits that financial institutions must maintain.

Varying the required reserve ratio does not change the total reserves of a depository institution, just the proportion of total reserves that the bank must have on hand, that are *required.* Therefore, it changes the proportion that is counted as excess.

For example, a commercial bank has $100,000 in demand deposits and $25,000 in total reserves. If the required reserve ratio is 20 percent, its required reserves would be 20 percent of $100,000 (the amount of demand deposits) or $20,000. Its excess reserves would be $5,000 ($25,000 minus $20,000). If the Fed were to reduce the required reserve ratio to 10 percent, the commercial bank's required reserves would be $10,000 (10 percent of $100,000) and its excess reserves would be $15,000 ($25,000 minus $10,000). In other words, if the Fed lowers the required reserve ratio, the commercial bank's excess reserves increase.

If the Fed were to increase the required reserve ratio from 20 percent to 25 percent, the commercial bank's required reserves would increase to $25,000 (25 percent of $100,000) and its excess reserves would decrease to zero ($25,000 total reserves minus $25,000 required reserves). In other words, if the Fed increases the required reserve ratio, the commercial bank's excess reserves decrease.

Clearly, the Fed's ability to vary the required reserve ratio is a very powerful tool, since it means that the Fed can readily change the excess reserves of the whole commercial banking system. The problem is that it is *too* powerful to be used often. Small percentage changes in the reserve ratio can have enormous effects on the reserve position of financial institutions. That is why the Fed varies its activity on the open market on an ongoing basis, giving the economy the ongoing changes in M_1 money that are needed to carry out its monetary policy. Only rarely and cautiously does it tamper with the reserve ratio. Changes in the reserve ratio usually signify major shifts in Federal Reserve policy.

A Review: How the Fed Nudges the Banking System

If the Federal Reserve wishes to *increase* the excess reserves of commercial banks to enable them to increase loans and create more demand deposits (the supply of money), it can do the following: (1) *buy* government securities on the open market, (2) *lower* the discount rate, or (3) *lower* the required reserve ratio.

If the Federal Reserve wishes to *decrease* banks' excess reserves, to reduce commercial banks' ability to make loans and create more demand deposits, it can do the following: (1) *sell* government securities on the open market, (2) *raise* the discount rate, or (3) *raise* the required reserve ratio.

Specific Powers of the Federal Reserve

No sooner had Congress passed the Federal Reserve Act of 1914, which brought the Federal Reserve Bank into existence, than people came forth with ideas to strengthen its authority. So, over the years Congress has passed amendments giving the Federal Reserve additional powers, especially in the areas of lending and credit. Powers added to the Fed over specific areas of lending are called **specific powers**.

Specific Powers
Additional authority of the Fed beyond the general power to control lending and credit.

Margin Requirements on Stocks

Margin Requirement
The percentage of cash required as a down payment on stock purchases.

The **margin requirement** is the percentage of cash required as a down payment on the purchase of a share of stock. The Bank Act of 1933 gave the Federal Reserve power to set the *margin* that buyers of stock in the various stock exchanges must pay when they buy corporate stock. The purpose of the margin requirement is to control speculation on the stock market.

If the Federal Reserve wants to reduce speculation on the stock exchange, it can increase the margin requirement. Let's say that the Federal Reserve increases the margin from 50 percent to 75 percent. This means that a person buying stock must pay cash equal to 75 percent of the value of the stock and can borrow only 25 percent of its purchase price. It works in reverse too. For example, in 1974 the stock market fell drastically from the high 900s to below 600. (These figures are from the Dow Jones Industrial Index, which measures changes in the prices of stock on the New York Stock Exchange) To stimulate demand for securities, the Federal Reserve dropped margin requirements from 65 percent to 50 percent. It did not do so in October, 1987, however, because the market recovered rather quickly and steadily.

The Federal Reserve's responsibility for watchdogging speculation in the stock market does not clash with its responsibilities for controlling excess reserves. Variations in stock-market margin requirements do not affect the total or excess reserves of commercial banks.

Regulation X
Empowered the Fed to control loans on consumer goods.

Regulation W
Empowered the Fed to control real estate loans.

Regulations X and W

Beginning in World War II, Congress gave the Federal Reserve the power to regulate consumer and real estate loans. **Regulation X** concerned loans on consumer goods, while **Regulation W** involved real estate loans. These regulations made the Federal Reserve responsible for determining the minimum down payment on a loan and the maximum length of time in which a loan could be repaid.

Regulation Q
Empowered the Fed to set maximum interest rates commercial banks could pay on savings accounts.

Regulation Q

Regulation Q empowered the Federal Reserve to set the maximum interest rates that commercial banks could pay on savings accounts (time deposits) and on demand deposits. While this authority existed, the Fed would not allow banks to pay interest on demand deposits and, also, set the maximum interest rates payable on savings accounts.

Deregulation and Financial Markets: The 1980s

A movement to reverse some of the regulatory controls established or expanded in the 1930s took hold in the United States in the late 1970s. Although deregulation began with the airline industry, financial markets, including commercial banking, were not far behind. Regulation Q had placed controls over banks regarding interest rates, the kinds of assets they could invest in, and the kinds of financial instruments they could issue. By the late 1970s, this regulation seemed to many, including many in the banking industry, to be anachronistic. Banks, by then, were only an (important) part of a much larger financial industry comprised also of savings and loan associations, mutual savings banks, brokerage houses and other thrift institutions. It seemed inequitable and inefficient to many that banks should be subject to regulations that did not apply to the other institutions. Perhaps more importantly, it seemed that the American economy and its people would benefit from allowing all the players in these markets to compete on an equal footing in an increasingly competitive industry.

The "Deregulatory Act" of 1980

The Depository Institutions Deregulation and Monetary Control Reform Act of 1980, which repealed Regulation Q, was seen by many as a move toward a more competitive set of financial institutions. The law provided that:

1. Controls over interest rates on deposits were to be phased out over five years.
2. All deposit-taking institutions could issue checking accounts.

3. Thrift institutions could now make a wider range of loans.

4. Reserve requirements were extended uniformly to all depository institutions.

5. All depository institutions would be able to avail themselves of the services of the Fed (clearinghouse, borrowing, etc.).

All in all, the 1980 Act went a long way toward creating a competitive, though not, as we shall see, a necessarily stable environment in American financial markets.

How well has deregulation worked?
The push for financial market deregulation ran up against a severe set of failures in such markets in 2008-2009. We examined some of those problems and government reaction to them in Application I (The Financial Crisis of 2008-2009: background, Causes and Effects) and recommend that you read that application again.

How Sound Are America's Financial Institutions?

In many respects, the 1980s were more turbulent for American financial institutions than any period since the 1930s. Major U.S. banks (including Continental Illinois) failed or were "bailed out." Others saw much of their loan portfolios (to underdeveloped nations, to farmers, etc.) on the verge of becoming non-performing or written off as bad debts. The Savings and Loan Associations had an even more rocky period with 17 percent of them disappearing in the first two years of the 1980s and continued failures with a massive "bail-out" of these institutions agreed to in the late 1980s. Partly in response to the perceived instability in the industry (more a threat to shareholders than to depositors who are insured), the Garn-St. Germain Act was passed in 1982. The legislation was designed primarily to increase the borrowing authority of savings and loan associations and thereby to avoid a wave of bankruptcies in that industry. At the same time the Act authorized all depository institutions to sell money market mutual funds, adding further to the competitiveness of financial markets.

In spite of the Garn-St. Germain Act, the years since 1982 have been turbulent ones for America's financial institutions, both its commercial banks and its thrift institutions (savings and loan firms, credit unions, and the like). Between 1982 and 1991, more than two thousand failed. Many more have failed in the financial crisis of 2008-2009. More than half of the failed thrift institutions were savings and loan associations, with the recession of 1990-1991 putting further pressure on marginal financial institutions. If the financial services sector was just another (big) industry in the American economy, this "shaking out" of weak firms might be seen as the ordinary working of an increasingly competitive marketplace. There are two basic reasons, however, for viewing the failure of so many financial institutions differently.

1. We have seen that banks and other depository institutions are key to the operation of our monetary system. They not only hold the money deposits of businesses and individual households, but as we have seen, create most of America's money supply through making loans. Some of the institutions that failed were large; only quick intervention prevented a serious threat to regional economies, perhaps even the larger national economy.

2. The intervention, though substantially successful, has been at a huge cost to taxpayers. Recall that we earlier said that beginning in the 1930s, the Federal Government provided its full backing to protect checking and savings deposits in banks and thrifts. The Federal Deposit Insurance Corporation (FDIC); and the Federal Savings and Loan Insurance Corporation (FSLIC); were pledged to pay for most of the losses in the more than 2,000 insured financial institutions. By 1995, the estimate of this cost to taxpayers has risen to over $500 billion including interest payments.

Are the Nation's Financial Institutions Still in Trouble?

At first, it appeared that many of the Nation's commercial banks were in peril and more than 1,300 did fail between 1982 and 1991. Even a few large banks failed with one (the Bank of New England) becoming insolvent in the recession of 1990-1991. However, the Federal Deposit Insurance Corporation (FDIC) was authorized in 1991 to borrow from the Federal Government, many banks were reorganized or acquired by sounder ones, and the improved economy in 1993 and 1994 brought renewed financial health to most banks. Since 2000, many mergers and acquisitions further strengthened remaining banks. The wave of failures in 2008-2011 has re-exposed the unacceptably of firms to engage in highly risky additions of poor quality loans to their portfolios. The rate of bank failures continued to drop in 2012 from its 2010 peak of 2.09%. The failure rate was .71% in 2012 down from 1.24% in 2011. It appears that at this time that the banking industry is becoming stronger and moving away from higher failure rates coming out of 2008 - 2009. Savings and loan associations (S&Ls), however, have not fared as well. More than one-third of all S&Ls in business since 1987 have gone out of business or merged with commercial banks (a process that continues on 2008-2011). There are three main reasons why failure in this area of our financial services industry continues to be a serious concern.

1. Deregulation. Deregulation, as we have noted, has substantially increased competition among financial institutions. The Savings and loan association (S&Ls) had, since the 1930s, enjoyed a virtual monopoly on home mortgage loans. These relatively long-term, well-secured assets helped to create a stable, low-risk industry. With deregulation, other financial institutions could compete for home mortgage loans and could also attract savings deposits with higher interest rates since deregulation had removed interest rate caps. S&Ls, stuck with low interest rate mortgages and the need to attract savings deposits with higher interest rates, shifted their loans toward high risk loans of all types.

2. *Problems of Insuring Against Risk.* In 1980, the Federal Deposit Insurance Corporation (FDIC) insurance was raised to $100,000 per account with no limit on the number of individual accounts. In 2009 this insurance was raised to $200,000. Though FDIC's original purpose in the 1930s was to stabilize financial markets through averting panics, the ironic result of deposit insurance in the 1980s and 1990s was able to reduce stability. This seems to be at least partially the result of the **problem of moral hazard**, the problem that insuring individuals (depositors) against risk reduces the individual's incentive to prevent the occurrence of losses. The strategy of the S&Ls to offer extraordinarily high interest rates to attract deposits worked in part because depositors took no risks in putting their funds in shaky financial institutions. Insurance also permitted S&Ls to make higher risk loans than they would otherwise have done. After all, if the loans were successful, S&L shareholders would benefit; if the borrowers defaulted and the S&Ls became bankrupt, the FDIC, not the shareholders, would cover the losses of depositors.

Problem of Moral Hazard
The problem that insuring individuals against risk reduces their incentive to prevent losses.

3. *Fraud and Loan Defaults*. There were many defaults and S&L failures in oil-producing states (especially Texas). Defaults on many loans escalated as oil prices fell sharply in the 1990s. At the same time, less restrictive oversight by bank regulators led to widespread fraud by some S&L officers. One estimate in the 1990s is that there were fraudulent practices in about 40 percent of the failed S&Ls.

Further Reform of Financial Services

Resolution Trust Corporation (RTC)
A federal agency created in 1989 to preside over the dissolution of insolvent S&Ls

The 1990s saw further substantial reforms. In 1989, the Financial Institutions Reform, Recovery, and Enforcement Act (FIRREA) established the **Resolution Trust Corporation (RTC)** to preside over the dissolution of insolvent S&Ls. We mentioned earlier that by one estimate, the cost to taxpayers of the RTC's activities was estimated to be $500 billion. FIRREA's other changes included: (1) putting all deposit insurance under FDIC control, (2) increasing insurance premiums for banks and thrifts, (3) raising capital requirements for S&Ls, (4) permitting S&Ls to receive deposits from businesses, and (5) directing the Fed to allow bank holding companies to acquire financially sound S&Ls. Since the mid-1990s, further reforms have occurred including allowing banks to enter the insurance business.

A Further Movement Toward Competition? Interstate Banking

Bank Holding Companies
Corporations that may own several banks, even in different states.

Throughout American history, the number of banks has been large relative to that of other industrial nations such as Canada and Great Britain. The reason for the disparity has lain in the tradition and often legal insistence on branch banking. Some states have even insisted on unit banking, the requirement that a bank have one location and no branches even within the same state. Interstate branches are forbidden by Federal law, though permitting the practice would probably increase the competitiveness of the industry. Resistance to changing the restrictions on interstate banking led to the formation of **bank holding companies**, corporations that may own several banks, even banks in different states. Nearly all big banks in the United States today are owned by holding companies who not only offer diversified banking services but also such collateral activities as leasing and credit cards. In 1995, the Congress passed legislation that removed restrictions in interstate banking.

Financial Institutions: A Summing Up

We witnessed a number of fundamental changes in American financial institutions in the 1980s and 1990s. It became easier to enter financial markets, and as a result they have become more broadly defined. At the same time, it became easier to fail. Many questions remain to be resolved. Should deposit insurance continue to encourage depository institutions to take excessive risks? Are regulatory functions adequate to protect society's interests? How do we measure the money supply so that, once defined, a supply exists that can be closely correlated with changes in income and unemployment. As Keynes wrote, "We can draw the line between "money" and "debt" at whatever point is most convenient for handling a particular problem." Even in the early 2000s, we are still trying to draw that line.

The Powerful Fed: A Summary of Its Functions

We have seen that the Fed is a powerful agency and that its authority over the financial institutions of America in many respects, grew in the 1980s. Although we have mentioned some of its powers before, let's summarize them.

The Fed Regulates the Supply of Money

Through its control over the excess reserves of depository institutions, the Federal Reserve regulates the supply of M_1 money. By means of its operations in the open market, and its variations in the discount rate and in the required reserve ratio, the Federal Reserve may increase or decrease excess reserves. Depository institutions must have excess reserves in order to make loans and create new demand deposits, which are the main form of money.

A great economist, Joseph Schumpeter, once said that whoever controls credit or access to financial capital is akin to the judges (ephors) of ancient Egypt who had power of life or death over all that nation's citizens except for the Pharaoh. To Schumpeter, bankers who controlled access to credit exercised this power in a modern capitalist society. If Schumpeter is right, is the Fed their Pharaoh? After all it controls the ephors (bankers and lenders at all depository institutions) in the United States.

The Fed Acts as a National Clearinghouse for Checks

When a depository institution receives a check written against an account in another financial institution, it gets paid by sending the check to the Federal Reserve Bank. The Federal Reserve Bank, when it receives the check, increases the deposits with the Federal Reserve of the institution sending the check and reduces the deposits of the bank on which the check is drawn. The Federal Reserve institution then sends the check to the depository institution on which it is drawn. *That* institution reduces the amount of demand deposits in the account of the person who wrote the check.

The Fed Issues Paper Currency

The Federal Reserve issues all the paper money in circulation. The Federal Reserve does not use the issuance of currency as a device to control the overall supply of money, but it must make certain that there is enough currency around to meet the economy's needs. For instance, the need for currency varies from season to season.

Before Christmas, people want to hold cash to buy Christmas presents so demand for paper currency increases. As people withdraw currency from their demand-deposit accounts, depository institutions run low on cash in their vaults. They therefore order more currency from the Federal Reserve, which fills their currency order and reduces their deposits with the Fed by an equal amount. In this way the Fed increases the supply of currency in the economy each Christmas season.

After Christmas, business falls off and people become uneasy about holding more currency than they actually need, so they deposit the excess in their demand-deposit accounts. The depository institutions now have more cash in their vaults than they want, so they send the excess back to the Federal Reserve, which stashes away the cash and increases the banks' deposits with the Fed. In this way the Fed withdraws currency from circulation. This high elasticity in the supply of currency helps take care of seasonal changes in the volume of business.

The Fed Regulates and Examines Member Banks

Congress has given the Federal Reserve the power to regulate many of the activities of depository institutions. To check whether these institutions are obeying the rules, the Fed periodically examines their books. Some believe that this regulatory function needs further strengthening.

The Fed Acts as a Banker's Bank

When depository institutions want to go to the bank, they go to the Federal Reserve, which loans them money by accepting, at a discount, to be sure, their short-term debt instruments. The Federal Reserve also holds deposits of depository institutions, deposits that form part of their total reserves.

The Fed Is a Fiscal Agent and Bank for the U.S. Treasury

The U.S. Treasury itself keeps deposits at the Federal Reserve and writes checks on them. Furthermore, the Federal Reserve handles the national debt for the government. When the Treasury issues the federal debt, the Federal Reserve sells the debt instruments and collects the proceeds for the Treasury. When this debt *matures* (is due for payment), the Federal Reserve pays what is owed out of the Treasury's account.

The Fed Is a Fiscal Agent for Foreign Central Banks and Treasuries

A number of foreign central banks and treasuries use the Federal Reserve as their bank in the United States. The Federal Reserve treats them as impartially as it does its own member banks or the U.S. Treasury. It loans money, buys and sells debt instruments, and in general acts as their fiscal agent.

Monetary Policy

Monetary Policy
Decisions of the Fed regarding changes in the money supply and interest rates.

Monetary policy consists of the decisions of the Fed regarding changes in the money supply and interest rates to achieve economic goals. The most important goal is to reach acceptable levels of growth, employment and price stability. Therefore, in order to understand monetary policy, one needs to know how changes in the money supply affect interest rates and influence income, employment, and prices.

Varying the Supply of Money

Earlier we looked at the effects of changes in the money supply on employment and prices. We saw that increases in the supply of money expand effective demand, while contractions reduce it. Therefore, to counter unemployment, a nation's monetary policy should be to expand the money supply. On the other hand, to counter inflation, a nation's monetary policy should be to cut back the money supply.

Table 13-1
The Federal Reserve's Monetary Policy

What should the Fed do about unemployment?	What should the Fed do about inflation?
Increase excess reserves	*Decrease excess reserves*
Buy government securities	Sell government securities
Lower the discount rate	Raise the discount rate
Lower the required reserve ratio	Raise the required reserve ratio

Varying Interest Rates

What happens to an economy when interest rates vary? When interest rates go up, people do not want to borrow as much to buy consumer goods, because the cost of borrowing money has risen. Businesses do not want to buy as much new plant and equipment, for the same reason. So investment decreases. (Remember that investments need to have an expected rate of return equal to or greater than the interest rate.) Also, when interest rates go up, government expenditures at the state and local levels that are financed by borrowing tend to go down. State and local governments must be concerned about their taxpayers moving to other locales, with lower tax rates. So state an local governments are more sensitive than the federal government about raising taxes to pay increased interest costs on borrowed money. (You knew, didn't you, that state and local governments have to borrow heavily in order to see themselves through the fiscal year?)

All in all, raising interest rates decreases aggregate demand by decreasing consumption based on consumer borrowing as well as investment, and debt-financed expenditures by state and local governments.

What happens when interest rates go down? Just the reverse of what happens when they go up. People more readily borrow money to buy consumer goods because credit is cheaper. Businesses increase their investment spending because there are more investments that yield a return equal to or greater than the cost of the interest. And state and local governments increase their deficit-financed expenditures, too, because the price of money is low.

Some Recommendations on Monetary Policy

During a recession, when there is a lot of unemployment, monetary policy should aim at expanding total spending by increasing the supply of money and decreasing the interest rate. During an inflation, monetary policy should aim at decreasing total spending and discouraging price increases by reducing the supply of money and increasing the interest rate. Table 13-1 outlines the methods the Federal Reserve can use to combat unemployment or inflation.

What to Do When Recession Hits

Suppose there is a recession. Aggregate demand is low, unemployment is high and nobody is buying much. What can be done? The monetary policies that increase the supply of money also lower interest rates and combat unemployment.

During a period of high unemployment, the Federal Reserve should follow policies that increase excess reserves. In the discussion of the Fed, you learned how this can be done. The Federal Reserve should do one or more of the following:

1. *Buy government securities on the open market.* The proceeds are used to increase the deposits of commercial banks with the Federal Reserve; that is, the commercial banks' total and excess reserves rise, so that they can lend out more money.

2. *Lower the discount rate.* This encourages commercial banks to discount acceptable short-term debt and increase their total and excess reserves.

3. *Lower the required reserve ratio.* This does not change commercial banks' total reserves, but it does lower the percentage of reserves that are required, and thus it creates mor excess reserves.

Figure 13-6
Credit Market Equilibrium

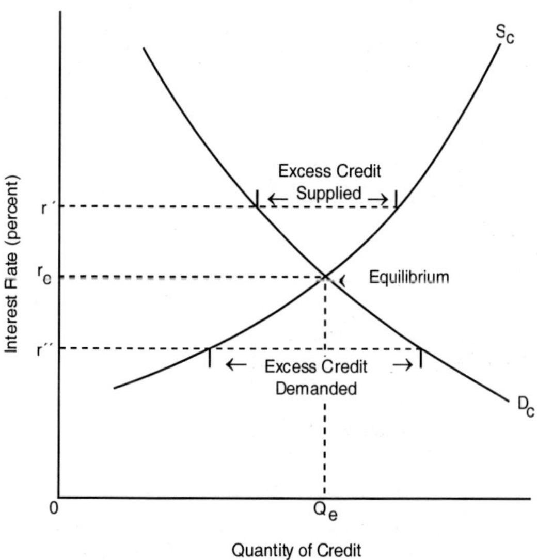

The Supply of Credit (S_c) is upward sloping, and the demand for credit is downward sloping as functions of interest rates. Equilibrium is established at interest rate r_e, where quantity demanded = quantity supplied. Other interest rates (such as r′ and r′′ are disequilibrium rates associated with excess supply or excess demand.

The Monetary Transmission Mechanism: Credit Markets in a Recession

Let's suppose the monetary policy task is to increase real income and reduce unemployment while minimizing inflationary pressures on prices. Whichever of the three "tools" or combination of them it employs, the effects of Federal Reserve action will be felt in credit markets. Let's trace through how those effects occur.

In Figure 13-6, we see the workings of a credit market. Remember that most of our money is in the form of credit (interest bearing loans), created by depository institutions. There are, thus, many credit markets. For convenience, however, let's aggregate them into a hypothetical credit market as in Figure 13-6. The supply of credit (S_c) slopes upward (holding everything else but interest rates constant); as interest rates rise more credit is offered because savings move from non-interest bearing form (e.g., stocks) into interest bearing deposits at banks, savings and loan associations and the like. The demand for credit (D_c) is downward sloping (holding everything else but interest rates constant). The quantity demanded rises because firms, consumers, and even governments borrow more at lower interest rates. Equilibrium is established where the quantity demanded equals the quantity supplied of credit at interest rate r_e. Any other interest rate than r_e would lead to either excess quantity supplied (at r′) or excess quantity demanded (at r′′).

Figure 13-7
Credit Market Response to an Increased Supply of Credit

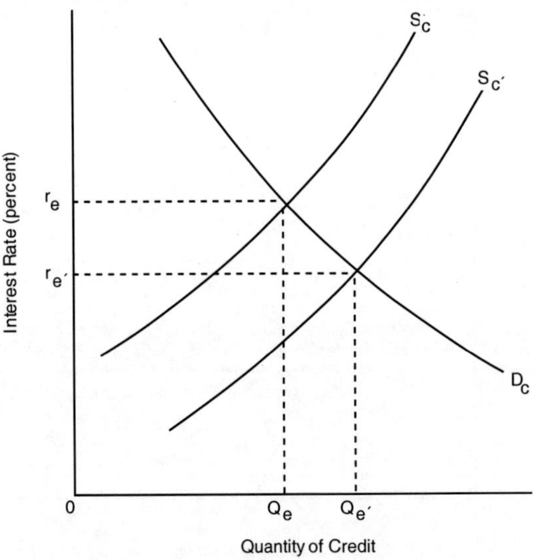

The Fed follows an "easier" monetary policy and the supply of credit (S_c) increases to (S_c'). The equilibrium interest rate falls and the quantity of credit demanded (borrowing) rises from Q_e to Q_e'.

A Recession: Enter the Fed

Let's suppose that credit markets are in equilibrium with market clearing interest rates but that the economy is in recession. The Fed (FOMC, Board of Governors) decides to fight the recession with an "easier" monetary policy. Through whatever means (discount rate, reserve requirements, open market purchases of government securities, etc.), the Fed, acting through depository institutions, creates an increase in the supply of credit as in the shift of supply from S_c to S_c' in Figure 13-7. As a result interest rates fall from r_e to r_e'.

Short-run Effects

As the above happens, we see in Figure 13-8 that short-run equilibrium real income is affected. As depository institutions expanded credit in Figure 13-7, interest rates fell. In 13-8 that leads to investment increases that shift aggregate demand in the short run from AD to AD.′ Real income grows from Q_e to Q_e' and prices rise modestly from P_e to P_e'.

Note: There would have been no upward pressure on prices if aggregate supply had been horizontal at price level P_e. That aggregate supply assumption, however, is the Keynesian assumption. Monetarists do not necessarily agree with the idea that resource idleness is so widespread that increases in aggregate demand that cause real income growth always occur with no short-run upward pressure on prices.

Figure 13-8
Short-Run Aggregate Demand Increase from the Increased Investment Effect of Monetary Policy Easing

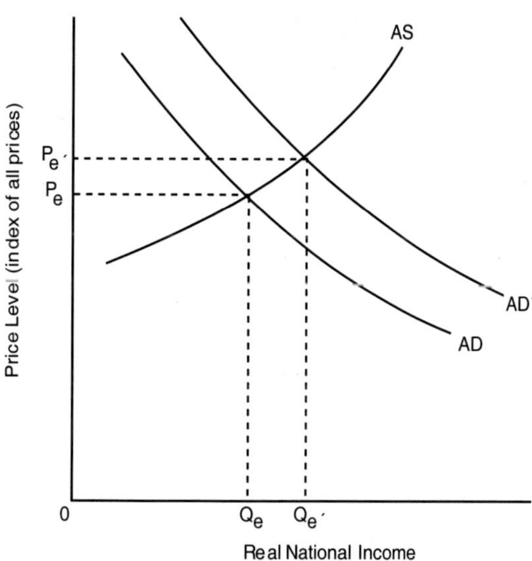

As interest rates fall with an easing of monetary policy, investment increases cause a growth of aggregate demand (AD to AD´). Real income rises from Q_e to Q_e' and prices rise modestly from P_e to P_e'.

Long-run Effects

What about the long-run effects of easing monetary policy? We see these in Figure 13-9. What we have seen so far is a monetary policy transmission mechanism that looks like this when put in Keynesian terms.

Easing of Monetary Policy → Increase in Supply of Credit → Decrease in Interest Rates → Increase in Investment → Increase in Aggregate Demand in Short Run → Increase in Real Income and Prices.

Now we must factor in the long-run supply effects of the investment increases resulting from lower interest rates. In Figure 13-9, we see that in the long run, further shifts that occur in aggregate supply from AS to AS´ resulting in a growth in real income from Q_e' to Q_e''. Note that the supply increase results in lowering prices from P_e' back to P_e. Note also that it is not necessarily a monetarist assumption that money supply growth is price neutral in the long run. Rather, the important point is that increasing aggregate supply in the long run will reduce the upward pressures on prices from increased spending or increased aggregate demand. Completing the transmission mechanism (in Keynesian terms), it becomes:

Easing of Monetary Policy → Increase in Supply of Credit → Decrease in Interest Rates → Increase in Investment → Increase in Aggregate Demand in Short Run → Short-run Increase in Real Income and Prices → Long-run Increase in Aggregate Supply → Further Growth in Real Income and Reduced Pressure on Prices.

Figure 13-9

Long-Run Aggregate Demand and Aggregate Supply Effects of Monetary Policy Easing

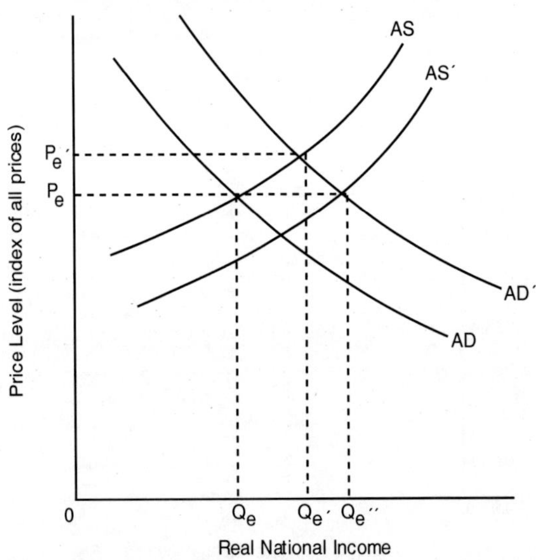

The short-run increase in real income (Q_e to Q_e') and increase in prices (P_e to P_e' from Figure 13-8) leads to the long-term increase in aggregate supply (AS to AS′) that restores price equilibrium at P_e and further increases real income (Q_e' to Q_e'').

What to Do When Inflation Hits

Suppose there is an inflation. Aggregate demand is high, and prices are rising fast. What can be done? During a period of rising prices, the Federal Reserve should follow policies that decrease the supply of money and increase interest rates. From the discussion of the Fed, you know how this can be done. The Federal Reserve should do one or more of the following:

1. *Sell government securities on the open market.* This has the effect of reducing the financial institutions' deposits at the Federal Reserve, which means that their excess reserves go down by a like amount, and they have fewer loanable funds.

2. *Raise the discount rate.* This makes it more expensive for financial institutions to borrow from the Federal Reserve, and, therefore, discourages them from increasing their reserves by means of short-term debt.

3. *Raise the required reserve ratio.* This leaves financial institutions' total reserves untouched, but makes them hold a higher percentage of their total reserves as required reserves, which leaves a smaller percentage of excess reserves.

Remember that each of these general powers has different effects. Open-market operations can increase excess reserves or decrease them, and they are also more selective than the other powers. For ordinary monetary policy operations, the Federal Reserve uses mainly open-market operations. Varying the discount rate cannot decrease excess reserves, but it does have a strong immediate impact on interest rates. It causes the interest rates for various kinds of debt instruments (mortgages, personal loans) to fluctuate readily. Varying the required reserve ratio, as we noted before, is too strong and unselective a weapon for the Federal Reserve to use often. The use of this weapon generally signals a major change in Federal Reserve policy.

The Monetary Transmission Mechanism: Credit markets in Inflation

Let us suppose now the economy we are looking at has a serious (demand-pull) inflationary problem. Imagine that it is like the American economy in 1979-1980 with "double-digit" inflation. The job of the Fed, using any of the above "tools" is to "cool-off" the economy with a restrictive monetary policy. Go back to Figure 13-6 and imagine that equilibrium interest rates are too low, that is they are creating inflationary levels of aggregate demand. How can the Fed get interest rates up? Look again at Figure 13-7, but let's have the Fed decrease the supply of credit (S_C' to S_C in 13-7), which reduces the quantity demanded of credit (Q_e' to Q_e) and cause interest rates to increase from r_e' to r_e. Put again in Keynesian terms, the transmission mechanism in the short run is:

A "Tightening" of Monetary Policy; → Decrease in Supply of Credit → Increase in Interest Rates → Decrease in Investment → Decrease in Aggregate Demand → Lower Level of Prices.

Figure 13-10
The Effects of Restrictive Monetary Policy on Aggregate Demand, Real Income, and the Price Level When the Economy is Operating at Capacity

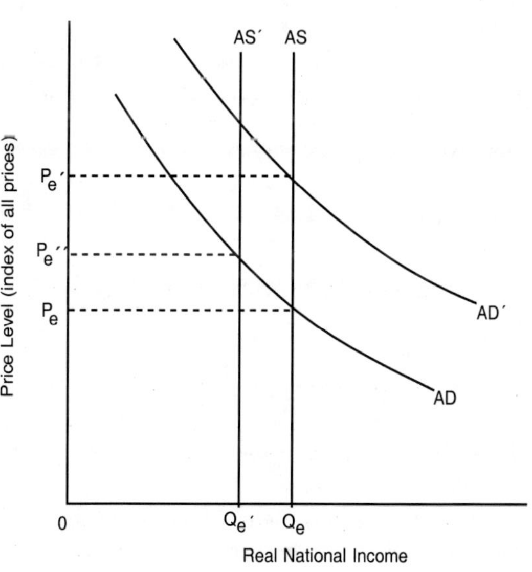

The inflationary economy is operating at capacity with an aggregate supply that is vertical at real income Q_e. Increasing AD is causing demand-pull price pressures that raise prices from P_e to P_e'. The Fed reduces the supply of credit, interest rates rise and aggregate demand decreases from AD′ to AD. Prices are stabilized at P_e and real income maintained at capacity, Q_e.

The effects of the decrease in investment can be seen in a reduction of aggregate demand such as from AD′ to AD in Figure 13-8. As AD falls, price levels diminish as from P_e' to P_e, and real income will fall. Of course, if the inflation is pure demand pull, aggregate supply may have a vertical (capacity range) look as in Figure 13-10. Here the economy has reached its maximum (capacity) real income at Q_e and is operating with its natural rate of unemployment. Increasing aggregate demand cannot cause a growth in real income so, instead, with "too many dollars chasing an unchanged quantity supplied of goods" prices are pushed up from P_e to P_e'. The Fed decreases the supply of credit by the proper amount, interest rates rise and aggregate demand decreases from AD′ to AD. The economy in the short run then enjoys both full employment and price stability (established as a target level of prices).

What happens in the long run? The higher interest rates would be expected to lead to a short-run decrease in investment and a long-run decrease in aggregate supply (as from AS to AS′ in Figure 13-10). The consequence of the supply effects of restrictive monetary policy might be less than full employment with lower real income (Q_e to Q_e') and higher prices (P_e to P_e''). A falling level of real income and rising prices would probably be seen as a slowing of productivity growth and a call, as we witnessed in the 1980s, for stimulating the supply side of markets. To do that, of course, the Fed would have to reverse course, ease up in credit markets, and let interest rates drift downward.

The Main Point

The main point of the preceding discussion is to emphasize the complexity of the cause-and-effect relationships in monetary policy. These depend on: (a) credit markets, (b) interest rates as signals to borrowers and lenders, (c) investment effects of changing interest rates, (d) demand effects of investment decisions and, in the long run, (e) the supply effects of investment decisions.

There are some who say that in view of all these complexities, discretionary monetary policy is a job for a "philosopher king," not a Federal Reserve chairman. In this regard, some would argue for a simple monetary rule (increase the supply of credit by X percent per year) as opposed to discretionary changes from week to week. It is no easy job being Chairman of the Fed. If you are right about direction and magnitude of choice, you may get some credit (Paul Volcker in the 1980s). If you are wrong about direction and amount, you may be blamed for a recession or depression (ironically, the same Paul Volcker for the 1981-1982 recession).

Weaknesses of Monetary Policy

Monetary policy cannot be expected to provide solutions to all economic problems. Here are six reasons why:

1. *Inadequate demand for credit.* During a serious recession or a depression, monetary policy may be quite ineffective in stimulating the economy. Depository institutions may already have all the excess reserves they need. (a) As business goes into a slump, people may shy away from borrowing to such an extent that more loans are paid off than are made. So excess reserves increase without the help of the Federal Reserve. (b) With the economic outlook so gloomy, lending institutions are often unwilling to run the risk of lending. So no matter what the Fed does to increase excess reserves, lending institutions refuse to increase loans and the supply of money. (This is what the commercial banks did during the Great Depression of the 1930s.) (c) The depository institutions may have money they are willing to lend, but people are just not borrowing. During a mild recession, however, monetary policy aimed at increasing excess reserves may work well, as it did in the recession of 1954. That recession was caused by the decline of defense expenditures at the end of the Korean War. At that time, people's confidence in the economy was strong. There was a tax cut; and an easy-

money policy increased excess reserves, thus stimulating bank lending, increasing the supply of money, and reducing interest rates.

2. *Non-demand-pull inflation.* Monetary policy may curb inflation, provided that it is a demand-pull inflation of the type in Figure 13-10. The Federal Reserve can dry up excess reserves so much that depository institutions cannot make loans. Then people cannot get money to buy things with. However, if the inflation is caused by factors *not* susceptible to control by the lowering of aggregate demand (cost-push and administered-price inflation), monetary policy may not be the cure. For example, the inflation of 1973-1974 was caused in part by the raising of oil prices by OPEC (Organization of Petroleum Exporting Countries) and the rise in agricultural prices. The Federal Reserve tried to use monetary policy to decrease prices. But its tight-money policy, that is charging very high interest rates on the money it lent, only led to commercial banks raising *their* interest rates to 12 percent. A liquidity crisis (that is, a shortage of assets that could be easily converted into money) in the banking system was predicted. The Fed was forced to back off from its tight-money policy before the double-digit inflation could be contained.(*Double-digit* meaning at any rate of 10 percent or more per year.)

3. *Recognition and Implementation Lag.* Only a philosopher king has perfect foresight. A Fed chairman (and board) rely on data that is always lagged and that may or may not be an accurate measure of current economic activity. Monetary policy changes, thus, may be a reaction to an incorrect perception of problems, akin to giving someone a dose of medicine for an ailment that the patient no longer has!

Even a philosopher-king cannot have orders carried out instantly. While some Fed policies can be changed quickly (open-market operations) others take 30 months or more to fully implement. Lower interest rates may find a few firms with investment plans on the shelf waiting for the right present value; many other firms will only *begin* planning new investments as interest rates fall. Implementation lags can seriously slow the workings even of correct monetary policy.

4. *Distributive effects.* During inflation, a tight-money policy of raising interest rates does not affect the economy *evenly.* It hits some groups harder than others. For instance, in the construction industry, high interest rates cause the demand for new houses to plummet. Each time there has been a period of tight-money policy and high interest rates, the construction industry has experienced serious cutbacks, with consequent layoffs of workers.

Depository institutions, as their excess reserves dwindle, do not lend their reduced supply of money evenly. Safe customers get loans, but risky ones do not. The more risky firms (generally smaller-scale, new firms) not only face higher interest rates, but also have difficulty getting loans. Larger corporations do not have this problem. They are isolated from the tight-money situation because, when *they* want money, they can dip into their own retained earnings and depreciation funds.

Figure 13-11
Expectations Effects on the Demand for Credit Result in perverse effects of Monetary Policy

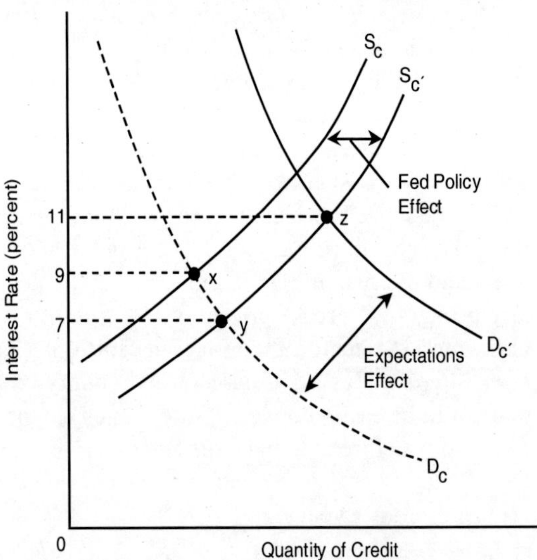

The Fed seeks to lower interest rates from their initial equilibrium at X (D_c intersects S_c) and nine percent. The target interest rate is seven percent, which can be attained by increasing the supply of credit from S_c to S_c' (S_c' intersects D_c) at point Y. The public, expecting higher inflation to result, attempts to lock in the lower interest rate and increases its demand for credit from D_c to D_c'. At the new equilibrium, point Z, (D_c' intersects S_c') interest rates rise to 11 percent.

5. *Changes in Velocity.* As the Federal Reserve increases the money supply during a recession and decreases it during an inflation, changes in the velocity of exchange may partially counteract these trends. During a recession the velocity of exchange may decrease, which reduces the impact of an increased supply of money. Pessimistic consumers and businesses try to hold on to their money. During an inflation, the velocity of exchange, V, may increase, which reduces the impact of a decreased supply of money. Optimistic consumers and businesses, expecting that prices will go up still higher, continue to buy at an ever greater rate. Although monetary velocity, as we saw earlier, has been relatively constant in recent years, it can change as it did in the 1970s.

6. *Changes in Inflationary Expectations.* To execute its monetary policies through credit markets, the Fed must set up equilibrium interest rate targets. Suppose, for example, that the Fed wants to expand the economy and decides to try to get interest rates down from an average of nine percent to seven percent. To do this, it uses some set of the previously discussed policy tools to increase the supply of credit as in Figure 13-11 from S_C to S_C'. With demand D_C, the Fed's target would be achieved. The public, however, expecting this increase in the quantity demanded of credit to cause a higher rate of inflation, tries to lock in the seven percent rate and increases its demand for credit from D_C to D_C'. In the new credit market equilibrium, the interest rate effect of the Fed's action is not to lower interest rates to seven percent but to raise them to 11 percent!

Monetarism

Monetarism
An approach to macroeconomic policy in which the supply of money is the dominant factor.

Monetarism is an approach to macroeconomic policy in which the supply of money plays the dominant role. Nobel Laureate Milton Friedman, the economist who founded the monetarist school, maintains that both fiscal policy and monetary policy based on Keynesian analysis are wrong. He and other monetarists charge that the Keynesians underestimate the effects of the supply of money on the economy. Friedman, as well as newer monetary theorists, says that people have a stable and predictable demand for money, a demand related to the size of the economy. Therefore, the supply of money and its relationship to national income should be the key to government policy, both fiscal and monetary. To control unemployment and inflation, the monetarists say, the government should follow a policy of increasing the supply of money at a proper and constant rate.

In the mid-1990s, some economists suggested that discretionary monetary policy was becoming less and less effective. One important reason cited was that international capital markets had become so large and so efficient that a single central bank, even one as powerful as the Fed could have little overall influence on credit supplies and interest rates. These issues plus the monetarist attack on Keynesian fiscal and monetary policy deserves full treatment. So, in the following application we will explore these controversies.

Application I: How Much Does Money Matter? Monetarists Versus Keynesians

The most serious challenge to Keynesian theories of economics, especially to the monetary and fiscal policies, has come from Milton Friedman and the monetarist school of economics. These economists say that monetary policy is more important than fiscal policy, and that in order to stabilize an economy, a steady rate of growth in the supply of money must be ensured. The monetarists do not simply say that money matters, as would Keynesians, they go further, and say that money supply policy matters more than any other economic policy.

The Monetarists' Position

The basic tenet of the monetarists is that the biggest single factor in determining money income, real income, and the level of prices is the *rate of growth of the money supply.* They contend that people want to keep a fixed percentage of their assets in the form of money, a percentage that depends on their real incomes, their standards of consumption, and the composition of their other assets. As you know, if the supply of money increases too quickly, people find themselves holding more money than they wish. They try to re-establish the old equilibrium, by demanding more nonconsumption assets, such as land, machinery, stocks, and bonds; and/or more consumer goods, either of which causes the economy to expand. If the supply of money shrinks, the reverse happens, and the economy contracts.

This variation in the supply of money also affects prices. Monetarists do not accept the Keynesian view that an economy with growing expenditures can expand indefinately with stable prices. Beyond some point, as the economy expands, demand-pull inflation sets in. Conversely, as the supply of money and the economy contract, excess capacity and excess inventory drive prices down.

Some but not all monetarists are critical of discretionary policy. They recommend that the Federal Reserve concentrate on monetary rules maintaining a steady increase in the money supply, at about two to four percent per year. This, they say, would force the economy into a stable growth with low inflation.

The 4 percent growth in the money supply would provide enough expansion to accommodate the three percent increase in productivity that some economists feel is historically what can be sustained. It would also provide enough flexibility to reinforce sectors of the economy that have less capacity than others, so that inflation would be mild.

Monetarists challenge the assumption that by means of continuous adjustments in fiscal policy and monetary policy, one can cause the economy to grow with relative stability. He says that changes in fiscal policy are ineffective and that the monetary policy of changing the interest rate also accomplishes little, since it is the *percentage rate of change in the supply of money* that is most closely correlated with changes in levels of income and employment. Furthermore, because nobody can accurately predict future business trends, it is dangerous to use changes in the rate of growth of the money supply for fine-tuning purposes.

Thus, monetarists who support decision by rule make simple and direct recommendations for government economic policy: Let the monetary authority (the Federal Reserve) increase the supply of money at a fixed rate of two to four percent per year and the economy will adjust itself. Although this will not eliminate all economic instability, it will avoid extreme variations. As Friedman notes: "We do not know enough to avoid minor fluctuations. The attempt to do more than we can will itself be a disturbance that may increase rather than reduce instability."

Discretionary monetary policy has at times seemed to complicate stabilization rather than solve the problems of economic fluctuations. After World War II the Federal Reserve used its open-market operations to peg the price of government securities, and neglected the postwar inflation. In 1957 the Fed enforced such a tight policy, in an attempt to fight inflation, that it contributed to the 1958 recession. Often just before or during an inflation, the Fed has increased the supply of money by greater amounts than the four percent recommended by Friedman. This has fed the inflation; 1973 is a good example.

It is somewhat ironic that the sharply restrictive monetary policy practiced by the Fed in 1981-1982 has been both hailed as a triumph of correctly timed monetary restraint and pointed to as an example of overreaction by some monetarists. While the decrease in money supply growth did, as we have already seen, lead to a reduction in inflation, it also caused a fall in real GDP and a sharp increase in unemployment.

The Keynesian Defense

While Keynesians do not deny the importance of the money supply, they regard it as a complementary tool to fiscal policy. Commenting on the rapid growth in income and jobs in the mid-1980s, a leading Keynesian and Nobel Laureate James Tobin[1] remarked that "the patent success of fiscal stimulus in promoting recovery in the United States in 1983-1984 reinforces the Keynesian side of this old debate."

A flaw in the monetarists' theory is the implied assumption that velocity of exchange remains constant. (The monetarists say that V is constant in the short run, but not in the long run.) As you saw earlier, V can change in the long run. These variations indicate the economy's responses to changes in many factors, including fiscal policy (taxes and government expenditures). Variation in the supply of money, say the Keynesians, is not the main stimulus that brings

---

1. Tobin, James. "Monetarism, An Ebbing Tide?" *The Economist*, April 27, 1985.

about changes in money income and real income. It is only one of a number of factors, including variations in fiscal policy and interest rates, that cause such changes. Critics of monetarism claim that the rigid link that the monetarists would forge between money and economic activity just does not exist.

A leading economist and former chairman of the Council of Economic Advisers, Martin Feldstein[2], says, however, that perfectly stable or predictable trends in velocity are not necessary, merely that "controlling monetary aggregates is better than the alternative bases for guiding monetary policy."

The monetarists' demand for a rigid monetary rule opens up several areas of debate. What money are they talking about? Is it to be just demand deposits plus all currency and coin in circulation (M_1)? Or does it also include various forms of near money (M_2)? If near money is excluded, don't variations in these highly liquid assets affect the situation?

Debates about whether to include M_2 elements of near monies and which to include explain some theoretical differences. This explains also some of the conflict in policy recommendations.

Also, how much time elapses between an increase in the supply of money (however one defines it) and the effect of that increase in the form of improved economic activity? The data that Friedman presents show great variability in time lags.

If, as is questionable, there is any validity to the Phillips Curve and if there is some trade-off between inflation and unemployment, what clue does one get from the monetarists that can be used to decide at what level the trade-off should be with this fixed growth in the money supply? If the Federal Reserve should increase the money supply at a certain fixed annual rate, this would force into the open certain changes in the economy. There might be fluctuations in interest rates that might be too large for comfort.

Table 13-2
Keynesian Versus Monetarist Views

Item	Keynesian View	Monetarist View
Demand for Money	Determined by people's incomes, (opportunity) cost of holding money, interest rates.	Determined by inflationary expectations, people's incomes, the level of prices, rates of returns on various forms of wealth and institutional factors.
How Money Affects the Economy	Increases in money supply lower interest rates, increase investment, and raise aggregate demand.	Increases in money supply cause increases in consumer spending as well as investment, which raise real income.
Discretionary Fiscal Policy	Very important as a tool to raise aggregate demand, lower unemployment, and raise real income.	Ineffective if not counterproductive in reaching real income targets because deficits lead to crowding out and politicians are short sighted.
Discretionary Monetary Policy	Useful, but not as potent a tool as discretionary fiscal policy.	Seen as very powerful and important by many monetarists while other prefer a fixed monetary rule.

A Conclusion

Milton Friedman and the monetarist school have affected the thinking of many economists and public policy makers. People have begun to pay a lot more

2. Feldstein, Martin. "Monetarism: Open-Eyed Pragmatism?" *The Economist*, May 3, 1985.

attention to the role of the money supply and monetary policy. These factors have assumed greater importance in government economic policy, even if making monetary policy effective is more difficult in a world of huge and efficient international capital markets. Nearly everyone agrees that money does matter. However, many economists are unwilling to concede that money is the only, or even the only major, thing that matters. Nor are they willing to completely abandon discretionary fiscal policy as a tool to affect the economy, although, its use is much more restricted today than in earlier decades. Many continue to espouse correcting for ups and downs in economic activity by making periodic adjustments in fiscal and monetary policy, a little of this and a dash of that, and prefer this on-the-spot approach to the measured-recipe method of following the rigid monetary rule and adding four percent to the money supply each year.

Keynesian and Monetarist Views: A Summary of Differences

The Keynesian-Monetarist debate is far from over. Both see the growth of the 1980s as providing supporting evidence for their views. Table 13-2 gives a summary of their contrasting views.

Monetary practitioners (e.g., Paul Volcker at the Fed in the 1980s) see discretionary monetary policy as a powerful and effective force. Milton Friedman sees the problem with discretionary policy as being people inadequate to a task. (Friedman: "Clearly the problem is not the person who happens to be chairman, but the system.") Thus, the crux of the debate *among* monetarists.

Keynesians see both views as too narrow, believing that discretionary fiscal and monetary policies can be linked together to achieve macroeconomic targets of growing real income and stable price levels. James Tobin regards the pure monetarist view as an "ebbing tide: which enjoyed its heyday in the 1960s and 1970s". The debate, in other words, is far from over.

Monetary Policy and International Markets Monetary Policy

Whatever the eventual outcome of the Keynesian-Monetarist debate, its importance has diminished from a policy standpoint. As we have seen, aggregate demand management, however effective or ineffective it might be, is severely constrained by the reality of the large federal debt together with the acceptance of the view that a natural rate of unemployment makes demand management ineffective or even counterproductive in the long run. That same debt and the necessity to finance it, together with the extreme ease with which capital funds move internationally, seems also to be making discretionary monetary policy more difficult to administer.

Much of the federal debt is held by foreigners. The Japanese are the largest holders of this debt. In order to attract foreign capital in these amounts, U.S. long-term interest rates have to be competitive with those in other major capital markets, such as Germany and Japan. When those rates rise, U.S. rates have to be kept high also even if domestic concern for a recession might otherwise cause the Fed to move toward monetary ease.

An article in *The Wall Street Journal* in March, 1990 relates a case in which the Fed acted in December 1989 to increase the money supply (buying treasury bills) to act against a possible recession: Although long-term interest rates fell briefly, they quickly moved upward and were soon *above* the rate existing before the easing of the money supply.

Then-Fed Chairman Alan Greenspan, asked whether the powerful Central Bank could still do its job of managing the money supply in a contracyclical manner, responded to a congressional committee: "To what extent have we lost control over our economic destiny? The Fed can still do its job but it's more difficult." Former New York Fed Chairman Anthony Solomon compares the difficulty with trying to juggle three balls at the same time: (1) economic growth, (2) inflationary pressures, and (3) foreign holdings of U.S. debt together with the need to attract long-term capital from abroad. At this point, few doubt that the Fed *can* do so, but it certainly is a more difficult task in the early twenty first century.

SUMMING UP

1. The Federal Reserve System (the Fed) is organized as follows: (a) There are 12 Federal Reserve Banks in 12 districts. (b) All *national* commercial banks must be members of the system, while *state banks* may join if they wish. (c) Each member bank must buy some stock in its particular district Federal Reserve Bank. (d) A seven-member board of governors in Washington controls the system. Its members are appointed by the President, with the advice and consent of the Senate, for terms of 14 years. (e) The Open Market Committee and the Federal Advisory Council are the two main committees under the board of governors. (f) Each Federal Reserve Bank has nine people on its board of directors: three appointed by the board of governors, three elected by the member banks, and three from the local community.

2. The so-called "general powers" of the Federal Reserve, including those granted in the Deregulatory Act of 1980, entitle it to control the excess reserves of all depository institutions, bank and non-bank alike by the following devices: (a) *Open-market operations.* To increase all institutions' excess reserves, the Fed buys government securities in the open market; it buys them from the commercial banks and pays for them by increasing deposits with the Federal Reserve. To reduce excess reserves, the Fed sells government securities on the open market to the depository institutions and deducts the amount of the sale from their deposits (reserves). (b) *Varying the discount rate.* When the Fed wants to encourage an increase in excess reserves, it lowers the *discount rate,* so that money becomes cheaper for the depository institutions to borrow. The institutions therefore borrow more, which increases their deposits with the Fed and increases their excess reserves. When the Fed wants to discourage the discounting, it increases the discount rate. (c) *Varying the required reserve ratio.* The Fed can lower or raise the percentage of a depository institution's total reserves that are considered "required," which in turn raises or lowers the reserves that are counted as "excess."

3. The Federal Reserve has or has had *specific powers* over certain aspects of lending. (a) The Fed sets the *margin requirement* for stock purchases. The *margin* is the percentage of cash required as a down payment on a purchase of corporate stock. The balance may be borrowed. (b) Regulation Q, the authority of the Fed to set maximum interest rates, was repealed in 1980. The act made all depository institutions subject to uniform reserve requirements and gave all such institutions access to the Fed's services. In general, it created a much more competitive American financial industry.

4. Financial markets were substantially deregulated in the 1980s. Controls over interest rates were removed, all depository institutions were permitted to create checkable deposits, loans by thrifts were expanded, and the Fed became available as a lending agency to all depository institutions.

5. The 1980s and early 1990s were turbulent for American financial institutions. Many banks and S&Ls failed. Two important concerns are (a) such institutions are primarily responsible for making loans and, thereby, creating most of America's money supply, and (b) taxpayers have absorbed a huge cost through the FDIC and Federal Savings and Loan Insurance Corporation (FSLIC) of guaranteeing depositors in the failed institutions.

6. The banking industry recovered in the 1990s because of reorganization and improved lending conditions. The S&L industry remains a problem. This seems to be because (a) deregulation has increased competition for savings and loan associations, which caused them to pay higher interest rates to attract depositors, and (b) insuring depositors against risk results in the *moral hazard problem* in that it reduces incentives by depositors to prevent losses.

7. Financial reform legislation; in 1989 created the *Resolution Trust Corporation (RTC)* to preside over the dissolution of failed S&Ls. The legislation also broadened FDIC authority over deposit insurance and allowed bank holding companies to acquire sound S&Ls while raising capital requirements for S&Ls to the same levels as that of banks.

8. The functions of the Federal Reserve are the following: (a) It regulates the supply of money. (b) It acts as a national clearinghouse for checks. (c) It issues all paper currency. (d) It regulates and examines member banks. (e) It acts as a banker's bank. (f) It acts as a fiscal agent and bank for the U.S. Treasury. (g) It acts as a fiscal agent for certain foreign central banks and treasuries.

9. Monetary policy works through credit markets that are controlled by interest rates. Using any one or a combination of its powers, the Fed can increase or decrease the supply of credit in these markets and, thereby, cause interest rates to rise or fall. As they rise, the quantity demanded of credit falls. As they fall, the quantity demanded of credit rises.

10. A lowering of interest rates, seen in Keynesian terms, leads to an increase in investment. As investment increases, aggregate demand grows, leading to an increase in real income and prices in the short run. In the long run, there is also an increase in aggregate supply that will cause further growth in real income and may partially or entirely offset the short-run price increase.

11. Increasing interest rates leads to a reduction in investment. Seen in Keynesian terms, as investment decreases, aggregate demand falls, leading to a decline in the short run real income and prices. In the long run, the decline in investment may lead to a decline in aggregate supply and a reduction in real income.

12. Discretionary monetary policy is based on complex relationships involving credit markets and interest rate targets. Some argue that it is so easy to be wrong about direction and magnitude of policy change that it would be better to have a monetary rule or fixed rate of increase in the supply of money and credit.

13. *Monetary policy* involves manipulating the supply of credit and interest rates so as to achieve low unemployment and only slight price increases. The Board of Governors of the Federal Reserve is the group responsible for administering monetary policy.

14. To overcome unemployment, one should increase the supply of credit and decrease interest rates in order to increase investment, aggregate demand, and income. In the long run, this should increase aggregate supply and further increase real income. To increase excess reserves, and thereby increase the money supply, the Fed should: (a) buy government securities on the open market, (b) lower the discount rate, or (c) lower the required reserve ratio.

15. To overcome inflation, one should decrease the supply of credit and increase interest rates; this should decrease aggregate demand and reduce prices. To decrease excess reserves, and thereby decrease the money supply, the Fed should: (a) sell government securities on the open market, (b) raise the discount rate and (c) raise the required reserve ratio.

16. The weaknesses of monetary policy are: (a) Inadequate demand for credit. During a severe recession, the policy may not work. People are afraid to invest, so they pay off loans and shy away from further borrowing. As a result, excess reserves increase without Fed interference. (b) Non-demand-pull inflation. During an inflation, monetary policy may be ineffective in dealing with kinds of inflation that are not susceptible to the lowering of aggregate demand (cost-push and administered-price inflation). (c) Monetary policy becomes ineffectual when inflation accompanies high unemployment. (d) Lags of recognition and implementation. (e) Changes in inflationary expectations may offset the plans of the Fed about interest rate changes.

17. Milton Friedman and some other economists of the monetarist school of thought reject discretionary fiscal and monetary policy aimed at stabilizing aggregate demand. They believe that a constant and proper level of increase in the supply of money is the key to containing both inflation and unemployment.

18. The monetarists claim that the rate of growth of the money supply is the primary factor that influences the level of economic activity (employment and prices). Some argue that deliberate (discretionary) monetary policy that changes the money supply may have a perverse effect on economic activity. This, plus the fact that no one can accurately predict future business affairs, makes discretionary, monetary, and fiscal policy ineffective and dangerous. Some monetarists therefore advocate a simple monetary rule: Let the government increase the supply of money by a fixed rate of two to four percent per year. Other monetarists regard discretionary monetary policy as effective and important in achieving economic growth and stability objectives.

19. The Keynesians point to the following weaknesses in the monetarist position: (a) The velocity of exchange is not constant, either in the short or long run. Therefore, there is no rigid link between the economy and the supply of money. (b) The monetarists leave a number of questions unanswered: What do they define as being money? What about variations in time between changes in the supply of money and changes in the economy?

20. Keynesians believe that discretionary monetary and fiscal policies can be devised to achieve real income and price-level goals.

21. The debate between Keynesian and monetarist views continues. All economists, nonetheless, regard the supply of money as an important macroeconomic variable.

KEY TERMS

Bank holding companies
Central bank
Discount rate
General power
Margin requirement
Monetarism
Monetary policy
Moral hazard problem
National banks
Regulation Q
Regulation W
Regulation X
Required reserve ratio
Resolution Trust Corporation
Specific powers
State banks

QUESTIONS

1. What is a central bank? How does it differ from private banks?

2. Which is more important, the pure public element or the quasi-public element of the structure of the Federal Reserve?

3. Given that the required reserve ratio is 20 percent, describe the way the following transactions would affect the following accounts: Required Reserves, Excess Reserves, Total Reserves, and Supply of Money.

   a. A commercial bank *buys* $10,000 in government securities from the Federal Reserve Bank.
   b. A commercial bank *sells* $10,000 in government securities to the Federal Reserve Bank.
   c. A commercial bank discounts a $1,000 note at 8 percent for 90 days at the Federal Reserve.
   d. The Federal Reserve raises the required reserve ratio to 25 percent.
   e. The Federal Reserve lowers the required reserve ratio to 15 percent.

4. What are the general powers of the Federal Reserve? How do they work? Why are they called general powers?

5. How do federal reserve policies affect credit markets?

6. What would you advise the board of governors of the Fed to do in case of an inflation? of a recession? What would you have advised them to do in the 1981-1982 inflationary situation?

7. When the Federal Reserve practices a policy of tight money in order to combat inflation, who pays the cost? Give reasons why these groups bear the cost.

8. How does non-demand-pull inflation complicate monetary policy?

9. You have just been appointed to the Board of Governors of the Federal Reserve System. The chairman has asked you to review monetary policy and present your recommendations on:

   a. Federal Reserve policy to counter inflation or unemployment.
   b. the groups in the economy that obtain advantages or disadvantages from your recommendations.
   c. the economic justification for your recommendations.
   d. how you would deal with significant amounts of inflation and unemployment at the same time.

10. How may changes in inflationary expectations complicate reaching Fed policy objectives?

11. What were the major changes since the 1980s in American financial institutions? What is the present role of the Fed vis-a-vis these institutions?

12. What seems to have caused widespread failures of banks and S&Ls in the 1980s and early 1990s?

13. What was the original purpose of deposit insurance? What is the problem of moral hazard and how was it related to financial failures in the 1980s and 1990s?

14. What was the purpose of the Resolution Trust Corporation?

15. What are the basic elements of the monetarists' position? Do they seem justified? Why?

Chapter 14: Economic Policy Controversies Supply-Side Economics, Rational Expectations, New Views by Keynesians;, Classical Economists, and the Post-Keynesians

As America entered the 1980s, its economy seemed to face some unprecedented challenges. Having survived the supply shocks of the early to mid-1970s, (OPEC I) and the late 1970s (OPEC II), it found itself in 1981 with an inflation rate of almost nine percent (briefly over 10 percent), an unemployment rate rising to almost 10 percent (in 1982), and a growth in real GDP declining sharply through much of the early 1980s. As often happens in periods of economic difficulty, the nation looked for new ideas or old ideas re-expressed to fit the times.

Supply-Side Economics
Arguments about efforts and incentives to stimulate growth in aggregate supply.

In electing Ronald Reagan as President, the country, at least in part responded to his promise of new policies to reinvigorate the American economy. Prominent among Reagan's arguments and those of his advisers was that of using **supply-side economics**, arguments about efforts and incentives to stimulate growth in aggregate supply. These efforts were designed to ensure real income growth at stable prices. Growth was to occur rapidly enough to create jobs at a rate that would bring down unemployment. In this chapter we are going to look at some of these supply-side arguments, arguments that are again being advanced in the early twenty first century, and the evidence regarding policies undertaken in their support. We will also look at some of the reservations expressed by those who argue that such discretionary government policies can have little or no macroeconomic effect. Finally, we will look at new views about macroeconomic theory, including those of rational expectations, new Keynesians, new classical economists, and the post-Keynesians.

Figure 14-1
Changes in Aggregate Demand, Aggregate Supply and Prices

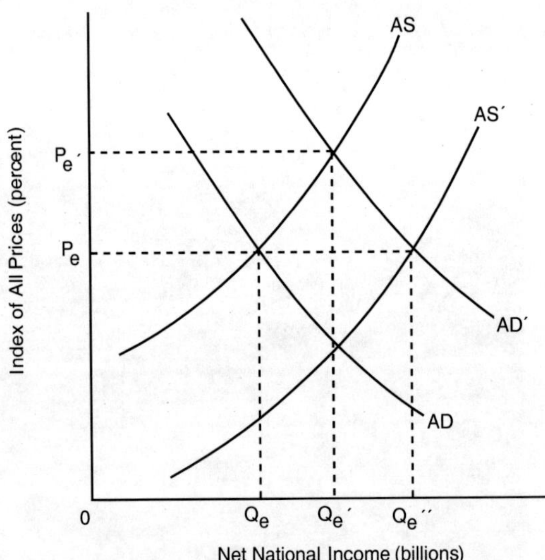

The initial equilibrium real income is Q_e with price level P_e (AD = AS). If aggregate demand is increased through fiscal or monetary policy, the short-run effect is to shift AD to AD′. The new equilibrium real income (AD′ = AS) is Q_e' with price level P_e'. In the long run, if aggregate supply grows, AS shifts to AS′ and prices reequilibriate at P_e with real income Q_e''.

Aggregate Supply and Aggregate Demand: A Review

Recall from a previous chapter that equilibrium real income and the equilibrium price level are established where aggregate quantity demanded equals aggregate quantity supplied (the level of output and prices at which the plans of those making expenditure decisions are made equal to the plans of those making production decisions). The initial equilibrium in Figure 14-1 is at real income Q_e and price level P_e, where aggregate quantity demanded equals aggregate quantity supplied. Now suppose that aggregate demand grows to AD′ as the result of stimulative fiscal (tax cuts, etc.) or monetary policy. With aggregate supply unchanged, real income grows to Q_e' but prices rise to P_e'. In the interest of price stability, an increase in aggregate supply is called for such as from AS to AS′. It would then be possible to establish a new higher level of real income at Q_e'', where a new aggregate quantity demanded equals a new aggregate quantity supplied. Prices, then, stabilize at the old level P_e.

How Do We Stimulate Aggregate Supply?

The shift of aggregate supply in Figure 14-1 could be a reaction to long-run investments that occur because of the larger aggregate demand. That simple Keynesian view of aggregate supply changes as responses to changes in aggregate demand is disputed, however, by "supply-side" economists. These economists assign aggregate supply a much more important and autonomous role in achieving the macroeconomic objectives of real income growth and price stability. Let's look, then, at the foundations of supply-side economics.

Fundamentals of Supply-Side Views

F. Thomas Juster[1] has argued that supply-side economics is based on four elements or hypotheses:

1. Entitlement programs (unemployment compensation, social security payments, etc.) have lowered work incentives; reducing such programs will, therefore, restore incentives and cut the tax burden on tax payers and investors.

2. America's system of taxes is biased against effort, saving, and investment. Lowering taxes, thus, will increase labor supplies and savings and investment.

3. Public regulation designed to protect consumers and employees raises costs and reduces investment. Many such activities offer few benefits relative to their costs. The view of supply-side proponents is that this applies both to (1) industrial regulation of particular industries that often creates monopolies or cartels with less efficiency and higher costs, and (2) social regulation such as pollution control health and safety regulation that raises costs and prices without being subjected to a cost/benefit calculation.

4. The long use of monetary and fiscal programs to stimulate aggregate demand has created a climate of inflationary expectations. Changing those expectations (through, for example, a commitment to balanced budgets) will help, therefore, to reduce inflationary pressures.

While Juster expresses sympathy for some of these four propositions, he expresses serious doubt about the linkage between tax reductions, labor supplies and the volume of savings. One should not forget, though, that supply-side policies are founded not only in economic theory but also in political philosophy. As President Reagan said in his *Economic Report* of 1987: "Government should play a limited role in the economy, It should encourage a stable economy in which people can make informed decisions. It should not make those decisions for them or arbitrarily distort economic choices...."

Tax Policy, Keynesian Expenditure Reductions or Supply-Side "Wedges?"

Tax Wedge
The supply-side view that taxes are a wedge between resource prices and the prices of final goods and services.

To Keynesians, tax increases are seen as a reduction of the ability of consumers and firms to purchase goods and services. Tax increases, thus, reduce aggregate demand and are contractionary. Supply-siders, on the other hand, believe that most tax increases ultimately are incorporated as higher costs by producers and finally are shifted forward to consumers by way of higher prices. Tax increases, therefore, create a cost-push effect on aggregate supply. In the decades of the 1970s and 1980s, for example, federal payroll taxes (primarily social security taxes), as well as state and local government excise and sales taxes were boosted substantially. Supply-siders see such tax increases as a "**tax wedge**" between the prices of resources and the prices of final goods and services. In other words, as government taxes have increased, costs of production and prices have risen and aggregate supply has been reduced (shifted to the left). To supply-siders, rever-

1. Juster, F. Thomas. "The Economics and Politics of the Supply-Side View." *Economics Outlook USA*, Autumn, 1981.

sal of this trend of rising taxes would lower production costs and prices and lead to an increase in aggregate supply (a shift to the right).

The Tax Cuts of 1981: How Well Did They Work?

We witnessed numerous changes in Federal taxation in the 1980s. The 1981 changes reduced the highest marginal income tax rate from 70 percent to 50 percent (by 1984). Income taxes were indexed to prevent "bracket creep," rising marginal tax rates associated with growth in nominal but not real income. In line with article (2) of the supply-side propositions, this was expected to increase savings and investment, as well as to encourage a larger supply of labor. It might also be added that it was expected to encourage legal transactions as opposed to the **underground economy**, those transactions that give rise to taxable income but are not reported for tax purposes. In 1985, Reagan proposed a further reduction in the highest marginal tax rate to 31 percent; a proposal that went into effect in 1987 (although, in 1993, it was raised to 33 percent).

Underground Economy
Economic transactions that give rise to taxable income but are not reported for tax purposes.

It is still difficult to assess the long-term relative aggregate supply and aggregate demand effects of the 1981 tax cuts. It is, of course, still too early to forecast the long-run effects of the 1987 tax law. President Reagan, in his 1987 *Economic Report*, regarded the 1981 cuts as a clear success, reporting that "businesses fixed investment set records as a share of real gross domestic product in 1984 and 1985 and remains high by historical standards." Some economists have criticized the correlation saying that increased investment rates were merely a reaction to the extraordinarily low investment rates during the severe recession of 1981-1982 rather than a long-term improvement in savings and investment. Benjamin Friedman[2], a Harvard economist, says that attacking the deficits will be necessary before such a long-term change in savings and investment rates can occur. That argument was joined forcefully in the intense debates in the mid-1990s over reducing federal deficits and is being renewed in the wake of the deficits of 2002 to the present.

Supply-Side Economics: Why So Controversial?

That there was a significant recovery of the American economy between 1982 and 1990 is unquestionable. That it constitutes the second longest sustained recovery in the economy's peacetime history is also correct, as is the statement that relatively stable prices (inflation rates of two to four percent) and declining unemployment (5.2 percent in early 1990) accompanied the expansion. In many respects, this would seem to validate the idea that proper coordination between changes in aggregate demand and changes in aggregate supply can produce sustained real income growth *and* relative price stability. Why, then, the controversy over supply-side economics? In substantial measure, the controversy (at least at the macroeconomic level) derives from the large budget deficits of the 1980s that we examined in another chapter. Many supply-siders argued that real income growth could occur with no need to incur such deficits because federal revenues would grow in spite of tax cuts as the economy expanded.

---

2. Friedman, Benjamin M. "Did Regan's 1981 Tax Incentives Work? The Vaunted Investment Boom Is a Bust." *New York Times*, July 7, 1985.

The Laffer Curve: Too Much Taxation Reduces Revenue

Laffer Curve
A theoretical association between various tax rates and the tax revenues collected at each rate.

An early precept upon which supply-side economic arguments were founded was a proposition named for economist Arthur Laffer and called the **Laffer curve**. This is a theoretical association between various tax rates and the tax revenues collected at each rate. We see a hypothetical Laffer curve in Figure 14-2. Note that as tax rates rise from point 0 to point B, tax revenues rise and reach a maximum of $1,000 billion ($1 trillion) at point B. As rates rise above 40 percent, revenues decline. Cutting tax rates from 75 percent to 40 percent could, thus, increase revenues (from $500 billion to $1 trillion). It follows from the curve that there is more than one rate that will generate a specific amount of revenue. Notice that points A and C correspond to the same revenue ($500 billion) but to very different tax rates (25 percent and 75 percent). The reasoning underlying the Laffer curve is that of point (B) in our supply-side elements: taxes are biased against effort, saving and investment. Beyond some point, as they rise, they lead to reduced effort (or diversion of resources to the underground economy) as well as reduced saving and investment. As they are cut, the supply of effort increases as does savings, investment, income, and the tax base.

Figure 14-2
A Hypothetical Laffer Curve for an Economy

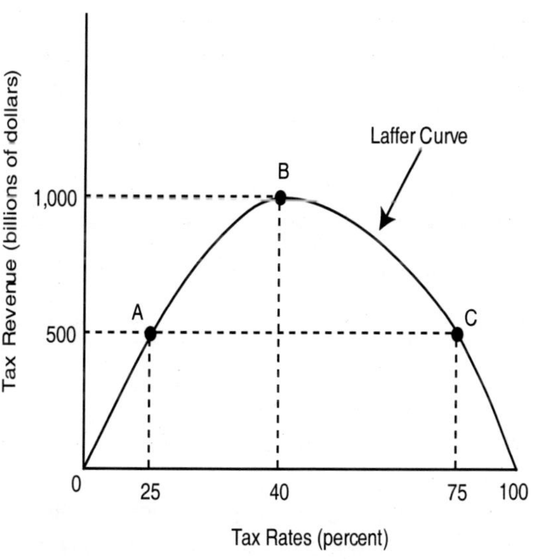

As tax rates rise, tax revenues rise. At (A), a tax rate of 25 percent yields revenues of 500 billion dollars. That same revenue would be yielded however at Point C with a tax rate of 75 percent. Tax revenues are at a maximum ($1,000 billion) at Point B.

A major problem with the Laffer curve is in making it operationally testable. How can we know where point B lies in reality? If we want to produce a certain amount of tax revenue, how can we structure taxes in advance and in the proper way to avoid the disincentives of proceeding past point B? President Reagan and others were apparently persuaded of the validity of the Laffer argument in the case of the 1981 tax cuts. Although there may be some who say investment lags simply postponed the revenue inflow, many others point to the deficits and question the Laffer curve concept itself. A second problem with the Laffer curve is the sensitivity of incentives to work and save and invest when tax rates are reduced. Some empirical studies by critics suggest that these incentive effects will be smaller than supply-siders believe. Thus, tax cuts in a growing economy may primarily expand aggregate demand and may result in budget deficits and inflation. What effects will the tax cuts of 2003 have on aggregate demand and aggregate supply?

Can Discretionary Policy Changes Alter Growth Anyway? Rational Versus Adaptive Expectations

Economists of whatever view agree that expectations play an important role in private economic decision making. Consumers must form expectations about the future including such things as incomes, prices, taxes, interest rates, and inflation rates. Firms must form expectations about future events including many of the same things. Neither group can make informed present decisions without some perspective on the future.

Adaptive Expectations Hypothesis
The argument that decision makers form their view of the future on the basis of actual events that have occurred in the recent past.

Differences exist among economists as to how expectations are formed. A traditional idea is that called the **adaptive expectations hypothesis**, which holds that decision makers form their view of the future on the basis of actual events that have occurred in the recent past. Consider the question of inflation rates. As we noted earlier, annual inflation rates since 1983 have generally ranged from two to four percent. Adaptive expectationists would argue that this range is probably the prevailing view that we have of the immediate future. Suppose now that the monetary authority increases the supply of credit and inflation rises to 10 percent. Wage demands of labor (and other costs) will not likely rise immediately to offset the difference between expected and actual inflation rates. As a result, firms' (real) costs fall, profits rise and investments are likely to increase. In the long run, of course, resource suppliers will adapt to the new inflation rate and adjust their resource price demands upward to offset the change in inflationary expectation. In the short-run, though, monetary (or fiscal) policies could work to stimulate the economy.

Rational Expectations Hypothesis
The argument that decision makers form their view of the future partly on the basis of events in the recent past but also on the basis of present events.

A more recent view associated in particular with Robert Lucas, Jr. and Thomas Sargent of the University of Minnesota, is called the **rational expectations hypothesis**[3]. This hypothesis is that private decision makers form their inflationary expectations partly on the basis of events in the recent past but also on the basis of present events. People not only learn from what *has* happened but from what *is* happening. Combining the two sources of information, they anticipate future events including inflation rates and changes in inflation rates. Suppose that this view is accepted. If the monetary authority increases the supply of credit, private decision makers quickly build this information into their view of the future. If they now expect (without the lag of adaptive expectations) that inflation rates will rise, they adjust their wage and other price demands upward, raising costs, reducing the profitability of investment, and offsetting the investment effects of the macroeconomic efforts to stimulate the economy.

Rational expectationists would argue, thus, that discretionary macroeconomic policy, especially monetary policy, is not only ineffective but even destabilizing. Only if the macroeconomic policy change was greater than expected by firms and consumers would it work. If one accepts this idea, it would seem almost impossible to fool all private decision makers in some systematic way. Discretionary macroeconomic policy would seem to be ruled out, and macroeconomic policy by rule would be called for.

---

3. In McCallum, Bennett. "The Significance of Rational Expectations Theory." *Challenge,* November-December, 1980.

How Influential is Rational Expectations Theory?

There is no doubt that rational expectations theory is some what influential. It has caused some economists to rethink and even question some of their beliefs about the degree of effectiveness of various macroeconomic policy tools (money supply changes, tax cuts, etc.). Many economists, nonetheless, are not prepared to abandon their view that the macroeconomy can successfully be nudged toward more rapid growth or price stability through selectively applied policy changes. As recently as 1981-1982, a powerful dose of monetary restraint did moderate inflation as well as impel the economy into recession. In 1992-1993, a powerful series of monetary growth stimuli does seem to have helped foster an economic recovery. Policy changes, in other words, may work; they just may not work as well as adaptive expectations conclude, but not as poorly as rational expectationists conclude.

Beyond Traditional Keynesian and Classical Policy Arguments

Let's sum up some of the policy controversies that continued throughout the 1970s and 1980s, and continue today between the Keynesians and the classical schools of economic thought. These policy differences focus on three aspects of the modern macroeconomy.

1. ***How well do markets work?*** Are they competitive, and, if so, competitive enough so that flexibility of resource and product prices will tend to create a tendency toward full employment? Classical economists believe that the answer to both questions is yes. Keynesians, on the other hand, doubt that there is enough flexibility in market prices to eliminate the necessity for discretionary government fiscal and monetary policies designed to increase the economy's move toward full employment.

2. ***Will markets eliminate excess supply and excess demand?*** Even if there are flexible prices, will markets work efficiently, that is move resources with sufficient mobility to achieve macroeconomic equilibrium quickly? Classical economists, while realizing that there is not perfect mobility (there are barriers such as monopoly, discrimination, and lack of information), argue that there is sufficient mobility to move toward market clearing uses of resources in socially acceptable periods of time. Keynesian economists, by contrast, believe that the barriers to mobility are sufficiently great that excess supply and excess demand can exist in markets for significant periods of time. In their view, this justifies use of government fiscal and monetary policies to eliminate these "bottlenecks" in the macroeconomy.

3. ***Expectations, rational or adaptive?*** Many classical economists accept the view that consumers and producers in the modern macroeconomy are so knowledgeable about the effects on the aggregate price level of government demand management that such Keynesian policies can have no systematic affects on aggregate demand/ aggregate supply equilibrium. There is, after all, much effort to forecast such effects and react to them. Keynesians, however, argue that such forecasts are imperfect and that there are major variations from the forecasted results. There is room, therefore, say Keynesians, for government policies to affect the macroeconomic equilibrium in a systematic way.

The Post-Keynesians, Today's Contrarians

Keynesians and classical economists continue to argue about the scope and effectiveness of discretionary macroeconomic government policies. Neither group, however, argues that the private macroeconomy is so clogged with monopoly and market imperfections that it simply cannot work. Rather, the two groups argue about how serious the imperfections are and whether particular kinds of market intervention by government are warranted and effective. A third small, but vocal group of economists do, however, argue that the modern private macroeconomy is subject to so many such large-scale *structural* problems that recurrent crises characterize its operations. This group called **Post-Keynesians** argue, thus, for permanent government intervention to offset the private market failures they believe to be widespread. They cite price rigidities, monopolization of product and resource markets, and concentrated financial markets as evidence that the economy is "sick" and that their concerns are warranted. Rather than deal with the symptoms, as they believe Keynesians would do, post-Keynesians, in a position akin to that of Marxians, argue for systematic government intervention in the economy. This intervention would take the form of direct regulation of industries and use of tax and expenditure policies to alter the system of incentives about resource usage. Many post-Keynesians argue for an **incomes policy** that would move government's role to one of (1) wage, price and profit controls, and (2) substantial economic planning. Post-Keynesians differ from Marxians in that the former support a private market system that is extensively "managed" by government, while the latter group support direct government ownership of the means of production. Prominent post-Keynesians include the late English economist Joan Robinson and the prominent American economist, the late John Kenneth Galbraith.

Post-Keynesians
A school of economists who argue the need for widespread government intervention in the economy because of private market failures.

Incomes Policy
An argument of post-Keynesians that government intervention should include wage and price controls as well as extensive economic planning.

SUMMING UP

1 As America entered the 1980s, it had high inflation, rising unemployment and a declining rate of growth in real GDP.

2. Macroeconomic policy under the Reagan administration was partly based on supply-side economics, policies designed to stimulate growth in aggregate supply at stable price levels.

3. The equilibrium level of real income and prices is established where aggregate quantity demanded equals aggregate quantity supplied. In the face of growing aggregate demand, price stability requires incentives to increase aggregate supply through savings and investment.

4. "Supply-siders" have argued that macroeconomic growth and stabilization policy, which had long focused on aggregate demand changes, should shift emphasis to treat changing aggregate supply as an autonomous variable.

5. Supply-side views seem to be founded in four ideas: (a) entitlement programs reduce incentives; their reduction will raise incentives and cut tax burdens, (b) taxes are biased against saving and investment: lower taxes will mean more effort as well as savings and investments, (c) much public regulation to protect consumers and employees, both directly of industries and also social regulation such as pollution controls, has high costs and relatively few benefits,

(d) stimulating aggregate demand through monetary and fiscal policies has created high inflationary expectations and there is a need to lower these expectations.

6. The tax cuts of 1981 were intended to stimulate saving and investment and to redirect resources away from the underground economy of non-taxed transactions Marginal tax rates were cut in 1981 and again in 1987. The tax cuts of 2001, 2002 and 2003 are similar in structure.

7. There was an increase in investment rates after 1982; it is unclear how much of that increase is attributable to the tax cuts.

8. The main controversy over supply-side economic policies is not in the post-1981 sustained growth or relative price stability but rather in the large federal deficits that have resulted.

9. According to the Laffer curve, tax rates can be so high that disincentives to work, save and invest set in and actually reduce tax revenues as rates rise beyond some level. The Laffer curve apparently had some influence in the 1981 tax cuts.

10. A major problem with the Laffer curve is implementing it. We do not know whether the cuts in 1981 raised tax revenues through incentive effects or through aggregate demand effects. What we have observed is that revenues did not rise as rapidly as expenditures and large deficits resulted. Another problem is with the sensitivity of work and savings incentives to tax cuts. Supply-siders believe the incentives to be very sensitive, critics disagree.

11. Expectations play an important role in private decisions by consumers and by firms. The adaptive expectations hypothesis holds that expectations are formed by people on the basis of recent events. Macroeconomic policy changes, thus, can be influential in affecting savings and investment in the short-run because resource prices are based on current expectations and are not immediately adjusted upward in the face of rising rates of inflation.

12. Expectations, say some economists, are formed according to the rational expectations hypothesis, that is, on the basis not only of recent events but also current events. Combining both sets of information, private decision makers anticipate the consequences of current macroeconomic policy changes such as the higher inflation that may result from a growing money supply. Thus, resource prices adjust quickly and negate any stimulative effect from the policy change. Discretionary policy does not work; policy by rule is called for.

13. Rational expectations theory has been influential. It still appears to many economists, however, that discretionary policy changes such as the 1981 curtailment of the money supply and the monetary policy changes of the early 1990s worked, at least in the short run.

14. Keynesians and classical economists argue about the scope and effectiveness of government macroeconomic policies. Post-Keynesians, however, argue that widespread failures in the private economy make necessary permanent and extensive government intervention in a modern macroeconomy. This intervention, they argue, should take the form of direct and detailed regulation of industries as well as an incomes policy which would involve wage, price and profit controls. Post-Keynesians differ from Marxists in that they do not argue for public ownership of the means of production.

KEY TERMS

Adaptive expectations hypothesis
Incomes policy
Laffer curve
Post-Keynesians
Rational expectations hypothesis
Supply-side economics
Tax wedge
Underground economy

QUESTIONS

1. What were the general macroeconomic conditions of the American economy in the early 1980s?

2. What is meant by the term "supply-side economics?" What kinds of macroeconomic policies do supply-siders argue for?

3. In the face of growing aggregate demand, what is necessary to ensure price stability?

4. On what four propositions are supply-side economic views founded?

5. What were the intended effects of the 1981 tax cuts? What are the intended effects of the tax cuts of 2002, and 2003?

6. Were the 1981 tax cuts successful? If so, in what sense?

7. What is the source of the major controversies surrounding the supply-side policies of the 1980s?

8. In the figure below a hypothetical Laffer curve is drawn. Answer the following questions about the curve.

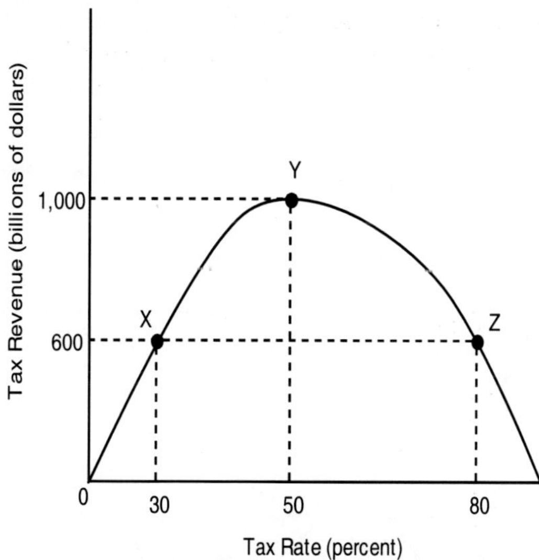

a. What is the Laffer curve argument about the association between tax rates and tax revenues?
b. At what tax rate do revenues reach a maximum?
c. Why are there two tax rates (30 percent, 80 percent) that yield the same revenue?
d. What causes tax revenues to decline beyond point Y?
e. What are the principal problems with using the Laffer curve as a basis for tax policy?

9. Explain the difference between the rational expectations hypothesis and the adaptive expectations hypothesis? Under which of the two may short-run charges in discretionary macroeconomic policy be successful?

10. What is the view of Keynesians and classical economists about the role of government in direct management of the economy?

Chapter 15: Economic Growth

Except for the earliest formative years of its colonial period, the United States has enjoyed one of the most impressive economic growth records among the world's nations. A small but prosperous nation in the late eighteenth century, it had, by the early twentieth century, become the world's leading industrial society. That process of industrialization, which came to be called the "American system of manufactures," produced a rate of growth in output that, even in the face of very rapid population growth, assured that each new generation of Americans enjoyed a higher standard of living than its predecessor. Indeed, each generation came to think of economic growth as the norm and to assume, justifiably, that its children would be better educated and more prosperous than themselves. Now, in the early twenty first century, troubling questions have arisen as to whether that long growth trend will continue and whether the resulting sanguine view of the future is still warranted. While we cannot forecast with precision the future of the nation's economy, we can, in this chapter, assay what constitutes economic growth and what were the factors that contributed to America's successful growth record. In doing that, we may gain some insights into what will be necessary to insure that the long-term trend is maintained.

Statics versus Dynamics

Until now, we have dealt with macroeconomic and microeconomic principles that are primarily *static.* That is, they are like a snapshot of a situation at a point in time, rather than like a motion picture showing the situation changing with the passage of time. Static principles of economics, such as supply and demand and national income determination, have helped us analyze problems as diverse as how to view the effects of rent control laws, and whether monetary policy is an effective tool against inflation.

Dynamic Framework
A framework that explains how things change over time.

We are about to explore some problems that, at least in some of their aspects, require a **dynamic framework**, one that explains how things change over a period of time. We will examine, for example, the growth record of the U.S. economy and its prospects for the future. In this chapter we will discuss several theoretical explanations of economic growth, and in the second application, we will present the following related problem: Do we have to choose between more growth and a clean environment?

Extensive Growth
The process by which the output of an economy grows through the use of more resources

Intensive Growth
The process by which productivity, output per hour of labor increases.

Let's begin by making a distinction between expansion and growth. We'll use **extensive growth** to refer to the process by which the output of an economy grows as it uses more and more resources. **Intensive growth** refers to the process by which productivity, output per hour of labor (or income per capita), increases.

Sources of Extensive Growth

Extensive growth can be thought of as an outward shifting of a nation's production-possibilities curve. An economy can achieve such growth by using more resources. First, it might achieve extensive growth because of an increase in the supply of total resources (land, labor, capital, and entrepreneurship). Let's look at each of those resources to see how, and how much, each might contribute to expansion.

1. *Land* represents all the natural resources of a nation, not only the surface soil but the subsoil minerals, the timber, and the water. It is tempting to think of all resources as being fixed: so many acres of land, so many acre-feet of water, tons of minerals, and so forth. Although it is useful to know (or estimate) the economy's resources at a particular time, you should realize that they can and do change as time and technology change the ways of producing things as well as the things that can be produced. It is very important, also, to remember the role of prices in defining the supply of natural resources. At a price of $10 a barrel a nation may have so many billions of barrels it is profitable to use as a resource (to produce goods and services). At $65 a barrel, the amount that is profitable to recover and use will certainly be greater.

Consider the case of offshore oil, under the continental shelf: A few decades ago no one was even sure it was there and even if knowledge of it existed, at then-existing oil prices, it was not profitable to explore and recover it. Even after geologic surveys confirmed its existence, it was still only a potential resource that might be tapped someday. Now, technology and price changes have made a difference. With new oil-drilling technology, and with world oil prices much higher than in 1971, offshore oil, as well as oil in Alaska and other places, has become a resource, something available to use in producing goods.

Another example of technology creating a resource occurred in iron mining. In the Mesabi iron range, the richest iron ore was mined and the second-grade ore, called *taconite,* was thrown aside because it was too expensive to refine. Now, with new technology, the mining companies are working the Mesabi range again, this time getting iron from the taconite. The price of iron makes it economical, definitely worth the trouble.

We should note here that technology and changes in technology affect not only extensive growth, through making resources out of previously unusable potential resources. They also, as you shall see shortly, increase the productivity of resources that are employed and, thereby, are themselves a major source of intensive growth.

2. *Labor* represents the human resources of a society. In a sense, labor is the most basic of all resources. Without labor, nothing happens. The whole process of intensive and extensive growth depends on human motivations, work, aspirations, and skills. An increase in population or an increase in participation in the labor force (for example, labor force participation by women during and since

World War II) increases a society's total output (that is, it creates extensive growth).

3. *Capital* is the physical result of investment. Capital consists of the plant and equipment and tools with which people work. Capital's productivity rises with specialization, and specialization is limited by the size of the market. In a small town in a largely rural (perhaps low-income) area of the United States, there's not much specialization of either labor or capital. If you get sick, you go to the town doctor, who is almost certainly a general practitioner. If you have a leaky roof, you go to the town's general handyman, a jack-of-all-trades. If your car's engine is idling badly, you take it to the town mechanic, no matter whether the car is a Chevy or a Nissan.

Now, what happens if you live in a city and have the same problems? If your medical problem is a skin rash, you go directly to a dermatologist or you are referred to one. If you have a roof leak, you call in a firm of roof specialists. If you have car trouble, you probably find a garage that specializes in that particular make of car.

Whether in small town or city, the kind and amount of capital that people have to work with has a lot to do with their productivity. The more capital, and the more sophisticated the capital available to workers, the greater their output.

The differences in these two earlier situations are due to *different market sizes.* The small (poor) town has few consumers and relatively little aggregate demand. The city has many consumers and much more aggregate demand. In the city there are enough people with enough purchasing power to warrant the investment that results in specialized tools, machines, and plant facilities. Without this capital, jobs for those in the (increasing) labor force will not be created and the society will not be able to use its (potential) natural resources.

4. *Entrepreneurs* (enterprisers) constitute a critical resource to any society. Indeed, entrepreneurial activities involve seeking out the best opportunities, especially *new* opportunities for using resources to produce goods and services. Often, such activities involve *innovation*, the creation of new firms, new products, new markets, as well as applying new technology to produce existing products in more efficient ways. In doing these things, entrepreneurs take differential risks and, when successful, not only shift the production-possibilities curve outward, but also raise productivity. They decisively influence, thus, not only extensive growth but also intensive growth.

Increasing Productivity and Growth

There is a link between productivity and growth. As more and more resources are used in production, growth may occur because as productivity increases the cost per unit of output goes down. As the economy uses existing plants, or builds more plants, and as it employs more people and uses more land (natural resources), output may increase more rapidly than input. In other words, a five percent increase in the use of inputs may generate more than a five percent increase in output. Let's examine the reasons for this.

According to Adam Smith and other early classical economists, *specialization* is a major reason for such increases in output. In an economy whose market size is growing, there is more and more specialized use of labor and capital, which leads to more and more output. In fact, large market size, as we mentioned a bit earlier, is necessary if specialization is to become widespread in an economic society.

Technological Change
The growth in knowledge or advances in techniques that result in more productive capital goods and more efficient organization.

Technological change, the growth in knowledge or advances in techniques that result in more productive capital goods and more efficient organization, is perhaps the main thing that holds out hope for future growth. If all our prospects for growth depended on the static benefits of specialization, the future might prove as gloomy as the classical economists (Adam Smith, David Ricardo, and others) predicted. Their dismal view prevailed through much of our industrial history. To see why, examine Figure 15-1.

Let's suppose that the economy shown in Figure 15-1 has met various preconditions for growth: attitudes favorable to growth, financial institutions to receive and channel savings into productive investments, a government to establish and enforce commercial rules, people drawn into the market system, all the things we have discussed in previous chapters. Suppose also that it has at least one industry that has a high growth potential whose effects seem likely to spread throughout the economy.

What will happen first as the economy starts to grow and expand? In the early years, its productivity and per capita income may rise rapidly. The part of the growth path (Y/P) from zero up to time t_0 represents this period. As the size of its market gets larger (as reflected in its growing per capita income), it begins to enjoy all the efficiencies of increased specialization. The slope, or rate of change, of (Y/P) increases, indicating that real per capita income is growing faster and faster.

Then, after time t_0, the slope of (Y/P) becomes less steep, which means that if the economy remains on this growth path (even at full employment), growth will be slower. (As time passes, the increments in growth will get smaller and smaller.) This implies that there are barriers or resistances to rapid growth. What are they? Why can't the economy simply keep on growing at the same rate?

Decreasing Productivity and Growth

Let's answer the question of why there has been a slowdown in the growth rate:

1. In the short term, some resources may be relatively fixed in usage. For example, the Atlas Company makes stereo sets, for which plant and equipment are the fixed inputs. Now it naturally takes longer to put new plant and equipment into use than it does to vary the use of other inputs (labor, land, and materials). So if Atlas wants to make more stereos, and if it starts using more labor and land without increasing its use of capital (plant and equipment), then its productivity (output of stereos per unit of additional input) will ultimately decline. Why? Basically, because of overcrowding. With a fixed number of machines and a fixed amount of plant space, workers may start having to wait to use machines. They may finally get in each other's way and disrupt the specialized routines of the plant.

2. As an economy begins to suffer diminishing productivity growth, the rate at which per capita income grows slacks off. At some point (t_0 in Figure 15-1), diminishing efficiency (due to the slowness of increase in plant and equipment) begins to more than offset the increased amount of efficiency resulting from specialization. The slope of the (Y/P) curve becomes less and less steep. When it reaches zero (past t_1), the society is in a *stationary state*. Real per capita income is at a maximum and will not grow further until something in the economy changes.

Figure 15-1
Growth Paths of an Economy

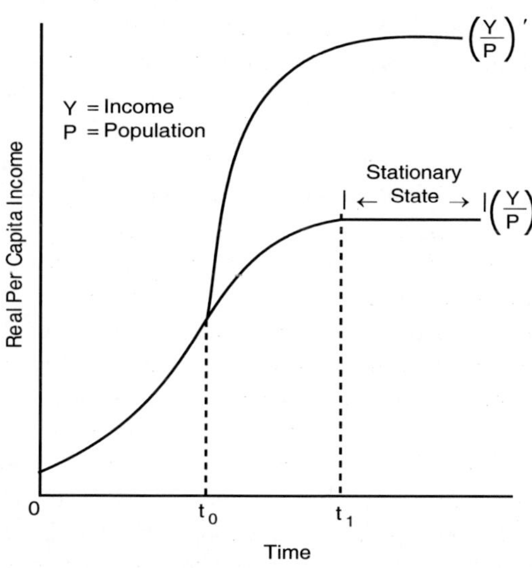

The Classical View

The classical economists (Adam Smith, et al.) who talked about the stationary state disagreed about how high the upper limit to (Y/P) might be. Smith was among the most optimistic. Unlike others, Smith refused to look upon technology as containing a fixed number of choices. Some classical economists gloomily predicted that a society would use techniques that added less and less to productivity as time went on and that it would finally run out of new technological choices. They felt that this gradual disappearance of new technology, combined with the need to produce more and more food for a growing population on a fixed supply of land, would ultimately produce the stationary state at a fairly low level of real per capita income. But Smith had slightly more optimistic hopes for the future. He believed that population growth might be held in check because as people become accustomed to more goods and services, they might develop a taste for more goods rather than more children.

Malthusian Specter
The view of Thomas Malthus that because of slower growth in food supplies than in population, starvation, wars, plagues, and famines would result.

The most pessimistic of the classicists was the English economist, Thomas R. Malthus. Parson Malthus (he was a preacher) originated what has become known as the **Malthusian specter**. His grim view of the future derived from two influences: the supply of people and the supply of food to maintain them. Malthus argued that the supply of people (the population) will increase at a geometric rate (1, 2, 4, 8, 16, and so on), that is, double each generation, or every twenty-five years. On the other hand, the food supply will increase only at an arithmetic rate (1, 2, 3, 4, 5, and so on). Finally, widespread starvation will result unless people are able to restrict the population. According to Malthus, there will be wars, plagues, and famines that ultimately will bring population into line with the means of sustaining people.

Has the Malthusian Nightmare Occurred in Some Places?

We said in an earlier chapter that a small but growing part of the world's population lives in high-income countries. For this lucky minority, the ominous predictions of the classical economists have obviously not come to pass. For the majority, however, the scenario, especially Malthus's version, has real meaning. Everyone reads about starvation, plague, famine, and war in such countries as Congo and Somalia. The photographs from those areas are heart-rending. Real per capita income in such countries is extremely low. For example, in India, each year population growth presses ever harder on the means of sustaining India's more than one billion people. In spite of the green revolution (that is, the growth in agricultural productivity), countries such as Bangladesh and Rwanda sometimes need foreign relief in the form of massive shipments of grain and other foodstuffs to prevent widespread starvation. For such countries, the low-level stationary state is a grim reality.

But what about that one-third of the world's people who live in Europe, North America, Australia, Japan, and the newly industrializing nations such as Taiwan and Korea? Why have they escaped? Look again at Figure 15-1, and let's use the United States as an example. The United States has experienced, at least over the last 25 years, a continuous shifting of Y/P, our growth path. In fact, real growth over that period has averaged 3.25 percent per annum. Each time, before the economy actually reached a point of declining growth (such as t_0), it has moved into a higher growth path, such as $(Y/P)'$. A series of such shifts has kept the U.S. economy from entering a stationary state. A study of our industrial history suggests that there are two major reasons for this: technological change and population increase.

Technological Change

A large part of U.S. productivity growth and increase in real income is due to the fact that U.S. industry has constantly changed the techniques by which it produces things. There is an old but true story about the clerk in the U.S. Patent Office who resigned, in the early nineteenth century, because he was sure that most of the important inventions had already been made. But Americans as a rule are optimistic about the future and count on technological change to increase their incomes and their productivity. To a great extent, their optimism is justified. Except for cyclical variations in investment in new forms of technology (such as the depression of the 1930s), U.S. industry has kept pushing ahead, using new methods as fast as people invent them. Beginning with the cotton gin in the late eighteenth century and continuing through the glamorous devices made possible by the aerospace technology and computer technology of the last three decades or so, U.S. industry has employed better and better machinery and tools, which have raised the productivity of American laborers right into the twenty first century. The United States has also made larger and larger investments in people themselves, spending billions on such things as education, health programs, and slum clearance, all of which have helped raise the productivity of the American worker.

Technologicial change can be thought of as improvements in the *quality* of capital. A new, faster computer, for example, raises the productivity of labor because it embodies the latest technology. Not all technological change however, is so embodied. A second form of technological change is through **disembodied technological change**, or change that is only partly, if at all, embodied in the quality of labor or capital resources. For example, a new transportation or communications network may lower the costs of many firms even if those firms continue to use the same capital and labor resources. Supply of the firms, thus, may increase without any embodied technical change.

Disembodied Technological Change
Technological change that is not completely reflected in improved quality of labor or capital.

Population Increase

In 1930 there were 123 million Americans. In 2013 there are about 314 million, more than a two-and-a-half-fold increase. This increase in population has been favorable to growth in the United States. Until people began to question the idea in recent years, Americans believed that growth in numbers would make them better off in the long run, which naturally influenced their willingness to have children. During the nineteenth century, when we were an agricultural society, large families were like money in the bank. Children started working on the farms at an early age and were active producers.

Likewise, when the United States was becoming an urban industrial society in the late nineteenth and early twentieth centuries, large families (together with waves of immigrants) were a good thing because they produced the labor force needed to build and operate mass-production factories.

But now that the United States is a mature industrial, or post-industrial, society, large families are no longer an *economic* asset (at least to individuals), although we continue to benefit from a large influx of immigrants. Children are consumers, not producers. So now, in the early years of the twenty first century, America has a relatively low rate of natural population growth. Though controversial to many, birth-control information is free in most states, and the advent of the Pill, plus the passing of laws and court decisions to legalize abortion (which are even more controversial) have combined to reduce the number of births from 27.7 live births per thousand in 1920 to 13.8 live births per thousand in 2009, a drop of more than 50 percent in eighty years.

"Now will you have the vasectomy?"

Capital-Intensive
Techniques that use relatively more capital than labor or land.

Labor-Intensive
Techniques that use relatively more labor than capital or land.

Capital Deepening
When the capital/labor ratio rises for the economy.

Capital Broadening
When capital grows at the same rate as labor and the capital/labor ratio remains constant.

Instead of trying to expand its labor force, the United States is trying to expand its capital. This means that industry produces things through techniques that are ever more **capital-intensive** (using relatively more capital than labor or land) rather than through techniques that are **labor-intensive** (using relatively more labor than capital or land). As this is done generally, **capital deepening** occurs, that is, relatively more and more capital is used (raising the capital-to-labor ratio for the economy).

By contrast, **capital broadening** occurs when capital instruments (tools, plant, and the like) grow at the same rate that labor grows.

There is a lesson to be learned from the economic history of the U.S. and other industrial nations: The Malthusian nightmare need not come true at all. Technological change, both that which is embodied as well as that which is disembodied, can rapidly increase a nation's ability to produce all things, including food. Population increase need not be a drag on industrial growth. In fact, an educated populace *can* slow population growth to zero.

But the extent to which the experience of the United States (and other industrial nations) will be repeated in other nations as they attempt to industrialize, or whether the grim Malthusian scenario will indeed come to pass for some of the world's poorer countries, remains to be seen.

The Importance of an Educated Populace: Human Capital Formation

Human Capital
The improvement in labor skills attributable to investment in education.

Beginning with Nobel Laureate Theodore Schultz, economists in recent decades have identified and focused on the growth impact of a fifth factor of production, **human capital.** Recall that it is defined as the improvement in labor skills attributable to investment in education. Michael Walden[1] puts the impact this way, "Clearly, better educated and skilled workers are more productive workers, and more productive workers increase the long-run economic growth rate." Robert Barro[2] estimates that a 10 percent increase in educational levels of the labor force is associated with a 0.2 percent increase in the annual long-run growth rate. Remember that increase, while it may seem modest, is a *permanent* increase. Robert Barro has compared the long-run rates of economic growth across many countries, rich and poor. A fundamental conclusion of Barro is that it is underinvestment in human capital, rather than physical capital that explains the failure of poor countries to catch up with the rich ones.

These are but a few of the important options to the United States if, in the early twenty first century, it decides to consider ways to enhance its long-run growth rate and projected standards of living.

Slowing Productivity Growth in the United States?

Edward Denison[3], a leading authority on productivity in the American economy found that the growth of potential output (shifting of the American production-possibilities frontier) declined between 1948 and 1983. For the period 1948-1973 this potential grew at an annual rate of 3.9 percent per year. Between 1973 and 1979, this rate fell to 3.0 percent. From 1979 to 1983, it fell dramatically to

1. Walden, Michael. *Economic Issues: Rhetoric and Reality.* Englewood Cliffs, N. J. Prentice Hall. 1995.
2. Barro, Robert. "Economic Growth in a Cross Section of Countries." *Quarterly Journal of Economics,* 106. 1991.
3. Dennison, Edward. *Trends in American Economic Growth, 1929-1982.* Washington, The Brookings Institution. 1985.

1.8 percent, less than half of the 1948-1973 rate. Growth in output per worker fell over the same period from 2.3 percent per year to zero or less. Why the dramatic slowdown or virtual elimination of the shifting of the production-possibilities curve? At least five basic explanations have been offered:

1. **A change in the composition of the American Labor Force**. People who have had years of on-the-job experience have higher levels of productivity than new entrants. As the proportion of the labor force made up of new entrants has risen, productivity growth has slowed. This change, however, does not appear to be a major explanatory factor.

2. **The Composition of Output in the American Economy Has Changed**. As America's demand for output shifts more and more to labor-intensive services, productivity will grow more slowly than it did when a larger part of the GDP was produced by more capital-intensive manufacturing industries. Almost all students of the productivity growth problem agree that this factor has contributed to the slow down. Some say it has had little effect, others say almost half of the slow down can be explained by this change.

3. **Growth in Government Regulation:** Costs to firms of complying with government regulations fell in the early 1980s but rose again in the late 1980s and 1990s. Resources are required not only to regulate industries but also to meet standards of compliance with regulations. Neither of these resource usages is directly productive. While such diversions of resources may improve our quality of life or standard of living, as in the case of much environmental regulation, they reduce the (full-employment) growth of our productive potential. Thomas Hopkins[4] has shown that as regulatory costs rise, long-run economic growth declines. Milton Friedman[5] argues that, "dismantling the regulatory state would foster a return to the long-run capacity of the U.S. to grow at roughly 4 percent a year...."

4. **Rising Resource Prices**. Some have particularly suggested that OPEC I and OPEC II made fuel inefficient capital less productive to use and encouraged the substitution of labor for capital. Denison found, however, that rising prices for energy in the 1970s accounted for only about one-tenth of one percent of the reduction in productivity growth. If so, we might have expected little positive effect in this regard from falling real energy prices after 1987. Since 1995, energy prices have risen substantially.

5. **A Decline in the Rate of Capital Formation.** Capital formation and productivity growth are closely related. Economies that use relatively more capital have higher levels of productivity. Imagine a choice between solving data processing problems with (1) pen and paper, (2) mechanical calculators, (3) modern computers. Obviously (3) is the most capital intensive and also the most productive. Denison found, however, that only a small part of the productivity growth slowdown could be explained this way.

---

4. Hopkins, Thomas. *Cost of Regulation.* RIT Working Paper, Rochester Institute of Technology. 1991.
5. Freidman, Milton. "Getting Back to Real Growth." *The Wall Street Journal*, August 4, 1995.

What is the Implication: A Contrary View

A leading American economist, William Baumol[6] of Princeton, argues that the U.S. economy is *not* losing its productivity edge. Writing in the *Wall Street Journal* in March, 1990, Baumol cited the following: (1) Although the productivity growth rate has fallen, it has simply adjusted back to its historic rate (the 1950s and 1960s, with U.S. dominance of the world, were abnormal, says Baumol), (2) the productivity growth rate has slowed in all industrial nations (That of Japan has decreased as much as that of the U.S.), and (3) the "absolute productivity level of U.S. labor in general, and manufacturing in particular continues to be the highest in the world".

U.S. domination of manufacturing output, says Baumol, is growing along with that of Japan and in contrast to the European economies. Between 1975 and 1988, the share of the U.S. in world manufacturing output rose from 25.5 to 27.0 percent (Japan's from 11.5 to 17.5 percent). Service sector employment ("flipping the hamburgers") has grown because of rapid population growth between 1962 and 1985. U.S. labor is moving into services less rapidly than that of any U.S. trading partner except New Zealand. That the U.S. has become increasingly a service economy has resulted from "the outstanding productivity achievements of both industrial and agricultural section, there is nothing disturbing about the U.S. record."

While conceding that some U.S. industries have lost their competitive edge (including consumer electronics, automobiles, and such), and that this has created tragedies, especially for older workers, this process of rise and decline in industries, has been, according to Baumol, a "hallmark of technological progress accompanied by international competition". Views to the contrary, he says, are "a melange of half-truths" and the implications drawn from them false.

Technological Change Again: The Answer to Faster Growth?

A Nobel Laureate, Simon Kuznets[7], said that about 90 percent of growth came from a qualitative improvement in resources or from technological change. For this reason, many feel that more should be done in America to stimulate research and development activities (R&D). While R&D by private firms has been fairly constant since the 1960s, government support fell although it partially recovered in the 1980s. The repeal of investment tax credits in the 1987 law was regarded as unwise by some economists who believe that a government subsidization is warranted in view of the declining rate of growth in productivity. Still, high-tech industries have grown in the U.S. In 1980, they produced 20 percent of U.S. manufacturing output; in 1990, they produced 30 percent of that output. Real expenditures by U.S. firms on R&D increased in the same period from 1.7 percent of GDP to 2 percent in 1989. Thus, many other economists believe that investment tax credits are unnecessary and simply distort resource usage.

Has the U.S. Growth Rate Really Fallen?

We began this chapter by noting that troubling questions have arisen about the long-term growth rate of the American economy. Yet, as Baumol notes, Ameri-

---

6. Baumol, William J. "Americas' Productivity "Oasis: A Modest Decline Isn't All That Bad." *New York Times*, February 15, 1987.
7. Kuznets, Simon. "Economic Growth Explaining the Mystery." *The Economist*, January 4, 1992.

cans have not lost their productivity edge. Recent data show that American workers are still the most productive in the world. If productivity is measured by economic output per full-time employed person, U.S. workers in 1988 were 10 percent more productive than French workers, 16 percent more productive than German workers, 30 percent more productive than British workers, and 39 percent more productive than Japanese workers. While these "edges" are not uniform across all industries, they do not suggest an American manufacturing economy that is in decline.

Growth Rate Implications

Many studies of American economic growth have focused on recent performance in comparison to that of the 1950s and 1960s. DeLong, and Summers[8] say that on that basis, the average long-run growth rate in the 1970s and 1980s was only 0.9 percent whereas it was 2.3 percent on average during the 1950s and 1960s. Michael Walden[9] argues, however, that this comparison is not valid for two reasons: (1) all industrialized nations have witnessed a long-run growth rate decline in the 1970s and 1980s, and (2) the U.S. is one of only two industrial nations (Canada, the other) to witness an increase in its long-run growth in the 1980s over the 1970s.

Table 15-1

Long-Run Per Capita Economic Growth Rates in the United States

Period	Real Average Annual Growth Rate (%)
1840 – 1860	1.8
1860 – 1880	3.3
1880 – 1900	1.1
1900 – 1920	1.9
1920 – 1940	1.1
1940 - 1960	1.7
1960 - 1980	2.0
1980 – 1990	1.6
2001 - 2005	1.46
2006 - 2010	.07

Source: The World Bank, 2012.

Robert Barro[10] says that there are two reasons for skepticism about the studies that purport to show a decline in America's long-run growth rate

8. DeLong, J. Bradford and Lawrence Summers. "Macroeconomic Policy and Long-Run Growth." *Economic Policies for Long-Run Economic Growth*. Kansas City, MO. Federal Reserve Bank of Kansas City, 1992.
9. Walden, Michael. *Economic Issues, Rhetoric and Reality*. Op. Cit.
10. Barro, Robert. "Economic Growth in a Cross Section of Countries." *Quarterly Journal of Economics* 106, 1991.

beginning in the 1970s: (1) they focus on aggregate rather than per capita growth, and (2) they assume that the 1950s and 1960s are the appropriate time frame for comparison. Barro corrects for this by measuring average growth rates on a per person basis and takes an historical (1840 – 1990) time period as the basis of comparison. We can see the results of Barro's research in Table 15-2.

You can see that there have been fluctuations in the long-run per capita growth rate of the U.S. economy since 1840 (as far back as we can go using census data). Barro concludes that there has been no significant decrease in the growth rate since the 1970s. Barro estimates the average growth rate for the entire period since 1880 at 1.6 percent per annum. The growth rate in the 1980s was exactly equal to the long-run post-1880 average. The 1950s and 1960s may have been abnormally high for two reasons: (1) an unusually high population growth rate, and (2) the recovery of the American economy from the depression of the 1930s and World War II.

What Could We Do to Increase the Growth Rate?

The research of Robert Barro suggests that there has been no long-term slowing of this country's growth rate. That does not mean, however, that an increase in the growth rate is undesirable or that it would not convey great benefits. Remember that the growth rate of the 1980s was about 1.6 percent. Suppose it could be raised by 50 percent to 2.4 percent per annum. While an enormous task, the increased rate of growth would mean that Americans thirty years from now would have more than 75 percent more goods and services than they would with the (historic long-term) rate of 1.6 percent! What could be done to raise America's growth rate? Here are just some of the suggestions that have been made in recent years.

1. ***Increased savings and investment*** in R&D, implementing new technologies, and building "state-of-the-art" plant and equipment. While the U.S. does have a relatively low rate of savings (especially by comparison with Japan), spending on plant and equipment has not declined; in fact, it rose in the 1980s.

2. ***Increased investment in human capital***,– We looked at this earlier and know of the contribution it can make to a faster growth rate. There are major concerns about the nation's educational system in the early twenty first century. Additional effort to reform are being undertaken, though it is not clear how much of the problem is due to underinvestment.

3. ***Regulatory and tax reform*** – We mentioned earlier that recent research shows a negative effect of increased regulatory cost on the long-term growth rate. A proposal in the Congress in 1995 to require that cost/benefit analyses be applied to government regulatory programs was defeated. We may find that both direct and indirect regulation has exceeded the optimal level in terms of its effects on long-term growth.

4. ***The size of government*** – Robert Barro and others have found that larger government spending, especially on transfer programs that redistribute income, tends to lower the long-run growth rates of countries. It does so through lowering incentives to individuals to work.

Application I: Will Declining Military Spending Cut Our Growth Rate?

Do Wars Keep the Economy Healthy?

With the "Cold War" over, many Americans in and out of political life have called for reduced Federal government spending on defense. This is especially true in 2011 with a push to reduce federal deficit and the federal debt. While opinions vary greatly on what to do with this "peace dividend" (reduce the deficit, reduce taxes, spend more on ________), an appropriate question to ask is: "What will happen to the growth of the American economy if we reduce defense spending?"

Must thc Amcrican cconomy, in other words, have heavy injections of government spending for war and defense in order to achieve full-employment, full-capacity growth? Opinions vary greatly. Let's look at two contrasting views.

Writing about the period since World War II, Douglas Dowd[11], an economist critical of many aspects of the American economy, says, "The key to this process of sustained growth, i.e., the absence of even a serious recession, let alone a depression, is to be found in the record of federal purchases, and in that category, the key factor is purchases geared to the military." Dowd says that between 1946 and 1971, 80 percent of the $1.4 trillion of federal expenditures was in some way connected with defense. This, he argues, is the primary reason for the stability and growth of our post-World War II economy.

Other observers claim that the connection between defense spending and the growth of the American economy is not at all clear; indeed, say some, the connection does not exist. It is true, they say, that defense spending has helped to create jobs and stimulate consumption and investment spending, and that massive war expenditures beginning in 1941 had a lot to do with reducing unemployment from 14.6 percent in 1940 to 1.2 percent in 1944. It is also true that unemployment reached its lowest postwar point (2.9 percent) in 1953 when Korean War expenditures were at their peak. Yet the unemployment rate swung up and down widely between 1946 and 1986, and defense spending was probably only one of several factors affecting employment and growth.

To put these two positions in perspective, see Table 15-2. From the mid-1940s to the end of the 1960s, unemployment; varied from 1.9 percent to 6.8 percent of the civilian labor force. The high points in unemployment (1949-1950, 1958-1963) reflect downturns in the economy. They do not, however, correspond to downturns in military spending either in absolute terms or in terms of a percentage of GDP. (Military spending includes military purchases and military salaries, but not interest on the national debt associated with deficits attributable to war or defense spending.) The low points in unemployment (1946-1948, 1951-1953, 1955-1957, 1965-1969, 1989-1990) also reflect upturns in the economy, not upturns in defense spending. These conclusions generally follow even if one introduces a time lag of a year or so between changes in defense spending and changes in the rate of unemployment.

11.In Walden, Michael. *Economic Issues, Rhetoric and Reality.* Op. Cit.

Table 15-2
The Federal Government's Purchases of Goods and Services for the Military and there Relation to GDP, 1945-2012

Year	Amount of Military Spending (billions of dollars)	Percentage of GDP	Unemployment as a Percentage of Civilian Labor Force
1945	73.7	34.5	1.9
1955	39.0	9.6	4.4
1965	51.0	7.2	4.5
1975	86.5	5.5	8.5
1985	245.1	6.6	7.2
1995	259.4	3.5	6.1
2005	585.3	4.0	5.1
2009	640.9	4.7	9.3*
2012	703	4.06	8.1

Source: CIA World Fact Book, 2012.

The single exception appears to be 1953-1954, when the percentage of the GDP consumed by national defense fell from 13.5 percent to 11.3 percent (in absolute terms, it fell by about $8 billion) and unemployment rose from 2.9 percent to 5.6 percent. Even if the income (and employment) multiplier was large, say two or three, a decline of $8 billion in defense spending in 1954 should not by itself have produced a near doubling of unemployment. In fact, GDP rose in 1954, and it appears that a rise in people's spending for personal consumption, together with a rise in net exports, more than offset the decline in defense spending. The rise in unemployment was probably largely due to industry's having to make a transition from producing military to producing civilian goods.

On the basis of these data and the relationship between defense spending and employment, we can say two things with a fair amount of confidence:

1. The United States has apparently not used *variations* in defense spending as a strategic weapon to combat unemployment.

2. Military spending, up to the 2000s, constituted a large, relatively stable portion of GDP (Aggregate demand). As a percentage of GDP it hit a low point of 3.5 percent in 1995. Since then it has risen slowly to 4.7 percent by 2009.

If there had been no military spending and no other compensating expenditures in the United States since 1946, unemployment would have been much higher. The same thing could be said, however, about *other* federal expenditures. As Arthur Okun[12], a former chairman of the Council of Economic

12.In Walden, Michael. *Economic Issues, Rhetoric and Reality.* Op. Cit.

Advisers in the Johnson administration, put it, "Ever since Keynes, economists had recognized that the federal government could stimulate economic activity by increasing the injection of federal expenditures into the income stream or by reducing the withdrawal of federal tax receipts."

If any net increase in GX or decrease in T in the $C + I + G = C + S + T$ equilibrium is stimulative, then there is nothing unique about defense spending. Lord Keynes himself expressed it well in 1936 in an essay entitled "Economic Possibilities for our Grandchildren", when he wrote about societies that lower unemployment by engaging in government spending:

> *Ancient Egypt was doubly fortunate, and doubtless owed to this its fabled wealth, in that it possessed two activities, namely, pyramid-building as well as the search for precious metals, the fruits of which, since they could not serve the needs of man by being consumed, did not stale with abundance. The middle ages built cathedrals and sang dirges. Two pyramids, two masses for the dead, are twice as good as one.*

In other words, the government might have spent the same amount of money on developing the world's best system of mass transit or on some income-maintenance scheme to supplement the earnings of the nation's poorest citizens, and achieved the same aggregate demand effect on the economy. It might also have lowered taxes with a stimulative effect on private sector expenditure.

What About Reaching Potential?

In the 1980s, the government began to shy away from using fiscal policy (both expenditures and tax cuts) as a "fireman's tool" to cure unemployment fires already burning. The emphasis turned instead to stimulating the economy toward its productive potential (with only frictional or transitional unemployment). This change was based on the belief that, in the long run, and especially if the economy could move toward full capacity as well as full employment, this would bring forth the continued investment (aggregate supply) needed to increase productivity and create new jobs as well.

To see how close the United States has come to reaching its potential GDP, examine Figure 15-2. Since 1955, the performance has been uneven. In the late 1950s, the gap between actual and potential GDP widened. Yet during this period, defense spending was growing, though slowly, and it remained nearly constant as a percentage of GDP. Beginning in the early 1960s, the United States moved toward reaching its potential GDP, with the pace quickening after the tax cut of 1964. By 1966, the economy was running just about at or slightly above potential, and continued to do so through 1969. Note in Table 15-2 that in this period there was no significant change in the percentage of GDP spent on defense.

So you can see that the following occurred: (1) Defense spending from 1951 to 1970 was a stable component of government spending and therefore provided a floor under aggregate demand, income, and employment. (2) Movement toward full-potential growth in the sixties was caused by fiscal (tax) policy, not change in defense spending. (3) Defense spending from 1975 and 1990 varied only between 5.5 percent and 6.6 percent. While since 1990, it fell in 1995 to 3.5 percent and in 2012 was 4.06 percent of GDP.

Figure 15-2
Actual and Potential Gross Domestic Product

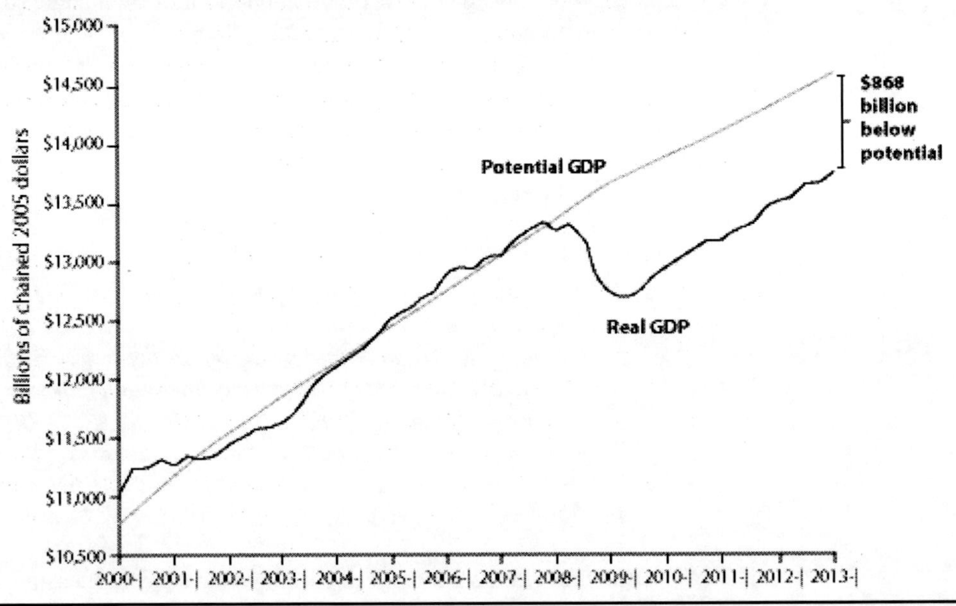

Source: Bureau of Economic Analysis National Income and Product Accounts and Congressional Budget Officet, updated April 26, 2013.

Defense Spending: Does It Encourage or Retard Technological Change?
Some economists argue that large defense expenditures actually reduce our full capacity rate of growth. They feel that research and development skills and resources which are put to military uses do little to increase the nation's industrial capacity. As a result, the United States gives up larger increases in capacity that could be used to help solve not only employment problems but also a host of other problems such as income-distribution problems, problems of the cities, of racial problems, and of poverty and education problems.

"All right, suppose we abolish war, and the entire world is at peace, then what?"

There is another way of looking at this. A good many people feel that the government's expenditures for defense (and space exploration) have helped increase our full capacity growth through fostering technological change (in communications equipment and in many other things).

Who is right? It's hard to say; both viewpoints may be right. The unanswered question is: What is the net effect, the relation between what the economy gives up in technological change in the private sector versus what is gained? One cannot estimate this at present.

What About the Early Twenty First Century?

Let us repeat: "Will reduced defense spending lower our growth rate?" Calls for such reductions were intensified by the large deficits of the 2000s. Will such reductions trigger a recession or other undesirable economic effects? While there is no absolute answer, the evidence we have examined suggests that unfavorable results would not follow from such cutbacks. Defense spending continued to rise from 2009-2013. Whether the economic growth of the 1990s continues throughout the first and second decades of the 2000s and following the recession of 2008-2009 would appear to depend on a set of factors far more complex than simply defense spending or even of government spending in general. Indeed, as we have seen, the answer will depend at least as much on stimulating aggregate supply, as on aggregate demand.

Application II: Must We Sacrifice Growth to Have a Clean Environment?

More than a century has passed since the era of the "dismal science" and its grim Malthusian predictions. Optimism about the material future of human beings has grown even in the recession of 2008-2009. Improved technology and better organization, plus growing supplies of resources (including labor), have caused more and more countries to follow Britain and the United States toward ever higher levels of real income and better standards of living. Evidently the economist's assumption about growing output chasing rising aspirations was correct.

In the 1970s, however, the optimists began to qualify their optimism. (As Don Marquis said, "An optimist is a guy who has never had much experience.") Some argued that growth was inconsistent with environmental quality.

The Economists' View

Economists in general will not concede that pollution of the environment is the result of economic growth *per se.* Many also believe that the market system can offer solutions to the problems of pollution. In addition, many economists believe that continued growth is necessary, not as an end in itself, but as a means of solving a Pandora's box full of economic problems. Walter Heller[13] (chairman of the council of Economic Advisors during the Kennedy and Johnson administrations) summarized these views as follows:

13.Heller, Walter W. "Economic Growth and Ecology, an Economist's View." In *Economics Mainstream reading and Radical Critiques,* 2nd ed. Random House, New York, 1973.

> *In the starkest terms, the ecologist confronts us with an environmental imperative that requires an end to economic growth, or a sharp curtailment of it, as the price of biological survival. In contrast, the economist counters with a socioeconomic imperative that requires the continuation of growth as the price of social survival....Like it or not, economic growth seems destined to continue.*

Heller goes on to say the following: (1) Ecologists disagree with economists about whether real growth (improvement in the quality of life) has occurred, considering negative externalities. (2) Ecologists envision absolute bans and absolute limits to growth: economists envision marginal trade-offs and cost-benefit relations. (3) Ecologists want to rely on government to solve ecological problems; economists would rely on the price system to create solutions. Walter Heller says that growth could be checked, but that this "would throw the fragile ecology of our economic system so out of kilter as to threaten its breakdown."

Most economists would probably agree with Heller that it is the *pattern* of growth of the U.S. economy, not growth itself, that has created environmental pollution. Heller makes the point that scares about the environment (based on a static view of resources) occur periodically. He also says that our attempts to solve problems such as adequate defense, poverty, discrimination, and pollution have so mortgaged future GDP growth that there is no choice left; the economy *has* to grow.

Economists generally agree that good environmental quality is a scarce commodity. Most of them acknowledge that the market system does not adequately incorporate externalities, such as pollution of the nation's water supply by industry, into its pricing system. However, this problem cannot be solved by limiting growth or by eliminating it.

Let's examine the problem of water. The world is running short of clean water, yet our need for it is growing with each passing year. Industries use millions of gallons of it hourly, for quenching steel ingots, for washing paper pulp, for cooling nuclear power plants, for cleaning newly slaughtered animals being readied for market, for washing away the chemicals from textile mills, and for thousands of other uses. The *effluent*, that is, the used water that flows out of factories, is often dumped into nearby rivers or streams. The water itself is not used up in this process. Rather, we have to clean it so that we can use it again, for bathing, swimming, cooking, and drinking.

To solve this problem, we could do several things: (1) *set minimum standards for industrial effluents* (though this would circumvent the market, and create large bureaucratic costs), (2) *tax industrial effluents* (this would make firms, and ultimately consumers, internalize the costs of pollution) or (3) Sell the rights to pollute water and raise the revenues to clean it up.

How Population Enters the Picture

Both economists and ecologists point out that the problems of economic growth are inextricably tied in with the problems of population growth. However, as industrialization and urbanization take place, population growth tends to level off, even to decline. Families that live in urban, industrial societies acquire education and realize that children are consumers, not producers. Also, since a pollution-free environment is a "luxury" good, demand for it rises with income. As the economy continues to grow, people may be expected to demand more of this luxury (income superior) good and substitute it for the relatively less desirable (income inferior) good, in other words, more children.

It is mainly ecologists who present the anti-growth view, but some economists join in. Fundamentally, the arguments are founded on the belief that it is nature that imposes the limits to growth. As the distinguished historian Arnold Toynbee[14] put it:

> *More and more people are coming to realize that the growth of material wealth, which the British industrial revolution set going, and which the modern British-made ideology has presented as being mankind's proper paramount objective, cannot in truth be the "wave of the future." Nature is going to compel posterity to revert to a stable state on the material plane and to turn to the realm of the spirit for satisfying man's hunger for infinity.*

Economist Kenneth Boulding[15]has argued that we must move from viewing the economy as an open system, with unlimited resources and growth (the cowboy economy"), to a "spaceship earth" closed economy (the "spaceman economy"). Boulding says that in the latter system, consumption and production that use up finite (nonreproducible) resources is not "good." Society must distinguish between reproducible and nonreproducible resources.

As Some Ecologists Have Seen It

Others, such as Herman Daly[16], argued for many years that "growthmania", the insistence that growth is the solution to economic problems, had outlived its usefulness. This view was reinforced by certain famous computer studies (the 1971 Club of Rome study is the most famous one) that predicted disaster unless growth trends were reversed. Daly and others argued not only for **zero economic growth (ZEG)**, *no* increase in GDP, but also **zero population growth (ZPG)**, no increase in population. To alleviate any hardships that this reversal of industrial history would cause, they wanted to see constant controls on physical wealth and distribution of income.

Zero Economic Growth (ZEG)
The argument that GDP growth should be stopped.

Zero Population Growth (ZPG)
The argument that population growth should be stopped.

Such ecologists reject the market solution, which would entail forcing industries to internalize the externalities. Two observers, Richard England and Barry Bluestone, maintained, however, that this would require *total recycling* of wastes, with an accompanying "astronomical cost."

As Many Economists Have Seen It

Few economists have favored ZEG. Those that have argued that using selective means, such as tax cuts, to stimulate consumer spending is *not* necessary to maintain full employment. They say that a guaranteed annual income can maintain a full-employment level of spending just as well, and accomplish many of the same objectives.

---

14. In Hailstones, Thomas J. and Frank V. Mastriana. Contemporary Economic Problems and Issues. Cincinnati. Southwestern Publishing Co. 1988.
15. Boulding, Kenneth E. "The Economics of the Coming Spaceship Earth." In *Environmental Quality in a Growing Economy.* Baltimore, Johns Hopkins, 1966.
16. Daly, Herman E. "The Steady State Economy: Toward a Political Economy of Biophysical Equilibrium and Moral Growth." In *Toward a Steady State Economy.* Freeman, San Francisco, 1973.

In rebuttal, economists who oppose ZEG generally (1) attack the idea (which is implicit in the computer models) that the supply of resources is static, that the world will soon run out of oil, coal, and other essentials; (2) argue that leaving resources unused so that future generations may use them may not be as important as the capital and technology that would result from using them in the present; (3) feel that the ZEG and ZPG groups underestimate the ability of the price system to ensure efficient use of resources, to cause substitutes to be developed, and to force industry (when required to) to internalize the externalities that may have been ignored in the past.

Growth and the Environment: A New Consensus?

As America enters the twenty first century, concerns for achieving an acceptable level of environmental quality seem to be growing. At the same time, few people now seem inclined to advocate stopping economic growth to solve problems such as acid rain or the greenhouse effect. Indeed, as political scientist Robert Slavins has argued: "A new environmentalism has now emerged that embraces market-oriented environmental-protection policies." Both economists and ecologists now see that there are major environmental problems and, unlike the earlier era, many ecologists now believe market forces can be harnessed to help solve these problems in ways consistent with maintaining economic growth.

SUMMING UP

1. The United States has enjoyed a long-run economic growth rate that, including growth by the 20th century, made it one of the most prosperous of the world's nations. In order to be able to analyze many economic problems, one needs a *dynamic* rather than a *static* framework, that is, a structure that shows change through time.

2. *Extensive growth,* a process by which total output increases, comes about through the use of more resources, land, labor, and capital. *Intensive growth* is a process by which productivity, output per hour of labor (or income per capita), increases and becomes more complex.

3. According to Adam Smith and other classical economists, growth takes place because of the increased productivity that accompanies specialization in the uses of resources. This specialization is limited by the size of the market. As the market grows, more and more specialization takes place. But because of limited supplies of land and, ultimately, diminishing efficiency (diminishing returns), an economy's growth will diminish beyond some point and will ultimately reach a *stationary state.*

4. The stationary state may be high or low in terms of real per capita income. Smith envisioned it as becoming high, since with the development of better technology, people might prefer more goods to more children. Malthus thought it was likely to be low, since population increase would outstrip the food supply, and famine, plagues, and the like would result.

5. The classical scenario (the Malthusian version in some cases) has come true in many poor countries, whose growth has been very slow, or nonexistent, and whose investment in education has been slight.

6. Industrial nations and newly industrializing nations have escaped the stationary state, for two reasons: (a) Technological change has shifted their growth paths upward and overcome the long-term tendencies toward stagnation. (b) As growth has occurred, the rate of growth of their populations has tapered off.

7. Even a growing economy's growth is not necessarily accompanied by full employment. Therefore, a society's *actual growth path*, the change in its real per capita income as time goes by, may be less than its full-employment potential.

8. The *aggregate production function* is the relationship between total output and the labor force employed. It tells us how much output an economy produces at various levels of employment.

9. According to Edward Denison, productivity growth in the United States slowed over the period from 1948 to 1983, especially from 1979 to 1983. Some of the reasons for this slowing appear to be: (a) A change in the composition of the American labor force, (b) A change in the composition of the output of the economy, (c) Growth in government regulation, (d) Rising resource prices, (e) A decline in the rate of capital formation.

10. An important ingredient that contributes to economic growth is investment in *human capital*, the improvement in labor skills due to investment in education.

11. Most productivity growth is due to improvements in the quality of resources or to technological change. There are calls in the United States to create greater incentives to research and development and the resulting improvements in applied technology. Technological change represents an improved *quality* of capital. It may be embodied in better plants and equipment or it may take the form of *disembodied* technological change, that which is not completely reflected in an improved quality of labor or capital.

12. The United States has a long record of growth. Over the last one hundred years its output has increased at a compound annual rate of 2.1 percent. But it has had long periods of less than full employment, and therefore its growth path has often been below the full-employment level. Thus, the United States has lost a great deal of per capita income.

13. According to William Baumol, a slowing rate of growth in productivity is not a reflection of economic failure. For the U.S. this slowing reflects what has happened in most other industrial nations. Growth in services was caused by rapid population growth and, though severe dislocation have resulted in some industries, this has been so throughout modern U.S. history.

14. Americans are still the world's most productive workers. They are more productive than French, German, British or Japanese workers, though not uniformly so across all industries.

15. Some studies have concluded that there was a slowing of America's long-term growth rate in the 1970s and 1980s. Michael Walden argues that (a) this was true of all industrial nations, and (b) America's growth actually rose in the 1980s above that of the 1970s.

16. Robert Barro's research on America's growth rate focuses on (a) per capita growth and (b) a very long-term (1840 – 1990) historical view of growth. Barro concludes that there has been no significant decline in that growth rate. The 1950s and 1960s were higher because of (a) high population growth, and (b) recovery from World War II and the depression of the 1930s.

17. Increasing the nation's growth rate would convey significant long-term benefits in terms of the real standard of living.

18. Some ways by which the country's growth rate could be increased include (a) increased savings and investment in R&D, implementing new technologies, and building "state-of-the-art" plants and equipment, (b) increased investment in human capital, (c) a reassessment of the *costs and benefits* of government regulation, and (d) assessing what the trade-offs are between government size and the country's long-term growth rate.

19. Some economists, including Douglas Dowd, have argued that defense spending since World War II has been the key to growth and stability in the American economy. Other economists, however, dispute that connection.

20. The economic record for the 1950s and 1960s seems to show that (1) *variations* in defense spending were not used to reduce unemployment, and (2) that military spending was a large but stable portion o aggregate demand.

21. Military spending, like other federal expenditures, adds to aggregate demand and, thereby, to the stimulation of economic activity and to a reduction in unemployment.

22. The 1980s saw a major increase in defense expenditures. While there was a decline in unemployment after 1983, increased defense spending was only one of several factors including tax reductions that may have contributed to a lower rate of joblessness.

23. Reductions in defense expenditures in the 1990s did not necessarily raise unemployment. Unemployment trends, as well as growth depended on many factors, including those affecting aggregate supply as well as aggregate demand.

24. Until recently, twentieth-century economists, unlike their nineteenth-century forerunners, generally held an optimistic view of economic growth and its potential for solving economic problems. In the early twenty first century, optimism is tempered by the need to maintain environmental quality.

25. Certainly it is not economic growth alone that is responsible for polluting the environment. In fact, many economists believe that economic growth and the free market can solve the problems of the environment in the future.

26. Walter Heller said that economic growth seems destined to continue and that (a) economists and ecologists disagree over whether the quality of life has improved in recent years; (b) ecologists see absolute limits to growth and to resources, while economists do not; and (c) ecologists want government to solve environmental problems, while economists rely heavily on the market system.

27. The market system does not fully incorporate externalities, such as pollution of the nation's water supply by industry, into its pricing system. The solutions to this might be (a) to set minimum standards for industrial effluents, or (b) to tax industrial effluents so that producers (and ultimately consumers) would have to pay the full social costs of polluting the water.

Cartoon Feature Syndicate

28. Economic growth is inextricably intertwined with population growth. However, population growth declines with economic growth, since children in an urban, industrial society are nonproducers and people begin to prefer higher *per capita* income as well as environmental improvement to more children.

29. Arnold Toynbee argued that growth is not the wave of the future, but that natural forces will force the world's people to revert to a stable state, that is, no growth.

30. Some economists and ecologists have decried "growthmania" and argued for both *zero economic growth* (ZEG) and *zero population growth* (ZPG). They argued that obtaining these would necessitate government controls over physical wealth and distribution of income.

31. Some ecologists rejected for many years the idea of the free market offering the solution to environmental pollution, on the grounds that the cost of total recycling of wastes would be astronomical.

32. The few economists who favor ZEG say that a guaranteed annual income (with its income redistribution effect) would be a good substitute for economic growth. A guaranteed annual income, they say, would sustain consumption demand and thereby keep employment at an acceptable level.

33. In rebutting the gloomy arguments of the ecologists, most economists oppose ZEG on the grounds that (a) resources are not static, (b) it is better to leave capital, technology, and productive capacity to posterity than to leave unused resources to posterity, (c) proponents of ZEG and ZPG underestimate the ability of the price system to change patterns of resource use and to induce people to use and find substitutes for nonreproducible resources.

34. In the early 2000s, there appears to be a growing consensus among economists and ecologists that environmental problems are severe and that market solutions to many of these problems are possible without sacrificing economic growth.

KEY TERMS

Capital broadening
Capital deepening
Capital intensive
Disembodied technological change
Dynamic framework
Extensive growth
Human capital
Intensive growth
Labor intensive
Malthusian specter
Technological change
Zero economic growth (ZEG)
Zero population growth (ZPG)

QUESTIONS

1. Why is a dynamic framework more useful than a static one for analyzing growth relationships and problems?

2. Is extensive growth or intensive growth more important to improving the material well-being of people? Why?

3. What are resources? What is the role of prices in creating and identifying the resources of a nation?

4. What is entrepreneurship? What is its important role in long-run economic growth?

5. What is the impact of technological change on growth? What is meant by disembodied technological change?

6. What was the classical view of long-run economic growth for a nation?

7. Why is investment in human capital so important to long-run economic growth?

8. To what did Edward Denison attribute the slowing of America's growth rate?

9. What does William Baumol conclude about the causes and effects of a slowing rate of growth in productivity?

10. Is 1950 – 1970 the appropriate base period of determining whether America's growth rate has slowed? What period does Robert Barro use and what are his conclusions?

11. What are some of the important ways through which America's growth rate could be increased?

12. Suppose that you are chairman of a special task force on employment. The President of the United States calls you in and says that he is going to propose an extraordinary increase of $50 billion in federal spending in order to create one million new jobs. He can't decide, though, whether to increase the spending of the Defense Department (which maintains that it needs a new manned bomber system) or the Department of Health and Human Services (which wants to expand educational benefits, medical care benefits, and other such programs). The President wants to know whether there will be different aggregate demand effects from the two types with expenditures of equal size. What would you tell the President?

13. The long-run growth future of the American economy depends as much on stimulating aggregate supply as on stimulating aggregate demand. Do you agree? Why?

14. What is the relationship between economic growth and the solutions to such ills as poverty, discrimination, and the welfare situation?

15. Is pollution of the environment *necessarily* the result of economic growth? If not, what else might it result from?

16. How may the market system, either with or without additional government control, develop solutions to problems of pollution?

17. What does Boulding mean by the "spaceship earth" concept?

18. State what you think of the arguments for and against ZEG.

SECTION IV:

International Trade And Finance

Chapter 16: Patterns of International Trade

Closed Economy
An economy that engages only in domestic economic activities.

Throughout this book, we have looked at the many facets of a single market economy. For the most part, we treated that economy as ***closed*** or as one that engages in domestic economic activities only. The purpose of this was part of the larger approach of the text; to begin with simple principles and then gradually to make them more general and more complex until they could shed light on a wide range of economic problems

Open Economy
An economy that engages in both domestic and international activities

Now, let us look at the American economy as ***open*** or as one that engages in both domestic and international economic activities. This means that America not only trades with other nations, but also must finance that trade. In the early years of the twenty–first century, international trade by the United States is not only growing, but also becoming a more important part of its economy. Arguments have flared again, as they have any times in our history, over the conditions under which this country should trade with others. One thing is clear, however: with combined exports and imports, in the year 2000, of more than two and one third *trillion* dollars, the U.S. is the world's largest trading nation and a nation for which trade has again become a key sector of its economy.

What Makes Up Trade?

Exports
Commodities and services sold to other nations.

Imports
Commodities and services bought from other nations.

Trade consists of **exports**, commodities and services sold to other nations, and **imports**, commodities and services bought from other nations. Suppose that a dealer in San Francisco imports a Toyota. The price the importer pays (plus any shipping charges paid to foreign shippers) is added to the total of U.S. imports. Similarly, when a Japanese grain dealer imports American wheat, the payments that U.S. wheat sellers receive (plus any payments to our own shippers) are added to the total of our exports.[1]

1. Although the 2008-2009 financial downturn temporarily slowed this growth.

Visible Items
Those physical commodities that are exported or imported by a nation.

Invisible Items
The services including financial services associated with exports and imports by a nation

International trade, thus, is made up of both **visible items** and **invisible items**. The visible items are the commodities (cars, wheat, television sets, petroleum, machinery, and so on) that are exported and imported. Invisible items are the services, including financial services (services of exporters and importers, ship rentals, cost of financing, and so on) which are exported and imported.

How Important is Trade to America?

Only a few decades ago many might have said: "Look, the U.S. is a big nation; it produces a great variety of goods and services and has vast natural resources. Surely trade with other nations isn't all that important to us. Why devote a whole chapter to it?" Now, hardly a day passes without reference in the media to the importance of foreign trade to our economy and to the jobs of its people. Deficits in trade (imports > exports) are front page news to which stock markets react. Negotiations between the U.S. and China over further opening of Chinese markets to American exports are both economically and politically sensitive. Arguments about "free trade" versus "fair trade" are not merely academic issues. International trade and the financing of that trade have, by the early 21st century, become vital issues and seem likely to increase in importance as the nation continues to progress into the remaining part of the century.

America's Balance of Trade and Net Foreign Trade

Commodity Balance of Trade (X-M)
The value of commodity exports less the value of commodity imports.

It is worthwhile to repeat that both commodities and services are traded internationally. Commodity exports (X) (wheat, computers, and the like) and commodity imports (M) (autos, textiles, and the like) determine the **commodity balance of trade** so that when only commodities are considered:

$$X - M = \text{Commodity Balance of Trade}$$

When the commodity balance of trade is positive ($X > M$), a nation is selling more of its goods and services abroad than it is purchasing from other nations. This positive balance is commonly referred to as a "favorable" balance of trade. When the commodity balance is negative ($X < M$), the nation is purchasing more goods and services from abroad than it is selling to other economies; the negative balance is commonly referred to as an "unfavorable" balance of trade. While one should be cautious about reading too much into the terms "favorable" and "unfavorable," it is well to remember that differences between exports and imports (sales and purchases) must be financed each year by every nation.

Net Foreign Trade (NFT)
A measure of the trade balance that includes services. It is measured by taking the commodity balance and adding in net services (service exports – service imports).

When services (transportation, insurance, financial services, and the like) are included in the balance, however, we arrive at a measure of **net foreign trade**, or one which subtracts imports from exports ($X - M$), but adds in net services (S_N) (service exports – service imports). Thus net foreign trade is:

$$(X - M) + S_N = \text{Net Foreign Trade (NFT)}$$

NFT, thus, is a measure of the balance on both goods and services. Clearly, one way in which a deficit in the commodity balance ($X < M$) may be financed is through a positive net services (service exports > service imports) balance.

Table 16-1
U.S. Exports, Imports, Net Services, and Net Foreign Trade, 1960-2012 (billions of dollars)

Year	Merchandise Exports (X)	Merchandise Imports (M)	Net Services (S_N)	**Net Foreign Trade* $(X – M) + S_N$**
1960	19.7	14.8	-1.4	3.5
1965	26.5	21.5	-.3	4.7
1970	42.5	40.0	-.3	2.2
1975	107.1	98.2	3.5	12.4
1980	224.3	249.8	6.1	-19.4
1985	215.9	338.1	0	-122.1
1990	389.3	498.3	31.0	-78.8
1995	575.8	749.5	73.9	-99.8
1996	612.0	802.6	82.8	-107.8
1997	678.4	876.5	63.2	-107.8
1998	670.4	917.1	68.1	-178.6
1999	684.6	1,030.0	73.9	- 261.8
2001	718.7	1,164.1	62.5	- 382.9
2008	1,276,994	2,117,245	142	-698.2
2012	1,564.1	2,299	195	540.3

Source: *Economic Report of the President*, 2012.

*Merchandise plus Services (may not add because of rounding)

www.oecd.org
For more information on foreign trade visit this web site.

What has been the record of the American economy in recent decades regarding the commodity balance and net foreign trade? From Table 16-1, several trends may be seen in both the commodity balance and in net foreign trade. From 1960 to 1975, America had a "favorable" commodity balance (X > M), even though there were typically small deficits in net services (service exports < service imports). Overall, net foreign trade, though typically small, was positive, reaching $12.4 billion in 1975. After 1975, America had consistently "unfavorable" commodity trade balances (X < M) reaching nearly 700 billion in in 2008. At the same time, after 1985, it began experiencing large positive net service balances (service exports > service imports), which partially offset the commodity deficits. In 2002, however, the NFT deficit grew to $406.9 billion and by 2004 had reached $665.4 billion. Exports, however, grew after 2004 as the declining value of the dollar stimulated exports. The dramatic growth of the average NFT deficit (after 1980) seems to have come about because of: *Changes in exchange rates.* Between 1980 and mid 1985, U.S. dollar/foreign currency exchange rates soared. Against the currencies of America's major trading partners, the dollar increased in value almost 70 percent. Goods imported into the U.S. became relatively cheaper while American exports became relatively more expensive. Our rising quantity demanded of imports and the declining quantity demanded of our exports pushed X – M to ever larger negative figures. After mid 1985, the dollar declined against the currencies of our major trading partners, a trend that has continued into 2009. Because of this, export growth was strong, more than doubling between 1985 and 1993. From 2003 into 2009, the dollar again declined but export growth has been weak because of low economic growth among many US trading partners.

Table 16-2

Export of Goods and Services as a Percentage of GDP, Selected Countries, 2012

Country	Exports as Percentage of GDP 2012
Netherlands	83
Canada	31
Germany	50
New Zealand	30
Spain	31
Italy	37
France	27
United Kingdom	32
Japan	15
United States	14

Source: IMF, International Financial Statistics, 2012.

Real Income Growth. In the face of the tax changes and other stimulative actions from 1982 on, the American economy and the real incomes of its citizens grew (except for the recession years of the early 1990s, the early 2000s and the recession years of 2008 and 2009). Since Colonial days, Americans have had a strong (income-related) taste for imported goods. A growing demand for imports, even in the face of rising prices, added fuel to the large deficits, which were only partially offset by positive net service balances.

But is Trade as Important to us as to others?

Perhaps you are saying, "All right, granted that foreign trade *can* have an effect on the U.S. economy, and will continue to do so in the twenty-first century; is the effect really important compared to the other factors that influence jobs and the welfare of Americans?" One way to answer the question is to look at how large a part exports or sales abroad are of the GDP or final value of all goods and services produced in America. Table 16-2 shows that for the U.S., exports make up a smaller percentage of GDP than they do for many of the other nations. Trade today constitutes only about 14 percent of U.S. total output, but for the other nations, which account for a large part of the world's trade, the figure ranges up to 83 percent (Netherlands).

Do these figures mean that trade is relatively unimportant to the U.S.? The answer, emphatically, is *no*, for the following reasons:

Growth in importance. The percentage of total output made up of exports has almost doubled since 1970. The 14 percent represents an important part of the demand for U.S. output and thus the derived demand for labor (jobs) and other resources. If this foreign market for U.S. goods were to disappear, it would mean not just an 14 percent reduction in GDP, but a much larger reduction.

Greater firm efficiency. The additional demand created by trade enables American firms to operate more efficiently and to achieve economies of scale that might not otherwise be possible. Because of this international trade, manufacturers are able to lower their costs. This means not only potentially lower prices to consumers (both for exported goods and for goods produced in the U.S. from exported inputs), but also more profitable investment opportunities and demand for labor (jobs).

Reversal of historical decline. The growth of export importance is interesting historically. Early in U.S. history, trade was very important to the economy of the U.S. Then as the U.S. came of age the importance of foreign trade declined. Now there is a clear resurgence of international trade as a mainstay of the U.S. economy.

Importance of raw material imports. One big reason for the increased importance of trade is the growing dependence of the U.S. on imports of raw materials. The U.S. now imports more than 50 percent of the petroleum it uses (as late as the 1950s it was an exporter of oil). And although the U.S. has huge mineral resources, it must import 100 percent of the chromium and tin it uses, as well as between 90 and 100 percent of such minerals as cobalt, manganese, platinum, and nickel. In other words, the U.S. *needs* foreign trade for the sake of our industrial economy.

Of course the U.S. must, as we noted earlier, pay the countries from which it imports in their own currencies. Japanese business firms want yen, not dollars, so that they can pay their workers and other costs. In turn, to earn these foreign currencies, the U.S. must export its own goods and services as well as import capital.

The Gains from Trade

Earlier in our history there were those who argued for isolationism, both politically and economically. Today, we are seeing a resurgence of such arguments. Today there might be some who would say: "Apart from those needed minerals (and we can probably find substitutes even for many of them in the long run), I fail to see that we are necessarily better off because of trading. After all, we can use macroeconomic policy to achieve full employment, even without trade. Surely if we made the effort, we could produce just about everything we want. Let's keep the jobs at home in the U.S. Where is the advantage to be had from trade?"

The answer to the above question is not obvious. The U.S. is among a few fortunate nations that probably could, from a technical point of view, achieve **autarky**, economic self-sufficiency. Most food can be grown in the U.S., even tropical fruits. The nation could achieve self-sufficiency in energy too, if it chose to do so. But is complete self-sufficiency necessarily desirable for

Autarky
Economic self-sufficiency.

the U.S. or for any nation? Virtually all economists say no, for reasons we shall now examine.

Trade and Comparative Advantage

In discussing the reasons for trade among nations, one immediately encounters two terms: the **absolute advantage** and the **comparative advantage** that each nation has in producing things. We can best define these terms by example.

Absolute Advantage
The ability of a given nation to produce all commodities more cheaply (that is, using up few resources per unit of output) than any other nation with which it might trade.

Comparative Advantage
A situation in which a nation is relatively more efficient at producing some goods than at producing others, compared with the production capabilities of other nations with which it trades.

Let's say that you are a graduate engineer, and you set up a personal small business of your own. You have an assistant named Pat Bloggs, who does the filing and other routine jobs in your office. You pay Bloggs $30 a day to perform these tasks, while you, as a professional engineer, earn $100 a day. After a particularly hellish week, in which drawings have gone to the wrong firm, you review the operation of the office. You realize that you can do these routine chores much more efficiently than Bloggs. Thus you have an *absolute advantage* over Bloggs. Should you fire Bloggs and do the job yourself? Comparative advantage says no. The $100 a day you earn as an engineer reflects your marginal revenue productivity (MRP); the $30 reflects Bloggs' *MRP*. Therefore, you should stick to your specialty of engineering, because in this you have a *comparative advantage*. In other words, you are relatively more productive as an engineer than as an office assistant. There is a lesson to be learned here. Even a person with an absolute advantage in doing *every* task should specialize in that field in which her or his comparative advantage lies.

We demonstrated how this principle works when we were discussing the market system of a single country: for efficiency's sake, resources should move to their most productive alternative uses. A city could hire engineers to sweep the streets, and they would probably do a great job. But it would be foolish for a society to employ its engineers in this way, since their comparative efficiency is greater when they are building roads, bridges, and offshore drilling rigs.

Now let's apply this idea of comparative advantage to trade between nations. In the real word, international trade involves many nations and thousands of commodities and services. To keep things simple in this illustration, though, we shall deal with only two nations, the U.S. and Honduras. We will examine the trade in only 2 commodities that each country can produce, tractors and bananas.

Discussing additional goods and countries would not change the basic principles; it would just make the relationships more complex.

Table 16-3 shows the production-possibilities (PP) schedules for the U.S. and Honduras. Each country is capable of producing both bananas and tractors. However, note that the rate at which tractors can be traded off for bananas (that is, the rate at which the output of tractors decreases as the output of bananas increases) is very different for the two countries. The reason is that there are different resource endowments in the two countries including climate and human capital.

Figure 16-1 illustrates the PP for the two countries. Unlike the PP curves we saw earlier, these "curves" are straight lines. That is, they reflect a constant rate of exchange of tractors for bananas (we are assuming that the cost of producing each item is constant). Later in this chapter we will discuss PP curves that are concave to the origin and reflect increasing real cost.

Table 16-3
Production-Possibilities Schedules, United States and Honduras (hypothetical)

United States		Honduras	
Units of Tractors	Units of Bananas	Units of Tractors	Units of Bananas
50	0	0	100
40	5	5	80
30	10	10	60
20	15	15	40
10	20	20	20
0	25	25	0

Figure 16-1
Production Possibilities for the United States and Honduras

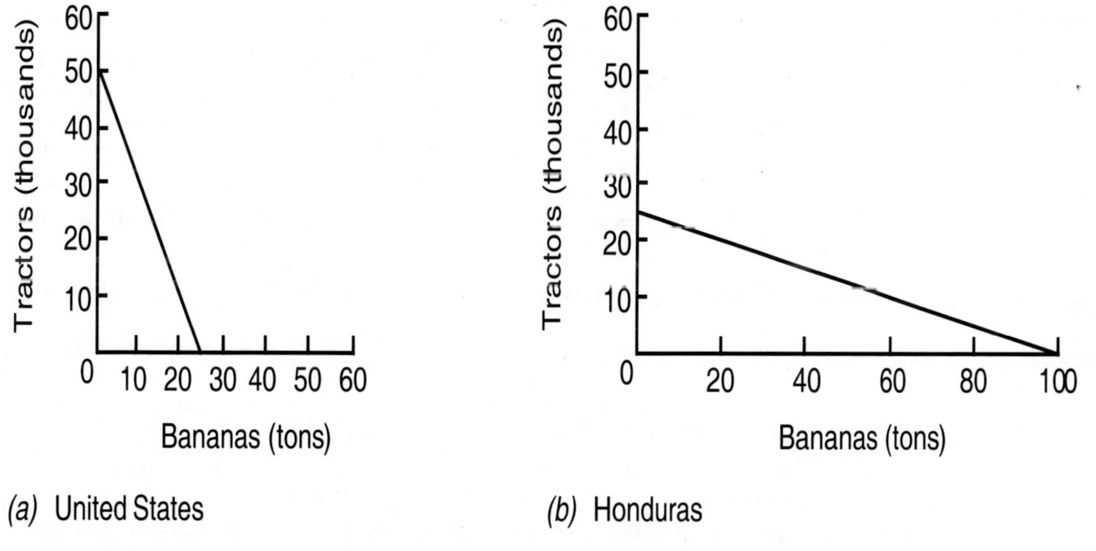

The Terms of Trade

Terms of Trade
The rate at which a nation's exports and imports exchange. In real terms, the number of its exports necessary to obtain its imports. In financial terms, the ratio of export prices to import prices x 100.

From the tables above it can be seen that the U.S. should, for the sake of trade gains, specialize in producing tractors, and Honduras should specialize in bananas. Now the real **terms of trade** (the relation for a nation at which its exports exchange for imports) must be decided. That is, a ratio must be determined at which Honduran bananas will be exchanged for U.S. tractors. There must be an advantage for each country. The Americans must get more than 1/2 unit of bananas for each unit of their tractors, and the Hondurans more than 1 unit of tractors for 4 units of their bananas.[2]

Each country must get more for its products in the world market than it would if it had sold them domestically. If both countries are to benefit, the actual exchange rate must lie between 1T = 1/2 B (preferred by Honduras) and 1T = 4B (preferred by the U.S.).

Figure 16-2
Production-Consumption Possibilities for the United States and Honduras (after trade)

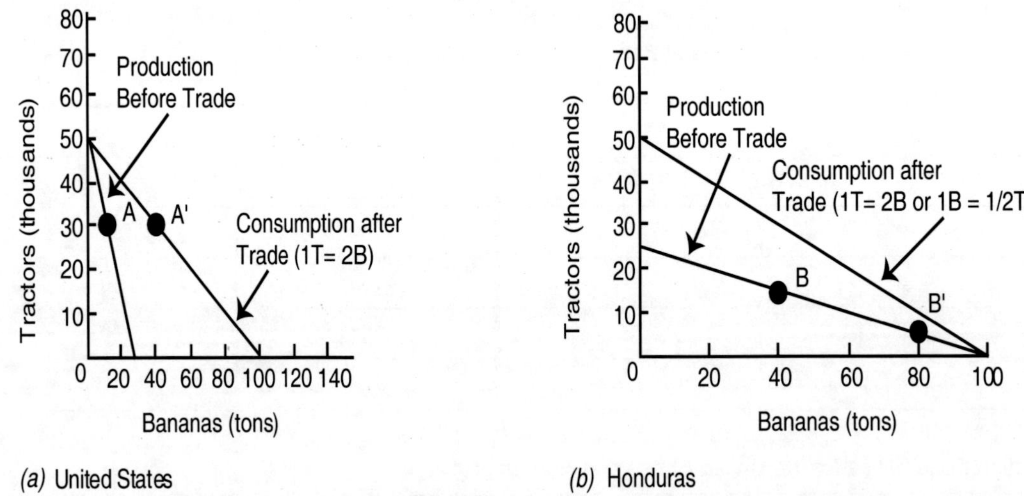

The exact terms of trade will depend on the market demand for both products. Market demand depends on the degree to which one can substitute other products for either commodity, and on the relationship of demand to supply. If there are no good substitutes for tractors, and if demand for them is large relative to supply, the exchange rate (terms of trade) will be in favor of the U.S. If conditions are reversed, the terms of trade will be favorable to Honduras.

Gains from Trade

Suppose that the exchange rate moves to 1T = 2B. Figure 16-2 shows what happens to production and consumption in both countries. Look at the replotted PP curves of both countries. The dark lines (called consumption-possibilities curves), indicating consumption after trade, show what each country can consume if it specializes in the good in which it has a comparative advantage and exports part of its output. We can see first how this process of mutually beneficial exchange occurs through an arithmetic example. Table 16-4 shows what happens when one tractor can be exchanged for two tons of bananas (1T=2B). That exchange rate is the same as one ton of bananas for one half a tractor (1B=1/2T). Each country benefits by taking some of the output of the good in which it has a comparative advantage (tractors for the U.S., bananas for Honduras) and exchanging with the other country for the good in which it does not have a comparative advantage (bananas for the U.S., tractors for Honduras).

If instead of consuming the 50 units of tractors it can produce, the U.S. exports 10 to Honduras, it can consume 40 units of tractors and 20 tons of bananas (instead of the 40 units of tractors and 5 tons of bananas possible without trade). If, at the same time, Honduras, instead of consuming the 100 tons of bananas it can produce, exports 20 tons to the U.S., it can consume 10

2. We are working here with the real terms of trade. In reality, of course, it is the prices of exports and imports that determine a nation's (financial) terms of trade.

units of tractors (instead of the 5 units possible without trade). Let us take one other consumption with and without trade point. If the U.S. consumes 30 units of tractor and exports 20 to Honduras, it can consume 40 tons of bananas (instead of the 10 tons without trade shown in Table 16-3). Honduras, on the other hand, can export 40 tons of bananas to the U.S. and consume 20 tractors instead of the 10 it could consume without trade.

Table 16-4
(Hypothetical) Consumption Possibilities Schedules after trade, United States and Honduras

United States		Honduras	
Units of Tractors	Units of Bananas with trade	Units of Tractors with trade	Units of Bananas
50	0	0	100
40	20	10	80
30	40	20	60
20	60	30	40
10	80	40	20
0	100	50	0

The important result that Table 16-3 together with Table 16-4 and Figure 16-2 enables us to see is:

As long as a nation has a comparative advantage in producing some things, it should specialize in producing those things. It should then export part of the goods for which it has a comparative advantage and import goods in which it has a comparative disadvantage. By so doing, it will increase the total utility of both nations.

This is true even if the nation has an absolute advantage in producing everything it consumes.

What Determines Comparative Advantage?

Since we have shown that comparative advantage is a mutually advantageous basis for trade, we need to identify the factors that determine a nation's comparative advantage. Also we want to ask the question: Are nations locked into a particular comparative-advantage position, or do their positions change?

First, *nations have differing comparative advantages,* for the following reasons:

Different endowments. Different nations have different endowments of natural resources, both in quantity and quality. For example, nations such as the U.S., Canada, Russia, and the People's Republic of China have large quantities (although different proportions) of relatively high-grade resources (petroleum, mineral deposits, topsoil, and so on).

Different physical features. Different nations have different physical features (mild or extreme climate, many or few natural harbors).

Different stages of development. Different nations are at different stages of development of markets. For example, the U.S., Japan, and the countries in Western Europe have well-developed capital markets, reflecting large supplies of savings that can be transformed through investment into capital, including human capital (skills and abilities resulting from investment in education). In other countries, markets may be either rudimentary or nonexistent.

Different supplies of productive factors. Different nations have different supplies of factors of production, including labor. For example, China and many other less-developed countries have large supplies of labor relative to capital. A country tends to specialize in products (or services) that intensively use those resources in which it is relatively rich.

Second, the *comparative advantages of nations change*. Nations are not locked into a position with respect to comparative advantage. For example, the U.S. began as a nation rich in land and short of capital and labor. Today, it is relatively rich in capital and land, and relatively short of labor. (This has nothing to do with our unemployment rate. It means that as the U.S. presently produces things, even at full employment, capital and land are abundant relative to labor.) Up until the Civil War, the U.S. specialized in land-intensive agricultural exports (cotton, tobacco, rice, and so on). Today, it specializes in exports that are capital-intensive and land-intensive. For example, in 2000 more than 45 percent of U.S. exports were comprised of capital (non-automotive) goods. Another 10 percent were grains and cereals, which are land-intensive. Thus, almost half of U.S. exports were derived from processes that were capital- and land-intensive. On the other hand, the U.S. imports many things (coffee, cocoa, inexpensive textiles, handicrafts) that are relatively labor-intensive. (Although automobiles, steel, and other such goods are exceptions.)

Demand Considerations

As we have seen, domestic economic trade is based on the benefits of voluntary exchange. International trade, whether between nations or, as is most often the case, between individuals, is also based on the expected benefits of voluntary exchange. We saw in Figure 16-2 that supply (cost-based) considerations make it possible for nations, through exchange, to consume more with trade. There are also important benefits to trade that derive from demand considerations. The structure of demand differs greatly from one country to another as well as from one part of the world to another. The primary reason for these differences lies in the diversity of tastes and preferences that exists among individuals within countries as well as between different nations. Consider tastes in food and clothing. Americans (both North Americans and Latin Americans) prefer coffee; the English and many Asians prefer tea. The Japanese prefer fish; Americans have a much stronger taste for beef, pork and chicken. Out of these differences arises a willingness to pay prices for goods and services that differs substantially from one area to another and thus gains to be had in exporting.

There are many arguments about changing the comparative advantages of countries, especially about whether comparative-advantage trade tends to help the poor-trading nations to develop. In the application in this chapter, we will examine some of these arguments.

Increasing Costs and Other Cautions

In the case involving the U.S. and Honduras, we concluded that each would produce only its most advantageous good, tractors or bananas. We showed that bilateral exchange between the two nations would make both better off in terms of the quantities of the 2 goods available for consumption. There are some qualifications to the argument, however.

Increasing costs. As each country reallocates its resources from the disadvantageous good to the advantageous one, it will run into *increasing costs*. For example, as the U.S. produces more tractors, the cost (in bananas not produced) may rise, until it reaches a point at which it would be better off if it produced some bananas of its own rather than always exchanging tractors for Honduran bananas. Honduras, whose costs of producing bananas also rise, may be better off producing some of its own tractors. The point is that increasing costs cause international specialization to be less than complete.

Employment effects. When two countries specialize in making things in which they have a comparative advantage and then trade with each other, achieving the greatest possible production, we assume that there is full employment in the trading nations. However, at times this trade means reallocating resources and, when this results in unemployment, the countries' output may fall below the PP curve. So there are some possible undesirable effects for a country from trade. But there are various macroeconomic (fiscal and monetary) tools that a nation can use to achieve its employment goals, and there are microeconomic tools that can be used to reallocate resources in efficient resource markets (job retraining, for example). Thus, many economists feel that the risk of creating temporary unemployment is not a compelling reason to forego trade.

Assumption of competitive trade. The principle of comparative advantage depends heavily on *competition* in international trade. If the tractors are produced by a monopolistic firm but the bananas are exported by competitive firms, Honduras may not fully reap the benefits of trade. If monopolistic export boards (perhaps government ones) negotiate the terms of trade (American wheat for Russian oil, for example), one cannot tell what the outcome will be. This is also true of bilateral monopoly. The end result depends on the relative skills and bargaining strengths of the participants.

Externalities. If there are *externalities*, the terms of trade may not reflect the real costs of production. The countries may produce and exchange either too little or too much. (Suppose that the tractor factories pollute the water and air and that their costs do not reflect the added social costs of cleaning up the environment.)

Prices may not reflect relative scarcity. The principle of comparative advantage depends on the fact that relative prices (the American price of tractors and the Honduran price of bananas) reflect relative scarcities of resources in each nation. If the prices do not reflect these scarcities, an international (as well as domestic) misallocation of resources occurs. Suppose that the U.S. subsidizes the tractor industry. Then international prices of tractors (the terms of trade) would not reflect underlying relative scarcity and companies would produce more tractors than is efficient (and trade them). (Americans would, in effect, be producing tractors when they should be producing bananas.)

Figure 16-3
How a Protective Tariff Works

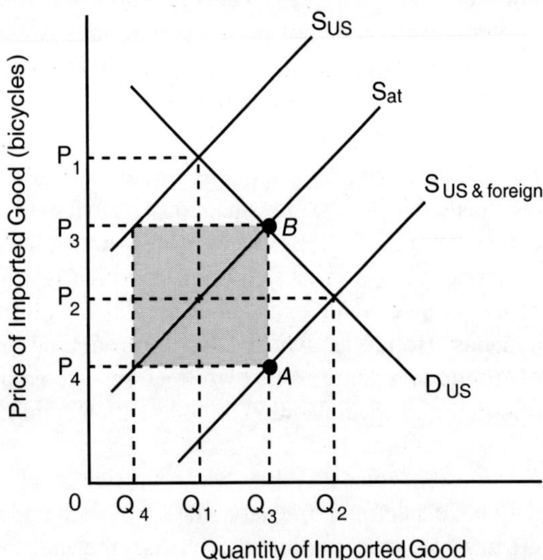

Figure 16-3 illustrates the effects of a protective tariff. The domestic supply of the good is S_{US} and the domestic demand is D_{US}. Without trade equilibrium price is P_1 and Q_1 of the good is sold. If free trade in the good occurs, imports increase the domestic supply to $S_{US\ \&\ foreign}$. As a result of trade, price declines to P_2 and Q_2 of the good is sold. Both the decline in price and the increased consumption of the good ($Q_2 - Q_1$) are benefits to consumers attributable to trade. If a protective tariff of *AB* is imposed, supply declines to S_{at}, with the tariff, price rises to P_3 and quantity sold declines to Q_3. Both the increase in price (P_2 to P_3) and the decrease in consumption of the good ($Q_2 - Q_3$) are costs to consumers attributable to protectionism.

Protectionism
Efforts by governments to protect domestic firms and industries from the competition of imported goods

Protectionism. The biggest obstacle to trade being conducted according to comparative advantage is **protectionism**, the efforts of governments to protect domestic firms or industries from the competition of imported goods. Consequently, there has been little completely free trade in modern times (or indeed at any time). Let us now look at how nations may protect trade and the arguments surrounding these practices.

The Means of Protection

There are two principal means by which countries usually intervene to protect their own industries from overseas competition: tariffs and quotas.

Tariffs
Taxes levied on imported goods

Tariffs

The most common means of protection are **tariffs**, which are taxes levied on imported goods. Figure 16-3 shows how a protective tariff works and also shows its effects on trade and prices. Before trade begins, the U.S. demand for bicycles is D_{US} and the supply is S_{US}. Equilibrium price is P_1 (Q_1D_{US} = Q_1S_{US}). At this price, Q_1 of bicycles are sold. (Presumably, bicycles are goods in which this country has a comparative *dis*advantage.) Now trade opens up. The U.S. begins to import foreign bicycles (from Japan, Italy, and France). The supply of bicycles increases to $S_{US\ \&\ foreign}$. Equilibrium; price falls to P_2, and Q_2 bicycles are sold. The supply increases until the price of bicycles in the U.S. is equal to the price of bicycles abroad (not including transportation costs). As long as the American price is higher, foreign producers will continue to export bicycles in order to sell in the more profitable American market. Now suppose that the bicycle manufacturers complain to Congress, as the Bicycle Manufacturers' Association did in the 1970s. They argued as follows:

> *A deluge of imported bicycles into the U.S. has increased imports from 19.8 percent of our market in 1964 to 37.1 percent in 1972. We don't feel our business should go down the drain. Standards must be established that would automatically impose restrictions on imports competing with American products.... This is not protectionism.*

Let's say that the bicycle lobby convinces Congress that this argument is valid, so that Congress and the President levy a tax, a tariff, on imported bicycles. The tax which is equal to *AB* in Figure 16-3 increases the cost of importing bicycles and reduces the supply to S_{at} (supply after tariff). The new equilibrium price is P_3, which is higher than the pre-tariff price (by $P_3 - P_2$). The number of bicycles sold goes down (by $Q_2 - Q_3$) to Q_3. Note that part of the gain to consumers from all the foreign bicycles coming into the country is eliminated. If the tariff had been higher, imports might have ceased altogether, and supply might have fallen back to S_{US}. Then price would have gone back up to P_1 (with only Q_1 sold).

So the tariff hurts consumers, because now they must buy bicycles at a price higher than the free market international price, and they are getting fewer bicycles. The tariff also hurts foreign bicycle manufacturers, because the net price they receive (after paying the tariff) is P_4. In addition, the tariff hurts U.S. firms that may use the product as an input (messenger services and the like). The total revenue to the U.S. government from the tariff is shown by the shaded area. This is the unit tariff per bicycles ($P_3 - P_4$) times the number of bicycles imported ($Q_3 - Q_4$). (At price P_3, American manufacturers supply Q_4.)

Cartoon Feature Syndicate

"He wasn't even warm, was he, Mom?"

Figure 16-4
The Burden of a Tariff with Inelastic Demand

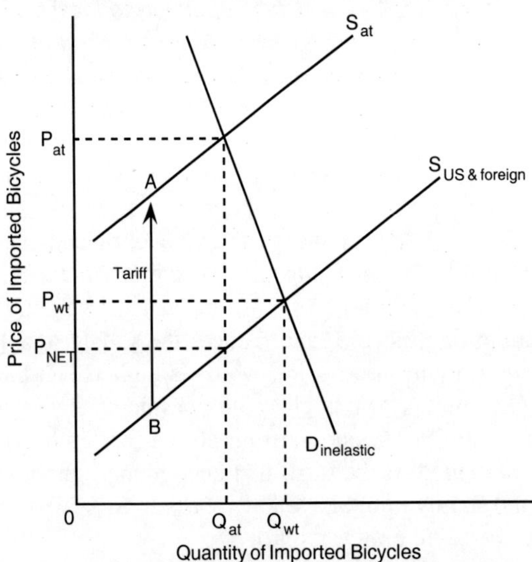

The burden of a tariff is related to the elasticity of demand for the imported good. Figure 16-4 illustrates the relationship for the case in which demand is price *in*elastic. Without a tariff, supply is S US & foreign, price without tariff is P_{wt}, and quantity sold before the tariff is Q_{wt}. A tariff of AB on the imported good decreases supply after tariff to S_{at}. As a result, price rises to P_{at} and quantity sold declines to Q_{at}. There is a large increase in price (P_{wt} to P_{at}) relative to the decline in sales ($Q_{wt} - Q_{at}$). Most of the burden of the tariff is borne by consumers in the form of higher prices, though foreign producers also are burdened by the lower net price (P_{NET} as opposed to P_{wt}).

Figure 16-5
The Burden of a Tariff with Elastic Demand

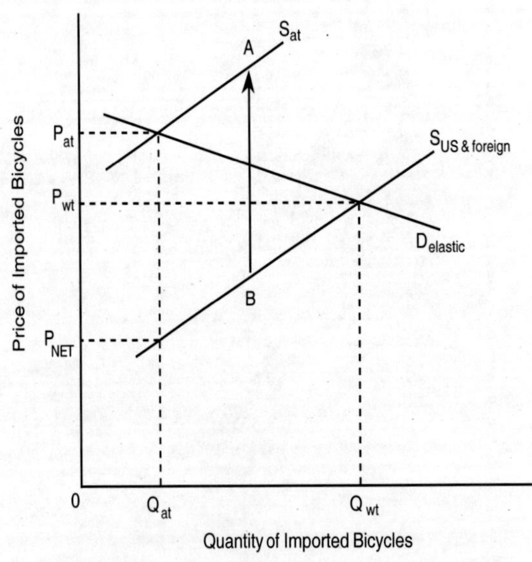

Elasticity and the Burden of the Tariff

You may recognize that the burden of the tariff (either the higher price to consumers or the lower net price to sellers) is distributed on the basis of the price elasticity of demand for the imported good. We see in Figure 16-4 and Figure 16-5 how the distributive burden of the tariff is related to elasticity. There may be both a *consumer burden*, the portion of a tariff paid by consumers in higher prices, and a *producer burden,* the portion of a tariff paid by importers in a lower net price and reduced sales of the imported good.

In Figure 16-4 the demand for the imported good is price inelastic, implying that poor substitutes exist for the good or that consumers spend relatively little of their incomes on it. With unrestricted trade, the bicycle market clears at Q_{wt} (quantity without tariff) and at price, P_{wt} (price without tariff). After tariff AB is levied, supply is reduced from $S_{US\ \&\ foreign}$ to S_{at} (supply after tariff). Now the market is cleared at Q_{at} and P_{at} (quantity and price after tariff). Most of the market burden ($P_{at} - P_{wt}$) is borne by consumers in the form of higher prices but part, $Q_{wt} - Q_{at}$ is borne by producers in the form of reduced sales and a lower net price (P_{NET}). Consumers absorb most of the burden. We see in Figure 16-5 how the burden of a tariff is distributed when the demand for the imported good is price elastic. Before the tariff, with elastic demand $D_{elastic}$ and supply $S_{U.S.\ \&\ foreign}$, price is P_{wt} and the quantity sold of the good is Q_{wt}. When the same amount of tariff AB is now imposed, costs of importing the good rise, and supply declines to S_{at} resulting in a higher price (P_{wt} to P_{at}) and a decrease in the quantity of the good sold (Q_{wt} to Q_{at}) and a lower net price (P_{NET}) to foreign producers. There is a large decrease in quantity sold relative to the increase in price and most of the burden of the tariff falls on firms importing the good. The demand for the imported good is price elastic; implying that relatively good substitutes for the imported good exist or that consumers spend a significant part of their income on it. With unrestricted trade, the market clears at Q_{wt} and P_{wt}. After tariff AB is imposed, supply falls from $S_{US\ \&\ foreign}$ to S_{at} and the market clears at Q_{at} and price P_{at}. The consumer burden ($P_{at} - P_{wt}$) is relatively small while the producer burden ($Q_{wt} - Q_{at}$) and the lower net price ($P_{wt} - P_{NET}$) is relatively large. Clearly, when demand is elastic, most of the burden falls on producers in the form of reduced sales and lower net prices.

Is anyone better off as a result of the tariff? Yes, the American bicycle manufacturers are. They do not have to pay the tariff, so they keep the full price (P_{at}) of their product. This is higher than P_{NET}, which is the price foreign makers have after they pay the tariff. The federal government is better off by the amount of revenue. The tariff, in other words, represents a loss in income by consumers, which is transferred to the government and to protected domestic firms.

Beyond the burden, two points about tariffs should be emphasized: (1) When the government imposes a tariff, it makes a *net addition to domestic monopoly power.* In our example, bicycle manufacturers had been getting a competitively set international price for their product. Now they are getting a more monopolistically established price instead. (Though in this case the government, rather than private business, is the agent that creates the monopoly influence.) Thus, tariffs defeat our objective of having a competitive market system. (2) When the government imposes a general tariff (or other trade restriction), it *reduces the number of good substitutes that consumers have for domestically produced goods.* This, in turn, may make the demand *more price inelastic* and (because it increases monopoly power) may cause prices in the long run to rise by an even greater amount than the amount of the tariff itself.

Import Quotas

Import Quotas
Restrictions imposed by governments on the quantity of a good that may be imported.

The second major means governments use to protect their industries against competition from abroad is **import quotas**, that is, restrictions on the quantity of goods that may be imported. In one way, the effects of quotas are much like those of tariffs. Look again at Figure 16-3. Suppose that Congress, instead of enacting a tariff, had said that only $Q_3 - Q_4$ bicycles could come into the U.S. Supply would still have dropped to S_{at} (or we could call this S_{aq} to stand for supply after quota). Total supply (Q_3) would have been domestic supply (Q_4) plus foreign supply ($Q_3 - Q_4$). Consumers would be affected just as adversely and U.S. bicycle makers would still get the higher price, P_3. The difference is that *a quota is not a revenue-producing device* (the shaded area would not exist), so the government would not get any extra tax revenue. Foreign bicycle makers would get the same price as domestic makers, P_3 (less transportation costs, of course), and domestic consumers would carry the burden of the quota.

Import Embargo
A prohibition, imposed by government, against importing certain goods.

The most extreme form of a quota is an **import embargo**, which is an absolute prohibition against importing a good. If Congress had imposed an embargo on foreign bicycles, supply would have reverted to S_{US}. Price would have risen to P_1 (domestic producers would have been restored to whatever monopoly power they originally had).

Embargoes are relatively rare in American history. In 1808, during the Napoleonic wars, President Jefferson imposed one. After 1962, the U.S. government embargoed trade with Cuba (no Cuban cigars, sugar, or rum). Until the 1970s, there was a U.S. embargo on trade with the People's Republic of China. It is worth noting that when embargoes are lifted, they are usually lifted in the interest of political expediency (détente, for example) rather than in the interests of free trade. Embargoes are usually short-term political penalties against antagonistic nations. In 1996, the decades long embargo against Cuba was intensified after tensions rose between the two governments.

Export Quotas: Rational Ignorance by Consumers?

As we have seen, quotas have effects similar to tariffs except that they do not generate revenues for governments. In protecting domestic producers, governments sometimes assign shares of their domestic markets to foreign exporters. Examples of this in the U.S. include imports of textiles, apparel, and sugar. The American government assigns quotas to foreign governments (Dominican Republic, Taiwan, etc.), and those governments, recall, assign the quotas to their own producers. In all cases, of course, American consumers pay prices above the world price (for example, more than twice the world price of sugar). Clearly, American sugar producers have benefited as well as foreign producers who are able to obtain quota shares. By one estimate, the value of these monopoly rights (rents) to foreign producers in 1993 was over $11 billion.

Rational Ignorance
The argument that when the benefits of a public choice are highly concentrated and its costs highly diffused, it is rational for those who bear its costs to ignore them.

Why, you may ask, do such clear and obvious impediments to free trade exist when millions of consumers are harmed and a few thousand (domestic and foreign) producers reap the benefits. Why should consumers ignore these added costs rather than inform themselves fully and attempt to resist efforts by government to impose such costs? Many economists believe that the explanation lies in the concept of **rational ignorance**, the rationality of consumers in ignoring many proposals of government in view of the large costs of informing themselves about such proposals and the small individual benefits of doing so. It is worth reminding ourselves of this idea. Take the case of sugar quotas which were renewed in 1996. Would you, for example, as a consumer of sugar, bother to inform yourself about monopoly sugar prices in the U.S. and lead a campaign to overturn the public decision to impose a quota system? Even if you were successful in eliminating quotas (a very unlikely result for one voter), the benefit/cost ratio of this activity to you would be unfavorable. Notice, though, that the same calculus would not apply to most private consumption decisions. Would you inform yourself about the private choice between a Chevrolet Corvette and a Nissan 350-Z? In the latter instance, the benefits and costs would be quite different and most likely would make it irrational to ignore the information needed to be fully informed.

Many economists would argue that quotas are clearly less preferred to tariffs where governments intend to restrict international trade. Notice that tariffs create tax revenues whereas quotas generate benefits only to private producers. At least with tariffs, the revenues *could* be used to reduce other taxes as well as to fund public expenditure programs. It is for this reason that some economists, faced with the political difficulties of eliminating quotas, have proposed auctioning the rights to export quotas. Presumably, the rights would bring something close to the $11 billion referred to earlier.

Arguments in Favor of Protection

As already noted, the U.S. has rarely if ever practiced completely free trade. (Neither have most other countries.) Americans frequently say they believe in competition. But many, including many of their elected representatives, seem to argue against it when it is to their financial advantage. Economists in general, most U.S. economists, that is, sing the praises of free trade. But apparently, the economists who make public policy cannot completely convince the government. In the mid 1990s, we again saw efforts to impose new restrictions on trade between the U.S. and other nations. Similar arguments for protectionism have arisen during the sharp economic downturn of 2008-2010. In view of these continuing efforts to push for protectionism, let's examine the arguments most commonly advanced in favor of restricting trade.

The Infant-Industry Argument

The infant-industry argument is as follows: Industries that are just starting cannot meet the pressures of competition by similar, already established industries located in other, more industrially mature countries. Such infant industries deserve the protection of a tariff or other protective device, and they should be sheltered until they have become big enough to take advantage of economies of scale.

This argument may seem reasonable. However, there are opposing arguments: (1) Tariffs and other forms of protection, once enacted, are extremely hard to abolish. For example, the bicycle industry still enjoys tariff protection. So do the automobile and steel industries and many other U.S. industries that are hardly infants. (2) If an industry needs to be protected before it is mature, direct government subsidies are preferable, since they make the costs of such protection explicit. (3) The logic of the infant-industry argument is difficult to apply, since it is hard to know (in either a developed or underdeveloped nation) *which* infant industries will (and should) survive. Short of pursuing a goal of autarky, a nation must choose, without any clear guidelines, *which* infant industries to put into its protective and expensive incubator. The protecting nation runs the risk not only of distorting its uses of resources but even of ending up with an industry that fails anyway, especially if the protection is finally withdrawn.

The National-Security Argument

The national-security argument is as follows: The U.S. can never really be certain of the supply of a good produced in a foreign country. The nation cannot even depend on its present friends to help in a tight spot. This means that, when it comes to defense goods, U.S. security must take precedence over U.S. economic efficiency.

This argument is difficult for economists to judge, since there are no objective criteria by which to evaluate the trade-off between increased national security and decreased industrial efficiency. Economists can only identify the costs involved in (1) levying tariffs, or (2) directly subsidizing firms that make defense goods. Most economists would say that direct subsidies are preferable, because they more clearly identify the costs involved.

Figure 16-6
History of American Tariffs, 1820-1980

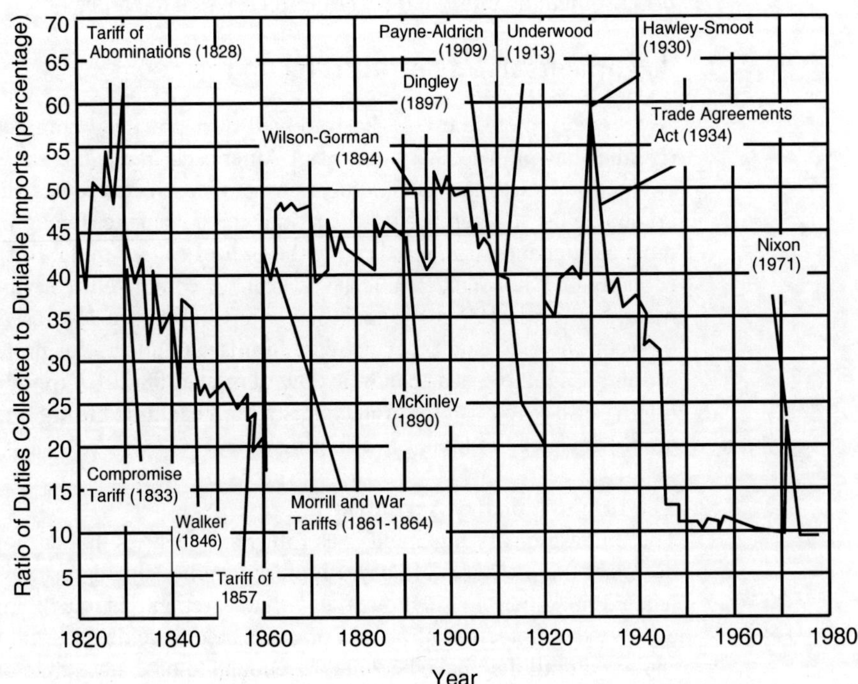

Source: U.S. Department of Commerce, Historical Statistics of the U.S. and Statistical Abstract of the U.S., 1982.

Figure 16-6 shows the wide variations in American tariffs between 1820 and 1980. Since 1980, tariffs have declined with the free trade agreements such as those with Canada, Mexico and other nations increasing the volume of goods not subject to import duties.

The Cheap-Foreign-Labor Argument

The cheap-foreign-labor argument can best be summed up in two examples. The American textile industry, say proponents of protection, must be protected from imported textiles from nations such as Malaysia, Thailand, and the Peoples Republic of China. Wages in Thailand and other such nations are so low that American firms cannot price their textiles low enough to compete. Florida farmers must be protected from the winter produce of Mexican farms where much agricultural labor is paid $3 per day. How, say some Florida farmers and their elected representative, can they possibly compete with Mexican farmers whose labor costs are only 3 to 5 percent of their own? Although this argument is persuasive to many people, it is irrelevant to economists because (1) the higher wages of Americans presumably reflect higher marginal productivity; (2) it is socially inefficient to have an American firm that cannot compete with labor-intensive imports try to do so; and (3) it is less costly to retrain labor and reallocate resources to more efficient uses than it is to protect an inefficient industry (however, remember the exception: the national-security argument.); and (4) wage costs are only part of the costs of production. Costs per unit of product produced depend not only on prices paid for labor but on labor's productivity. Much of the seeming advantage of low wage countries seemed to disappear in the 1990s. Much of this advantage has been in "blue collar" labor cost, which is declining and will continue to decline as a portion of total cost in the twenty-first century. Already, as Peter Drucker[3] has observed, this no longer provides a competitive edge to low wage countries. As a result, in spite of the continued movement of some industries to low wage countries and the continuing controversy over "outsourcing" of U.S. jobs, we are witnessing a net return of industries to the U.S. to take advantage of lower transport costs.

The Macroeconomic-Employment Argument

The macroeconomic-employment argument is that during hard times the U.S. can "export" some of its unemployment. (This is sometimes called a *beggar-thy-neighbor* argument.) Large segments of the business community (except big importers) and of labor often support this idea. The principle is to create more jobs at home by excluding, or sharply restricting, imports. Such an increase in domestic demand for formerly imported goods causes the U.S. to move toward full employment. Has the U.S. followed the beggar-thy-neighbor principle? Figure 16-6 shows what has happened to tariffs during our "hard-times" periods. You can see that tariffs have been high during most recession and depression periods, such as the mid-1870s, 1890s, early-1900s (though they were falling then), and 1921. They were especially high in the early years of the Great Depression (the Hawley-Smoot tariffs, in 1930, were the highest in modern American history). The purpose of the so-called Tariff of Abominations (1828) was to protect U.S. infant industries such as textiles and iron. Tariffs have from time to time protected American makers of every sort of commodity. Cheese, watches, cameras, musical instruments, and machinery are some that come to mind.

Economists usually feel that a beggar-thy-neighbor action is not likely to succeed. Even if it does work initially, the cost is great because such actions invite retaliation in the long run by other countries. (If the U.S. raises its tariff on bananas, Honduras will raise *its* tariff on tractors.) A trade war is likely to result and every nation will be hurt.

The reason why nations will be hurt is that as tariff walls go up, governments try to stimulate domestic demand, through tax cuts, increased government spending, and lowered interest rates. Assuming that previous international trade has reflected a comparative advantage, the U.S. will increase its domestic output, substituting homemade products for imported ones, at the expense of efficiency. Without trade, even if the U.S. reaches full employment, there will be relative inefficiency in the industries producing these products. Thus, the level of U.S. production of goods and services will be lower than if the tariff had not been introduced.

---

3. Drucker, Peter J. "Low Wages No Longer Give Competitive Edge." *The Wall Street Journal*, March 16, 1988.

Retaliation for "Unfair" Trade Practices

Proposals to restrict trade are often based on the view that they are necessary to punish unfair trading practices by other nations. Such proposals frequently include the following reasoning: "Since free trade does not, and perhaps cannot exist, trade restrictions can be used as leverage against unfair traders to create a system of fair trade." This rationale is found in the provisions of the Trade Agreement Act of 1979. Among the provisions of the act is one prohibiting foreign firms from dumping or selling products in the U.S. at prices lower than those in their own domestic markets. The act provides that, on a finding of dumping by the International Trade Commission, the President may impose penalties against foreign producers.

Economists are divided on the question of penalizing dumping. Some say that dumping is merely a subsidization of domestic consumers by foreign producers. Why turn down a gift? Others say that dumping may be predatory, an attempt to suppress competition or prevent its development through entry into an industry. The problem with this rationale for trade restrictions is that it supposes that dumping may create monopoly. Many economists would say that if it does, the monopoly profits will serve as a stimulus to entry anyway, and tend to eliminate the benefits of dumping. We will see more about retaliation in the Applications section of this chapter.

The Rustbelt: Protecting Declining Industries

Many of the arguments for trade restriction in recent decades have came from elected officials of areas with declining industries or industries containing antiquated plants and equipment. An argument advanced was the reverse of the infant-industry argument. Such industries, it is said, need temporary protection while they phase out or cut back production and during the period in which jobs are found for workers in other industries. While plausible, the argument suffers from many of the same problems as the infant-industry argument. Which industries should be protected? How much cost is reasonable? An illustration will suffice. About 75 percent of all shoes sold in the U.S. are imported (mainly from Brazil, Taiwan, China and The Republic of Korea). In an effort to protect this declining industry, Congress, in 1985, studied imposing import restrictions that would have saved more than 30,000 jobs in the industry. The cost *per job*, however, in terms of higher prices and other costs, would have been about $68,000! Publicity about the costs led to the demise of the proposal.

An equally serious problem is in choosing the industries that are declining and face ultimate elimination. Only a few years ago, the American steel industry seemed a candidate with the closing of much of its older plants and equipment and the consequent loss of jobs in the Mid-west. With the exchange rate changes of 1987–1988, however, the steel industry again became more competitive and operating at high levels of capacity. The "rustbelt" prospered in the 1990's and had low unemployment rates. In the early 2000s, exchange rates moved against the dollar and the American steel industry sought and received temporary protection. Was this protection either necessary or economically wise?

International Trade Policy Since World War II

General Agreement on Tariffs and Trade (GATT)
An international organization created in 1947. Its objectives included fostering freer trade throughout the world.

As we have seen, tariff levels have fluctuated greatly throughout American history. After World War II, the U.S. was instrumental in creating the **General Agreement on Tariffs and Trade (GATT)** in 1947. From 23 original members, it has grown to more than 159 nations in 2013 and now includes much of Eastern Europe and even such nations as the People's Republic of China and Russia. Dedicating itself to fostering trade and lowering tariffs, GATT has held a series of meetings, or "rounds." Three of the more recent rounds, the Kennedy Round (1967), the Tokyo Round (1979), and the Uruguay Round (1994), resulted in major tariff reductions. The Uruguay round alone reduced tariffs world-wide by 40 percent. Further GTO meetings have, however, been less successful.

World Trade Organization (WTO)
A successor organization to GATT whose primary purpose is to further liberalize world trade.

The Uruguay round also resulted in the creation of a new international organization, the **World Trade Organization (WTO)**. The WTO is the successor to GATT and has the same basic objective, that of further liberalizing trade. All member states have rights and obligations within this organization. A difference between the WTO and GATT, however, is that developing nations, like the industrial nations, have an obligation to liberalize trade. Indeed, in2002, preferential trade policy treatment for the developing nations was eliminated. A new legal system now exists within the WTO to resolve trade disputes among the member nations.

Regional Trade Agreements

While GATT and WTO grew after 1947 as organizations that are global in scope, a parallel pattern emerged in which nations have joined to form regional agreements also designed to liberalize trade among their members. These agreements have taken three different forms:

1. Common markets
2. Customs unions
3. Free trade agreements

Common Markets
Agreements for free trade, common tariffs and free movement of capital and labor.

Customs Unions
Agreements for free trade and common tariffs.

Free Trade Agreements
Agreements for free trade among members.

The most comprehensive of the three are **common markets**, which provide for (1) free trade among the members, (2) common tariffs for trade with non-member states, and (3) free movement of capital and labor among the members. A **customs union**, on the other hand, is less comprehensive and provides for free trade among members and common tariffs for trade with non-members. Finally, a **free trade agreement** is least comprehensive providing only for free trade among member states.

Current Regional Trade Arrangements

The most successful free trade agreement since World War II is the European Union (EU). Many nations that did not wish to join the EU formed the European Free Trade Association (EFTA) in 1960, and have since negotiated free trade agreements with the EU. The combination of EU-EFTA nations forms a free trade area which encompasses a population of over 300 million and constitutes the largest free trade market today.

North American Free Trade Association (NAFTA)
An agreement among the U.S., Canada, and Mexico to create a free trade area among the three nations over a period of 15 years.

Western hemisphere nations are moving to create a free trade market that may be even larger than that in Europe. In 1988, the U.S. and Canada signed a free trade agreement that eliminated tariffs on all goods and virtually all services by 1999. The *bilateral* free trade flows are the largest in the world. In 1993, the agreement was expanded with the inclusion of Mexico and an agreement to phase out all tariffs in this trilateral trade over a period of 15 years. The **North American Free Trade Association (NAFTA)** included a provision to ultimately include all western hemisphere nations. This goal has proved difficult to achieve, however, in view of the continuing controversies surrounding NAFTA and the narrow margin of its congressional approval in 1993.

Multilateral Free Trade: Its Future

The period since 1947 has seen impressive gains in free trade through much of the world. World trade today is probably freer (though not yet fully free) than it has ever been. Does this mean that the culmination of the trade liberalization of the past half century will be truly global free trade? While most economists would wish the answer to be yes, the answer is not that clear. There are at least two alternatives to free trade that will contend for dominance over the next 10 to 20 years.

Regional trading blocs. Growth of regional trading blocs that erect barriers to external trade while furthering free trade among members (for example, a European bloc contending with a western hemisphere bloc.)

State-directed trade. Growth of state-directed trade: in spite of the seeming demise of central planning (the old Soviet Union, the "old" People's Republic of China, etc.), forces may already be seen urging at least a partial return to state economic direction. That urge seems strongest in parts of Latin America.

Economists are sure only of this: Although both of the above arrangements may produce some short term gains for some states, both will produce greater real losses in contrast with global free trade. If this conflict of trade policy philosophies or ideas is compared to a prize fight, world trading history since 1947 seems to have free trade ahead on points, but no knock-out is in sight!

Free Trade: A Reprise

Before 1947, the U.S. and other trading nations were free to impos iffs. Tariff increases frequently lead to retaliation and, at times, with major reductions in the volume of trade. The 1930s, as we ha especially characterized by these conditions. Many economic h clude that protectionism contributed significantly to the lengtheni depression.

Lowering of tariff and other trade barriers since World doubtless increased stability and reduced the effects of trade wars su the 1930's.

Application I: Does Trade Create Development?

From 1960 through the early 2000s, it became apparent that nations such as Mexico, Brazil, Korea, Taiwan, Singapore, Malaysia, India and China were developing major manufacturing sectors and that international trade was playing a key role in this process. Indeed, these nations came to be known as the newly industrializing countries (NICs), in contrast with the less-developed countries (LDCs). The emergence of the NICs seemed to reignite a long-standing debate among economists and others, not only about the future course of economic development, but also about the role of international trade in fostering such development.

In the 1980s, the "debt crisis" of some of the NICs and many of the LDCs further complicated efforts to assay the relationship between trade and development. In the early twenty first century, pressures to move away from free trade have arisen again, especially, as pointed out above, in Latin America. Opponents have even rioted during meetings designed to promote free trade. That these issues will continue to be important to all nations, rich, poor and in between, seems nearly certain. Development cannot begin or continue without capital and other imports, and importing cannot occur unless nations have export earnings with which to finance imports. Likewise, debt cannot be serviced, much less repaid except out of export-derived revenues. In an increasingly interdependent international economy, few issues take on more importance than the relationship between trade and development. Few also are likely to be more contentious.

The Relation Between Trade and Development

To establish this relationship, we must find a relation between exporting-importing and the increase in productivity that is the key to development. Opinions are divided about whether trade, especially trade based on comparative advantage, enhances economic development. In this application we will examine some of the controversies surrounding this subject.

The Classical View

Early economists, including Adam Smith and David Ricardo, believed that trade was essential to economic development, or to what Smith called "The Wealth of Nations." Writing about the country's efforts to produce things that it could import more cheaply, Smith said, "The value of its annual produce is certainly more or less diminished, when it is thus turned away from producing commodities evidently of more value than the commodity which it is directed to produce."

This idea of maximizing the wealth of a nation through trade, however, is based on a static situation (*static* meaning timeless). Much of the argument over its validity arises from the distinction between the static economic position of a country at a point in time, and the improvement (or deterioration) in the country's position that occurs over time. Let's illustrate the difference between these two perspectives.

At its beginning, the U.S. started out with a certain endowment of land, labor, capital, and entrepreneurship. For simplicity, assume that all its resources were integrated into the market system. Now ask yourself the following questions: (1) In any given year, for instance, 1940, would the per capita national income be higher if the U.S. followed a policy of free trade? Or would it be higher if it imposed restrictions on trade? (2) Which policy, restricted trade or unrestricted trade, would cause income to grow faster from one date to another (for instance, from 1940 to 2000)?

Figure 16-7 will help you visualize the answer. It shows that in 1940 the U.S. could have two levels of per capita income: $1,300 or $1,350. The $1,300 figure corresponds to the level if the government enforced protective practices (such as tariffs or quotas). It represents many possible levels of income resulting from different combinations of trade restrictions. Each of the combinations causes resources to be used in ways that are *less* productive than would be the case if there were free trade, or if there were comparative-advantage trade. The $1,350 represents the *free*-trade (comparative advantage) case.

Therefore, the answer to question 1 is that at any point, its process of development, a nation will have a higher income if it engages in free trade and utilizes all its resources on the basis of comparative advantage.

Figure 16-7
Hypothetical Growth Paths of the United States: Free Trade and Protectionism, 1940 to 2000

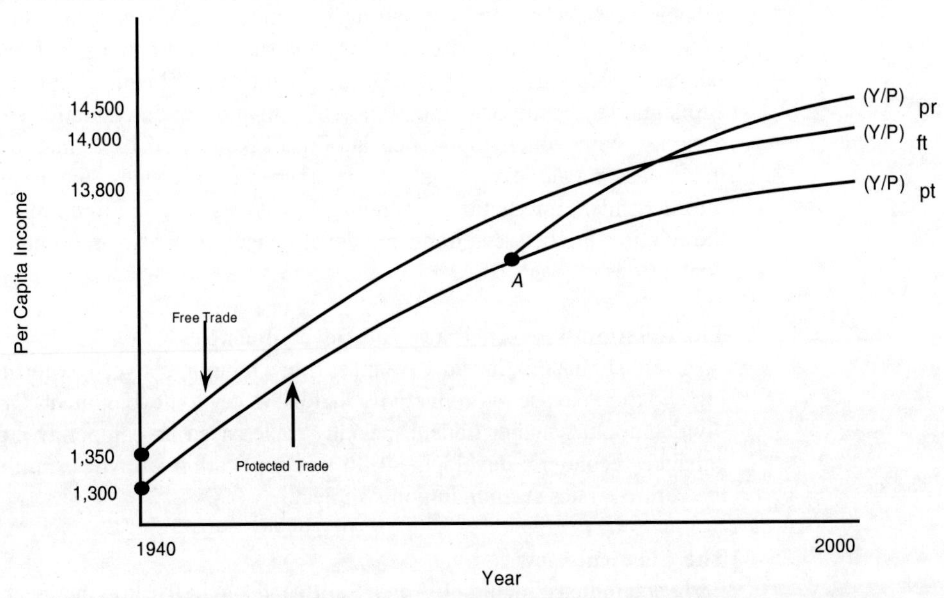

Now what about *growth* as it relates to international trade? Which policy, comparative-advantage (free) trade or some sort of protective tariffs or quotas, would yield the U.S. the greater growth in income during the period from 1940 to 2000? Adherents of the classical economic view say that comparative-advantage trade would give the greatest growth, because a nation that trades according to the principle of comparative advantage allocates its resources to their most productive uses. Thus, the nation is maximizing its productivity. With free trade, as income grows over time, along $(Y/P)_{pt}$ in Figure 16-7, the size of the nation's market grows. There is specialization and division of labor. Capital increases and productivity increases as well.

The growth path with protected trade $(Y/P)_{ft}$, begins at a lower level ($1,300) in 1940 and in 2000 results in a lower level of per capita income ($14,500) as well. This is because even with full employment of its resources, allocation is less efficient and productive with protection than with (comparative advantage) free trade. This is the traditional view of the relationship between trade and development and the reason why many economists espouse free trade as the desired policy objective of developing nations.

Reservations About the Traditional View

There are objections to the above scenario. Some economists feel that a policy of comparative-advantage trade is not, in the long run, the best policy for developing nations. They feel that one cannot prove an explicit relationship between growth and free international trade. Economist Hollis Chenery[4] has been one of the doubters. Chenery, a long time official of the U.S. Agency for International

Development (USAID), has argued that there are five reservations that point to the wisdom of modifying comparative advantage as a policy to enhance economic development for NICs and LDCs:

1. *Factor costs.* The benefits of comparative advantage trade depend on factor markets producing equilibrium prices of resources. This means that the prices reflect "true" relative costs of production. Consider the imperfections in labor or capital markets that one sees in developing countries (for example, the U.S. in the 19th century or in virtually all LDCs today). As development takes place, markets perform more efficiently. There are often dramatic changes in factor costs, and thus in comparative advantage.

2. *Export markets.* Comparative-advantage trade gives rise to specialization. NICs and LDCs frequently come to specialize in producing, and exporting, just one, or a very few, raw materials. Then they must import food and raw materials that they do not produce along with manufactured (and semi-manufactured) products. The result is an unstable economy, which is tied to the fluctuating prices of raw materials. (For example, the world price of copper plunged 65 percent in the early 1970s. Chile, which produces one-eighth of the world's copper, suffered acutely.) You can see that following a policy of comparative-advantage trade makes it hard for an underdeveloped nation to keep its economy stable. In addition, price and income elasticities of demand for these countries' raw materials are low, though data are conflicting. (When the price of copper falls on the world market, and a country's chief export is copper, it cannot make up in export earnings for the drop in price by selling a greater quantity to its industrialized neighbors.) So the terms of trade, the ratio of export prices to import prices, may turn against the exporter of the raw material. The reason is that the developing nation, for example, Chile, must continue to import manufactured goods, whose prices (compared to the price of the exported copper) are now relatively much higher.

Many economists fail to see factors 1 and 2 as being necessarily valid arguments against a developing country's specializing in its comparative advantage raw-material exports. In their view, a developing nation's rate of return on investment in its raw material is greater than the rate of return it *would* receive if it tried to build up other internal projects, such as factories, even after correcting for factor costs and fluctuating world prices.

3. *Productivity changes.* Manufacturing, by its very nature, may enhance the skills of labor and management more than agriculture does. So some economic advisers urge a developing nation to stress manufacturing, even at the expense of comparative-advantage exports. Some of the NICs appear to have done so. Others disagree, asking whether such an advantage exists. Perhaps, they say, the developing nation could make as much headway by concentrating on agriculture as by concentrating on manufacturing. Some of the LDCs are attempting to reemphasize agriculture. All agree, however, that the nation must make allowances for productivity changes in allocating its resources, even if it does not, in the long run, opt for manufacturing as the area of concentration.

4. *Dynamic external economies.* As an industry grows, its costs fall. Or demand for its output increases. As a result, the costs of other industries may also fall. There may, in fact, be a whole group of investments that are profitable *only if*

---

4. Chenery, Hollis B. "Comparative Advantage and Development Policy." *American Economic Review,* 51:1 March, 1961.

they are undertaken together. Comparative advantage, manifested in market signals such as equilibrium prices, does not under these conditions indicate to a nation how it should allocate its resources. Suppose, for example, that the underdeveloped nation increases its investment in industry and realizes certain of these external economies. This will reduce the costs of more than one industry. But, some economists say, perhaps it would have realized even more external economies if it had allocated its capital to comparative-advantage agriculture. For example, it could have built fabricating plants, including expanding the production of the raw material.

5. *Uncertainty and flexibility.* Some economists feel that changes in markets can happen so quickly, and are so hard for policy makers to foresee, that a diversified economy, one that can quickly adjust to changes in supply and demand, is better (and certainly more flexible) than one that relies on a single product, or only a few products. Economists Peter Lindert and C. P. Kindleberger[5] have argued that the terms of trade now discriminate against the raw-material-exporting nations and favor the industrialized nations, because the raw-material-exporting nations lack flexibility. So it seems that a developing nation might be well advised to sacrifice some short-term efficiency in the interests of longer-term flexibility, and a capacity to adjust more rapidly to changes in world supply and demand.

A serious problem with this, though, is that inefficiency often involves creating monopoly privileges and rents that are very difficult to eliminate in the long run. Many examples of this problem can be found in some of the NICs and LDCs. A report in the Wall Street Journal in November 1986 indicated that in Indonesia, a country possessed of many exportable natural resources including oil, export revenues have done little to finance broadly based economic development programs. Principal among the reasons for this has been the substitution of bureaucratic import controls and corruption for free trade. A small oligarchy, including the then President's family, received monopoly rights over imports and control over access to import quotas along with (monopoly) distribution rights to products within the country. Such monopoly pricing might ordinarily attract investors into these industries but investment licensing has prevented that. Higher monopoly prices made Indonesian exports less competitive and reduced export earnings, thereby reducing the ability to finance developmental imports. In the 1990's, a proposal was made in Indonesia to develop an expanded automobile industry. A member of the President's family was given monopoly rights and partly as a result, an efficient competitive automobile industry did not materialize. It is not surprising that bureaucratization and corruption have made the export position of many LDCs less competitive. Indeed, their share of world exports has been falling since the 1950s.

Those With Reservations: Modify Free Trade

Those who have reservations about comparative-advantage trade and its ability to insure or accelerate growth argue for modifications in trade policy. Such modifications may involve significant departures from free trade. Some of the measures adopted include (1) rationing of trade (foreign exchange) earnings either direct controls or through multiple pricing (exchange rate) controls, (2) providing direct subsidies or tax incentives to firms that produce import sub-

---

5. Lindert, Peter H. and Charles P. Kindleberger, *International Economics.* Homewood, Illinois, Richard D. Irwin. 1998.

stitute products, and (3) creating import-export monopoly agencies to obtain lower prices for imports and capture revenue from domestic producers for governmentally determined development uses. To the extent that these noncompetitive market interventions are effective, proponents say that the growth path with protection, $(Y/P)_{Pr}$ in Figure 16-7, can accelerate at some point (point *A* in Figure 16-7), utilizing dynamic externalities and other advantages to propel the nation onto a new path that will generate higher real income at the end of the period ($14,500 versus $13,000) than would be the case with free trade.

Debt Problems of the LDCs and NICs

With the dramatic exception of the "Asian Tigers" (South Korea, Taiwan, Hong Kong, Singapore, Malaysia, Thailand and in recent years China and India), the trade positions of the LDCs and NICs deteriorated in the 1970s and 1980s. Most of the LDCs exports continue in the early twenty first century to consist of primary commodities. For many of them (Indonesia and Venezuela excepted), agricultural primary commodities dominate their exports. Such products have declined in value from more than one-third in 1955 to less than 14 percent in 1986. While those that export fuels benefited (until the mid-1980s) from rising prices, this added, ironically, to the financial problems of others. The dramatic increase in manufactured engineering products has benefited some NICs (especially the "Asian Tigers") while it has had little effect on many LDCs whose manufactured products are not competitive in world markets.

Faced with rising import prices (especially fuels) and softening primary commodity export prices, many NICs and LDCs turned to international capital markets and borrowed heavily in the 1970s. In some instances, the long-term investment credits were wisely invested and resulted in dramatic productivity growth and growth in exports (e.g., South Korea). In other instances, the long-term credits appear to have been less wisely employed, often in the bureaucratic controls and corruption to which we referred earlier. Some countries, especially in Latin America (Brazil, Argentina, Peru) have, at times, appeared to be on the verge of inability to even service the interest payments on their debts (often 50 percent or more of their GDPs). Liberalization of economic policy in the 1980s and 1990s, especially in Argentina and Chile, eased some of these concerns in the 1990's, but serious problems reappeared in 2002, especially in Argentina.

Implications for Trade Policies

For many years, representatives of the LDCs and, to a lesser extent, the NICs, argued for creating a special system of trading and financial preferences for the "developing nations." At times, especially at the United Nations Conference on Trade and Development (UNCTAD), they lobbied for a system under which there would be guaranteed export prices for primary commodities, easier access to markets in industrial nations and long-term capital flows to LDCs and NICs at preferential interest rates. Those pressures, however, seemed to abate until the debt crisis of the 1980s.

In the 1980s and 1990s, we heard again arguments for trade preferences. One NIC (Brazil) temporarily suspended interest payment on its debt. An LDC (Peru) announced it would pay no more than 15 percent of its GDP in interest payments on its external debt. Two American Secretaries of the Treasury argued for more public and private capital flows to LDCs and NICs at below market interest rates. Arguments in support of these policies have reemerged in the early twenty first century. Which shall it be in the future, free trade in commodities services and capital or a "new (non-free trade) order" of trading relationships? As we indicated in the preceding chapter, free trade has gained, but there are real concerns about the future. Economists are not of one mind about which trade policies are consistent with sustained growth and development. Many would agree with Arnold Harberger[6] that free trade, and a minimum of government involvement in domestic and international economic affairs, is preferable. Other economists would agree with Hollis Chenery that free (comparative-advantage-based) trade may be stacked against the LDCs and NICs. For them, government action is called for to encourage the real and financial trading relationships that will permit more and more LDCs to become NICs and for the NICs to become major industrial countries.

Application II: Steel Tariffs

The United States is generally perceived as having a free market economy. Within this structure, competitive markets, self sufficiency, and individualism are highly valued. This is why former President Bush's imposition of tariffs on imported steel-products came as a surprise to many Americans.

On March 5, 2002, the President announced that the U.S. would impose tariffs of up to 30 percent on 15 imported steel products, starting March 20 and lasting 3 years. These import tariffs were placed on the selected products in an effort to protect the U.S. steel industry from lower cost foreign producers.

Some of the President's liberal political opponents criticized the plan for not going far enough. They believed the U.S. steel producers were being treated unfairly by other nations' illegal "dumping" of steel in the U.S., below the cost of production in their home countries. Conservative allies of the President and many economists said this was a step away from the commitment to freer trade that had characterized foreign economic policy of both democratic and republican administrations since World War II.

It appears politics played an important part in President Bush's' decision to impose steel tariffs. The tariffs were good news for several Rust Belt swing states such as Pennsylvania and West Virginia.

These economic sanctions ignited an enormous international controversy. The European Union announced that it planned to immediately impose retaliatory tariffs on the U.S. to be started on June 18, 2002. Many people feared this would inevitably be the start of a major trade war. The retaliatory tariffs never materialized but in the fall of 2003, the World Trade Organization (WTO) stated that dumping was not a significant problem and that these American tariffs represented an illegal barrier to trade.

In late 2003, with trade wars still looming, President Bush decided to lift the tariffs which, by this time, had been drawing criticism at home from several industries, including automobile manufactures and other large steel users. This early withdrawal of the tariffs drew criticism from many steel producers, but was applauded by steel importers and free trade proponents.

The steel tariffs of 2002-2003 demonstrate again not only the tug and pull of our economic relations with other nations but also the clear nexus between economic policy and domestic politics.

---

6. *World Economic Growth: Cases of Developed and Developing Nations*. San Francisco: Institute for Contemporary Studies, 1984.

SUMMING UP

1. In this chapter, we looked at a market economy as one that is open, or that trades (exports, imports) with the rest of the world. For the U.S., international trade has grown in its importance to its economy.

2. Trade consists of *exports*, commodities and services sold to other nations, and *imports*, commodities and services purchased from other nations. Exports and imports consist of both *visible items* (commodities) and *invisible items* (services).

3. The *commodity balance of trade* measures the difference between commodity exports and commodity imports (X - M).

4. *Net foreign trade (NFT)* is the commodity balance (X – M) difference between exports (X) and imports (M), plus net services (service exports – service imports):

$$NFT = (X - M) + S$$

Foreign trade is important, even to a diversified economy such as that of the U.S.

5. NFT can exert a significant macroeconomic influence on the level of income and employment, the demand for goods, services and the creation of jobs. This is so even in the U.S., in which exports (and NFT) form a smaller percentage of output than they do in many other major trading nations. (However, in dollar volume, the U.S. is by far the largest international trader and the percentage of its output made up of exports has nearly doubled since 1980.)

6. Between 1960 and 1980, the U.S. usually ran a small trade surplus or trade deficit (X < M). Since1983, the U.S. has run up increasingly large trade deficits that seem to be due to exchange rate changes and the income taste of Americans for imported goods.

7. Trade is important to the U.S. for several reasons: (a) Trade constitutes an important part of demand for U.S. output, and hence demand for labor (that means more jobs) and other resources. (b) Demand that results from trade enables many U.S. industries to operate more efficiently and on a larger scale. (c) The percentage of U.S. GDP represented by trade has grown in recent years. This reflects a greater interdependence with other nations. (d) The U.S. needs imports of raw materials, such as certain key minerals, in order to operate many industries.

8. *Autarky* (economic self-sufficiency), although it may be technologically possible for the U.S., is economically unwise, because the U.S., by specializing in items in which it has a comparative advantage, can realize gains from trade.

9. *Absolute advantage* refers to a nation's ability to produce all of a good it consumes more efficiently than any other nation. (Some nations may have an absolute advantage in all goods.) *Comparative advantage* refers to a nation's being more efficient in producing some good or goods than in producing others (even though the nation may also be absolutely more efficient than its neighbors in producing everything).

10. At any given time, nations have certain production possibilities. These are reflected in their PP curves (assuming full employment and a given technology level). So long as any two nations have different internal rates of exchange (trade-offs) between producing the same 2 goods, it is mutually beneficial for each to specialize in producing the good in which it has a comparative advantage.

11. By specializing in producing those things in which it has a comparative advantage, and by trading what it does not consume to other nations for goods in which *they* have a comparative advantage, a trading nation can have more goods to consume (the consumption-possibilities curves will be above the domestic PP curve). Differences in tastes and preferences of consumers in different countries also create utility gains from trade.

12. Comparative advantage derives from (a) different endowments of natural resources, (b) different physical features (climate, harbors, and so on), (c) different states of development of markets (for example, some nations have well-developed capital markets), and (d) different supplies of labor.

13. Comparative advantages change, sometimes dramatically. The U.S. began with a comparative advantage in land-intensive commodities, which it exported. Today it has a comparative advantage in capital-intensive as well as land-intensive goods.

14. If nations run into a certain level of increasing costs as they specialize, the specialization may not be complete. That is they will produce a wider variety of goods. (For example, Honduras will produce some of its own tractors, the U.S. will produce some of its own bananas.)

15. Some people disapprove of foreign trade because of the unemployment that occurs when resources (especially labor) must be reallocated as a result of that trade. To economists, this is not a compelling argument against an open economy. They point to the macroeconomic tools that can be used to increase employment, and the microeconomic tools that can be used to reallocate resources (for example, job retraining).

16. Comparative advantage depends on competition. When competition does not exist, or when nations with equal advantage do not trade competitively with each other, some of the benefits of comparative-advantage trade are lost.

17. Trading nations that are burdened by *externalities* may produce and trade too much or too little for comparative advantage to work. Prices for goods exported should accurately reflect relative scarcity of resources.

18. The theory of comparative advantage depends on relative prices reflecting relative scarcities of resources in each nation. If prices do not reflect these scarcities, an international misallocation of resources occurs.

19. The major obstacle to free trade is *protectionism,* the effort to protect farmers and industries from the competition from lower-priced goods imported from foreign countries when there is free international trade.

20. The two major means of protectionism are (a) *tariffs,* which are taxes levied on imported goods, and (b) *quotas,* which are limitations on the quantity of imports.

21. Tariffs and other trade restrictions reduce the supply of goods and raise the prices charged consumers. They may also add to the monopoly power of domestic producers, and they may reduce the number of good substitutes available to consumers, making domestic demand for a good more inelastic. One thing in their favor is that they produce revenue for the importing governments.

22. The burden of a tariff consists of a *consumer burden,* that part of the tariff paid by consumers in a higher price, and the *producer burden*, that part paid by sellers in a lower net price and reduced sales. The more inelastic is the demand for the imported good, the greater is the consumer burden. The more elastic is the demand for the imported good, the greater is the producer burden.

23. Quotas do not produce revenue for governments. Otherwise the effects of quotas are similar to those of tariffs. They reduce supply, raise prices to consumers, and enhance the monopolistic position of domestic producers. The most extreme form of quota is an *embargo,* an absolute prohibition against importing a certain good or trading with a certain country. Export quotas are sometimes assigned not only to protect domestic firms but to favor foreign countries and firms. Voters (consumers) may not resist the higher prices of these quotas because of rational ignorance.

24. Some arguments in favor of protectionism are as follows: (a) the *infant-industry argument* (firms that are new and small need to be protected until they are large enough to compete with more established firms in foreign industries); (b) the *national-security argument* (uncertainty of foreign supply, plus need for a reliable source of military hardware, means that domestic producers must be protected, even if they are inefficient); (c) the *cheap-foreign-labor argument* (domestic firms that must pay high wages should be protected against imports from countries in which wages are low); (d) the *macroeconomic-employment argument* (recessions and depressions can be "exported" if a nation puts up barriers to trade that reduce imports without reducing exports); (e) retaliation for "unfair" trading practices (make them trade fairly) and; (f) protection of declining industries (help such industries temporarily) during phasing out.

25. Economists generally reject these arguments that favor protectionism, with the exception of the national-security argument, for which there is little objective basis for evaluation. However, even in the case of protection given to industries producing goods needed for national security, economists feel that there should be direct subsidies instead of tariffs, so that the costs of protection are clearly identified.

26. Beggar-thy-neighbor tariffs are likely to be ineffective, even counterproductive. When one nation sets up high tariffs, other nations retaliate. As a result, without specialized trade, nations have fewer goods and services to consume, even when they have full employment.

27. In 1947, the world's major trading nations created GATT, the *General Agreement on Tariffs and Trade*. By 2013, it had grown to over 159 nations dedicated to liberalizing trade.

28. The Uruguay round of GATT talks (1994) created a new trade organization, the *World Trade Organization (WTO)* which seeks to further increase trade liberalization in both developing countries and industrial nations.

29. Regional trade agreements have grown since World War II. They have taken the form of (a) common markets, (b) custom unions, and (c) free trade agreements.

30. *Common markets* provide for free trade, common tariffs, and free movement of capital and labor. *Customs unions* provide for common tariffs and free trade. *Free trade agreements* provide only for free trade.

31. The future of free trade is being clouded by (a) the growth of regional trade agreements and (b) the re-emergence of state-directed trade.

32. Major free trade arrangements include the European Union-European Free Trade Association (EU-EFTA) Agreement and NAFTA (North American Free Trade Association).

33. Policy makers today must face a major question: Can international trade provide the primary basis for the economic development of poor nations? Evidence since the 1960s of growth of the newly industrialized countries (NICs) seemed to suggest yes.

34. Views differ as to the relation between trade and development. Classical economists (Adam Smith, David Ricardo) felt that comparative-advantage trade was essential to increasing output and maximizing the wealth of a nation.

35. Much of the debate over the relation between trade and development involves the distinction between the static principles of comparative-advantage and the dynamic principles of growth.

36. One can show that, in a static sense (that is, at a point in time), a nation can maximize its output if it allocates all its resources to their most productive uses. However, there is no certainty that if a nation does this, the growth of its output over a period of time will be greater than it would have been if it had departed, selectively, from comparative-advantage trade.

37. Those who argue for restricting comparative advantage, as the basis for trade, argue on the basis of: (a) *Factor costs.* Imperfections in the factor markets of underdeveloped nations cause their factor costs not to reflect their real relative cost. (b) *Export markets.* Comparative-advantage specialization on the part of the poor nations may result in unstable economies. Low income and price elasticities of demand for raw-material exports may turn the terms of trade against the nation that specializes. (c) *Productivity changes.* In an economy based on manufacturing, the skills of labor and management increase and diversify more rapidly than they do in an economy based on agriculture. (d) *Dynamic external economies.* Several investments, a whole package of them, may have to be made simultaneously in order to make them succeed, or pay off. This is more likely to happen in an industry-based economy than in an agriculture-based economy. (e) *Uncertainty and flexibility.* A diversified economy is more flexible, and can adjust more readily to changes in supply and demand, than an economy that specializes in a few raw-material exports. Thus, it can better resist the effects of worsening terms of trade.

38. Economists generally discount points (a) and (b), from the above paragraph as reasons to abandon comparative-advantage trade. However, they should take into account factors (c), (d), and (e) when they are working out trade policy.

39. Deviations from free trade seem often to give rise to bureaucratic red tape in LDCs and to monopoly grants and corruption. These impediments to productivity growth raise prices and make LDC exports less competitive in world markets

40. Faced with rising import (especially fuel) prices in the 1970s and falling primary commodity prices, LDCs and some NICs borrowed heavily in world capital markets. Where the capital was not wisely invested, a "debt crisis" arose in which threats to default or limit payments created serious problems in financial markets.

41. For years LDCs and NICs have argued for a "new international economic order" with restrictions on free trade involving guaranteed export prices, easier access to markets, and below market interest rates for capital.

42. Economists generally espouse free trade. Many, probably most American economists, argue that free trade is preferable to trade restrictions as a means to create productivity growth and minimize the distortions of bureaucracy and corruption. Some, however, argue that free trade is stacked against LDCs and NICs and that trade preferences should be considered.

KEY TERMS

Absolute advantage, comparative advantage
Autarky
"Beggar-thy-neighbor" argument
Burden of a tariff (consumer burden, producer burden)
Cheap foreign labor argument
Commodity balance of trade
Common markets
Customs unions
Exports, imports
Free trade agreements
General Agreement on Tariffs and Trade (GATT)
Infant-industry argument
National security argument
Net foreign trade
Open economy, closed economy
Protectionism
Rational ignorance
Tariffs, quotas, embargoes
Terms of trade
Visible items, invisible items of trade
World Trade Organization (WTO)

QUESTIONS

1. What is meant by the term "open economy?" "Closed economy?"

2. What imported goods do you often buy? How would you be affected if the U.S. restricted international trade or stopped trading with other nations entirely?

3. Why are most production-possibilities curves *not* straight lines? What happens to international specialization when such curves are truly curves?

4. Consider the following hypothetical production-possibilities schedules for the U.S. and Honduras:

United States		Honduras	
Units of Tractors	Units of Bananas	Units of Tractors	Units of Bananas
50	0	0	100
40	5	5	80
30	10	10	60
20	15	15	40
10	20	20	20
0	25	25	0

a. Plot the production-possibilities curves.
b. Is there a basis for mutually beneficial trade between the two countries?
c. What will determine the terms of trade that are established between the two countries?

5. Based on the arguments advanced in this chapter, why, in your opinion, did the beggar-thy-neighbor tariff (Smoot-Hawley tariff) of 1930 perhaps slow the American recovery between 1930 and 1934?

6. What happens to the trade from either developed or underdeveloped nations when monopoly export and import agencies are set up? Why?

7. Evaluate the following statements:

a. "Free trade forces domestic producers to pay attention to consumer tastes and preferences."
b. "Free trade would be desirable, but we can't afford to rely on the Russians, or the French, or even the British, for our military hardware."
c. "High tariffs to create more jobs will work for the U.S. because other, less powerful nations wouldn't dare retaliate."
d. "In several recent years, the U.S. has run a large commodity trade deficit. What we should do to counteract this is to buy less from abroad."
e. "In several recent years, the U.S. has run a large commodity trade deficit. We don't need to worry, though, because exchange rate changes will eliminate the deficit."

8. In the following graph, we see the demand for and supply of an imported good. D_d is the domestic demand, S_d is the domestic supply. S_{ft} is the supply with free trade of both domestic producers and imports, and S_{at} is the supply after a tariff is imposed.

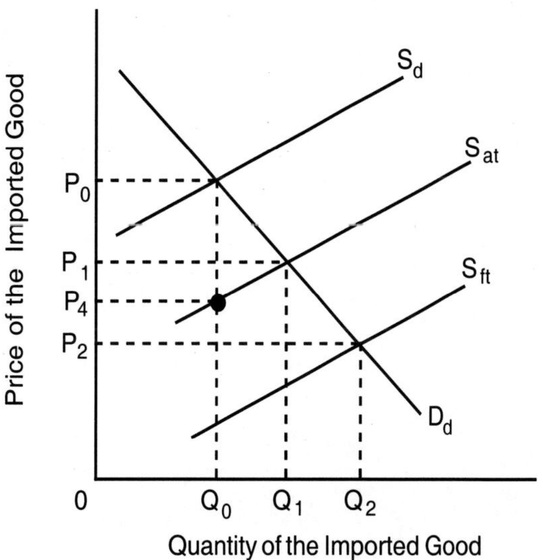

a. What is the price and quantity of the good without trade? With free trade? After a tariff is imposed?

b. Who bears most of the burden of the tariff, consumers or importing firms? What is the burden of each?

c. Who benefits from the tariff? What is the price benefit?

9. What are the differences between common markets, customs unions and free trade agreements? Which of these is the most comprehensive form of trade agreement.

10. What was the basic role of GATT? What is the basic objective of the WTO?

11. What are the major threats to further world trade liberalization?

12. What are the differences between the static view of comparative advantage and the dynamic view of growth?

13. If you were recommending economic policy to a developing low-income country, at what point would you recommend that it follow a policy of comparative-advantage trade, and at what point would you recommend that it sacrifice a certain amount of efficiency in the use of its resources in order to achieve more growth?

14. Consider an underdeveloped country (for example, Chile), and suppose that it primarily exports one raw material (for example, copper). How can low price and income elasticities of demand for copper affect Chile's export earnings, its ability to import other necessary goods, and its terms of trade?

Chapter 17: *Paying for International Trade*

In the previous chapter we developed the logic of international trade and saw why, based on comparative advantage, nations that engage in trade are better off than those that practice autarky. As a part of that same argument, we saw further evidence that the freer trade is, the greater are its benefits when compared with protectionist trade practices. Now we will examine the role of money in international trade.

It is true, of course, that nations can engage in barter or, in other words, exchange goods for goods. If they do so, there is no need for money. Occasionally, this practice is still carried out, usually when trade between two governments is involved. Like domestic exchanges, however, nearly all international exchanges of goods and services require an exchange of money. A key difference, though, is that international exchanges involve more than one currency. For international trade to work smoothly requires not only markets to price the goods and services that are exported and imported, but also markets to establish the exchange values of the different currencies used in that trade. The latter are called **foreign exchange markets**, or markets in which the exchange values of different domestic currencies are established. Let's now see why these foreign exchange markets are so important to world trade. Then we will see how they work to establish exchange rates.

Foreign Exchange Markets
International money markets in which the exchange values of domestic currencies are established.

www.x-rates.com
For more information on currency exchange visit this web site.

An Example of Trade Involving Different Domestic Currencies

Suppose that the American Steel Company agrees to sell $500,000 worth of rolled steel to the Japanese Automobile Company. Suppose also that the *rate of exchange*, the price at which Japanese yen can be exchanged for American dollars, is 100 yen per dollar. (Later we will see how this rate is established.) The Japanese importer, in other words, owes 50 million yen (500,000 x 100) to the American Steel Company. Let's follow this transaction through the banking system in both countries:

1. Japanese Auto writes a check on its Tokyo bank for 50 million yen, and mails the check to American Steel.

2. American Steel cannot pay its workers and creditors in Japanese yen; it needs dollars. Therefore, it sells the check to a New York bank that has a correspondent relation with a Japanese bank.

3. Now American Steel has a $500,000 deposit in the New York bank. The New York bank deposits the check from Japanese Auto in its correspondent bank in Tokyo and becomes the owner of a claim to 50 million Japanese yen.

Note. Nearly all of this is now accomplished by electronic transfers. In other words, an American company's exports of a commodity create a demand for dollars. When this demand is fulfilled, more foreign currency is available to people in the U.S. who will demand it to pay for their own (Japanese) imports.

When a U.S. company imports something, the process is reversed. The American company must obtain a supply of the currency of the country from which it is buying the goods. The supply comes from foreign currencies that American firms have earned through their exports. Thus, Japanese yen are available to pay for U.S. imports of Toyotas because Americans have exported wheat (and many other commodities) to Japan. The very important point to remember is this: *In order to be able to pay for its imports, a country must also export or sell its goods to other countries.*

A Workable International Monetary System

This two-country illustration, although it is correct, makes the financing of international trade seem simpler than it is. Financing trade is quite complex, and involves intricate relationships between the domestic economies of more than a hundred independent nations, each with its own domestic currency, that exchange goods and services. In short, it involves an elaborate international monetary system.

Let's examine the characteristics of a workable money system in an *international* economy. One feature that is essential is that the system expedite the trading of goods and services. (After all, barter, as we noted earlier, is no more feasible in international trade than it is in domestic trade.) By what criteria is a workable system of payments judged?

1. *The system must strike a reasonable balance between stability and growth in international trade and stability and growth in the individual nations that engage in it.* The economy of the U.S. (or Britain, or any other nation) should not have to absorb large shocks to its own employment and investment situation in order to accommodate changes in its international trade position, or that of other nations. This doesn't mean that nations need not make long-term adjustments in their domestic economies as their trade positions change, only that these adjustments should be gradual and not overly disruptive. The present set of monetary arrangements, although it is a great improvement over the gold standard in these respects, may still force some countries, especially those with large external debts denominated in other currencies, to make major adjustments in their internal economies in order to handle their international payments. This is a problem for many less-developed countries (LDCs) and newly industrialized countries (NICs).

Essential to this requirement of reasonable balance is consistency of action. Once the rules for international financial transactions have been made, all the participating nations must play by the rules. The system may force a nation to make adjustments that conflict with its political and economic objectives, or even threaten the political survival of its government. (For example, it may have to raise interest rates, lower investment, and create unemployment.) If the system demands too many adjustments of this sort, nations may not adhere to it consistently. Then the system may become unstable.

2. *The system of payments must be seen to be equitable.* It is hard for nations to agree on how the costs and benefits of a system are to be distributed so that there is equity for all. Many nations, especially the developing ones, feel that present international financial arrangements are inequitable. They claim that they do not have enough control over decisions about the availability of capital and credit, and about who is to bear the costs of financing. At the same time, the system must facilitate the repayment of capital whose movement is essential to the finance of exports and imports. Proposals for further capital flows to the LDCs and even some NICs must incorporate this principle.

3. *The system of payments must be efficient,* just as any other system of markets must. The efficiency of an international system of payments is measured in terms of the effect of that system on the cost of trade. An efficient system encourages trade by making the means of financing exports and imports readily available and low cost, and by reducing the risks of trade (unanticipated changes in exchange rates, for example).

Let's now look at how foreign exchange markets work. Fundamentally, they work like other markets to establish equilibrium or market clearing results. Like other markets, their results depend on their competitiveness or lack of competitiveness.

Foreign Exchange Markets: Determining Equilibrium Exchange Rates

Equilibrium Exchange Rates
Rates of exchange between currencies that clear currency markets or that eliminate excess supply or excess demand.

An **equilibrium exchange rate** is the rate of exchange between two currencies that clears the market or eliminates excess supply or demand. This rate will change only as the supply of or demand for the currencies changes. Like any other price, the exchange rate may be established in one of two ways: (1) It may be freely floating, that is established by impersonal market forces (competition), or (2) It may be fixed, that is, administered (determined by certain individuals or agencies). We will illustrate both approaches in this section.

Freely Floating Exchange Rates

Freely Floating Exchange Rate
A competitive rate of exchange, one that is free to move to any equilibrium level that will clear currency markets.

Let's take as an example the exchange rate between the dollar and the deutsche mark (the currency of the Federal Republic of Germany). With a **freely floating exchange rate**, the exchange rate is established through the interplay of supply and demand. Figure 17-1 illustrates this interplay. The curve D_0 is the American demand for marks. It slopes downward because as the dollar price of marks falls (as a dollar buys more marks), German goods (Volkswagens, Rhine wine, cameras, binoculars, and so on) become cheaper for Americans to buy. When that happens, the quantity demanded by Americans of German goods increases and Americans demand more marks, so they can pay for those goods. The demand for marks, in other words, is a *derived demand*, a demand derived from the demand for German imports.

The curve S_1 is the supply of marks. It slopes upward because as the dollar price of marks rises (as marks buy more dollars), American exports become cheaper for Germans to buy. When that happens, Germans increase the quantity demanded of imported American goods and demand more dollars, so they can pay for those goods (cars, computers, wheat, and so on). The Germans pay for their purchases with checks drawn on German banks.

Figure 17-1
Foreign Exchange Market with a Freely Floating (Competitive) Exchange Rate (dollars versus marks)

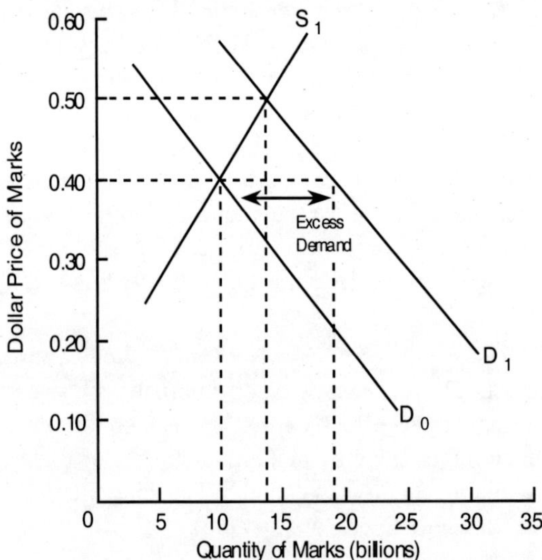

In Figure 17-1, D_0 represents the initial American demand for marks. It is derived from the American demand for German goods and services. The supply of marks is S_1 and slopes upward because, as the mark/dollar rate rises, American goods are cheaper in Germany and more marks are supplied to pay for these German imports. With a competitive exchange rate market, the equilibrium (market clearing) rate is 0.40 where the quantity supplied of marks equals the quantity demanded of marks. Ten billion marks are exchanged. If a disequilibrium occurs, a new equilibrium exchange rate must be established. An increase in the demand for marks (D_0 to D_1) leaves excess demand at a rate of.40 dollars to the mark (2.5 dollars per mark); to eliminate the excess, demand requires a new exchange rate of.50 (2 dollars to the mark). At the new exchange rate, there is no excess demand or supply.

Since the exchange rate is free to seek its market level, the equilibrium level is the one at which quantity supplied equals quantity demanded. We see in Figure 17-1 a foreign exchange market, the market in which exchange rates and exchange rate charges are established. Here, equilibrium is established at 0.40, which is 2.5 marks to the dollar ($^1/.40 = 2.5$). In other words, a mark will buy four-tenths of a dollar. The equilibrium quantity of marks in Figure 17-1 is 10 billion.

Now what if a disequilibrium, a variation in supply or demand that throws things off balance, develops in this market? Suppose that Detroit automakers, in a surprise move, announce a big increase in prices. (If the price increase had been anticipated, it would have been reflected in D_0, the original demand for marks.) Higher prices for Detroit-made cars mean that German cars are now cheaper by comparison. As a result, the demand for marks shifts upward to D_1 (people want to buy more Volkswagens and Mercedes Benzes). But now there is disequilibrium. At the present exchange rate (0.40), only 10 billion marks are supplied, but foreign-exchange buyers now want nearly 20 billion.

When the exchange rate is freely floating, the excess demand of 10 million marks is taken care of by dealers in foreign exchange markets who bid up the dollar price of the mark. (There are foreign exchange markets and dealers in nearly every major city in the world.) The mark then costs more to buy. When the rate of exchange rises to 0.50 ($1/0.50 = 2$ marks to the dollar), excess demand is eliminated. Remember that the additional quantity of marks supplied is forthcoming because, as the mark appreciates in value, Germans buy more of relatively cheaper American goods (ironically, they even buy more of the now relatively cheaper American cars if exchange rate changes more than offset the original price increases), thus creating claims to marks by American exporters.

Advantages and Disadvantages of Floating Exchange Rates

Let's look at the advantages and disadvantages of allowing the value of currencies to float freely. The *advantages* are those of a competitive market: (1) The system responds quickly to changes in supply and demand. (2) Disequilibria in payments are readily resolved; for example, the excess demand that appeared when Americans wanted to buy more German goods (Figure 17-1).

The *disadvantages* of the system are as follows: (1) The rate of exchange may be very unstable. This instability may inhibit trade, because a buyer who orders an imported article will soon stop buying if large changes in the exchange rate make the article cost more when it is delivered than when it is ordered. (2) Some countries depend heavily on international trade to provide jobs and investment capital (especially the LDCs and NICs, in which the foreign-trade sectors dominate the economies). In these countries, wide swings in exchange rates can cause very destabilizing changes in exports and imports. (3) A nation's financial terms of trade can change quickly and sharply. The terms of trade, recall, refer to the ratio of export prices to import prices. In a sense, they measure the value of exports a nation must have in order to maintain a given level of imports. Wide variations in the values of currencies can cause either variations in imports or disruptive efforts to adjust exports. In either case, destabilization may result.

Freely floating exchange rates have been common since 1971 with President Nixon's decision to "float" the U.S. dollar. Some economists have reservations about such fluctuations. Arthur Burns[1], former chairman of the Federal Reserve Board, gave four reasons for his skepticism: (1) Freely floating rates are an academic dream that cause people to demand protection through government controls or government intervention in the money market. (2) Floating rates may lead to political friction. If other nations suspect that the rates are being manipulated, they will take retaliatory steps. (3) Floating rates increase people's uncertainty and thus inhibit both commodity trade and capital flows. (4) Floating rates make it harder for the government to implement suitable domestic fiscal and monetary policies.

Arbitrage
A practice under which exchange dealers buy currencies in one market and sell them at a higher price in another.

Other economists (such as Milton Friedman[2]) believe that fears such as these about the dangers of floating rates are exaggerated. They say the following: (1) Where the policy of floating rates has been tried, there have not been enormous swings in rates. The apparent reason for this is that speculators in foreign exchange, those who engage in **arbitrage** or who buy and sell currencies in different markets to make profits, stabilize the market. (2) Although freely floating rates do increase business uncertainty, this is thought by many economists to be a price worth paying in exchange for the above-mentioned benefits of the system.

---

1. In Baldwin, Robert E. and David Richardson, Jr. (eds). *International Trade and Finance Readings*. Boston, Little Brown. 1981.
2. Friedman, Milton, "Outdoing Smoot-Hawley." *The Wall Street Journal*, April 20, 1987.

Fixed Exchange Rates

Fixed Exchange Rates
A system in which the rates of exchange between currencies are established by government and not allowed to vary with changing currency market conditions.

By contrast with floating exchange rates, some rates of exchange between currencies are based on **fixed exchange rates**, a system of payments involving agreed-upon relationships between the world's currencies. Even today, some nations fix the rate at which their currencies exchange. Some have a two-tiered system with fixed rates for some transactions and flexible rates for others. For much of the post-World War II period fixed exchange rates prevailed. To see how a fixed rate system works, refer again to Figure 17-1. Suppose that at the fixed rate of 2.5 marks to the dollar, there is an excess demand of 9 billion marks. The U.S. and German governments (perhaps dealing through an international agency) are committed to maintaining the 2.5:1 rate. The additional marks come from somewhere. Since the market will not supply them at the fixed rate, governments or international agencies must. (Note that this is hypothetical: the dollar/mark exchange rate is, in fact, not fixed and has not been since 1971.)

International Reserves
Assets available to central banks and other agencies that are accepted in payment of international debts.

The additional marks can come only from **international reserves**, assets available to central banks and other agencies that are acceptable in payment of international debts. (In the past it was gold.) It is possible, of course, that the German central bank (the Deutsche Bundesbank) might lend the marks to the Federal Reserve (Fed) System. The Fed, in turn, would make them available to American commercial banks. Alternatively, there might be an international agency such as the *International Monetary Fund (IMF)*, which has reserves of dollars, deutsche marks, Swiss francs, British pounds, claims to gold, and all other major currencies. The IMF makes loans to the Fed and through the Fed to our commercial banks.

Note: Fixed exchange rates require large currency reserves. In the face of growing world trade, they require *increasing reserves,* if banks are to be able to take care of fluctuations in demand for currencies.

The chief advantage of fixed exchange rates is that they lend stability to world trade. Fixed rates reduce uncertainty about international prices. If you want to buy a German car or import German machinery, and you know that the banking system is committed to a 2.5:1 exchange rate, you can plan your purchase even if the goods are not actually delivered to you until months later. This stability provides a favorable climate for the growth of trade, especially for long-term capital flows.

Even fixed exchange rates are not necessarily fixed forever. For example, the German government may decide that subsidizing German exports to the U.S. is not in Germany's best interests. The U.S. government may decide that at the 2.5:1 rate its exports to Germany are too low. The international reserves needed to finance this trade imbalance may run dangerously low. The countries, by mutual agreement, may change the rate to 2 marks to the dollar (which will equilibrate the exchange market shown in Figure 17-1).

Exchange Rate Market Intervention

Managed or "Dirty" Float
A system in which exchange rates are "pegged" or allowed by central banks to move within certain limits.

We have posed the exchange rate policy choice of governments as either: (1) allow exchange rates to float freely (flexible rates) or (2) fix rates and adjust them occasionally by mutual agreement (fixed rates). For both political and economic reasons, governments, including that of the U.S. have not been willing consistently to follow one path or the other. When they have not, they have chosen to intervene but only selectively in exchange markets. In doing so, they have created a system of managed exchange rates on what is often called the **managed or "dirty" float**. Essentially, it means that the Fed allows the dollar to float but only within certain "pegs" or limits. While these pegs are rarely clearly defined, their expectation does send a (poorly defined) signal to exchange rate dealers about the limits of rate changes.

Why, in the absence of fixed exchange rates, do governments intervene in this way? It is sometimes said that nations intervene out of national pride to keep their currency high and stable in value against other currencies. There is no evidence to support this and it seems that there are much stronger reasons that can be shown for intervention. Consider the case of the U.S. dollar, which is a key currency in international finance. Much of the reserves of America's trading partners (reserves of their central banks) consist of holdings of U.S. dollars. Thus, when the U.S. dollar declines sharply, so do the value of the assets of those banks (Bank of Japan, Deutsche Bundesbank, etc.). The Fed then, perhaps under pressure from our allies, may intervene if the dollar drops too sharply. The U.S. dollar is sometimes the only currency accepted in payment for certain international transactions. OPEC, for example, accepts only U.S. dollars in payment for its oil exports. If the U.S. dollar rises sharply against the pound sterling or French franc, those countries must spend more to buy the dollars to pay for their oil imports. Again, the Fed may intervene to moderate the growth in the exchange value of the dollar.

Market intervention by different governments may, of course, be contradictory. When the dollar falls against other currencies, U.S. exports become cheaper and the Fed may do nothing to support its currency. This was generally the case in the late 1980s, because stimulating export growth was U.S. national policy. Other nations such as Japan, however, saw the dollar falling against their currencies and their own exports becoming more expensive. To avert a decline in its export industries, Japan intervened at times to buy dollars and keep the yen from falling further against the dollar. It is not surprising in view of the potential for conflicting interventionist policies that there are numerous meetings and other efforts by central banks to agree on exchange rates.

Adjusting Economies to Fluctuations in the Exchange Rate

One can trace the origin of an exchange-rate disequilibrium (such as the excess demand in Figure 17-1) to changes in economic conditions in the exporting and importing nations. Figure 17-2 gives you the situation at a glance.Suppose that the dollar-mark exchange market is initially in equilibrium. The demand for marks is D_0, supply is S_1, and the exchange rate is 2.5:1 (that is, the mark is equal to 0.40 dollars). Ten billion marks are exchanged. Now, suppose that inflation hits the U.S. The rapidly rising prices of American goods make German imports relatively cheaper. As a result, American demand for marks to finance purchases of German goods rises to D_1. At the old exchange rate, there is an excess demand of 6.5 billion marks. If the dollar-mark rate is *not* freely floating, and if there is no system of international reserves to finance the payments deficit at existing exchange rates, two things may happen.

Means of Adjustment

Exchange Controls
A system by which a nation rations foreign currency when there is excess demand for that currency.

1. Excess demand may be treated as a rationing problem. People demand more marks than the amount of marks available at the going exchange rate. So to "ration" marks, a nation might set up a system of **exchange controls** (perhaps an agency acting through its central bank). The agency could establish priorities to determine who should get the available marks. In effect, this would mean determining what kinds and quantities of German goods could be imported into the U.S. (perhaps Volkswagens, but no Mercedes Benzes, or perhaps machinery, but no cars at all). Presumably, these priorities would reflect certain national goals.

The main advantage of this approach to managing fluctuations in the exchange rate is that it enables countries to hold to a fixed exchange rate (with the aforementioned stability of trade), while at the same time ensuring that national import priorities are consistent with domestic economic priorities. The main disadvantages are that it does not allow the market to work, and that it imposes public tastes and preferences in place of private ones. (No matter how much you might like to import a Mercedes, you cannot, because the government regards it as more important to the country to import farm machinery.) It can also lead to corruption through granting special access to foreign exchange on the part of those favored by the government.

1. Neither the U.S. nor other major trading nations use exchange controls, although many LDCs do. Low-income countries must import much of their capital. They do not have the domestic markets to provide it, and their governments do not wish to import expensive consumer goods at the same time.

2. The deficit in payments (or the excess demand) shown in Figure 17-2 may be taken care of by adjustments in income and employment in the economy of the country that is demanding "too much" foreign currency.

Deflation
A general lowering of prices in an economy.

In this case, inflation in the U.S. is causing the excess demand for marks. To counter this demand, the U.S. may use the macroeconomic adjustment of **deflation**, which is a general lowering of prices. To accomplish this, the government may reduce aggregate demand by increasing taxes. It may also reduce government spending and raise interest rates. Or it may adopt any of the combinations of means that you will/or have already learned in your Macroeconomics course. (Of course, a tax on imports could correct the relative imbalance in prices between the two countries, but this would be at the price of free trade.)

Figure 17-2
Exchange-Rate Equilibrium Maintained Through Macroeconomic Adjustment

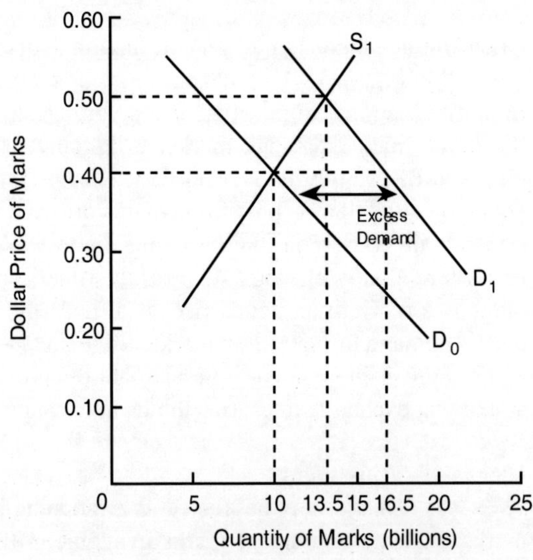

In Figure 17-2, the dollar-mark exchange rate is in equilibrium with demand D_0 and supply S_1. The equilibrium exchange rate is 0.40 dollars per mark (or it takes 2.5 marks to buy a dollar). As a result of U.S. inflation, rising domestic prices make German imports cheaper and the demand for marks increases to D_1 to finance additional imports. At the new demand D_1 there is excess demand for marks at the old rate of 0.40. With a freely floating rate, the exchange rate would rise to 0.50 where quantity demanded of marks would equal quantity supplied. To maintain the old (fixed) exchange rate of 0.40, governments would (1) have to ration the exchange available (10 billion marks) to prevent the excess demand (6.5 billion marks) from raising the rate, or (2) deflate the American economy, reducing the total demand for imports and reducing the demand for marks back to D_0.

If the U.S. follows a deflationary policy and aggregate demand does decrease, money incomes will certainly decrease also. Now let's assume that the demand for imports has a strongly positive income elasticity. (Americans, like many people, have a strong taste for imported goods.) Demand for imports, and for German marks, will fall. If the decline is strong enough, D_1 in Figure 17-2 may shift back to D_0, and the dollar-mark ratio may again find its equilibrium at 2.5:1.

The main advantage of tying a nation's economy to its exchange-rate position is that it practically guarantees stable rates of exchange. (Remember that stable exchange rates are desirable because they enhance trade and make possible longer term planning for trade.) The main disadvantage of such a policy is that the nation has to pay a price for this stability of exchange rates and equilibrium of payments. Most economists believe this price is out of proportion to its worth. It is truly letting "the tail wag the dog." In the example here, the U.S. would have to deflate its economy deliberately, with all the effects it would have on income distribution, jobs, savings, and investment. Even if the U.S. had been at full employment before the government introduced the fiscal and monetary measures necessary to bring about deflation, there would soon be some significant changes in prices, incomes, and employment. But suppose that the U.S. had been suffering significant unemployment coupled with inflation, as it did in the early 1980s, and the government came along and put through these measures. Then, deflating the economy would just add to the unemployment problem, thus curing an external problem by worsening an internal one. Few countries would be willing to pay such a price for stability of exchange rates, though some LDCs and NICs have done so as part of a program to lower inflation and refinance external debts.

The Gold Standard

Gold Standard
An international system under which currencies are valued in terms of gold content. Nations are obligated to exchange their currencies for that amount of gold.

During the nineteenth and much of the twentieth centuries, the system of fixed exchange rates was tied to the **gold standard**. The gold standard provided for the rates of exchange of most of the world's currencies for about 50 years before World War I, in varying degrees until the Great Depression of the 1930s and, to a lesser extent, to 1971. Under the freely convertible gold standard, nations could be sure of two things:

1. Each trading nation permitted unrestricted exports and imports of gold.

2. Each nation defined its own currency in terms of a specific quantity of gold, and guaranteed to convert any claims to that currency into gold at the defined rate.

Under the gold standard, each currency was defined to be worth so many grains of gold. For example, the German mark might be defined as 10 grains of gold and the American dollar as 25 grains of gold. Therefore, the dollar would be worth 2.5 marks. No one would pay more than 2.5 marks to get $1, or sell a mark for less than 40¢, because the dollars (or marks) could always be converted into gold at the official rate. People could take their dollars or marks down to the bank and get gold for them. (Here we are ignoring the cost of moving gold, actually physically moving it, from one nation to another: transporting, insuring, and handling it.)

Suppose that the U.S. was operating on the gold standard with an initial equilibrium at demand D_0, supply S_1, and a dollar price of marks of 0.40 (point *A* in Figure 17-3). A disequilibrium of payments occurs (see Figure 17-3). Demand increases first to D_1 and then shifts leftward to D_2. The U.S. is committed to exchanging dollars for gold at 25 grains of gold per dollar. But it is *not* bound to keep the dollar-mark exchange rate constant. At first, therefore, the excess demand for marks at 40¢ apiece (distance *AB,* or 10.5 billion marks) causes the dollar price of marks to be bid upward (depreciating the dollar). At some price, let's say 40¢ per mark plus the cost of transferring gold (shown arbitrarily as 45¢ to the mark), it becomes cheaper to buy gold in the U.S., at the fixed price, and ship it to Germany to pay for imports than to buy marks with dollars to pay for the imports. This price is called the **gold-flow point**.

Gold-Flow Point
Under the gold standard, the disequilibrium price at which it is profitable to convert currency into gold and ship the gold as payment.

Let's suppose that the dollar price of the mark (Figure 17-3) rises beyond the gold-flow point. Gold begins to flow from the U.S. to Germany. Under the gold standard, the U.S. government backs its dollars by gold and must redeem them for gold. Since there is now less gold to back the currency, the money supply in the U.S. must be reduced.

The contraction in the money supply leads to a decline in the volume of transactions. Banks call in their loans, refuse to renew loans, and tighten credit. In effect, there is a deflation. Assuming a positive income elasticity of demand for German goods, the demand for imports (and German marks to pay for them) diminishes. The American demand for marks (D_1) will shift to the left to D_2

Now let's switch to Germany, where the gold is flowing in. More gold means a larger supply of money (M). Either prices (P) will rise, or quantities of goods sold (Q) will rise, or both. In either case, the German economy is inflated toward full employment. This will increase German demand for American imports, and thereby increase the supply of marks available to the U.S. The supply of marks (S_1) shifts to the right to S_2 in Figure 17-3.

In the long run, equilibrium is restored at point *C*. The changed supply of marks again intersects the demand, at the previous exchange rate of 40¢ to the mark. The equilibrium quantity of marks exchanged must be between *A* and *B*: in this instance at *C* (15.5 billion marks).

The U.S. and other leading trading nations have not, in any strict sense, used the gold standard since the 1930s and have not used it at all since 1971. Yet there are still those, including some economists, who advocate its return. In the 1970s, the government of France came out in favor of it. The gold standard thus remains a source of controversy, particularly among those who believe it would restore discipline not only to international trade, but also to domestic economic policies.

The advantages of the gold standard are the following: (1) It is automatic; any imbalance in relations between currencies sets in motion corrective gold flows. (2) It stabilizes exchange rates, and thereby makes possible long-term planning for trade. (3) Some economists maintain that gold flows make a nation practice economic self-discipline, live within its own (gold-determined) means, and refrain from forcing other nations to subsidize its consumption of goods.

The disadvantages of the gold standard are the following: (1) It causes domestic economic policy to be tied to international trade (the tail-wagging-the-dog argument). (2) It causes the volume of trade to be tied to the supply of an exhaustible resource, gold, which is in inelastic supply.

Figure 17-3
Exchange-Rate Equilibrium Under the Gold Standard

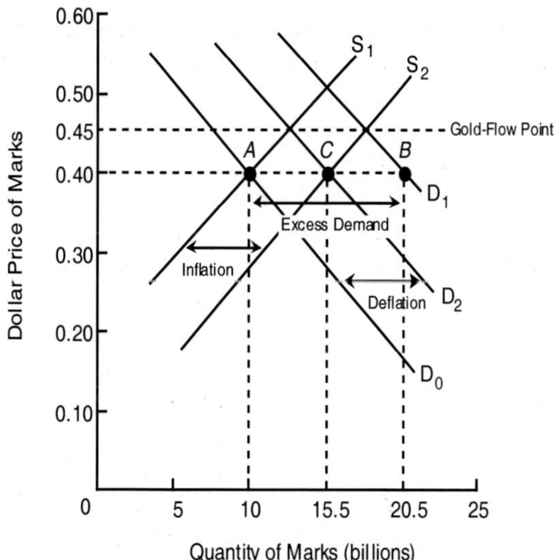

Under the gold standard, gold may move if an exchange rate is significantly different from the official (gold-determined) rate. In Figure 17-3, there is an initial equilibrium at point *A* where demand D_0 and supply S_1 intersect. Because of demand increases (D_0 to D_1) there is ultimately a disequilibrium or excess demand for marks at the old exchange rate (0.40) of 10.5 billion marks (*AB*). At some exchange rate (0.45) the gold-flow point is reached and gold moves to Germany from the U.S. As this happens, the U.S., with less gold to back to its currency, must reduce the money supply and *deflate* the economy. This in turn reduces the demand for marks. The influx of gold into Germany increases the supply of marks and *inflates* the German economy, enlarging the demand for U.S. goods and shifting the supply of marks to S_2. In a new equilibrium with demand for marks (D_2) and supply of marks (S_2) the old equilibrium of 0.40 is established at *C*.

Postwar International Exchange Arrangements

The International Monetary Fund (IMF)
An international agency designed to administer the adjustable peg system of post-World War II monetary relationships. It makes loans to nations with problems of exchange rate disequilibrium.

www.imf.org
For more information on the IMF visit this web site.

Most present-day arrangements for financing trade stem from a meeting that the allied nations (the U.S., Britain, and France) held at Bretton Woods, New Hampshire, in 1944. Although there were many other nations present as well, Britain and the U.S. dominated the meeting. The Bretton Woods conference set up two basic trade features: (1) a system of adjustable pegs for exchange of currencies, a system that lasted until the 1970s, and (2) the **International Monetary Fund (IMF)**, an intergovernmental agency designed to administer the post-World War II monetary system and enhance its stability. It administers the operation of the *adjustable-peg system*, a system of exchange in which currencies are pegged, or are not allowed to change in value by more than a specific percentage. It can use its capital to make bridge loans to nations experiencing exchange-rate disequilibrium problems.

The nations that met at Bretton Woods sought to create relatively fixed exchange rates, which could be maintained. Each currency was to be valued in terms of both gold *and* U.S. dollars. Currencies could vary from these parities by no more than 1 percent. Exchange rates could be changed, however, when countries found that there was a "fundamental disequilibrium" in their payments position. But the Bretton Woods conference failed to define the term *fundamental disequilibrium.*

So, beginning in the 1950s, countries such as the U.S. began to run long-term deficits in payments, with no changes in exchange rates. They did this by drawing on gold reserves, reserves held by the IMF, and by borrowing from the central banks of other countries. Thus, they were without the automatic, self-correcting, adjustment mechanism that had existed under the gold standard (a good feature, for all its other flaws). This went on until 1971, when President Nixon devalued the dollar and set it free from the pegged rate.

During the 1960s, pressure for change in the international money system began to develop. The countries that had to absorb the excess dollars created by U.S. balance-of-payments deficits began to be dissatisfied with the terms of the Bretton Woods agreement, and with good reason: Speculators in the late 1960s were moving huge amounts of money out of dollars and into strong currencies such as German marks.

Special Drawing Rights (SDRs)
A kind of "paper gold" or lines of credit that nations may borrow from the IMF to cover exchange-rate disequilibrium.

One modification of the system was the creation by the IMF of **special drawing rights (SDRs)**. By using SDRs, countries with deficits could borrow so-called paper gold from the IMF to finance their imbalances of payments. This made it possible for the exchange system itself to finance trade. But it did nothing to establish equilibrium relations between the world's major currencies. A second modification was to allow currencies to establish a supply-demand equilibrium through freely floating against each other. The dollar, as you know, led the way in doing this in 1971.

The system of freely floating rates, even if it is accompanied by the managed or "dirty" float, that is presently in force seems to work reasonably well. It does not satisfy those who want more stability in the exchange rate for dollars. Other people, who want a competitive exchange-rate system, praise the system.

The Managed or "Dirty" Float: Whither the Future?

There are some economists who say the Bretton Woods exchange-rate system with its fixed but adjustable pegs died in late 1971 with the floating of the dollar against other major trading currencies. That assessment is warranted at least to the extent that there is no longer a governmental or intergovernmental agreement on the ratios at which (or even within which) international currencies will be allowed to trade.

The present international monetary system is a hybrid version of those (gold standard and fixed exchange rates with adjustable pegs) that preceded it. SDRs in some measure have provided the liquidity that might have been supplied by gold flows. The managed (dirty) float seems to be workable in the face of multi-country central bank cooperation. Dissatisfied with a dollar subject to wide swings in price, efforts have been made to create alternatives to it as *the* international currency. Some European nations have formed the European monetary system under which they value their currencies against each other. This group has also created a new unit of money called ECU (European currency unit), the Euro, which has become a rival to the U.S. dollar in international trade and finance.

For the near-term, it seems unlikely that there will be major changes in the present system of international finance. The managed or "dirty" float seems likely to continue. What long-term effect the 1992 integration of Europe and the expansion of free trade areas, such as NAFTA, will have on the system of international payments is, at this juncture, impossible to assay. The IMF seems likely to increase in importance as industrial nations, LDCs, and NICs alike attempt to come to grips with debt crises, threats of repudiation, and balance-of-payments problems that, for some nations, threaten domestic economic growth.

The Mexican Peso in December 1994: How the International System Works in Crisis

An illustration of how the international financial system may work in crisis was provided in Mexico in December 1994. During the 1980s, Mexico's economy moved toward becoming more free-market. Under the regime of President Carlos Salinas, government ownership of industries was reduced (banks, for example, were reprivatized), import restrictions were lifted, foreign capital investment was encouraged, and a stable Mexican peso was promised.

For much or the 1980s and into the first years of the 1990s, the Mexican economy boomed, enjoying one of the highest growth rates and lowest inflation rates in the western hemisphere. The peso, pegged at.29 to the U.S. dollar, was stable until December 1994. Although Mexico ran substantial deficits in its current account, foreign (especially American) capital inflows permitted their financing with little inflationary threat. Although the peso was thought by some to be overvalued, it remained strong throughout the period.

In late 1994, Mexico's political and economic situation changed dramatically. A combination of a peasant uprising in Southern Mexico and two major political assassinations (including that of the nation's presumptive next president) produced pessimism and uncertainty not only among Mexicans, but among foreign investors as well. As a result, what had been a strong inflow of foreign capital became a net outflow, putting great pressure on the exchange rate between the Mexican peso and other currencies (especially the U.S. and Canadian dollars).

In late December 1994, Mexico's new president, Ernesto Zedillo, unexpectedly devalued the peso by 13 percent and allowed the currency to float freely in foreign exchange markets. As a result, the value of the peso fell to about 18 pesos to the U.S. dollar. The results were predictable: (1) Foreigners with investments; in Mexico (those holding securities, or those whose mutual funds had invested there) took huge losses; (2) U.S. exports to Mexico were drastically reduced; (3) Many Mexican firms faced bankruptcy (Mexico raised domestic interest rates to reduce capital outflows); (4) A "spread effect" to other Latin American countries (their stock markets, for example) occurred as far south as Argentina and Brazil).

What could stop the free fall of the (floating) Mexican peso? Political decisions were taken at the highest levels of the U.S. and Canadian governments to provide Mexico with large quantities of U.S. and Canadian dollars. Mexico's central bank (Banco de Mexico) intervened with those dollars, together with a large loan from the International Monetary Fund (IMF), to stop the free fall, finally stabilizing the peso.

While the rescue (critics called it a bailout) of the Mexican peso remains controversial, it was, in retrospect, predictable. Earlier, we said that trade policy is based as much on political considerations as on economic ones. A decision to intervene by Mexico's trade partners was surely impelled by considerations of political instability as much as by calculations of the effects on trade among three countries. Those considerations were probably influential with the IMF, as well. Though some said Mexico should have solved its problems alone through macroeconomic adjustments (drastic spending cuts, and the like), would Mexico's political system have survived this economic medicine?

The Balance of Payments

Balance of Payments
A statement of a nation's transactions with all other nations.

Thus far in dealing with international trade, we have treated it as a process of exporting and importing goods and services and paying for them directly with currency. Now, we need to factor in other aspects of international trade including the capital flaws between nations.

Each nation puts together (annually or quarterly) an accounting of all its trading transactions with other nations. This accounting statement is called the **Balance of Payments (BOP)**. Any transaction that creates claims by Americans to foreign currencies (causes money to flow into the U.S.) is a credit to the nations balance of payments. Any transaction that causes foreigners to gain claims to U.S. dollars (causes money to flow out of the U.S.) is a debit to the U.S. balance of payments. These trading transactions are not only between individuals and businesses but also include government agencies in the U.S. and in the rest of the world.

It is important to remember that each international transaction results in a credit to one country's BOP and a debit to another country's BOP. Let's illustrate how this works. If someone in Canada buys a South Korean automobile, the purchase is a debit to the Canadian BOP and a credit to the BOP of South Korea. If an Argentine company sends an interest payment to a bank in the U.S., the transaction is a debit to the BOP of Argentina and a credit to that of the U.S.

The Accounts of the Balance of Payments

Current Account
All transactions involving goods, services and earnings on investments.

Capital Account
Shows capital flows or transfers along with the acquisitions and disposal of financial assets.

Financial Account
Shows transfers of financial capital and non-financial capital.

There are three basic accounts in a country's BOP, the ***Current Account***, the ***Capital Account***, and the ***Financial account***. The current account includes all trade in goods and services and also earnings on investments. The capital account includes capital flows or transfers together with the acquisition and disposal of non-produced non-financial assets. The financial account shows transfers of financial capital and non-financial capital. Each of these accounts is divided into sub-accounts.

The Current Account

The current account is divided into four sub-accounts.

- **Merchandise trade** includes all raw materials and manufactured goods bought, sold, or given away. Since 1993, this account has been combined with services to determine the balance of trade total.
- **Services** is a broad category comprising tourism, transportation, engineering and business services (such as management, law, consulting, software, books and movies).
- **Income payments** include incomes from ownership of assets including dividends on stock holdings and interest on securities.
- **Unilateral transfers** are one-way transfers including worker remittances from abroad and direct foreign aid or gifts. The donor nation receives a debit in its capital account and the receiving nation a credit.

The Capital Account

- **Capital transfers** include many things such as forgiveness of debt and goods and financial assets that accompany people migrating to or from the country. Also, transfers include transferring of titles to fixed assets and funds transfers associated with the sale of fixed assets, death duties, inheritance taxes, and legacies.

- **Acquisition and disposal of non-produced non- financial assets.** In this category, one finds such financial transactions as sales and purchases of non-produced assets such as rights to national resources and sales and purchases of intangible assets such as trademarks, patents, copyrights, leases, and franchises.

The Financial Account

This account is a record of the trade in assets such as business firms, stocks and bonds, and real estate. The financial account is divided into two categories:

- **U.S.-owned assets abroad** consist of official reserve assets, government assets, and private assets. Such assets include gold, foreign securities, foreign currencies, the reserve position in the International Monetary Fund, U.S. credits and other lon-term assets, direct foreign investment, and U.S. claims reported by U.S. banks.
- **Foreign-owned assets in the United States** consist of foreign official assets and other foreign assets in the U.S. Such assets include U.S. government, agency, and corporate securities, direct investment, U.S. Currency, and U.S. liabilities reported by U.S. banks.

The Balance of Payments: Deficits and Surpluses

You may wonder about this heading. After all everything that is bought must be paid for. Theoretically, therefore, the current account should balance with the capital plus the financial account. The sum of the (three account) balances of payments should, therefore, be zero. If the United States buys more goods and services than it sells (a current account deficit which has characterized our BOP in recent times), it must finance the difference by borrowing, or by selling more capital assets than it buys (a capital account surplus also characteristic of the U.S. BOP in recent times).

What does it mean for a nation such as the United States to run a persistent deficit in its current account? Effectively the nation is exchanging capital assets for goods and services. A large trade deficit means that the U.S. is borrowing from abroad. In our BOP, this appears as an inflow of foreign capital.

Recall that we said above that the current account, theoretically, should balance with the capital account plus financial account. Because the accounts do *not* exactly offset each other in reality, a "balancing" entry entitled statistical discrepancy must be added to ensure that the overall balance, subtracting minuses from pluses equals zero. There are actually several reasons why this is necessary including 1) statistical discrepancies (items not entered or entered wrongly), 2) accounting convention differences, and 3) exchange rate changes that change the value of recorded transactions are the most common reasons.

An Actual BOP: The U.S. in 2008

To trace through an actual U.S. balance of payments, refer to Table 17-1 which shows the nation's total trading relations with other nations for the year 2008.

In 2008, the U.S. exported approximately $2,591.2 million of merchandise and services (line 1) and imported approximately $3,168.9 million of merchandise and services (line 2). This left the country with a deficit in the trade balance of approximately (-) $577.7 million (line 3). The U.S. received net income receipt (credits plus debits) and payments of $577 million. It also made unilateral transfers (debit) of $8.6 million. The deficit on goods and services, therefore, was about $128 million. Interest payments from the U.S. to other countries and U.S. income from payments abroad (unilateral current transfers) were $128.3 million and about $646.4 million, respectively. There was therefore, a positive figure of $11 million in interest, profits, and dividends (line 5) plus a net outflow of (-) $86 million in unilateral transfers (line 6). Overall, the current account showed a deficit of approximately (-) $577.7 million.

The balance of payments must, like any balance sheets, have offsetting credits and debits. How then was this $577.7 million deficit financed or balanced? For the financial and capital account, U.S. investors acquired more assets abroad [all credits in (B)] than foreign investors acquired in assets of the United States [all debits in (B)]. There was a net financial account plus capital account surplus of about $473.6 million. That $473.6 million balanced most of the $577.7 million deficit in the current account. The overall balance (line 13), the difference between (A) and (B) is $173 million, an amount which must be financed. The compensating transactions total of $878,891 million (line 14) exactly offsets the overall imbalance in the capital and current accounts (line 13) of (-) $878,891 million. The final balance (line 15), thus is and *must be* zero (line 13-14).

Table 17-1
The United States Balance of Payments, 2008 ($million)
[Credits (+), debits (-)]

A. Current Account	
1. Exports (X) of goods and services and income receipts	+ $2,591,233
2. Imports (M) of Goods and Services	- $3,168,938
3. Balance of Trade (X-M)	- $577,705
4. Unilateral Net Transfers	- $128,363
5. Income Payments	- $646,406
B. Capital Account and Financial Account	
6. Net Transactions	+ $953
7. U.S. Government assets	- $529,615
8. Government net assets, non-official	+ $332,012.
9. U.S. Treasury securities	+ $543,496
10. U.S. currency	+ $126,737
11. Foreign owned assets in the United States	- $534,971
12. Capital and Financial Account Balance	+ $473,583
13. Overall Balance, Current Account + Financial Account	- $878,891
14. Compensating Transactions	+ $878,891
15. Final Balance (13 - 14)	- 0 -

Source: Department of Commerce, Bureau of Economic Analysis, 2009.

Figure 17-4
Balances on the U.S. Current and Capital Accounts, 1981 to 2012

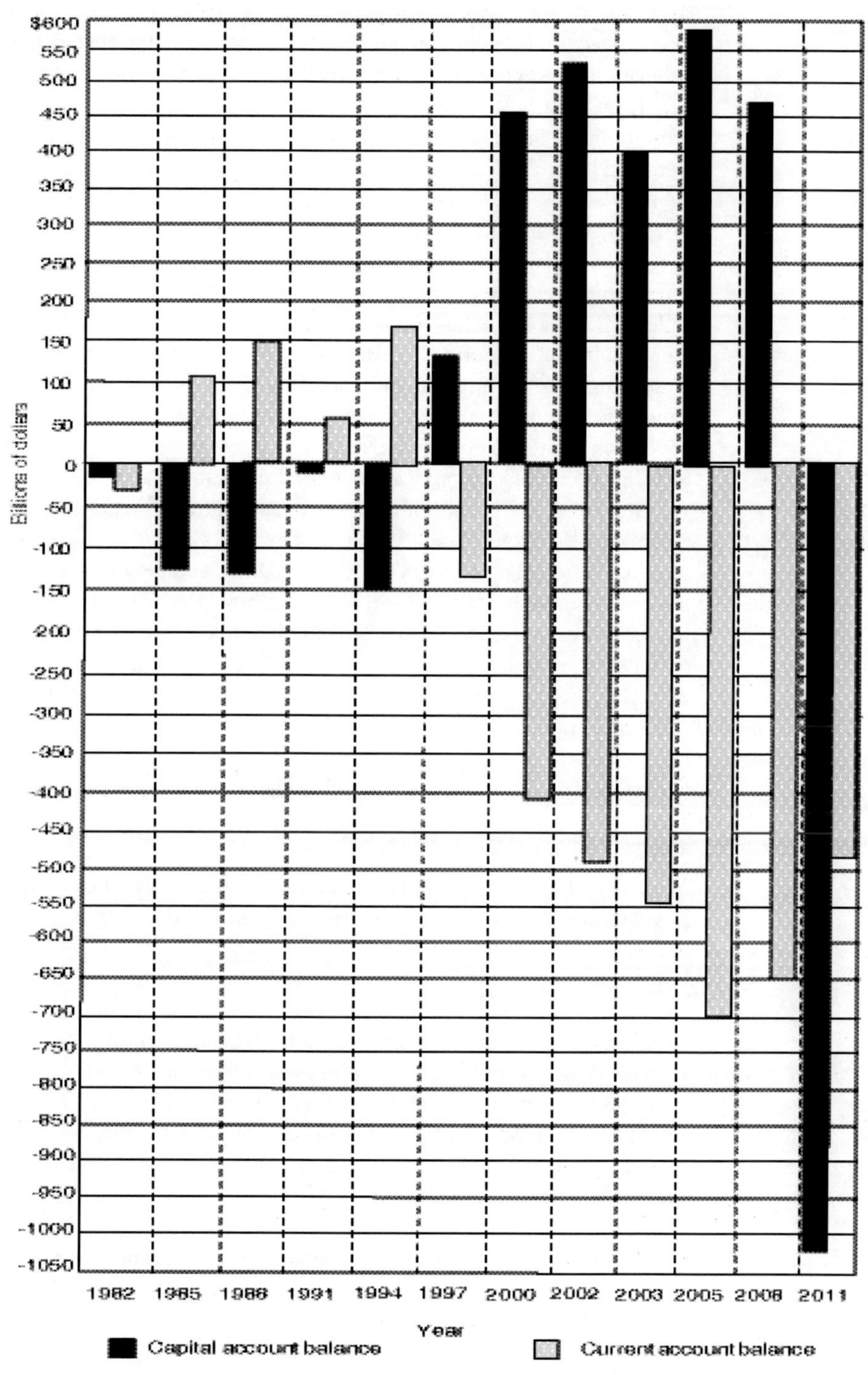

Sources: Adapted from the *Economic Report of the President, 2009, and the Department of Commerce and the The World Bank, 2012.*

In 1981, the U.S. had a very small surplus in its current account and a small deficit in its capital account. In 1982, both accounts showed small deficits. Since 1983, it has had consistent deficits in its current account and surpluses in its capital account.

Deficits to be Financed: Current and Capital Account Balances

Figure 17-4 shows that, since the early 1980s, the U.S. has had deficits (amounts to be financed) in its current account balances. The problem seems to be primarily in the merchandise export-import position, Because the dollar's exchange rate is free to float (at least a "dirty" float), and because American goods, between 1980 and 1985, became relatively more expensive and difficult to export (at least until 1985), the trade (merchandise) deficits from 1980 to 1985 grew rapidly. Since 1985, however, the dollar has fallen against the yen, the Euro and other currencies, and, as we saw earlier, America's exports have grown substantially. We see that the large deficits in the current account are partially offset by substantial surpluses in the capital account.

The deficits to be financed since 1980 have largely been accommodated, as we have seen, through capital inflows into the U.S. that are reflected in the capital account surpluses. While some people have seen this as the "buying of America," these inflows of capital have not only financed America's taste for imports but also, through enlarging the supply of financial capital, have permitted credit markets to be equilibrated at what otherwise might have been higher interest rates. In this sense, they have stimulated the domestic American economy through encouraging domestic investment.

If the dollar continues to fall against other currencies and the deficits to be financed decline, "trade" deficits may decline or even disappear. This will require major readjustments in trade patterns and flows of capital. Financing trade deficits with the U.S. will again become a problem for many nations. At this juncture, any such forecast is difficult to make with confidence. Whether the deficits are eliminated and whether trading relationships will continue to be essentially free are political as well as economic questions as we will see in the following application.

Application I: Politics and the Balance-of-Payments Problem

Reasons Behind Import Restraints

Whenever the U.S. buys more goods and services from other countries than they buy from us there is a deficit in our balance of trade, (current account or goods and service's balance) and a resulting cry to "buy American!" Various people, union leaders and business executives alike, exhort the citizenry to either buy products made in the U.S. or to impose restrictions on imports. In fact, firms or industries may urge this at any juncture, whenever foreign producers begin to take away any sizable share of domestic sales from American industry. In the mid 1980s for instance, lobbyists for both the steel and automobile industries worked hard in Washington trying to get Congress to impose import restrictions on European and Japanese steel and cars. (Detroit watches with gloom the import figures on Toyotas and Nissans, Volvos and Saabs, Renaults and Peugeots, Hyundais and Hondas.)

From early years of independence to the mid-twentieth century, the U.S. ran deficits on its current account. Up until the Great Depression of the 1930s, however, there was rarely much attention paid to the buy-American slogan. A country's nervousness about excessive imports usually comes out when some if not most of its industries are enduring hard times. But as we have seen, since the early 1980s, there have been large deficits in U.S. goods and services and U.S. current account (including U.S. government grants). The U.S. has had such continuing deficits in its balance of trade only twice since 1893 (also in the early 1970s).

In the early 1980s, the cries for protectionism, which had been muted since the mid 1970s, again became loud. In apparent response to the threat of protective legislation, the executive branch of the government negotiated "voluntary" export agreements with some foreign manufacturers, especially with Japanese auto makers. Like quotas, these restraints limited imports but, unlike quotas, were imposed or at least agreed to by foreign manufacturers. While such firms (Nissan, Toyota, etc.) may have agreed to the export limitations to prevent more restrictive action by U.S. Congress, they may also have agreed because they benefit from the higher net price on automobiles in the American market that resulted from the reduced supply.

Voluntary export agreements, alone, did not seem to satisfy the proponents of protectionism including those who believed that America should work more aggressively to open the markets of other nations to its exports. Many argued that the U.S. should retaliate against those who engaged in "unfair" trading practices such as **dumping** goods in U.S. markets. Dumping is the practice of selling goods in foreign markets at prices below their cost of production. Indeed the Trade Agreements Act of 1979 provides for severe anti-dumping penalties. The Trade and Tariff Act of 1984 did little to allay the fears of those who have argued for "fair" as opposed to "free" trade. The act extended the Generalized System of Preferences (GSP) adopted in 1974, which provides duty-free access to U.S. markets for many "non-import sensitive" items from the LDCs and NICs. In a policy statement in 1985, the AFL-CIO argued that such preferences, especially for many of the successful NICs (Korea, Taiwan, Singapore, Hong Kong) are no longer necessary, and argued as well that they have even been extended to some Communist countries. The 1984 act authorized the President to negotiate bilateral free-trade agreements with other nations, with NAFTA,[3] the free trade agreement with Canada and Mexico, being the first major fruit of that activity.

Dumping
The practice of selling goods in foreign markets at prices below their costs of production.

The trade-offs between trade policy and policy toward the LDCs and NICs promise to be difficult. As distinguished economist Bella Belassa[4] has argued: "The more advanced developing economies would, thus benefit from liberalizing their imports in exchange for reductions in the trade barriers of the developed countries." Perhaps such bilateral "free trade" agreements will become a more prominent feature of U.S. policy. The 1984 act also extended the authority of the President to negotiate further voluntary export agreements, especially with foreign steel producers and these, too, may become a more prominent feature of our trade policy.

Protectionism: Costs and Benefits

Restrictions in the form of tariffs or quotas have usually been imposed for the purpose of saving the jobs of workers in the U.S. In 1985 the AFL-CIO put it this way:

> *"...positive governmental action is needed to reverse the erosion of America's industrial base, (between 1982 and 1985) it is estimated that more than 3 million jobs have been lost or not created due to America's continued trade decline."*

---

3. "International Trade and Investment." *The National Economy and Trade* Report of the Executive Council of the AFL-CIO, October, 1985.
4. Belassa, Bella. "The Importance of Trade for Developing Countries." *Banca Nazionale Del Lavaro Quarterly Review* No. 163 Rome, December, 1987.

In the mid 1970s, a major labor leader in the U.S. argued that the costs of free trade ("low-wage imports") were borne by American workers but that "international operators" not U.S. consumers got the benefits. Economists, on the other hand, have estimated that the cost of both tariff and nontariff restrictions (including voluntary export controls) is between $20 billion and $45 billion per year. This figure reflects the consumer burden of higher prices resulting from import duties (for example, there is a 12 percent import tax on cars). It also reflects the higher prices resulting from a lowered supply and a less competitive market in the U.S. for cars, steel, cattle, meat, dairy products, and all the other goods protected by high tariffs. For example, economist William Albrecht[5] says:

> *Between 1969, when the quota system was first introduced, and 1972, steel companies increased their prices 5 times as much as they had in the preceding 8-year period, despite the fact the industry was experiencing declining demand and had unused capacity of 25 to 50 percent.*

To the extent that this heightened price structure may be generalized to apply to many industries, one could say that it is indeed the American consumer who suffers as a result of import restrictions. Even a consumer who has lost a job because of competition from cheap imports is worse off. After all, the jobless consumer, who very much needs bargains, cannot buy inexpensive shirts made in Taiwan or inexpensive shoes made in Korea or low-price beef from Argentina.

America's Trade Problem: The Myths

Murray Weidenbaum[6], a former chairman of the Council of Economic Advisers, argues that much of the rhetoric surrounding our trade problems is based on misconception. Weidenbaum identifies five myths that he believes are fairly common:

1. *Japan is the problem, and if it would only open its markets, much of the problem would disappear.* As Weidenbaum points out, our trade deficit extends to Canada, Mexico, Europe, and in the early twenty first century to the Peoples Republic of China. It must be "our problem," not a "Chinese problem."

2. *The U.S. is alone in practicing free trade.* In fact, says Weidenbaum, we have an elaborate system of preferences, even apart from quotas (sugar, beef, etc.); only 30 percent of our imports are allowed in duty free (though NAFTA has requested the U.S. to raise this percentage).

3. *Imports depress the American economy, especially in terms of manufacturing jobs.* Imports, says Weidenbaum, have little to do with the structural decline in relative importance of manufacturing; services have been larger than manufacturing in the U.S. since 1929. Manufacturing production, in an absolute sense, has never been as high as it is today.

---

5. Albrecht, William. In Baldwin, Robert E. and David Boston Richardson, Jr. (eds). *International Trade and Finance Readings,* Boston, Little Brown, 1981.
6. Weidenbaum, Murray L. *Foreign Trade and the U.S. Economy: Dispelling the Myths*. CATO Policy Report, January/February, 1986.

4. *The way to save American jobs is through trade protection.* On the contrary, says Weidenbaum, "protectionism is the most inefficient welfare program ever devised." Saving a job in the steel industry, for example, may cost 3 to 4 jobs in steel using industries (due to higher costs).

5. *Workers in import-sensitive industries deserve better treatment than other workers.* As Weidenbaum says, "I know of no reason why the one group is more meritorious than the other."

Protectionism: Will It Triumph or Fail?

It is not difficult to imagine some form of protectionism triumphing in the political arena. After all, NAFTA passed with the smallest of margins in the U.S. Congress. If it does triumph, a likely explanation is that offered by Weidenbaum who says that "Protectionism is a politician's delight because it delivers visible benefits to the protected parties while imposing the costs as a hidden tax on the public." This public choice explanation, seems compelling. After all, a higher tariff or a quota on automobiles, for example, will clearly and significantly benefit a particular industry (its owners and managers) as well as particular groups of American workers (the members of the United Automobile Workers Union). The costs, on the other hand, will be spread over many millions of would-be automobile buyers in the form of higher automobile prices. Which group has the more intense and intensely expressed preferences: the protectionists or the free traders? Before we too hurriedly proclaim the likely demise of freer trade, however, let us remember the following:

1. For more than 50 years, America has moved toward lower tariffs and freer trade as reflected in Reciprocal Trade Agreements Acts and other forms of legislation as well as through bilateral agreements, the renewal of GATT, the creation of the World Trade Organization (WTO) and the extension of NAFTA. Many industries and workers in this country are well served by lower priced imported goods and services. In addition, many industries and jobs depend on American exports and would surely suffer in the retaliation that American protectionism would engender. Resistance to protectionism may be strong from those with preferences for freer trade.

2. The push for increased protectionism has stemmed in large measure from U.S. balance of trade deficits since the early 1980s. If the dollar continues to decline against the currencies of its major trading partners further into the twenty-first century, we are likely to see a growth of American exports, and decline in imports. Historically when this has happened, the push for protectionism has abated, and we may see this again.

Lessons to Be Learned

There are several things one can learn from the recent unusual balance-of-trade situation. First, the U.S. should not formulate foreign economic policy on the basis of short-term variations in its trade position. This position can change so quickly, and the changes are so hard to forecast, much less control, that the situation may change by the time the policy is implemented. Second, protectionism is nearly always self-defeating. If the U.S. enacts a drastic import-quota system, Western Europe and Asian countries assuredly will retaliate. They will put import quotas of their own on the things the U.S. wants to sell to *them.* U.S. exports will decline and the projected balance-of-trade turnabout will never take place. Tariffs and quotas have a way of boomeranging.

In general, then, economists rarely espouse the cause of protectionism. When industries find that they can no longer maintain a competitive cost position with respect to foreign suppliers, economists' advice is usually "Retrain labor! Reallocate resources!"

SUMMING UP

1. Today very little international trade is carried out by means of barter. Nearly all of it requires a means of monetary payment, a money exchange system. *Foreign exchange markets* provide the essential function of establishing exchange rates, the rates at which different domestic currencies exchange.

2. The conversion of currency of one nation to that of another is carried out by the international banking system and by specialized dealers. For example, a person importing a pair of shoes from Italy can mail a check to the Italian exporter. The exporter deposits it in a bank in Italy and gets a certain amount of lire for it. The Italian bank gets a claim to dollars from its correspondent bank in the U.S. Such transactions now almost always occur electroniclly.

3. The money exchange system enables exporters and importers to end up with the kind of national currency (dollars, marks, yen, and so on) that they need.

4. Exports by the U.S. create a demand overseas for dollars to pay for them. When a French firm imports American goods, for example, it creates a supply of claims to francs with which Americans may pay for their imports from France. In other words, *a country that wishes to export must import, in order to create the claims to currency necessary for it to trade.*

5. A workable international monetary system has the following characteristics: (a) It establishes a balance between stability and growth in international trade and stability and growth in each of the trading nations. (b) It is equitable and ensures that each nation will have access to foreign exchange, and that each will help bear the costs of operating the exchange system. (c) It is efficient and thus lowers the cost of trade and enhances the growth of international trade.

6. Exchange rates established in foreign exchange markets may be of two basic types of systems: (a) freely floating exchange rates and (b) fixed exchange rates.

7. A *freely floating exchange rate* is determined by the supply of a currency and the demand for it. The *equilibrium exchange rate* is the rate at which quantity supplied and quantity demanded are equal. This means that there is no excess demand or excess supply.

8. The advantages of a freely floating rate are that (a) the rate responds quickly to changes in supply and demand, and (b) imbalances or disequilibria in payments are readily resolved. The disadvantages are that (a) there can be great instability in rates, (b) there can be great instability in savings, investment, and prices in countries that depend heavily on foreign trade, and (c) there can be sudden changes in *terms of trade,* requiring a country to make a reallocation of resources so that it can export more, in order to continue to import.

9. Economists differ on the merits of freely floating exchange rates, though most favor their competitive characteristics. For the time being, the U.S. seems committed to letting the dollar continue to float within ill defined limits.

10. *Fixed exchange rates* mean that the currency of a country keeps the same value with respect to the currencies of other countries. The main advantage of fixed rates is stability; they permit longer term planning for trade. The main disadvantage is that supply and demand are not allowed to work freely. Also, fixed exchange rates require a system of *international reserves* to fill excess demands.

11. Most governments do not consistently follow the principle of freely floating or fixed exchange rates. They intervene selectively in what is called a *managed or "dirty" float*.

12. Fluctuations of exchange rates derive from changes in economic conditions in the exporting and importing nations. Excess demand can be handled by (a) introducing *exchange controls* (rationing of currencies) or (b) by adjusting the economy of the country suffering the disequilibrium so that the domestic cause is eliminated.

13. LDCs often use exchange controls. They determine who shall have access to the limited foreign exchange available. The advantage is a stable exchange rate; the disadvantage is that exchange controls impose a set of public tastes on what would be the private tastes for imports. The government decides what is best for the country to import. Such controls may also give rise to corruption or favoritism in access to foreign exchange.

14. Adjusting a country's domestic economy to eliminate excess demand for foreign exchange means adjusting domestic prices, incomes, and employment. Although a nation may use such means to establish exchange-rate equilibrium, it is a drastic solution. Most economists feel that it creates a major problem (unemployment) in order to solve a lesser problem for which other solutions exist.

15. Under the freely convertible *gold standard,* which has not been used since the 1930s, currencies are valued in terms of grains of gold. Each currency has a value in terms of gold as well as in terms of other currencies. In order for the gold standard to work, the exchange value cannot deviate much from the gold value. If it does, people buy gold and ship it overseas to pay for traded goods, rather than using currencies to pay for them.

16. The *gold-flow point* is the exchange rate at which it is cheaper to ship gold in payment for traded goods than to buy currency.

17. The advantages claimed for the gold standard are that (a) it operates automatically, (b) it stabilizes exchange rates, and (c) gold flows impose an economic self-discipline on nations. The disadvantages claimed for the gold standard are that (a) it ties a nation's internal economic policy to the balance of its foreign payments (the tail wags the dog), and (b) it ties the world's volume of trade to the inelastic supply of an exhaustible resource.

18. The Bretton Woods Conference in 1944 established (a) an *adjustable-peg system* for international currencies, and (b) and the *International Monetary Fund (IMF)* to administer the system.

19. The system of pegging currencies meant that exchange rates could change in value by no more than 1 percent. The world no longer uses this currency-pegging system. However, the IMF still exists. It administers a system of *special drawing rights (SDRs),* (or *"paper gold")* through which countries with balance-of-payments problems can borrow from the IMF.

20. The debt crisis of Mexico in late 1994 illustrates how (1) economic trade policy; is driven by political considerations, and how (2) nations (U.S., Canada) and international organizations (IMF) will intervene to prevent the continued free fall of a floating currency (the Mexican peso).

21. The freely floating exchange rates now in use appear to work reasonably well. Actions of private speculators, who buy and sell currency (arbitrage), may have helped to prevent exaggerated fluctuations.

22. Each nation annually prepares a *balance-of-payments statement,* an accounting of its international purchases and sales, plus an explanation of how it has financed any deficit payments.

23. A balance-of-payments statement lists (a) current account (visible and invisible items of trade), (b) current account balance (balance on current account including unilateral transfers), (c) capital account and financial account which show both capital outflows and capital inflows (d) balance to be financed, and (e) *official reserve transactions balance* (what the nation borrows from other nations, changes in its gold holdings, and so on). A nations' official reserves change when it has a payments deficit or surplus. The balance of payments *must* balance.

24. Since the late 1960s, the U.S. has usually had a deficit to be financed in its balance of payments. More recently (after 1980), this deficit has been due mainly to a *balance-of-trade deficit* (merchandise exports minus imports), and partly to military commitments abroad and our foreign aid program. Our export position since the late 1980s has improved somewhat. Prices of things we exported have fallen relative to prices of other nations' export items. Even so, the deficit in our balance of payments continues.

25. When any nation experiences a deficit in its balance of trade (that is, when it exports less than it imports), citizens may be urged to buy locally made products, and people may call on the government to impose either voluntary or mandatory controls in order to limit imports of foreign goods.

26. Nations that run persistent balance of trade deficits are, in effect, exchanging long-term capital assets for commodities and services.

27. A strong push for protectionism reemerged in the 1980s and 1990s. To head off protective legislation, "voluntary" export agreements to limit foreign sales, especially of Japanese autos, were negotiated. The AFL-CIO, however, argued for a new trade policy including the elimination of many of the preferences given to the LDCs and NICs. The Trade and Tariff Act of 1984, however, authorized more voluntary export agreements and other bilateral trade agreements

which may become an increasing feature of American trade policy. Under this 1984 law, agreements between Canada, the U.S. and Mexico have led to the creation of the North American Free Trade Association (NAFTA). In addition, free trade agreements with other countries, especially in Latin America, have been created.

28. Labor leaders maintain that protectionism is necessary to guard American workers against competition from low-wage areas of the world. They also claim that low-priced foreign imports do not benefit American consumers; they benefit international (multinational) manufacturers. Economists, however, estimate that direct and indirect controls cost American consumers between $20 and $45 billion per year. They maintain that such import controls not only add to the costs of goods, but also enhance the monopoly power of domestic producers.

29. Support for protectionism seems in part to be based on some myths about America's trade problem. These include: (a) Japan, China and others and their protectionism are the problem. (b) Only the U.S. practices free trade. (c) Imports have caused the decline of manufacturing industry in the U.S. (d) American jobs can be saved through protectionism. (e) Workers in import-sensitive industries deserve better treatment than other U.S. workers.

30. One can learn from the recent U.S. balance-of-trade experience: (a) The U.S. should not base its foreign economic policy on short-term changes in its trade position, because its trade position can change dramatically and is difficult to predict. (b) Protectionism is almost bound to be self-defeating, since it invites retaliation by foreign customers for U.S. exports.

31. Economists rarely support protectionism. Most feel that retraining of labor, plus reallocation of resources, is the way out for an industry that cannot compete with cheaper imports from low-wage areas of the world.

KEY TERMS

Balance-of-payments statement
Basic balance
Current account balance
Capital account balance
Deflation
Dumping
Equilibrium exchange rates
Exchange controls
Fixed exchange rates
Foreign exchange markets
Freely floating exchange rates
Gold standard
Gold-flow point
International Monetary Fund (IMF)
International reserves
Managed or "dirty" float
Official reserves transactions account
Special drawing rights (SDRs)

QUESTIONS

1. What are foreign exchange markets? Why are they essential to a modern system of international trade and finance?

2. Do you think the U.S. should continue to let the American dollar float against other currencies, or should it go back to some sort of pegged or fixed exchange rate system? Why?

3. Evaluate the following statement: "A nation cannot for long export (sell its goods to others) unless it imports (buys from others)."

4. What were the problems associated with the gold standard? What were its advantages?

5. Why is it correct to say that a nation's balance of payments *must* balance even though its balance of trade need not? What are the main balancing items?

6. What is the managed or "dirty" float? Why do nations try to manage their exchange rates?

7. What are the advantages and disadvantages of fully floating exchange rates? What is the role of arbitrage in such a system?

8. In the figure below, the exchange rate between the U.S. dollar and the Japanese yen is initially in equilibrium with demand for yen D_0 and supply of yen S_0 at 120 yen = 1 dollar. An increase in the demand for yen D_1 occurs to finance imports from Japan:

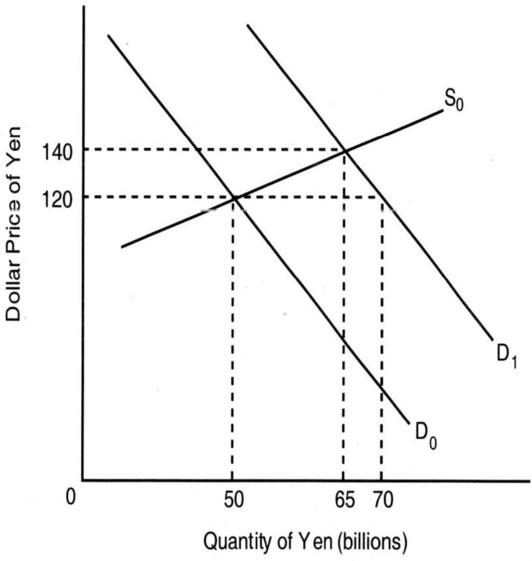

a. If the exchange rate of the dollar to the yen is freely floating, what will be the new equilibrium exchange rate?
b. If the U.S. and Japan want to restore the old equilibrium rate (120), how many yen will have to be supplied to eliminate excess demand?
c. If the excess demand is treated as a rationing problem, what might be the solution?
d. If the U.S. sought to reduce demand for yen by deflating the economy, what might it do?

9. What are the advantages and disadvantages of fixed exchange rates?

10. Suppose that the Secretary of the Treasury calls you in and says, "I have to go before the Joint Economic Committee of Congress and present a good argument for why the dollar should not be allowed to float on world currency markets. What's the best argument I can make?" What would your response be?

11. From the standpoint of value, the U.S. has a greater volume of international trade than any other nation. In the face of this, why would a protectionist policy with respect to imports almost certainly cause other nations to retaliate?

12. Evaluate this statement: "American workers earn high wages. The government must protect them against the imports of goods that are from low-wage countries."

13. What is the role of the IMF in international trade and finance? What are SDRs?

14. In what ways does the Mexican debt crisis of 1994 illustrate the likely future of international financial relationships?

15. What is dumping?

16. What groups are likely to pay the bill for protectionism?

17. In what ways is a policy of retraining workers and reallocating resources preferable to a policy of protecting (by tariffs and quotas) a firm or an industry that is inefficient, relative to foreign firms or industries?

18. What are some of the myths about America's trade problems?

Chapter 18: Economic Systems—How Many in the Twenty-First Century?

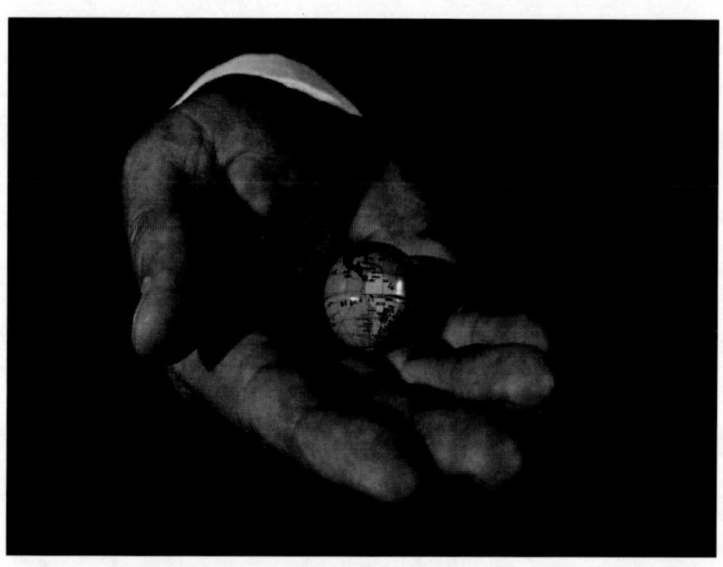

As we saw at the outset of our introduction to the study of economic societies, scarcity, the inability to satisfy all human wants with limited resources, imposes on every society the necessity to create institutions that result in choices about how to use those limited resources. As well, decisions about *which* wants to satisfy must be made. These institutions created to bring about these choices are called an **economic system**.

Economic System
The institutions a society establishes to deal with choices imposed on it by scarcity.

Throughout history, economic systems have competed against one another, both intellectually and politically. Those judged inferior, especially in terms of efficiency and growth, have given way to those judged superior on one or both grounds. In perhaps no period of history was that competition more intense than in the twentieth century. The two main rival systems from the mid to the late twentieth century were planned socialism and market capitalism. We will look at each in turn, but let us first look again at the kinds of choices all societies throughout history have been forced to make because of scarcity.

Basic Economic Choices: A Reminder

Let's remind ourselves of the choices imposed by scarcity. Regardless of the philosophical or ideological preferences of a society, these are the questions about using resources that *must* be answered. By way of quick review, these choices are:

1. *What* shall be the composition of output? Since everything that is desirable cannot be produced in the quantities desired, choices, often difficult ones, must somehow be made about allocating resources to produce one good as opposed to another. Shall these choices be made by individual consumers or shall government planners make the decisions? Whose tastes and preferences, in other words, shall dominate the choice about output?

2. *How* shall goods be produced? At any particular time, there is a menu of choices about producing goods. Shall we, for example, produce information for making economic decisions with typewriters and telephones or

with computer hardware and software? An answer to this question is necessary; shall it come from individual managers and entrepreneurs or from central planners?

3. *Who* shall receive the output (real income) of the society? This question of distribution is perhaps the most difficult and potentially divisive one for all nations. Shall markets, responding to productivity signals, ration output on the basis of (market-earned) incomes and tastes or shall planners set prices and factor incomes according to some set of "social" objectives? What is equitable or fair? Since, as we have noted at various points, there is no unique definition of distributive equity, each society must not only find a means or process to distribute income, but must also agree on the results of that process.

Evaluating an Economic System

There are many dimensions to the evaluation of an economic system and economic, along with moral and political criteria may be used. An economic criterion inevitably used is that of efficiency in resource usage. Rich society or poor, socialist or capitalist, the ability to provide solutions to economic problems now and in the future depends heavily on **efficiency.** We shall look at efficiency questions in two dimensions.

Static Efficiency

Static Efficiency
At a point in time, using resources in ways that produce the most desired mix of output.

Since resources are scarce, they should, to be used efficiently, be allocated to produce that mix of goods and services that the society prefers. While the answer to what is preferred depends on whose preferences are considered, no society in a static (timeless) sense is efficient if it produces one good (for example, pet rocks) where doing so causes it to produce less of another good (microcomputers for example) that is more preferred.

Dynamic Efficiency

Dynamic Efficiency
Over a period of time, using resources in ways that maximize the long-term benefits from their employment.

Dynamics involves looking at a process over time. Present uses of resources will have consequences for the future and for future consumers. Efficiency over time requires that scarce resources be used in ways that maximize the stream of long-term benefits from their employment.

Whether from the standpoint of static or of dynamic efficiency, the successful use of resources critically involves control over those resources or, in other words, the location and security of property rights.

Property Rights: Should They be Vested in Individuals or in the State?

Property Rights
The rights to own, control, and profit from the use of resources.

Property rights, the rights to own, control, and profit from the use of resources, must be vested somewhere in any society. Without secure property rights and the control they carry with them, choices about resource usage would be nearly impossible. There are two basic ways these rights may be assigned in an economic system:

Private Property Rights

Property rights in resources may be assigned exclusively to individuals who not only control their use but also have the right to transfer control to others through a process of exchange. In such a system, the individual owns not only his own labor, but also any other real or financial assets to which title is held. Homes and land, for example, are owned by individuals and families who are free to sell them, rent them, or make any other lawful use of them.

Public Property Rights

Public property rights are not assigned to individuals but are held in some kind of communal ownership. Though individuals own their own labor, other resources including land and housing are not individually owned and cannot, therefore, be sold or rented to others by their occupants. Collective ownership of resources implies that the state through some means must decide who shall have access to a society's resources.

No society today assigns property rights entirely in one way or the other. In the U.S. there are some goods such as parks as well as many schools that are collectively owned. There are also public goods such as military weapons that have indivisible benefits. In the former Soviet Union, there were some goods, such as automobiles, that were privately owned, and much agricultural output came from privately controlled plots of land. In addition, there was a large informal or "underground" economy. Still, each present society has an *emphasis* about the location of property rights with some such as the United States emphasizing private property rights and others such as Cuba emphasizing public property rights.

Why Do Property Rights Matter?

Property rights are important to an economy in two separate but interrelated ways. To begin with, such rights or their lack, create incentives or disincentives on the part of individuals to supply effort and to create innovations. If I do not own the home in which I live, what incentive have I to keep it up or improve it? If I cannot patent a new process, what incentive have I to develop it? A society with secure widespread private property rights is, therefore, one in which individuals will be likely to supply effort voluntarily and one in which innovation is likely to be forthcoming.

Property rights also heavily influence the distribution of income in a society. Those who own more resources or more productive kinds of resources will be likely to receive a greater part of the income and real product of the economy. If individuals such as inventors or innovators are given exclusive use to their new processes, they will enjoy monopoly returns and incomes. If, on the other hand, individuals are completely denied such ownership rights, disincentives to effort and innovation are created. Trade-offs, thus, are created in all societies when property rights choices are made.

Housing may well be one of the best examples of these trade-offs. If privately owned, incentives exist to maintain and improve it. At the same time, the best housing will go to those with the most income, while those with lesser incomes will have less desirable housing. Some may actually be homeless. If housing is publicly owned, disincentives exist for individuals to maintain and improve it but there may be more widespread access to it (assuming enough of it is produced).

With this background in mind, let us turn to look at each of the two major twentieth century benchmark economic systems, market capitalism and planned socialism, in turn. First, we will examine market capitalism, a system whose detail has been examined throughout this book. Now, however, we want to examine its systemic fundamentals.

Market Capitalism

Market Capitalism
An economic system characterized by (1) private assignment of property rights and (2) decision making about uses of resources is expressed through a system of product and factor markets.

A system of **market capitalism** has two *essential criteria*:

1. Most of the means of production are privately owned. Property rights are vested in individuals. As a result, economic decision making is relatively decentralized, and

2. Economic decisions about uses of resources are expressed through a system of interrelated product and factor markets.

By private ownership of the means of production, we mean that the legal owners of real capital (machines, buildings, and so on) used to produce goods and services in an economy are *individuals* in that society. This definition allows for the existence of corporations, since they are owned by stockholders. In addition, it allows for some government ownership. But the amount of capital owned by the government is a small percentage of the total means of production. The fact that, in the U.S., governments own some schools, hospitals, parks, and so on, does not, therefore, mean the U.S. economy is not *capitalist.*

Markets in a capitalist economy may be organized in many ways ranging from highly competitive to monopolistic in structure. The key feature of capitalism, though, is not the structure of these markets, but the fact that *markets exist.* Market capitalism is not necessarily the same thing as a competitive-free-enterprise market system. Nor, in the political realm, does capitalism *necessarily* translate into a representative, democratic system of government. We will come back to this point later.

Necessary Legal Features of Market Capitalism
(1) right of private ownership, (2) legal enforceability of contracts.

For a capitalist economy to function well, two **necessary legal features of market capitalism** must exist. The two basic elements of this legal framework are (1) *the right of private ownership or, in other words, secure private property rights* and (2) *the legal enforceability of contracts*.

Economic Advantages of Market Capitalism

Because choices about what to produce and what to buy are made by private individuals, choice making under capitalism, as we noted, is relatively decentralized. This is true even in a capitalist economy in which significant elements of monopoly may exist in product and factor markets. Voluntary exchange based upon mutual advantage is perhaps the most important distinguishing characteristic of capitalism. The role of government in such an economic system, while important, is relatively limited.

As noted before, a principal advantage of a capitalist economy lies in the incentives to efficiency created by private property rights. Because private owners of resources keep the gains of their use and have the right to sell their property, there is a strong incentive to maximize the value of those rights by using resources efficiently. Those who take risks receive whatever profit is created; to use the term economists prefer, there are no "**free riders**," individuals who can lay claim to the benefits from resource usage for which they bore none of the costs.

Free Riders
Individuals who can lay claim to the benefits of using resources while bearing none of the costs of their usage.

A second advantage of capitalism is that the costs of decision making are likely to be low relative to societies without private property rights. The administrative costs of firms and private decision makers in general may be sizable but there is an incentive to minimize them since profit is the residual after subtracting costs from revenue flows. In a centrally planned economy, on the other hand, the planning mechanism must be relatively large and costly. Those who manage it have less clear incentives to minimize its costs since they have no property rights in the resources and must share any productive gains with numerous "free riders."

Economic Criticisms of Capitalism

Even though a capitalistic system allocates resources with efficiency, its critics argue that it has two drawbacks:

1. The tastes of some consumers, those with greater incomes; are given more weight than those of others in determining what to produce. Output is rationed, therefore, on the basis of how much money each consumer has to spend. For those with less income, who have needs but less purchasing power, the market does not as readily supply goods. These output results trouble those who regard them as inequitable and frequently lead to arguments in capitalist societies for "income transfer programs."

2. Business firms, in setting output and prices, fail to include in their calculations the external costs (and benefits) that result from production but that are not part of the private costs or benefits of production or consumption. The most notable of these external costs are pollution and other forms of damage to the environment. *Note:* Socialist countries are by no means untarnished in this respect. The same kinds of externalities tend to occur in socialist economies such as the former Soviet Union as was seen in the nuclear plant disaster at Chernobyl in 1987 and in the pollution of many of that nation's major lakes and waterways.

In order to deal with the problems of poverty and ecological damage, societies, often acting through governments, must devise means of interfering with or supplementing market decisions. Inevitably, such interferences involve abridgments of private property rights.

Planned Socialism

Because of the diversity of socialist theory, it is difficult to give a precise definition of socialism that can encompass all its forms. Here we will describe the most important one in modern times: all forms of planned socialism.

What is Planned Socialism?

Planned Socialism
An economic system in which property rights are largely held publicly, and choices about resource usage are made by central planners.

Of the many varieties of socialism found in the late twentieth and early twenty-first centuries, **planned socialism** is the one with most direct ties to Marxist thought. Property rights are largely held publicly and choices about resource usage are made centrally by a group of planners. If one created a spectrum of economic systems, this one would be at the opposite end in terms of resource decisions and rewards from the pure form of market capitalism discussed earlier.

Advantages of Planned Socialism

Unlike the results of pure capitalism, planners in socialism can create any distribution of real income desired. By allocating resources and by setting prices, all distributional "inequities," at least in theory, can be eliminated. By planning, all externalities (theoretically) can be incorporated into those prices and resource allocations.

Criticisms of Planned Socialism

The major disadvantage of planned socialism is that with public property rights, there are, as indicated earlier, disincentives to individual effort. If all laborers, for example, are to be paid the same, why would one work harder than any other? Distribution, in other words, can be made more "equitable," but there may be less to distribute since productivity differentials are not rewarded. The second major disadvantage of planned socialism is more technical. Since there are no private markets to guide the allocation of resources (no "market tests"), how do the planners figure out where financial capital and other resources should go? All must be done by plan, an enormously more difficult and costly task than the "invisible hand" direction of capitalism. If to this is added the fact that managers who actually produce goods are given quotas, the incentives to quality as opposed to quantity may be low as well. Resource wasteage may be high.

Figure 18-1
An Example of Marxian Analysis

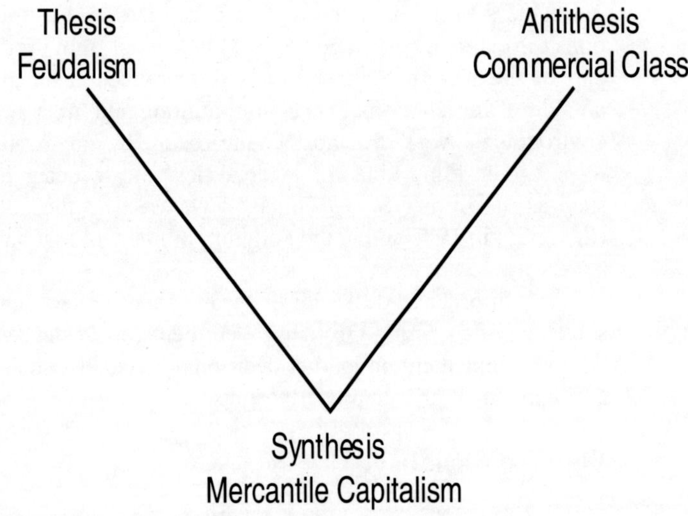

Another example would be: thesis = industrial capitalism; antithesis = the proletariat, or laboring class; synthesis (what Marx predicted would occur) = socialism.

Marx and Socialism

Just as Adam Smith created much of the foundation for capitalist thought, Karl Marx is responsible for the foundation of planned socialism. Marx's theory of history sought to explain the evolution of socialism and, for that reason, we will briefly examine the principles he set forth. This is true even though Marx wrote mostly about Capitalism rather than socialism. Indeed, his most important work, *Das Kapital*, is an analysis of capitalism and a forecast by Marx of its ultimate demise.

Dialectical Materialism

Dialectical Materialism
A view that material things are the subject of all change and that technology, and the natural environment are the causes of that change.

The philosophical foundation of Marxism is **dialectical materialism**, a philosophy that views material things as the subject of all change and technology, and the natural environment as the main forces that cause human society to change continually. Let's examine this philosophy one step at a time.

Dialectics emphasizes that all phenomena, natural and human, involve processes of development. The seed grows into the plant. The infant grows into the child, the child into the youth, the youth into the adult. (Darwin's theory of evolution is another example of this dialectical process of reasoning.)

Marx analyzed this process of development of human society, and used it, as he came to understand it, as the scientific basis for socialism. The first law of this argument is that the foundation of society is materialistic. Technology and the natural environment (climate, resources, geography) are the dominant forces in society's development. The rest (culture, institutions, social classes, and the relations between them) are linked to the economic (materialist) base, and are shaped by that base.

Historical Materialism
The view that human society undergoes a continual process of change from one form to another.

Dialectical materialism is the basic idea behind Marx's concept of **historical materialism**, which holds that human society throughout history has undergone a continual process of change, or development from one form to another: this change results from conflict between classes in a society. In ancient times, there was slavery; in medieval times, serfdom; then came handicraft and cottage industry, which gave way to factory-oriented capitalism. The guiding factors in this process are changing technology and the natural environment.

Figure 18-1 illustrates this process of social change or class conflict for the transition from feudalism to the beginnings of capitalism. The *thesis* (the class system that is dominant at a given time) is feudalism, in which the ruling class is the landed aristocracy. The *antithesis* (the class that is the main force in changing the thesis) is the emerging commercial class. The *synthesis* (the system that evolves after the antithesis has forced changes) is mercantile capitalism, in which the commercial class replaces the landed aristocracy as the dominant class.

Class Conflict

Karl Marx, as we indicated before, believed that the most dramatic feature of this process of change was the conflict of classes at each stage of development. In ancient Rome, the slaves were in conflict with their masters. In medieval Europe, the serfs and the emerging merchant class were in conflict with the landed aristocracy. With the development of factories, a new class, the *proletariat* (the workers in the factories), came into conflict with the capitalists, the owners of the factories. The basis of these conflicts is the effort of one class to dominate and exploit other classes. A basic tenet of Marxism is that as long as there are private property rights classes will continue to exist, and conflict will result. Marx argued for a **labor theory of value**, that is that all value is created by labor, but that wages under capitalism tend toward a subsistence level. The difference between the value of products created by labor and the wage payments to labor constituted what Marx called **surplus value**.

Labor Theory of Value
The Marxist argument that the entire value of a product is made up of its labor cost.

Surplus Value
In Marxist theory, the difference between the value created by labor and its wage payments.

Falling Profits and the Reserve Army of the Unemployed

According to Marx, competition between firms and the increasing scarcity of profitable investment opportunities would cause profits in a capitalist economy to eventually fall. Capitalists could counter this fall in two ways: (1) They could get employees to work longer hours, and in this way increase surplus value and the degree of exploitation of labor. But the opportunity to do this was limited. (2) They could invest more and improve technology further, thus increasing output per worker and surplus value. However, improving technology meant that more and more machines replaced more and more workers, and this increased unemployment.

The rising number of unemployed caused by increased use of capital and improved technology was called the **reserve army of the unemployed**. This reserve army, Marx said, competed with the employed workers, and this competition had the effect of keeping wages down.

Reserve Army of the Unemployed
Marxist idea that capitalist societies displace labor in favor of capital and create a growing number of unemployed workers.

Recurring Business Cycles

Marx also maintained that as capitalists increase investment to ward off falling profits, the productive capacity of the economy expands and output increases. But because wages are kept low, workers do not have the ability to buy this expanded output. So, although the economy expands for a while, eventually industry's ability to produce output far outstrips consumers' ability to buy that growing output. (If you tool up your factory with all the latest equipment, so that you can make 10,000 washing machines a month, but the public has enough purchasing power to buy only 5,000 of them, you will eventually go broke.) Excess capacity is generated, which causes economic crisis and then collapse. Along comes a depression, and firms are forced out of business. Eventually, enough firms are forced out of business so that capacity contracts to a point at which expansion can be renewed, and the process repeats itself. Marx identified the business cycle and the exploitation of labor as two hallmarks of the capitalist system. Marx was one of the first to introduce the idea of recurring business cycles, and his theory of them constituted a significant contribution to economic theory.

Marx's Prediction: The Collapse of Capitalism

Marx concluded that capitalism (the thesis) contained within it inherent contradictions (capitalism's antithesis) that would bring about its end and a movement toward the next stage of development, socialism. He predicted that economic crises would recur, and would become progressively more serious. With more investment and continuing technological change, the reserve army of the unemployed would become larger and larger. Because of their increased investment and ever-greater need to compete against others, firms would get bigger. As this occurred, those among the bourgeoisie who owned smaller firms would be forced into the proletariat and into the reserve army of the unemployed.

Eventually, Marx predicted, economic crisis and unemployment would become so large that revolution would take place, and capitalism would be overthrown. The proletariat would come to realize that capitalism was against their self-interest; the wastes of resources due to recurring crises would become apparent. The proletariat would therefore seize political power and establish a socialist society which would ultimately evolve into a classless communist society.

What Happened to the Collapse?

Marx argued that the overthrow of capitalism would take place in the most advanced countries. Marxist socialism, however, was established almost entirely in economically backward societies. In addition, in the late 20th century, many

Marxist economies have moved toward the establishment or reestablishment of capitalist economic institutions. Has history proved Marx wrong?

Whether the Marxist prediction would have ever been fulfilled had capitalist economies remained unchanged is unclear. What is evident is that since Marx's prophesy, there have been fundamental influences at work in capitalist societies that have increased their vitality and made their predicted collapse fundamentally wrong.

1. Contrary to the labor theory of value, labor's wage depends, in a market economy, on its productivity. As more capital is employed, labor's productivity rises as does its wage. Indeed, labor's (wage-salary) share of national income, at least in the U.S., has grown to around 70 percent and has been remarkably steady since World War II. The Marxist view of increasing exploitation seems unwarranted. The very (labor) theory of value on which it was based has been repudiated.

2. Since the 1930s, governments in market economies have taken an active role in trying to stabilize their economies. To many economists, this seems to have reduced the severity of recurring business crises. Also, it is not at all clear that crises in such economies were becoming ever more severe.

3. Modern capitalist states have developed extensive social welfare programs to redistribute real income. Whatever its growth effects and incentive effects, redistribution is seen by some as having taken the "sting" out of pure market capitalism.

4. Many workers have themselves become capitalists in a small way. In the U.S., nearly 67 percent of the population either own or are buying their own homes, and over 50 percent own stocks or bonds, either as individuals or through pension and retirement funds. In other words, larger numbers of workers are sharing in the property rights of capitalism.

Efficiency of Central Planning: The "Fatal Conceit" Problem

Over time, centrally planned economies in the twentieth century ultimately seemed to suffer from "economic sclerosis." Some of these economies, especially that of the Soviet Union, experienced substantial growth during periods in which they were building basic industries such as steel. As they matured, however, an inability to reallocate resources to their most productive uses became increasingly severe. As we know, in market economies, this process of reallocation depends on a myriad of changing supply and demand signals that emanate from both consumers and producers. The market pricing system, thus, provides generally reliable information to resource owners about the most profitable uses of those resources in the face of changing consumer tastes as well as changing technology.

In a centrally planned economy, on the other hand, such flows of information do not "bubble up" from the interaction of buyers and sellers. Rather, central planners, in deciding on uses of resources, their prices, and the prices of both producer and consumer goods must try to estimate all that information. A Nobel Laureate, Frederick Hayek[1], referred to the presumption by planners that they could generate and efficiently use this information without allowing markets to exist as the "fatal conceit" of centrally planned economies. It led Hayek to conclude that, ultimately, centrally planned economies would grow less and less efficient and would fail. This remarkable insight by Hayek occurred decades before the collapse of the Soviet Union.

The End of Planned Socialism?

Ironically for Marxists, by the late 1980s, it was the planned socialist states that were on the brink of collapse. In the amazingly brief period of less than a decade following 1989, the Soviet Union collapsed (1991) and split into ten independent republics, most of which moved in varying degrees to try to create capitalist economies. In addition, all the planned socialist states of Eastern Europe moved to recreate capitalist economies with Eastern Germany becoming a part of a reunited German capitalist society. In Asia, in the 1980s, China, the world's most populous society, began a steady movement toward a capitalist economy. While proclaiming its devotion to socialism, the nation began basic economic reform first in agriculture where private property rights were restored and then to create private firms and private stock ownership throughout special economic zones. In 1997, a decision was made to either privatize or close many of the huge, inefficient state-owned firms in basic and consumer goods industries. As we start the twenty-first century, there are few economic societies left that can be called planned socialist. North Korea and Cuba are two that cling to a rejection of markets in favor of central planning, Even Cuba, though, is experimenting with limited market reforms though seeking to find ways to do so while maintaining its commitment to a socialist economy.

Has history proved Marx wrong? Impressive evidence suggests that the answer is Yes. In recent years, some writers have argued that we are witnessing an "end to history," a termination of the contest among competing economic systems. We are skeptical of this argument, for systems evolve and the future, by definition, is unknown. Additionally, Marxism-Leninism provides a rationale for dictatorship as we see in Cuba, Zimbabwe and elsewhere. What seems clear at the beginning of the twenty-first century, however, is that the contest between economic systems based on markets and those based on central planning has been resolved in favor of markets. This does not mean that ideological contests have come to an end.

Transition from Planned Socialism to Market Capitalism: How Long and How Difficult?

Major questions exist about how to accomplish a transition from planned socialism to market capitalism and about the length of time required for such a transition. Even in Eastern Europe, which had market economies until the 1940s, major problems of transition occurred. While it might seem relatively simple to privatize a socialist economy, in fact, it has proved complex even in Poland, whose pace of reform has been among the most rapid in the region.

Key Reforms

There is no simple "recipe" of reforms in the transition from planned socialism to market capitalism. Nonetheless, there is widespread agreement, based especially on the experience of Eastern Europe, that among the most important key reforms are:

---

1. In Friedman, Milton. *Capitalism and Freedom,* Chicago, University of Chicago Press, 1972. Also Hayek, Friedrich. *The Constitution of Liberty.* University of Chicago Press, 1970.

1. Creation of private property with secure property rights

2. Creation of a system of prices that reflect relative scarcity

3. A monetary system that permits price stability and the achievement of the price goals in (2) above

4. A system of institutions, both economic and political, that facilitates the first three reforms

Command Economy
An economy in which the problems created by scarcity are dealt with by a central planning bureaucracy.

Market Economy
An economy in which the problems created by scarcity are dealt with by market signals that allocate and reallocate resources.

Let's look at each of these four interrelated reforms to see why they form a package of changes necessary to transform a **command economy**, *one in which the problems created by scarcity are dealt with by a central planning bureaucracy*, into a **market economy**, *one in which the problems arising from scarcity are dealt with by market signals*. These signals allocate and reallocate resources to their (changing) most productive uses.

Secure Private Property Rights

A key feature of a market economy is the ability of private individuals, acting on the incentive to maximize the value of their property rights, to choose how to use resources, including financial capital, under their control. As we said before, secure private property rights minimize free rider problems and permit an expectation on the part of property owners that they will be able to appropriate the benefits of their maximizing efforts. Under planned socialism, this type of private gain was officially discouraged, if not prohibited. Today, in some former socialist states, especially the former Soviet Union, private property rights remain restricted. As an example, Russia is just beginning to permit unrestricted private ownership of land. Partially as a result of this delay, agriculture remains a major problem in terms of productivity.

Prices that Reflect Relative Scarcity

Under planned socialism, prices were set by central planners to accomplish "social" objectives. Heavily subsidized prices, particularly of basic staples such as bread, electricity and housing were seen as "equitable." The two main problems that resulted, however, were that (1) not nearly enough of the goods were produced to clear markets, thus creating unfilled demand (long waiting lines, in many cases), and (2) the distorted prices created perverse incentives to use goods that were produced. As an example, in the 1980s, administered bread prices were so low in Poland that farmers reportedly fed bread, rather than more expensive grain, to their cattle and hogs! Many formerly socialist states have reformed prices (it was a first action of the democratic Polish government in 1990), but Russia is just starting to undertake the politically painful rationalization of its entire pricing system.

A Monetary System that Permits Price Stability

Price reform and monetary reform go hand in hand. When prices are reformed and subsidies eliminated, governments in newly-forming market economies are tempted to expand the money supply to "take some of the sting" out of price reform. The result in Russia in the mid 1990s, for example, was an inflation rate of over 1,000 percent per year. A currency of determinate and stable value is also necessary for foreign trade and as an incentive to attract long-term foreign capital to the former socialist states. Still, the temptation to ease the pain of price reform with increased supplies of money is intense. Russia's central bank announced in 1999 that it planned to do just that.

Institutional Reform

The economic and political institutions created by a society are nothing less than the set of means by which all economic activities are governed. These institutions determine the cost of economic transactions. If the institutions are reliable and efficient, the volume of transactions increases and the size of the economy is enhanced. If the institutions are unreliable and inefficient, the reverse happens and economic growth slows. Where institutions are unreliable, economic activities are subject to corruption and many are diverted to an "underground economy." The institutions created by long-standing market economies took long to create. It remains to be seen whether they can easily be transferred to some formerly planned socialist economies. This is especially true of such economies that had never been fully evolved market societies.

Mixed Economies: A Third System?

There is no economy in the early twenty-first century that falls neatly into one of the two systems that we have outlined. Private property rights are dominant in some, public property rights in others; almost all have a mixture of the two assignment methods. In some economies choices about using resources are very decentralized; in others, central planning of those choices continues; in almost all there is some mixture of these levels. Nations at this time are, thus, **mixed economies**, those that combine elements of private and public property rights along with centralized as well as decentralized choice making about resources.

Mixed Economies
Economic systems that combine elements of private and public property rights and centralized as well as decentralized choices about resource usage.

Many Western European economies have evolved what is known as *democratic socialism*. Sweden, Belgium and other economies come to mind. One may question whether such modern "welfare states" are really a distinct economic system. Almost all, though, rely, in practice, on private property rights to create incentives for resource usage while permitting decentralized private markets to allocate resources. Democratic socialism, in other words, seems more a political than an economic system, one in which the state has distributional goals which it achieves through political means while relying on a decentralized market economy for the resources with which to achieve those goals.

The End of Socialism: A Disclaimer

Does the end of the Cold War mean that capitalism has won out over socialism and that the latter will disappear as an economic system? The argument *has* been advanced that ideological contest and the evolution of economic systems is over. Contrary to Marx's prophecy, say proponents of this view, capitalism has proved to be the ultimately successful economic system. Others, such as the well known American socialist economist, Herbert Gintis[2], conclude that "reports of the death of socialism are premature." Gintis concedes that "markets work because they are disciplinary devices," thus they avoid shirking, reveal price information and produce high-quality goods under the threat of losing buyers. In turn, managers have incentives to invest in profitable activities and employees incentives to work hard to avoid loss of jobs.

---

2. Gintis, Herbert. "Is Socialism Dead?" *The Margin,* March/April, 1991.

Nonetheless, says Gintis, Eastern Europe (including the Soviet Union) was never the socialism envisioned by its philosophical founders. Nor, according to Gintis, are modern capitalist economies, the models envisioned by Conservatives because they have "incorporated socialist goals and structures into their institutional fabric." Both systems, he argues, must continue to evolve and incorporate the features of each that have merit.

Economic and Political Freedom: Are They Related?

As planned socialist economies began their transition to market capitalist economies, a question that became common was: *Will the increased freedom associated with capitalism lead to faster growth as well as greater political freedom?* These are, in fact, two *interrelated* questions. One appears to have a fairly clear answer, the other is more arguable.

Faster Growth

Recent studies seem to confirm the view that greater economic freedom is associated with higher levels of GDP and faster growth. In a 1994 study by the *Heritage Foundation*, free and mostly free nations (relatively free of government economic controls), such as Hong Kong, the U.S., and the U.K., dominated the list of nations with high per capita GDP. Mostly unfree and repressed nations, such as Zimbabwe, Vietnam, Cuba, and N. Korea (all of which remain planned socialist economies), dominated the list of nations with low GDP per capita. GDP growth rates continued this pattern. It would seem, thus, that as economic freedom increases in formerly planned societies, their growth rates will increase. But, will this, in turn, lead to greater political freedom as well?

Political Freedom: Does it Follow from Economic Freedom

In the 1994 article in *The Wall Street Journal*, Kim R. Holmes[3] argues that policy makers have paid inadequate attention to economic freedom while concentrating on political freedom in the movement away from planned socialism. She suggests a change of emphasis not only because "a free economy can lift itself, and its people, out of poverty," but also because "economic freedom is a breeding ground for political freedom." Should we expect, then, that economic liberalization, with its increased freedom of choice, will be accompanied by political liberalization and increased freedom to choose political leaders.

Proponents of this economic-political liberalization argument feel that as consumers and producers exercise economic freedom they will press for freer political choice as well. This is especially true, argue some political scientists, as a middle class develops and grows with faster growth in per capita GDP. Those skeptical of the argument counter that economic and political freedom are not that well correlated. Skeptics point, for example, to Singapore and Hong Kong as examples of high income countries with great economic freedom that have significantly lesser levels of political freedom.

---

3. Holmes, Kim R. "In Search of Free Markets." *The Wall Street Journal*, December, 12 1994.

Cartoon Feature Syndicate

"I forget whether he calls himself a conservative radical or a radical conservative."

China: A Test Case?

Nowhere has the argument about economic and political freedom crystallized more than in arguments about U.S. economic policy toward the People's Republic of China. Though China still is not among the World's most free economies (it ranked 136 in the 2013 Index of Economic Freedom), it moved in the 1990s *toward* creation of the requisites of a market economy. Nonetheless, China, at least at the national level, remains politically monolithic. Only the Communist party is permitted to exist. In 1999, dissidents who attempted to form a new political party were imprisoned. Critics of the "economic-freedom-leads-to-political-freedom argument" cite this as evidence, not only of the incorrectness of the argument, but also of the need to change U.S. economic policy toward China. Proponents, on the other hand, point to increased political freedom at local levels in China and argue it will ultimately translate into political liberalization at the national level.

Who is right? At this point, there is no clear answer. In the twenty-first century, however, China may well be the clearest test case of the arguments about the relationship between economic and political freedom.

SUMMING UP

1. An economic system consists of the institutions created by a society to deal with the problems created by scarcity.

2. The basic questions that all economic systems must address because of scarcity are: (a) What to produce, (b) What shall be the technology of production, and (c) Who shall receive the real income of the society.

3. Any economic system can be evaluated in terms of its (a) static efficiency, (does it produce what is desired?), and (b) dynamic efficiency, (are resources used to maximize the long-term stream of benefits from their use?).

4. The placement of the *property rights*, rights to own, transfer and profit from the ownership of resources, may be public or private. All societies have some mix of these two assignment methods.

5. Property rights are important to societies in two ways: (a) they create incentives for innovation and (b) they heavily influence the distribution of income.

6. A system based on *market capitalism* has two essential criteria: (a) The means of production are privately owned and property rights are vested in individuals. (b) Economic decisions are expressed through a system of interrelated markets and are decentralized. The two legal features necessary to achieve these essentials are (a) the right of private ownership and (b) the legal enforceability of contracts.

7. Two major economic advantages of market capitalism are (a) the incentives to efficiency by private property owners seeking to maximize the value of their rights along with the absence of *free riders*, those who benefit from using resources but bear none of their cost, and (b) incentives to minimize decision-making costs.

8. The criticisms of market capitalism are: In a society in which there is pure capitalism, the needs of poor people who have less purchasing power are given less weight in establishing market demand. In addition, firms may fail to consider external costs and benefits, especially the costs to the populace of pollution and other forms of environmental damage. The economic advantages of capitalism include: (a) the efficiency that private property right incentives creates, and (b) the low costs of decision making that decentralized decision making creates.

9. *Socialism* has various forms but there is a common belief in each that resources other than labor should be socially owned and there should be few private property rights.

10. *Planned socialism* involves public property rights with centralized choices about using resources. Theoretically, it can create any distribution of real income chosen and can incorporate externalities. However, it tends to create disincentives to efficiency and lacks an appropriate and low-cost way to allocate resources. It is also far from clear that planned socialism in practice leads to the incorporation of externalities.

11. Karl Marx, the intellectual father of modern planned socialism wrote about capitalism and predicted its ultimate demise. *Dialectical materialism*, the basic principle behind Marx's concept of *historical materialism*, holds that human society throughout history has undergone a continual process of change or development. The social structure evolves from one form to another; the guiding factors in this process of evolution are changing technology and the natural environment.

12. It is basic to Marxist thought that as long as there is private ownership of the means of production, there will be differing classes. As long as classes exist, conflict will exist, as one class exploits another.

13. According to Marx, surplus value, the difference between the value of products created by labor and its wage payments will create a problem of inadequate demand for growing output under capitalism. A declining rate of profit will lead to recurrent depression according to Marx.

14. Marx argued that the falling profits would lead capitalists to increase their investment to improve technology, and this in turn would increase unemployment. The result would be a *reserve army of the unemployed,* with the effect of keeping wages down.

15. Because Marx based his theory of value on labor, he failed to integrate the fact that labors' payment depends on its productivity. As more capital, and other factors are used, that productivity rises and so does labor income. He also failed to foresee that (a) governments in market economies, would step into the picture and reduce the severity of business cycles by manipulating interest rates, taxes, and government spending, (b) that modern capitalist states would develop extensive social welfare programs and, (c) that many workers would themselves become capitalists, through ownership of property or stocks and bonds.

16. Most economies today are mixed economies. They involve various mixes of property rights and levels of resource usage decision making. *Democratic socialism* seems to be a system in which private property rights exist but in which states intervene after decentralized choices about resource usage are made to achieve distributional goals.

17. Over time, many planned socialist economies suffered from the "problem of fatal conceit," a term of Frederick Hayek. Hayek predicted the ultimate failure of such economies because of their inability to generate the information necessary to reallocate resources in the face of changing tastes and technology.

18. By the late 1980s, planned socialist economies began to fail. Many, including the former Soviet Union and the People's Republic of China, began to create or recreate market capitalist institutions.

19. In the twentieth century contest between market capitalism and planned socialism, it appears that planned socialism lost out, although some nations continue with planned socialism.

20. The four main reforms necessary in the transition from planned socialism to market capitalism are (a) creation of secure private property rights, (b) creation of a system of prices that reflect relative scarcity, (c) a monetary system that

produces price stability and relative scarcity prices, and (d) political and economic institutions that facilitate (a), (b), and (c).
21. Arguments continue about the relationship between economic freedom and political freedom. Some argue that in the transition from planned socialism to market capitalism the greater economic freedom of capitalism will engender greater political freedom. Studies indicate that economically freer societies grow more rapidly than planned societies. Arguments continue about whether greater political freedom will accompany increased economic liberalization.

22. Arguments remain about the continuing viability of socialism in the post-cold war era. Some conclude that ideological evolution has ended and that capitalism has been proved the only viable economic system. Others, such as Herbert Gintis, argue that a new socialism true to its intellectual origins will evolve and that each system will adopt the best features of the other.

KEY TERMS

Command economy
Dialectical Materialism
Dynamic efficiency
Economic System
Essential Criteria of Capitalism
Free riders
Historical Materialism
Market capitalism
Mixed economies
Planned Socialism
Property rights
Reserve Army of the unemployed
Static efficiency
Surplus Value
The problem of "Fatal Conceit"

QUESTIONS

1. What is an economic system?

2. As a reminder, what choices *must* any economic system create answers to? Why must it do so?

3. As a student of economics, what arguments would you advance for market capitalism as a desirable economic system?

4. What is *planned socialism*? What are its main differences from market capitalism?
5. Sketch the main points of Marx's model of history and explain why Marx's prediction about the collapse of capitalism has not come true.

6. What is meant by the Marxist term, "surplus value"? What is the labor theory of value on which it was based?

7. How is the "free rider" problem resolved in a market capitalist economy?

8. Why do property rights and the level at which choices about using resources occur matter to an economic society?

9. What seems to be the explanation for the fact that most economies in the early twenty-first century are "mixed economies"?

10. What is the problem of "fatal conceit" that has afflicted planned socialist economies in the 20th century? What causes the problem?

11. Why has planned socialism largely lost out in the contest with market capitalism?

12. What are the major reforms necessary in the transition from planned socialism to market capitalism?

13. What is the argument of Herbert Gintis about the future of socialism?

Glossary

Ability-to-pay principle A principle of taxation under which those who have a larger income are deemed capable of paying not only a larger tax but a larger percentage of their income in taxes.

Absolute advantage The ability of a given nation to produce all commodities more cheaply (that is, using up few resources per unit of output) than any other nation with which it might trade.

Abstinence theory of interest A theory that people prefer to consume goods and services now, rather than later; therefore, people will save (postpone consuming) only if they are given a reward. That reward is called interest.

Accelerator principle The general rule that changes in the rate of change of consumer demand cause much larger changes in induced investment. The accelerator is positive if a change in the increase in consumer demand causes induced investment to increase. It is negative if the change in induced investment decreases.

Accounting profit The difference between total revenue and total explicit cost.

Adaptive expectations hypothesis The view that decision makers form their inflationary expectations on the basis of events of the recent past.

Adjustable-peg system A system of exchange in which currencies are pegged, or are not allowed to change in value by more than a specific percentage. The pegs themselves, however, may be changed from time to time.

Administered-price inflation A kind of inflation that occurs when firms with some control over price use that power to raise prices more rapidly than cost increases.

Administered pricing A term used by some economists to refer to prices that are set by the administrators of firms rather than established by independent influences of supply and demand.

Age-earnings profile A profile that shows the relationship between annual incomes and age for groups with various levels of education.

Aggregate-demand-equals-aggregate-supply approach (Keynesian) An approach to the problem of finding equilibrium income in a simple economic model without government and foreign trade. According to this approach, the equilibrium is at that level at which *aggregate supply*, consumption plus savings (C + S), is equal to *aggregate demand*, consumption plus intended investment (C + I).

Aggregate-demand-equals-aggregate-supply approach (General) An approach that holds that equilibrium real income is established where aggregate quantity demanded equals aggregate quantity supplied.

Aggregate demand shock A term used to describe a shift in aggregate demand.

Aggregate production function The relationship in physical (nonmonetary) terms between output and employment for a given economy (at a specific time). A "recipe" for output.

Aggregate supply shock A term used to describe a shift in aggregate supply.

Allocative inefficiency The tendency for monopoly firms to set prices above marginal costs and to allocate fewer resources to producing their products than consumers prefer.

Antithesis In Marxist theory, the force arising from a social contradiction that compels a change in the existing thesis (or set of social arrangements).

Arbitrage The practice of buying international currencies at low prices and quickly selling them at high prices.

At factor prices Method of computing national income using the prices paid in the factor markets. This measuring practice excludes indirect business taxes.

At market prices Method of computing national economic accounts using the prices paid in the markets for goods and services. This measuring practice must utilize all market costs incurred in production.

Autarky Economic self-sufficiency.

Automatic stabilizers Structures built into the U.S. economy that have a moderating influence on recessions and inflations. They are automatic in that they operate without being invoked by government policy makers. They are not considered strong enough to prevent, by themselves, the occurrence of business fluctuations. The progressive personal income tax is an example.

Autonomous investment Investment that is not affected by changes in the nation's overall level of income and consumption.

Average propensity to consume The percentage of their incomes that people at a given level of income tend to consume:

$$APC = C/Y$$

Average propensity to save The percentage of their incomes that people at a given level of income tend to save:

$$APS = S/Y$$

Average revenue Total revenue divided by output.

Average total cost Average fixed cost plus average variable cost.

Backward-bending labor supply curve A graphic illustration of a situation in which the quantity of labor supplied decreases as the wage increases beyond a certain level.

Balance-of-payments statement The annual accounting statement disclosing the status of a nation's foreign trade, including its capital transactions. The statement reveals what was bought and sold, and how any difference between the two was financed. (The balance-of-payments account must balance.)

Balance of trade The monetary value of exports minus imports:

$$X - M.$$

Balance to be financed In the balance-of-payments statement, the combination of the basic balance plus the short-term capital account.

Balanced-budget multiplier The multiplier that makes itself felt when a balanced-budget change in government expenditures and taxes (that is, government expenditures and taxes moving in the same direction and by the same amount) causes the level of national income to change in the same direction and by the same amount as the expenditure-tax change. *See also* Multiplier effect.

Bank holding companies Corporations that own one or more banks.

Barriers to entry Factors that prevent other firms from entering a market.

Barter A system of exchange that does not involve money; the trading of goods directly for other goods.

Basic balance In the balance-of-payments statement, the balance in the current account plus the balance in the long-term capital account.

Benefits-received principle of taxation The theory of taxation according to which people pay taxes that are commensurate with, or in line with, the benefits they receive from government services.

Bilateral monopoly A market situation in which a single seller bargains with a single buyer.

Bonds Instruments of debt, guaranteeing payment of the investment (face value) plus interest by a certain date. Interest on bonds is a cost of production to a business firm that raises capital by selling bonds.

Break-even point or price Occurs when a firm just covers its opportunity costs. A price that equals average cost and marginal cost is a break-even price.

Bretton Woods Conference International monetary conference held in 1944, which established the International Monetary Fund (IMF) and the International Bank for Reconstruction and Development (IBRD).

Budget restraint The limits on purchases of goods imposed by a consumer's income and by the prices of the goods bought.

Business cycles Variations in a nation's general economic activity; fluctuations in output, income, employment, and prices.

Capital account The account, in a nation's balance-of-payments statement, that is made up of long-term and short-term capital flows.

Capital broadening (constant capital-to-labor ratio) The situation in which capital instruments grow at the same rate as the amount of labor employed.

Capital consumption allowance *See* Depreciation.

Capital deepening The situation in which a nation's employers use more capital relative to the amount of labor used, thus raising the capital-to-labor ratio for the economy.

Capital gains tax A tax placed on the increase in the value of an asset, which is realized on the sale of the asset. It is considered a tax loophole because the tax rate on such gains tends to be lower than on other forms of income.

Capital-intensive process A production process that uses relatively more capital than labor or land.

Capitalism An economic system with two essential ingredients: (1) the private ownership of the means of production, and (2) the expression of economic decisions through a system of interrelated markets.

Capture hypothesis The view that regulatory agencies are often captured by the industries they regulate and serve industry interests rather than those of the public.

Cartel A group of producers who join forces and behave like a monopoly with respect to price and output.

Ceteris paribus In economic analysis, the practice of holding certain variables constant and permitting other *key* variables to change.

Change in demand A shift in a demand curve (by which more or less of a good is bought at all prices) that results from a change in (1) income, (2) tastes, (3) prices of other goods, (4) number of consumers, or (5) consumers' expectations of future prices.

Change in quantity demanded A movement along a demand curve that results from a change in the price of that good.

Change in quantity supplied A movement along a supply curve that reflects a change in the amount of a good offered for sale as only the price of that good changes.

Change in supply A shift in a supply curve that reflects that more or less of a good is offered for sale by a firm at all prices.

Check An order to a bank from the holder of a demand deposit to transfer money from that demand-deposit account and pay it to someone else.

Checking accounts *See* Demand deposits.

Closed market economy A market economy consisting of interrelated product and factor markets that does not trade products, services, or resources with other economies.

Closed shop An employment situation in which workers *must* join a union in order to get or hold a job.

Coins Metal tokens minted by the Treasury and issued through the Federal Reserve Banks.

Command economy An economy in which the problems generated by scarcity are solved by a system of central government planning.

Commercial bank Any bank that holds demand deposits.

Common property resources Those that are open to use by everyone. They have, thus, no individual owners (also called common access resources).

Common rent *See* Quasi-rent

Common stock Instruments of ownership of a corporation. People who own shares of common stock can vote on all matters requiring stockholders' consent, and there are no limitations on the amount of dividends they can receive. However, they receive dividends only after all prior claims against the company (interest on bonds, and so on) have been paid.

Comparable worth A proposal under which wages would be based on the intellectual and physical demands of various jobs. Points would be created for each job and jobs with the same numbers of points would receive equal wages.

Comparative advantage A situation in which a nation is relatively more efficient at producing some goods than at producing others, compared with the production capabilities of other nations with which it trades.

Compensatory fiscal policy *See* Functional finance.

Competing interest laws Those in which special interest groups on both sides of a legislative issue vie for favor in order to obtain concentrated benefits.

Competition The market form in which no individual buyer or seller has influence over the price at which she or he buys or sells. *See also* Pure competition.

Complementary investment An investment that increases the productivity of other investments.

Complements Products used in conjunction with each other.

Concentration ratios A measure of the combined market shares of an industry's largest firms.

Conscious parallelism A practice in which a dominant firm sets its prices and other firms set theirs in a way that parallels those of the price leader.

Constant capital-to-labor ratio *See* Capital broadening.

Constant-cost industry An industry in which the cost curves of individual firms remain the same as the output of the industry varies.

Constant GNP *See* Real GNP.

Constant returns to scale The condition for a firm when all inputs are increased at the same proportion and output increases by this same proportion.

Consumer choice A theory of demand that rests on four assumptions about consumers: (1) Consumers buy competitively. (2) Consumers have limited money incomes and full information. (3) Consumers are rational. (4) Consumers maximize their utility or satisfaction.

Consumer price index An index that measures price changes for a certain market basket of goods likely to be purchased by a family of four living in an urban area. Compiled and published monthly by the Bureau of Labor Statistics.

Consumers' surplus The difference between what consumers would be willing to pay for a good and what they actually pay for it.

Consumption function Schedule of the quantities that people are willing and able to consume at different levels of income during a given time period.

Contestable market One in which there are no significant losses from entry or exit due to sunk costs.

Contraction phase That part of the business cycle in which the level of economic activity falls.

Control through the ruble Control that the Soviet Union exercises over business firms through the medium of the Gosbank (central bank). A business firm's account at the Gosbank is credited with the value of its assigned production goal. As the firm uses resources, it pays for them by checks on its account. If the firm uses up its account before it achieves its assigned goal, it fails in its assignment.

Corporate profits The return to entrepreneurship in firms that are incorporated. Corporate profits equal dividends plus retained earnings (undistributed corporate profits) plus corporate taxes.

Corporation A legal entity or form of business enterprise, created by the process of incorporation, which functions separately from its owners.

Cost-plus pricing A form of administered pricing in which a firm first computes its variable cost, then its overhead or fixed cost, and finally adds its expected profit per unit. The result is the price it charges to consumers.

Cost-push inflation The kind of inflation that occurs when suppliers of resources increase their prices faster than productivity of manufacturers increases. Costs of production then go up, which forces prices up.

Countervailing power The idea that monopoly power often exists on both sides of a market. The monopsony power of buyers is counterbalanced by the monopoly power of sellers.

Coupon economics The system by which a government rations the output of the economy by issuing ration coupons to consumers, which consumers must redeem in order to buy rationed products.

Covert collusion A situation in which representatives of various firms in the same industry meet and decide on prices, shares of the market, and other conditions of the market.

Creeping inflation A kind of inflation in which there is a moderate rise in prices that continues for an extended period of time.

Criticism and self-criticism program A program in the Soviet Union that requires individual citizens to identify and report deviations from the government's economic plan.

Cross price elasticity of demand The percentage change in the demand for one good divided by the percentage change in the price of another good.

Crowding theory A theory that explains the effects of discrimination by tracing the impact that discrimination has in forcing women, blacks, or other minorities into certain kinds of employment and out of others.

Cultural Revolution A mass social movement that took place in the People's Republic of China in 1966-1969, supported by the Chinese government and aimed at rooting out bourgeois and antirevolutionary thought and action.

Currency in circulation Currency (both paper money and coins) that is actually in use, not in the vaults of banks or in the Treasury.

Current account An account in the balance-of-payments statement that is like the income and expense statement of a nation. It includes all current transactions, but excludes short-term and long-term movements of capital.

Current account balance The balance in the interpayments accounts obtained by adding exports of goods and services minus imports of goods and services plus net unilateral transfers.

Customer discrimination Job and wage discrimination resulting from tastes of buyers (for example, diners in restaurants preferring to be served by men or whites).

Cyclical deficits component That part of the federal deficit which arises from automatic stabilizers.

Deadweight loss of monopoly A welfare loss to society of consumers' and producers' surplus that results from monopoly. It is a loss not captured by someone else.

Decreasing-cost industry An industry in which external economies cause costs of all individual firms in the industry to fall as the output of the industry as a whole increases.

Deflating current GNP The act of decreasing current GNP to take into account a rise in prices; expressing GNP in terms of dollars of constant purchasing power.

Deflation A general lowering of prices in an economy.

Deflationary gap The increase in aggregate demand necessary to make aggregate demand equal to aggregate supply at full employment.

Demand A set of relationships representing the quantities of a good that consumers are willing to buy over a given range of prices in a given period of time.

Demand curve A graphic plotting of the demand schedule, or a set of relationships between various prices of a good and the quantities of it that the public will buy at each of those prices in a given period of time.

Demand deposits Deposits in commercial banks that can be withdrawn "on demand" by one who presents a check.

Demand-pull inflation A rise in prices that occurs when demand for goods exceeds the ability of the economy to supply these goods at existing prices. The result is that the market rations this short supply through the medium of increased prices.

Demand schedule Indicates the quantity demanded at each price level.

Democratic socialists Those who believe in using democratic procedures to gain political power and curtail capitalism.

Dependent variable The factor in a two-variable system that changes as a result of changes in the independent factor.

Deposit multiplier That formula for determining the multiple that demand deposits may be of the required reserve ratio.

Depreciation An account allowance for the capital that "wears out" (either through use or obsolescence) while being used to produce the final goods and services of an economy in a given period of time.

Derived demand A demand for one thing that depends on the demand for something else. (For example, the demand for labor depends on the demand for the goods produced by labor.)

Dialectical materialism A philosophy in which material things are viewed as the subject of all change, and technology and the natural environment as the main forces that cause society to change continually.

Diminishing marginal utility of income The theory that people get less and less satisfaction from each increase in their incomes.

Diminishing rate of transformation The idea that the rate at which one good may be traded off, or transformed, into another decreases.

Direct The relationship between the independent variable and the dependent variable is direct if the dependent variable changes in the same direction as the independent variable.

Direct democracy A governmental system in which citizens directly choose the rules under which they will be governed.

Dirty float A system of managed exchange rates in which exchange rates are "pegged" or allowed by central banks to move with certain limits.

Discommunication The problems that a large organization encounters in trying to communicate in order to achieve effective decision making; due in part to large size.

Discount rate The rate of interest that the Federal Reserve charges depository institutions when it discounts acceptable short-term debt at the Federal Reserve, to enable the institutions to obtain reserves.

Discretionary fiscal policy Day-to-day fiscal policies established by government officials, designed to cope with changing economic conditions.

Diseconomies of scale The disadvantage a firm may encounter when it increases the size of its plant and increases its output, only to find that the cost of each unit produced is greater than before.

Dissavings Consuming more than is produced, or consuming more than one's income.

Double coincidence of demand In a system of barter exchange the requirement for a mutuality of needs; each party to a transaction must want what the other has.

Double taxation A situation that arises when a corporation pays taxes on its gross receipts. Then it distributes its dividends from these receipts to its stockholders, who must then pay income tax on the previously taxed money.

Duopoly An industry dominated by two interdependent major sellers, although there may be a number of fringe firms as well.

Durable goods Commodities (such as automobiles) that are used up at a very slow rate; that is, it takes a long time (years) to use them up.

Dynamic efficiency Over a period of time, using resources in ways that maximize the long-term benefits from their employment.

Dynamic framework A concept or set of relationships by which one can explain the way certain things change through time.

Economic capacity The level of long-run production that is achieved with the lowest per-unit cost at the optimal plant size.

Economic determinism Assuming that all actions are reactions to changing economic reality.

Economic development The long-term process by which the material well-being of a society's people is significantly increased.

Economic dualism The coexistence within a society of two or more different economies (frequently, one with markets and cash incomes and the other with barter).

Economic imperialism A Marxist concept according to which capitalists ward off a fall in profits and lessen the severity of economic crises by exploiting the underdeveloped countries. Supposedly, capitalists do so by using the underdeveloped countries as a source of demand for their output and supply of cheap raw material and as places to invest capital.

Economic integration The degree to which an economy's resources are employed in their most productive uses.

Economic institutions Social institutions through which economic decisions are made (for example, the Federal Reserve System).

Economic loss The excess of total costs over total revenues.

Economic loss with production A situation in which a firm's short-run total revenue is less than its total costs, but greater than its total variable costs. The firm minimizes its loss by continuing to produce.

Economic loss with shut down A situation in which a firm's short-run total revenue is less than its total costs, but greater than its total variable costs. The firm minimizes its loss by continuing to produce.

Economic loss without production A situation in which a firm's short-run total revenue is not only less than its total costs, but also less than its total variable costs. The firm loses less by closing down altogether.

Economic profit Profit that is above normal profit. When there is economic profit, total revenue is greater than total cost (including the opportunity cost of entrepreneurs).

Economic rent The payment made to a resource whose supply is perfectly inelastic.

Economics The social science that deals with the analysis of material problems, how societies allocate scarce resources to satisfy human wants.

Economies of scale Achieved by a firm when the cost of each unit produced falls as output increases with larger plant size.

Effective demand The total aggregate demand for commodities and services in an economy.

Elasticity of (product) supply A measure of the rate of change in quantity supplied divided by the rate of change in price.

Elasticity of resource demand The rate at which the quantity of a resource demanded changes as its price changes:

$$\%\Delta Qd / \%\Delta P$$

where Q = quantity of the resource demanded, P = price of the resource, and (Greek delta) = "change in."

Elasticity of resource supply The rate of change in the quantity of an input supplied as its price changes:

$$\%\Delta Qs / \%\Delta P$$

where L = amount of labor, W = wage rate, and (Greek delta) = "change in."

Elasticity of supply of labor The rate of change in the quantity of labor supplied divided by the rate of change in the wage or:

QsQs/ WW,

where W equals the wage rate.

Embargo An absolute prohibition against importing certain goods.

Employment The situation in which a unit of resource (labor, land, capital, entrepreneurship) is used in some economic activity.

Entrepreneurship The function of organizing labor, land, and capital into a firm capable of producing and marketing a commodity or service.

Entry limit pricing The practice by monopoly and oligopoly firms of setting prices below profit maximizing levels in order to deter entry of new firms.

Equation of exchange MV = PQ, where M = supply of money, V = velocity of exchange (number of times M changes hands), P = price level, and Q = number of transactions.

Equilibrium exchange rate The rate of exchange between two currencies that clears the market or eliminates excess supply and demand.

Equilibrium income The level of income that results from the central tendency of a model. This level will be maintained as long as the factors in the model (savings and investment) remain the same.

Equilibrium price The market-clearing price, or the price at which quantity demanded equals quantity supplied.

Equity stock *See* Common stock.

Ex-ante investment The amount of investment firms plan to make.

Ex-post investment The investment that firms actually undertake (not simply plan to undertake).

Excess demand The excess of quantity demanded over quantity supplied at a price lower than the equilibrium price.

Excess reserves Assets that depository institutions hold in the form of reserves, but which are over and above that required by Federal Reserve regulations.

Excess supply The excess of quantity supplied over quantity demanded at a price higher than the equilibrium price.

Exchange controls Devices governments use to ration foreign currencies or eliminate excess demand for those currencies.

Exclusive unions Bargaining agents that agree to restrict union size and maximize the wage gains of their members.

Expansion The process by which a society's output grows as it uses more and more resources.

Expansion phase That part of the business cycle in which economic activity rises.

Expenditure approach A method of computing national income accounts that is concerned with the kinds of goods people buy, with what kinds of expenditures they make.

Explicit costs Those costs of a firm that result from contracting for resources in the markets.

Exploitation In neoclassical economic theory, a payment to a resource that is less than its value of the marginal product.

Exports Commodities and services sold to other nations.

External diseconomies of scale An increase in a firm's costs caused by changes in the output of the industry as a whole.

External diseconomy A cost increase originating outside of the individual firm.

External economies of scale A decrease in a firm's costs caused by increases in the output of the industry as a whole.

External economy A cost decrease originating outside of the individual firm.

Externalities The differences between privately expressed (market) costs and benefits and publicly expressed (nonmarket) costs and benefits. *See also* Spillovers.

Factor markets Those in which the prices of resources like land, labor, capital, and entrepreneurship are established and in which these resources are allocated.

Fascism An economic system combining private property rights with centralized choices about what to produce.

Featherbedding A practice in which unions require a certain number of jobs for the production of goods or services, and there is no need for that number of jobs.

Federal funds market The market in which banks lend their excess reserves to each other over night at the federal funds rate.

Fiat money Money that has greater value as a monetary instrument than as a commodity. It is money because the government issued it and says that it is money, and because people accept it as such.

Final goods and services Goods and services sold to the ultimate user.

Final-value method Method of computing GNP that sums up the prices to final buyers of all goods and services produced by the economy. Avoids double counting by eliminating intermediate production, and leads to the same statistical result as the value-added method of computing GNP.

Financial capital Capital in the form of money; savings that are available for investment in physical capital.

Fine tuning Discretionary changes in fiscal and monetary policy leading to counterchanges in the state of the economy.

Fiscal policy Manipulation of the expenditures and taxes of the federal government to achieve certain economic goals.

Fixed costs Costs that do not vary with output.

Fixed exchange rates A system of international exchange in which the currency of each nation has a certain fixed relationship to the currencies of other nations that is established by government decision. Rates are not allowed to vary with changing market conditions.

Foreign-trade multiplier effect (FTM) The change in GNP resulting from a change in net foreign trade:

$$FTM = GNPX - M'$$

where X = exports, M = imports, and (Greek delta) = "change in."

Fractional reserve requirement The percentage of deposits that depository institutions must hold as reserves. As a result, such institutions can lend out amounts that are a multiple of their reserves.

Free good A good with a price of zero. Supply is greater than demand at any price above zero.

Free rider problem Refers to the fact that once public goods are produced, they are available for consumption by individuals who may have contributed nothing to the cost of producing them.

Freely-floating exchange rate A competitive system of international exchange in which the currencies of the various nations are valued according to supply and demand in the international money market. The exchange rate is free to move up or down to eliminate excess supply or excess demand.

Frictional unemployment Short-term unemployment resulting from workers moving from one job to another.

Full capacity A situation in which a firm or industry is at the low point on its long-run average-cost curve.

Full economic integration When all resources of a society are employed and used in their most productive uses.

Full employment A situation in which everyone in the labor force is employed except those who are frictionally unemployed.

Full-employment budget The budget that balances government expenditures against the level of receipts (taxes) that the government would receive if the economy were at full employment.

Functional distribution of income An approach to the distribution of income that emphasizes the *sources* of income: wages, interest, rent, and profit.

Functional finance A policy that aims at compensating for changes in aggregate demand in the private sector by varying the public sector's expenditures and taxes.

General powers of the Federal Reserve System Powers that enable the Federal Reserve to increase or decrease the amounts of excess reserves that commercial banks need in order to make loans.

General price index Index construction by the Commerce Department to convert current GNP to constant GNP.

Giffen goods Those inferior goods with an income effect that moves in the same direction as price and for which the income effect is larger than the substitution effect.

GNP gap The difference between potential GNP and actual GNP achieved.

GNP implicit price deflator *See* General price index.

Gold-flow point The disequilibrium exchange rate at which it is cheaper to buy and ship gold in payment for trade than to buy currencies.

Gold standard The system of international exchange used up until the 1930s, according to which currencies were valued in terms of gold and were convertible into gold, and each nation was obligated to exchange its currency for gold.

Gold tranche position The amount of gold a member nation can borrow from the International Monetary Fund (IMF).

Gosbank The state bank in the Soviet Union, used to control and audit individual firms' activities. All firms have accounts with Gosbank, and all their purchases and sales go through the bank.

Gosplan An agency in the Soviet Union that translates overall goals into a comprehensive plan for the economy. Gosplan is the central planning committee of the Soviet Union.

Government expenditures In the national economic accounts, the measure of all government purchases of goods and services.

Great Leap Forward Second 5-year plan of the people's Republic of China (1958-1962). Execution of the plan was such a disaster that it was abandoned in 1960.

Gross national income (GNI) Total income at market prices generated in the production of all final goods and services during a specific time period. GNI = wages and salaries + rent + interest + proprietors' income + corporate profits + depreciation + indirect business taxes.

Gross national product (GNP) Total dollar value of all final goods and services produced in a given time period. GNP = consumption + gross investment + government expenditures + net foreign investment (export - imports).

Gross private domestic investment Investment including depreciation or capital consumption allowance. *Private* means counting only nongovernment investment; *domestic* means counting only investment made in the U.S. Investment is the act of creating capital, manufactured producer goods that aid in producing consumer goods and other capital goods.

Growth The intensive process by which the productivity (output per hour of labor employed or income per capita) increases.

Hedonism A philosophical school that argues that self-satisfaction is the primary goal of individuals.

Hedonist One who argues that people act to achieve self-satisfaction.

Herfindahl index A measure of market concentration obtained by summing the squared percentage market shares of firms in an industry.

Historical materialism The view that society throughout history has undergone a continual process of change and development from one form to another. The guiding factors in this process are the natural environment and changing technology.

Historical period A period of time in which technology changes.

Homo communista Communist or communal man.

Homo economicus A term meaning "economic person."

Homogeneous product A product so standardized that buyers do not differentiate between the output of different firms.

Horizontal mergers Are mergers between firms in the same industry.

Human capital The improvement in labor skills (marginal physical product) attributable to education or other training, innate ability and acquired skills.

Implicit costs Those costs associated with using self-owned resources.

Import duties *See* Tariffs.

Imports Commodities and services bought from other nations.

Inclusive unions Bargaining agents that seek to expand the number of jobs offered, and thus, the size of the union.

Income approach Computation of the national income accounts based on measuring the kinds of income generated in producing the output of the economy.

Income effect In demand analysis, the change in the quantity of a good that consumers demand as a result of a change in its price and thereby the consumers' purchasing power, or real income.

Income elasticity of demand An estimate of the rate at which the demand for a good varies as consumer incomes vary:

$\%\Delta Q/\%\Delta Y$

where Q = output and Y = income

Income-inferior goods Those goods that consumers tend to buy less of as their incomes increase, and more of as their incomes fall.

Incomes policy A policy that frequently involves wage and price controls by the government. In general, a cooperative effort of labor, management, and government to find mutually agreeable goals for the economy and the means to achieve these goals.

Increasing-cost industry An industry in which individual firms experience increasing costs caused by increases in output by the industry as a whole.

Increasing marginal utility of income The assumption that people get more and more satisfaction from each additional increase in their incomes. (This is not generally accepted as true).

Increasing opportunity cost The assumption that as a nation chooses to produce more of one good, it must (ultimately) give up increasing amounts of the other good.

Incremental capital-output ratio The additional capital needed to produce additional output.

Independent variable In a set of relationships, the variable that changes first.

Indicative planning The kind of planning one finds in France, where the government draws up targets for the economy and brings together employers and unions to discuss and modify the proposals. Firms and workers, with government support, move to implement these plans.

Indirect business taxes Taxes on goods and services passed on to consumers in the form of higher prices (for example, excise and sales taxes).

Induced investment Investment generated by changes in income and in quantity consumed. An increase in income leads to greater quantities consumed. Then there is an increase in investment to expand capacity in order to satisfy the new demand.

Inferior goods Goods that you cut back consumption of as your income increases.

Inflating current GNP Increasing current GNP to take into account a fall in prices; expressing GNP in terms of dollars of constant purchasing power.

Inflationary gap The excess demand at full employment that causes prices, rather than output, to increase.

Innovation Introduction of new products or processes.

Input-output relationships The complex set of interrelated requirements for inputs needed by the economy to produce various combinations of output (arranged by industries).

Instantaneous multiplier A multiplier effect that takes place without an intervening period of time. *See also* Multiplier effect.

Interdependency A situation in which economic actions depend on each other (for example, when firms in an industry act on the assumption that their price and output policies are dependent on the actions of other firms in that industry).

Interest The return to the owners of capital. Only interest paid by businesses is included in gross national income. (Interest on the national debt or interest on consumer loans is not included.)

Interlocking directorates A practice in which individuals serve on the boards of directors of more than one firm in the same industry.

Internal economies of scale Decreasing costs from a firm's increased output in the long term. These decreasing costs are due to changes made within the firm.

Internalizing costs and benefits The process through which the prevention of spillovers or externalities is accomplished by having all costs, private and public included in the price of a good.

Internal rate of exchange The rate at which a nation gives up one good in order to produce another.

International monetary fund (IMF) An organization set up at the Bretton Woods Conference in 1944 to facilitate international trade, especially to assure the financing of such trade and to administer the adjustable peg system of post-World War II exchange rates.

International reserves Assets available to central banks and other agencies that are accepted in payment of international debts.

Inverse The relation between independent and dependent variables is inverse if the dependent variable changes in the opposite direction from the independent variable.

Investment function A schedule of the quantities that people are willing and able to invest at various levels of income during a given period of time.

Invisible hand argument The idea attributable to Adam Smith that self-interest based voluntary exchanges can make all those involved in the exchanges better off.

Invisible items The services, including financial services (as opposed to physical commodities), that are exported or imported by a nation. Items not normally reflected in merchandise exports and imports.

Involuntary additions to inventory *See* Unplanned additions to inventory.

Involuntary reductions to inventory *See* Unplanned reductions in inventory.

Jawboning The use of persuasion on the part of the government to get business and industry to comply with government guidelines.

Job discrimination A situation in which workers are employed on the basis of some consideration other than their productivity, such as race or sex.

Kibbutz A community that operates on the principle of complete income equality. In Israel in 1973, there were 240 kibbutzim, with more than 85,000 members.

Kinked-demand curve A demand curve that is based on the assumption that firms in an oligopoly follow suit when competitors' prices decrease, but ignore other firms' price increases.

Labor-intensive process A production process that uses relatively more labor than capital or land.

Laffer curve A theoretical association between various tax rates and the tax revenues collected at each rate.

Law of demand The general rule that consumers buy more at lower prices than they do at higher prices; that price and quantity demanded are inversely related.

Law of diminishing marginal utility The general rule that as more of a particular good is consumed in a given time period, the additional utility of each additional unit of the good will ultimately decrease.

Law of diminishing returns *See* Law of variable proportions.

Law of supply The general rule that the quantity supplied rises as price rises, and falls as price falls; that price and quantity supplied are directly related.

Law of variable proportions (diminishing returns) The general short-run rule that as a firm uses successive equal units of a variable input in conjunction with a fixed input, additions to output (marginal output) derived from the variable input begin to diminish beyond some point.

Leading indicators Certain kinds of economic activity that lead the business cycle by increasing or decreasing before the rest do. Measurements of these indicators are "weather vanes" for the economy.

Leakages Factors in the multiple creation of demand deposits that reduce the ability of depository institutions to expand the supply of money or demand deposits.

Legal tender Anything that the law requires be accepted in payment of a debt.

Limited liability A legal term that means that those who own the corporation (stockholders) are not responsible for its debts. Stockholders' liability (or the amount stockholders are liable for if the firm goes bankrupt) is limited to the purchase price of their stock.

Liquid assets Assets, such as savings accounts or government bonds, that can be quickly converted into money with little risk of loss.

Liquidate To sell a firm or to convert its plant capacity to producing other goods.

Logrolling The practice of trading votes or trading support for one issue in order to obtain support for another.

Long-run period A planning period of a firm or industry, in which all inputs are variable. During this period, the firm can choose any plant size permitted by present technology and by its financial limitations.

Lorenz curve A curve that shows the degree of inequality in the distribution of income for a specific year. The percentage of people in different groups is shown on the horizontal axis, and the percentage of income going to each group is shown on the vertical axis.

Loss minimization *See* Profit maximization.

M1 money A measure of the money supply that consists of currency, coin and checking deposits and travelers checks.

M2 money A measure of the money supply that consists of all components in M1 plus savings deposits, small time deposits and money market mutual funds.

M3 money A measure of the money supply that consists of all the components of M2 plus large value certificates of deposit.

Macroeconomics The study of the forces that determine the level of income and employment in a society.

Malthusian specter The nineteenth-century view, advanced by Thomas R. Malthus, that the supply of people (increasing at a geometric rate) would outrun the supply of food (increasing at an arithmetic rate), and that widespread starvation would result.

Margin requirements Regulation by the Federal Reserve of the percentage of the selling price of stock that a purchaser must put down in cash in order to buy a stock. The purchaser may borrow the rest from a bank or a stockbroker.

Marginal cost The cost of producing an additional unit of output.

Marginal efficiency of capital The expected rate of return on capital; the stream of income a business expects to obtain over the life of a piece of capital in relation to the price of that capital.

Marginal physical product The additional amount of product that a firm can produce as a result of hiring an additional unit of input (labor, capital, and so on).

Marginal private cost or benefit Cost or benefit that individuals derive from producing or consuming an additional unit of a good.

Marginal propensity to consume The percentage of any change in income that people tend to spend:

$$MPC = \Delta C/\Delta Y$$

where C = consumption, Y = income and (Greek delta) = "change in."

Marginal propensity to save The percentage of any change in income that people tend to save:

$$MPS= \Delta S/\Delta Y$$

where S = savings, Y = income and (Greek delta) = "change in."

Marginal resource cost The amount it costs a firm to hire one more unit of a resource or factor.

Marginal revenue The change in total revenue due to a small or one-unit change in output.

Marginal revenue product The addition to total revenue attributable to using an additional unit of a resource. One finds it by multiplying the marginal physical product of the resource times the marginal revenue from selling the additional units of product it produces.

Marginal social cost or benefit Cost or benefit to society caused by producing and consuming an additional unit of a good.

Marginal tax rates The rates on additional taxable income.

Marginal utility The additional satisfaction derived from the consumption of the last unit (or additional unit) of a good purchased.

Marginal utility of income The change in satisfaction derived from a change in income.

Marginal utility of leisure The change in satisfaction derived from change in leisure time.

Market period The period of time in which a firm has already produced its output. All costs are fixed costs.

Market system The set of means by which exchanges between buyer and seller are made.

Marxist socialism A system of philosophy of government and economics that grew out of the writings of Karl Marx in the nineteenth century.

Materials-balance approach An explanation of environmental problems based on the amount of input used in production and the disposal of waste products created in the consumption of that output.

Means of deferred payment The function of money that is concerned with facilitating lending and the repayment of loans.

Medium of exchange The function of money that deals with exchanging goods for money and money for goods.

Mercantilism A system of economic thought, at its peak from the sixteenth to nineteenth centuries, according to which governments were responsible for the welfare of the economy.

Microeconomics The study of disaggregated economic activities or how a market economy allocates resources through prices.

Midpoint formula A device used in calculating the price elasticity of demand by dividing the average rate of change in quantity demanded by the average rate of change in price.

Mixed economies Economic systems that combine elements of private and public property rights and centralized as well as decentralized choices about resource usage.

Model A device economists use to create a systematic analogy to actual economic behavior.

Monetarism An approach to economic policy that emphasizes the dominant role of the supply of money. It calls for a fixed and appropriate increase in the money supply each year as the basic policy for economic stabilization.

Monetary policy A government's manipulation of the money supply to achieve economic goals.

Money Anything that performs the functions of a medium of exchange, standard of values, store of value, and standard of deferred payment.

Money (current) GNP Output of a given year valued at the prices of that year. Data on GNP before being adjusted for price changes.

Money income The number of dollars received in income; does not reflect purchasing power.

Monopolistic competition A market situation with three main characteristics: (1) many firms, (2) differentiated products, and (3) relative ease of entry into and exit from the market.

Monopoly power A firm's ability to influence the price of its product.

Monopsony A market situation in which there is only one buyer.

Monopsony profit *See* Technical factor exploitation.

Moral suasion The use of persuasion by the Federal Reserve to get depository institutions to do what it wants.

Multinational corporations (MNCs) International firms that buy raw materials, sell finished products, and have production facilities in many countries.

Multiplier effect The multiple change in income due to a given initial change in aggregate demand. *See also* Balanced-budget multiplier.

Multiplier formula

$$M = 1/\ MPS \text{ or } 1/1\text{-}\ MPC$$

where MPC = marginal propensity to consume and MPS = marginal propensity to save.

National banks Commercial banks chartered by the federal government.

National income (NI) Net income of a country using factor prices generated in the production of all goods and services in a given period of time. NI = wages and salaries + rent + interest + proprietors' income + corporate profits.

National income at factor prices Net income of a country obtained by using only market prices of factors rather than market prices of finished commodities or sales on the commodity markets.

Natural monopoly A market situation for an industry in which there are economies of scale up to the output rate that fills the market. A single firm is more efficient than any larger number of firms.

Natural rate of unemployment The difference between what economists consider full employment and a zero level of unemployment. Basically it is frictional unemployment.

Near money Assets that have all the characteristics of money except that they are not used as a medium of exchange.

Negatively sloped A curve sloping downward, to the right, on a diagram.

Negative net investment A situation in which gross investment is less than depreciation. In such a case, the capital stock of the economy is contracting.

Negative savings *See* Dissavings.

Negative sum game When losses exceed the winnings in a game.

Neoclassical economics School of economic thought developed during the late nineteenth century. Many aspects of this thought are considered valid today, and others have been changed and expanded. For example, Keynesian economics (named after John Maynard Keynes) evolved from a basic change in one aspect of neoclassical economics.

Net foreign trade (NFT) The difference between exports and imports:

$$NFT = X - M,$$

where X = exports and M = imports.

Net national income (NNI) A nation's net income at market prices generated in the production of all final goods and services during a given period of time (excluding depreciation) NNI = wages and salaries + rent + interest + proprietors' income + corporate profits + indirect business taxes.

Net national product (NNP) The net value of all final goods and services a nation produces during a given time period (excluding depreciation), NNP = consumption + net investment + government expenditures $\pm$ net exports.

Nomenklatura The term used to describe the Soviet elite whose special entitlements increase their real incomes.

Nondurable goods Commodities, such as food, that are used up fairly quickly.

Nonprice competition Forms of competition between businesses that do not involve price. May include competition in styling, services, advertising, and quality.

Normal goods Those that consumers buy more of as their real incomes rise and less of as their real incomes fall.

Normal profit A profit just large enough to keep the firm producing in the long run. Normal profit equals the entrepreneur's opportunity cost (what entrepreneurship could earn in other uses). A normal profit is included in total cost.

Normative economics Economic discussions that make judgments about the way things should be.

Official reserve transactions account An account of those sources such as borrowing from other official agencies that finance the basic balance.

Official reserve transactions balance In a nation's balance of payments, the account showing how a payment deficit is financed.

Oligopoly An industry characterized by (1) the existence of a few firms that dominate an industry, each of which can affect the actions of others in the industry; (2) either homogeneous or differentiated products; and (3) significant barriers to entry.

Oligopsony A situation in which there are few buyers in the market.

OPEC An acronym for the Organization of Petroleum Exporting Countries, an international oil export cartel that sets the price of (most) exported oil.

Open market economy A market economy that does exchange products, services, or resources with other economies or nations.

Open-market operations The buying and selling, by the Federal Reserve, of highly liquid, short-term, low-risk government debt.

Opportunity cost The best alternative good one gives up when one chooses to produce a certain thing.

PACs or political action committees Organizations that channel funds from special interest groups to the election campaigns of politicians.

Paradox of thrift An ironic situation in which, during a recession, if people all try to increase their savings, the equilibrium level of income of the nation and the actual quantity saved decrease.

Paradox of value That some goods have great total utility in use (e.g.; water) but little in exchange while other goods have relatively little value in use (e.g.; diamonds) but great value in exchange. The price we are willing to pay for a good is based on its value in exchange.

Pareto optimal A situation that makes at least one person better off while making no one else worse off.

Parity A level for farm-product prices, maintained by governmental support and intended to give farmers the same purchasing power for each product sold as they had in some designated base period.

Partnership A business arrangement in which two or more individuals combine to operate an unincorporated business enterprise.

Per capital real GNP The figure obtained by dividing real GNP by the size of the population.

Per se rule A rule in law that certain acts are illegal in and of themselves, no matter what their intent.

Perfect economic integration The situation in which units of a resource are paid the same amount in all uses of that resource.

Perfect elasticity The situation in which price elasticity of demand approaches infinity. This means that as the quantity demanded changes, there is no change in price. The demand curve is horizontal.

Perfect inelasticity The situation in which price elasticity of demand equals zero. This means that as price changes, there is no change in quantity demanded. The demand curve is vertical.

Perfect integration The situation in which units of a resource are paid the same amount in all uses of that resource.

Perfect price discrimination The situation in which a firm charges the same consumer a different price for each unit sold. The price is the maximum that the consumer will pay for each unit.

Perfectly contestable market One in which there are no losses from entry or exit due to sunk costs.

Periodic multiplier A multiplier effect that takes place over time. *See also* Multiplier effect.

Personal disposable income The portion of personal income that people may either spend or save. PDI = personal income - personal taxes.

Personal income All income received by people, whether from production or from transfer payments. PI = national income + undistributed corporate profits + corporate taxes ± net transfer payments.

Phillips curve A curve that shows the trade-off between unemployment and price changes. If employment increases, prices will increase; if unemployment increases, price increases will go down.

Physical capital Capital in the form of tools and instruments of production.

Pigou effect An economic reaction whereby, as prices fall, people with savings have greater purchasing power; therefore, savers increase their demand for goods and services.

Positive economics Economic discussions that consist of pointing out what *is*, positive economics contains no value judgments.

Positive net investment A situation in which gross investment exceeds depreciation; this means that the capital stock of the economy is expanding.

Positive sum game When winnings exceed losses in a game.

Positively sloped Sloping upward, to the right on a diagram.

Precautionary purposes One reason why people want to hold money; they want cash in hand in case of emergencies.

Preferred stocks Stocks that have preference status when it comes to receiving dividends and assets of a given corporation, in case the corporation should have to liquidate. Preferred stocks usually do not carry voting privileges, and the amount of dividends is usually limited.

Present discriminatory activity Basing jobs and wages on goods other than productivity.

Price discrimination The charging of different prices for a good to different consumers. A situation in which the price of a unit of some good, divided by the marginal cost of that unit, is not the same for all customers. The seller of the good discriminates against some customers.

Price elastic A term describing a market situation in which the quantity of a good demanded changes at a faster rate than the price of the good:

$$\%\Delta Q/\%\Delta P > 1$$

where Q = quantity, P = price, (Greek delta) = "change in, "and > = "greater than."

Price elasticity of demand (E_d) An estimate of the rate at which the quantity demanded of a good varies in response to its price:

$$E_d = \%\Delta Q/\%\Delta P$$

where Q = quantity demanded, P = price, (Greek delta) = "change in."

Price elasticity of supply An estimate of the rate at which the quantity of a good supplied changes as the price of the product changes:

$$Es = \%\Delta Qs/\%\Delta P$$

where Q = quantity supplied, P = price, (Greek delta) = "change in."

Price floor A target price, usually established by government, below which the market price is not allowed to move.

Price index A measure of changes in a price level.

Price inelastic demand A term describing a market situation in which the quantity of a good demanded changes at a slower rate than the price of the good:

$\%\Delta Q/\%\Delta P < 1$ where Q = quantity demanded, P = price,
(Greek delta="change in," and < = "less than."

Price leadership In an oligopoly, a form of implicit collusion in which a leader firm sets prices that are observed and followed by others in the industry.

Price rivalry The contest in which sellers watch what prices others charge and then react to those prices.

Price seeker A firm that must set the price of its product(s) as well as determine its most profitable output rate.

Price taker A firm which acts on a price that is beyond its control. This generally occurs in perfect competition.

Primary demand Demand for a commodity (such as cars or refrigerators) by those who have not owned that commodity before: first-time owners.

Private equilibrium The *market* equilibrium between the buyer's privately and noncollusively determined benefits from the sale of a commodity and the seller's privately determined costs (including the profit necessary for entrepreneurship).

Private rates of return Rates of return on investment that do not take into account indirect social costs and benefits (called external costs and benefits).

Producers' surplus The difference between the actual selling price of a good and the marginal cost of producing it.

Product differentiation An attempt to make your product different, or appear to be different, from your competitors product.

Production-possibilities curve A graphic representation of the production-possibilities function. *See also* Production-possibilities function.

Production-possibilities function A relationship expressing those combinations of goods that the full-employment use of a society's resources can produce during a particular period of time (using the best available technology).

Profit A return or payment to the entrepreneur.

Profit maximization To produce an output level where profits are maximized. Profit is said to be maximized or loss minimized when production is at the level at which marginal cost is equal to marginal revenue.

Profit-push inflation *See* Administered-price inflation.

Profits of unincorporated businesses. *See* Proprietors' income.

Progressive tax A tax with a rate that increases as the tax base increases.

Proletariat Workers in the factories of the industrial societies developed since the eighteenth century.

Property rights Rights of ownership to use, to transfer, and to benefit from the employment of factors of production.

Proportional tax A tax with a rate that remains the same as the tax base changes.

Proprietors' income The return to entrepreneurship in firms that are not incorporated.

Protectionism The government's effort to protect domestic firms or industries from free (competitive) international trade by imposing tariffs or quotas on imported commodities.

Public goods Goods that can be used by a person without reducing the amount available for other people to use.

Pure competition A market form that has the following characteristics: (1) No single firm can influence price. (2) There is no collusion. (3) Products are homogeneous. (4) There are no barriers to entry or exit. (5) Prices are flexible. (6) Buyers and sellers have full information.

Pure economic determinism The assumption that the actions of people and institutions are reactions to changing economic reality.

Pure economic rent The payment to a resource whose supply is perfectly inelastic.

Pure monopoly A market form in which (1) there is just one firm, and (2) the firm's product has no close substitutes.

Pure monopsony A labor market situation in which there is one employer that sets wage rates.

Pure number A number that is independent of the units of measure of the factors involved in compiling it.

Quantity adjuster A firm that has no control over the price at which it sells its product. It decides only how much to produce.

Quasi-rent or common rent The difference between the actual payment to a resource in relatively inelastic supply and its opportunity cost.

Quotas Restrictions on the quantities of goods that may be imported into, or exported from, a country.

Random variations Variations that cannot be accounted or planned for, since they do not follow any regular pattern.

Rational expectations hypothesis The view that decision makers form their inflationary expectations on the basis of current and recent past events and thus anticipate future events.

Rate of exchange The price at which one nation's currency is exchanged for that of another.

Rate of transformation The rate at which one good is traded off for another.

Rational ignorance The argument that when the benefits of a public choice are highly concentrated and its costs highly diffused, it is rational for those who bear its costs to ignore them.

Real GNP The output of a nation for a given year, adjusted for price changes between that year and given base year.

Real income The value of what one can buy with one's money income.

Regressive tax A tax with a rate that declines as the tax base increases.

Regulated monopoly A market situation in which one firm usually has a franchise from government, but a government regulatory commission sets prices and other conditions that the firm must follow.

Regulation Q A government regulation that empowered the Federal Reserve to set the maximum interest rates that commercial banks can pay on savings accounts and demand deposit (checking) accounts. This regulation was abolished in the early 1980s.

Regulations X and W Government regulations that empowered the Federal Reserve to set minimum down payments and maximum length of loans for consumer lending and real estate lending; expired in the 1960s.

Relative rent Differences in rent payments to a resource in different uses.

Rent (national income measures) In the calculation of gross national income, the payments to owners of land. Includes an estimated rent on homes occupied by their owners.

Rent (resource market payments) A payment to resource owners above that which would just induce them to employ resources in a particular use.

Rent seeking activities Those activities undertaken by special interest groups to obtain privileges from governments that will raise their return above opportunity cost.

Replacement demand *See* Secondary demand.

Representative democracies Systems of government in which voters choose elected representatives to make public choices.

Required reserve ratio The percentage of depository institutions' demand deposits that the Federal Reserve requires these banks (financial institutions) to keep in the form of assets called reserves.

Reserve army of the unemployed A Marxist term denoting the number of people who are unemployed in capitalistic societies because of the increased use of capital and improved technology (that is, machines replacing labor).

Reserves Eligible assets (their eligibility determined by the Federal Reserve) that must be held by depository institutions.

Resource externalities Changes in the costs of resources that are not attributable to the actions of a single firm but are due to changes in the industry, or in the natural or political environment.

Resources The inputs (land, labor, capital, entrepreneurship) used to make consumer and producer goods.

Results of historical discrimination The effects on present patterns of jobs and wages attributable to previous economic discrimination.

Retained earnings Undistributed corporate profits.

Rule of reason A rule under which there is a broad judicial determination of the reasons for a firm's conduct and the effects of that conduct on restraint of trade.

Sales maximization hypothesis The argument that firms seek to maximize sales or the size of the firm rather than the firm's profit.

Satisficing A decision to seek an acceptable or satisfactory level of profit as opposed to a maximum level of profit.

Savings-equals-intended-investment approach An approach to the problem of finding equilibrium income, in a model without government and foreign trade, according to which the intended investment curve is placed above the x axis (measured income) in relation to the savings function (S = II).

Savings function Schedule of the quantities that people are willing and able to save at different levels of income during a given period of time.

Say's law Supply creates its own demand

Scarcity The relation between limited resources and unlimited wants which results in the inability to satisfy all human wants for goods and services.

Seasonal variations Fluctuations in employment, money supply, and cash flows that occur regularly at certain periods each year.

Second degree price discrimination The practice of charging different prices to different groups of buyers.

Secondary demand Demand by consumers for commodities to replace consumer goods.

Secular trend The expansion or contraction of an economy over very long periods of time. The long-term trend in any time series.

Services Those products of an economy (haircuts, medical attention, and so on) that are not commodities. The value of services is included when GNP is computed.

Short-run period The period of actual production, in which some resources used by a firm are variable and at least one resource is fixed.

Shut down point or price The rate of output that corresponds to a price equaling average variable cost. Total revenue equals total variable cost and the firm's loss is no greater with than without production.

Signaling The idea that employers pay higher wages to more educated workers because the education is a signal of other aspects of productivity increasing behavior.

Single-tax movement A school of thought in the late nineteenth century, led by Henry George, which proposed taxing away all land rents and using the revenues to fund governments. Henry George believed this would be the only tax needed to finance an economy.

Social costs Private costs plus spillovers (externalities). *See also* Externalities; Spillovers.

Socialism A social system in which there is collective or governmental ownership of the means of production and distribution of goods. There are many brands of socialism, encompassing many gradations of political and economic thought. Common to all of them is the idea that control of the means of production should be in public, not private, hands.

Sole proprietorship A form of business enterprise in which one person is the owner, and is solely responsible for that enterprise.

Special drawing rights (SDRs) A system of international reserve assets, the so-called "paper gold"; a market basket of currencies established by the International Monetary Fund (IMF). Nations that are members of the IMF may borrow these SDRs to ease currency crises.

Special interest laws Those that confer concentrated benefits but impose diffused costs on voters.

Specific powers of the Federal Reserve Powers of the Federal Reserve to regulate particular areas of lending, such as margin requirements on stock purchases; Regulation Q, W, and X were part of these powers.

Speculative purposes One reason why people wish to hold some of their assets in the form of money: they want to be able to take advantage of unforeseen opportunities to invest, to buy bargains, and so forth.

Spillovers Differences between *private* costs and benefits and *public* costs and benefits. *See also* Externalities.

Standard of value The function of money that enables people to place values on goods and services.

State banks Commercial banks chartered by the various state governments.

Static efficiency At a point in time, using resources in ways that produce the most desired mix of output.

Stationary state A condition in which a given society has reached the upper limit to its growth in per capita income.

Store of value The function of money that enables holders of money to save by a process of transferring value from the present to the future.

Structural deficits component That part of the federal deficit that arises from discretionary fiscal policy.

Structural unemployment A kind of unemployment caused by changes in the structure of the economy, either in the composition of demand or in technology. Either one of these types of changes may cause changes in the composition of the demand for labor.

Substitutes Products that may be consumed in place of each other.

Substitution effect An effect that appears when there is a change in the quantity of a good demanded resulting from a change in its price relative to other goods' prices. This effect comes to light during analysis of demand in a given market. A relatively cheaper good is substituted for relatively more expensive goods.

Sunk costs Outlays on resources that have already been made. Also called fixed costs.

Superior goods Those whose consumption varies in the same direction as but at a greater rate than real income. The elasticity of income is greater than 1.

Supply A set of relationships representing the quantities of a product that a firm (or all firms in an industry) will offer for sale at each possible price in a given period of time.

Supply curve A graphic plotting of the supply schedule, or a set of relationships between various prices of a good and the quantities of it that a firm supplies.

Supply of M_1 money All demand deposits in commercial banks, plus all currency and coin in circulation.

Supply of resources The quantities of a resource offered for sale at various prices in a given period of time.

Supply side economics Efforts and incentives to stimulate growth in aggregate supply.

Surplus value Marxist term for the differences between the wages paid to workers and the market value of what workers produce. Surplus value, to Marxists, measures the degree of exploitation of the proletariat (working class).

Synthesis In Marxist theory, the system that evolves after the antithesis has forced social changes.

Tariffs Taxes on imported goods.

Tax avoidance The process by which tax obligations are minimized by lawful use of the provision of tax laws.

Tax evasion The illegal process by which tax obligations are either not reported or incorrectly reported in order to evade tax payment.

Tax rate With respect to income, the percentage of income a citizen must pay annually in taxes. With respect to property, the percentage of the value of property the owner must pay to the government annually in taxes.

Technical factor exploitation In factor markets, the failure of a monopsonistic employers to pay resources their value of marginal product or marginal revenue product (also called monopsony profit).

Technocrats Term used by John Kenneth Galbraith to describe those who hold power in large corporations (also used to apply to those who would "manage" the economy).

Technological change Growth in knowledge or advances in techniques that result in more productive capital goods and more efficient organization.

Technostructure Term used by John Kenneth Galbraith to describe the many interlocking committees of people with technical expertise in large corporations, who make the essential corporate decisions.

Terms of trade Relationship between a nation's export prices and its import prices:

$T = PxP_I$ where P_X = prices of exports and P_I = prices of imports.

Thesis In Marxist theory, the set of social arrangements existing at a given time.

Tight money policy A policy of a nation's central banking authority that aims at reducing aggregate demand by decreasing the supply of money in an economy.

Time deposits Savings accounts for which depository institutions can require prior notice before the account holder can withdraw the funds.

Total cost Total fixed cost plus total variable cost.

Total utility The entire satisfaction from consuming a good.

Transactions purposes One reason for holding some assets in the form of money. People do not receive their income at exactly the same time that they need to pay out money. Thus, they want to hold money to be able to meet these day-to-day payments.

Trust An organization that controls the voting shares of an industry and thus can set output rates and prices like a multi-plant monopoly.

Turnover tax A tax on goods as they pass through the various stages of production. The Soviet Union uses turnover taxes to increase prices so that the quantities of goods available (quantity supplied) will be equal to the quantities demanded. It is also employed in some Western European countries.

UNCTAD United Nations Conference on Trade and Development.

Underemployment An employment situation in which units of resources are not employed in their most productive uses.

Unemployment A situation in which a unit of a resource is unable to find use as an input.

Underground economy Transactions that occur and give rise to taxable income but are not reported for tax purposes.

Union shop A labor market in which individuals who are employed by a firm must then join the union.

Unions Organizations formed by employees for purposes of collective bargaining with employers.

Unit elastic demand A term describing a market situation in which quantity demanded of a good changes at the same rate as its price:

$$\%\Delta Q / \%\Delta P = 1$$

where Q = quantity demanded, P = price, and (Greek delta) = "change in."

Unit of account *See* Standard of value.

Unlimited liability A situation in which there is no differentiation between the assets of the business and the personal wealth of its proprietor. If the business suffers reverses, the owner is personally liable for all its debts.

Unlimited life A situation in which a corporation can continue to exist no matter who owns its stock.

Unplanned additions to inventory A situation in which a business firm produces more of its product than the public is willing or able to buy, which must then be added to inventory. The result is that the business acts to reduce supplies and reduce amounts produced; income moves toward equilibrium.

Unplanned reduction in inventory A situation in which a business firm does not produce as much of its product as the public is willing and able to buy. The result is that the business acts to increase its orders and increase the amounts produced; income moves toward equilibrium.

Utility theory A theory of demand that assumes that consumers buy things on the basis of their evaluation of the satisfaction to be derived from various combinations of goods, and of their effort to maximize that satisfaction.

Value-added method A method of computing GNP in which one adds all additions to the value of a product made at each stage of production; the total of these additions for a given product equals the final value of that product.

Value of marginal product The value to consumers of the output produced by using an additional unit of a resources. One computes this value by multiplying the marginal physical product of the resource times the price of the good produced by the resource.

Variable costs Costs of factors of production (such as labor, raw materials, and so forth) that vary according to variations in the firm's output.

Veblen good A good whose appeal is greater at higher prices than at lower prices.

Velocity of exchange The number of times the supply of money changes hands in a given period of time.

Vertical mergers A merger of firms producing inputs to be used in the production of a final product.

Visible items Those commodities (such as cars, food, and machinery) that are exported or imported by a nation.

Wage and price controls Mandatory limits on wages and prices established by a regulatory authority and enforced by law.

Wage and price guidelines Suggested rules for levels of wages and prices. The government suggests these rules, but compliance with them is voluntary.

Wage discrimination A form of price discrimination in which employers use, as criteria to determine the wages they pay to their employees, certain characteristics that have nothing to do with the productivity of the employees, such as race or sex. They may pay lower wages to blacks than to whites, to women than to men, and so forth.

Wages and salaries The money income, including social security taxes, that is the return to labor; figured into the computation of gross national income.

Waste of monopolistic competition The failure of monopolistically competitive firms to produce at minimum long-run average cost or, in other words, the tendency to product with excess capacity.

Wholesale price index An index that measures change in wholesale prices.

Zero economic growth (ZEG) The idea or belief that an economy's GNP should not increase. ZEG is usually based on a concern for preserving or improving the physical and cultural environment.

Zero population growth (ZPG) The slogan advanced by people who feel that the birth rate should equal the death rate so that population will not increase.

Zero sum game When winnings are equal to losses in a game.

Index

A

Ability-to-pay principle 73, 84
Abstinence theory of interest 172, 175, 189–190
Accelerator 209
    Negative 209, 228, 235
    Positive 209, 235
Accelerator effect 209, 228–229
Accelerator principle 208–209, 226, 235
Account balance
    Capital 430
    Current 430
Account budget
    Capital 254
    Current 254
Acid rain 368
Actual investment 199
Actual savings 199
Adaptive expectations 342–343, 345
Adjustable-peg system 423
Administered-price inflation 136, 325, 333
Advertising 108
Aggregate consumption 184
Aggregate demand 141, 143, 145, 205
    Shifts in 149
Aggregate demand curve 145–146, 150, 162–163
Aggregate demand shift 149, 163
Aggregate demand shock 149, 163
Aggregate price level 88, 145–147, 152, 161, 242
Aggregate production function 369
Aggregate quantity demanded 143, 156, 158, 161–162, 178, 214, 218, 234–236, 338, 344
Aggregate quantity supplied 143, 152, 161–162, 178, 214, 218, 234–236, 278, 338, 344
Aggregate Supply 338
Aggregate supply 141, 146
    Ranges of 151
    Shifts in 149
    Short-run 177
Aggregate supply costs 156
Aggregate supply curve 147, 150–151, 162–163, 177
Aggregate supply function 200
Aggregate supply shift 149–150, 163
Aggregate supply shock 149, 163
Aggregate-demand-equals-aggregate-supply
    Approach 188, 192, 211, 234
Aggregate-quantity-demanded-equals-aggregate-quantity-supplied
    Approach 214–215, 217
Aggregate-quantity-demanded-equals-aggregate-quantity-supplied approach 218
Aggregate-supply-equals-aggregate-demand
    Approach 201
Albrecht, William 432
American goods 146
American Revolution 270
Antimonopoly laws 69
Antitrust laws 69, 76
Arbitrage 417
Autarky 381
Automatic fiscal policy 242
Automatic stabilizers 242, 258, 262
Autonomous investment 185–186, 188–189, 191, 197, 205–206, 208–209
Availability of credit 143, 162
Availability of resources 146–147, 162
Average propensity to consume 201–203, 234, 274
Average propensity to save 202, 234

B

Balance of payments 231
    Politics and the 434
Balance of Payments (BOP) 426
Balanced budget 236, 243, 245, 250, 252, 339
Balanced Budget Amendment of 1995 250
Balanced-budget multiplier 221–222, 236
Bank Act of 1933 311
Bank holding companies 315
Bankers' bank;"bankers' bank." 306
Bankruptcy
    Federal 248
Barro, Robert 247, 356, 359–360, 370
Barter 268
Barter economy 269
Barter system of exchange 268, 280
Baumol, William 358, 369
Beggar-thy-neighbor argument 395
Belassa, Bela 431
Benefits-received principle 72–73, 84
Blinder, Alan 256–257, 261
Bonds 68
    Government 90, 184, 229
Bottlenecks 151, 163
Boulding, Kenneth 367
Budget
    Balanced 236, 243, 245, 250, 252
    Capital 254, 260
    Current 254, 260
    Federal 222, 245, 253, 259
    National 222
Budget deficit 232, 242, 245, 249, 251–252, 255, 258–260, 340, 342
    Federal 249, 251
Budget Enforcement Act of 1990 252
Budget Reconciliation Act of 1990 252
Budget surplus 242
Budgetary procedure 253
    Federal 241, 253–254, 260
Bureau of Labor Statistics 97
Business 66

Business cycle 116–118, 120, 122–123, 125, 135–136, 229, 243, 256–257, 260
Business cycles
Recurring 448
Business firms 3
Business fluctuation 117, 122, 136, 226
Business investment 198, 229
Business tax 106
Indirect 102, 111

C

Capital 351
Foreign 330
Human 356
Physical 356
Capital account 430
Capital account budget 254
Capital broadening 356
Capital budget 254, 260
Capital consumption allowance 96, 101, 110
Capital deepening 356
Capital gains tax 73
Capital goods 59, 249, 352
Capital investment 226, 246
Capital market 330
Capital resources 354
Capital stock 182
Capital surplus 305
Capital-intensive 356–357
Capitalism
Collapse of 448
Capitalist system 255
Cartel 157, 164
Central Bank 288, 290, 304, 306
Certificates of deposit (CD)
Negotiable 273
Non-negotiable 273
Ceteris paribus 145–146
Cheap-foreign-labor argument 395
Chenery, Hollis 400, 404
Circular flow 60
Circular-flow model 57–58
Complex 59, 171, 175, 189
Simple 57, 59, 82, 170–171, 175, 189
Circular-flow model with only a private sector
Simple 58
Circular-flow model with private and public sectors
Complex 60
Civilian goods 362
Classical 195, 225, 237
Classical economics 170, 189
Classical economists 337, 343, 346
Classical economists, and the post-Keynesians.
New 337
Classical theory 169–170, 175, 189
Closed economy 249
Coins 271–272, 280
Advantages of 272
Disadvantages of 272
Command economy 451
Commodity balance of trade 378–379, 405
Commodity exports 378, 405
Commodity imports 378, 405
Common market 397, 408
Common stock 68
Comparative advantage 386
Trade and 383
Compensatory fiscal policy 242, 253–254, 258
Competition
International 358
Congress 306, 433
Constant GDP 97–99, 111
Consumer debt 95
Consumer demand 66, 104, 173, 176, 188, 199, 209–210, 212, 229–230, 235
Consumer durable goods 230
Consumer durables 100, 118, 230
Consumer expenditures 143
Consumer goods 60, 65, 72, 145, 176, 185, 188, 198, 201, 206, 209, 227, 229–230, 279, 312, 317–318, 327
Durable 143
Consumer income 257
Consumer price index 97, 230, 232
Consumer price index (CPI) 153–154, 164
Consumption 59, 82, 90, 94, 100, 103, 110–111, 117, 127, 135, 143, 170–176, 178, 181–186, 191–192, 196–199, 201–205, 208–211, 213–215, 217, 219–221, 228–229, 233–236, 246, 251, 259–260, 279, 281, 318, 327, 361, 367
Aggregate 184
Change in 183
Current 246
Intended expenditures 178
Personal 62, 82, 93, 362
Present 246, 259
Private 246
Consumption curve 180
Consumption demand 178, 196, 199, 217, 279, 371
Consumption expenditures 94, 143, 145, 162
Consumption function 179–184, 188, 191–192, 203, 205, 211–212, 214–215, 236
Consumption schedule 180–182
Contraction phase 117, 135
Corporate income tax 68, 76
Corporate profit 95, 102, 106, 110–111
Undistributed 102
Corporate stock 228, 311, 331
Corporate tax 102, 111
Corporation 66–71, 76, 78, 82, 102, 187
Advantages of 68, 83
Disadvantages of 68, 83
Multinational 71
Cost of credit 143, 162
Cost of resources 146–147, 162

Cost-of-living adjustments 155
Cost-push inflation 127, 136, 325, 333
Costs
  Aggregate supply 156
  Opportunity 109, 135
  Production 151, 156, 164
  Social 371
Cowboy economy 367
Credit
  Availability of 143, 162
  Cost of 143, 162
  Demand for 319, 326, 333
  Supply of 320–321, 323–324, 326, 332–333, 342
Credit cards 274, 281
Credit market 319–320, 323–324, 326, 332
Credit market equilibrium 326
Credit markets 251, 259–260
Credit union 313
Creeping inflation 130, 137
Crowding-out effect 246–247, 251, 259
Currency 272, 280
  Advantages of 272
  Disadvantages of 272
Currency in circulation 271
Current account 430
Current account budget 254
Current budget 254, 260
Current GDP 97–98, 111
  Deflating 99
  Inflating 99
Curve
  Aggregate demand 145–146, 150, 162–163
  Aggregate supply 147, 150–151, 162–163, 177, 190
  Consumption 180
  Demand 179
  Laffer 341, 345
  Lorenz 62–63, 82
  Phillips 131–135, 137, 329
  Production-possibilities 65, 357
  Progressive 74
  Proportional 75
  Regressive 74
  Supply 147
Customs union 397, 408
Cyclical unemployment 122

D

Debt 241–245, 251
  Federal 243–246, 317, 330
  Federal government 306
  Foreign 251, 259
  Issuance of 266
  National 228, 317, 361
  Non-interest-bearing 272
  Opportunity cost of 249, 259
  Private 271
  Public 271
  Refinancing of 248
  Repayment of 249
  Sale of 244, 246
Declining income 144
Defense expenditures 72, 109, 123, 230, 254, 324, 364, 370
Defense goods 249
Defense spending 361, 365
Deficit 241–253, 255, 258–260, 430
  Budget 232, 242, 245, 249, 251–252, 255, 258–260, 340
  Federal 219, 228, 232, 245–246, 248–249, 251–252, 258–259, 345
  Federal budget 266
  Trade 232, 251, 259–260
Deficit expenditures 228
Deficit finance 241–242, 246, 260
Deficit reduction 252, 255
Deficit-financed expenditures 318
Deflating current GDP 99
Deflation 128–130, 133–134, 136, 269, 420
Deflationary gap 220, 222, 236, 274
Demand 33
  Aggregate 146, 149, 205, 338
  Consumer 66, 104, 173, 176, 188, 199, 209–210, 212, 229–230, 235
  Consumption 178, 196, 199, 217, 279, 371
  Derived 415
  Double coincidence of 268, 280
  Effective 178, 191, 317
  Excess 218, 220
  Government 213, 230
  Investment 176, 199, 247, 279
  Law of 145
  Primary 226–227
  Public 213–214, 235
  Replacement 227
  Secondary 227
  Total 274
Demand curve 179
Demand deposits 270, 272, 280
  Advantages of 272
  Disadvantages of 272
Demand for loanable funds 172
Demand shocks 155
Demand-pull inflation 125, 127, 131, 136, 230, 246, 323, 325, 327
Democratic socialism 452
Denison, Edward 356–357, 369
Department of Agriculture 77
Department of Health and Human Services 77
Department of Housing 77
Department of Transportation 77
Deposit insurance 314–315
Deposit multiplier 295–296
Depository institution 270, 313
Depository Institutions Deregulation and Monetary Control

Reform Act of 1980 305, 312
Depreciation 96, 100–102, 106, 108, 185, 229
Depression 101, 117, 127, 144, 174, 182, 227–229, 233, 235, 324, 361
Deregulation 147, 303, 314
Deregulatory Act of 1980 312, 331
Derived demand 415
Development
  Economic 3
Dialectial materialism 447
Dirty float 418, 424
Discount policy 310
Discount rate 306, 309–311, 316, 318, 320, 322, 331, 333
Discount-rate policy 310
Discouraged-worker effect 123
Discretionary expenditures 259
Discretionary fiscal policy 242, 330, 333
Discretionary government policy 337, 343
  Discretionary government 343
Discretionary macroeconomic policy 303, 342
Discretionary monetary policy 324, 328, 330, 333
Discretionary policy 327, 330, 333, 342, 345
Discrimination
  Racial 135
  Sexual 135
Disembodied technological change 354
Disequilibrium 143
Disposable income 103, 105, 110–111, 143, 152, 162, 215
  Personal 103–104
Dissavings 181–183
Distribution
  Income 252
Distribution of income 62–63, 65–66, 215, 367, 371
  Actual 62–63
  Changes in 184–185, 191
  Perfectly proportional 62–63
Dividends 102, 129
Dollar
  Appreciation of 251
  Decline of 250, 259
Dollar appreciation 259
Domestic economy 251
Domestic goods 146, 162
Domestic income 110
Domestic investment 93, 251
Domestic savings 250–251, 259
Double coincidence of demand 268, 280
Double taxation 68
Double-digit inflation 323, 325
Dow Jones Industrial Index 311
Dowd, Douglas 361, 370
Dumping 431
Durable consumer goods 143
Durable goods 82, 93, 117–118, 136, 184, 230, 279
  Consumer 230
Durables
  Consumer 100, 118, 230
  Producer 118
Dynamic efficiency 442
Dynamic framework 349, 368

E

Economic
  Development 17
  Policy 403, 422
  Trade policy 436
Economic activity
  Domestic 377
  International 377
Economic development 3
Economic efficiency 66
Economic equity 66
Economic growth 65–66, 122, 125, 130, 235, 254, 331, 333, 349, 356–357, 359, 365–366, 368–372
  Zero 367–368, 371
Economic growth rate 358–360
Economic policy 266
  Government 222
Economic recovery 343
Economic role of government 254, 258
Economic systems 441
  Evalutating 442
Economics
  Classical 170, 189
  classical 170
  Neoclassical 266
  Supply-side 152, 337–340, 344
Economists
  Classical 337
Economy 241–242, 246–247, 249–251, 254–256, 259, 261, 313, 377
  Barter 269
  Closed 249
  Cowboy 367
  Domestic 251
  Individual 2
  Market 2, 88, 222, 255
  Mixed 452
  Modern 267
  Money 269
  Share 255–257, 260–261
  Spaceman 367
  Underground 340
Effective demand 178, 191, 317
Efficiency
  Dynamic 442
  Static 442
Embargo 156, 392
Emergency expenditures 252
Employment
  Full 121, 241
  Self 241
Employment Act of 1946 241

English Common Law 69
Entitlement programs 254, 260
Entrepreneurs 351
Entrepreneurship 95, 106, 170
Environmental pollution 81, 83, 366, 371
Environmental regulation 357
Equation of exchange 276, 278–279, 281
Equilibrium 88, 133, 141–143, 148, 161, 163, 195–201, 206, 211–214, 217–218, 224–225, 233–236, 319–320, 327, 338, 363
    Credit market 326
    Product 141
Equilibrium exchange rates
    Determining 418
Equilibrium income 147–148, 150, 162–163, 178, 198–199, 212, 214, 217–218, 221, 233–234
Equilibrium interest rate 189, 323, 326
Equilibrium level 197
Equilibrium level of income 148–149, 161, 163, 178, 188, 196–201, 205, 208, 211, 213–215, 217–219, 221–222, 233, 235–236
Equilibrium level of prices 143, 149, 161–162, 344
Equilibrium level of real income 149, 162, 165, 344
Equilibrium level of real national income 143, 156, 164
Equilibrium price 196
Equilibrium real income 163, 178, 338
    Short-run 320
Evons, Paul 247
Ex-ante investment 233
Ex-ante savings 233
Excess demand 218, 220
Excess income 90
Excess reserves 290–296, 300, 305–312, 315–316, 318, 322, 324–325, 331, 333
    Role of 296
Excess supply 218, 236
Exchange controls 419
Exchange rate 425, 434
    Floating 417
Exchange rates 413
    Equilibrium 418
    Fixed 418
    Fluctuations in 421
    Freely floating 417
Excise tax 96, 102
    Federal 73
    State 73
Expansion phase 117, 135
Expectations
    Adaptive 342–343, 345
    Inflationary 342, 345
    Rational 337, 343, 345
Expenditure approach 91–92, 100, 102–103, 110
Expenditures 245, 248, 253, 258, 260
    245, 258
    Consumer 143
    Consumption 143, 145, 162
    Defense 72, 109, 123, 230, 254, 324, 364, 370
    Deficit 228
    Deficit-financed 318
    Discretionary 259
    Emergency 252
    Export 94
    Federal 243, 249, 252, 254–255, 361–363, 370
    Import 94
    Investment 59, 93–94, 144–145, 162
    Korean War 361
    Military 229–230
    National security 72
    Private 246
    Special-interest 253
    War 361
Export expenditures 94
Export goods 229
Export quotas 393
Exports 94, 144, 162, 228–229, 377, 380, 383
    Commodity 378, 405
    Military 229
    Net 94, 110–111, 144–145, 162, 362
Ex-post invesment 199, 233
Ex-post savings 233
Extensive growth 350, 368
External aggregate demand shocks 155

F

Factor market 58
Factors of production 96
Failure
    Financial institution 313–314
Family income 62
Federal Advisory Council 305, 331
Federal bankruptcy 248
Federal budget 222, 245, 259
Federal budget deficit 266
Federal Communications Commission 77
Federal debt 241, 243–246, 248–250, 252–253, 255, 258–259, 317, 330
Federal deficit 219, 228, 232, 245–246, 248–249, 251–252, 258–259, 340, 345
Federal excise tax 73
Federal expenditures 243, 249, 252, 254–255, 361–363, 370
Federal fiscal system 252
Federal funds market 296, 300, 306–307, 310
Federal funds rate 296, 300
Federal government 59, 68, 72, 75–76, 84, 93, 102, 104, 110, 228, 305–306, 318, 363
Federal government debt 306
Federal income tax 74
    Graduated 84
Federal Open Market Committee (FOMC) 305–306, 320, 331
Federal Reserve 271–272, 277, 280, 288–289, 291–293, 295–296, 299–300, 303–312, 315–319, 322–329, 331–333

General powers of 306, 322, 331
Specific powers of 311, 331
Structure of 304
Federal Reserve Act of 1914 304, 311
Federal Reserve Board 256
Federal Reserve Districts 304
Federal Reserve Note 272
Federal Reserve; that is, the commercial banks' .iB.total reserves 318
Federal revenue 340
Federal revenues 75
Federal tax receipt 363
Federal taxation 340
Federal Trade Commission 77, 79
Feldstein, Martin 329
Fiat money 271, 280
Final-value method 105–106, 111
Finance
Deficit 246
Functional 242
Financial institution 313–314, 332
Financial Institutions Reform, Recovery, and Enforcement Act (FIRREA) 315
Financial market 273, 277, 303, 312–315, 332
Deregulated 303
International 303
Fiscal policy 222, 241–242, 250–251, 254–255, 258, 266, 327–330, 333, 338, 342–343, 345, 363
Compensatory 242, 253–254, 258
Discretionary 242, 258, 330, 333
Fixed exchange rates 418
Fixed income 128, 136
Fixed interest rate 273
Food and Drug Administration 77
Foreign capital 330
Foreign exchange markets 413, 415, 434
Foreign goods 146, 162
Foreign investment 250
Foreign savings 250
Fractional reserve principle 275, 281
Fractional reserve requirement 291
Free market 370–371
Free riders 444
Free trade 145, 397–398, 403, 424
Free Trade Agreement 397–398, 408, 431
Freely floating exchange rate 417
Frictional unemployment 122, 133, 136, 138, 148, 162, 363
Friedman, Milton 327–330, 333, 417
Full Employment 133
Full employment 121
Functional distribution of income 61, 82
Functional finance 242

G

Galbraith, John Kenneth 344
Garn-St. Germain Act 313
GDP
Constant 97–99, 111
Current 97–98, 111
Money 97–99, 111, 227
Per capita 97
Real 97–99, 111, 120, 158, 231–232, 328, 337, 340, 344
GDP deflator 153, 164
GDP gap 123–124, 136, 148, 162
GDP growth 366
GDP implicit price deflator 98
GDP money 226
GDP price index 153, 158, 164
General Agreement on Tariffs and Trade (GATT) 397, 407, 433
General price index 98
Generalized system of preferences 431
Gintis, Herbert 452
Gold standard
Advantages of 422
Disadvantages of 422
Gold-flow point 422
Goldsmith banking 274
Goods
American 146
Capital 59, 130, 249, 352
Civilian 362
Consumer 60, 65, 72, 145, 176, 185, 188, 198, 201, 206, 209, 227, 229–230, 279, 312, 317–318, 327
Defense 249
Domestic 146, 162
Durable 82, 93, 117–118, 136, 184, 230, 279
Export 229
Foreign 146, 162
Illegal 99, 111
Investment 100, 229, 246
Military 62, 229
Non-consumer 145
Non-defense 249
Nondurable 82, 93, 117–118, 136
Nonmilitary 127
War 101
Gordon, Robert J. 135
Government 3, 88, 266
Federal 59, 68, 72, 75–76, 84, 93, 102, 104, 110, 228, 305–306, 318, 363
Local 59, 72, 75, 93, 226, 318
Role of 241, 254, 260
State 59, 68, 72, 75, 84, 93, 226, 305, 318
Government bonds 90, 184, 229, 248, 250
Government debt 95, 103
Government demand 213, 230
Government economic policy 222, 328, 330
Government Expenditures 212–214, 235–236
Government expenditures 59, 62, 72, 93–94, 104, 110–111, 124, 126, 133, 144–145, 162–163, 171, 175, 178–179, 189, 191, 196, 199, 211–212, 214–215,

217, 219–222, 235–236, 241–242, 246–247, 249, 258–259, 266, 317, 328, 365
Government intervention 81, 83, 222, 257, 260
Government investment 93
Government policy 266, 327
    Discretionary 337
Government regulation 79–80, 288, 296, 299
    Costs and benefits of 370
    Growth in 357, 369
Government sector 221
Government securities 245, 307–309, 311, 318, 320, 322, 328, 331, 333
Government-debt securities 306
Gramm-Rudman-Hollings Act (1985) 252, 260
Great Depression 227, 398, 421, 430
Great Depression of 1930 117, 124, 174, 324, 354
Greenhouse effect 368
Gresham's Law 272
Gross Domestic Income (GDY) 92, 95–96, 101–102, 110
    Formula for 96
Gross domestic income (GDY) 96, 110
Gross Domestic Product 243–244, 253–254, 258, 260
Gross Domestic Product (GDP) 89–90, 92, 230–231, 361
Gross domestic product (GDP) 92–95, 97–99, 102, 107–111, 123, 136, 148, 156, 222, 272, 357, 362–364
    Actual 124
    Formula for 94
    Potential 124
Gross income 143
Gross investment 93, 101, 108
Gross national product (GNP) 110
Gross private domestic investment 93, 101, 186
Growth
    Economic 65–66, 88, 122, 125, 130, 235, 254, 331, 333, 349, 356–357, 365–366, 368–372
    Extensive 350–351
    Full-capacity 361, 365
    Full-potential 363
    GDP 366
    Income 107
    Industrical 356
    Intensive 350–351
    Macroeconomic 344
    Monetary 343
    Money supply 321
    Population 186, 353–356, 358, 366, 369, 371
    Productivity 147, 324, 352, 354, 356–358, 369
    Real income 337–338, 340

H

Harberger, Arnold 404
Hawley-Smoot tariffs 395
Heilbroner, Robert 109
Heller, Walter 365–366, 370
Historical materialism 447
Home mortgage loan 314
Hopkins, Thomas 357
Household income 59, 61–62
Households 3, 72
Human capital 356, 360, 369–370
    Investment in 147, 162
Human resources 350
Humphrey-Hawkins Act of 1978 133, 152

I

IInflation 231
Illegal goods 99, 111
Import embargo 392
Import expenditures 94
Import quotas 392
Import restraints
    Reasons behind 431
Imports 94, 144–145, 162, 377, 383
    Commodity 378, 405
Income
    Actual distribution of 62–63
    Aggregate level 88
    Classical theory of 170, 174–175
    Consumer 257
    Declining 144
    Disposable 103, 143, 152, 162, 215
    Distribution of 62–63, 65–66, 215, 367, 371
    Equilibrium 147–148, 150, 162–163, 178, 198–199, 212, 214, 217–218, 220–221, 233–234
    Equilibrium level of 148–149, 161, 163, 178, 188, 196–201, 205, 208, 211, 213–215, 217–219, 221–222, 233, 235–236
    Excess 90
    Family 62
    Fixed 128, 136
    Functional distribution of 61, 82
    Gross 143
    Household 59, 61–62
    Inequality of 62
    Interest 61, 82
    Keynesian model of 143
    Money 61, 63, 127–128, 136, 220, 327, 329
    National 98–99, 102–103, 107, 111, 143, 178, 212, 242, 327
    National level of 217–218, 242
    Net 73, 101–102, 111
    Noncash 63
    Per capita 350, 352, 369, 371
    Perfectly proportional distribution of 62–63
    Personal 68, 102–103, 111, 229
    Personal (PY) 102
    Proprietors' 61, 82, 95, 111

Real 88, 127
Rental 82
Semifixed 128, 136
Taxable 73–74, 340
Tax-base 74–75
Total 91, 95, 101
Variable 136
Varied 128
Velocity of 276
Income approach 91–92, 110
Income distribution 252
Inequality in 65
Income growth 88, 107
Income inequality 63
Income inferior 366
Income multiplier 362
Income redistribution 360
Income security 72
Income superior 366
Income tax 340
Corporate 68, 75–76
Federal 74
Graduated 73
Marginal 340
Personal 75–76, 84, 103
Income tax rate 73, 252
Income taxes 248
Incomes policy 223
Index
Price 152
Index of leading indicators (ILI) 120
Indirect business tax (T) 96, 102, 111
Induced investment 185, 191, 208–209, 228, 235
Industrial growth 356
Industrial revolution 175
Inequality of income 62
Infant-industry argument 393
Inflating current GDP 99
Inflation 2, 60, 73, 90, 120, 125, 127–130, 132–137, 143, 148, 150–152, 156, 162, 176, 178, 184, 191, 219–220, 229–233, 241–243, 248, 254–256, 261, 269, 274, 278, 317–318, 322, 325–329, 333, 337, 340, 342–345, 349
Administered-price 136, 325, 333
Cost-push 127, 136, 325, 333
Credit market in 323
Creeping 130, 137
Demand-pull 125, 127, 131, 136, 230, 246, 259, 323, 325, 327
Double-digit 323, 325
Non-demand-pull 325, 333
Worldwide 127
Inflationary expectations 130, 133, 135, 137, 326, 333, 339, 342, 345
Inflationary gap 220, 222, 236, 274
Instantaneous multiplier 207
Institution
Depository 313
Financial 313–314, 332
Thrift 313
Intended consumption 178, 191
Intended investment 188, 190–192, 197–199, 209–212, 214, 217, 233–236
Intended investment function 185, 188, 192, 196–198, 235
Intended savings 190–191, 210
Intensive growth 350–351, 368
Interest 95, 172, 244, 246
Abstinence theory of 172, 175, 189–190
Interest income 61, 82
Interest payments 243–245, 259
Interest rate 172–173, 175, 184–187, 189–191, 210–211, 220, 228, 235, 246, 296, 300, 310, 312, 314, 317–326, 328–333, 342
Equilibrium 189, 323, 326
Fixed 273
Varying 317
Interest rate cap 314
Interest rates 246–247, 251, 259–260
Internal Revenue Service 275
International competition 358
International exchange market 231
International market 231, 330
International Monetary Fund 418, 423, 425
International monetary system 415
International reserves 418
International trade 228, 284, 299
Terms of 385
International trade policy 397
Interstate Commerce Commission 77
Investment 171, 185
Actual 199
Autonomous 185–186, 188–189, 191, 197, 205–206, 208–209
Business 198, 229
Capital 226, 246
Domestic 93, 251
Ex-ante 233
Ex-post 233
Foreign 250, 425
Government 93
Gross 93, 101, 108
Gross private domestic 93, 186
Induced 185, 191, 208–209, 228, 235
Instability of 186
Intended 188, 190–192, 196–199, 209–212, 217, 233–236
Long-run 338
Net 101, 246, 259
Net private investment 228
Nongovernment 93
Planned 175–176, 199
Private 93, 146, 228, 247
Public 246
Rational 183
Investment demand 176, 199, 247, 279
Investment expenditures 59, 93–94, 144–145, 162
Investment function 180

Intended 185
Investment goods 100, 229, 246
Investment in human capital 147, 162
Investment spending 246
Investment tax credit 144, 186, 219, 232, 358
Invisible hand 78–81, 83–84
Invisible items 378
Involuntary accumulation of inventory 198, 236
Involuntary additions to inventory 198, 213, 233, 235
Involuntary reduction in inventory 198
Involuntary reductions in inventory 198, 213, 233, 235

J

Juster, F. Thomas 339

K

Keynes, John Maynard 170, 174–176, 178, 190–191, 222, 255, 315, 363
Keynesian 195, 211, 223–225, 236, 242, 255–258, 261
Spending, taxes 211
Keynesian argument 242, 247, 260
Keynesian assumption 242, 258
Keynesian critique 174
Keynesian demand management 255
Keynesian effects 259
Keynesian fiscal policy 254
Keynesian model 88, 143, 169, 177, 190, 241, 251, 266
Keynesian multiplier effects 246
Keynesian revolution 255, 260
Keynesian system 226
Keynesian theory 169, 177, 189
Keynesians
New 337
Kindleberger, C. P. 402
Korean War 324
Korean War expenditures 361
Kuznets, Simon 90, 358

L

Labor 350
Labor market 256
Labor resources 354
Labor skills 356
Labor theory of value 447
Labor unions 76, 127, 174, 176
Labor-intensive 356–357
Laffer curve 341, 345
Laffer, Arthur 341
Law of demand 145
Laws
Antimonopoly 69
Antitrust 69, 76
Minimum wage 123, 135, 176
Say's 170, 174, 189
Say's; 170–171, 174–175, 190
Leading economic indicators 136
Leading indicators 120
Leakages 296
Legal tender 271, 280
Limited liability 68, 83
Line-item veto 253, 260
Liquid assets 184, 279
Liquidity 274
Loanable funds
Demand for 172
Supply of 172–173
Local government 59, 72, 75, 93, 226, 318
Local revenue 75
Local tax 76
Long-run investment 338
Lorenz curve 62–63, 82
Low rate of unemployment 256
Lucas Jr., Robert 342

M

M1 money 272–275, 277, 280, 283, 286, 288, 311, 315, 329
Supply of 286, 296, 299–300, 315
M2 money 273, 280, 329
M3 money 273, 281
Macroeconomic growth 344
Macroeconomic policy 255–256, 327, 342–345
Discretionary 303, 342
Macroeconomic theory 337
Macroeconomics 2, 88, 133, 141, 156, 163, 266, 349
Macroeconomy 241, 250
Maisel, Sherman 123
Malthus, Thomas R. 353, 368
Malthusian specter 353
Margin requirement 311–312, 331
Marginal efficiency of capital 185–186, 191
Marginal income tax 340
Marginal propensity to consume 202–204, 206, 215, 221–222, 234, 236, 274
Marginal propensity to save 202, 204, 206, 215, 234, 236
Marginal tax rate 340, 345
Market 3
Capital 330
Credit 319–320, 323–324, 326, 332
Federal funds 296, 300, 307, 310
Financial 273, 277, 303, 312–315
Free 370–371
Individual 266
International 231, 330

International exchange 231
Labor 256
Open 306, 310–311, 316, 318, 320, 322, 331, 333
Private 88
Stock 228, 311–312
Market Capitalism 445
Economic advantages of 445
Economic criticisms of 445
Necessary legal features of 444
Market economy 2, 88, 222, 255, 266, 377, 451
Closed 377
Market system 352, 365–366, 370–371
Markets
Credit 251, 259–260
Marx, Karl 446, 448
Marxians 344
Marxists 346
Materialism
Dialectical 447
Historical 447
McCracken, Paul 249–250, 259
Mercantilism 178
Microeconomics 2, 70, 349
Military expenditures 229–230
Military exports 229
Military goods 62, 229
Minimum wage laws 123, 135, 176
Mixed economy 452
Model
Circular-flow 57–58
Complex circular-flow 59–60
Keynesian 169, 190
Simple circular-flow 57–59, 82
Modern economy 267
Monetarism 327
Monetary growth 343
Monetary policy 222, 250, 266, 303, 311, 317–330, 332–333, 338, 342–343, 345, 349
Discretionary 324, 328, 330, 333
Restrictive 328
Weaknesses of 324, 333
Monetary system 270
International 415
Money 268
Characteristics of "good" 270, 280
Coins 271–272, 280
Currency 272, 280
Demand deposits 270, 272, 280
Demand for 279, 327
Effective supply of 276
Fiat 271, 280
Functions of 269
M1 272–275, 277, 280, 283, 286, 288, 296, 299–300, 311, 315, 329
M2 273, 280, 329
M3 273, 281
Near 273–275, 280–281, 296, 329
Supply 266
Supply of 267, 269–272, 275–281, 283–288, 291, 300, 305, 309, 316–318, 322, 324–329, 332–334
Varying the supply of 317
Money economy 269
Money GDP 97–99, 111, 226–227
Money income 61, 63, 127–128, 136, 220, 327, 329
Money market 170
Money market fund account 273
Money market mutual funds 273, 280, 313
Money markets 171
Money supply 248
Money supply growth 321
Money system of exchange 268, 280
Monopoly 80, 157, 228, 314, 402
Monopoly power 76, 78, 83, 118, 176
Multinational corporation 71
Multiplier 205–207, 209, 214, 221, 234, 300
Balanced-budget 221–222, 236
Deposit 295–296
Income 362
Instantaneous 207
Periodic 207
Multiplier effect 205, 207, 209, 226, 229, 234
Multiplier effects
Keynesian 246
Multiplier formula 206, 234
Municipal bonds
Tax-free 76

N

National bank 305, 331
National budget 222
National debt 72, 228, 317, 361
National economic account 90–91, 97, 99, 103, 110, 200
Formula for 105
National economic accounting 89–90
National income 143, 145, 178, 218, 242, 327
National income (NY) 98–99, 101–103, 107, 111
National level of income 217, 242
National security argument 394
National security expenditures 72
Natural rate of unemployment 133–135, 137–138, 148, 162–163, 256, 261, 323, 330
Natural resources 350–351
Near money 273–275, 280–281, 329
Supply of 296
Negative accelerator 209, 228, 235
Negative net investment 101, 182
Negative savings 181, 183
Neoclassical economics 266
Net exports 94, 110–111, 144–145, 162, 362
Negative 144
Positive 144
Net factor income 96–97

Net foreign trade 378–379
Net income 73, 101–102, 111
Net investment 101
Negative 101, 182
Positive 101
Net investment spending 259
Net national income (NNY) 100, 102, 110
Net national product (NNP) 100, 102, 110–111, 276–277
Net private domestic investment 101, 111, 228
New technology 351
New York Stock Exchange 312
Noncash income 63
Non-consumer goods 145
Non-defense goods 249
Non-demand-pull inflation 325, 333
Nondurable goods 82, 93, 117–118, 136
Nongovernment investment 93
Nonmilitary goods 127
Nonreproducible resources 367, 371
North American Free Trade Association (NAFTA) 431, 433, 437

O

Obsolescence 96, 100, 229
Okun, Arthur 110, 154, 362
Open economy 77–78
Open market 306, 310–311, 316, 318, 320, 322, 331, 333
Open market operations 305, 310
Open-market operations 306, 322, 325, 328, 331
Open-wallet system 254, 260
Opportunity cost 249
Opportunity cost of debt 249, 259
Opportunity costs 109, 135
Organization of Petroleum Exporting Countries (OPEC) 127, 325

P

Paradox of thrift 210, 235
Partnership 66–69, 82–83
Advantages of 67, 82
Disadvantages of 67, 82
Payroll tax 73, 75
Per capita GDP 97
Per capita income 352, 369, 371
Per capita real GDP 98, 107, 111
Periodic multiplier 207
Personal consumption 62, 82, 93, 362
Personal consumption enditures 93
Personal disposable income 104
Personal income 68, 102–103, 110–111, 229
Personal income tax 75–76, 84, 103
Personal savings 103, 183, 229
Personal tax 103, 111
Phillips curve 131–135, 137, 329
Physical capital 356
Pigou effect 174, 190
Pigou, Arthur 174
Planned investment 175–176, 199
Planned savings 210, 235
Planned socialism 445
Advantages of 445
Criticisms of 446
Policy
Fiscal 241–242, 250–251, 254–255, 258, 343
Macroeconomic 255–256
Monetary 250, 343
Tax and expenditure 242
Pollution
Environmental 81, 83, 366, 371
Population growth 186, 353–356, 358, 366, 369, 371
Zero 367–368, 371
Population increase 355
Population increase.iB.Population increase 355
Positive accelerator 209, 235
Positive net investment 101
Positive savings 181
Post-Keynesian 346
Post-Keynesians 337, 344
Preferred stock 68
Present consumption 246, 259
Price
Equilibrium 196, 344
Price index 88, 97–99, 111, 152–153, 163, 226
Consumer 97, 154, 230, 232
GDP 153, 158
General 98
Wholesale 98
Price level
Aggregate 242
Stable 242, 255–256, 258
Price ratio 153
Primary demand 226–227
Private consumption 246
Private debt 271
Private expenditures 246
Private investment 93, 146, 228, 247
Private property rights 442
Privatization of federal programs 253, 260
Problem of moral hazard 314
Producer durables 118
Product equilibrium 141
Product market 58
Production costs 151, 156, 164
Production-possibilities curve 65, 350–351, 357
Productivity 351
Productivity growth 147, 324, 352, 354, 356–358, 369
Productivity of capital 185
Profit
Corporate 95, 102, 106, 110–111
Undistributed 175
Profit sharing 255–256

Progressive curve 74
Progressive tax 74, 76, 84
Property rights
    Importance of 443
    Private 442
    Public 443
Property tax 68, 75–76, 84, 103
Proportional curve 75
Proportional tax 74, 84, 215
Proprietors' income 110–111
Protectionism 395, 433
    Costs and benefits of 432
Proxy card 69
Public debt 242, 271
Public demand 213–214, 235
Public investment 246
Public property rights 443
Public regulation 339, 344

Q

Quantity demanded 141–142, 144–146, 157, 165, 183, 189, 208, 214, 319, 323, 326, 332
    Aggregate 143, 156, 158, 161–162, 178, 214, 218, 234–236, 338, 344
    Excess 319
Quantity supplied 141–142, 147, 157, 165, 189, 214, 219, 319, 324
    Aggregate 143, 152, 161–162, 178, 214, 218, 234–236, 278, 338, 344
    Excess 319
Quotas 157
    Export 393

R

Racial discrimination 135
Random variations 117, 135
Rate of exchange 413
Rational expectations 342–343, 345
Rational investment 183
Real 145
Real GDP 97–99, 111, 120, 158, 231–232, 328, 337, 340, 344
    Per capita 98, 107, 111
Real income 127
    Equilibrium 163, 178, 338
    Equilibrium level of 149, 162, 165, 344
Real income growth 250, 337, 340
Real national income 142, 145
    Equilibrium level of 143, 156, 164
Real per capita income 352–354, 368
Recession 226, 318–319
    Credit market in 319
Recession of 1937-1939 228
Recession of 1949 117
Recession of 1954 230
Recession of 1958 230
Recession phase 117
Reciprocal Trade Agreements Acts 433
Recovery
    Economic 343
Recovery phase 117, 120
Refinancing of debt 248
Regressive curve 74
Regressive tax 74, 76, 84
Regulation Q 312, 331
Regulation W 312
Regulation X 312
Rent 95
Rental income 82
Repayment of debt 249
Replacement demand 227
Reproducible resources 367
Required reserve ratio 289, 291–293, 295–296, 300, 306, 310–311, 316, 318, 322, 331, 333
Required reserves 290–291, 293–294, 296, 300, 306, 310–311, 322, 331
Reserve army of the unemployed 448
Reserve requirements 289
Reserves 289, 299
    Decreasing 308
    Excess 290–296, 300, 305–312, 315–316, 318, 322, 324–325, 331, 333
    Increasing 306
    International 418
    Required 290–291, 293–294, 296, 300, 306, 310–311, 322, 331
    Total 290–291, 300, 307–312, 317–318, 322, 331
Resolution Trust Corporation (RTC) 315, 332
Resources 3, 88
    Availability of 146–147, 162
    Capital 354
    Cost of 146–147, 162
    Human 350
    Labor 354
    Natural 350–351
    Nonreproducible 367, 371
    Reproducible 367
Revenue
    Federal 75, 340
    Local 75
    Tax 341, 345
Reverse supply shock 158, 165
Ricardian Equivalence Theorem 251, 260
Ricardo, David 352, 399
Robinson, Joan 344
Role of government 241, 254, 260
    Economic 254, 258
Rustbelt 396

S

S&L, see Savings and loan association
Salary 95
Sales tax 74–76, 84, 96, 102
Samuelson, Paul 108
Sargent, Thomas 342
Savings 171
    Actual 199
    Change in 183
    Domestic 250–251, 259
    Ex-ante 233
    Ex-post 199, 233
    Foreign 250
    Intended 210
    Negative 181, 183
    Personal 103, 111, 183, 229
    Planned 176, 210, 235
    Positive 181
Savings and loan 313
Savings and loan association 314
Savings deposits 273
Savings function 180, 182–183, 188, 191, 196–198, 210–211, 215–216, 235–236
Savings schedule 182–183
Savings-equals-intended-investment
    Approach 192, 196–197, 211–212, 234
Say, Jean Baptiste 190
Say's law 170–171, 175, 190
Say's law, Abstinence theory of interest 189
Scarcity 3, 17
School tax 72
Schultz, Theodore 356
Schumpeter, Joseph 316
Seasonal unemployment 123
Seasonal variations 116, 135
Secondary demand 227
Secular trend 116, 135
Securities
    Government 245
Securities and Exchange Commission 77
Semifixed income 128, 136
Sexual discrimination 135
Share economy 255–257, 260–261
Shephard, William 80
Sherman Antitrust Act of 1890 69
Short-run aggregate supply 177
Short-run equilibrium real income 320
Single proprietorship 69
Smith, Adam 78–79, 81, 83, 351–353, 368, 399, 446
Social costs 371
Social security tax 95, 102, 106
Social Security Trust Fund 245, 249, 259
Socialism
    Democratic 452
    Marx and 446
    Planned 445
Society
    Economic 352
Sole proprietorship 66–68, 82–83
    Advantages of 66, 82
    Disadvantages of 66, 82
Spaceman economy 367
Special drawing rights 424
Special-interest expenditures 253
Stable price level 242, 255–256, 258
Stagflation 132, 151, 231–232
Stagnation 369
State bank 305, 331
State excise tax 73
State government 59, 68, 72, 75, 84, 93, 226, 305, 318
State tax 76
Static efficiency 442
Static framework 349, 368
Stationary state 352–354, 368–369
Stock
    Capital 182
    Common 68
    Corporate 228, 311, 331
    Margin requirements on 311
    Preferred 68
Stock exchange 311
    New York 312
Stock market 228, 311–312
Stone, Richard 90
Structural unemployment 122–123, 134, 136, 138
Summers, Lawrence 256, 261, 359
Supply 33, 88, 266
    Aggregate 88, 177
    Excess 218, 236
    Money 248
Supply curve 147
Supply of loanable funds 172–173
Supply shift
    Aggregate 150
Supply shock 147, 156, 158, 164–165, 232, 337
    Minimizing 157
    Reverse 158, 165
Supply shocks 155
Supply-side argument 241, 254
Supply-side economic policy 345
Supply-side economics 152, 266, 337–340, 344
Surplus value 447
System of exchange
    Barter 268, 280
    Money 268, 280

T

Tariff 398
Tariff of Abominations 395
Tariffs 144, 162, 228, 391
Tax 266
    Business 106

Capital gains 73
Corporate 102, 111
Excise 96, 102
Income 340
Local 76
Payroll 73, 75
Personal 103, 111
Progressive 74, 76, 84
Property 68, 75–76, 84, 103
Proportional 74, 84, 215
Regressive 74, 76, 84
Sales 74–76, 84, 96, 102
School 72
Social security 95, 102, 106
State 76
Turnover 106
Value-added 106–107
Tax and expenditure policy 242
Tax credit
Investment 144, 186, 219, 232, 358
Tax increase 339
Tax loopholes 73, 76
Tax policy 266
Tax rate 73–75, 84, 152, 162, 318, 341, 345
Marginal 340, 345
Tax receipt
Federal 363
Tax revenue 341, 345
Tax wedge 339
Taxable income 73–74, 340
Taxation 72–74, 84, 186
Double 68
Federal 340
Principles of 72
Tax-base income 74–75
Technological change 352, 354, 356, 358, 365, 369
Disembodied 354
Technologicial change 354
Technology 146
New 351
Terms of trade 384–385
Thrift institution 313
Tight-money policy 325
Time deposits 273
Tobin, James 328, 330
Total demand 274
Total income 91, 95, 101
Total reserves 290–291, 300, 307–312, 317–318, 322, 331
Trade 377
Comparative advantage and 383
Free 145, 398
International 228, 284, 299, 377, 405, 413, 422
Net foreign 378–379
Terms of 384
Trade Agreement Act 396
Trade and Tariff Act 431
Trade deficit 232, 251, 259–260
Trade policy 144, 397–398, 425
Economic 436
International 397
Transfer payments 94
Transitional unemployment 122, 135, 138, 363
Turnover tax 106

U

U.S. Treasury 271, 317
Underground economy 340
Undistributed profit 175
Unemployment 121, 123
Frictional 122, 133–134, 136, 138, 148, 162, 363
Low rate of 256
Natural rate of 133–135, 137–138, 148, 162–163, 256, 261, 323, 330
Structural 122–123, 134, 136, 138
Transitional 122, 135, 138, 363
Unemployment compensation 94
Unions
Labor 76, 127, 176
United Nations Conference on Trade and Development 403
Unlimited liability 66–67, 82
Unlimited life 68
Unplanned additions to inventory 197, 200, 233, 235
Unplanned reductions in inventory 198–199, 217, 233, 235

V

Value-added method 105–106, 111
Value-added tax 106–107
Variable income 136
Varied income 128
Velocity of exchange 276–279, 281, 326, 328
Velocity of income 276
Visible items 378

W

Wage 95
Wage-price flexibility 173–174, 176, 190
Lack of 176, 255
Theory of 170, 189
Walden, Michael 254, 359, 369
War expenditures 361
War goods 101
War on Poverty 230
Wealth of Nations 78
Weidenbaum, Murray 433
Weiner, Stuart 134–135
Weitzman, Martin 255–257, 260–261
Wholesale price index 98
World Trade Organization (WTO) 397, 407, 433

Z

Zero economic growth (ZEG) 367–368, 371
Zero population growth (ZPG) 368, 371

Student Study Guide to Accompany

Explorations In Macroeconomics

Chapter 1: Getting Started

Chapter Highlights: We sincerely want you, the student, to "Join us in the Fun," and have written this workbook with that in mind. Of course, this is not all. Economics is important as well as fun. Economics can be tough, and surely at times you will wonder why your instructor is putting you through all this. It is because we know economics is important. We also know that economics can be difficult for the student. It is analytical, for one thing, and many students have not been exposed to much of that type of reasoning. Also, many students start with the misconception that economics is about business. This turns some students on, as they see dollar signs flash before their eyes, and it turns some students off, as they envision the greedy capitalist partaking in the fruits of life while others live in squalor. But, the "Economics is Business" is a misconception. Economics is a social science dedicated to mitigating the problem of scarcity. So shed your misconceptions, open your mind to some challenges, and do, "Join us in the Fun."

This Chapter is intended to do just what the title implies, "Get Started." We try to get you to see what Economics is about by describing some of the things professional economists do, by briefly describing the methodology economists use, and to bridge the gap between an algebraic/graphic presentation and a more mathematical approach. There are no **Solved Problems** and only one **Problem for Practice** in this chapter. We urge you to spend some time going through this problem and the examples presented in the text under the section **Mathematical Skills**. If you have difficulty going through these pages, you probably need to ask your instructor for other exercises to work through. The tools described in these pages will be used time and time again throughout the semester.

Problems for Practice, Ch.1:

Name ____________________
Section ____________________

1-1. Allocation of Time and the Importance of Marginal Analysis --- Joie Miner is a good student, but she finds herself in a predicament–next Friday, tomorrow, there is an exam in Econ and in Physics. Both courses were difficult for her and she needs to do well on both tests to get a decent grade in the course. Unfortunately, she only had a limited amount of time to study. Let's assume she has 5 hours to allocate to study for the two exams, each exam has 100 points, and she considers a point on the Econ exam to be as important as a point on the Physics exam. That is, she wants to maximize the sum of the scores on the two tests. Let's also assume she is able to estimate the relationship between hours of study in each course and her expected grade. The table below specifies these relationships.

Hours Study	Econ Pts	Marginal Pts	Hours Study	Physics Pts	Marginal Pts
0	10	----	0	20	----
1	40	______	1	43	______
2	65	______	2	64	______
3	75	______	3	79	______
4	80	______	4	86	______
5	83	______	5	90	______
6	85	______	6	92	______

We want to find the optimal allocation of time using Marginal Analysis. cost (benefit) is simply the increase in total cost (benefit) resulting from a one-level increase in the activity (e.g., from 3 to 4 hours of study in Economics).

a. First, fill in the two columns headed Marginal Points. Marginal Points is simply the change in points associated with an additional hour of study.

b. Using data in the Marginal Points columns, how many hours should Joie allocate to the study of econ? To the study of Physics? What is the sum of her points on the two tests?

c. What is the cost to Joie if, rather than allocate her time efficiently, she were to allocate all of her five hours to the study of economics? What would be the cost to Joie if she had already studied economics for four hours and decided to study a fifth hour? In answering, remember in economics cost always means the benefits given up. Also, remember that the question is about the costs of her decisions, not the net effect.

d. What do you get if you were to sum the marginal points in econ? Include in your summation the points associated with zero hours. We can interpret these points as marginal points if we consider time to be continuous rather than hour by hour.

e. What is the most important lesson Joie can carry away from this experience?

f. Suppose we can estimate the relationship between Marginal Points, MP, and the Hours of Study, H, in Calculus for another student, Bill, as:

$$MP = f(H) = 30 - 5H$$

In the quadrant to the right, plot this relationship.

MP

H

g. Use the information provided by the graph and determine Bill's score if he were to study calculus for four hours.

Note: In this problem we have used marginal analysis to find the efficient allocation of time between two activities. We defined the marginal concept, e.g., marginal points (MP) as the increase in total points (TP) resulting from a one-level increase in the hours of study (H). That is,

$MC = \Delta TP/\Delta H$ where $\Delta H = 1$ when the relationship was discrete as given in the table.

We will often find it convenient to assume continuous functions and find the derivative of a function. The derivative of a function, $y = f(x)$, at a given point is the limit of the slope of the function as the change in x approaches zero (that is, Δx T 0), and is written dy/dx. These derivatives are often referred to as first derivatives. In the example here, the dependent variable, y, is marginal points, MP, and the independent variable, x, is hours of study, H. We assume $MP = f(H)$ and $MP = dTP/dH < 0$. When we work with continuous functions, we will give you the marginal equation rather than expect you to determine the first derivative.

Chapter 2: SCARCITY, EFFICIENCY, AND GROWTH

Chapter Highlights: In this chapter we learn about a model that describes the possible combinations of goods a country could produce with its given resources and technology, when those are fully and efficiently used. In this model, a country that makes full and efficient use of its resources and technology is said to be producing on its Production Possibility Frontier (PPF), a frontier between what is inefficient and what is unattainable. Only points on the frontier are efficient. The model shows growth in a country's economy as outward shifts of the PPF, which occur when technology improves, resources increase and/or more investment in capital is made. Similarly, shrinkage in a country's economy is represented by shifts inward of the PPF. This can occur when inputs to the production process are destroyed or made less productive, such as, through natural disasters or wars. The model we present illustrates the notion of scarcity, because it shows how, when a country is producing efficiently (on its PPF), given the resources and technology, producing more of one good implies giving up some of another good. This "giving up" is what we call opportunity cost. There is an opportunity cost attached to any action when resources are limited, assuming the country is producing ***on*** (not ***inside***) its PPF. This per unit opportunity cost is generally assumed to increase or decrease.

The concept of opportunity cost is not limited to entire economies-- it's applicable to any activity an individual undertakes, since time is a limited resource. By spending time attending the university, you give up the opportunity to earn income at a job. To attend the Tuesday night movie, you must give up some other activity that could occupy that time. And to attend your Principles of Microeconomics class, you give up something that was not quite as valuable.

The PPF model only tells what combinations of goods produced are efficient, which are inefficient, and which are unattainable. It does not decide for us which combination a country will choose to produce at a particular point in time. For that, it is necessary to study how the consumers and producers interact in the country. This model is applicable to the possible alternatives in any situation of limited resources. For example, you could look at the combination of grades you would get in your classes, given the time you have to study, your intelligence, your background, etc.

Solved Problems:

2-1. Frontierland produces wheat (W) and all other goods (AOG). The country's production possibilities are given by the following equation:

$$W = 4K^2 + 2L^2 - 3AOG$$

where K is units of capital and L is units of labor.

a. Suppose that Frontierland has L = 22 and K = 9 today. Are resources equally productive in the production of wheat and all other goods in Frontier land? How do you know? Explain and prove numerically. Then draw the PPF and explain the relation between its shape and the extent to which resources are equally productive.

Resources are equally productive in the two uses since the PPF is linear. Another way to say this is the slope of the PPF is a constant (= -3), so one more unit of AOG requires the sacrifice of three units of W, regardless of how many units of W and AOG are produced. The marginal cost of AOG is 3 units of W, and the marginal cost of W is 1/3 unit of AOG.

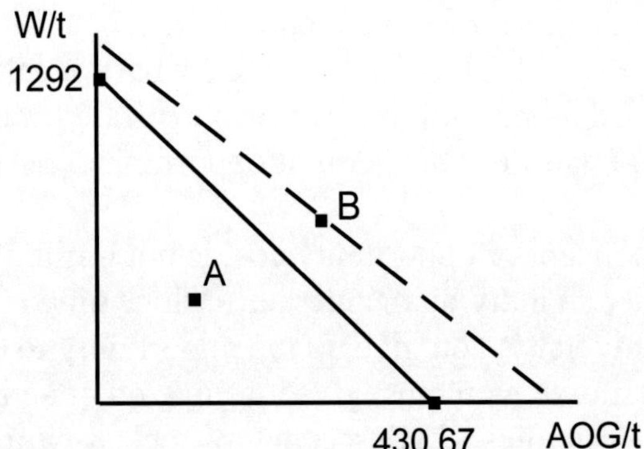

b. Write down and mark in your graph a combination of W and AOG for whose production the country is not using 100% of its resources. What circumstances in a country like Frontierland may lead to that situation? Mark this situation in your diagram and denote it by "A."

See Graph, point "A." Production at "A" may be due to unemployment and/or underemployment of resources.

c. Write down a combination of W and AOG that is unattainable today; denote it by "B". What could Frontierland do today in order to be able to reach that combination in the future? How will those things that Frontierland does to reach "B" be reflected in the equation for the PPF given above and in the diagram?

See Graph, point "B." To reach "B", Frontierland would have to increase its stock of resources and/or improve technology. A technological advance would change the coefficients in the PPF equation, while an increase in just the resource stock would shift the PPF outward. The dashed line shows an improvement in technology as well as an increase in resource stock.

Problems for Practice, Ch. 2:

Name ____________________

Section ____________________

2-1. Suppose the production possibilities for steel (S) and all other goods (AOG) are as follows:

Choice	Steel	All Other Goods
A	0	100
B	25	95
C	50	85
D	75	50
E	100	0

a. Graphically illustrate the production possibilities. Put Steel on the horizontal axis and All Other Goods on the vertical axis. Label each choice, and use a straight line to connect the dots.

b. What is the cost of moving from choice **C** to choice **D**?

c. What is the cost of producing 95 units of All Other Goods?

Problems for Practice, Ch. 2:

Name ____________________
Section ____________________

2-2. Foreverland produces only rice (R) and silk shirts (S). The country's production possibilities are given by the following equation:

$$R = 2K^2 + 3L^2 - 4S$$

where K is units of capital and L is units of labor.

a. Suppose that Foreverland has L = 20 and K = 20 today. Are resources completely substitutable in Foreverland? How do you know? Explain and prove numerically. Then draw the PPF and explain the relation between its shape and the extent to which resources are substitutable.

b. Write down and mark in your graph a combination of R and S for whose production the country is not using 100% of its resources. What circumstances in a country like Foreverland may lead to that situation? Mark this situation in your diagram and denote it by "A."

c. Write down a combination of R and S that is unattainable today; denote it by "B". What could Foreverland do today in order to be able to reach that combination in the future? How will those things that Foreverland does to reach "B" be reflected in the equation for the PPF given above and in the diagram?

Problems for Practice, Ch. 2:

Name ____________________
Section ____________________

2-3. Economists often say that there is no free lunch, which means that we must give up something we want to get more of something else we want. But when society is producing inefficiently, it is possible to produce more of all goods. In that sense, there is a free lunch; nothing need be lost by producing one more lunch.

a. Describe the circumstances under which there is no free lunch and explain why there is no free lunch under those circumstances. Show an example of such a situation in a PPF diagram.

b. Assume that the general equation for the PPF is: x = f(y). Use this to give a general algebraic description of the set of points for which there *is* a "free lunch." (Hint: You will have to use an *inequality* expression to do this. The answer is actually fairly simple.)

Chapter 3: RESOURCE ALLOCATION THROUGH THE FORCES OF SUPPLY AND DEMAND-AN OVERVIEW

Chapter Highlights: In a market economy decisions regarding "What do we want?," "How shall we acquire what we want?" and "Who will enjoy what we have?" are determined by forces of supply and demand. This chapter introduces you to these forces. You may have seen the skit by comedian Father Guido Sarducci: "How to Get Advanced Degrees with Minimum Cost and Effort." One degree he offers is in Economics. According to Father Sarducci, all you have to say is "Supply and Demand," perhaps twice for emphasis. As you might expect, this is too easy, but it is a start, and that is what this chapter is intended to provide--a start.

Buyer's behavior is represented by demand, seller's behavior by supply. Together, supply and demand determine price, and we take these prices into account in the decisions about "What," "How," and "For Whom." We start by developing demand and supply by a single person, a single buyer and a single seller. These demands and supplies for a given commodity are "added" to form market demand and market supply which, through an adjustment process, determine the commodity's price and quantity exchanged per period. The adjustment process is assumed stable so an "equilibrium" price and quantity result, e.g., $10 per unit with 10 million exchanged over a year. Equilibrium is neither good nor bad; it is just a state of rest, or balance, between two sets of opposing forces, demand and supply. Later, we will look at circumstances when the equilibrium is "good" and "bad" in the sense of attaining an efficient result rather than an inefficient result.

Commit the general demand and supply shifters to memory, and take care in making the distinction between shifts in demand (or supply) and changes in quantity demanded (or supplied).

Solved Problems:

3-1. Assume a market demand equation for X per month is estimated as

$$\mathbf{D_x = 100 - 0.25P_x + 0.10I - 0.05P_w + 1.0P_z}$$

a. Is X a normal good or inferior? How do you know?

X is a normal good. The sign of the estimated income coefficient, if statistically different from zero, tells us whether X is normal or inferior. The income coefficient, 0.10, is positive; thus, X is normal.

b. Are X and W substitutes or complements? What about X and Z? Again, how do you know?

X and W are complements, but X and Z are substitutes. Again, the sign of the estimated coefficients, if different from zero, tells us the market relationship between goods. If the price of Z increases by one unit, ceteris paribus, the demand for X increases by one unit. By definition, this positive relationship means the two goods are substitutes. By similar reasoning, the negative coefficient attached to the price of W means X and W are considered by consumers as complements.

3-2. Solve for the equilibrium price and quantity given the following demand and supply equations:

$$\mathbf{Q_{Dx} = 100 - 4.5P_X, \text{ and } Q_{Sx} = -15 + 2.0P_X}$$

The supply equation applies for $\mathbf{P_x \geq \$7.50}$. The qualification on the supply curve, $\mathbf{P_x \geq \$7.50}$ means that for prices greater than or equal to \$7.50, the quantity supplied is described by the equation, $Q_{Sx} = -15 + 2P_x$. If P_x is less than \$7.50, $Q_{Sx} = 0$. Provide answers to the nearest cent and unit of X. Quantities are in 100's of millions of units per year.

First set $Q_{Dx} = Q_{Sx}$ *and solve for the equilibrium price. Substitute the price into the demand or supply equation to find the equilibrium quantity. Check to see if your calculated values satisfy both equations.*

$$Q_{Dx} = 100 - 4.5P_X = Q_{Sx} = -15 + 2.0P_X$$

$$115 = 6.5P$$

$$P_e = \$17.69$$

$$Q_{Dx} = 100 - 4.5(17.69) = 100 - 79.606$$

$$Q_e = 20.395 \text{ per year}$$

3-3. Graphically show the solution to question 3.

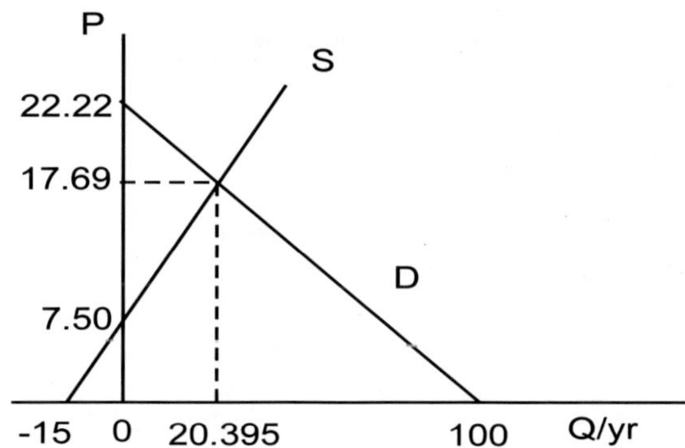

3-4. Suppose society decides to support the price of the good in problem 3-2 at $20 per unit (**$P_F$ = $20**). From the demand and supply equations given in 3-2, **$Q_{Dx} = 100 - 4.5P_X$, and $Q_{Sx} = -15 + 2.0P_X$.** for **$P_x \geq \$7.50$**, we found: $P_e = \$17.69$ and $Q_e = 20.395$ per year. If the price support, or price floor, is enforced, what is the quantity demanded? What is the quantity supplied? How many units will be bought and sold in the market? Is there a shortage or surplus? How large is the shortage or surplus? What quantity will be bought and sold? Illustrate the problem graphically.

Since we already have the market equilibrium without the price support, we can see the price floor will be effective since $P_F = \$20 > \$17.69$. To find the quantity demanded, or quantity supplied, substitute the price floor into the appropriate demand or supply equation.

$Q_{Dx} = 100 - 4.5P_F, = 100 - 4.5(20) = 10$ million units per year
$Q_{Sx} = -15 + 2.0P_F, = -15 + 2.0(20) = 25$ million units per year

The surplus ($Q_{Sx} > Q_{Dx}$) is the difference between the quantity supplied and the quantity demanded at the supported price.

$Q_{Sx} - Q_{Dx} = 25 - 10 = 15$ million units per year.

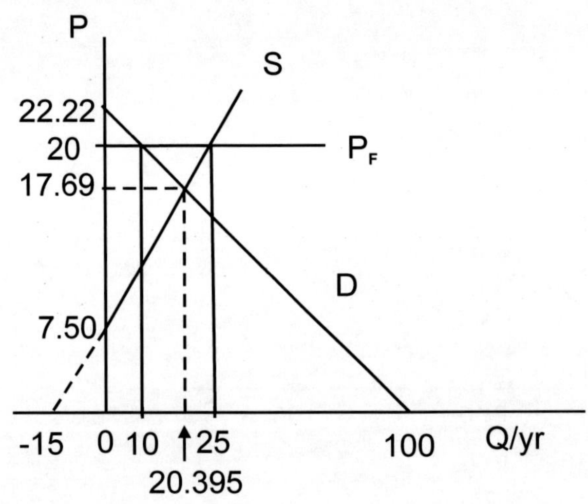

Problems for Practice, Ch. 3:

Name ____________________

Section ____________________

3-1. Assume a market demand equation for **x** per year is estimated as

$Q_{Dx} = 2000 - 50P_x + 0.005I + 20P_w - 10P_Z$

where **I** is income per year, $\mathbf{P_W}$ is the price of **W**, and $\mathbf{P_Z}$ is the price of **Z**.

a. Is **X** a normal or inferior good? How do you know?

b. Are **X** and **W** substitutes or complements? What about **X** and **Z**? Again, how do you know?

c. Assume **I** is $40,000 per year, $\mathbf{P_W}$ is $10, and $\mathbf{P_Z}$ is $5. Plot to scale below, the demand for **X** per year. Be sure you correctly label the axes and $\mathbf{Q_{Dx}}$.

d. Assume $\mathbf{P_W}$ increases to $40. Now redraw, *on the same graph*, $\mathbf{Q_{Dx}}$, but label it $\mathbf{Q_{Dx1}}$. Is this an increase or decrease in demand?

Problems for Practice, Ch. 3:

Name ____________________
Section ____________________

3-2. Solve for the equilibrium price and quantity given the following yearly demand and supply equations: $\mathbf{Q_{Dx} = 225 - 0.5P_X}$, **and** $\mathbf{Q_{Sx} = -50 + 5P_X}$. The supply equation applies for $\mathbf{P_x >=}$ **\$30.00**; otherwise, supply is zero. Units are in millions per year. What are consumer expenditures per year assuming supply and demand conditions do not change? Provide answers to the nearest dollar and unit of X and show the solution graphically. Be careful to label the axes and the curves.

Problems for Practice, Ch.3:

Name ____________________
Section ____________________

3-3. Often the government, usually at the request of a special interest group, imposes price controls such as price floors or ceilings. For a price ceiling to be effective, it must be below the market equilibrium. Assume yearly demand is given by $\mathbf{Q_{Dx} = 120 - P_x}$ and yearly supply by $\mathbf{Q_{Sx} = -30 + 2.0P_x}$ for $\mathbf{P_x > \$20.00}$. Now set a price ceiling of \$45. What is the quantity demanded? What is the quantity supplied? How many units will be bought and sold per year? What are consumer expenditures for the year? Is there a shortage or surplus? How large is the shortage or surplus? Show the problem and solution graphically.

Problems for Practice, Ch. 3:

Name ____________________
Section ____________________

3-4. Often the government, usually at the request of a special interest group, imposes price controls such as price floors or ceilings. For a price floor to be effective, it must be above the market equilibrium. Assume yearly demand is given by $\mathbf{Q_{Dx} = 120 - P_x}$ and yearly supply by $\mathbf{Q_{Sx} = -30 + 2.0P_x}$ for $\mathbf{P_x > \$40.00}$. Now set a price floor of \$60. What is the quantity demanded? What is the quantity supplied? How many units will be bought and sold per year? What are consumer expenditures for the year? Is there a shortage or surplus? How large is the shortage or surplus? Show the problem and solution graphically.

Chapter 4: Components of an Economic Society- Households, Business Firms, Governments, the Rest of the World

Part 1

First, read the section entitled "Summing Up" at the end of Chapter 4 for thorough summary of the material presented in the chapter.

Things to Watch For

Chapter 4 is divided into five main sections. The first four deal with a closed macroeconomy, one that does not trade with other economies. In the first one, there is a discussion about circular flow models of how our economy functions. (These aren't the first models we've presented. Remember the production-possibilities curve in the discussion of scarcity in Chapter 2.) The circular-flow model brings out the interrelationships between the components of the economy and the economic activities of each in factor and product markets. You could compare the interconnecting or circular nature of economic activity to the case of the chicken and the egg. There is no beginning or end to economic activity.

The remainder of Chapter 4 points out some important aspects of the three main components of the economy: households (or the people), business firms, and governments, and introduces the question about social responsibility of business.

The chapter's second section, on households, deals with the way income is distributed to households and what the households spend that income on. In this part, be sure you can distinguish between functional distribution of income and personal distribution of income. Remember that a Lorenz curve measures the degree of equality or inequality in the personal distribution of income.

The third section, on businesses, talks about the three forms of business organizations (sole proprietorships, partnerships, and corporations) and identifies the major strengths and weaknesses of each. It's important that you keep in mind the distinctions introduced in this part. Part 3 closes with a discussion of some of the concerns created by large corporations.

The fourth section concerns governments: federal, state, and local. First this section gives some figures to show what governments spend money on. Then it discusses taxation, or where governments get their money. It is important that you understand the two principles of taxation-benefits received and ability to pay-and the three kinds of tax structures-progressive, regressive, and proportional. Equally important is the question of who pays the taxes (the incidence of taxation). When it comes to the question of how progressive our tax structure is, it's difficult to arrive at any hard-and-fast answers. In this section, we look at the distribution of income and how it is affected by taxes, transfer payments and payments in kind. This section concludes by looking at some of the many implications of the distribution of income and changes in that distribution.

Next, the chapter notes how governments also affect the economy by making laws that set the rules of the game, and by the activities of various regulatory bodies.

Finally, the chapter briefly deals with an open economy, or one that exports to and imports from other economies.

The most important conclusion on the question of social responsibility of business seems to be that it's very hard to define what the social responsibility of business really is. This suggests that even if business is socially responsible to the people, this cannot really solve the fundamental social problems of our economy. One may well ask, "Should social responsibility on the part of businesses even be expected to solve our problems?" The section deals with the responsibility of businesses to their shareholders and with the relationship between competition and socially responsible behavior by firms. A key question asked is: "When will markets punish or reward socially responsible behavior by firms?"

Part 2

Define the following terms and concepts.

1. Open economy
2. Closed economy
3. Factor markets, product markets
4. Functional distribution of income
5. Lorenz curve
6. Sole proprietorship
7. Partnership
8. Corporation
9. Unlimited liability
10. Limited liability
11. Unlimited life
12. Bonds
13. Preferred stock
14. Common stock
15. Double taxation
16. Multinational corporations
17. Benefits-received principle of taxation
18. Ability-to-pay principle of taxation
19. Progressive tax
20. Regressive tax
21. Proportional tax
22. Tax rates

Part 3

Answer the following questions and problems.

1. In Figure 4-1, label the boxes and the connecting lines with their appropriate titles. Use arrows to show the correct flows of economic activity for the complex circular-flow model.
2. Using the circular-flow diagram (Figure 4-1), start at any point and explain how the circular flow of economic activity works.
3. Using Figure 4-1 again, explain how the flow of economic activity can be decreased; how it can be increased.

Figure 4-1
Complex Circular-Flow Model

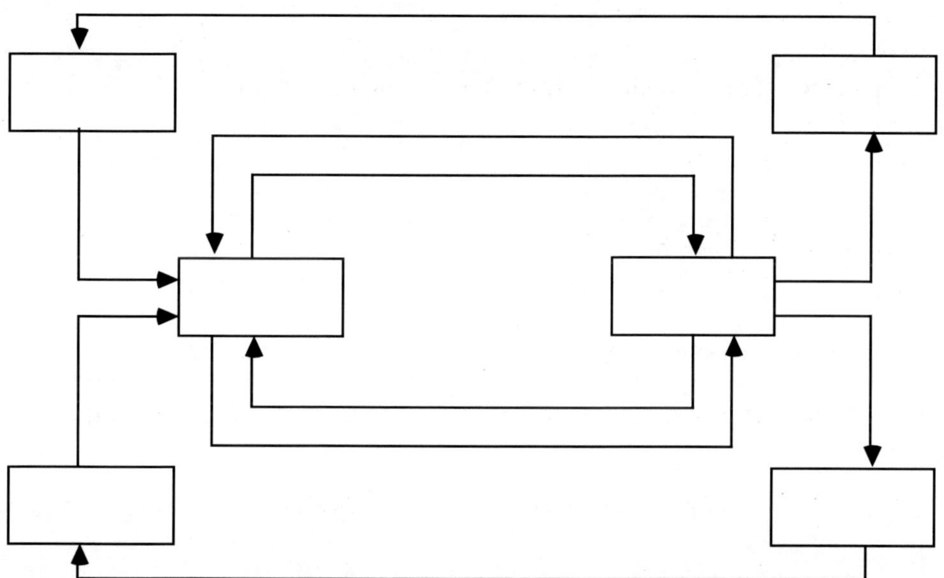

4. List, in order of increasing magnitude, incomes classified according to the functional distribution of income. Review factors that have affected this distribution.

5. Review the various factors that have affected the personal distribution of income since 1935.

6. Using Figure 4-2 and Table 4-1, draw a Lorenz curve for column A and also one for column B. Which distribution is more nearly equal?

Figure 4-2
Lorenz Curves for Distributions A and B

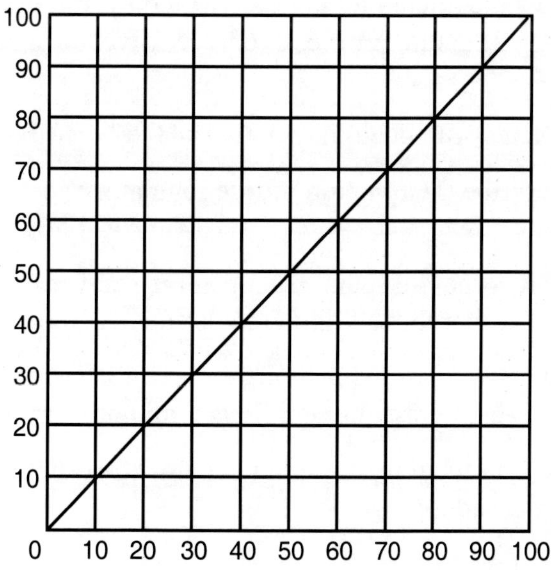

Table 4-1
Distribution of Personal Income

	A	B
Percentage of People	**Percentage of Total**	**Percentage of Total**
Lowest one-fifth	6	4
Second one-fifth	12	8
Third one-fifth	18	16
Fourth one-fifth	24	28
Highest one-fifth	40	44

7. Review the advantages and disadvantages of sole proprietorships, partnerships, and corporations.
8. Why are some economists concerned about the concentration of economic power in large corporations?
9. What economic and political problems and benefits are created by multinational corporations?
10. What are the principal kinds of expenditures made by the federal government? by state governments? by local governments?
11. Explain and criticize the benefits-received principle of taxation; the ability-to-pay principle.
12. What is the most important source of tax revenue for the federal government? for state governments? for local governments?
13. Taking taxes as a whole, including taxes collected by all levels of government combined, is our tax structure progressive, regressive, or proportional? Explain your answer.
14. What are the problems with deciding what is a "fair" distribution of income?
15. List and briefly describe the function of five regulatory commissions of the federal government.
16. Who should exhibit corporate social responsibility: governments, or the managers or the stockholders of corporations? Explain your answer; be complete.
17. What are the arguments of critics that profit maximizing behavior by firms is consistent with private interests but conflicts with public interests?
18. What factors have caused an increase in the competitiveness of the American economy in recent decades?
19. When will markets reward socially responsible behavior by firms? When will they punish such behavior?
20. What is the Lorenz curve trying to show us?

Part 4 Self-test

Section A True/false questions

T F 1. Increases in savings and taxes expand the circular flow of economic activity; increases in investment and government expenditures contract it.

T F 2. Data on the functional distribution of income indicate that since 1935 there has been a relative shift from wages and salaries to corporate profits.

T F 3. Between 1935 and the mid-1950s, the personal distribution of cash income became more nearly equal; from then to the early 1990s it did not change.

T F 4. Looked at from a demand point of view, saving contracts an economy because it decreases the demand for consumer goods.

T F 5. The form of business enterprise that is easiest to establish is the sole proprietorship.

T F 6. An advantage of partnership over sole proprietorships is that partnerships have unlimited life.

T F 7. Corporations may have limited liability.

T F 8. Common stock differs from preferred stock in that it offers greater voting rights but is limited in the amount of dividends its owners can receive.

T F 9. To say that taxes from all levels of American government are at most only mildly progressive is a correct generalization.

T F 10. The benefits-received principle of taxation supports the conclusion that taxes are best when based on the size of a person's income.

T F 11. The advantage of the benefits-received principle of taxation is that there is little difficulty in computing who receives the benefits from the goods and services provided by government.

T F 12. The best example of a proportional tax is the sales tax, because the same tax rate is applied no matter how large the purchase.

T F 13. Since corporate executives are professional managers of their enterprises, they have expertise in deciding what is socially desirable for our society.

T F 14. According to the chapter, socially responsible behavior by firms will never be rewarded by markets.

T F 15. According to William Shepherd, non-competitive forces have grown in the American economy in recent decades.

T F 16. For an individual firm, lack of information or perspective may make socially responsible behavior difficult to undertake.

T F 17. All government expenditures are productive.

T F 18. An advantage of a partnership over a sole proprietorship is that the partnership has unlimited life.

T F 19. A corporation may have limited liability.

T F 20. The distribution of cash income in the US is equal.

T F 21. The three main forms of business organizations are the sole proprietorship, the partnership, and the government.

Section B Multiple-choice questions

1. For a corporation, limited liability means that
   a. the corporation is limited in its obligation to pay its debts, up to a certain percentage of its net worth.
   b. the managers are limited in how much debt they can cause the corporation to incur.
   c. the corporation is limited in paying dividends to stockholders to periods in which it has made profits.
   d. the stockholder has no further financial obligation to the corporation beyond the money paid for the stock.

2. In comparison with taxes collected by the federal government,
   a. state and local taxes are both more progressive.
   b. state and local taxes are both more regressive.
   c. state taxes are more progressive, while local taxes are regressive.
   d. local taxes are more progressive, while state taxes are regressive.

3. The ability-to-pay principle of taxation is best illustrated by a
   a. property tax.
   b. sales tax.
   c. personal income tax.
   d. corporate income tax.

4. Through which of the following do governments affect economic activity?
   a. Expenditures and taxation
   b. Enactment of laws
   c. Use of regulatory agencies
   d. All of the above

5. Of the three forms of business enterprise discussed in the text, which can most effectively raise financial capital?
   a. Sole proprietorships
   b. Partnerships
   c. Corporations
   d. All are equally effective

6. In what aspect does the corporation not represent the dominant form of business enterprise?
   a. Share of wages paid
   b. Share of capital invested
   c. Share of number of firms
   d. Share of output

7. Which one of the following combinations of taxes and expenditures represents the major source of income and major type of expenditure for local governments?
   a. Property tax; education
   b. Sales tax; welfare
   c. Sales tax; education
   d. Personal income tax; highways

8. Which of the following statements is not true?
   a. Householders supply the resources and demand the consumption output.
   b. Firms supply both resources and output.
   c. Savings and taxes reduce households' demand for the output of firms.
   d. Investment and government expenditures increase the demand for the output of firms.

9. Which of the following combinations of expenditures and taxes represents the most important form of expenditures and taxes for the federal government?
   a. Defense expenditures; corporate income taxes
   b. Income security; personal income taxes
   c. Education; sales and excise taxes
   d. Defense expenditures; personal income taxes

10. Multinational firms are difficult for any one country to control because
    a. they are chartered and regulated by the United Nations.
    b. unions cooperate with them on an international scale.
    c. they can shift purchases and production from one country to another.
    d. they are incorporated in more than one country.

11. A weakness of the argument in favor of social responsibility on the part of corporations is represented by which of the following?
    a. Although corporate managers are trained to make profits, they have no expertise in determining what actions are socially responsible.
    b. There is no objective way to define social responsibility.
    c. Corporate executives are insulated from reality by their positions and have difficulty understanding what constitutes a socially responsible position.
    d. During a business contraction, profits contract, and firms may cut back socially responsible activities just when they are most needed.
    e. All of the above.

12. According to William Shepherd, the competitiveness of the American economy
    a. increased from 1960 to 1980 but has declined since.
    b. has declined significantly in the past three decades.
    c. has increased substantially in the past three decades.
    d. has not changed in recent decades.

13. According to Adam Smith, greedy behavior by firms is effectively limited by
    a. firms' desires to promote the public's welfare.
    b. public regulation of firms.
    c. the invisible hand of competition.
    d. the organization of consumers.

14. Critics of profit maximizing behavior by firms argue that governments should do which of the following?
    a. Ban socially undesirable products.
    b. Establish minimum standards for products.
    c. Regulate the marketing of products.
    d. All of the above.

Section C Matching questions

I. Match the terms in column B with related terms in column A.

Column A	Column B
1. Labor	(a) Rent
2. Capital	(b) Wages
3. Land	(c) Profits
4. Entrepreneurship	(d) Interest

II. For each of the terms in column A, write (if applicable) an S for sole proprietorship, a P for partnership, and a C for corporation in column B.

Column A	Column B
1. Existence as a legal entity	______
2. Unlimited liability	______
3. High level of incentive	______
4. Ease of formation	______
5. Unlimited life	______
6. Access to capital by use of special financial instruments	______
7. Limited life	______
8. Specialized management functions	______
9. Separation of management and ownership	______
10. Tendency to suffer from management inefficiency	______
11. Higher cost of formation	______
12. Possibility of being subject to special laws	______

III. Match the terms in column A with related terms in column B.

Column A	Column B
1. Progressive	(a) Property tax
2. Regressive	(b) Federal income tax
3. Proportional	(c) Sales tax

ANSWERS

Part 4

Section A 1, F; 2, F; 3, F; 4, T; 5, T; 6, F; 7, T; 8, F; 9, F; 10, F; 11, F; 12, F; 13, F; 14, F; 15, F; 16, T; 17, F; 18, F; 19, T; 20, F; 21, F

Section B 1, d; 2, b; 3, c; 4, d; 5, c; 6, c; 7, a; 8, b; 9, b; 10, c; 11, e; 12, c; 13, c; 14, a

Section C I.1, b; 2, d; 3, a; 4, c

II.1, C; 2, S and P; 3, S; 4, S; 5, C; 6, C; 7, S and P; 8, P and C; 9, C; 10, S; 11, P and C; 12, C

III.1, b; 2, c; 3, a

Chapter 5: Measuring Domestic Income and Product

Part 1

First, read the section entitled "Summing Up" at the end of Chapter 5 for a thorough summary of the material presented in the chapter.

Things to Watch For

Chapter 5 explains the concepts you need in order to understand the ways governments compute the level of aggregate activity in the economy. All of us hear these measures of national output and income continually bandied about. Not only economists and politicians but also the news media constantly refer to measures of national income and product, especially when they are discussing the state of the nation or the health of the economy. The subject is also important because these concepts will be used in building more sophisticated concepts and theories further along in the text.

The chapter is divided into three parts. The first part defines the five major measures of economic performance and shows how each is computed. To be able to understand discussions of the nation's economy, you need to remember the distinctions among these five measures beginning with Gross Domestic Product (GDP). The text leads you through them one by one, from the first measure, GDP/GDI, through NNP/NNI, NI, PI, and DI, showing what is excluded and what is added in each case. The chapter explains the difference between gross domestic product and gross national product. The chapter, as well, details the components of GDP, namely, personal consumption expenditures (C), gross private domestic investment (I), government (G), and net exports (XN).

Note that we use the terms output or product and income interchangeably. Since the expenditure and income approaches lead to the same numerical result, output and income are equal. It is important that you remember the reasoning behind that result.

The second part of Chapter 5 presents several topics that add depth to our understanding of the five national economic accounts. First, the distinction between gross domestic and gross national product is not only shown but the rationale for adopting GDP measures is explained. Statisticians use two approaches-the final-value method and the value-added method-to add the data to obtain these measures of output and income. You should know the distinction between money (or current) GDP and real (or constant) GDP. You should also be able to convert money GDP to real GDP by the use of a price index. The last section discusses the various forms of output and of economic transactions that are not included in GDP.

To complete the approaches to macroeconomics measurement, the components of gross domestic income (GDI) are explained. Those components are wages and salaries (W), rent (R), interest (PC), profit (P), capital consumption allowance (D), and indirect business taxes. In adding to the total GDI, we see that it is (must be) equal to GDP.

Lastly, there is a discussion on GDP as a measure of human well-being that concludes the inadequacies in the measurement of GDP are significant enough to make one question the validity of its use as a measure of human welfare. These inadequacies are: (1) GDP does not include most nonmarket forms of output; (2) GDP does not take into account external costs and benefits of production and consumption (especially pollution of various kinds); (3) GDP does include output that many people feel does not contribute to human welfare (output such as excessive advertising and defense expenditures); and (4) GDP cannot take into account the economic effects on future generations of the depletion of nonreproducible resources by present production. Note: Be sure you understand Arthur Okun's feelings on the subject.

Part 2

Define the following terms and concepts.

1. Expenditure approach to national economic accounting
2. Income approach to national economic accounting
3. Gross domestic product
4. Gross domestic income
5. Final goods and services
6. Private consumption expenditures
7. Durable goods
8. Nondurable goods
9. Net exports
10. Gross private domestic investment
11. Government expenditures
12. Income at market prices
13. Income at factor prices
14. Factors of production
15. Wages and salaries
16. Rent
17. Interest
18. Proprietors' income
19. Corporate profits
20. Capital consumption allowance (depreciation)
21. Indirect business taxes
22. Net national product
23. Net national income
24. Positive net investment
25. Negative net investment
26. National income
27. Personal income
28. Disposable income
29. Final-value method of income estimation
30. Value-added method of income estimation
31. Money (current) GDP
32. Real (constant) GDP
33. Consumer price index
34. Wholesale price index
35. General price index
36. Per capita real GDP
37. Inflating current GDP
38. Deflating current GDP

Part 3

Answer the following questions and problems.

1. What do we mean when we say that the national economic accounts are definitional concepts?

2. Why are the statistical results of the expenditure and income approaches of estimating national income accounts always equal?

3. Define and give a formula for computing the following national economic accounts:

   (a) gross domestic product, (b) gross domestic income, (c) net national product,

   (d) net national income, (e) personal income, and (f) disposable income.

4. Show how the value-added method of computing GDP equals the final-value method in terms of final results.
5. What is the difference between money GDP and real GDP? How do you convert money GDP to real GDP?
6. List the kinds of output that are not included in GDP for the United States. Why are they not included?
7. List the kinds of economic transactions that are not seperately included in GDP. Why are they not included?
8. From the data in Table 5-1, compute the five major accounts: GDP, NNP, NI, PI, and DI. (This one is easy.) The answers are given after Part 4.

Table 5-1
Data for Problem 8 (billions of dollars)

Consumption	300
Gross private domestic investment	75
Government expenditures	100
Net exports	-5
Depreciation	25
Indirect business taxes	10
Corporate taxes	15
Retained earnings	10
Net transfer payments	15
Personal taxes	25

9. Using all the formulas available plus the data in Table 5-2, compute the five major national economic accounts: GDP, NNP, NI, PI, and DI. (This one is more difficult.) Answers and hints are given after Part 4.

Table 5-2
Data for Problem 9 (billions of dollars)

Consumption	350
Rent	15
Gross private domestic investment	100
Personal taxes	75
Corporate taxes	15
Wages and salaries	400
Personal savings	30
Indirect business taxes	20
Net private domestic investment	75
Domestic business interest	20
Dividends	5
Proprietors' income	25
Retained earnings	10
Interest on consumer loans	10

10. In Table 5-3, fill in the column for real GDP. (The answers are given after Part 4.)

Table 5-3
Hypothetical Data for Problem 10

Year	Money GDP	Price Index	Real GDP
1950	55.6	50.6	
1960	284.8	80.2	
1970	684.9	110.9	
1980	974.1	135.3	

11. In Table 5-4, first compute the price index using 1962 as the base year for the hypothetical prices; then compute the price index using 1972 as the base year. (The answers are given after Part 4.)

Table 5-4
Hypothetical Data for Problem 11

Year	Price	Price Index (1962 = 100)	Price Index (1972 = 100)
1957	12		
1962	14		
1967	18		
1972	27		
1982	32		

12. GDP statistics fail to take into account costs that are outside the marketplace. What are these costs? Do you agree that they reduce the effectiveness of GDP as a measure of well-being?
13. Some people argue that large amounts of output included in GDP do not really contribute to material well-being. What kinds of output may fall into this category? Do you agree that they do not contribute to our well-being?
14. What was Okun's advice to those computing the accounts? Why?
15. Explain the distinction between gross domestic and gross national product.
16. Why do we need both real GDP and current GDP?
17, Why is some output excluded from GDP?

Part 4 Self-test

Section A True/false questions

T F 1. If the price level rose between one year and another, you must inflate the GDP figure for the latter year in order to compute real GDP change.

T F 2. When you convert money GDP to real GDP, you must divide real GDP by the price index.

T F 3. If gross investment is greater than depreciation, the economy has negative net investment, and as a result the economy contracts.

T F 4. The wages of used-car salesmen are included in gross domestic income.

T F 5. The market value of a car built and sold in 1987 and resold in 1989 is not included in 1989's GDP.

T F 6. Net investment is included in GDP, while gross investment is included in NNP.

T F 7. The value of total transactions in an economy exceeds the value of GDP.

T F 8. Capital gains from the resale of personal property are not included in GDP.

T F 9. Profits are part of national income, but all profits are excluded from personal income.

T F 10. When one is computing GDP, one excludes interest on the national debt from government expenditures; when one is computing GDI, one includes interest on the national debt as part of interest.

T F 11. No doubt exists that real GDP is not a good measure of material well-being because GDP does not include all output.

T F 12. Since one does not include external costs of production and consumption in the market calculation of price, such costs do not affect real GDP as a measure of material well-being.

T F 13. Because some people consider that certain types of output do not contribute to material well-being, they argue that real GDP, which includes these, cannot be considered a useful measure of material well-being.

T F 14. The opponents to economic growth argue that in the long run a high level of GDP decreases future well-being because it depletes the world supply of nonreproducible resources.

T F 15. Arthur Okun argued that real GDP was not designed to be a measure of material well-being and therefore should not be computed.

T F 16. Gross domestic product excludes imports and exports while gross national product includes them.

T F 17. The work of children doing household chores is counted a part of GDP.

T F 18. A car is a durable good.

T F 19. GDP measures the value of all intermediate goods and final services in a given period of time.

T F 20. Illegal goods and services are included in the GDP.

T F 21. The transactions involved in buying and selling of used items are included in the GDP.

T F 22. National income includes only wages and salaries.

Section B Multiple-choice questions

1. In the calculation of GDP, which of the following is not considered investment?

   a. Construction of a factory to produce widgets

   b. Construction of a house to be lived in by the owner

   c. An increase in inventory on the shelves of a supermarket

   d. Increased purchases of shares of stock in AT&T

2. Suppose that a CD player is produced in 1993 but not sold until 1994; it affects GDP

   a. as a consumption good only in 1993.

   b. as a net addition to inventory in 1994 only.

   c. as a net addition to inventory in 1994 and a consumption good in 1993.

   d. as a net addition to inventory in 1993 and a consumption good in 1994, with a net decrease in inventory in 1994.

3. Which of the following is not subtracted from national income to arrive at personal income?

   a. Personal taxes

   b. Retained earnings

   c. Corporate taxes

   d. Social security taxes

4. Suppose that the money GDP was $800 billion in 1988 and $900 billion in 1989. We may

   a. conclude that more was produced in 1988.

   b. not compare the real output of the economy in 1988 and 1989 without knowing changes in prices.

   c. conclude that prices were higher in 1989.

   d. conclude that real output was larger in 1989 than in 1988.

5. The difference between net national income and national income is

   a. proprietors' income.

   b. depreciation.

   c. social security taxes.

   d. indirect business taxes.

6. Interest on consumer loans is included in which one of the following?
   a. Gross domestic income
   b. National income
   c. Net national product
   d. Personal disposable income
7. To compare real GDP of one year with real GDP of another, we must
   a. correct for changes in the price level.
   b. divide by total population.
   c. correct for changes in the size and composition of the labor force.
   d. correct for changes in firms' accounting procedures.
8. Which of the following items is not calculated in national income?
   a. The rent a homeowner would have to pay if he or she did not own the home
   b. Social security payments to people over 65
   c. Tips received by a waiter
   d. Pay received by an army private
9. One of the following is included in GDP. Which?
   a. The work of housewives
   b. Illegal production
   c. The production of services
   d. Labor on do-it-yourself projects
10. Value added is computed by
    a. subtracting the figure for GDP for one year from the figure for GDP for the following year.
    b. adding up the values added at each stage.
    c. subtracting the amount allowed for depreciation of machinery from the amount of total production of the machinery.
    d. subtracting the amount of transfer payments received from the government from the amount of transfer payments paid to the government.

11. Some people say that real GDP fails to include all output and all cost, and that therefore it is not a measure of material well-being. Which of the following items does not support their argument?

    a. The contributions of housewives

    b. Air pollution

    c. Current production for military defense

    d. Water pollution

12. Some people say that real GDP contains output that fails to contribute to material well-being. Which of the following items does not support their argument?

    a. Intermediate products, such as steel that goes into an automobile

    b. Many forms of advertising

    c. Output of a chemical plant that contributes to pollution

    d. Unnecessary levels of defense expenditures

13. A main point in the argument that present economic growth reduces future material well-being is that

    a. full employment increases inflationary tendencies.

    b. increases in productivity lead to greater unemployment, since employers do not need to hire as many workers.

    c. economic growth reduces the supply of nonreproducible resources available for the future.

    d. GDP does not take into account an increase in leisure time.

14. Which of the following best states Arthur Okun's plea to the calculators of the national economic accounts?

    a. Real GDP is not an accurate measure of material well-being, and thus we should abandon it as an indicator.

    b. Real GDP is not an accurate measure of material well-being, and those who calculate it should do whatever is necessary to correct that deficiency.

    c. Real GDP is an accurate measure of material well-being, and we should ignore its critics.

    d. Real GDP is not an accurate measure of material well-being, nor is it meant to be. People who calculate real GDP should not try to meet the criticisms.

15. The difference between GDP and GNP is:

   a. depreciation is subtracted from GDP.

   b. all international trade is subtracted from GNP.

   c. personal taxes are subtracted from GNP.

   d. GDP is a measure of the value of output that is occurring in this country regardless of who owns the domestic resources that produces the output.

Section C Matching questions

Match phrases in column B to the terms in column A.

Column A	Column B
1. Final goods and services	(a) Gross investment exceeds depreciation
2. Factor prices	(b) Uses a price index
3. Positive net investment	(c) Does not take into account changes in prices
4. Money (current) GDP	(d) The price index is below 100
5. Real (constant) GDP	(e) Do not include intermediary products as separate items
6. Inflating current GDP	
7. Corporate profits	(f) Is equal to income approach
8. Rent	(g) Includes only domestic business interests
9. Expenditure approach	(h) Excludes indirect business taxes
10. Interest	(i) Includes rent on owner-occupied homes
11. Measured economic welfare	(j) Equals dividends + corporate taxes + retained earnings
	(k) NDP + leisure and non-market services - regrettable necessities and disamenities

ANSWERS

Part 3

8. GDP 470, NNP 445, NI 435, PI 425, DI 400
Problem 8 is relatively simple. To compute GDP, use the formula for GDP. Then compute the other accounts by using first the formula for NNP, then the one for NI, then the one for PI, and finally the one for DI.

9. GDP 535, NNP 510, NI 490, PI 465, DI 390
Problem 9 is harder. First compute disposable income by using the formula DL = C+ PS + ICL Compute personal income by adding PT to DI. Compute national income by using the formula NI = W&S + R+ I P Inc + CP; compute corporate profits by adding dividends and CT + RE; compute net domestic product by adding IBT to NI; compute gross domestic product by adding depreciation or capital consumption allowances to NNP; compute capital con-

sumption allowances by subtracting net domestic investment from gross private domestic investment.

10. 109.9, 355.1, 617.6, 720.0
Solve problem 10 by dividing money GDP by the price index and multiplying by 100 for each year.

11. 1962: 85.7, 100, 128.6, 192.9, 228.6 1972: 44.4, 51.9, 66.6, 100, 118.6
Solve problem 11 by dividing the price of each year by the prices of the base years and multiplying by 100.

Part 4

Section A 1, F; 2, F; 3, F; 4, T; 5, T; 6, F; 7, T; 8, T; 9, F; 10, F; 11, F; 12, F; 13, T; 14, T; 15, F; 16, F; 17, F; 18, T; 19, F; 20, F; 21, F; 22, F
Section B 1, d; 2, d; 3, a; 4, b; 5, d; 6, d; 7, a; 8, b; 9, c; 10, b; 11, c; 12, a; 13,c; 14, d; 15, d
Section C 1, e; 2, h; 3, a; 4, c; 5, b; 6, d; 7, j; 8, i; 9, f; 10, g; 11, k

Chapter 6: Economic Fluctuations

Part 1

First, read the sections entitled "Summing Up" at the end of Chapter 6 for a detailed and thorough summary of the material in the chapter.

Things to Watch For

Chapter 6 is not a difficult chapter. It consists primarily of descriptions and definitions. However, it is an important chapter, for it gives you a background for the study of a big problem in our economy: fluctuations in the level of business activity.

Chapter 6 is divided into four parts. The first part discusses business fluctuations in a general sense. It defines what fluctuations are and describes the various phases of the business cycle. The most important point made here is that each cycle differs in length and intensity, or in other words, use of the word cycles, does not imply regularity in occurrence or length. In fact, both the cycle as a whole and its various stages differ in length and intensity. Within a given cycle, all economic activity does not vary in the same direction at the same time. However, there is enough uniformity for economists to be able to identify certain leading indicators. These indicators are very useful to economists when they are trying to predict the course of a business cycle.

The second part is concerned with unemployment. It defines full employment as well as the various kinds of unemployment (frictional unemployment, cyclical unemployment, and structural unemployment) and discusses some implications of each. These definitions are very important. You'll run into them again later on, in the analysis of government economic policy. The concept of a GDP gap, the difference between full employment and actual GDP is developed. The part ends with a discussion of the costs of unemployment-economic, social, and psychological.

The third part analyzes inflation and the economic effects of variations in prices. It first defines the two kinds of inflation (demand-pull inflation and cost-push inflation) and discusses some economic problems of each. These definitions, too, are very important. In our analysis of government economic policy they'll be used frequently. There is next a discussion of the effects of price variations (decreases as well as increases) both on the distribution of real income and real wealth, and on output.

The fourth part deals with the interaction between employment and prices. This section stresses two main points: (1) Full employment and stable prices may be difficult to maintain at the same time. The closer an economy gets to full employment, the higher the rate of increase in prices becomes. (2) The Phillips curve indicates that there is a set of relationships between various degrees of unemployment and the rate of inflation. The fourth part winds up with an analysis of what happens when the Phillips curve shifts up to the right. At the same level of unemployment, a higher level of inflation exists. It is important that you keep these changing unemployment-inflation relationships in mind, because they are a key factor in the effectiveness of government economic policy.

The application within Chapter 6 surveys the problems of trying to establish an acceptable unemployment goal for the American Economy. Attention today is focused on identifying the economy's natural rate of unemployment, one at which the rate of inflation is not only acceptable but also neither accelerating or decelerating. The natural rate argument leads to the conclusions that (a) the actual unemployment rate may be impossible to push below the natural rate in the long run, and (b) efforts to push unemployment below the natural rate lead to higher inflation rather than less unemployment. The application surveys some of the evidence about what has happened to the natural rate for the U.S. (it seems to have risen) as well as some of the ways through which the natural rate might be reduced.

Part 2

Define the following terms and concepts.

1. Secular trend
2. Business cycle
3. Seasonal variations
4. Random variations
5. Contraction phase
6. Expansion phase
7. Leading indicators
8. Full employment
9. Frictional unemployment
10. Structural unemployment
11. Cyclical unemployment
12. GDP gap
13. Inflation
14. Cost-push inflation
15. Demand-pull inflation
16. Deflation
17. Real interest rate
18. Stagflation
19. Inflationary expectations
20. Okun's Law
21. Natural rate of unemployment

Part 3

Answer the following questions and problems.

1. Distinguish among secular trends, business cycles, seasonal variations, and random variations.

2. Name the four phases of the business cycle and note what happens to prices, output, and employment in each.

3. Why do some economists prefer the term business fluctuations to the term business cycles?

4. Over a business cycle, why do the prices and outputs of durable-goods industries behave differently from those of nondurable-goods industries?

5. What do economists mean by leading indicators? What function do these leading indicators perform?

6. Distinguish among the three kinds of unemployment and give an example of each. How would you go about reducing each of these kinds of unemployment?

7. Review the kinds of costs of unemployment.

8. Describe each of the types of inflation.

9. If we assume that total output is unchanged, how do price increases redistribute real income? What groups benefit? Who suffers? Apply the same questions to price decreases.

10. During an inflation, who benefits: debtors, creditors, or savers? Why? What happens during a deflation?

11. How may a high rate of inflation lead to recession and unemployment?

12. Why may a moderate rate of inflation be beneficial to output?

13. How do the authors justify viewing creeping inflation as a threat to economic stability?

14. Whereas a moderate deflation may be beneficial to economic expansion, a rapid decline in prices tends to reduce output. Why?

15. Why may the goals of full employment and stable prices be contradictory? Draw a Phillips curve as part of your explanation.

16. What does the line labeled Potential GDP in Figure 6-1 represent? What does the line labeled Actual GDP represent? From 1994 to 1998 line Actual GDP was on or below potential GDP. What does that Potential GDP mean? From 1986 to 1990 Actual GDP was on or above Potential GDP. What does that mean?

Figure 6-1
The GDP Gap

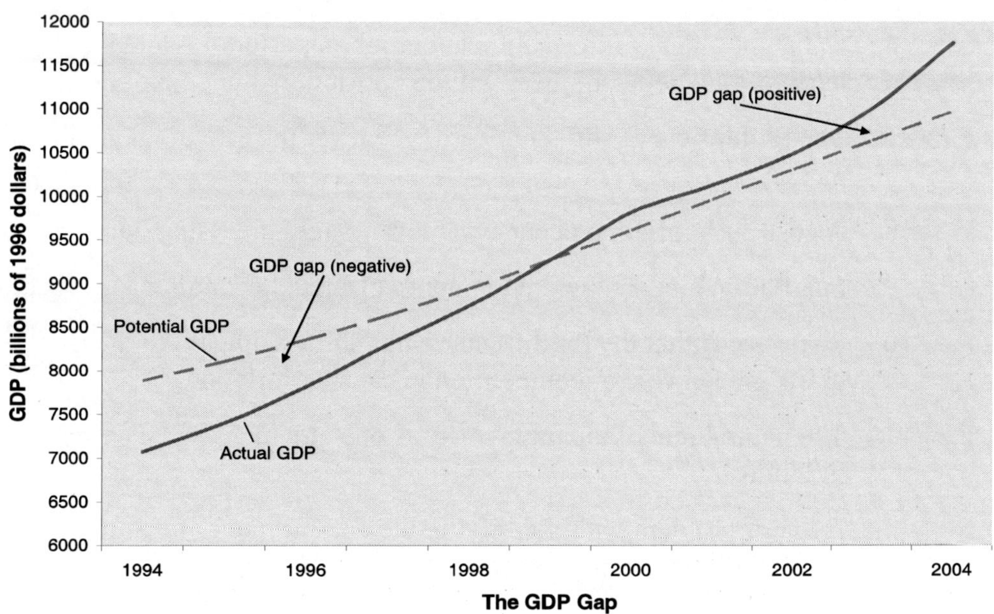

17. What is meant by the natural rate of unemployment?

18. Why is it difficult in the long run to push an economy's actual unemployment rate below its natural rate?

19. What seems to have happened to the natural rate of unemployment of the American economy? How might the natural rate be lowered?

20. How are unemployment and inflation related?

21. Why is understanding leading indicators important?

Part 4 Self-test

Section A True/false questions

T F 1. The nondurable-goods sector of the economy experiences wider fluctuations in price and smaller fluctuations in output than the durable-goods sector, because it is characterized by such high degrees of competition that no one firm has much control over the price.

T F 2. Before 1969, inflation and unemployment moved together during the business cycle; high unemployment was associated with high rates of inflation.

T F 3. When prices increase, savers benefit, while debtors do not.

T F 4. Business cycles are recurrent and nonperiodic variations in the level of economic activity.

T F 5. In a market-oriented economy, some level of frictional unemployment will always exist.

T F 6. If there is enough information about job opportunities and an adequate level of total demand, there will be no frictional unemployment.

T F 7. The Phillips curve shifts outward whenever the rate of unemploy-ment increases.

T F 8. A cost-push inflation occurs whenever wages are rising during an inflation.

T F 9. Stagflation hinders the government's efforts at economic stabilization.

T F 10. Some argue that the Phillips curve has shifted upward to the right because of the greater role of competition in causing inflation.

T F 11. The natural rate of unemployment is one at which there is a zero rate of inflation.

T F 12. A major problem with identifying the natural rate of unemployment is due to shifting inflationary expectations.

T F 13. The natural rate of unemployment for the U.S. has fallen in recent years.

T F 14. The changing composition of the American labor force has had a major effect on the nation's natural rate of unemployment.

T F 15. The natural rate of unemployment cannot be lowered.

T F 16. Okun's Law states that GDP will decline 2 1/2% for each 1% of employment above the natural rate.

T F 17. Leading economic indicators reflect how an economy has already changed.

T F 18. Inflation causes a decrease in the purchasing power of the dollar.

T F 19. Business cycles are regular in length and average between 2 to 4 years.

T F 20. During a recession phase inflation tends to move downward.

T F 21. In the long run, an economy cannot be pushed below its natural rate of unemployment.

Section B Multiple-choice questions

1. Which one of the following may be interpreted as demand-pull inflation?
   a. At full employment, demand exceeds the ability of the economy to produce at existing prices.
   b. Prices increase slowly over a long period of time.
   c. Costs of resources rise more rapidly than productivity rises.
   d. Prices increase very rapidly due to a rapid increase in the supply of money.
2. If OPEC quadruples the price of crude oil in 2005, the resulting inflation will be called
   a. creeping inflation.
   b. hyper-inflation.
   c. cost-push inflation.
   d. demand-pull inflation.
3. Which of the following is true?
   a. Business cycles tend to be recurrent and periodic.
   b. All phases of the business cycle tend to take an approximately equal length of time.
   c. All phases of the business cycle tend to be about equal in intensity.
   d. All the above are false.

4. In which industry do the most substantial variations in output and employment occur during a business cycle?

   a. Medical services

   b. Automobiles

   c. Food

   d. Furniture

5. If we assume that real output is unchanged, which generalization is not true about the effects of inflation?

   a. Debtors benefit.

   b. Savers benefit.

   c. Lenders are hurt.

   d. Both lenders and debtors are hurt.

6. Over a business cycle, prices in nondurable-goods industries tend to fluctuate widely while output tends to be relatively stable, because

   a. these industries are concentrated industries in which certain firms have the power to control output.

   b. consumers are limited in their ability to postpone new purchases from these industries because of the nature of the product.

   c. firms in these industries are small and therefore cannot get enough resources to keep output stable.

7. The shift outward of the Phillips curve can be attributed to

   a. increased amounts of structural unemployment.

   b. increased importance of cost-push inflation.

   c. increased impact of international inflationary forces beyond the control of domestic stabilization policies.

   d. all of the above.

8. The Phillips curve measures the tradeoff between

   a. unemployment rate and price level changes.

   b. wages and profits.

   c. quantity demanded and quantity supplied.

   d. employment rates and rates of inflation.

9. Which of the following generalizations about the relationship between price changes and output is usually true?

   a. A strong inflation can lead to a recession.

   b. A mild inflation tends to encourage economic expansion.

   c. A strong deflation tends to lead to economic contraction.

   d. All of the above are usually true.

10. Government economic policy may not achieve full employment and stable prices at the same time because

    a. full employment is impossible, since some workers are always unemployed as people move from one job to another.

    b. business groups within the country will not allow the achievement of this objective because it cuts down on their profits.

    c. some kinds of resources are in shorter supply than others.

    d. all of the above explain why both goals cannot be achieved.

11. Which of the following best describes the natural rate of unemployment concept?

    a. The unemployment rate associated with no unemployment.

    b. The unemployment rate associated with no change in the rate of inflation.

    c. The unemployment rate associated with creeping inflation.

    d. The unemployment rate associated with mild deflation.

12. Which of the following is not a way to lower the natural rate of unemployment?

    a. Creating a better match between job locations and available workers.

    b. Enhancing barriers to resource mobility.

    c. Creating a better match between skills of available workers and job openings.

    d. Reducing barriers to labor mobility such as economic discrimination and union membership requirements.

13. An attempt to reduce the actual rate of unemployment below the natural rate will likely result in which of the following?

    a. A short-run rise in the rate of unemployment.

    b. A short-run increase in the rate of inflation.

    c. A long-run decrease in the rate of unemployment.

    d. A short-run decrease in the rate of inflation.

Section C Matching questions

Match the phrases in column B to the terms in column A.

Column A	Column B
1. Secular trend	(a) A situation in which actual output is less than potential output
2. Leading indicators	(b) Depends on degree of mobility of labor
3. Frictional unemployment	(c) Savers suffer
4. Structural unemployment	(d) A situation in which demand exceeds supply
5. GDP gap	(e) Fall before economy falls, rise before economy rises
6. Demand-pull inflation	(f) Expresses what money income can buy
7. Cost-push inflation	(g) Depicts the tradeoff between price changes and unemployment
8. Price increases	(h) A situation in which prices of resources increase more than productivity
9. Real income	(i) Long-term movements in the economy
10. Phillips curve	(j) Depends on changes in technology and composition of demand for output
11. Natural rate of unemployment	(k) Has risen in the U.S. in recent decades

ANSWERS

Part 4

Section A 1, T; 2, F; 3, F; 4, T; 5, T; 6, F; 7, F; 8, F; 9, T; 10, F; 11, F; 12, T; 13, F; 14, T; 15, F; 16, T; 17, F; 18, T; 19, F; 20, T; 21, T

Section B 1, a; 2, c; 3, d; 4, b; 5, b; 6, b; 7, d; 8, a; 9, d; 10, c; 11, b; 12, b; 13, b

Section C 1, i; 2, e; 3, b; 4, j; 5, a; 6, d; 7, h; 8, c; 9, f; 10, g; 11, k

Chapter 7: Aggregate Demand and Aggregate Supply

Part 1

First, read the sections entitled "Summing Up" at the end of Chapter 7. They offer a thorough review of the chapter.

Things to Watch For

Chapter 7 introduces a very important series of chapters; those discussing how the level of income, output, employment, and prices are determined. This chapter shows how the equilibrium level of real income and prices is determined through the interaction of aggregate demand and aggregate supply.

First, the chapter introduces and defines the concept of aggregate demand and explains the factors that determine it. Then the downward-sloping nature of the aggregate demand curve is explored. Second, the concept of aggregate supply is introduced, defined and its determinants are detailed. The upward-sloping nature of aggregate supply is then examined. Finally, the two curves are put into the same diagram with prices on the vertical axis and real income/output on the horizontal axis. Equilibrium, where aggregate quantity demanded equals aggregate quantity supplied, will establish the level of prices and real income in the economy. You should remember that although the analysis seems much like the supply-and-demand model presented in Chapter 3, it has important differences. Know these differences. Furthermore, the student is cautioned that equilibrium and full employment are not necessarily the same.

Rounding out the discussion, the chapter analyzes the effects of changes in aggregate demand and aggregate supply under conditions in which there are demand shocks and supply shocks. It is also important to remember the three ranges of aggregate supply in its relationship between prices and employment.

Before the application, the chapter concludes with two further subjects. First, is a brief comment on supply-side economics-the main point here is that policy advocates of it concentrate on policy that would increase the ability of the economy to produce. More on supply-side policies will be included in a later chapter. Second, is a discussion of price indexes including the Consumer Price Index and computing the GDP price deflator.

The application reviews the economic effects of the (oil-price determined) supply shocks of 1973 and 1979 in terms of the aggregate demand-aggregate supply model introduced in Chapter 7. The application continues with an examination of the reverse shocks of falling oil prices in the 1980s and 1990s. In conclusion, the application looks at the economic effects of terrorist attacks on the United States in 2001 and how those attacks may influence the recovery from recession of an economy mobilizing to fight terrorism.

Part 2

Define the following terms and concepts.

1. Equilibrium level of prices and real income
2. Aggregate demand
3. Aggregate supply
4. Aggregate demand shock
5. Aggregate supply shock
6. Supply-side economics
7. OPEC I, II, III
8. Investment in human capital
9. Ranges of aggregate supply
10. Price indexes
11. GDP price index or deflator
12. Consumer price index
13. External aggregate demand shocks
14. External aggregate supply shocks

Part 3

Answer the following questions and problems.

1. Draw a diagram representing aggregate demand and aggregate supply.
   a. Label all curves and axes.
   b. Show equilibrium and indicate and explain an excess supply or excess demand.
   c. Explain how equilibrium is achieved.
   d. Show the results of a demand shock.
   e. Show the results of a supply shock.
2. Explain why the aggregate demand curve slopes downward. Why does aggregate supply slope upward?
3. State each of the determinants of aggregate demand, and explain what happens when they shift.
4. State each of the determinants of aggregate supply, and explain what happens when they shift.
5. Explain how equilibrium employment and full employment may differ.
6. What is an aggregate demand shock? Show by use of a diagram how it affects prices and real income.
7. What is an aggregate supply shock? Show by use of a diagram how it affects prices and real income.
8. Using a diagram, show the three ranges of aggregate supply. What causes these different ranges to exist?
9. What are external demand and supply shocks?
10. What were the external oil supply shocks of the 1970s and 1980s and how did they affect the economy?

11. What is supply-side economics? What government policies do you think would be consistent with it's arguments?
12. Make up a numerical problem that illustrates how a 2000 GDP price index would be computed using a market basket price in 2000 and a market basket price in 1987.
13. Why is the CPI considered such an important index? How may it overstate aggregate price changes?
14. Summarize the possible aggregate demand and aggregate supply effects of the "war on terrorism." What caveats apply to those effects?
15. If the economy is not in equilibrium, how does it get back?
16. What is the largest component of aggregate demand (AD)?

Part 4 Self-test

Section A True/false questions

T F 1. As with the supply-and-demand model of a particular market, the equilibrium price level and equilibrium real income are determined by the intersection of aggregate demand and aggregate supply.

T F 2. The aggregate demand curve slopes downward for the same reason as does the demand curve for a particular commodity.

T F 3. Among other factors, aggregate demand is determined by consumption, investment, and government expenditures.

T F 4. Expectations about future economic events become more optimistic as the aggregate demand curve shifts down to the left.

T F 5. Aggregate supply curves slope upwards so that real income increases as prices increase.

T F 6. Among other things, the aggregate supply curve is determined by cost of resources, technology, and productivity.

T F 7. If our expectations about future economic activity become more optimistic, the aggregate supply curve shifts to the right.

T F 8. Equilibrium between aggregate supply and aggregate demand is always at full employment.

T F 9. When there is an aggregate demand shock due to increased demand, the aggregate demand curve shifts to the right with both real income and the price level increasing.

T F 10. The aggregate supply curve has three ranges:

1. No increases in prices as real income increases.

2. Increases in the price level as real income increases.

3. Increases in the price level with no increases in real income.

T F 11. OPEC I (1973-74) increased prices as the reduced supply of oil decreased real income.

T F 12. The increase in oil supply known as OPEC III (early 1980s) caused a reduction in the price level and an increase in real income.

T F 13. Supply-side economics is concerned with how the ability of the economy to produce can be increased.

T F 14. The consumer price index is used as the GDP price deflator.

T F 15. A war on terrorism is likely to reduce aggregate demand.

T F 16. The aggregate supply curve has a positive slope.

T F 17. Aggregate demand is a measure of the entire planned spending on final goods and services at each level of prices and real incomes.

T F 18. The CPI consumer price index is one of the most widely used indexes of the federal government.

T F 19. Supply shocks have only positive effects on the economy.

Section B Multiple-choice questions

1. When diagramming aggregate demand and aggregate supply

   a. real national income is placed on the vertical axis and the price level on the horizontal axis.

   b. the price level is placed on the vertical axis and real income on the horizontal axis.

   c. employment is placed on the vertical axis and the price level on the horizontal axis.

   d. government expenditures are placed on the horizontal axis and employment on the vertical axis.

2. Which one of the following is not a determinant of aggregate demand?

   a. Consumption expenditures

   b. Investment expenditures

   c. Technology

   d. Net exports

3. Which one of the following is not a determinant of aggregate supply?
   a. Cost and availability of resources
   b. Capacity and investment plans
   c. Productivity
   d. Disposable income
4. Which one of the following does not cause the aggregate demand curve to slope downward?
   a. Changes in real output
   b. Interest rate changes
   c. Wealth effects
   d. Changes in relative prices between foreign and domestic goods
5. Which of the following relationships is correct?
   a. Equilibrium employment and full employment may not be the same.
   b. Equilibrium employment and full employment are always the same.
   c. Equilibrium employment and full employment are never the same.
   d. Equilibrium employment and full employment are unrelated.
6. Which of the following is not correct?
   a. Real income will increase without increases in prices when there is substantial unemployment.
   b. Both real income and prices will increase when there are bottlenecks in the supply of some resources.
   c. When full employment is reached, only prices can increase.
   d. When full employment is reached, only increases in real income can occur.
7. With aggregate demand shocks
   a. the aggregate demand curve moves up the aggregate supply curve and increases prices and real income.
   b. the aggregate supply curve moves up the aggregate demand curve and increases price but reduces real income.
   c. the aggregate supply curve moves down the aggregate demand curve and reduces prices and increases real income.
   d. the aggregate demand curve moves down the aggregate supply curve and increases both prices and real income.

8. An improvement in technology will

   a. increase aggregate demand.

   b. decrease aggregate demand.

   c. increase aggregate supply.

   d. decrease aggregate supply.

9. Which of the following was not a factor limiting the severity of the effects of the oil supply shock of 1979-80?

   a. More efficient use of energy.

   b. Increase in use of alternative sources of energy.

   c. Increased suppliers of non-OPEC oil.

   d. More rapid worldwide economic growth.

10. The oil shock in 1979-80 was an example of

    a. an external demand shock increasing prices and real income.

    b. an external supply shock increasing prices and decreasing real income.

    c. an external supply shock decreasing prices and increasing real income.

    d. an external demand shock decreasing prices and real income.

11. Oil price changes in 1985 and 1986 are an example of

    a. an external supply shock decreasing prices and raising real income.

    b. an external demand shock increasing prices and reducing real income.

    c. an external supply shock increasing prices and reducing real income.

    d. an external supply shock increasing prices and reducing real income.

12. The negative effects of a war on terrorism are likely to be

    a. a decrease in aggregate supply and an increase in aggregate demand.

    b. an increase in aggregate supply and an increase in aggregate demand.

    c. an increase in aggregate supply and a decrease in aggregate demand.

    d. a decrease in aggregate supply and a decrease in aggregate demand.

13. The positive effects of a war on terrorism are likely to be

    a. an increase in aggregate supply and a decrease in aggregate demand.

    b. a decrease in aggregate supply and a decrease in aggregate demand.

    c. an increase in aggregate supply and an increase in aggregate demand.

    d. an increase in aggregate demand and a decrease in aggregate supply.

Section C Matching Questions

Match the phrases in Column B to the terms in Column A

Column A	Column B
1. Aggregate demand	(a) Reduced aggregate demand
2. Aggregate supply	(b) Downward sloping curve
3. Increased cost of credit	(c) Increased aggregate demand
4. Increased disposable income	(d) GNP gap is zero
5. Equilibrium real income	(e) OPEC oil price increases of the 1970s
6. Equilibrium income = potential income	(f) Less real income demanded at each price level
7. Aggregate supply shocks	(g) Aggregate quantity supplied = Aggregate quantity demanded
8. Aggregate demand shock	
9. Full-employment aggregate supply	(h) Upward sloping curve
10. External aggregated demand and supply shocks.	(i) No increase in real income
	(j) Influences outside the domestic economy
11. Colas	(k) Determined by the consumer price index

ANSWERS

Part 4

Section A 1, T; 2, F; 3, T; 4, F; 5, T; 6, T; 7, T; 8, F; 9, T; 10, T; 11, T; 12, T; 13, T; 14, F; 15, F; 16, T; 17, T; 18, T; 19, F
Section B 1, b; 2, c; 3, d; 4, a; 5, a; 6, d; 7, a; 8, c; 9, d; 10, b; 11, a; 12, d; 13, c
Section C 1, b; 2, h; 3, a; 4, c; 5, g; 6, d; 7, e; 8, f; 9, i; 10, j

Chapter 8: Aggregate Spending in the Macroeconomy: Classical and Keynesian Theories

Part 1

First, read the section entitled "Summing Up" at the end of Chapter 8. It offers a thorough review of the chapter.

Things to Watch For

You may find Chapter 8 rough going, but if you are willing to work your way through it step by step, you will be rewarded. Chapter 8 is the first of three chapters that will lead you through the Keynesian model of income determination. This model is named after the economist John Maynard Keynes (whose name rhymes with gains). This chapter will give you a theoretical foundation for our later discussion of economic policies that governments use to stabilize a nation's economy and for some of the controversies surrounding those policies..

The chapter is divided into three sections. The first explores the macroeconomic theory most widely accepted before Keynes formulated his model. This earlier theory is called classical income-determination theory. Classical theory held that a market economy, if left alone, would achieve a level of income and output that would bring about full employment. What was necessary, such economists believed, was a low and balanced government budget plus competitive markets. The three concepts that underlie their thinking are Say's law, the abstinence theory of interest, and wage and price flexibility.

The second section of Chapter 8 explains Keynes's ideas about income determination by analyzing his criticisms of the classical model. Keynes attacked the abstinence theory of interest by breaking the relationship between the interest rate and savings, and reducing the strength of the relationship between the interest rate and investment. He also challenged the effectiveness of wage and price flexibility as a device for eliminating a temporary oversupply of firms' inventories. If you want to understand the relationships discussed in the next chapters, it is important that you understand this reasoning. It is important to remember Keynes' assumption about aggregate supply, i.e., that supply is horizontal and increases in response to increased demand without increases in prices (the unemployment range of aggregate supply).

The third section of this chapter sets up the basic elements of the Keynesian model. Keynes said that the level of income may be such that the economy may be at full employment, above full employment (inflation), or below full employment (unemployment). The thing that determines the level of income in the Keynesian model is the level of effective demand or aggregate demand. The five factors that determine effective demand are consumption, savings, investment, government expenditures, and taxes. The latter part of the chapter explores the relationship between the first three factors and the level of income, and brings together in diagrammatic form the elements contained in the Keynesian model. It is essential that you thoroughly understand this section, because the next chapters build on it. The Keynesian theory of income determination is a key concept, and this chapter sets forth the crux of this theory.

Part 2

Define the following terms and concepts.

1. Classical theory
2. Say's law
3. Abstinence theory of interest
4. Wage-price flexibility
5. Pigou effect
6. Effective demand
7. Consumption function
8. Savings function
9. Investment function
10. Dissavings
11. Liquid assets
12. Autonomous investment, induced investment
13. Marginal efficiency of capital
14. Aggregate-demand-equals-aggregate-supply approach
15. Savings-equals-intended-investment approach
16. Keynesian theory
17. Mercantilism

Part 3

Answer the following questions and problems.

1. What do classical economists conclude about full employment in a market-oriented economy? Under what two conditions do they feel that unemployment can exist? What three concepts underlie their conclusions?
2. What is Say's law? Illustrate it with a simple circular-flow diagram.
3. When a complex circular-flow diagram rather than a simple one is used, what additional problems confront the classical economist with respect to income determination? How does the abstinence theory of interest solve those problems?
4. Explain the abstinence theory of interest. Explain how the interest rate links savings to investment.
5. Explain how, according to classical economists, wage and price flexibility does away with unemployment and a temporary oversupply of firms' goods. What role does the Pigou effect play in this process?
6. What arguments did Keynes use to refute Say's law? To refute the abstinence theory of interest? Explain how Keynes challenged the relationship between planned savings and the interest rate, and cast doubt on the relationship between planned investment and the interest rate.
7. Keynes denied the assumption that wages and prices are flexible enough to move the economy toward full employment. Explain the points he used to support his conclusion.
8. After he had refuted classical conclusions about the level of income, what did Keynes conclude about it? What did he say determines the level of income?
9. Draw the aggregate supply curve that is consistent with the Keynesian assumptions. What level of employment must be assumed? Why?

10. Name five factors that determine the level of effective demand. Which of these factors increase demand as they increase, and which decrease demand as they increase?

11. Draw a diagram showing the 45? line, the consumption function, and the savings function. What is the significance of the 45? line? Given the consumption function you have drawn, what are you assuming about the relationship between the percentage of income that people consume and the various levels of income? Between the percentage of income that people save and the various levels of income?

12. What does it mean when we say that individuals sometimes dissave?

13. Distinguish between a change in the quantity consumed and saved on the one hand and, on the other, a change in consumption and savings.

14. What are five factors that can cause a change in consumption or savings?

15. The level of autonomous investment is determined by the cost of investing and the expected rate of return. What determines the cost of investing? What determines the expected rate of return, or the marginal efficiency of capital?

16. Use a diagram to show how the quantity of autonomous investment is determined. (Be sure to label the diagram properly.)

17. Why is the quantity of investment so unstable? What factors have tended to reduce this instability?

18. Add intended investment to your diagram of the consumption and savings functions, using the following two approaches. What set of relationships does each approach emphasize?

    a. The savings-equals-intended-investment approach.

    b. The aggregate-demand-equals-aggregate-supply approach.

19. What is the difference between Classical and Keynesian economics?

20. Why is investment so volatile over time?

Part 4 Self-test

Section A True/false questions

T F 1. According to Say's law, supply creates its own demand, so that unemployment cannot long exist.

T F 2. Classical theory maintains that the economy can only temporarily deviate from full employment.

T F 3. Classical economists, knowing that saving reduces consumer demand, believe that demand will be equal to supply only if people do not save.

T F 4. Classical theorists considered unemployment a temporary problem because of considerable monopoly in both the product and the labor markets.

T F 5. Although Keynes agreed that the level of saving is determined by the interest rate, he felt that the level of investment is not deter-mined by it, because of business expectations.

T F 6. Keynes concluded that an economy's level of income may be such that the economy may be at full employment, or at inflation, or below full employment.

T F 7. The aggregate supply curve that is consistent with the Keynesian model slopes upward showing that increases in demand will increase both real income and prices.

T F 8. The position of the consumption function depends on the level of income, but the quantity of goods and services consumed depends on many other factors.

T F 9. If the interest rate decreases, the amount of investment also decreases because the profits investors expect to make decrease.

T F 10. An individual can dissave by decreasing his or her accumulated savings, but the economy as a whole cannot dissave.

T F 11. The marginal-efficiency-of-capital curve slopes down to the right because, as the interest rate falls, larger amounts of investment yield a return equal to or greater than the interest rate.

T F 12. Induced investment is the result of increased buying.

T F 13. Classical theory believes that the supply curve is vertical.

T F 14. Say's Law says that demand creates supply.

T F 15. Keynesian economists theorize that government intervention is not necessary to move to full employment.

Section B Multiple-choice questions

1. The classical conclusion that a market economy has built-in mechanisms that will keep income at the full-employment level is supported by which of the following assumptions?
   a. Wage and price flexibility
   b. Say's law
   c. The abstinence theory of interest
   d. All of the above

2. The abstinence theory of interest does not maintain that
   a. people would rather consume now than later.
   b. total demand equals total supply only when savings are zero.
   c. the higher the interest rate, the larger the quantity saved.
   d. the lower the interest rate, the smaller the quantity saved.

3. Wage and price flexibility will eliminate a temporary oversupply of goods and also unemployment by
   a. decreasing wages and prices and thus increasing quantity demanded.
   b. increasing the purchasing power of workers as wages fall more slowly than prices.
   c. increasing the purchasing power of entrepreneurs as wages fall faster than prices.
   d. decreasing wages and prices and thus decreasing quantity demanded.

4. Which of the following did Keynes present as an argument for maintaining that the interest rate does not equate desired savings and desired investment, and that the abstinence theory of interest is wrong?
   a. Those who save are not the same as those who invest.
   b. Motivations for saving are not entirely related to the rate of interest.
   c. Expectations about future economic activity weaken the relationship between investments and the interest rate.
   d. All of the above.

5. Which of the following arguments did Keynes use in challenging the idea that wage and price flexibility is sufficient to bring about a situation of full employment and no surpluses?
   a. Monopoly power is rare in the U.S. market economy.
   b. Wages always fall more rapidly than prices.
   c. Workers are more concerned with real income than with money income.
   d. None of the above.

6. After analyzing the classical conclusions about the level of income and employ-ment, Keynes concluded that
   a. the level of income will always be such that there is full employment.
   b. the level of income will always be such that there is less than full employment.
   c. the level of income may be such that there is full employment, or unemploy-ment, or inflation.
   d. the level of income is unrelated to the level of employment.

7. Which of the following is not correct about the aggregate supply curve consistent with the Keynesian assumptions?
   a. Prices do not increase with increases in output.
   b. Unemployment exists.
   c. Both prices and real income increases with increases in demand.
   d. The aggregate supply curve is horizontal.

8. Effective demand will increase if
   a. consumption, investment, and government expenditures increase.
   b. taxes and savings increase.
   c. consumption decreases and savings increase.
   d. government expenditures decrease.

9. The quantity consumed may change if there are changes in
   a. institutions or customs.
   b. the level of income.
   c. liquid assets or taxes.
   d. tax laws.

10. Which of the following is most correct? The quantity of autonomous investment changes when there are changes in
   a. interest rates.
   b. expectations about future economic activity.
   c. productivity of investment.
   d. interest rates, expectations, and productivity of investment.

11. Of all the factors that influence effective demand, the most unstable over time is
   a. consumption.
   b. savings.
   c. investment.
   d. government expenditures.

Section C Matching questions

Match the phrases in column B to the terms in column A.

Column A	Column B
1. Classical economics	(a) Investment in relation to savings
2. Say's law	(b) Income increases, quantity consumed increases
3. Abstinence theory of interest	(c) Income always tends toward a level at which there is full employment
4. Wage and price flexibility	(d) Consume now rather than save and consume later
5. Pigou effect	(e) Consumption exceeds income
6. Consumption function	(f) Supply creates its own demand
7. Autonomous investment	(g) Eliminates temporary oversupply
8. Dissavings	(h) Not affected by income
9. Marginal efficiency of capital	(i) Expected rate of return
10. S=II	(j) Savers feel wealthier as prices fall, and they demand more consumption

ANSWERS

Part 4

Section A 1, T; 2, T; 3, F; 4, F; 5, F; 6, T; 7, F; 8, F; 9, F; 10, F; 11, T; 12, T; 13, T; 14, F; 15, F
Section B 1, d; 2, b; 3, a; 4, d; 5, d; 6, c; 7, c; 8, a; 9, b; 10, d; 11, c
Section C 1, c; 2, f; 3, d; 4, g; 5, j; 6, b; 7, h; 8, e; 9, i; 10, a

Chapter 9: Equilibrium in the Macroeconomy

Part 1

First, read the section entitled "Summing Up" at the end of Chapter 9. This will provide a thorough review of the chapter.

Things to Watch For

Chapter 9 takes up the Keynesian model where Chapter 8 left off. It leads you diagrammatically through two approaches to the income-determination model. The first stage in constructing the model excludes the government sector. Thus you get an idea of the situation as it would be if there were no government expenditures and no taxes.

The first approach-savings equals intended investment-shows that the equilibrium level of income must be the point at which desired savings (which drains away demand for consumption) is offset by desired investment (which exactly replaces that demand). At any other level of income, the expectations firms have about the quantity that the public is going to buy are unfulfilled. When this happens, businesses must change their plans about investment. They take steps to bring their actual inventory in line with their planned inventory. This causes the level of income to move toward the equilibrium level.

The second approach-aggregate demand equals aggregate supply-uses the 45? line. (Aggregate demand consists of C + II) When aggregate demand and aggregate supply are not equal, there is either too much demand or not enough. Changes must be made in the level of inventories, and these produce changes in income.

The two approaches to income determination yield the same equilibrium level of income.

The second concept Chapter 9 introduces is the multiplier effect. The idea behind the multiplier is that, when there is a given change in aggregate demand, the national level of income changes by a larger amount. The strength of the multiplier depends on the size of the marginal propensity to consume. The formula for the multiplier (M) is:

$$\mathrm{M} = \frac{1}{1 - MPC}$$

It's important to remember the multiplier concept and also the average and the marginal propensities to consume. They help explain business cycles and enable people to estimate the effects of government stabilization policy.

Chapter 8 assumed that "investment" includes only autonomous investment. Chapter 9 discusses the concept of induced investment, or investment brought on by increases in employment and the GDP. The accelerator principle explains the movements of induced investment in response to variations in the rate of change in consumer demand. One can explain the importance of induced investment and the accelerator principle on the same grounds as the multiplier principle.

The paradox of thrift explains the unexpected effects on an economy in recession when many people start saving more money. Increased savings at the same level of income may be a good thing for individuals, but it may not be a good thing for the economy as a whole if everyone does it at the same time. At the same time, it is important to remember that an adequate supply of savings is important to establish a level of investment consistent with high real income.

Stage two of our model building, in Chapter 9, is divided into two sections. In the first section the government sector is added to the simple model. When government expenditures are added, S = II becomes S = II + GX and aggregate demand now consists of C + II + GX. The analysis is the same as the analysis of the simple model. Then taxes are added to the model. Remember that people pay taxes partly out of income that they would have consumed and partly out of income that they would have saved. Therefore, the inclusion of taxes shifts consumption downward, and along with it aggregate demand. Savings is also shifted downward. The equilibrium level is now the point at which S + T = II + GX and, of course, the level at which aggregate quantity demanded equals aggregate quantity supplied.

The chapter, then, presents a simple problem that illustrates the concept of the balanced-budget multiplier. When government expenditures and taxes change in the same direction and by the same amount, the equilibrium level of income also changes in the same direction and by the same amount. In other words, income changes even when there is a balanced-budget change in federal expenditures.

Stage three of our model building involves adding the international economy. What needs to be remembered is that imports reduce, while exports increase, the demand for output of the economy.

The equilibrium level of income may occur when there is full employment and relatively stable prices, or when there is unemployment, or when there is inflation. Therefore, the concepts of deflationary gap (the deficit in aggregate demand represented by the difference between actual demand and the demand necessary to achieve full employment) and inflationary gap (surplus aggregate demand, which causes inflation) are very important. You will encounter these concepts throughout all discussions of government stabilization policy.

Lastly, the chapter deals with government fiscal policy-policies that involve varying expenditures and taxes in order to stabilize the economy. The chapter includes an application that describes the fluctuations of economic activity from the 1920s through the beginnings of 2004. A careful reading of this section will give you some understanding of the factors that expand or contract the economy.

Part 2

Define the following terms and concepts.

1. Instantaneous multiplier
2. Periodic multiplier
3. Accelerator principle
4. Deflationary gap
5. Inflationary gap
6. Balanced-budget multiplier
7. Discretionary fiscal policy
8. Net Exports
9. Primary demand
10. Secondary (replacement) demand
11. Stagflation
12. Multiplier
13. Unplanned or involuntary additions to inventory
14. Unplanned or involuntary reductions in inventory
15. Ex-ante investment
16. Ex-post investment
17. Average propensity to consume
18. Marginal propensity to consume
19. Average propensity to save
20. Marginal propensity to save
21. Multiplier effect
22. Multiplier formula
23. Post-Keynesians

Part 3

Answer the following questions and problems.

1. Draw the appropriate functions (Sf, II, 45° line) for the simple model of national income determination, using the savings-equals-intended-investment approach. Show why an economy cannot maintain a level of income above the equilibrium level. Also show why an economy cannot maintain a level of income below the equilibrium level.

2. What is the key relationship between savings and investments?

3. What makes ex-post investment always equal to ex-post savings? Why must ex-ante investment equal ex-ante savings if equilibrium income is to be achieved?

4. Draw the appropriate functions (Cf, Cf + II, 45° line) for the simple model of national income determination, using the aggregate-demand-equals-aggregate-supply approach. What determines the equilibrium level of income? Why can it not be higher? lower?

5. Distinguish between

   a. the average propensity to consume and the marginal propensity to consume.

   b. the average propensity to save and the marginal propensity to save.

6. Why is the change in income always greater than any change in aggregate demand that precedes it? Make up your own example of the multiplier. Use as an example some contemporary form of change in aggregate demand, and choose your own marginal propensity to consume.

7. Distinguish between instantaneous and periodic multipliers. Why is it important to make this distinction?

8. When would you find induced investment decreasing while the quantity of consumption was still rising. Why?

9. In the earliest phase of recovery from a recession, why doesn't the accelerator principle operate?

10. During a recession (when there is unemployment), it may well be to the best interests of an individual to increase savings. For the society as a whole, however, an increase in people's savings may be detrimental to the economy. Why? Use a diagram to support your reasoning.

11. Here's a simple problem. The marginal and average propensities to consume are 35 . The equilibrium level of income is 500. What is the level of consumption, savings, and investment? (Government expenditures and taxes are both zero.) Now, suppose investment increases by 10. What is the new level of income, consumption, savings, and investment? (The answer is given after Part 4.)

12. Using Figure 9-1, complete the following statements. (The answers are given after Part 4.)

    a. The equilibrium level of income is _________ .

    b. At income level C, involuntary (additions to/reductions in) inventory are _________ or _________ .

    c. At income level A, involuntary (additions to/reductions in) inventory are _________ or _________ .

Figure 9-1
Graph for Problem 12

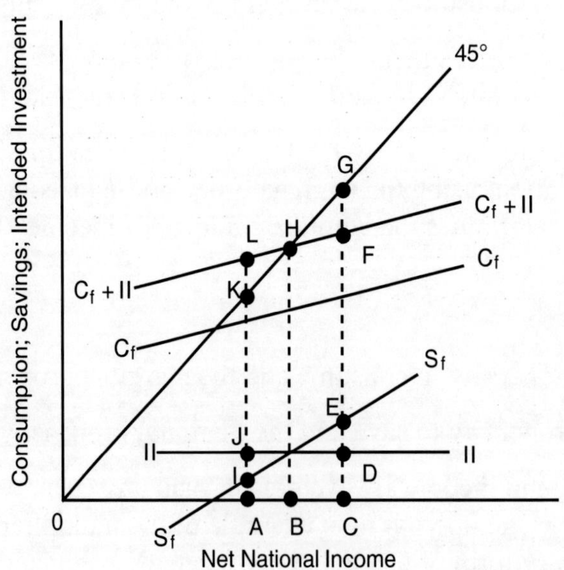

13. On the graph provided as Figure 9-2, draw the simple Keynesian model of savings equals intended investment. (Be sure your diagram uses all of the space available.) To that model, add government expenditures, so that the approach becomes S = II + GX Mark which is the equilibrium level of income, and explain why it is the equilibrium level. Then indicate a level of income above the equilibrium, and explain why it cannot be the equilibrium level. Do the same for a level of income below the equilibrium.

14. Add to Figure 9-2 an intended-investment function, above the consumption function, and finally a government-expenditure function, so that aggregate demand equals C + II + GX. Again mark the equilibrium level of income, and explain why it is the equilibrium level. If this equilibrium level is not the same as the one you obtained in your answer to problem 13, you have made an error in drawing your diagram. Try to find it. Use the same above-equilibrium income level that you used in answering problem 13, and explain why it cannot be the equilibrium level. Also, use the below-equilibrium income level that you used in answering problem 1, and explain why it cannot be the equilibrium level.

Figure 9-2
Graph for Problems 13 and 14

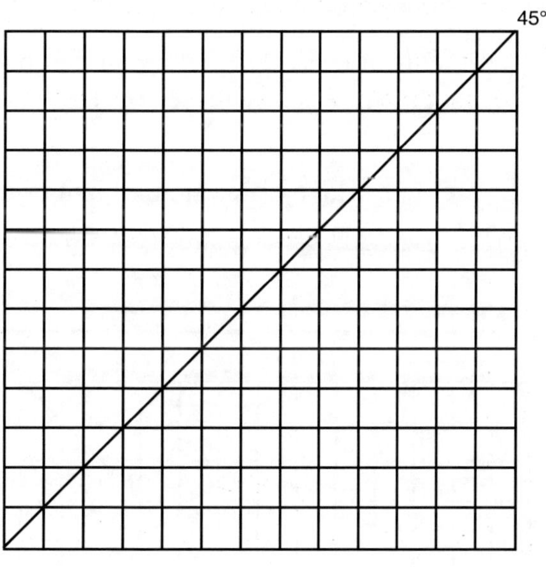

15. On Figure 9-3, redraw your diagram of problems 13 and 14; be sure that the functions are far enough apart so that you will have room to draw in the functions after taxes are introduced. Now assume some specific amount of taxes and some specific marginal propensities to consume and save. Using either dashed lines or colored pencils, draw in all the relevant functions, including taxes.

First, use the approach of savings plus taxes equals intended investment plus government expenditures. Indicate the equilibrium level of income, and explain why it is the equilibrium level. Then indicate a level of income above the equilibrium, and explain why it is not the equilibrium level. Do the same for a level of income below the equilibrium.

Second, use the approach of aggregate demand equals aggregate supply, and do the same as you did above. (Do not copy the figures in the text; but do refer to them if you get stuck. Also use them to check for the general correctness of your own diagram.)

16. On the graph provided as Figure 9-4, illustrate a deflationary gap. What does it mean? How would you eliminate a deflationary gap?

17. On the graph provided as Figure 9-5, illustrate an inflationary gap. What does it mean? How would you eliminate an inflationary gap?

18. Assume a marginal propensity to consume of 2/3 and an average propensity to consume of 2/3. The equilibrium level of income is 300, consumption is 200, savings is 100, and intended investment is 100. Government expenditures and taxes are both zero. (This is really a simple problem. Answers are given after Part 4.)

    a. Now government expenditures become 10. What is the new level of income, consumption, savings, and investment?

    b. Now taxes become 10. What is the new level of income, consumption, savings, investment, government expenditures, and taxes?

    c. When you compare the income level at the end of part b with income at the beginning, you see that income has increased by 10. What is this called? Why did it occur?

    d. Try computing the problem with a different marginal propensity to consume. Are the results the same?

Figure 9-3
Graph for Problem 15

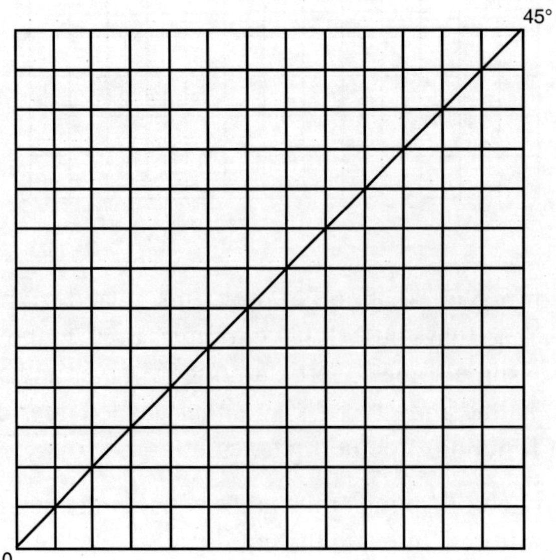

Figure 9-4
Graph for Problem 16

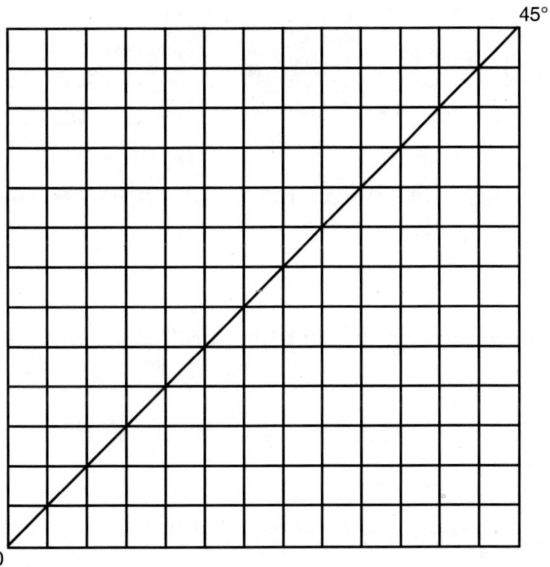

Figure 9-5
Graph for Problem 17

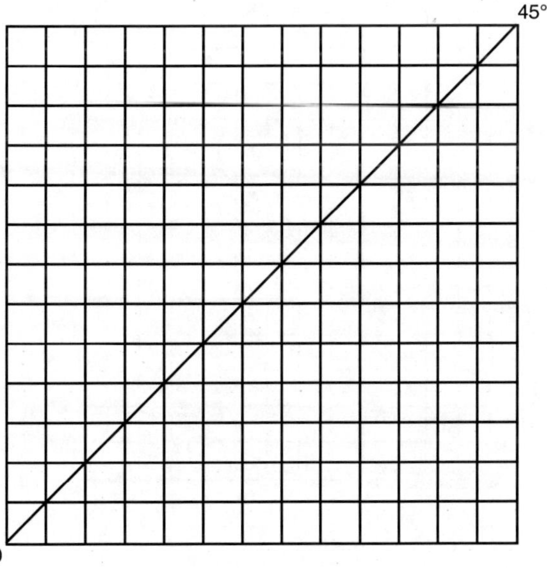

19. You are an economic adviser to the federal government. The big problem the economy has at the moment is unemployment accompanied by falling incomes and falling output. Prices are not rising. What would you recommend that the federal government do to remedy the problem?

20. You are an economic adviser to the federal government. The big problem the economy has at the moment is inflation. What would you recommend that the federal government do?

21. What is propensity?

22. If the government can change taxes and spending why aren't we always at full-employment?

23. Figure 9-6shows the entire complex model of an economy, including government expenditures and taxes. Examine the figure. Be sure you understand all the functions or curves in it. If you have any confusion about any aspect of it, reread the appropriate part of Chapter 9. Use Figure 9-6 to answer the following questions. (The answers are given after Part 4.)

    a. The equilibrium level of income is ________.

    b. At a level of income above the equilibrium level, unplanned addition to inventory is __________ or _________.

    c. At a level of income below the equilibrium level, unplanned decrease in inventory is _________ or _________.

    d. The marginal propensity to consume is equal to __________________.

Figure 9-6
Graph for Problem 21

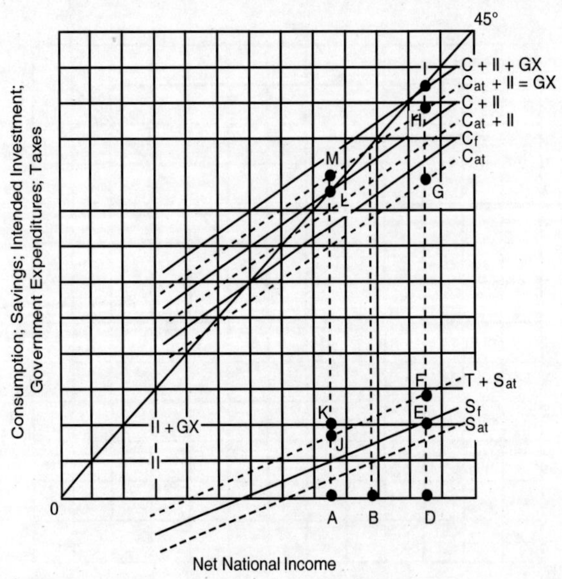

PART 4 SELF-TEST

Section A True/false questions

T F 1. Planned (ex-ante) investment always equals planned (ex-ante) savings.

T F 2. Actual (ex-post) investment always equals actual (ex-post) savings.

T F 3. When aggregate supply exceeds aggregate demand, planned (ex-ante) savings exceed planned (ex-ante) investment; unplanned increases in inventories result.

T F 4. A family has a disposable income of $16,000 and spends $12,000 on consumption. Its average propensity to save (APS) is .25, or one-fourth.

T F 5. The average propensity to consume is the key to the size of the multiplier.

T F 6. The larger the marginal propensity to save, the larger the multiplier.

T F 7. The periodic multiplier impresses economists with the need to keep prior increases in aggregate demand in mind when planning government policy.

T F 8. In an economy's initial phases of recovery from a recession, the accelerator does not operate because manufacturing plants have excess capacity.

T F 9. As long as income and the quantity of consumption increase, induced investment-and therefore the accelerator-will increase.

T F 10. When unemployment is on the rise, an increase in savings (people at every income level saving more) benefits both the individual and the economy as a whole.

T F 11. An increase in taxes has two effects on our model of income determination. It (a) shifts the consumption function down and (b) shifts the savings function down.

T F 12. If the equilibrium level of income is less than the full-employment level of income, there is a deflationary gap. This deflationary gap is equal to the additional aggregate demand that is needed to achieve full employment.

T F 13. One can eliminate an inflationary gap by increasing aggregate demand through increases in consumption, investment, and government expenditure.

T F 14. The size of the balanced-budget multiplier varies, depending on the marginal propensity to consume.

T F 15. Keynesian fiscal policy focuses solely on changes in aggregate demand as the factor that determines changes in income and employment.

T F 16. Imports increase demand, while exports decrease demand for output of our economy.

T F 17. The prosperity of the 1920s uniformly helped the entire economy.

T F 18. In 1937, for the first time in the history of U.S. business cycles, the U.S. economy experienced a recession before it had recovered from a prior depression.

T F 19. The first postwar recession, in 1949, was caused primarily by excess inventory, as output temporarily outstripped demand.

T F 20. "Stagflation"-that is, an inflation accompanying a recession-is the best situation for a recession.

T F 21. In the simple economy, equilibrium occurs when saving equals investment.

T F 22. When savings exceed intended investment, inventories build up.

T F 23. The multiplier formula is M = 1/MPC

T F 24. When businesses experience unplanned or involuntary reductions in inventories the results are increased output, employment, and income.

T F 25. When aggregate demand shifts, income does not change.

T F 26. Taxes shift both the consumption function and the savings function downward.

Section B Multiple-choice questions

1. The equilibrium level of income is the level at which

   a. aggregate demand equals aggregate supply.

   b. savings equals intended investment.

   c. ex-ante investment equals both ex-post investment and ex-post savings.

   d. all of the above apply.

2. In a situation in which there is unemployment and aggregate demand exceeds aggregate supply,

   a. economic activity will continue unchanged.

   b. economic activity will expand and unemployment will decrease.

   c. economic activity will contract and unemployment will increase.

   d. All of the above will occur.

3. The marginal propensity to consume indicates

   a. what percentage of their incomes people will consume.

   b. what percentage of any change in income people will save.

   c. what percentage of income at any specific level of income people will consume.

   d. None of the above.

4. In a situation in which planned (ex-ante) investment exceeds planned (ex-ante) savings,

   a. unplanned increases in inventory will take place, and the economy will contract.

   b. unplanned decreases in inventory will take place, and the economy will expand.

   c. nothing will accrue to the economy, because actual (ex-post) investment will equal actual (ex-post) savings.

   d. planned changes in inventory will not take place.

5. Which of the following is correct?

   a. MPC + MPS = 1

   b. MPC + MPS > 1

   c. MPC + MPS < 1

   d. MPC + MPS = 0

6. The multiplier reveals the degree to which

   a. the quantity consumed changes with changes in the level of income.

   b. the quantity of investment changes with changes in consumption.

   c. the level of income changes with changes in either consumption or investment.

   d. All of the above occur.

7. If the marginal propensity to consume is 45 and investment increases by $10 million, the level of income will

   a. increase by $40 million.

   b. increase by $10 million.

   c. decrease by $50 million.

   d. increase by $50 million.

8. Which of the following best states the accelerator principle?

   a. Changes in the rate of change in quantity consumed generate equal changes in investment.

   b. Changes in the rate of change in quantity consumed generate greater changes in investment.

   c. Changes in the rate of change in quantity consumed generate smaller changes in investment.

   d. None of the above accurately states the accelerator principle.

9. Induced investment will increase if

   a. the quantity consumed increases at a steady rate.

   b. the quantity consumed increases at an increasing rate.

   c. the quantity consumed increases at a decreasing rate.

   d. the quantity consumed decreases.

10. The paradox of thrift is that during a recession

    a. an increase in savings is beneficial to both the individual and the economy as a whole.

    b. when savings increase (that is, when the savings function shifts up to the left), the equilibrium level of savings and income increases.

    c. when savings increase (that is, when the savings function shifts up to the left) because of induced investment, the new quantity of savings falls.

    d. an increase in savings can never be beneficial to the economy.

11. When taxes increase, which one of the following things does not happen?

    a. The consumption and savings functions shift down.

    b. Aggregate demand shifts down.

    c. The equilibrium level of income decreases.

    d. Autonomous investment increases.

12. At full employment, an economy's consumption equals 300, its investment equals 60, and its government expenditures equal 40. Now its government expenditures increase by 10. Which of the following happens?

    a. A deflationary gap appears.

    b. An inflationary gap appears.

    c. Equilibrium income decreases.

    d. Equilibrium income is unchanged.

13. At full employment, an economy's consumption equals 300, its investment equals 60, and its government expenditures equal 40. Now its government expenditures decrease by 10. Which of the following happens?

    a. A deflationary gap appears.

    b. The equilibrium level of income decreases by 40.

    c. To maintain full employment, taxes are increased by 13-1/3.

    d. All of the above occur.

14. At the equilibrium level of income, the expenditures of the government increase by 10 and taxes also increase by 10. Which of the following happens?

   a. Income increases by more than 10.

   b. Income increases by 10.

   c. Income increases by less than 10.

   d. Because we do not know what the marginal propensity to consume is, we do not know what happens to income.

15. An economy is at the full-employment equilibrium level of income, and investment decreases by 10. What would be appropriate fiscal policy for the government to adopt?

   a. Decrease taxes and increase government expenditures.

   b. Increase taxes and decrease government expenditures.

   c. Increase taxes and leave government expenditures unchanged.

   d. Do not vary either taxes or government expenditures.

16. An economy is at the full-employment equilibrium level of income, and investment increases by 10. What would be appropriate fiscal policy for the government to adopt?

   a. Increase taxes and increase government expenditures.

   b. Increase taxes and decrease government expenditures.

   c. Decrease taxes and leave government expenditures unchanged.

   d. Do not vary either taxes or government expenditures.

17. Which of the following is most correct about imports and exports?

   a. Imports increase demand for U.S. output, while exports decrease it.

   b. Imports decrease demand for U.S. output, while exports increase it.

   c. Imports and exports both decrease demand for U.S. output.

   d. Imports and exports both increase demand for U.S. output.

18. The prosperity of the 1920s was not based on which one of the following?

   a. Expansion of demand for the products of a number of "new" industries, especially automobiles

   b. Rising prices that increased profits

   c. Sustained expansion of construction until 1927

19. The expansion of 1955-1957 was characterized by

   a. a boom in residential construction and in demand for consumer durables in 1955

   b. a high level of demand for producer durables and nonresidential construction that continued the expansion into 1956 and 1957.

   c. recurrence of inflation as prices increased.

   d. All of the above.

20. Economic conditions from 1980 to 1989 were characterized by

   a. declining aggregate supply and a sharp long-lasting recession.

   b. increasing aggregate supply, a supply shock, and a prolonged depression.

   c. a sharp recession in 1982 -1983 followed by sustained growth.

   d. continuous growth in income and stable prices from 1980 to 1989.

Section C Matching questions

I. Column B lists distances graphed in Figure 9-1. Match the distances in column B to the terms in column A.

Column A	Column B
1. Equilibrium income	(a) LK
2. Intended investment	(b) CE
3. Unplanned accumulation in inventory	(c) OB
4. Unplanned decreases in inventory	(d) OG
5. Savings	(e) DE
6. Consumption	(f) AJ

II. Match the phrases and formulas in column B to the terms in column A.

Column A	Column B
1. Unplanned additions to inventory	(a) Planned investment
2. Unplanned reductions to inventory	(b) SY
3. Ex-ante investment	(c) The more you attempt to save, the less savings result
4. MPC	(d) Income changes more than aggregate demand changes
5. APS	(e) Investment exceeds savings
6. The multiplier formula	(f) 1(1-MPC)
7. Induced investment	(g) Income and employment will decrease
8. Accelerator	(h) ?C?Y
9. Paradox of thrift	(i) To be positive, it requires an increase in the rate of change of consumption
10. Multiplier	(j) Changes in income and consumption

ANSWERS

Part 3

11. 300, 200, 200, 525, 315, 210, 210
12. (a) B; (b) additions to, ED, GF; (e) reductions in, IJ, KL
18. (a) With an MPC of 2/3, the multiplier is 3. If GX increases by 10, then income increases by 10 x 3 (the multiplier effect), or 30. Income equals 330. When the APC is 2/3, then C is two-thirds of income, or 220. APS is 1/3, and S is one-third of income, or 110. Investment is unchanged at 100, and (as stated) GX is 10. S = II + GX, or 110 = 100 + 10.
(b) When taxes increase by 10, C shifts down by 10 X 2/3 (the MPC), or 6 2/3. Aggregate demand (C + II + GX) also shifts down by 6 2/3. The multiplier is 3 (MPC equals 2/3). If aggregate demand decreases by 6 2/3, income decreases by 6 2/3 x 3, or 20. Income equals 310. All this decline was in C, so C is 200. S declines by 10, to 100, because the S function shifts down with taxes by one-third (the MPS) of taxes (10), or 3 1/3. The multiplier 3 caused S to decrease by 3 1/3 x 3, or 10. II is unchanged at 10, GX is 10, and T is 10. Remember that T + S = II + GX, or 10 + 100 = 100 + 10.
21. (a) B; (b) EF, HI; (c) JK, LM; (d) two-thirds

Part 4

Section A 1, F; 2, T; 3, T; 4, T; 5, F; 6, F; 7, T; 8, T; 9, F; 10, F; 11, T; 12, T; 13, F; 14, F; 15, T; 16, F; 17, F; 18, T; 19, T; 20, F; 21, T; 22, T; 23,F; 24, T; 25, F; 26, T
Section B 1, d; 2, b; 3, d; 4, b; 5, a; 6, c; 7, d; 8, b; 9, b; 10, c; 11, d; 12, b; 13, a; 14, b; 15, a; 16, b; 17, b; 18, b; 19, d; 20, c
Section C I. 1, c; 2, f; 3, e; 4, a; 5, b; 6, d
I. 1, g; 2, e; 3, a; 4, h; 5, b; 6, f; 7, j; 8, i; 9, c; 10, d

Chapter 10: Fiscal Policy, Deficit Financing, and the National Debt

Part 1

First, read the section entitled "Summing Up" at the end of Chapter 10. It provides a thorough review of the material in the chapter.

Things to Watch For

The first part of Chapter 10 deals with the fiscal policy implications of the Keynesian model. Fiscal policy consists of variations in government expenditures and taxation. The policy based on that model is called compensatory fiscal policy or functional finance. First, be clear on the distinction between discretionary policy and automatic stabilizers. Second, be able to explain how functional finance would work in theory. The result of this policy is that a budget deficit would tend to result in its use during a recession and a surplus during inflation.

The second part is concerned with budget deficits and the rapidly increasing federal debt. First presented, are relevant statistics on the relationship between federal debt, GDP, interest on debt, total and per capita debt. Understand which of these are most relevant to an understanding of the seriousness of the debt. Next, there is a discussion of the major concerns that economists have about the size and growth of the federal debt. Be sure you can distinguish between relevant and unfounded concerns about the debt. In this discussion the crowding-out effect is most important and should be given close attention.

The question of the burden of thc federal debt is also very important. Be sure to understand the income redistribution effects and the possible opportunity cost effects of the debt. Another area where budget deficits may affect the economy is through its affect on the balance of trade and payments. Be sure to understand both the traditional arguments and alternatives to the traditional view.

Beginning in the 1970s, efforts have been made through legislation and legislative proposals to reduce the growth in the federal debt and to reduce the budgetary deficits. The Gramm-Rudman bill of 1985 is one early example. Be familiar with these efforts. Finally, include the balanced budget amendment controversy, the line item veto controversy, privatization of federal programs, and changes in budgetary procedures.

The chapter ends with Martin Weitzman's proposal for a share economy to reduce the reliance on Keynesian demand management. Understand the workings of the two-wage system. Also, understand the various critiques of the system, both pro and con. The chapter concludes an application on the national debt and where we are headed

Part 2

Define the following terms and concepts.

1. Fiscal policy
2. Discretionary fiscal policy
3. Automatic stabilizers
4. Compensatory fiscal policy
5. Budget deficit
6. Budget surplus
7. Crowding-out effect
8. Ricardo Equivalence Theorem
9. Share economy

Part 3

Answer the following questions.

1. Explain the difference between discretionary policy and automatic stabilizers.
2. Explain how functional finance or compensatory fiscal policy would work according to the Keynesian model.
3. What are the concerns about the growing federal debt discussed in the text? Explain why they should be of concern to you.
4. Explain the "crowding-out" effect. What factors would tend to offset the crowding-out effect?
5. Discuss the fallacies of the concern over the federal government going bankrupt.
6. In what various ways are the burdens of the debt increased? For the present generation? For future generations?
7. What is the traditional view about the relationship between budget deficits and the balance of trade? What alternative view is presented in the text?
8. Name and discuss four pieces of legislation, passed or proposed, aimed at resolving the large federal budget deficit.
9. Discuss the pros and cons of the share economy proposal of MartinWeitzman.
10. What are the potential problems if a rapidly growing national debt?
11. What does discretionary mean?

Part 4 Self-test

Section A True/false questions

T F 1. Automatic stabilizers are structures in our economy that were designed specially to moderate inflations and recessions.

T F 2. Discretionary fiscal policy involves varying the supply of money and the interest rate.

T F 3. During a recession, functional finance would increase government expenditures and or decrease taxes.

T F 4. A more valid measure of the significance of the national debt, thus the absolute total of debt, is the amount of interest as a percentage of per capita income.

T F 5. There is little difference between the economic impact of private debt and the economic impact of federal debt.

T F 6. Since the economic cost of a war is financed by government debt, it is passed on to the generation that has to pay off the debt.

T F 7. When it comes to the problem of redistribution of income, it makes little difference who owns the national debt.

T F 8. The traditional view of the relationship between federal budget deficits and the balance of trade is that deficits increase interest rates that appreciate the dollar, reducing exports and increasing imports.

T F 9. The Gramm-Rudman bill was a last ditch effort of legislation to increase the power of discretionary fiscal policy.

T F 10. The share economy is based on a two-tier wage system with one tier based on the firms profits.

T F 11. Automatic stabilizers are discretionary factors that reduce the likelihood of recession.

T F 12. Crowding out is when government receives funds that would otherwise go to private users.

T F 13. Taxing and spending are both part of fiscal policy.

T F 14. Budget Deficits are defined as the amount by which government expenditures exceed government revenues.

Section B Multiple-choice questions

1. Compensatory fiscal policy, or functional finance, during a recession would
   a. compensate for low levels of aggregate demand by increasing government expenditures and or reduce taxes.
   b. compensate for high levels of aggregate demand by decreasing government expenditures and or increase taxes.
   c. increase the interest rate and reduce the supply of money.
   d. decrease the interest rate and increase the supply of money.

2. Who pays the economic cost of a war financed by federal debt?

   a. the generation that pays taxes to pay off the debt resulting from the war

   b. the generation that fights the war, since resources are siphoned away from consumption and investment to the production of military goods

   c. no one, in that there are no economic costs to wars, since they stimulate the economy

   d. all of the above

3. Under a share economy wages would be

   a. entirely tied to the profitability of employing firms.

   b. entirely separated from the profitability of employing firms.

   c. unrelated to the profitability of employing firms.

   d. partially tied to the profitability of employing firms and partly determined by fixed wage contracts.

4. Which of the following is true about compensatory fiscal policy?

   a. It operates automatically and is one of the automatic stabilizers.

   b. During a recession, it would decrease the deficit in the federal budget.

   c. It would use fiscal policy to counteract inadequate levels of demand to achieve full employment and stabilize prices.

   d. It would compensate for improper changes in the interest rate.

5. Which of the following is not a major concern of economists about the federal debt?

   a. The federal government would go bankrupt if it had to pay off the debt.

   b. The interest on the debt is so high that it reduces the ability to move towards a balanced budget.

   c. The crowding-out effect reduces investment.

   d. Large deficits during low levels of unemployment increases the fear of inflation.

6. Which of the following does not tend to counter the argument about the crowding-out effect?

   a. Increased demand for output due to deficits stimulates demand for investment.

   b. Government debt, due to deficits does not have a direct affect on the interest rate.

   c. Part of government expenditures are for investment purposes, such as roads and schools.

7. It is generally assumed that deficits in the federal budget would
   a. have no affect on the balance of trade.
   b. tend to increase exports and decrease imports.
   c. tend to increase imports and decrease exports.
   d. tend to increase both exports and imports.
8. Which one of the following is not a proposal to impose some fiscal discipline that would restrain debt growth?
   a. The Employment Act of 1946
   b. Gramm-Rudman-Hollings Act of 1985
   c. Balanced budget amendment to the constitution
   d. Line-item veto

Section C Matching questions

I. Match the phrases in column B to the terms in column A.

Column A	*Column B*
1. Fiscal policy	(a) Expenditures exceed taxes
2. Discretionary fiscal policy	(b) A two-tier wage system
3. Automatic stabilizers	(c) Varying taxes and government expenditures
4. Compensatory fiscal policy	(d) The same results occur from debt increase or tax increase
5. Budget deficit	(e) Work without policy action
6. Budget surplus	(f) Interest increases and investment decreases
7. Crowding-out effect	(g) Need policy action
8. Ricardo Equivalence Theorem	(h) Compensates for improper levels of aggregate demand
9. Share economy	(i) Taxes exceed expenditures

ANSWERS

Part 4

Section A 1, F; 2, F; 3, T; 4, T; 5, F; 6, F; 7, F; 8, T; 9, F; 10, T; 11, F; 12, T; 13, T; 14, T
Section B 1, a; 2, b; 3, d; 4, c; 5, a; 6, b; 7, c; 8, a
Section C 1, a; 2, g; 3, e; 4, h; 5, a; 6, i; 7, f; 8, d; 9, b

Chapter 11: Money in the Modern Economy

Part 1

First, read the section entitled "Summing Up" at the end of Chapter 11 for a thorough review of the chapter.

Things to Watch For

Chapter 11 is an introduction to money and its importance to an economy. (Chapter 12 will discuss the banking system and Chapter 13 monetary policy.)

This chapter first tackles the question of what money is. It analyzes a barter economy (in which there is no money) and then a money economy. It states the four functions of money and gives the characteristics of a good money along with emphasizing the fact that money is debt. Next the chapter discusses the supply of money and analyzes the three kinds of money that make up this supply: demand deposits, currency in circulation, and coins in circulation. It contains a number of definitions (Part 2 gives a complete list of new concepts) so that you can distinguish between money and near money (for example, the money in savings accounts and government debt) and also credit cards. Finally, the chapter distinguishes between, M1, M2, and M3 money as alternative measures of the money supply.

Keep in mind that money is money because people accept it as money. Money becomes money because people accept it in exchange for goods and services. It is a social convention to reduce the real costs of exchanging goods and services.

To give you a glimpse of the banking system and its role in the supply of money, Chapter 11 offers a brief look at goldsmith banking in seventeenth-century England. The goldsmith system had most of the elements of the modern commercial bank: demand deposits, checks, fractional reserves, loans, and the creation of demand deposits. The next chapter will lead you again (but this time very slowly) through the workings of the commercial bank system as it affects lending and the supply of money.

The last question Chapter 11 deals with is: How do changes in the supply of money affect output and prices? The chapter gives two approaches: (1) the equation of exchange (MV = PQ), the velocity of exchange and (2) the demand for money. Both lead to the same conclusions. If you increase the supply of money, the economy expands. If there is full employment, this expansion is shown only in increases in prices. If you decrease the supply of money, the level of demand declines. It is important that you understand this last section, because the chapter on monetary policy will bring you back to the equation of exchange and the problem of the effect on the economy of changes in the supply of money.

Part 2

Define the following terms and concepts.

1. Barter system of exchange
2. Double coincidence of demand
3. Money
4. Medium of exchange
5. Standard of value or unit of account
6. Store of value
7. Means of deferred payment
8. Checking accounts or demand deposits
9. Depository institution
10. Fiat money, legal tender
11. Near money
12. Fractional reserve principle
13. Equation of exchange
14. M1 money
15. M2 money
16. M3 money
17. Legal tender
18. Gresham's Law

Part 3

Answer the following questions and problems.

1. Contrast a barter system of exchange with a money system. Which is more efficient? Why?
2. What makes something money? What are the functions of money in an economy?
3. Pick something that you think would serve as a good form of money and list characteristics that would favor its use as a money. Also list any characteristics that might make it unfavorable.
4. What are the advantages and disadvantages of the three forms of M1 money in the U.S. economy?
5. Define M1, M2, and M3 money. What do you think are the advantages and/or disadvantages of each as measures of the money supply?
6. The text maintains that money in our economy is debt. What does the text mean by that?
7. Why aren't credit cards considered money? Why are traveler's checks considered money?
8. The text describes seventeenth-century goldsmith banking as the origin of today's commercial banking system. How did goldsmiths in those days affect the supply of money?
9. State the equation of exchange and explain what each letter symbol in the equation stands for.
10. Use the equation of exchange to show what would happen during a recession if the supply of money increased. What if there were full employment?
11. What is a double coincidence of wants?

12, If fiat money is not backed by gold, why does fiat money have value?

Part 4 Self-test

Section A True/false questions

T F 1. Money is anything that people accept as an asset.

T F 2. Savings deposits are near money but are not regarded as M1 money.

T F 3. Checking-account deposits are not money, because not everyone will accept a check.

T F 4. Money is not wealth, since it is almost costless to produce.

T F 5. The purchase of goods with a credit card is an illustration of money serving as a medium of exchange.

T F 6. Because prices can vary, money is sometimes not a good store of value.

T F 7. During an inflationary period, increases in the velocity of exchange tend to hold down increases in prices.

T F 8. According to the quantity theory of money, a ten-dollar bill that circulates five times has the same effect as fifty dollars circulating once.

T F 9. If we assume that Q increases and MV is constant, we can safely conclude that prices will decrease.

T F 10. The major weakness of the barter system of exchange is that it requires double coincidence of demand.

T F 11. M2 money is smaller in quantity then M1 because it does not include M1 money.

T F 12. M3 money is the narrowest of the alternative measures of the money supply.

T F 13. Batter is a system in which goods and services are exchanged for other goods and services.

T F 14. Demand deposits are also known as savings accounts.

T F 15. Gresham's Law states that gold and silver will be taken out of circulation and fiat money will circulate.

T F 16. Money is only acceptable in the form of paper or metal.

T F 17. Credit cards are not money.

T F 18. Travelers checks are considered part of the money supply.

Section B Multiple-choice questions

1. The chief difference between near money and money is
   a. near money is fiat money, whereas money is not.
   b. near money consists of all deposits in commercial and savings banks, whereas money does not include deposits.
   c. near money is not directly spendable, whereas money is directly spendable.
   d. None of the above.
2. If people hold money because they need to spend money before their next paycheck, this is an example of
   a. the transactions demand of money.
   b. the quantity theory of money.
   c. the velocity of exchange.
   d. None of the above.
3. Which one of the following generalizations can be derived from the equation of exchange?
   a. In deflationary periods, creditors gain at the expense of debtors.
   b. At full employment, any increase in the money supply tends to increase prices.
   c. In inflationary periods, producers increase prices to counter rising costs.
   d. All of the above can be derived from the equation.
4. Fiat money is
   a. money backed by gold.
   b. something more valuable as a monetary instrument than as a commodity.
   c. anything that the government says is money.
   d. All of the above.
5. The largest single component (in terms of total value) in the M1 money supply is
   a. coins.
   b. currency.
   c. demand deposits.
   d. savings deposits.

6. When we are talking about money in an economy, it is incorrect to say that

   a. money is anything that is accepted as a medium of exchange, as a standard of value, as a store of value, or as a means of deferred payments, even if there is no gold to back it up.

   b. the stock of money does not include government bonds.

   c. demand deposits are by far the largest part of the supply of money in the United States.

   d. an economy's supply of money is a good measure of its wealth.

7. People hold money

   a. to have money for purchases in between receipts of income.

   b. to have money in case of unforeseen emergencies.

   c. to have money to take advantage of economic opportunities as they arise.

   d. for all of the above purposes.

8. If income and GDP rise and the supply of money remains constant, economic theory would predict

   a. a rise in the velocity of exchange if prices are constant.

   b. a fall in prices if the velocity of exchange remains constant.

   c. a rise in the demand for cash balances and reductions in demand for consumer goods.

   d. All of the above.

9. Which of the following combinations does not go together?

   a. Medium of exchange and means of deferred payments

   b. Barter system of exchange and double coincidence of demand

   c. Demand deposits and near money

   d. All are valid combinations.

10. In which of the following situations would money function as a store of value?

    a. The husband checks the prices at the local supermarket.

    b. The wife checks the balance in the family savings account.

    c. You take out a loan at the local bank.

    d. In all of the above, money functions as a store of value.

11. M2 money is:

    a. All demand deposits plus all currency and coin in circulation.

    b. M1 money plus near money.

    c. M3 money plus near money.

    d. M3 money plus all currency and coin in circulation.

12. Which of the following is not included in the M3 money supply?

    a. Currency and coins.

    b. Check deposits and time deposits.

    c. Large value certificates of deposit.

    d. All of the above are included in M3 money.

Section C Matching questions

Match the phrases in column B to the terms in column A.

Column A

1. Fiat money
2. Near money
3. Store of value
4. Equation of exchange
5. Demand deposits
6. Velocity of exchange
7. Standard of value
8. Depository institution
9. Double coincidence of demand
10. Precautionary purposes
11. M3 money

Column B

(a) The rate of turnover of the money supply
(b) Any bank that holds demand deposits
(c) The function of money as a unit of account
(d) He wants what I have and I want what he has
(e) Money deposited in checking accounts
(f) Holds money in case of emergencies
(g) Expresses the quantity theory of money
(h) The function of money as a means of saving
(i) More valuable as a monetary instrument than as a commodity
(j) Savings accounts
(k) Large value Certificates of Deposit

ANSWERS

Part 4

Section A 1, F; 2, T; 3, F; 4, F; 5, F; 6, T; 7, F; 8, T; 9, T; 10, T; 11, F; 12, F; 13, T; 14, F; 15, T; 16, F; 17, T; 18, T
Section B 1, c; 2, a; 3, b; 4, b; 5, c; 6, d; 7, d; 8, d; 9, c; 10, b; 11, b; 12, d
Section C 1, i; 2, j; 3, h; 4, g; 5, e; 6, a; 7, c; 8, b; 9, d; 10, f; 11, k

Chapter 12: Commercial Banking and the Creation of M1 Money

Part 1

First, read the section entitled "Summing Up" at the end of Chapter 12. It offers a thorough excellent review of the chapter.

Things to Watch For

Chapter 12 leads you step by step through the workings of the depository banking system, especially as they relate to the process of increasing and decreasing the supply of M1 money.

The chapter begins with the simplest of models, which assumes the following: (1) There is only one bank. (2) There is no government control. (3) There is no currency and no coin. (4) There is no international trade. In this simple model, you learn that the supply of money (demand deposits) is increased when the commercial bank extends a loan and creates a demand deposit in payment. The supply of money is decreased when the loan is paid off and there is a necessary reduction of demand deposits.

Then the text introduces currency and coin into the model. You learn that currency and coin perform two main functions: (1) they provide a more efficient form of money for small-value purchases, and (2) they provide a check on the ability of the commercial bank to expand loans and the supply of money.

Next government regulation is introduced. In its regulations, the government has an efficient method of controlling the bank's lending activities and the effects of these activities on the supply of money. The regulations require the bank to keep reserves equal to a certain percentage of its demand deposits. (This is called the required reserve ratio.) In order to make loans and thus increase demand deposits (money), the bank must have more than the required amount of reserves (excess reserves). If the required reserve ratio is less than 100 percent (if a fractional reserve requirement is in effect), the commercial bank can lend more than a dollar for each dollar of total reserves, thus increasing demand deposits. If the bank is a monopoly bank, it can lend a multiple of its total reserves, because it is the banking system and checks cannot flow to other banks.

We all know, though, that other banks do exist. When we drop the assumption of there being only one commercial bank in the banking system, our model approaches that of the U.S. banking system, with its more than 15,000 commercial banks. The Federal Reserve must now function as a national clearinghouse for checks. When someone deposits a check in a bank other than the one the account is in, the check goes to the clearinghouse (the Federal Reserve) and demand deposits and reserves (the commercial bank's deposits at the Federal Reserve) are transferred. Because of this, the individual commercial bank within this multibank system does not lend a multiple of its excess reserves. Instead it lends only up to the amount of its excess reserves, thereby increasing demand deposits by that amount. As these excess reserves work through the commercial banking system, the whole system creates loans and demand deposits that are a multiple (reciprocal of the required reserve ratio) of its excess reserves. This multiple is known as the deposit multiplier. The multiplier effect is reduced, however, by the effects of leakages and the desire of lending institutions to maintain excess reserves. Those excess reserves can be loaned to other banks at an interest rate called federal funds market rate.

Bear in mind that although the Federal Reserve controls this process, it is commercial banks (and other financial institutions) that are the primary instrument through which the supply of money is changed. Commercial banks vary the money supply by making loans and having loans paid off, transactions that increase and decrease demand deposits.

The application, "First Steps in Banking," is a reprint from the British humor magazine Punch. In a lighthearted vein the application discusses many of the basic characteristics of commercial banking, and the process of increasing and decreasing the supply of money.

Part 2

Define the following terms and concepts.

1. Required reserve ratio
2. Excess reserves
3. Fractional reserve requirement
4. Deposit multiplier
5. Leakages in money creation
6. Federal funds market

Part 3

Answer the following questions and problems.

1. Using the simple model of Chapter 12 (assuming that there is only one bank, no government regulation, no currency and coins, and no international trade), explain how the supply of money is increased and how it is decreased.
2. Now add currency and coin to the simple model (but keep the other assumptions). What two functions do currency and coin perform? Explain how they are carried out.
3. Now add government regulation to the simple model (but keep the assumption that there is only one bank). Show how the rule that a bank must keep reserves equal to a percentage of demand deposits restricts the monopoly bank's ability to expand loans and demand deposits (the supply of money).
4. In a banking system with only one bank (a monopoly bank), why is that bank able to expand the supply of money by an amount that is a multiple of its excess reserves?
5. Explain what occurs in a multibank system in which the Federal Reserve acts as the collection process, when checks written on accounts in one bank are deposited in another bank. Make up a numerical example.
6. Why would an individual bank in a multibank system use the conservative rule of making loans and creating demand deposits only up to the amount of its excess reserves? Make up a numerical example to illustrate your answer.
7. What is the deposit multiplier? How can a multibank system increase the supply of money by a multiple of its original excess reserves? Again use a numerical example to illustrate.

8. Although technically a multibank system can expand the supply of money by a multiple of the original excess reserves, it is rare that the system does so. There are leakages in this process of expansion of the money supply. Explain what these leakages are, and indicate how they reduce the ability of the banking system to expand the supply of money.

9. Suppose that the changes detailed below take place in the following accounts: demand deposits, loans, total reserves, excess reserves, and required reserves. Show what happens to these accounts. Use Table 12-1 and Table 12-2 to record your answers. Work the transactions separately; they are not cumulative. Indicate whether the accounts affected increase or decrease, and by how much. Do this for Bank A in Table 12-1 and also for the whole banking system in Table 12-2, which includes Bank A. The required reserve ratio is 20 percent. (The answers are given after Part 4.)

    a. Bank A is established with a capital of $100,000. For its stock, the bank receives $25,000 in currency and $75,000 in checks drawn on other banks. All checks are cleared. (Remember that total reserves consist of all deposits at the Federal Reserve, plus all currency and coin in the vaults of the bank.)

    b. Mr. Lopez deposits a check for $1,000 to his account at Bank A. That check is drawn on a deposit at another bank. All checks are cleared.

    c. Ms. Clark borrows $10,000 from Bank A and deposits the proceeds in Bank A.

    d. Ms. Jones withdraws $500 in currency from her account in Bank A.

    e. Mr. Lopez writes a check for $500 on his account in Bank A and deposits it in another account in Bank A.

    f. Ms. Clark pays off her $10,000 loan at Bank A with a check from another bank. All checks are cleared.

Table 12-1

Bank A

	Required Reserves (RR)	Excess Reserves (ER)	Total Reserves (TR)	Loans	Demand Deposits
a.					
b.					
c.					
d.					
e.					
f.					

Table 12-2
The Whole Banking System

	Required Reserves (RR)	Excess Reserves (ER)	Total Reserves (TR)	Loans	Demand Deposits
a.					
b.					
c.					
d.					
e.					
f.					

10. Table 12-3 lists three balance sheets for Bank A, a commercial bank. The required reserve ratio is 20 percent for balance sheet A, 25 percent for balance sheet B, and 50 percent for balance sheet C. Use the table to do the following problems. (The answers are given after Part 4.)
    a. For Bank A, compute the required reserves for each of the three balance sheets.
    b. Compute the excess reserves for each of the three balance sheets.
    c. How much could Bank A safely extend in new loans if it were one bank in a multibank system?
    d. How much could Bank A safely extend in new loans if it were the only bank in the commercial banking system?

Table 12-3
Balance Sheets for Bank A (thousands of dollars)

	A	B	C
	RRR 20%	**RRR 25%**	**RRR 50%**
Assets			
Reserves	80	100	150
Loans	200	150	200
Government bonds	70	60	50
Liabilities			
Demand deposits	300	240	300
Net Worth			
Capital	50	50	100
a. Required reserves			
b. Excess reserves			
c. New loans, multibank system			
d. New loans, monopoly bank system			

11. In the application, identify the questions and answers that apply to loans, demand deposits, and reserves.
12. What is the reserve requirement?

Part 4 Self-test

Section A True/false questions

T F 1. When a commercial bank extends a loan and increases demand deposits in payment, it increases the supply of money. Once created, this money cannot be decreased.

T F 2. The two functions of currency and coin are (a) to provide an effi-cient form of money for small-value purchases, and (b) to provide a check on the ability of a bank to extend loans and expand the supply of money.

T F 3. When borrowers from a commercial bank accept currency rather than a demand deposit, the potential for money expansion increases in the whole banking system.

T F 4. A commercial bank in a fractional reserve system is required to hold reserves equal to its demand-deposit liabilities, in case people withdraw currency.

T F 5. A single bank in a multibank system can make loans and create demand deposits only up to an amount equal to its excess reserves. However, the commercial banking system as a whole can make loans and expand demand deposits by a multiple of its excess reserves. If there are no leakages, the size of the multiple depends on the size of the required reserve ratio.

T F 6. When a check written on an account in Bank A is deposited in Bank B and cleared through the Federal Reserve, demand deposits flow from Bank A to Bank B, while reserves flow from Bank B to Bank A.

T F 7. The banking system may not expand loans and demand deposits by their greatest multiple because banks may fear larger-than-usual withdrawals.

T F 8. Total reserves equal all deposits made at the Federal Reserve by member banks, plus currency and coin in the vaults of banks; total reserves also equal excess reserves plus required reserves.

T F 9. Although the Federal Reserve controls the process, privately owned, profit-motivated corporations called commercial banks are the primary instruments through which the supply of money is increased or decreased.

T F 10. The most important reason for the legal reserve requirement is to prevent harm to depositors and stockholders if the bank should fail.

T F 11. Banks can create M1 money by making loans from their required reserves.

T F 12. Leakages limit the creation of money by the banking system.

T F 13. The deposits multiplier is 1/excess reserves.

T F 14. The Required Reserve Ratio is the minimum ratio of reserves to deposits that depository institutions are required to maintain.

T F 15. Banks that have excess reserves lend them to other banks that need reserves.

Section B Multiple-choice questions

1. Commercial banks increase the supply of money
   a. whenever they accept currency and coins in circulation in exchange for a demand deposit.
   b. whenever they extend loans and create demand deposits.
   c. every time they pay out currency or coin from the vaults when a depositor presents a check for payment.
   d. under all of the above circumstances.
2. The reserve requirements that the law imposes on commercial banks
   a. are primarily for protection of depositors in case customers make excessive withdrawals.
   b. are primarily to protect the stockholders against business losses by management.
   c. are primarily to set limits on the supply of money.
   d. serve all of the above purposes.
3. Suppose that Bank A, the only commercial bank in the economy, has no excess reserves and that the required reserve ratio is 20 percent. Sylvia Bloggs empties many years' spare change out of her cookie jar and deposits $500 in currency into the bank. Now Bank A can expand the supply of money by
   a. $2,000.
   b. $400.
   c. $500.
   d. $2,500.
4. Now suppose that Bank A of question 3 is only one bank of many in a multibank system. The right answer would now be
   a. $2,000.
   b. $400.
   c. $500.
   d. $2,500.

5. If the $500 deposit in question 3 had been a check drawn on another account in Bank A of a multibank system, the answer would now be

   a. $0.

   b. $2,000.

   c. $400.

   d. $500.

6. Which one of the following transactions leads to a change in the supply of money?

   a. Harry Smith deposits his paycheck in his checking account at his bank.

   b. Bertha Jones obtains a loan from her commercial bank and receives a demand deposit in return.

   c. Sally Robinson pays cash for a tool set at the local hardware store. The manager of the store deposits the cash in the store's checking account.

   d. All of the above affect the money supply.

7. Suppose that the required reserve ratio is 20 percent and that a given bank's total reserves are $1,000, with $200 in excess reserves. The total amount of demand deposits is

   a. $4,000.

   b. $5,000.

   c. $800.

   d. None of the above amounts.

8. Suppose that the amount of excess reserves in a commercial bank increases. One can conclude

   a. that the bank is making more profits from the loans made.

   b. that the amount of loans-and thus of demand deposits-will increase.

   c. that the potential for expanding loans and the money supply has increased.

   d. None of the above.

9. A commercial banking system does not expand loans and the supply of money by its full multiple effect because of which of the following leakages?

   a. Some borrowers may choose to get currency rather than a demand deposit in payment for a loan.

   b. Some banks may hold excess reserves because they fear that deposits and reserves may be lost by a greater-than-normal flow of checks to other banks.

   c. Economic conditions may be so uncertain that commercial banks may not lend out as much as they could.

   d. All of the above act as leakages.

10. The ability of an individual commercial bank in a multibank system to lend and create demand deposits is limited by

   a. possible withdrawals of currency by its depositors.

   b. possible flow of checks to other banks, which would transfer demand deposits and reserves to those banks.

   c. the need to maintain the amount of reserves required by law.

   d. All of the above.

11. The federal funds market is a financial market in which

   a. the federal government sells its new bond issues.

   b. depository institutions borrow from the fed.

   c. banks lend each other their excess reserves for long periods of time.

   d. banks lend each other their excess reserves for short periods of time.

Section C Matching questions

Match the phrases in column B to the terms in column A.

Column A	Column B
1. Federal Reserve	(a) Can extend loans and create demand deposits only equal to its excess reserves
2. Excess reserves	(b) Percentage of demand deposits required to be kept in reserve
3. Monopoly bank	(c) Creates demand deposits
4. Individual bank	(d) Functions as a national clearinghouse for checks
5. Currency and coin	(e) A better form of money for small-value purchases
6. Extending loans	(f) Excess reserves plus required reserves
7. Required reserve ratio	(g) Amount of reserves above that required
8. Total reserves	(h) Can expand credit and supply of money by a multiple of excess reserves
9. Deposit multiplier	(i) Short-term loans from one bank to another
10. Federal funds market	(j) Another potential growth in money supply from excess reserves

ANSWERS

Part 3

9. (a) The first transaction depicts the creation of a bank through the sale of capital stock. For Bank A, no deposits or withdrawals are made, and there are no loans. Bank A's total reserves increase by $100,000: $25,000 because of the increase in currency in Bank A's vault, and $75,000 because of the checks drawn on other banks, which are sent to the Fed for collection. This increases Bank A's deposits at the Fed. Required reserves are not affected, because demand deposits are not affected. Excess reserves, therefore, increase by the increase in total reserves ($100,000).

For the banking system as a whole, demand deposits decrease by $75,000, because $75,000 worth of checks are written to buy Bank A's stock and are not transferred to a demand deposit in Bank A. Loans are not affected. Total reserves increase by only $25,000, the currency taken out of circulation and now in the vault of Bank A. The $75,000 in checks simply transfers deposits at the Fed from the banks they were written on to Bank A, canceling the effect on the whole banking system. Required reserves decrease by 20 percent of the decrease in demand deposits, or $15,000. Excess reserves increase by $40,000 (TR = ER + RR).

(b) In transaction b, Bank A's demand deposits increase by $1,000 as the deposit is made. Loans are not affected. Bank A's total reserves increase by $1,000 when the check is sent to the Fed for collection, and Bank A's deposits at the Fed are increased. Its required reserves increase by $200, or 20 percent of the increase in demand deposits. Excess reserves increase by $800: TR (1,000) = ER (800) + RR(200).

There is no change for the banking system as a whole, since the increase in Bank A is offset by the decline in the bank the check was written on.

(c) In transaction c, Bank A's demand deposits increase by $10,000, because the proceeds of the loan are deposited in Bank A. Loans increase by $10,000 because a loan is made. Total reserves are unaffected, because neither cash in the vault nor deposits at the Fed are affected. Required reserves increase by $2,000 (20 percent of the increase in demand deposits); this must come from excess reserves, which decrease by $2,000.

Changes in the banking system as a whole as a result of transaction c are the same as the changes for Bank A. This transaction involves only Bank A, and thus there are no offsetting entries for other banks.

(d) In transaction d for Bank A, demand deposits decrease by $500 as the currency is withdrawn. Loans are not affected, since no loan is made or paid off. Total reserves decrease by $500, because now there is $500 less in Bank A's cash in vault. Required reserves decrease by $100 (20 percent of the decrease in demand deposits), and excess reserves decrease by $400: TR(-500) = RR (-100) + ER (-400).

For the banking system as a whole, transaction d brings the same changes as it does for Bank A, since only Bank A was involved in this transaction and there were no offsetting entries by another bank.

(e) Transaction e involves no change in any of the accounts for Bank A or for the banking system as a whole. It is merely a transfer of deposits from one account to another in the same bank.

(f) In transaction f for Bank A, no deposit or withdrawal is made, so demand deposits are unaffected. A loan is paid off, so Bank A's loans decrease by $10,000. Its total reserves increase by $10,000, since Bank A's deposits at the Fed increase due to the clearance of the check. Its required reserves are unaffected, since demand deposits are unaffected. Its excess reserves increase by $10,000, which is the same as its increase in total reserves.

For the banking system as a whole, demand deposits in the bank the check was drawn on decrease by $10,000. That check is used to pay off a loan and thus is not deposited in Bank A. Loans decrease by $10,000, the amount of the loan paid off at Bank A. Total reserves are unaffected, since, as the check is cleared, reserves (deposits at the Fed) are merely transferred from the account of the bank the check was written on to the account of Bank A. Required reserves decrease by $2,000 (20 percent of the decrease in demand deposits). Excess reserves increase by $2,000: TR (0) = RR (-2,000) + ER (2,000).

10. (a) Required reserves: A, 60; B, 60; C, 150.

(b) Excess reserves: A, 20; B, 40; C, 0.

(c) New loans, multibank system: A, 20; B, 40; C, 0.

(d) New loans, monopoly system: A, 100; B, 160; C, 0.

Part 4

Section A 1, F; 2, T; 3, F; 4, F; 5, T; 6, F; 7, T; 8, T; 9, T; 10, F; 11, F; 12, T; 13, F; 14, T; 15, T

Section B 1, b; 2, c; 3, a; 4, b; 5, a; 6, b; 7, a; 8, c; 9, d; 10, d; 11, d

Section C 1, d; 2, g; 3, h; 4, a; 5, e; 6, c; 7, b; 8, f; 9, j; 10, i

Chapter 13: Monetary Policy-Central Banking in Financial Markets that are Deregulated and International

Part 1

First, read the sections entitled "Summing Up" at the end of Chapter 13. It offers a thorough review of the material presented in the chapter.

Things to Watch For

Chapter 13 discusses the workings of the Federal Reserve System and examines the government's policy toward money.

The first part of the chapter sketches the structure of the Federal Reserve System. Note: The Fed is a combination of public and private structures. It is not simply an instrument to be used by those in power in the government.

The chapter analyzes the general powers of the Federal Reserve System. The Fed has the power to increase or decrease its member commercial banks' excess reserves. (Remember that excess reserves are the main ingredient necessary for loans and for the creation of demand deposits.) You should understand the workings of the Fed's general powers, because it is these powers (control over excess reserves and thus over the supply of money) that are the foundation of the government's monetary policy. A major component of these powers is the discount rate, or the rate charged, by the Fed in making loans to member banks. A second component is the required reserve rate, which determines the amount of reserves lending institutions must maintain.

In addition to its general powers, the Fed has specific powers-powers, for example, over specific areas of lending, including the power to set the margin requirement-the percentage of a cash down payment that a person must pay in order to buy stock. This means that the Fed can control to some extent speculation on the stock market. There was also Regulation Q, which gave the Fed control over interest rates on demand and savings deposits in commercial banks, and thus some control over the volume of funds available for mortgages. Remember the Deregulation Act of 1980; it repealed Regulation Q and, amongst other things, reduced regulation of banks. The now-lapsed Regulations X and W gave the Fed influence over consumption and real estate lending.

The discussion of the workings of the Federal Reserve closes with a section on the functions of the Fed. We have talked about most of these functions before: the fact that the Fed acts as a clearinghouse for checks, the fact that it regulates the supply of money, and so on. Here we introduce the facts that the Fed issues currency and that it functions as fiscal agent and bank for the U.S. Treasury, as well as for some foreign central banks and treasuries.

The next part deals with the Deregulatory Act of 1980. First, it lists the main features of the act and then discusses some of the consequences. Especially important, is the material dealing with the savings and loan crises of the 1980s and the problems of moral hazard exposed by these crises.

The sections of Chapter 13 dealing with monetary policy are very important. Like fiscal policy, monetary policy is a main tool by which the federal government can fight unemployment and inflation. Thus it is vital that you understand this area of economics thoroughly. In brief: To fight unemployment during a recession, the monetary policy of the government is to increase the supply of money and lower the interest rate. To achieve this, the Fed uses its general powers to increase the amount of excess reserves in commercial banks. To counter inflation, the government needs to decrease the supply of money and raise the interest rate. To achieve this, the Fed uses its general powers to decrease banks' excess reserves.

The effects of monetary policy are felt in credit markets. Chapter 13 illustrates how these markets react both in cases of unemployment and inflation to changes by the fed in the amount of excess reserves held by depository institutions. It is important that you understand the short-run as well as the long-run effects in both economic situations. Doing so will give you an appreciation of the complexity of implementing monetary policy in ways consistent with the government's macroeconomic objectives.

Monetary policy, in spite of its advantages, does have its weaknesses and limitations. One perplexing is the weakness it shares with fiscal policy: How should it function when significant inflation and unemployment exist at the same time? In addition, as Chapter 13 illustrates, changing inflationary expectations can affect monetary policy, even neutralize it, and, in some instances, even create perverse results for that policy. In addition, monetary policy can not assure adequate demand for credit.

The application considers the controversy between the monetarists and the Keynesians, especially as to the relative importance of monetary and fiscal policy. The monetarists maintain that money is the primary influence on a nation's output, income, and prices. These believers in monetarism feel that the supply of money should increase at a fixed and appropriate rate. They further maintain that fine tuning the economy through continual adjustments of fiscal and monetary policy is ineffective and maybe even dangerous.

Defenders of Keynesian policy say that there are a number of flaws in the monetarists' theory. (1) Monetarists' assumption that the velocity of exchange is constant is not valid. (2) Monetarists do not make it clear what they mean by "money supply," nor what time lag they consider to exist between a variation in the supply of money and the effect of that variation on the economy. (3) If inflationary forces other than demand-pull forces exist, monetarism is too indirect to work.

Part 2

Define the following terms and concepts.

1. National banks
2. State banks
3. General powers
4. Central bank
5. The discount rate
6. Specific powers
7. Margin requirements
8. Resolution Trust Corporation
9. Regulations X and W
10. Regulation Q
11. Required reserve ratio
12. Monetary policy
13. Monetarism
14. Bank holding companies
15. Moral hazard problem
16. Monetary policy

Part 3

Answer the following questions and problems.

1. The structure of the Federal Reserve System is a combination of public and private elements. Identify and briefly describe both the public and the private elements.
2. Explain how the Fed would use open-market operations to

   a. increase the amount of excess reserves of its member banks.

   b. decrease the amount of excess reserves of its member banks.
3. How does the Fed use the discount rate to affect the excess reserves of its member banks? Among the Fed's devices for controlling the money supply, why is the discount rate not as important as open-market operations?
4. How does a lowering of the required reserve ratio affect banks' excess reserves? What about an increase in the required reserve ratio? Make up a numerical example of how a lowering of the required reserve ratio affects banks' excess reserves.
5. Why does the Fed, in controlling excess reserves, rarely use its power to vary the required reserve ratio?
6. In four areas of lending, the Federal Reserve has (or has had) specific regulatory powers, called the specific powers of the Federal Reserve. List these specific powers and explain how they have functioned.
7. Why do you think there were so many failures of savings and loan banks in the 1980s?
8. What are the major provisions of the Deregulation Act of 1980?
9. The text lists seven functions of the Federal Reserve. Name and explain them.
10. During a recession, what monetary policy would you recommend with respect to the supply of money? with respect to the interest rate? Why? During an inflation, what monetary policy would you recommend with respect to the supply of money? with respect to the interest rate? Why? What should the Fed do to implement these recommendations?
11. Trace the monetary transmission mechanism for a recession. For an inflation.
12. The text lists weaknesses of monetary policy. Name and explain them.
13. Briefly describe what is meant by the monetarist school of economic policy.
14. Assuming that the required reserve ratio equals 20 percent, consider the following transactions. What changes occur in the accounts of commercial bank Alpha (given in Table 13-1) with respect to demand deposits, government securities, total reserves, excess reserves, and required reserves? Assume that each transaction is separate and not cumulative, and that all checks are cleared. (The answers are given after Part 4.)

Which of these transactions involve changes in the supply of money? By how much does the money supply change?

a. Alpha Bank buys $10,000 in government securities from the U.S. Treasury and deposits the proceeds in Alpha Bank.

b. Alpha Bank buys $10,000 in government securities from the Federal Reserve.

c. Mary Bloggs sells $10,000 in government securities to the Fed and deposits the proceeds in Alpha Bank.

d. Alpha Bank discounts $20,000 of prime commercial paper at the Fed.

Table 13-1
Accounts of Commercial Bank Alpha

	Required Reserves	**Excess Reserves**	**Total Reserves**	**Government Securities**	**Demand Deposits**
a.					
b.					
c.					
d.					

15. What role do inflationary expectations play in monetary policy? How may they interfere in monetary policy?

16. Assume that you belong to the monetarist school of thought. Defend your recommendation that the constant growth of the supply of money at an appropriate fixed rate should be a main component of government stabilization policy.

17. Why do the monetarists oppose fine tuning of the economy?

18. Discuss the various arguments the Keynesians present in opposition to Milton Friedman's monetarist position.

19. How can a bank create money?

20. Where do the bonds come from that the federal Reserve buys and sells to adjust interest rates?

Part 4 Self-test

Section A True/false questions

T F 1. The government owns and controls the Federal Reserve.

T F 2. The board of governors of the Federal Reserve is not under the direct control of the executive branch of the government.

T F 3. The Fed uses its general powers to control the amount of the basic ingredient needed for the extension of credit and the creation of demand deposits: excess reserves.

T F 4. An important general power of the Federal Reserve is its power to vary the discount rate, because by using this power the Fed can either increase or decrease total reserves.

T F 5. During a recession the Federal Reserve should buy securities in the open market, increase the discount rate, and increase the required reserve ratio.

T F 6. As one method of controlling the supply of money, the Fed varies the amount of currency in circulation.

T F 7. M2 money consists of all demand deposits, currency, and coin in circulation plus near money.

T F 8. A basic function of the Fed is to act as a national clearinghouse for checks, shifting reserves from one bank to another as checks flow between banks.

T F 9. Monetary policy was not effective in helping to cure the depression of the 1930s. The reason was that banks accumulated excess reserves without the help of the Fed, because the depression caused banks to lend less and borrowers to borrow less.

T F 10. During an inflation, when there is a tight money policy, certain groups suffer more from that policy than others. They include small and new firms, the construction industry, and borrowers for consumer purchases.

T F 11. The monetary policy transmission mechanism for a recession would be easing of monetary policy increase in supply of credit decrease in interest rates increase in investment increase in demand increase in real incomes and prices.

T F 12. Although the monetarists call for a fixed and appropriate rate of growth of the supply of money, they agree that there should also be fine tuning in other areas of fiscal and monetary policy.

T F 13. The increasing ease with which capital moves internationally has made monetary policy easier to implement.

T F 14. The increased holdings of federal debt by non-residences increased the case of implementing monetary policy.

T F 15. During the 1980s the Savings and Loan Association prospered because of the Deregulatory Act of 1980.

T F 16. Regulation X deals with loans on consumer goods.

T F 17. Regulation Q was used to set the minimum interest rate banks could pay on savings accounts.

T F 18. The fed can control the supply of money.

T F 19. All national banks are required to be members of the Federal Reserve System.

T F 20. To overcome unemployment, one should decrease the supply of credit and increase interest rates.

Section B Multiple-choice questions

1. Which of the following statements about the Federal Reserve System is true?

   a. All commercial banks are members of the Federal Reserve System, since the law says that they must join it.

   b. All commercial banks have an option to join the Federal Reserve System if they wish.

   c. National banks must be members of the Federal Reserve System, but state banks may join or not, as they wish.

   d. Any commercial or savings bank may join the Federal Reserve System.

2. Which of the following is not one of the Fed's general powers over excess reserves?

   a. Carrying out open-market operations

   b. Varying the discount rate

   c. Varying the margin requirements on stock trading

   d. Varying the required reserve ratio

3. When the Fed buys government securities on the open market, the effect is to

   a. decrease demand deposits in depository institutions.

   b. reduce depository institutions' deposits at the Fed, that is, reduce total and excess reserves.

   c. decrease the price of government securities.

   d. increase depository institutions' deposits at the Fed, that is, increase total and excess reserves.

4. A decrease in the required reserve ratio

   a. increases excess reserves but does not affect total reserves.

   b. decreases both total and excess reserves.

   c. decreases excess reserves only.

   d. increases both total and excess reserves.

5. Which of the following is not a function of the Federal Reserve?

   a. To issue all currency

   b. To act as a national clearinghouse for checks

   c. To be a banker's bank: that is, to hold deposits of member banks and to extend loans to member banks

   d. To manage the debt of the federal government

6. During a recession, the monetary policy of the Federal Reserve should be to

   a. increase the supply of money and reduce the interest rate.

   b. decrease the supply of money and increase the interest rate.

   c. increase both the supply of money and the interest rate.

   d. decrease both the supply of money and the interest rate.

7. During an inflation, the monetary policy of the Federal Reserve should be to

   a. increase excess reserves by selling securities on the open market, lowering the discount rate, and decreasing the required reserve ratio.

   b. increase excess reserves by buying securities on the open market, raising the discount rate, and increasing the required reserve ratio.

   c. decrease excess reserves by buying securities on the open market, lowering the discount rate, and decreasing the required reserve ratio.

   d. decrease excess reserves by selling securities on the open market, raising the discount rate, and raising the required reserve ratio.

8. One of the following statements does not describe a weakness of monetary policy. Which?

   a. During a serious depression, monetary policy will not work because banks' excess reserves may increase without the help of the Fed.

   b. Monetary policy may not be effective against an inflation that is due to causes other than demand pull.

   c. Monetary policy cannot readily deal with a situation in which high inflation and high unemployment occur at the same time.

   d. Variations in the supply of money do not affect prices during an inflation.

9. Which of the following is not a weakness of monetary policy?

   a. During inflation, a tight money policy does not affect all groups in the economy equally; some suffer more than others.

   b. During an inflation, the policies needed to reduce the supply of money are just the opposite of those needed to increase the interest rate.

   c. The velocity of exchange can vary; when it does, this may counteract monetary policy to some extent.

   d. Monetary policy cannot readily counter inflation and unemployment at the same time.

10. Which of the following statements is true of monetarism?

   a. Monetarism is another term for monetary policy.

   b. Monetarism is a viewpoint that fiscal policy is more important than monetary policy because monetary policy is weak.

   c. Monetarism is a viewpoint that the supply of money is extremely important and should be increased at a constant and appropriate rate.

   d. Monetarism is a viewpoint that the monetary policy and fiscal policy are equally important and effective.

11. The basic recommendation of the Friedman monetarists is

   a. a constant and appropriate rate of increase in the supply of money and fine tuning of the economy in other areas of fiscal and monetary policy.

   b. a constant and appropriate rate of increase in the supply of money and no fine tuning of the economy in other areas of fiscal and monetary policy.

   c. a vigorous use of both fiscal and monetary policy to control inflation.

   d. A vigorous use of discretionary monetary policy.

12. Which one of the following statements would not be used by Keynesians to refute the beliefs of the monetarists?

   a. Velocity of exchange can vary. Such variations can counteract the effects of a constant increase in the supply of money.

   b. The stabilizing mechanisms of a free-market economy are not as "automatic" as the monetarists assume.

   c. Money itself-or the amount of it in circulation-does not have any effect on the economy.

   d. The monetarists are unclear on which supply of money is important to control.

13. According to James Tobin, the experience of the American economy in 1983-1984 leads to the conclusion that

   a. monetary policy is the most effective tool in stimulating an economy to recovery from recession.

   b. fiscal policy was poorly timed and ineffective in stimulating the economic recovery.

   c. fiscal policy was very successful in promoting economic recovery.

   d. combined monetary and fiscal policy was successfully timed to promote economic recovery.

14. Which of the following is not a reason why the Keynesian-Monetarist debate may become less important in the 1990s?

   a. The federal debt and budget deficits make Keynesian demand management less attractive as policy devices.

   b. U.S. interest rates have to be keyed to and competitive with those in other international capital markets.

   c. International capital movements are much larger and easier than in previous decades.

   d. The Keynesians and monetarists have agreed on the respective importance of the two policy approaches.

15. Changes in inflationary expectations may have which of the following effects on the effectiveness of monetary policy?

   a. They make monetary policy easier to implement.

   b. They may offset or even more than offset the policy effect of changes in the money supply.

   c. They always work to reinforce the desirable policy effects of changes in the money supply.

   d. They are unrelated to the policy effects of changes in the money supply.

16. During the 1980s which of the following was not true?

   a. Substantial numbers of banks and savings and loans experienced sever financial difficulties.

   b. All banks could have demand deposits at their bank.

   c. Banks could establish branches anywhere in the U.S.

   d. All banks had access to the Fed clearinghouse.

Section C Matching questions

I. Match the phrases in column B with the terms in column A.

Column A

1. National banks
2. State banks
3. General powers
4. Open-market operations
5. The discount rate
6. Required reserve ratio
7. Regulations X and W
8. Regulation Q
9. Margin requirements on stocks
10. Deregulation Act of 1980
11. Monetary policy
12. Monetarists
13. Board of governors
14. Currency

Column B

(a) Buying and selling of government securities
(b) Variations in it do not change total reserves, but the combination of required and excess reserves does change
(c) Issued to meet the needs of the general public
(d) Chartered by state governments
(e) Critical of Keynesian monetary and fiscal policy
(f) Controlled the interest member banks could pay on savings accounts and demand deposits
(g) Varies the supply of money and the interest rate
(h) Control over excess reserves
(i) Semi-independent of the President
(j) All banks can hold demand deposits
(k) Chartered by the federal government
(l) Control speculation in the stock market
(m) Controlled lending in consumer and real estate markets
(n) The rate at which the Federal Reserve lends to its member banks

II. Column A lists things the Federal Reserve can do to counteract recession and inflation. Put an R in column B if the action listed would help to fight a recession, or I if the action listed would help to fight an inflation.

Column A	Column B
1. Buy securities in the open market	______
2. Sell securities in the open market	______
3. Raise the discount rate	______
4. Lower the discount rate	______
5. Raise the required reserve ratio	______
6. Lower the required reserve ratio	______

ANSWERS

Part 3

12. (a) When the government deposits the proceeds in Alpha Bank, Alpha Bank's demand deposits increase by $10,000. Due to the purchase by Alpha Bank, government securities increase by $10,000. The bank's total reserves do not change, because neither its deposits at the Fed nor its cash in vault is affected. Its required reserves must increase by 20 percent of the increase in demand deposits ($2,000). This increase comes from excess reserves, which in turn decrease by $2,000.

Notice that the bank's purchase of a government security from the Treasury has the same effect as the bank's loan to an individual.

(b) Alpha Bank buys $10,000 in government securities from the Fed. The Fed does not want money; it wants to reduce total and excess reserves. So there is no change in demand deposits. Government securities increase by $10,000. Since the Fed decreases Alpha Bank's deposits at the Fed, total reserves decrease by $10,000. Required reserves are not affected. All the decrease in total reserves comes from excess reserves, which decrease by $10,000.

(c) Mary Bloggs deposits in Alpha Bank the proceeds of her sale to the Fed of $10,000 in government securities. Alpha Bank's demand deposits increase by $10,000. The government securities in Alpha Bank are unaffected. Total reserves increase by $10,000 as Blogg's check is cleared and the Fed increases Alpha Bank's deposits at the Fed. Alpha Bank's required reserves must increase by $2,000 (20 percent of the increase in demand deposits). Excess reserves increase by $8,000 (since there is a $10,000 increase in total reserves and $2,000 is transferred to required reserves).

(d) Neither demand deposits nor government securities are affected. The Fed adds the proceeds of the discount to the deposits of Alpha Bank at the Fed, and total reserves increase by $20,000. Alpha Bank's required reserves are unaffected, but its excess reserves increase by $20,000.

Part 4

Section A 1, F; 2, T; 3, T; 4, F; 5, F; 6, F; 7, T; 8, T; 9, T; 10, T; 11, T; 12, T; 13, F; 14, F; 15, F; 16, T; 17, F; 18, T; 19, T; 20, F

Section B 1, c; 2, c; 3, d; 4, a; 5, d; 6, a; 7, d; 8, d; 9, b; 10, c; 11, b; 12, c; 13, c; 14, d; 15, b; 16, c

Section C I. 1, k; 2, d; 3, h; 4, a; 5, n; 6, b; 7, m; 8, f; 9, l; 10, j; 11, g; 12, e; 13, i; 14, c; II.1, R; 2, I; 3, I; 4, R; 5, I; 6, R

Chapter 14: Economic Policy Controversies: Supply-Side Economics, Rational Expectations, and New Views of Keynesians and Classical Economists, and the Post-Keynesians

Part 1

First, read the section titled "Summing Up" at the end of Chapter 14. It offers a thorough review of the material presented in the chapter.

Things to Watch For

Chapter 14 reviews the policy recommendations of supply-side economics. Referring back to the aggregate supply-aggregate demand model of Chapter 7, it is theoretically possible to increase real income at stable prices by increasing aggregate supply. This is the premise of supply-side economics, and it is important that you understand it.

Next the chapter presents the fundamental supply-side views. While learning these fundamentals, remember that they are both political philosophy and economic theory. Also you should understand the intent and reality of the 1981 tax cut. To understand the 1981 tax cut, you should understand the Laffer Curve, which relates tax rates to various levels of total tax revenue. One of the tenets of tax cuts was that lowering tax rates would reduce the number of transactions in the underground economy. You should also understand why the concept is controversial as a basis for economy policy.

Chapter 14 also raises the question of whether discretionary policy changes can achieve the objectives predicted for them. Here serious consideration must be given to the concepts as well as to their effectiveness in view of expectations that are formed rational or adaptive. Those expectations may be either. Finally, the chapter deals with the views of the Post-Keynesians who argue for greater government intervention to affect market failures through an incomes policy.

Part 2

Define the following terms and concepts.

1. Supply-Side Economics
2. Laffer Curve
3. Adaptive Expectations Hypothesis
4. Rational Expectations Hypothesis
5. Tax Wedge
6. Post-Keynesians
7. Incomes Policy

Part 3

Answer the following questions and problems.

1. Review the aggregate supply and aggregate demand model presented in Chapter 7. What happens when aggregate supply increases?

2. Draw the Laffer Curve. What are its policy implications?
3. What is the fundamental premise of supply-side economics?
4. What, according to F. Thomas Juster, are the basic elements of supply-side economics?
5. What is the Laffer Curve? What are its implications for tax policy? Why is it difficult to draw tax policy conclusions from the Laffer Curve?
6. From your perception of the material presented in Chapter 14, assess the effectiveness of supply-side economics. What are its most controversial aspects?
7. Discuss the Post-Keynesian policy problems from both a supply-side and Keynesian perspective.

Part 4 Self-test

Section A True/false questions

T F 1. When aggregate supply increases, both real income and prices increase.

T F 2. When aggregate supply decreases, real income falls and prices increase.

T F 3. Acceptance of the rational expectations hypothesis leads to te conclusion that discretionary monetary policy is ineffective in stimulating the economy.

T F 4. The Keynesian view is that increased demand will cause supply to increase in the long run, while the supply siders feel that aggregate supply is independent of aggregate demand and has an autonomous effect on real income and prices.

T F 5. The Laffer Curve relates tax rates to various levels of total tax revenues.

T F 6. Adaptive expectations are formed on the basis of what people have done both in the past and in the present.

T F 7. Rational expectations depend on both past experience and present events.

T F 8. Acceptance of the adaptive expectations hypothesis leads to the conclusion that monetary policy can only be effective in the long run.

T F 9. Keynesians maintain that obstacles in the market will prevent macroeconomic equilibrium.

T F 10. Classical economists believe that rational expectations would neutralize government discretionary policy.

T F 11. Supply-side economics was reflected in the economic views of the Reagan administration.

T F 12. Supply-side economics argues for stimulating demand by creating incentives to entrepreneurship.

T F 13. The Laffer Curve shows that as taxes increase, government revenue always grow.

T F 14. Underground economy involves those transactions that give rise to taxable income but are not reported for tax purposes.

Section B Multiple-choice questions

1. Which of the following happens when aggregate supply increases?
   a. Real income increases while prices decline.
   b. Real income increases while prices increase.
   c. Real income declines while prices also decline.
   d. There are no changes in income and prices.
2. Which of the following is not a fundamental element of supply-side economics?
   a. Entitlement programs lower work incentives.
   b. Taxes in the U.S. are biased against effort, savings and investment.
   c. Tax cuts to the poor will raise demand and thus supply.
   d. Regulations raise costs and reduce investment.
3. The Laffer Curve suggests that
   a. lowering of tax rates may increase tax revenues by increasing work incentives.
   b. increasing tax rates will always increase tax revenues.
   c. increasing tax rates always decrease tax revenues.
   d. lowering tax rates would always decrease tax revenue.
4. Adaptive expectations
   a. only take into account expected future events.
   b. only take into account expected present events.
   c. only take into account past events.
   d. take into account past and expected present events.

5. Which of the following is/are fundamental presumptions of supply-side economics?

   a. Public regulation raises costs, reduces investment, and has a low benefit/cost ratio.

   b. Programs designed to stimulate aggregate demand have created a climate of inflationary expectations.

   c. Entitlement programs lower work incentives and taxes are biased against saving and investment.

   d. All of the above are fundamental to supply-side economics.

6. Which of the following changes in federal taxation were contained in the tax legislation in the 1980s?

   a. Marginal tax rates were reduced from a high of 70 percent to 50 percent by 1984.

   b. Tax rates were lowered to discourage the growth of the underground economy

   c. Marginal tax rates by 1987 were lowered from a high of 50 percent to 35 percent.

   d. All of the above were contained in tax legislation in the 1980s.

7. According to the Laffer Curve argument, the relationship between tax rates and tax revenues is

   a. tax revenues always increase with increasing tax rates.

   b. tax revenues increase initially with increasing tax rates, then fall as tax rates continue to increase.

   c. tax revenues rise with rising tax rates, reach a maximum, then fall as tax rates continue to increase.

   d. Both (b) and (c) are correct.

8. The reasons for the shape of the Laffer Curve are

   a. rising taxes are biased against effort.

   b. rising taxes are biased against saving and investment.

   c. rising taxes ultimately create incentives to use resources in the underground economy.

   d. All of the above reasons explain the shape of the Laffer Curve.

9. The relationship between effective macroeconomic (monetary, fiscal) policy and the expectations of economic decision makers is that

   a. macroeconomic policy can only be effective if expectations are rational.

   b. macroeconomic policy can only be effective if, in the short run, expectations are adaptive.

   c. macroeconomic policy can be effective if expectations are either adaptive or rational.

   d. macroeconomic policy can never be effective in the short run if expectations are adaptive.

10. Much of the controversy surrounding supply-side economic policies in the 1980s is due to

    a. the decline in net national income between 1983 and 1989.

    b. the high rate of inflation between 1983 and 1989.

    c. the rising marginal federal tax rates in the 1980s.

    d. the large budget deficits that seemed to contradict supply-side predictions.

Section C Matching Questions

Match the phrases in Column B to the terms in Column A

Column A	Column B
1. Supply-side economics	(a) Reduce work incentives
2. Income-price level equilibrium	(b) Permanent government policy
3. Post-Keynesian	(c) Past and present events
4. Laffer curve	(d) Stimulating growth in aggregate supply
5. Entitlement programs	(e) Tax rates-tax revenues
6. Reduced regulation	(f) Aggregate quantity supplied = aggregate quantity demanded
7. Rational expectations	
8. Adaptive expectations	(g) Lower costs and raises incentives
	(h) Actual events in recent past

ANSWERS

Part 4

Section A 1, F; 2, T; 3, T; 4, T; 5, T; 6, F; 7, T; 8, F; 9,T; 10,T; 11, T; 12, T; 13, F; 14, T
Section B 1, a; 2, c; 3, a; 4, c; 5, d; 6, d; 7, d; 8, d; 9, b; 10, d
Section C 1, d; 2, f; 3, b; 4, e; 5, a; 6, g; 7, c; 8, h

Chapter 15: Economic Growth

Part 1

First, read the sections entitled "Summing Up" at the end of Chapter 15. They offer a thorough review of the material.

Things to Watch For

Prior to this chapter, the book has dealt primarily with static principles, those dealing with economic relationships at a point in time. Dealing with growth and thc problems relating to growth requires a dynamic framework-one that explains how economic relationships change as time goes by.

Chapter 15 begins by making a distinction between extensive growth and intensive growth. Extensive growth is the extensive process by which the total output of an economy grows as the economy has more and more resources. Intensive growth is the intensive process by which productivity, which is output per hour of labor (or income per capita), increases.

Since extensive growth comes about when the economy uses more resources, a nation's total supply of resources is the key to its expansion. Land represents natural resources. As we've seen before (in Chapter 2), resources are not fixed. They change, particularly as new technology makes it possible to use things previously not recognized as resources, or viewed only as potential resources. Labor is another resource. It represents the human skills and abilities of a society, without which there is no economic activity. Expansion via growth in the supply of labor can come about from an increase in population or from increased participation of people in the labor force (people working longer hours, more women entering the labor force, and so on). Capital, another resource, represents the results of investment. It may take the form of either an investment flow (financial capital) or a stock of plant and equipment (physical capital). Remember that capital basically affects the productivity of people. As workers have available more capital, and more sophisticated forms of capital, their productivity rises.

What determines the amount of capital people have to work with? One of the most important factors is market size. As a market grows, consumer purchasing power increases to the point at which aggregate demand warrants investment in plants, tools, and other forms of physical capital. Thus, areas or countries with low incomes and scanty populations employ less capital and have a less productive labor force than high-income areas or countries that have large populations.

Growth, the intensive process, is primarily the result of increasing efficiency. Relatively little of our increased output in the twentieth century has resulted from just increased use of resources. Most of it has resulted from increased output per unit of input (that is, increased productivity). Two developments account for this increase in productivity: (1) Specialization. As a market grows, it becomes possible to specialize in uses of resources within that market. (2) Technological change. Growth in technological knowledge results in greater productivity of capital goods and greater efficiency of organization.

Studies suggest that technological change has been the biggest cause of intensive economic growth. This is because it is the influence of technology that helps overcome the barriers to growth. There are at least two important barriers to growth: (1) The effect of diminishing returns (the law of variable proportions). There is a gradual decrease in efficiency associated with using more of certain inputs with a fixed amount of certain others. Many classical economists saw land as the fixed input. The effect of overcrowding-of more people on the same amount of land-is decreased efficiency. (2) Population pressures. If population increases more rapidly than the earth's capacity to sustain people (which mainly involves its capacity to produce food), the ceiling to growth will be very low. This pessimistic theory concerning barriers and population pressures is called the Malthusian specter, after T. R. Malthus.

Thus we say that technological change is a shift factor. It shifts the whole growth path of a society upward and prevents the above-mentioned barriers from producing stagnation, or a stationary state. Technological improvement has been the most important shift factor in the growth of the U.S. economy. One study concludes that between 1929 and 1957, 20 percent of economic growth in the United States resulted from improved technology and another 27 percent from improved education and training (in other words, greater investment in human capital).

Population growth retards the growth of low-income countries. However, it has been a significant factor in increasing demand and market sizes in the United States since 1900. The increase in U.S. population from 90,000,000 to more than 290,000,000 in the early twenty-first century has also increased the labor force and made possible the extension of mass production. Nowadays-especially because children in an urban industrial society are consumers, not producers, and because people prefer other goods to more children-we appear to be moving toward zero population growth.

In recent years U.S. economists have been interested less in a rapidly growing labor force than in expansion of capital. Production techniques have become more capital-intensive (increased capital/labor ratio) rather than more labor-intensive (increased labor/capital ratio). A situation of increased capital/labor ratio is referred to as capital deepening, in contrast to capital broadening, which is what happens when you have growth with a constant capital/labor ratio.

In a final section of the chapter, evidence regarding a slowing of productivity growth in the U.S. is discussed. According to Edward Denison, the rate of growth between 1973 and 1983 fell. Denison cites the reasons for this decline as (1) changing composition of the labor force, (2) changing composition of output, (3) growth in government regulation, (4) rising resources prices, and (5) declining rate of capital formation. A changing composition of output toward (labor intensive) services may be the most important of the causes.

William Baumol, on the other hand, argues that the American economy has not lost its productivity edge. Baumol cites the facts that, (1) productivity growth has simply returned to its historic rate, (2) productivity growth has declined in all industrial nations, and (3) productivity (output per unit of labor employed) of American labor remains the highest in the world.

The first application deals with the question of whether or not the growth of the United States depends on military spending. Some economists, such as Douglas Dowd, believe that since World War II the relative economic stability of the United States has indeed depended on defense-related purchases. Other economists, such as Arthur Okun, point out that military spending is like any other kind of federal spending in terms of its effect on GDP (that is, on aggregate demand). This is an extension of the point established by John Maynard Keynes in 1936.

Examining the record on military spending leads to the following conclusions: (1) If there had been no defense spending in this country since World War II, and if it had not been replaced by other spending, unemployment would have been much higher. (2) Defense spending has been a fairly stable part of government spending. (3) Changes in defense spending in the 1960s had much less impact on the growth of U.S. potential than did changes in monetary and fiscal policy.

As to the effect of military spending on technological change and industrial capacity, some feel that military spending does little to increase capacity and that we could better use our resources in ways that do increase capacity. Others feel that defense spending has helped bring about advances in technology (new processes, new techniques) and that this has enhanced our productivity. It is impossible to say which view is correct. If both are correct, we should try to find out what the tradeoff is between the technology we gain by military spending and the capacity we lose by it. One thing is clear. Defense spending in the 1970s, 1980s, and 1990s did not fill the gaps in either employment or capacity. The application concludes with a note that declining defense spending in the 1990s did not necessarily have undesirable effects on economic growth. Rising defense spending after 2001 may or may not have such effects.

Optimism about continued growth and improvement in material welfare has been tempered by recognition of the need to establish tradeoffs between more growth and protection of the environment. These tradeoffs are the subject of the second application. Economists generally don't believe that decay of the environment is due to growth, per se. They do, however, believe that economic causes are at the root of environmental problems; these causes are connected with the pattern of growth.

Economists have differed with some ecologists on the following points: (1) Given certain unfavorable externalities, ecologists dispute the amount of real growth that has occurred in the industrialized nations. (2) Ecologists see absolute limits to growth, whereas economists see tradeoffs and generally feel that growth must continue. (3) Ecologists usually see government action as the primary means of solving environmental problems, whereas many economists believe that the market system can provide solutions as well.

Economists feel that the market system can be made to incorporate the externalities (the costs of cleaning up air and water to acceptable levels of purity). Two ways to do this are (1) setting standards for industrial effluents, and (2) taxing industrial effluents. One would circumvent the market; the other would use market signals.

Ecologists feel that the limits of growth are established by nature. Economists such as Kenneth Boulding agree that we must take natural limits into account as we move from an open-frontier (unlimited-growth) society to a "spaceship-earth" society, where nature imposes limits. Some ecologists feel that growth itself is the source of the problem and must be stopped. Pressures for zero population growth (ZPG) and zero economic growth (ZEG) are continuing.

Economists rebut these ideas by arguing that (1) resources will continue to grow (not remain static, as assumed in "doomsday" models), (2) not using resources today will deny future generations the new capital that would result from their use, and (3) advocates of ZPG and ZEG underestimate the flexibility and usefulness of the market system in finding solutions to environmental problems.

The application concludes with a notation that improvement in environmental quality is an increasing concern. Economists and most ecologists have increasingly agreed that: (1) environment repair need not require elimination of economic growth, and (2) two market forces can be useful in accomplishing environmental goals that do not require sacrificing economic growth.

Part 2

Define the following terms and concepts.

1. Dynamic framework
2. Static framework
3. Extensive growth
4. Intensive growth
5. Disembodied technological change
6. Human capital
7. Technological change
8. Stationary state
9. Malthusian specter
10. Capital-intensive production
11. Labor-intensive production
12. Capital broadening
13. Capital deepening
14. Zero economic growth
15. Zero population growth

Part 3

Answer the following questions and problems.

1. In what ways has military spending played an important economic role in the United States since World War II? In what ways has this kind of spending been no more important than-or even less important economically than-other kinds of government expenditures?

2. What are the major differences between economists and ecologists when it comes to suggesting solutions to environmental problems? Is there a growing concensus between economists and ecologists about growth and environmental repair? Explain.

3. What is the "Malthusian Specter"? Why has it not occurred in industrial nations? What will be necessary to avoid it in less-developed nations?

4. Consider Figure 15-1, and do the following things.

   a. Draw a growth path that illustrates the classical view of an eventual "stationary state."

   b. Explain why the growth path is shaped the way you have drawn it.

   c. Explain what factors can shift this growth path upward (raise productivity and real per capita income).

Figure 15-1
Growth Path of an Economy

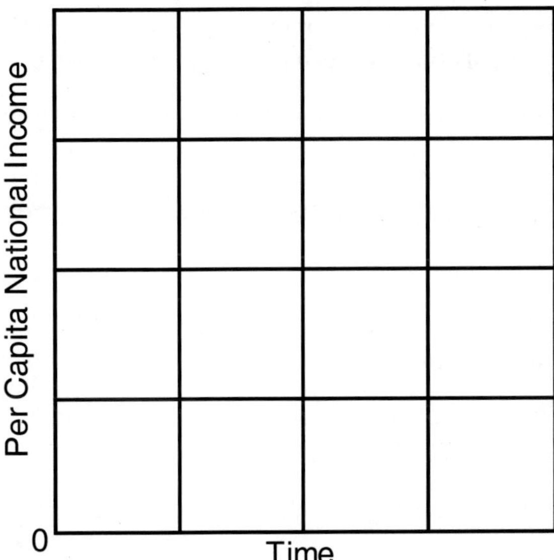

5. What role has population increase played in the economic growth of the United States? What role has immigration played in this growth?
6. What, according to Edward Denison, are the reasons for the declining growth of productivity in the United States since 1973? Which of these factors has/have been most important in decline?
7. William Baumol concludes that U.S. labor has not lost its productivity edge. What factors does he cite in reaching that conclusion?
8. What problems are associated with diverting investment to environmental-cleanup uses? What are solutions to these problems? Which solution do you favor? Why?
9. How important is the rate of growth?
10. How has the composition of the labor force changed?

Part 4 Self-test

Section A True/false questions

T F 1. Economists and ecologists seem to be coming to an agreement on the role of markets in finding solutions to environmental problems.

T F 2. Technological change has been the most important source of American growth since 1929.

T F 3. Growth and expansion are basically the same thing.

T F 4. Changes in military spending have done much to reduce unemployment since 1960.

T F 5. Economists generally believe that the market system can be used to force firms to incorporate externalities in their costs.

T F 6. When an economy is at a stationary state, this always means that it is at a level of near-starvation.

T F 7. Population increase always retards economic growth.

T F 8. Only dynamic theory is useful in economics.

T F 9. Economists believe that the pattern of growth, not growth itself, causes environmental pollution.

T F 10. According to Edward Denison, productivity growth has been faster than average since 1973.

T F 11. Technological change results in growth through increased efficiency.

T F 12. Human Capital consists of investment in the education of the workforce.

T F 13. Methus argued that food production grows geometrically.

T F 14. Military spending (federal expenditure) adds to aggregate demand.

T F 15. A growing economy's growth is always accompanied by full employment.

Section B Multiple-choice questions

1. According to Walter Heller, economists and ecologists disagree on all but which one of the following?
   a. Whether real growth has occurred
   b. Whether there are absolute limits to growth
   c. Whether growth can be stopped
   d. Whether markets can provide solutions to environmental problems
2. Ecologists believe in all but which one of the following?
   a. Zero population growth
   b. Zero economic growth
   c. Need for stimulants to private investment
   d. Government antipollution standards

3. Which one of the following courses of action open to government does not stimulate spending?

   a. Reducing federal expenditures

   b. Increasing federal expenditures

   c. Decreasing taxes

   d. Increasing government spending more than taxes

4. Which of the following represents capital?

   a. Offshore oil

   b. The building in which Congress meets

   c. A steel plant

   d. Your private automobile

5. Which of the following is the most important source of recent growth in the United States?

   a. Additional labor

   b. Additional land

   c. Better technology

   d. Wage and price controls

6. Which of the following does not help to explain the slowing of productivity growth in the United States since 1973?

   a. Decline government regulation

   b. Rising resource prices

   c. Decreases in the rate of capital formation

   d. A changing composition of output in favor of services.

7. William Baumol argues that U.S. labor has the highest productivity in the world and that it has not lost its productivity edge. What factors does he cite in support of this conclusion?

   a. Productivity growth has slowed in all industrial nations.

   b. Service sector employment in the U.S. has grown less rapidly than in almost all other industrial nations.

   c. Productivity growth in the U.S. has returned to its historic average.

   d. All of the above are cited by Baumol.

Section C Matching questions

Match the phrases in column A to the terms in column B.

	Column A		Column B
1.	Extensive process	(a)	Stationary state
2.	Fixed input(s)	(b)	Dynamic
3.	Classical economics	(c)	Static
4.	Capital/labor ratio rises	(d)	Growth
5.	Characterized by changes over time	(e)	Expansion
6.	Relation of employment to output	(f)	Malthus
7.	Specter of starvation	(g)	Diminishing returns
8.	Capital/labor ratio is constant	(h)	Capital broadening
9.	Existing at a point in time	(i)	Capital deepening
10.	Intensive process	(j)	Aggregate production function

ANSWERS

Part 4

Section A 1, T; 2, T; 3, T; 4, F; 5, F; 6, T; 7, F; 8, F; 9, F; 10, T; 11, T; 12, T; 13, F; 14, T; 15, F
Section B 1, c; 2, c; 3, a; 4, c; 5, c; 6, a; 7, d
Section C 1, e; 2, g; 3, a; 4, i; 5, b; 6, j; 7, f; 8, h; 9, c; 10, d

Chapter 16: Patterns of International Trade

Part 1

First, read the section entitled "Summing Up" at the end of Chapter 16. It provides an excellent review of the chapter.

Things to Watch For

In chapter 16 we relax the assumption that the economy examined is closed. Now we examine the impact of trade with other economies and how that trade is financed. Chapter 14 deals with exports (X, those things a nation sells to others) and imports (M, those things it buys from others). This trade is made up of visible items (the commodities) and invisible items (services, including financial services). The commodity balance of trade is the difference between exports and imports (X - M).

Net foreign trade (exports - imports + net services balance (SN)) can exert a powerful macroeconomic influence on a nation.

Trade is important for any nation except a nation that decides to pursue a course of autarky, or economic self-sufficiency. Autarky is economically disadvantageous, even for the United States, not in terms of absolute advantage (which exists when a given nation can produce all things more efficiently than any other nation can), but in terms of comparative advantage (which exists when a given nation can produce some things relatively more efficiently than others).

A production-possibilities schedule and a production-possibilities curve show that the internal rate at which a nation gives up one good to produce another ultimately increases. When one looks at these schedules and curves, the advantage to a nation of foreign trade becomes clear. By trading with one another, two nations that operate under comparative advantage can both have more of all goods and services than would be possible without trade.

The reason trade is beneficial is that the internal rate of exchange of one country (the slope of its production-possibilities schedule) is different from that of another country. Trade creates a new exchange rate, different from the internal rates of either nation. The actual exchange rate that is established is called the terms of trade. It is the rate at which one nation's goods are exchanged for the goods of another nation. (Later on in the chapter, we see that the terms of trade is also the ratio of the prices of exports to the prices of imports.)

Note these facts about comparative advantage: (1) Nations have differing comparative advantages based on varying endowments of resources, differing physical features, differing degrees of development of capital markets, and differing ratios of capital to labor. (2) As a nation develops, its comparative advantage changes. The main reason why specialization of trade on the basis of comparative advantage occurs is that a nation that does not practice such specialization encounters increasing costs. That is, a nation that wishes to produce both good A and good B finds that the necessary internal tradeoffs force it to give up larger and larger amounts of one of the two goods. Finally, it gets to the point at which it is cheaper to import some of the goods it would otherwise produce. Trade specialization is not, however, complete. This is so for a number of reasons: (1) International trade affects the internal level of employment. (2) There is a lack of competition in internal trade. (3) International trade carries certain externalities. (4) Relative prices between one country and another may not reflect scarcities. (5) There is protectionism, which means legal or government-established barriers to free trade.

The main devices governments use to practice protectionism are as follows: (1) Tariffs, or taxes on imports. Tariffs reduce the supply of the good that is being so taxed, raise the price of it, increase domestic monopoly power, and raise revenue for the government. (2) Quotas, or restrictions on the amounts of certain goods that may be imported. The effects of quotas are the same as those of tariffs, except that quotas do not raise revenue for the government. (3) Embargoes, or laws that prohibit the import of certain goods altogether. The effect of embargoes is to reduce the supply of the good to domestic sources, raise the price of the good, and enhance domestic monopoly power. Lack of effective opposition by consumers to import quotas may be attributable to rational ignorance.

The arguments in favor of trade protectionism are (1) the infant-industry argument, which holds that a newly begun, developing industry needs to be protected from mature foreign competitors; (2) the national-security argument, which holds that a nation should preserve its defense industries against competition from foreign defense materials, because it can never be sure of having a ready supply of any good that must be imported; (3) the cheap-foreign-labor argument; and (4) the macroeconomic-employment argument, which holds that protectionism restricts imports, stimulates exports, and as a result lowers unemployment.

Economists generally reject all these arguments as being fallacious and self-defeating, except for the national-security argument. Even in that case they feel that direct subsidies to defense industries are preferable to tariffs and quotas and embargoes, because subsidies give a clear picture of the costs involved. The United States has never allowed trade to be entirely free, but it also has only rarely set up extremely high tariffs or embargoes or other very restrictive trade rules. Those that it did enact were set up during wars, depressions, and other national emergencies.

GATT, the General Agreement on Tarrifs and Trade, was set up in 1947 to foster trade and lower various forms of obstacles to free trade.

In 1994, the Uruguay round of GATT created the World Trade Organization (WTO) to replace GATT. The WTO's purpose is to seek further trade liberalization. Various trade agreements have occurred since World War II. Their forms include common markets, custom unions, and free trade agreements. Be sure you understand the differences among them. Two present major free trade arrangements are the European Union-European Free Trade Association or EU-EFTA and the North American Free Trade Association or NAFTA.

The application deals with an issue very much in the forefront today. Does international trade help nations (especially the poor nations) to develop economically? The classical economists thought that it does. In fact, they felt that international trade is essential to a nation's economic development. The answer has been made more complicated by the appearance of a number of countries now called newly industrialized countries (NICs) and also the creation in the 70s and 80s and 90s of a very serious debt problem for many NICs and less developed countries (LDCs). The application shows that, if one takes a static approach (that is, if one ignores the changes that take place over time), this argument is compelling. Nations that trade will allocate their resources to their most productive uses, and thus will have a greater productivity and higher per capita income than nations that don't trade.

At least five points of doubt have been raised about whether international trade will have the same positive results over time. (1) Imperfections in the factor market. As these imperfections disappear, relative costs and comparative advantage change. (2) Unreliability of export markets. Some highly specialized raw-material economies are very unstable. They can't grow rapidly because of low price and income elasticities of demand for their products. The terms of trade are more unfavorable to them than to the developed industrialized nations. (3) Changes in productivity. Manufacturing, even when it is not dictated by comparative advantage, builds up supplies of resources and a pool of labor with sophisticated skills to a much greater degree than agriculture does. (4) Dynamic external economies. Equilibrium market prices do not indicate which investments must be taken together to be profitable. Thus, the market signals that emerge when nations trade under the comparative-advantage system may dictate the wrong investments. (5) Uncertainty and flexibility. An economy that is diversified in its trade relationships-one that does not base its trade strictly on comparative advantage-can respond more quickly and flexibly to changes in supply and demand (world prices) than an economy that is dependent on one or a few products.

Economists generally disregard the first two of these arguments. But they concede that the others may sometimes support an argument for a shift of economic policy away from comparative advantage. Recently, pressures have developed to create a "new economic order," one in which poor nations are given special trading arrangements and concessions. If such concessions are granted, they will probably involve a further move away from comparative advantage. Intense debate continues about whether free trade benefits the NICs and LDCs or whether special treatment should be afforded them to encourage growth. That the free trade argument seems to be winning is reflected in the rules of the new WTO that require both industrial nations and LDCs to follow the same free trade policies.

Part 2

Define the following terms and concepts.

1. Absolute advantage, comparative advantage
2. Autarky
3. "Beggar-thy-neighbor" argument
4. Burden of a tariff (consumer burden, producer burden)
5. Cheap foreign labor argument
6. Commodity balance of trade
7. Common markets
8. Customs unions
9. Exports, imports
10. Free trade agreements
11. General Agreement on Tariffs and Trade (GATT)
12. Infant-industry argument
13. National security argument
14. Commodity balance of trade
15. Net foreign trade
16. Open economy, closed economy
17. Protectionism
18. Rational ignorance
19. Tariffs, quotas, embargoes
20. Terms of trade
21. Visible items, invisible items of trade
22. World Trade Organization (WTO)
23. NAFTA
24. European Union-European Free Trade Association

Part 3

Answer the following questions and problems.

1. What problems would nations experience in trying to achieve autarky?
2. Consider the hypothetical production-possibilities schedule for the United States and Zaire shown in Table 16-1.

   a. What happens to the rate of exchange of trucks for copper in the United States? of copper for trucks in Zaire?

   b. What is the United States' initial rate of exchange of copper for trucks? Zaire's initial rate of exchange of trucks for copper?

   c. What causes the internal rate of exchange to change in each of the two countries?

   d. For trade to take place in this case (Zairian copper to the United States, American trucks to Zaire), what is the range within which the terms of trade must fall?

Table 16-1
Production-Possibilities Schedules: United States and Zaire

United States		Zaire	
Units of Trucks	**Units of Copper**	**Units of Trucks**	**Units of Copper**
100	0	0	100
80	10	5	80
60	20	10	60
40	30	15	40
20	40	20	20
0	50	25	0

3. In Figure 16-1, plot the production-possibilities schedules for (a) the United States and (b) Zaire from the data in Table 16-1. Then consider the following additions to this economic situation.

   a. What would the production-possibilities curves look like if resources were specialized in their uses?

   b. In Figure 16-1 plot the consumption possibilities after trade for both countries.

   c. What causes the internal rate of exchange to change in each of the two countries?

   d. For trade to take place in this case (Zairian copper to the United States, American trucks to Zaire), what is the range within which the terms of trade must fall?

   e. Would the United States benefit from trade with Zaire even if it had an absolute advantage in producing both trucks and copper? Why?

4. What are the major arguments for protectionism? Why do economists regard all but one as fallacious?

Figure 16-1
Production-Possibilities Curves

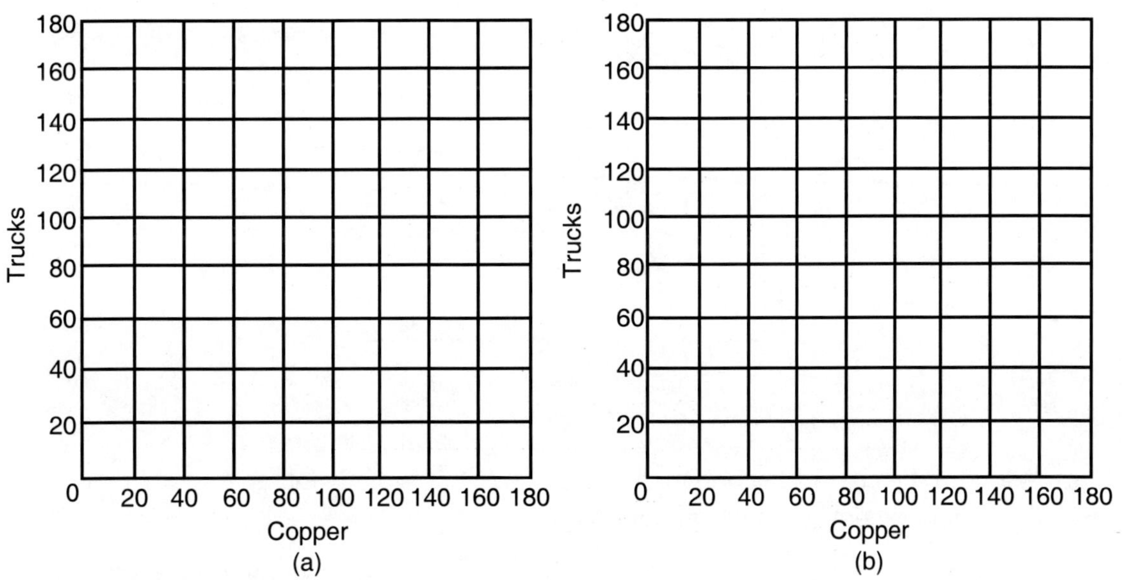

5. Consider Figure 16-2and then answer the following questions.

   a. What is the equilibrium price of the imported good (including foreign imports)?

   b. Draw a new supply curve reflecting a tariff on this good that partially reduces foreign supply. What happens to price? Who bears the burden of the tariff? Who benefits from the tariff?

   c. What will the price of this good be if an embargo is placed on imports of it from abroad? Who benefits from-and who "pays" for-the embargo?

Figure 16-2
Effects of a Tariff

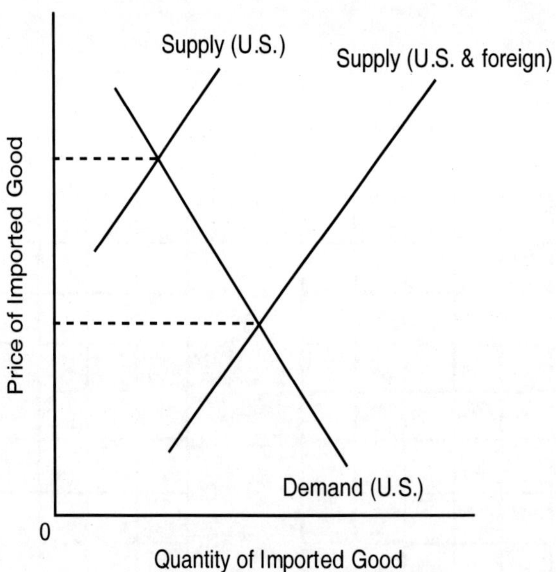

6. Why did the classical economists regard comparative-advantage trade as essential to the economic development of nations?
7. There are several arguments in favor of moving away from comparative advantage as the basis for a developing nation's trade policy. Which ones are regarded by some economists as valid?
8. What do you think is likely to happen in the future to free trade between rich and poor nations? What may the debt problems of NICs and LDCs have to do with this?
9. What is the difference between tariffs and Quotas?
10. What is absolute advantage?

Part 4 Self-test

Section A True/false questions

T F 1. The balance of trade measures the difference between exports, and imports, and services.

T F 2. Foreign trade is not important to the United States.

T F 3. The commodity balance of trade equals exports minus imports.

T F 4. Net foreign trade is equal to exports plus imports.

T F 5. The balance of trade affects the economy through its effects on GNP.

T F 6. A nation that has an absolute advantage in producing all its goods should not trade with other nations.

T F 7. In a real-world situation, production-possibilities curves are not likely to be straight lines.

T F 8. If internal rates of exchange are the same in two different nations, there is no advantage to be had from trade between them.

T F 9. The terms of trade express the prices at which the goods of one nation can be exchanged for the goods of another nation.

T F 10. The comparative advantage of the United States has changed little over the last century.

T F 11. Externalities may cause specialization of trade among nations to be incomplete.

T F 12. Tariffs decrease domestic monopoly power.

T F 13. The United States has never imposed an embargo in modern times.

T F 14. Economists accept all the arguments in favor of protectionism except the macroeconomic-employment argument.

T F 15. The classical economists saw little need for nations to trade with one another.

T F 16. At any given time, the nation that allocates its resources on the basis of comparative advantage is likely to have a greater output than the one that does not.

T F 17. One reason why nations should follow the principle of comparative advantage is the notion of dynamic external economies, which means that certain investments should be undertaken together.

T F 18. Price and income elasticities of demand may, according to some economists, weigh against raw-material-producing nations' use of trade as a basis for their economic development.

T F 19. A nation exporting one or just a few commodities is more likely to be able to adjust to changes in international supply and demand than a nation that exports many.

T F 20. The WTO was set up by the U.S. to protect U.S. industry from foreign competition.

T F 21. NAFTA is an agreement between the U.S., Canada, and Mexico to promote free trade.

T F 22. The World Trade Organization is the successor to GATT.

T F 23. The U.S. currently exports more than it imports.

T F 24. Imports are commodities and services bought from other nations.

T F 25. Tariffs and quotas are the two principle means by which countries usually intervene to protect their own industries from overseas competion.

Section B Multiple-choice questions

1. Which of the following is not a visible item of trade?

   a. Automobile exports

   b. Steel imports

   c. Petroleum imports

   d. Payments to foreign shippers

2. The commodity balance of trade is which one of the following?

   a. Exports minus imports

   b. Visible minus invisible items of trade

   c. Exports divided by imports

   d. The balance in the federal budget

3. Net foreign trade consists of

   a. exports plus imports.

   b. exports minus imports.

   c. exports minus imports plus net services.

   d. the value of services sold to other nations.

4. When imports increase which of the following occurs?

   a. the balance of trade increases

   b. the balance of trade decreases

   c. The balance of trade is unaffected

   d. GNP increases

5. The terms of trade express the relationship between

   a. exports and imports.

   b. total paid for exports and total paid for imports.

   c. prices paid for exports in relation to prices paid for imports.

   d. visible and invisible items of trade.

6. A nation's consumption-possibilities curve is probably affected by international trade in which one of the following ways?

   a. It is greater after trade.

   b. It is less after trade.

   c. It is unaffected by trade.

   d. The effect is indeterminate.

7. One of the following does not cause trade specialization to be incomplete. Which?

   a. Increasing costs

   b. Noncompetitive trading conditions

   c. Externalities

   d. Complete factor substitutability

8. Economists do not reject which one of the following arguments in favor of protectionism?

   a. Cheap foreign labor

   b. Infant industry

   c. Macroeconomic employment

   d. National security

9. A tariff is likely to do all but which one of the following?

   a. Reduce domestic prices

   b. Increase domestic supply

   c. Increase government revenues

   d. Increase domestic monopoly power

10. Economists generally accept all but which one of the following reservations about comparative-advantage trade among nations?

    a. Changes in factor cost

    b. Uncertainty and flexibility

    c. Dynamic external economies

    d. Changes in productivity

11. Which of the following changes seems least likely at this time to occur in international trade?

    a. Special trading privileges for poor countries

    b. Special borrowing privileges at the IMF for poor countries

    c. Movement in the direction of free trade

    d. Lower tariffs in rich nations for goods imported from poor nations

12. The World Trade Organization is

    a. a world customs union.

    b. a world common market.

    c. a free trade agreement between the United States and Europe.

    d. an organization to promote free trade.

Section C Matching questions

Match the phrases in column B to the terms in column A.

Column A	Column B
1. Autarky	(a) Exports minus imports + net services
2. Absolute advantage	(b) Excludes exports and imports
3. Internal rate of exchange	(c) Economic self-sufficiency
4. Terms of trade	(d) Producing all things more efficiently than others can
5. Net foreign trade	(e) Producing some things more efficiently than others can
6. Tariff	(f) Domestic tradeoff between goods for a nation
7. Embargo	(g) Price of exports ÷ prices of imports
8. Invisible items of trade	(h) Tax on imported goods
9. Dynamic external economies	(i) Prohibition against importing a certain good
10. Comparative advantage	(j) Return greater when a group of investments is taken together
11. Commodity balance of trade	(k) Exports minus imports

ANSWERS

Part 4

Section A 1, T; 2, F; 3, T; 4, F; 5, T; 6, F; 7, T; 8, T; 9, T; 10, T; 11, T; 12, F; 13, F; 14, F; 15, F; 16, T; 17, F; 18, T; 19, F; 20, F; 21, T; 22, T; 23, T; 24, T; 25, T
Section B 1, d; 2, a; 3, c; 4, b; 5, c; 6, a; 7, d; 8, d; 9, a; 10, a; 11, a; 12, d
Section C 1, c; 2, d; 3, f; 4, g; 5, a; 6, h; 7, i; 8, b; 9, j; 10, e; 11, k

Chapter 17: Paying for International Trade

Part 1

First, read the section entitled "Summing Up" at the end of Chapter 15. It provides a thorough review of the chapter.

Things to Watch For

Chapter 17 deals with the ways nations finance international trade. Almost all international trade requires a means for exchanging money; very little trade is done through barter. Exports create claims to the currencies of other nations; imports create claims to our currency. The rate of exchange is the ratio at which one currency can be exchanged for another. These rates of exchange are established in foreign exchange markets.

A workable system of exchange meets three requirements: (1) Balance. It strikes a reasonable balance between two needs-the need for stability and growth of trade, and the need for stability and growth of the economies that engage in trade. (2) Equity. It is based on a reasonable distribution of the costs and benefits of the financial system. (3) Efficiency. It encourages trade by operating at a reasonable cost.

An equilibrium exchange rate is one that clears foreign exchange markets. The various kinds of exchange rates are (1) freely floating exchange rates, in which supply and demand are free to move the various currencies up and down as the international market dictates, and (2) fixed exchange rates, in which governments and central banks are committed to maintaining a fixed relationship between currencies. Somewhat between fixed and floating is what is called the dirty float. Here the exchange rates are pegged within narrow ranges by the central bank.

Advantages of freely floating rates are that (1) they respond quickly to changes in supply and demand, and (2) they readily eliminate excess supply or demand. Disadvantages of freely floating exchange rates are that (1) they may be highly unstable, though arbitrage tends to minimize this instability, and (2) when they change, these changes may have a great effect on domestic economic conditions (income and employment).

Advantages of fixed exchange rates are that (1) they facilitate long-term planning for international trade, and (2) they encourage stability. Disadvantages are that (1) they require large international reserves, and (2) they prevent changes in supply and demand from nudging the market toward an equilibrium situation.

In many cases since 1971, governments have adopted a system of managed or "dirty" floats in which they intervene selectively to keep exchange rates within certain (ill defined) pegged rates.

An exchange-rate disequilibrium means that there is excess demand for or supply of a given currency. The problem may be dealt with by (1) rationing exchange (this eliminates the excess but by-passes consumer tastes for goods), or (2) making adjustments in income and employment-deflation in the country with the payments deficit, inflation in the country with the payments surplus.

A payments system that used to provide automatic adjustments to exchange variations was the gold standard. Under this standard, currencies were valued in terms of gold and could be exchanged for gold. When a currency disequilibrium occurred, the exchange rate would change. However, the gold value of currencies would not. Ultimately, currencies would reach the gold-flow point, the point at which it became cheaper to buy and ship gold than to exchange currencies. Taking gold out of one country caused deflation (lowered prices). Putting gold into another caused inflation. The deflated economy, with its lowered prices, increased its exports. The inflated economy, with higher prices, lost exports and increased imports. In this way the exchange rate automatically was driven back to equilibrium.

Adherents of the gold standard liked it because (1) it was automatic, (2) it gave stability to long-term planning for trade, and (3) it enforced an economic discipline on nations. Opponents disliked the gold standard because (1) it forced nations to tie their domestic economic policies to their trade positions, and (2) it tied trade to a resource (gold) that was in inelastic supply.

After World War II, the international financial system was built around the International Monetary Fund (IMF), an agency designed to oversee an adjustable-peg system of exchange rates. The IMF allowed currency values to vary from their established rates by no more than 1 percent. The IMF's policy in doing this was to foster stability and to encourage long-term planning of trade. Recently, dissatisfaction with the system (which permitted countries like the United States to run large deficits) led to the creation of SDRs, or special drawing rights. Nations with a deficit that are members of the IMF can borrow these SDRs. The IMF also has recently encouraged a system of floating exchange rates.

Finally, there is the balance of payments, the accounting statement that sets forth all a nation's trade transactions for a year. The statement must balance; all that is bought must be paid for. The statement consists of (1) the current account, a statement of all items currently bought or sold that includes the balance of trade (exports minus imports); (2) the capital account; including all capital flows (3) the basic balance (current account plus capital account); Also included in the balance of payments is the account that shows how any positive or negative balance is financed; this is called the official reserve transactions balance. A nation finances this balance by selling government liabilities to foreign official agencies or by selling reserve assets (gold, SDRs, and so on).

Briefly in the 1960s, some what more frequently in the 1970s and almost entirely throughout the period from 1980 to 1995, the U.S. economy experienced commodity balance of trade deficits. In the 1970s, but especially in the 1980s and 1990s, these deficits have created political controversy over how to deal with them. Representatives from both labor and ownership of those industries adversely affected by import competition pressed for various forms of restrictions on imports, especially from Japan. The economics profession almost universally has taken the position that comparative advantage trade should be adhered to. A number of studies have reiterated the position that interference in free trade hurts the economy as a whole including the adversely affected industries.

Part 2

Define the following terms and concepts.

1. Balance-of-payments statement
2. Basic balance
3. Current account balance
4. Deflation
5. Dumping
6. Equilibrium exchange rates
7. Exchange controls
8. Fixed exchange rates
9. Foreign exchange markets
10. Freely floating exchange rates
11. Gold standard
12. Gold-flow point
13. International Monetary Fund (IMF)
14. International reserves
15. Managed or "dirty" float
16. Official reserves transactions balance
17. Special drawing rights (SDRs)
18. Arbitrage
19. Official reserve transaction account

Part 3

Answer the following questions and problems.

1. What determines the supply of dollars the French have to purchase American exports? The supply of francs we have to purchase French imports?
2. What are the characteristics of a good international monetary system? Which, if any, of these characteristics are lacking in present international monetary arrangements?
3. How are freely floating exchange rates determined? What are their advantages and disadvantages?
4. Consider Figure 17-1, which represents freely floating exchange rates, and then answer the following questions.
   a. Let us say that D0 represents the U.S. demand for pounds and S0 represents the supply of pounds. What is the equilibrium exchange rate?
   b. Why does D0 slope downward? Why does S0 slope upward?
   c. Suppose that the demand for British pounds increases to D1 (Americans want to buy more British goods). (1) What does the distance AB represent? (2) What will the new equilibrium exchange rate be? How does it reach that level?
   d. Suppose that the exchange system is suddenly changed to one of fixed exchange rates (at $2.00 to the pound), and that D1 demand for pounds exists. To stabilize the exchange rate at its fixed value, how large will the reserve transaction have to be?

Figure 17-1
Freely Floating Exchange Rates

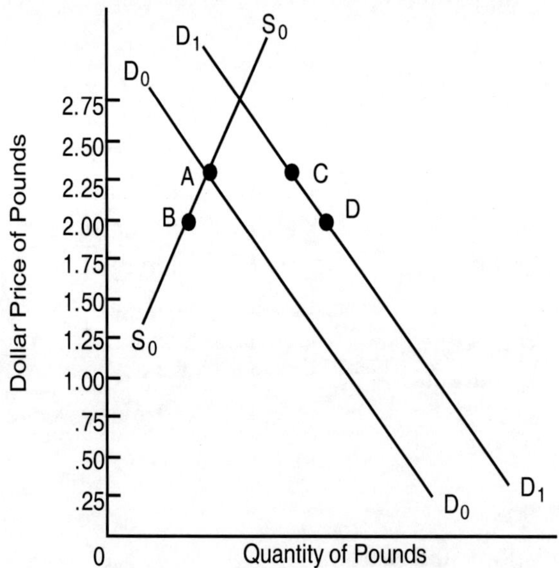

5. Consider Figure 17-2, which represents exchange rates under the gold standard, and answer the following questions.
   a. Suppose that D0 is the original demand for pounds and S0 the original supply of pounds. What is the original equilibrium exchange rate?
   b. When the demand for pounds rises to D1, what tends to happen to the exchange rate?
   c. Suppose (arbitrarily) that the gold-flow point is at $2.125. Once the exchange rate reaches that point, what happens in terms of the supply of gold and the price level in both Great Britain and the United States?
   d. What will happen to D1 and S0 once the gold flow is completed? What will happen to the exchange rate? to the quantity of pounds?

Figure 17-2
Exchange Rates and the Gold Standard

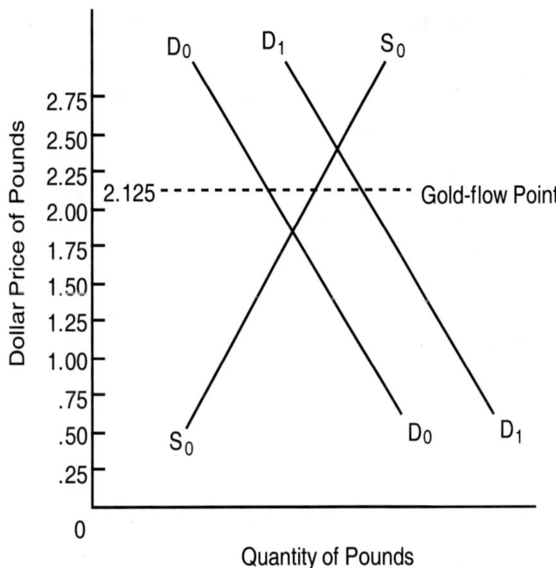

6. What basic features of the international monetary system have existed since 1946? What reforms have been made in the system since 1971?

7. Consider the hypothetical balance-of-payments statement for the United States shown in Table 17-1.

   a. Calculate the basic balance and the official reserve transactions balance. Then calculate the net balance of payments.

   b. What items in the official reserve transactions balance make it possible to finance the amount you calculated as balance to be financed?

Table 17-1
The United States Balance of Payments, 2005 (billions of dollars)

A.	Current account	+4.0
B.	Capital account	–7.8
C.	Basic balance	—
D.	Official reserve transactions balance	—
E.	Net balance of payments	—

8. What is an SDR?

9. What is the difference between floating exchange rates and fixed exchange rates?

10. Can we have a current account and capital account deficit?

Part 4 Self-test

Section A True/false questions

T F 1. In recent years the dollar has been allowed to float, to seek its market value in relation to other currencies.

T F 2. Foreign demand for American dollars is the result of American imports.

T F 3. An equilibrium exchange rate eliminates excess supply of or excess demand for a currency.

T F 4. American economists universally agree that freely floating exchange rates are preferable to fixed exchange rates.

T F 5. Fixed exchange rates promote long-term planning for trade.

T F 6. Freely floating exchange rates allow the independent influences of supply and demand to work themselves out.

T F 7. With the dirty float the government hides from the market the pegged rate.

T F 8. Many economists feel that a gold standard is undesirable because it causes the tail to wag the dog.

T F 9. The account that makes the international payments of a country balance is its capital account.

T F 10. Exchange controls by-pass the market system and impose public tastes on private tastes.

T F 11. The exchange-rate system introduced after World War II was called an adjustable-peg system.

T F 12. A freely floating exchange rate allows for immediate adjustment to a change in demand for a currency.

Section B Multiple-choice questions

1. All but one of the following are essential characteristics of a good international monetary system. Which one is not?

   a. A balance between the need for stability and growth of trade and the need for stability and growth in domestic economies

   b. Equity, or a reasonable distribution of costs and benefits

   c. Gold convertibility

   d. Efficiency

2. Which one of the following is not an advantage of a system of freely floating exchange rates?
   a. The system makes possible a quick response to changes in supply and demand.
   b. The system enhances long-term planning for trade.
   c. The system readily resolves a disequilibrium of payments.
   d. The system enables automatic adjustments to be made in the market to eliminate payments problems.
3. Which one of the following is not a characteristic of a system of fixed exchange rates?
   a. Supply and demand determine prices.
   b. The system promotes long-term planning of trade.
   c. Central banks manage large reserve accounts.
   d. With growing trade, international reserves increase.
4. A disequilibrium in exchange rates may be adjusted by all but which one of the following?
   a. Rationing access to foreign currencies
   b. Making macroeconomic adjustments in income, employment, and prices
   c. Lowering central bank reserves
   d. Letting the exchange rate float
5. As a result of problems connected with the balance of payments, since 1971 the United States has let the exchange rate between the dollar and foreign currencies be set by which one of the following?
   a. Fixed rates, with movement of central bank reserves
   b. Rationing of foreign currencies
   c. A return to the gold standard
   d. Floating of the dollar
6. Which one of the following is not an advantage claimed for the gold standard?
   a. It works automatically.
   b. It gives stability to the exchange rate.
   c. It frees domestic economic policy from foreign economic policy.
   d. It imposes economic discipline on nations.

7. One-time Federal Reserve chief Arthur Burns argued that a floating exchange rate would have all but which one of the following effects?

   a. It would engender political pressure for protectionism.

   b. It would lead to retaliatory policies on the part of other countries.

   c. It would make suitable domestic policies more difficult to implement.

   d. It would increase certainty and promote international trade.

Section C Matching questions

Match the phrases in column B to the terms in column A.

Column A

1. Gold standard
2. Adjustable peg
3. Floating exchange rate
4. Exchange-rate disequilibrium
5. Fixed exchange rate
6. Exchange rate
7. Exchange controls
8. Deflation
9. Managed or dirty float

Column B

(a) Price of one currency in terms of another
(b) Method by which various countries' currencies have been exchanged since 1971
(c) System of exchange that was used until 1930s
(d) Exchange-rate system established after World War II
(e) Excess demand for or supply of foreign currency
(f) A method the United States has never used to adjust an exchange-rate disequilibrium
(g) A general lowering of prices
(h) System that required large central bank reserves
(i) Exchange rates that move within certain pegs

ANSWERS

Part 4

Section A 1, T; 2, F; 3, T; 4, F; 5, T; 6, T; 7, F; 8, T; 9, F; 10, T; 11, T; 12, T
Section B 1, c; 2, b; 3, a; 4, c; 5, d; 6, c; 7, d; 8, d;
Section C 1, c; 2, d; 3, b; 4, e; 5, h; 6, a; 7, f; 8, g; 9, i